WORLD BANK OPERATIONS
Sectoral Programs & Policies

WORLD BANK OPERATIONS
Sectoral Programs & Policies

Published for
The International Bank for Reconstruction and Development
by The Johns Hopkins University Press, Baltimore and London
1972

Library of Congress Catalog Card Number 72-4032
ISBN 0-8018-1448-0 (clothbound edition)
ISBN 0-8018-1449-9 (paperbound edition)

PREFACE

Basically the World Bank's operations are shaped by the needs of the development programs of individual developing countries, and the part the Bank can play, with other development agencies, in satisfying those needs. For this reason our activities are usually examined on a country by country basis.

However, it is useful also to look at the aggregation of Bank operations by sector of activity (agriculture, industry, transportation, etc.) to determine the main problems and policy issues faced by the Bank in the various fields. The papers contained in this volume were originally prepared and printed over a period of twelve months as an internal exercise to meet those objectives. The papers describe the distinctive economic and developmental characteristics of each sector and review the approach and scale of Bank operations in each field.

The first of the papers deals with *Agriculture* which is becoming an increasingly important sphere of Bank activity, and in which the great majority of the population of less developed countries is engaged. *Industry*—the subject of the second paper—is the main alternative occupation; though it involves fewer people, it is a mainspring of rapid growth.

One way in which many of the less developed countries can earn foreign exchange from their richer neighbours is through providing tourist facilities. The paper on *Tourism* describes the problems the Bank has faced, and the solutions emerging in the four years it has been engaged in this new sector.

The "infrastructure" on which growth in agriculture, industry and tourism can be built is dealt with in four papers: *Transportation, Telecommunication, Electric Power, Water Supply*. Each gives an account of the emergence of Bank policy from long experience.

But development is not dependent on material growth alone. *Education*, or the lack of it, is recognized as a major constraint, and the paper on this subject indicates why the Bank has been placing increasing emphasis on this sector. Similarly it is increasingly being accepted that there cannot be social and economic progress without some check on the exponential growth of population; the paper on *Population Planning* lays out the global problem, as well as describing the first steps which the Bank has taken in cooperation with many other organizations, to assist Governments requesting help in this complex field.

In many parts of the developing world a critical human problem is the explosion of the cities, which attract an endless stream of immigrants from the countryside, for whom there are often neither homes nor jobs. These and other problems of *Urbanization* are examined, and the Bank's somewhat tentative policies in this new field of activity are described in the final paper in this volume.

But the end of the volume is not the end of the Bank's operational story. These papers themselves describe policies which are in evolution, being tested and changed as we learn more about the science of development.

It is our hope that, just as the preparation of these papers has concentrated our thoughts on the lessons of our experience, and our plans for the future, their publication will be useful for all those who are engaged in development, and who are trying to better the lives of the majority of the inhabitants of this globe.

President, World Bank Group

CONTENTS

THE WORLD BANK GROUP

The World Bank Group comprises the Bank itself, officially named the International Bank for Reconstruction and Development, and its two affiliates, the International Development Association and the International Finance Corporation. Each of the three institutions was established to fulfill a distinct function, but all are devoted to the same general objective—the provision of financial and other assistance for the economic development of member countries.

The World Bank was founded at the Bretton Woods Monetary and Financial Conference in 1944 and began operations in 1946. It is a Specialized Agency of the United Nations, as are its two affiliates. The Bank's principal role is the provision of loans to developing countries for a wide variety of productive projects in the various fields described in this volume. At present, the Bank is the largest multilateral source of development financing in the world. By the end of June 1972, the Bank Group had committed nearly $23 billion in over 100 countries.

The International Development Association (IDA) was established in September 1960. IDA performs the same function as the Bank and has the same staff, but its loans (known as credits) are on much easier terms and are made to the poorest member nations.

The International Finance Corporation (IFC), established in July 1956, finances most types of commercial enterprises through investments in equity, loans without governmental guarantee and underwriting commitments. Its mission is to supply venture capital to productive private enterprises, to stimulate the development of local capital markets, and to promote the international flow of private capital.

AGRICULTURE

AGRICULTURE
SECTOR WORKING PAPER

● This paper discusses the part that agriculture plays in achieving the key development goals of greater production and exports, more employment, and a better distribution of income. Some policy issues of wide relevance for less developed countries are singled out for attention. After a review of the Bank Group's past activities in agriculture, projections are made of its future work in the sector.

The paper is not intended to be comprehensive in its coverage. In order to be concise, it touches only briefly, and sometimes not at all, on several important aspects, such as agricultural credit, rural development, rural-urban migration, nutrition, international commodity stabilization schemes and ecological problems. Some topics that are of relevance to agriculture are discussed in companion working papers —particularly those dealing with population planning, transportation and water supply. The balance between rural and urban development is considered in the paper on urbanization.

The term World Bank Group as used in this paper refers to the International Bank for Reconstruction and Development (World Bank), the International Development Association (IDA) and the International Finance Corporation (IFC). References to the Bank include IDA, but not IFC. Money amounts are expressed in U.S. dollar equivalents. The Bank's fiscal year (FY) ends June 30.

CHALLENGES FACING AGRICULTURE

The importance of agriculture in the economic development of low-income countries has come to be recognized increasingly in recent years. A number of causes have contributed to this change. Rapid population growth has focused attention on the need to expand food production. At the same time, the success that has been achieved in obtaining dramatic increases in crop yields through the use of new agricultural technology has demonstrated that agriculture offers excellent investment opportunities. This combination of circumstances has meant that, for many countries, measures to raise agricultural production have become both more urgent and more feasible.

The renewed interest in agricultural development has been accentuated by a degree of disillusionment with the outcome of industrial growth. In particular, it is recognized that industrial growth has not succeeded in preventing rising unemployment and continuing poverty for the great mass of people. The creation of employment oppor-

3

tunities and the alleviation of poverty have thus tended to be raised to the status of important development goals in their own right. The challenge for agriculture is to combine an acceptable rate of growth of production with movement toward these goals.

In dealing with the related problems of poverty and unemployment, agriculture is of exceptional importance. It is the sector which provides employment for most—typically, 50% to 80%—of the work force, contains the majority of poor people, and is the birthplace of many of the urban poor. Food and fiber, the products of the agriculture sector, are prominent among the goods which poor people demand in greater quantities as their incomes rise. Furthermore, in countries not endowed with exploitable minerals, the foreign exchange earnings from agricultural exports are frequently of critical importance for development.

There is growing confidence that the development and application of new technology can solve many of the production problems in agriculture. But increasing concern is being expressed about the distribution of the benefits of economic growth. This reflects the fear that the technological revolution will itself have adverse distributional effects within the agriculture sector—in particular, that its benefits will be captured to a disproportionate extent by the landowners, and that labor will be "saved" to no purpose other than to swell the numbers of unemployed. If these consequences are to be avoided, much rethinking of the conventional wisdom is required.

Production

The performance of the agricultural sector is judged primarily by its ability to expand production of food and raw materials. Increased agricultural production is of critical importance when both population and income grow rapidly in low-income countries, particularly if the poorest segments of the population share in the income growth. For example, if the population grows by 3%, and per capita income also rises by 3%, the total demand for food could increase, typically, by about 5%. Rising incomes also generate a demand for a diet that is of higher quality and more varied, so that the pattern of agricultural production needs to be diversified.

During the 1960s, agricultural production in developing countries increased at an average rate of 2.6% per year, while food production alone grew by 2.8% per year (Annex 1). These rates were little more than sufficient to keep pace with population growth. As a result, per capita production increased at annual rates of 0.16% for all products and 0.20% for food alone. In Latin America and Africa, agricultural production per head actually declined. Although, if judged against the forecasts of widespread famine which were common in the mid-1960s, this performance may seem reasonably creditable, it is clear that agricultural production must accelerate if future demands are to be met.

According to the projections underlying the Provisional Indicative World Plan for Agricultural Development (IWP) prepared by the U.N. Food and Agriculture Organization (FAO), the total population of developing countries will rise from 1,720 million in 1970 to 2,515 million by 1985[1]. To meet the increase in domestic demand for food as populations grow and incomes rise, the IWP estimates that food production will have to expand by 4.3% per year for the period 1967-1985. The marketable portion will have to grow even more rapidly—by 5% to 6% annually—because of increasing urbanization. Even if the rise in incomes is smaller, the demand for food will increase rapidly, since the greater part (about 70%) of the increase will stem from population growth.

The growth in agricultural production has come from three sources: expansion of acreage, increase in yields, and shifts to more valuable crops. Expansion of acreage has been more important in Latin America and Africa, while yield increases have been more important in Asia. Although there are considerable areas of unused cultivable land in Latin America and Africa, and some in Asia, the expansion of arable and harvested area in developing countries is unlikely to exceed 0.7% and 1.3% per annum, respectively, over the period 1962 to 1985[2]. Since these rates are less than the expected rate of population growth, an increasing proportion of future agricultural growth will have to come from increased yields. The shift to higher value crops involves a greater degree of farm and regional specialization in production; this calls for improved communication and marketing facilities within countries and for trade policies which allow international specialization to take place.

It is necessary not only to increase agricultural production, but also to improve the productivity of labor in agriculture. The improvement in productivity is required to raise the incomes of those engaged in agriculture, and to meet the demand for agricultural products coming from the increasing proportion of the population engaged in non-farm activities. As Annex 2 shows, economic growth ordinarily involves a decline in the relative importance of agricultural production and of the agricultural work force, since other sectors expand more rapidly than agriculture. This means that the proportion of

---

[1] More recent projections by the United Nations raise these figures to 1,765 million and 2,675 million, respectively.

[2] FAO, *Provisional Indicative World Plan for Agricultural Development* (Rome, 1970), Vol. I, p. 39.

agricultural output that is marketed, rather than consumed on the farm, must rise.

If the marketed portion does not increase commensurately with the increase in demand, food prices rise. Since food expenditures represent half or more of the total expenditures of low-income people, the effects can be very disruptive, both economically and politically. Some of the possible consequences are inflationary wage demands which slow down industrial growth, expenditure of scarce foreign exchange on food imports, or resort to draconian—but frequently ineffective—measures to commandeer or ration food supplies.

Agricultural production per man varies considerably among countries but is low in most of the developing world (see Annex 3). There is a general tendency for low labor productivity to be associated with a high man/arable land ratio. But the main point conveyed by Annex 3 is that there is no simple explanation of low productivity in agriculture; it results from a complex of factors, such as poor natural resources, lack of accumulated capital and current inputs, technological backwardness, poorly-developed human skills, and the social environment.

Undoubtedly, many opportunities exist for increasing agricultural output through technological innovation involving relatively small amounts of investment per man and per unit of land. But identifying and exploiting these opportunities is not always easy. Nevertheless, a recent study (the results of which are given in Annex 4) showed that agricultural output per farm person increased in all but one of a group of developing countries, even though in some the crop area per person declined. The gains in productivity reflect partly an increased use of purchased inputs—and, indeed, it is this source which must be increasingly relied on in the future.

If it is assumed that the use of fertilizers is a rough measure of the use of purchased inputs of all kinds, the table in Annex 5 gives some idea of the probable scope for increasing the use of these inputs. Although fertilizer consumption in developing countries is very low in comparison with developed countries, it is expected to double between 1967/68 and 1972. But even the doubling will mean that the application of fertilizer per unit of cultivated area will remain relatively low. The actual availability of modern inputs such as pesticides, fertilizer, engines and piping will, of course, be an important determinant of gains in productivity.

New Technological Advances

Considerable improvements in agricultural technology have been achieved in the developing countries over the past 20 to 30 years. Initially the emphasis was on cash crops, particularly export crops,

6

where some quite remarkable technological successes have been achieved. Of particular importance have been the breeding of high-yielding oil palm varieties; the use of vegetative propagation techniques in rubber and tea production to allow the properties of high-yielding clones to be adopted widely; and the development of cotton varieties and their adaptation to the requirements of industrial processes. Cultivation practices have been greatly improved and there has been wide acceptance of chemical fertilizers, pesticides and herbicides, often specifically developed for particular crops in particular environmental conditions. In livestock production, too, there have been notable technological advances, even under tropical and semi-tropical conditions: production has been increased by improving animal health control, using tropical legumes for pasture improvement, and upgrading local cattle with improved disease- and insect-tolerant breeds.

More recently, there have been similar technological advances in the production of food crops under the tropical and semi-tropical conditions typical of many developing countries. Such advances are still largely restricted to wheat, rice and coarse grains grown under irrigation. The wheat and rice varieties of the "green revolution" are capable of high yields with the aid of fertilizers, pesticides and adequately controlled water supplies. They were produced by means of genetic and agronomic "engineering" carried out in international and national research centers, and were developed specifically for regions with an adequate supply of rainfall or irrigation water. Their wider use will require an expansion of reliably irrigated areas in various parts of the developing world.

But more work needs to be done to produce still better and more widely adaptable varieties, particularly for dry-land farming. The "green revolution," impressive as it has been, has left many parts of the world and many millions of farmers unaffected. A much bigger research effort is needed for crops such as millets, legumes, oilseeds, vegetables, tubers and fodder, if the advances made with wheat, rice and maize are to be matched. Similarly, more research is needed on livestock production and disease control—especially in the humid tropics—and on water management in irrigation systems[1].

The use of new, high-yielding cereal varieties has spread with remarkable speed in Mexico and parts of south and south-east Asia—and, to a lesser extent, in the Middle East and North Africa. Their use in Asia, the Middle East and North Africa commenced as recently as 1965-66, yet, by 1970, they covered 10 million hectares, or 22% of the

---

[1]The Bank's role in supporting such research is discussed on page 48.

wheat area of 14 major wheat-producing countries. In the same year, another 10 million hectares, representing 13% of the total rice area in 12 countries, were planted with high-yielding rice varieties[1]. Annex 6 gives the data for individual countries. It shows that adoption of the new varieties of wheat has proceeded furthest in Pakistan (46% of the total wheat acreage in 1970-71) and India (33%). Partly because less irrigated land is available, only 6% of the Turkish and 3% of the Iranian wheat areas were planted with the new varieties. Corresponding rates of adoption of the new rice varieties were 50% in the Philippines, 42% in West Pakistan, 19% in South Vietnam, 15% in India, and 11% in Indonesia.

While the expansion in area of high-yielding varieties can be measured, their precise effect on yields and production is more difficult to determine. In 1970-71, in the less-developed countries of Asia and the Middle East (excluding Mainland China), the estimated production of wheat was 71 million tons and that of rice (paddy) 163 million tons. These represented increases of 30% and 19%, respectively, over the tonnages produced in 1965. Not all of these increases are attributable to the "green revolution," of course, even though 1965 may have been a somewhat better-than-average year.

If one takes the total area planted to new varieties in the countries listed in Annex 6[2] in 1970-71, and uses estimated yield multipliers for the new varieties, it is possible to calculate roughly how much they may have contributed to production. For example, if it is assumed that use of the new varieties (in combination with complementary inputs), instead of the old, increases yields by 100% in the case of wheat, and 25% in the case of rice[3], wheat output has increased by 8.3 million tons (or 22%), and rice output by 4.6 million tons (3.25%) in 1970-71[4].

---

[1]There seem to be two main reasons why the new rice varieties have not been accepted as readily as the new wheat varieties. One is that they are less palatable than the old varieties of rice. The second is that they are less readily adaptable to a wide range of environments than the new wheat varieties.

[2]Note that not all countries where high-yielding varieties have had an impact are included in this list. Notable omissions are Mexico for wheat, and Taiwan for rice.

[3]These percentages do not imply that varietal improvement has been markedly greater in wheat than in rice. The difference in favor of wheat reflects the fact that the new wheat varieties are grown almost exclusively under irrigation; under these conditions, yields are well above average in any case since, unlike rice, a substantial part of wheat output is produced under dry-land conditions.

[4]Availability of the new varieties has led to an expansion of plantings, particularly in the case of wheat, as well as higher yields per unit area. The above calculations attempt to catch only the yield effect. However, they probably do not underestimate the net effect of the new varieties on agricultural output. Although they do not credit the new varieties with increased output resulting from expansion of areas sown to wheat and rice, neither do they debit them with the reduced production of crops—such as cotton and pulses—that were displaced by wheat and rice.

8

These estimates are very rough, because the yield multipliers used are of uncertain validity. Furthermore, they do not take into account the contribution of modern inputs used in conjunction with traditional crop varieties. Nevertheless it seems clear that the impact on total wheat production in these countries has been substantial, but that the effect on rice production has been relatively small in the aggregate, though quite significant in particular regions.

One result of the increased cereal production—as the FAO medium-term forecast on cereals (Annex 7) shows—is a trend toward greater self-sufficiency in countries which have traditionally relied on imports for part of their foodgrain requirements. However, there is reason to believe that grain production will not continue to increase as rapidly as hitherto unless stronger efforts are made to spread the use of improved technology, to intensify research, and to provide complementary inputs, particularly water. Not only will increased plantings of the new varieties be restricted by the lack of suitable environments; but the spread of disease and pests may become a problem too. For instance, in the Philippines both the traditional and the new varieties of rice were attacked by a serious virus disease in 1971, necessitating a resumption of rice imports. Even in wheat and rice, therefore, there is a need for continuous research to make the new varieties better able to resist disease and pests.

The availability of new technology was a necessary but not a sufficient condition for the "green revolution" to occur: changes in government policies and priorities were required to strengthen the incentive to modernize. In India, for example, the shock of two poor monsoons helped lift agriculture to the top of the government's development priorities; greatly increased amounts of foreign exchange were allocated for importing fertilizer, better price incentives were provided, and research, extension and input distribution facilities were expanded and made more efficient.

Agricultural production has been increased primarily by concentrating capital investments, purchased inputs and the new technology on a small segment of agriculture. While this is largely because land and water resources are better in some regions, it also reflects the uneven distribution of entrepreneurship, capital availability and public investment policies. Concentration of resources where output increases are most readily obtainable is a sound strategy if the aim is to increase marketed output as quickly as possible. But the less urgent this need becomes, the greater is the attraction of a policy whereby the limited supply of capital is combined with expanded use of labor and new technical knowledge over a much larger proportion of farms.

Such a strategy would help in a situation where production is constrained by lack of effective demand while a large proportion of the rural population continues to go hungry because it produces so little. Modernization on small farms will, however, require greater efforts to provide extension and credit services and possibly to develop techniques of production that are better adapted to the conditions prevailing in traditional agriculture.

The adoption of new techniques is likely to have significant effects on the geographical pattern of production, and also on the product composition. Developments to date have increased the comparative advantage of irrigated areas in the production of foodgrains. As production of these basic necessities increases and their prices fall, the real incomes of consumers will rise and they will increasingly demand other agricultural products—meat, milk, fibers, fruits and vegetables—and agricultural resources previously committed to foodgrain production will become available for meeting this demand. If economic growth is to be promoted through greater diversification of agricultural production, a good deal of investment in research, extension and the marketing infrastructure will be required.

Exports

Just as agriculture dominates the economies of most low-income countries, so also it provides the largest portion of the foreign exchange earnings that are so vital for their economic development. Although exports of minerals and manufactures have grown more rapidly over the last decade, agricultural primary products still account for over 80% of the export earnings of at least eight countries, 50-80% in the case of at least nine countries, and 30-50% in the case of another eight or more (Annex 8)[1]. The major customers for the developing countries' agricultural exports are the industrialized countries; consequently, agricultural production, income and employment for the majority of less developed countries are shaped in part by factors beyond their control. However, public policies in these countries sometimes discourage agricultural exports by reducing producer incentives and discouraging the reinvestment of earnings.

Despite some encouraging achievements, the record of less developed countries in expanding agricultural exports has been generally disappointing. The unit value of such exports from both developed and developing countries has more or less stagnated over the last ten years. But, in terms of volume, agricultural exports from developing countries have grown far more slowly than those from developed areas. As a result, the total value of developing countries' agricultural

[1]Based on a sample of 36 countries accounting for 65% of less developed countries' export earnings.

10

exports rose by only 30% between 1957-59 and 1970, compared to a growth three times as high in developed countries' exports (Annex 9). It is interesting to note that the more rapid growth in the latter case is accounted for in part by the lowering of trade barriers and expansion in trade among developed countries themselves.

The FAO forecasts that the agricultural exports of developing countries (excluding forestry and fish) will grow by about 3% annually over the next eight to ten years. In that case, the growth rate will be a little better than it has been during the past decade. It will need to be higher in order to make a greater impact on the employment problem in developing countries. The differences in labor and capital intensity in production indicate that if some agricultural production is shifted from the developed to the developing world, far more jobs would be created in the latter than would be lost in the former.

Demand prospects for many of the typical agricultural products of developing countries, such as rubber, palm oil, groundnuts, coffee, tea, cocoa, sugar, cotton and tobacco, often appear to be discouraging. If considered over the medium period of, say, ten years, the scope for increased exports is often limited by growing competition among developing countries, competition from synthetic substitutes, and sometimes competition from subsidized agricultural production in developed countries. Yet in the longer run the prospect of population increases and higher living standards must result in a growing demand for some of the commodities where surpluses now appear to threaten. Uncertainties inherent in making price projections for the longer term cause difficulties in making investment decisions, especially for tree crops with long economic lives.

While the export outlook for some agricultural products is not particularly encouraging, for others it is quite good. The latter category includes meat, feedgrains, certain types of fish, fruits and vegetables, timber and paper products. Some of these commodities might become scarce unless developing countries exploit their production potential effectively.

Another way in which developing countries could increase their export earnings is by doing more of the processing of raw materials themselves: meal and oil might be exported rather than oilseeds, cotton textiles rather than cotton lint, canned or frozen foods rather than fresh products. However, developments of this type require both better access to developed markets and increased investment in processing capacity. It would also be helpful if developed countries eliminated some of the existing structure of protection and subsidies, and thus encouraged their producers to shift away from products that can be imported more economically from developing countries. Finally,

Income per Capita, 1967, and Percent of Labor Force in Agriculture, 1965, Developed and Less Developed Countries

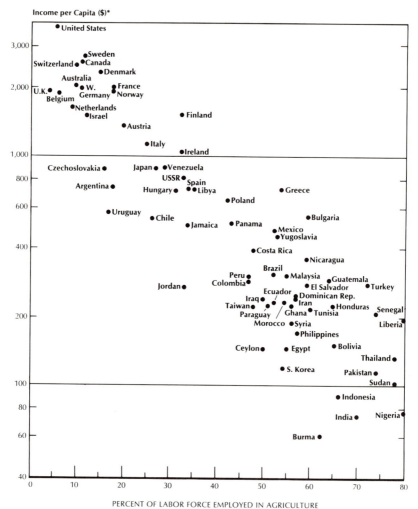

PERCENT OF LABOR FORCE EMPLOYED IN AGRICULTURE

*Gross National Product per Capita, 1966 Dollars.

Source: *Economic Progress of Agriculture in Developing Nations, 1950-68.* (Foreign Agricultural Economic Report No. 59, U.S. Department of Agriculture, Washington, 1970)

12

developing countries could stimulate trade among themselves by expanding their economies and adopting more liberal trade policies.

Although agricultural exports account for a substantial part of total exports of many developing countries, they often represent a much smaller percentage of total agricultural production. In India, for instance, agricultural exports are over 40% of total exports but less than 3% of total agricultural output. A similar situation prevails in Pakistan, where the respective figures are 50% and 5%; in Thailand (80% and 25%) and in Ethiopia (98% and 10%). On the other hand, these percentages are 90 and 50 for Argentina. A few countries may be able to sell a large part of the increase in their agricultural production in export markets. But most countries will have to rely mainly on the expansion of their domestic markets.

Employment

Developing countries face a pressing need to provide employment for a rapidly increasing population. In agriculture the problem is mainly one of underemployment, which is perhaps best defined as a condition in which irregular work of low productivity results in extremely low levels of earnings and consumption.

As mentioned earlier, and as indicated by the table in Annex 2, economic growth is ordinarily accompanied by a decline in the relative importance of the agricultural work-force. Further evidence of this tendency—but also of the existence of large departures in individual countries from the general relationship—is provided by the figure on the opposite page.

It would be unwarranted, however, to conclude that the task of employment creation must fall primarily to non-agricultural sectors of the economy. With rapid population growth, the absolute numbers of those available for employment in agriculture will increase, in many countries, for the foreseeable future. For example, as the table on the following page shows, the agricultural population of Asia will continue to increase until well into the twenty-first century, unless population growth is sharply reduced or the growth of urban employment is greatly accelerated.

Although the numbers employed in agriculture can be expected to increase in most developing countries, the rate of increase will differ among countries, depending mainly on the present size of their non-agricultural sectors. The latest FAO projections are that between 1970 and 1985 the agricultural population in East Africa will increase by 31% (from 80 million to 105 million); in South Asia by 24% (from 490 million to 606 million); and in Latin America by 14% (from 118 million to 135 million).

13

Agricultural Population Projections for Asia[1]

Assumed Rate of Growth of Population	Urbanization	Year in which Agricultural Population Reaches Peak	Size of Agricultural Population in Peak Year[2]
percent per annum			million
2.8[3]	3.8[6]	2052	2,790
2.5[4]	3.8	2025	1,310
2.3[5]	3.8	2011	950
2.8	5.0[7]	1993	820
2.5	5.0	1984	701
2.3	5.0	1979	640

[1]Excluding Communist countries and Japan.
[2]Agricultural population in 1962, the base period for these projections, was 583 million. By 1970 it had reached 701 million.
[3]U.N. high estimate.
[4]U.N. medium estimate.
[5]U.N. low estimate.
[6]IWP projected rate.
[7]"High" rate.
Source: FAO, Provisional Indicative World Plan for Agricultural Development (Rome, 1970) Vol. 1, pp. 32-33.

With few exceptions, agricultural production in developing countries is carried out by labor-intensive methods: traditional agriculture provides work for many hands, even if earnings are miserably low. The demographic prospect depicted in the table above implies that in many countries sustenance and work will have to be found for many more people in the coming decades. Fortunately, modern techniques that increase output can be introduced into traditional agriculture without changing its labor-intensive character. However, as is argued in detail later, if government policies and the structure of prices favor capital-intensive production techniques and if the small farm sector is neglected, agricultural growth will provide far fewer opportunities for productive employment than it could. Hence there is a need to re-examine existing policies and institutions to see whether they promote or discourage a pattern of development which utilizes labor resources.

A policy of creating employment in rural areas should reduce rural-urban migration and the social and private costs associated with it. Furthermore, it is very difficult to reduce urban unemployment by creating more jobs in urban areas if underemployment and low earnings remain characteristic of agriculture. For, as the urban unemployed are absorbed into the work-force, they will simply tend to be replaced by new migrants from the countryside, attracted by the chance of securing a high-paying urban job.

Effects of Technological Change on Employment

The introduction of modern agricultural technology has had mixed

14

effects on the demand for labor in Asia, and the net effect on employ-ment in regions where their use is spreading is not always clear. The high-yielding varieties of wheat and rice call for more intensive culti-vation. Moreover, the shorter growing season of the new varieties frequently permits double- or multiple-cropping, thus greatly increas-ing the number of cultural operations carried out in the course of the year. The use of improved seeds and fertilizers is therefore conducive to labor-intensive farming methods, and, of itself, tends to create more employment.

The use of the new varieties, however, has been accompanied, for various reasons, by an increasing degree of farm mechanization. Not all mechanization has an adverse effect on employment; the mech-anization of operations that can be performed only slowly or inade-quately using hand methods—or which take place at times of peak labor demand when labor is, in fact, a scarce resource—is often nec-essary in order to break the bottlenecks hampering production. Some examples are the use of tractors for rapid land preparation so as to permit increased double-cropping, of mechanical threshers to handle the greatly increased harvest, and of motor pumps to lift irrigation water. In these cases more intensive cultivation frequently raises the total requirement for on-farm labor.

However, once acquired for a particular purpose, some machines—and, in particular, tractors—can be used for other purposes as well, and it is usually economical so to use them. In addition, not all mech-anization that has occurred is of the sort that increases output. Some has been labor-saving in intent or in practice. For these reasons, and also because government policies in many countries often wittingly or unwittingly encourage indiscriminate mechanization, growing concern is being expressed about the extent to which mechanization is proceeding[1].

There is also a danger that the direct employment benefits of the new technology will, to some extent, be offset by changes in the cropping pattern. Areas planted to crops favored by technological advances tend to expand at the expense of other crops. If the former are less labor-intensive than the latter, the net effect on employment will be smaller; and, if the shifts in crop composition are large enough, employment could even decline. In South Asia some labor

[1]In an attempt to improve its knowledge of this matter, the Bank has arranged with the FAO/IBRD Cooperative Program for a pilot study of the employment and income distribution effects of the Muda Irrigation Project in Malaysia (which involved sub-stantial farm mechanization, including private machinery pools providing services to small farmers); and with some Indian research units for monitoring the employ-ment, income distribution and productivity effects of farm mechanization under two Bank-financed credit projects in India.

displacement has occurred as wheat acreage has expanded at the expense of more labor-intensive crops such as cotton—a tendency that has been accentuated by price incentives working in the same direction.

Looking to the future, however, the high-yielding grain varieties could contribute to employment by releasing land and water resources for producing other foods, such as vegetables and milk, where much more labor is required. Shifting away from monoculture with its seasonally-peaked demand for labor may also be the most practical solution to the problem of seasonal underemployment.

The "green revolution" also generates off-farm employment, in activities connected with supplying farm inputs and consumption goods and services and marketing the larger harvests. In parts of India, for example, there has been a clear rise in the earnings of village craftsmen, such as blacksmiths and carpenters, and small workshop industries have come into being, producing such things as simple mechanical threshers. However, quantitative evidence regarding these secondary employment effects is not available. There is also considerable potential for creating employment by the construction and improvement of irrigation facilities, the productivity of which has been greatly enhanced as a result of the new agricultural techniques.

In sum, the widespread adoption of the new, output-increasing agricultural techniques can significantly reduce unemployment and underemployment. However, if their full potential in this regard is to be realized, policies which favor almost exclusively the growth of a small capital-intensive "modern" agriculture sector will have to be modified. In particular, farm mechanization will have to be selective, the emphasis being on the type that is essential for increasing output per hectare. Of course, further development of yield-increasing technologies for a wider range of crops and environments—rainfed as well as irrigated—is as essential for generating employment opportunities as it is to meet the demands of the market.

As things stand, the fact that the new techniques are mainly applicable to irrigated agriculture means that their impact on employment is limited and is concentrated in particular regions. Because of low labor mobility, the expansion of output and employment in favored areas may be slowed by labor shortages, while chronic unemployment exists in other parts of the same country. Nor do the new techniques necessarily lessen the seasonality of farm labor-requirements: in fact, they sometimes accentuate the seasonal peaks. Depending on the overall availability of labor, the solution may lie in selective mechanization, in conducting some post-harvest processing, storing or marketing activities locally, in greater crop diversification, or in the

16

careful timing of programs for off-farm employment, such as rural public works.

Income Distribution

The progress of the agriculture sector—as the provider of subsistence and cash income to those engaged in it, and as producer of marketed foodstuffs and fibers—has a very direct bearing on the welfare of poor people in developing countries.

The rural poor consist of many millions of subsistence farmers, small farmers, laborers and their families. Their poverty reflects the fact that their productivity is low and that they own few assets in the form of either land or capital equipment. Programs for raising agricultural production by using modern techniques benefit the urban poor, since they tend to hold down the prices of their basic necessities. But they do not necessarily help the rural poor.

The effects on rural poverty depend on many factors, and are likely to be mixed. Initially, the benefits tend to go principally to the larger, more commercially-oriented farmers, who are better able to make the financial outlays required to purchase modern inputs and to assume the risks associated with trying something new. To secure acceptance, the new techniques are often subsidized. As they are accepted more widely, the burden of the subsidy weighs heavily on the exchequer, and it is sometimes reduced or removed just at the time when the smaller producers decide to adopt the techniques[1]. In addition, if the resulting production increases are not matched by rising demand, the prices of agricultural products tend to fall, so that those who have not managed to increase their production are left worse off than before.

Similarly, if the new techniques are, on balance, labor-saving, the lot of landless laborers, tenant farmers and owner-operators who supplement their incomes with outside employment is likely to worsen. In general, the effect of the new technology on income distribution will depend upon the pattern of adoption, the pattern of resource ownership, and on the net effect on the demand for labor. It will also depend upon existing redistributory devices, such as taxation of income or land.

Since the mass of the poor have few assets other than their capacity to work, they will be benefited by policies which increase the demand for labor; in this respect, the problems of poverty and unemployment are closely related. A development strategy which stresses paid employment will benefit small farmers: more of them or members of

---

[1] In some cases, instead of removing the subsidy, governments have limited the supply of the input.

their families will secure paid employment and there will be less underemployment of those who remain on the farm. But, in addition, specific programs designed to raise the productivity and the incomes of farmers and farm workers are needed.

One way of doing this is by giving them knowledge of new production methods, together with the means of putting the new methods into practice—for example, better credit and marketing facilities. Another approach is to provide them with more land, through land settlement (if unused land is available) or, in areas where the pattern of land ownership is highly skewed, land redistribution programs. The additional land raises the farmer's labor productivity; moreover, since the land is usually sold on concessional terms, he also benefits in his role of landowner.

Experience in a number of countries has shown that the second approach is unlikely to be successful unless it is accompanied by the first; that is, it is not sufficient to break up, through land reform, what is often a semi-feudal social structure and not put anything in its place. Similarly, in some situations, the first approach may make little headway without an admixture of the second, since the size and fragmentation of land holdings and tenure arrangements may discourage the adoption of new production techniques.

SOME MAJOR POLICY ISSUES

It is proposed now to focus attention on some important policy issues which many developing countries must face as they strive to promote agricultural development. It is realized, of course, that because of differences among countries in the physical, economic and social environment, the tasks facing governments will vary from country to country, as will the policy instruments that are feasible. However, a few of the issues that are of particular concern in many countries are singled out for attention here.

Government activities in relation to the economy fall into three main categories: first, the creation and/or maintenance of an institutional framework that is conducive to social stability and economic progress; secondly, the general management of the economy; and thirdly, the provision of public services and investments, particularly for purposes unlikely to be performed by the private sector. In agriculture, these public services and investments typically include research, technical extension services, general supervision of the cooperative sector, and provision of major infrastructure such as surface irrigation systems, systematic groundwater development and rural roads.

Governmental "management" of agriculture in most developing countries is weak—weaker than that of most other sectors of the economy. This is partly a result of past attitudes which gave low priority to agriculture. Although attitudes have been changing, government activities affecting agriculture still suffer from insufficient funds and a lack of skilled manpower, and economic policies often militate against agricultural development.

The concept of investment projects for agricultural development is still a fairly new one to some governments, and few are well equipped to identify, prepare and implement such projects. There is a reluctance to recognize that highly technical and specialized skills are as necessary in agriculture as they are in other sectors. For example, the fact that project management requires professional skills that might have to be hired from abroad is less readily appreciated in the case of agricultural projects than it is in the case of power and transport projects[1].

Resolution of the issues discussed below is the responsibility of the developing countries themselves. The Bank Group and other development agencies can assist through advice and objective commentary on the effects of existing and proposed policy options—for example, through the Bank Group's sector survey missions and in the course of project work. But the solution to one important problem will depend very much on policies adopted in developed countries. Agricultural exports from developing countries cannot increase significantly unless developed countries grant wider market access and offer less encouragement to high-cost production by their own agriculture. This conclusion follows from the fact that roughly three-fourths of developing countries' agricultural exports consist of commodities which compete directly with the same products or synthetic substitutes produced in developed countries (see Annex 10).

It is disturbing that despite the crucial importance of agriculture in most low-income countries, agricultural commodities remain the category where the least progress has been made after almost a quarter century of effort to achieve a worldwide reduction in trade barriers. A disposition to view the problem of agricultural development

---

[1]It is important to note that in the agricultural field there has been a significant improvement during the 1960s in the services which consultants can supply. Many consulting firms whose competence was formerly restricted to engineering have acquired agricultural expertise and in several cases have set up their own agriculture departments. A considerable number of new consulting firms have come into existence and it is now possible to hire suitable consultants for most agricultural work which may need to be done. This gives governments and development agencies much more scope and choice when they wish to undertake studies or when they need help in the execution of projects.

in a broader perspective is necessary in the interests of both the developed and the developing countries.

Making Better Use of the Price System

A considerable body of evidence is now available to demonstrate that peasant farmers respond to economic incentives. For example, the supply of many peasant-produced crops has been shown to have responded to changes in their relative prices. Also, it has been observed that small farmers are not indifferent to the income-increasing opportunities afforded by the adoption of new technology with a high pay-off. Traditional agriculture is recognized as being a good deal more efficient than it was once thought to be.

It follows that the price system can play an important role in allocating resources and products in the agricultural sector, and between it and the rest of the economy. If price signals are distorted so that they fail to reflect relative scarcities, resources may be misallocated, to the detriment of production, growth and employment. This is not to say that all distortions are bad—some, for example, may be justified on the ground that they improve the distribution of income; nor is it to say that the resulting misallocations are necessarily serious. However, it does mean that the possibility should be borne in mind that substantial misallocations may be occurring; price, trade and fiscal policies should be examined in that light.

Agricultural prices are often the subject of a good deal of government intervention designed to serve a variety of political, social and economic ends, and the resulting structure of relative prices may not encourage the efficient use of resources. Adjusting prices to bring them into line with relative scarcities and trading opportunities is a difficult task which calls for considerable political courage. It also calls for perceptive and informed economic analysis: in a situation where there are many discrepancies between the actual and an ideal price structure, it is not always apparent whether a particular discrepancy is harmful or, by offsetting another distortion, is beneficial. The task is further complicated by the existence of dynamic factors which cause production and trading opportunities to change, and by uncertainty regarding future trends—for example, in the market prospects for export commodities.

A few years ago, there was a general tendency for the price systems of developing countries to discourage agricultural investment and production. However, in the meantime, a number of countries have substantially revised, or are in the process of revising, their policies affecting agriculture. As a result, the situation is now much more mixed, and agricultural production in several countries is being actively encouraged through price support programs, investment incentives and so on.

But while price systems that are systematically biased against agricultural production are now less common, the problem of price distortions within the agricultural sector remains. This problem may, indeed, be more serious than it was, owing to the tendency of government intervention to be directed at specific products, or specific inputs, and also to a failure to adjust prices in directions indicated by technical advances. For example, the policy pursued by many countries of supporting foodgrain prices at levels above world prices deserves reconsideration in view of the fact that, as a result of the new agricultural technology, unexpected marketable surpluses of grain have been generated.

These surpluses give rise to a host of problems, including the strain on government budgets when surpluses are acquired at high support prices; loss of production of other crops, including export crops, because of diversion of resources to grain production; problems of storing grain stocks which cannot be moved at the high prices; and eventually, depression of world grain prices as former importers attain self-sufficiency or become exporters. The problem basically is to establish within the overall structure of market prices a level of price support for grains which appropriately reflects the decline in costs of production. This is a difficult task technically, and even more so politically.

Retention of high support prices is sometimes urged as being necessary to provide incentives for small farmers, even though small farmers are least likely to have marketable surpluses, and therefore least likely to benefit from the price supports. Similar arguments are invoked to justify the granting or retention of input subsidies. Price supports and subsidies are generally an inefficient way of assisting small farmers since, if payments are proportional to the volume of production, the benefits go mainly to well-off farmers.

Non-Price Rationing

In many cases, key resources necessary for agricultural development are allocated not so much by price, as by non-price rationing devices. Much of the credit available for agriculture goes to those who can provide acceptable collateral, i.e., to those with land or other forms of transferable wealth. Small farmers and landless laborers derive little or no benefit from low interest rates, low-cost inputs, cheap power rates, etc., when they cannot take advantage of them because they lack collateral or complementary resources. Ironically, such concessions are usually introduced supposedly to benefit these groups. The problem has been recognized, and the Bank is trying to find ways of dealing with it. But continuing efforts are required to devise allocative mechanisms that avoid the inherent biases associated with the traditional forms of subsidy within prevailing institutional frameworks.

Irrigation water is almost universally underpriced and allocated by physical rationing. Rules and practices governing the use of water often serve neither efficiency nor equity very satisfactorily, and their inflexibility hinders adjustments to changing production techniques and cropping patterns. Raising water charges to reflect opportunity costs would promote the more effective use of water and at the same time generate additional public revenues which could be used for other development projects. It is possible to devise water pricing systems that promote both equity and efficiency—for example, through discriminatory pricing, and by making water rights transferable, so that an allocation of rights on grounds of equity need not prevent an efficient allocation of water.

Price Distortions and Unemployment

Several types of price distortions which are commonly present in developing countries encourage producers to substitute capital for labor to a greater extent than is warranted by their relative scarcities. The fixing of interest rates at artificially low levels, trade policies that underprice imported capital equipment, such as farm machinery, and minimum wage and other social welfare legislation that raises the price of labor above its supply price, are cases in point. These distortions—since they do nothing to increase the aggregate supply of capital relative to that of labor—introduce rationing problems such as those mentioned above.

Entrepreneurs who are lucky enough to have access to cheap sources of credit or foreign exchange, or who are subject to minimum wage legislation, have an incentive to organize their economic activities in a capital-intensive manner. The labor that may be displaced either becomes unemployed or finds employment in those sectors—which may be traditional agriculture—that are not favored by access to cheap capital and in which the relative prices of labor and capital thus tend to be distorted in the opposite direction[1]. The effect is

[1]High urban wage rates induce unemployment not only through the displacement of labor by machines, but in a more direct manner. A large discrepancy between urban wage rates and rural earnings—provided it is not explicable in terms of higher skill requirements, high living costs, or similar factors—attracts rural people to cities in search of high-paying jobs. The number of such job seekers depends upon the urban-rural wage differential and on how they perceive their chances of getting a job. Creating more urban jobs may do little to reduce the total of urban unemployment, since the pool of job seekers is likely to be replenished by more migrants from the countryside. It can be reduced only by narrowing the wage differential.

22

therefore to accentuate the dualistic nature of the economy, i.e., to heighten the contrast between a technologically modern sector, with high capital-output ratios and labor productivity, and a traditional sector using labor-intensive techniques and providing extremely low labor incomes. The misallocation of resources restrains both total output and the demand for labor.

The policies just described are economy-wide in their impact. Being the main traditional sector, agriculture is affected if industrial employment does not expand as fast as it could: more people remain in the traditional sectors, resulting in lower labor incomes, underemployment and unemployment. But such policies also foster the growth of dualism within agriculture. As was pointed out above, it is the large commercial farmers who have the easiest access to cheap credit and cheap inputs. They are also frequently subject to minimum wage legislation—whereas traditional farmers are not, or can evade its provisions—and this has a direct effect on such decisions as replacing labor by machinery or chemicals (e.g., weed killers) and cultivating labor-intensive crops.

The present state of knowledge permits only impressionistic judgments concerning the effect of price distortions on the choice of technology; quantitative estimates are lacking. Nevertheless, the circumstantial evidence is too significant to be ignored. Furthermore, the use of capital-intensive methods of production is fostered by the ability of developing countries to borrow capital-intensive technology from developed countries. Often the developing country's needs would be better served by some intermediate type of technology, but the incentives to develop it are generally lacking[1].

Policy Implications

The best way of avoiding the resource misallocations associated with price distortions is to remove the distortions. This may involve the removal of taxes, subsidies, etc., or, in some cases, the imposition of "corrective" taxes, subsidies, etc. Thus countries should be encouraged to adopt realistic foreign exchange rates or, where appropriate, offset overvaluation with appropriate rates of import duties or special taxes; to adopt interest rates that adequately reflect the cost of capital; and, whenever they consider it essential to grant subsidies to agricultural production, to do it in such a way as to direct these to specific

---

[1] It is necessary to encourage research into labor-intensive agricultural production methods, as part of the increasing interest in agricultural research generally. When suitable opportunities arise, it should be possible to support applied research in this field. In the transportation sector, the Bank has recently begun a study of the substitution of labor for equipment in road construction. The results may have considerable significance for agriculture in terms of labor-intensive construction of minor agricultural roads and irrigation infrastructure.

high priority programs or enterprises in line with the optimal use of resources. Measures such as these could lead to political difficulties. This is, if anything, more true of correcting distortions in the price of labor, since it is not politically realistic to revoke existing minimum wage laws or to subsidize labor use directly, except perhaps to a limited extent—for example, by subsidizing the labor cost of local public works.

The best that can be done, perhaps, is to make the maximum practical use of the small farmer as a production unit. The small farmer (defined here as one who uses principally family labor) will tend to displace labor by other factors of production later than would other agricultural producers, since the price he places on his own and his family's labor will represent its opportunity cost, as he sees it. Unfortunately, there are practical limitations to expansion of small-farm production (see "Small Farm Sector" below). It is also theoretically possible to offset price distortions in the labor field by deliberately raising the price of labor-substituting inputs; but such action, unless generally applied to all sectors, would tend to discourage agricultural production.

The use of additional taxes or subsidies to correct price distortions is limited by the political difficulties which governments face in raising levels of taxation or public spending. Hence, close attention should be given to existing fiscal arrangements, to see if corrective taxes or subsidies can be substituted for distorting ones, within the given limits of governmental budgets.

Price Distortions and Public Investment

Price distortions particularly affect private investment decisions. They are, therefore, important in agriculture, where there are a large number of private producers. In the public sector, investment decisions need be less influenced by prices, since the desire to maximize profits or minimize costs is moderated by social considerations. Indeed, the influence of price distortions on public investment planning can be removed by the use of techniques such as shadow pricing, whereby prices intended to reflect the true relative scarcities of products and resources are used to assess the costs and benefits of investments.

There are some practical difficulties with this approach, however. A basic difficulty is that since many price distortions are the result of government policies, a high degree of sophistication is required of governments if they are to negate these policies in their public investment activities. Another difficulty is that while selecting and executing investment projects on the basis of shadow prices reduces the social

24

costs or increases the social benefits, it has the opposite effect on money costs and benefits, which depend on the prevailing market prices.

Governments facing severe budgetary constraints may, therefore, prefer to select projects and construction methods which are cheap in, terms of ruling prices. They may be reluctant to launch, say, labor-intensive public works programs the opportunity cost of which might be low because of unemployment in the economy, but which might be quite costly on a cash basis[1]. Project selection on the basis of shadow prices is likely—given a fixed budgetary constraint—to result in a smaller works program, but production elsewhere in the economy will suffer less since the program will tend to use resources, such as labor, that are underutilized in the private sector. Total output is thus likely to be greater than if the larger works program were implemented; furthermore, the use of labor-intensive works will improve the distribution of income.

In some cases the price distortions in the public sector may be more severe than in the private sector, since many public-sector agencies enjoy special concessions, such as duty-free imports, favorable exchange rates, and interest-free capital.

The price distortions are sometimes so great that although particular agricultural projects are financially attractive, they are nevertheless unsound for the economy as a whole. The Bank, therefore, requires that the projects it finances should provide a satisfactory rate of return to the economy, taking shadow prices into account. While this procedure can weed out some clearly undesirable projects, it does not assure the selection of the projects with the highest priority. This is particularly the case when labor resources are abundant.

The Bank is, therefore, increasing its sector work in order to help borrowers identify priority investments. It is playing a more active role in the identification and preparation of projects, so that relative resource endowments are considered at an early stage. The Bank's early involvement in project identification also presents the opportunity for introducing income distribution and employment as important criteria in the project selection process.

Small Farm Sector

A major policy issue in almost every developing country is how to raise the incomes of the rural poor—small farmers, landless laborers,

---

[1]In some instances, the budgetary cost of labor-intensive public works projects has been reduced by persuading local people to donate their labor services, or work for small rewards; and by drafting people, e.g., members of the armed forces, to work on them.

the unemployed, and their families. These groups represent a large proportion of both the total and the rural population; they constitute the poorest segment of society, and they have been largely bypassed by the progress of the past decade. Policies and techniques for raising their incomes and productivity have not yet been devised for application on a massive scale. Yet development cannot have much meaning if it does not include the alleviation of rural poverty.

The size of the problem is immense. About 700-800 million—about one-third of the total population of the developing world[1]—are economically deprived rural people. The gap between them and the rest of the population will continue to grow unless determined efforts are made to better their lot.

There is considerable potential in the small farm sector for reducing underemployment, alleviating poverty and increasing agricultural production. The marketable production of individual units is small, since most small farmers live at or near the subsistence level, but their combined output constitutes an important, and sometimes dominant, share of total agricultural production. Because productivity is low, incomes are low even though they may be supplemented by small farmers and their families undertaking off-farm work. Changes in technology and access to services would boost productivity and incomes, and serve to reduce underemployment. Even marginal increases in productivity in the small farm sector would make a substantial contribution to total output, though the total growth in output is constrained by the growth of effective demand.

There has been limited success in bringing the benefits of development to this economically-disadvantaged group. Several governments have initiated programs to combat poverty in rural areas; some examples of projects designed to help the small farm sector in which the Bank has participated are described later in this paper.

The scope of the problem is enormous in terms of the number of families involved and the capital and institutional services required. Moreover, the rural poor have the highest illiteracy rate, the worst health conditions and the poorest access to markets, all of which make innovation and investment more difficult. The average investment per farm family in a selected group of recent Bank-financed projects was $1,100. This investment level cannot be sustained in a world where there are more than 100 million small farm families. The total investment in agriculture in developing countries is estimated at $7,000-10,000 million per year, which would be equivalent to less than $100 per small farm family if all the investment was for them.

The analogy of the housing problem in developing countries may

[1]Excluding Mainland China.

26

be instructive. In that area, too, the capital cost of even minimum housing units far exceeds the available resources. The emerging solution is a "sites and services" approach, whereby governments provide the infrastructure but the urban poor have to construct their own dwellings. A comparable approach—substituting idle labor for capital—is indicated for the rural poor.

However, even the provision of extension, credit and other services to enable small farmers to increase their productivity requires massive resources. The total supply of trained personnel is grossly inadequate; moreover, only a small proportion of the staff available at present provides services for the rural poor. In addition, the rural poor are less well supplied with other public services, such as education, health, electricity and water.

Since growth in agricultural production is unlikely to exceed 4-5% per annum, and the rural population is expected to increase at about 1½% per annum for some decades, production per head in agriculture cannot be expected to increase by more than about 3-3½% per year. The increases in net income will be less since more purchased inputs will be required to boost production. But these are average figures. Unless new measures are devised, the increases will be concentrated among the larger farm units and the real incomes of the rural poor will change very little.

There are no ready-made, generally-applicable solutions to the problem. If maximum impact is to be achieved, programs will have to be devised which encourage initiative and self-help among small farmers and increase their productivity. However, increases in primary production alone cannot provide sufficient opportunities for increasing the incomes of small farmers and others among the rural poor.

It is proposed to outline here some of the difficulties and opportunities in the development of the small farm sector. While the problem is clear, the framing and implementation of programs to assist small farmers remain a major challenge to the ingenuity of those engaged in agricultural development.

Economies and Diseconomies of Scale

Many agricultural operations can be performed quite efficiently on a very small scale. For example, from the standpoint of crop biology there is no reason for yields to change according to size of field or of farm. However, some inputs require a certain minimum scale of operations if they are to be used efficiently. This is true of machinery of various types and of certain fixed investments, such as tubewells. Similarly, a certain minimum size of herd or flock is needed for efficient livestock breeding.

27

It is often possible for small farmers to share the services of these inputs by the creation of machinery pools, by contract hire, by setting up public or cooperative tubewell systems serving several farms, and by group ranching. However, such arrangements create organizational and managerial problems, and there have been many failures. Miniaturization of machinery is also possible, but usually at the cost of some loss of efficiency. In general, then, small farmers are at some disadvantage because of technological economies of scale, but usually the disadvantage is slight.

On the other hand, financial economies of scale in agriculture are often quite significant. For example, the small farmer suffers, sometimes considerably, from being able to purchase only small quantities of inputs, and to sell only small quantities of produce at a time. He also finds it hard to obtain credit on reasonable terms: he usually has little security to offer against loans and finds it difficult to make an initial down payment in cash. Banking institutions tend to find it too expensive to administer loans to small farmers because the amount of each loan is small. Since it is difficult to get credit on reasonable terms for storing their output, small farmers usually are forced to sell their produce at harvest time when prices are normally low.

The ratio of labor to land and capital on small farms tends to be high. Off-farm employment opportunities are often lacking, limited or inconvenient to exploit, so that family labor tends to be used on the farm, even if its marginal productivity is low. This tendency is reinforced by the willingness of small farmers to work hard, under the spur of poverty. The result is that labor-intensive production techniques tend to be used, and labor productivity is low. However, the productivity of land in small farms is frequently as high as, or even higher than, in large farms[1]. Provided that he is not too handicapped

[1]A number of studies have shown that the value of output per hectare, on average, is higher on small farms than on large farms. If this is because large farms tend to occupy the poorer land, or because small farms concentrate on labor-intensive high-value crops, the finding would be of little significance for agricultural policy: after all, subdividing large farms would not raise their natural fertility, nor could all land be devoted to intensive horticulture. However, when careful investigations have been made in which land quality and product-mix have been held constant, some difference in favor of small farms often remains, though in some cases it disappears. There is thus some evidence that small farmers use land more efficiently. However, the relevance of this evidence may be questionable since most such studies refer to earlier periods when the application of modern technology was not common practice.

A priori reasoning suggests—and experience tends to confirm—that yields per hectare may be greater on small farms for some particularly labor-intensive crops (such as fruits and vegetables and tobacco), but higher on large farms for crops (such as sugar, rubber and oil palms) where sophisticated technical management is required. Yields per unit area can be an ambiguous guide to intensity of land use, however, since as commonly quoted they do not take account of double-cropping or land left fallow.

by other disadvantages—in particular, as discussed below, by restricted access to modern technology—the small farmer can, through hard work and careful management, use land efficiently.

Adoption of Innovations

Small farmers tend to be slower to adopt innovations than large farmers. Such behavior does not imply that the profit motive is lacking; rather, it arises from the objective circumstances of the situation. Most innovations involve risks and a small farmer can ill-afford to take additional risks when the annual crop is all that stands between his family and starvation. The tactic of adopting the innovation on a small experimental scale, to see if it works, is hardly available to him when the scale of his whole operation is so small: it is far more rational for him to wait and see how others fare. New technologies also usually require increased expenditure on cash inputs, such as improved seeds, fertilizers and weedicides. The small farmer cannot always afford such expenditures, and his access to credit is limited. If he does secure credit it is likely to be from a moneylender and to carry a high interest charge, so that he will want to be reasonably sure of a high pay-off before he borrows.

For these reasons, large and medium-sized farmers are at an advantage in a period of rapid technological change. Some evidence from India illustrates the point. Before the "green revolution," small farms commonly showed higher yields per hectare, but subsequently the reverse relationship has been observed, owing to the larger farmer's greater propensity to adopt the new yield-increasing methods. The large farmer will have a permanent advantage if there is a continuing flow of potential innovations from research and development activity—even though the new technology itself is neutral to scale.

Extension services, credit agencies and similar institutions find it easier to deal with a few large farms than with many small ones. Apart from the fact that administrative costs are lower, large farmers tend to be more receptive to advice and more creditworthy; they are also less likely to be isolated by social barriers or by illiteracy. While large farmers can play an important role in demonstrating the effectiveness of new techniques, deliberate efforts are required if governments are to reach small farmers through extension services and credit agencies.

Policies which neglect the small-farm sector tend to widen income disparities, sharpen social tensions in rural areas, and do little to assist the bulk of the rural population. In a situation of population pressure and widespread unemployment, small farms have the not

29

inconsiderable social virtue of providing more employment per unit area than large farms. They are also capable of farming their land intensively. If they are offered the knowledge and the means to use new techniques, the social advantages of small-scale farming can be gained without harming production.

However, a substantial effort is required to plan and implement schemes for developing the small farm sector. It is seldom useful to offer only credit without also providing complementary facilities such as extension services and marketing infrastructure (including roads and physical facilities as well as marketing institutions). Such integrated schemes are thus apt to draw heavily on the financial and manpower resources of governments; and it is easy to succumb to the temptation to provide less than the minimum necessary for success (sometimes, on the other hand, such schemes are provided with an excessive share of scarce resources in order to push them through).

Land Policy

The pattern of land ownership and the contractual and customary relationships between landlords and tenants can have a considerable influence on production, employment and income distribution in agriculture. In developing countries, land represents a much higher proportion of total wealth than in developed countries, and inegalitarian patterns of land ownership are a major source of income inequality. Furthermore, the owners of land usually possess political and economic power which can be exercised in ways that harm the interests of the bulk of the rural people. Land reforms aimed at securing a more equal distribution of land have been prosecuted successfully in a number of countries, though in some cases at the cost of an initial drop in agricultural production. Some land reform measures have been little more than political gestures and have been ineffective, or even counterproductive.

Whether measures designed to break up large holdings—such as land distribution, progressive land taxes, or the imposition of ceilings on the size of individual holdings—will be undertaken depends on what society considers equitable, and on the balance of political forces. However, the need for productive efficiency and employment creation also has to be considered. Although a landholding is not necessarily the same thing as a farm operating unit, the pattern of land ownership does affect the way in which land is used, and does so in two main ways.

First, because the amalgamation or sub-division of owned parcels of land to form operating units involves transaction and coordination

30

costs[1], there is a tendency for landholdings and farm operating units to coincide. If the economies or diseconomies of scale are strong, operating units will tend to become of optimum size, despite the transaction and coordination costs. But the economies of scale generally are not very strong. It is the pattern of land ownership, therefore, that largely determines the size of operating units. Size, in turn, influences the character of farm operations. With small holdings, the agriculture is likely to be more labor-intensive, with lower output per man but probably no less output per acre. It will also require more publicly-provided credit and extension services but probably use less purchased inputs.

Second, the incentive to improve the land and use it efficiently depends in part on whether the person who cultivates the land also owns it; and, if not, on the contractual arrangements between the owner and the operator.[2] Ownership and operation will tend to be divorced if the size of the owned parcel of land is very different from the optimum-sized operating unit. (Absentee ownership also implies the separation of operation from ownership.) Under tenancy arrangements there is frequently little security of tenure, nor are there guarantees that the tenant will be compensated for the improvements he may make on the farm. His incentive to invest in farm improvements is thus blunted. Similarly, the tenant's or manager's incentive to farm efficiently is reduced if he does not share fully in the rewards of efficient operation.

These deficiencies in contractual relationships are usually not simply the result of landlords and tenants being thoughtless, but reflect the fact that there are difficulties and costs involved in devising tenancy contracts that preserve all the incentives. Tenancy reforms which give the tenant greater scope for exercising entrepreneurship usually reduce the landlord's entrepreneurial role correspondingly, so that the gain in efficiency is not clear-cut; there may, in fact, be a loss. Tenancy is a device whereby landlord and tenant combine their resources in a common enterprise: there are bound to be conflicts of interest and some blunting of incentives.

Owner-operated farming is often favored because it avoids the need to reconcile the interests of owners and operators through

---

[1]These include the cost of negotiating contractual arrangements, each party's uncertainty regarding the competence and good faith of the other, and, in general, all the monetary, psychic and time costs involved in the association of two or more persons in a single enterprise. These costs are the basic source of the disincentives to efficiency which inhere in many rental arrangements and which are discussed in the next paragraph.

[2]Communal ownership of land is not discussed in this paragraph. However, it should be noted that in some cases it provides sufficient incentives to cultivators.

rental and other contractual arrangements. It is also favored because, with the rent component of farm income accruing to the operator, a more egalitarian pattern of income distribution is generally promoted. The inclination to provide land to the largest possible number of small farmers means that the size of the operating unit tends to become as small as is compatible with reasonably efficient operation and the provision of a socially-acceptable minimum standard of living for the operators.

More recently, as the implications of demographic changes have become clearer, the principal virtue seen in small-scale family farming is that it can provide employment and, to a lesser extent, can economize on purchased inputs. If small holdings tend to be more socially-productive than large holdings—in that they produce as great an output per unit area using more of the abundant and less of the scarce resources—the conflict which many have perceived between an equitable distribution of land and efficiency in farming may be largely illusory.

Belief in the existence of this supposed conflict was often bolstered by an exaggerated idea of the economies of scale that could be realized in agriculture. Some governments therefore favored the establishment of large-scale cooperative or collectively-owned farm enterprises. However, the management of such enterprises has often been weak. Current approaches favor retaining owner-operated production units but assisting them through cooperative, collective or state-owned organizations that can realize economies of scale and exercise bargaining advantages in the provision of off-farm and some specialized on-farm services.

Whatever size of farm it is desired to promote, it is not merely a matter of breaking up large holdings; some farms are so small that they could never support a family, even if modern techniques are used to increase production. Such units can be viable if suitable opportunities exist for off-farm employment but, where they do not, land reform measures are required to bring farm sizes up to some minimum level.

This can sometimes be accomplished by combining small farms with land that is being redistributed: in Tunisia, for example, land taken over from *colons* was available for redistribution. But since it is politically difficult to enlarge holdings by dispossessing some smallholders (unless they can be induced to leave to take up other jobs), often the best that governments can do is to try to prevent the situation from getting worse. Inheritance laws which prohibit the subdivision of land below a certain size of holding can help in this respect.

32

Small farmers suffer from a number of disadvantages, of which perhaps the most serious are meager financial resources, restricted access to credit, and the consequent reluctance to adopt new techniques. Land redistribution therefore needs to be accompanied by the extension of credit, marketing and technical advisory services to small farmers. Often these services or functions were previously performed by landlords. If they are not provided, the impact of land reform on production, and possibly also on the welfare of the new smallholders, is likely to be adverse.

The Impact of New Technology

New agricultural technology which increases output per unit area is essentially land-substituting in character, since it enables a given output to be produced from fewer hectares of land. Its widespread adoption will tend ultimately to diminish the relative importance of agricultural land and the share of agricultural revenue attributable to land. On a global basis this tendency does exist. But in regions that have been favored by the new technology, land values have risen. For example, the introduction of the new high-yielding varieties has increased the value of wheat land in many parts of Asia.

However, in areas where the new technology has not been applied, the value of wheat land will tend to fall—since the overall increase in wheat production will tend to depress wheat prices. The danger therefore is that in regions where the new technology is being adopted, income inequalities may worsen—the tendency being reinforced by the fact that the larger farmers are usually the first to adopt the new techniques. Far from reducing social tensions in rural areas, the spread of the new technology is likely to sharpen them, and lead to greater demand for the implementation of measures, such as land reform, for the redistribution of income and wealth.

Use of the new technology may often be accommodated only with difficulty by existing tenancy arrangements. Although the latter are not without their deficiencies, they are often reasonably well adapted to the conditions of traditional agriculture. But they may need extensive revision if the new technology is to be adopted and its benefits equitably shared. For example, under crop-share tenancy —which, as compared with cash tenancy, or the use of hired labor, serves the purpose of dividing risks between the landlord and the tenant—each party has an incentive to supply too little of the inputs for which he is responsible. In practice, it appears that this tendency is often held in check so that each tends to adhere to customary norms of performance: at any rate, there is little evidence that share-rented farms are operated much less efficiently.

However, new technology, particularly since it involves increased

33

use of purchased inputs, will require a new set of commitments from landlord and tenant, and perhaps also changes in the customary shares into which produce is divided. Until the revisions are made, the incentives to adopt new techniques that depend on the use of purchased inputs may be seriously impaired.

Furthermore, it appears that rather than entering into revised tenancy agreements, landlords in areas favored by the new technology have been tempted to let their tenancy agreements lapse and to farm the land themselves, using hired labor and machinery. Several considerations probably explain this behavior: it may be easier for landowners to introduce new techniques by directly supervising hired workers; being uncertain about the yield increases that can be attained, they may have found it difficult to negotiate revised tenancy agreements; and legal protection of tenants—or the threat of it—may have prevented the negotiation of contracts acceptable to the landlord. Another possible explanation is simply that modern agriculture is intellectually more engaging and financially more rewarding than traditional farming.

There is a good deal of fragmentation of landholdings in some countries, especially in South Asia. Under traditional agriculture and with underemployment of labor, fragmentation probably does little to constrain production, and reduces risks to some extent. The effects of fragmentation are more serious under modern agricultural conditions since it increases the costs of distributing inputs, of appraising credit requests, and of arranging for custom services. It becomes highly inconvenient when labor is in short supply, as now happens in some areas at harvest time.

The inconvenience of fragmentation is greatest in irrigated areas, since it raises the costs of distributing water (both directly and through the loss of cultivable land to additional canals). Also, labor shortages at harvest time are more likely to occur in areas served by irrigation. Consolidation of land is difficult to arrange in practice; farmers are usually reluctant to participate voluntarily because they fear that the land they receive may be less valuable than the land they give up[1].

Implementation of Land Reforms

The historical record shows a tendency for land reforms to be enacted in law but not successfully—or only partially or slowly—

---

[1] Voluntary participation may be more readily encouraged if consolidation is accompanied by land improvement works, such as irrigation or land levelling within existing irrigation schemes. Since all participants are likely to benefit, each may be less concerned—so the argument runs—as to whether he receives precisely the same share of improved land as he had of the original unimproved land.

implemented in practice. Where the program has been vigorously prosecuted, the results have sometimes been adverse, in that agricultural output has fallen and the condition of those whom it was intended to benefit has not been improved, or has even deteriorated. The record is, in a sense, unfair to land reform in that it has often been implemented in times of great social tension, and against strong opposition, by radical governments. But even in a favorable environment, successful implementation requires a good deal of political courage and administrative finesse.

Land reform is expensive, both in terms of the fiscal cost of compensating the former owners, and of the human and material resources required to administer it properly and to provide services to the newly-created small holders or cooperative enterprises. It also suffers from perverse announcement effects: owners faced with the threat of losing their land—usually compensation is incomplete, so that a degree of expropriation is involved—cease to improve it and allow existing facilities to deteriorate; and laws which promise tenants security of tenure lead landlords to dismiss their tenants and replace them by hired laborers and/or machinery. Thus a difficult dilemma arises if the adverse announcement effects are to be minimized: the redistribution of land should be done rapidly, but a piecemeal approach is more in keeping with the limited fiscal and administrative resources of governments.

Attempts to bring about land reforms have sometimes been frustrated by vested interests, and governments may feel they have to proceed cautiously because production might be disrupted in the initial stages. In some cases governments, bowing to the pressure for land reform, but lacking the will to take effective action, have enacted token legislation. However, such political expediency usually worsens the existing situation, as landlords take evasive or defensive actions to the detriment of both production and the employment opportunities of tenants and rural workers.[1]

It is clear that agricultural development cannot do all it might to improve rural life if the distribution of land ownership is highly skewed. Despite the political and administrative difficulties involved, governments should pursue land policies which help disperse the benefits of agricultural progress widely rather than allowing them to

---

[1]A study of the impact of land reform legislation on two Indian villages showed that although laws were framed to improve the position of tenants (by limiting the amount of rent payable, and by giving them greater security of tenure and the right to purchase land) the results left them worse off. Owners were able to evade the legislation by various means, including the replacement of tenants by hired laborers. It is interesting to note that a new tenurial relationship—a form of quasi-tenancy (but not legally classifiable as tenancy)—was devised to meet the situation.

go to only a small segment of the population. Steps should at least be taken to tax the higher rental incomes arising from public investments, and to reinvest the proceeds in infrastructure so as to increase the income-earning opportunities of wider strata of the population. If this is not done, rising land values will make it increasingly difficult to redistribute the land later.

Although the Bank's overall influence on these matters is bound to be slight, it can take explicit account, in its appraisal work, of whether the benefits of a project are likely to be widely dispersed or captured by only a few individuals. The burden of financing the compensation paid to owners under land redistribution programs is the responsibility of the governments concerned, but the Bank can assist in financing other programs designed to raise the productivity of those to whom the land is distributed.

PAST BANK GROUP ACTIVITIES IN AGRICULTURE

The Bank Group's activities in the agricultural sector take various forms. The most obvious and easily measured is direct lending for agricultural projects. But a substantial proportion of the lending in other sectors—such as transportation, electric power, education and industry—also benefits agriculture indirectly. Analyses are made of the agricultural sectors of the economies of borrowing countries. Technical assistance is provided mainly, but not exclusively, through the preparation, appraisal, supervision and post-evaluation of projects. Finally, support is given for economic and agricultural research.

The agricultural sector is among the most difficult of any to "manage." It is thus a sector in which aid donors, including the Bank, have particular difficulty in agreeing with governments on satisfactory project lending programs. Decision-making at the farm level is in the hands of a very large number of small operators. The political repercussions of agricultural policies are usually wide, particularly in the case of food prices.

The Bank does not claim to have answers to the multifarious problems posed by agricultural development. The patterns of past agricultural lending described here are not a precise guide to the future. A great deal of innovation will be required, which may in time lead to considerable deviations from present patterns, and from the projections about future lending in the section entitled "The Bank Group's Future Role."

Capital Transfer

Direct Lending for Agriculture

The Bank's direct lending for agriculture has accelerated rapidly in recent years. By June 30, 1971, it had reached a cumulative total of about $2,500 million. A breakdown by subsector, area and period is given in Annex 11.

Until the early 1960's the importance of agriculture in overall economic development was not fully recognized. This tended to limit the scope for Bank operations in the sector. Thus, over the period FY1948-63, the Bank's lending for agriculture amounted to only $628 million for 71 projects; that sum represented 8.5% of its total lending. In 1963, the Bank decided to increase its support for agricultural development. The increase was facilitated by the fact that the International Development Association (IDA) had been established in 1960; with IDA, it became possible to expand activities in countries which were particularly poor and in which agricultural development was frequently of the highest priority.

The effort to increase support for agriculture was initially hampered by a shortage of well-prepared projects. The Bank began increasingly to provide assistance for the identification and preparation of projects. As a result, its direct lending for agricultural development over the five years, FY1964-68, amounted to almost as much as during the previous 16 years: about $600 million for 46 projects. The proportion of agriculture in the Bank's total lending rose to 12%.

In 1968, the Bank decided to accelerate its agricultural lending further. The target adopted was that over the five years, FY1969-73, it should total about $2,400 million, or four times as much as in the previous five years, FY1964-68. By the end of FY1971, 60% (or three years) of the time had elapsed, and around 50% of the target had been reached. About $1,200 million had been committed for 96 projects, which was almost equal to the total agricultural lending during the previous 21 years. In the period FY1969-71, the share of agriculture in total lending rose to almost 19%. Enough projects are now being processed to enable the FY1969-73 target to be met.

Lending in Indirect Support of Agriculture

A considerable amount of Bank Group lending in other sectors supports agriculture indirectly. While there are a number of conceptual difficulties in preparing precise data, some orders of magnitude can be given.

Of particular importance in this context are the investments in *road transportation,* especially in countries that are predominantly agricultural and where much of the traffic is therefore related to agriculture.

Over the past five years, the Bank has invested about $1,350 million in the highway sector. A large part of this investment is helping to finance the construction and improvement of some 30,000 km of roads. Over two-thirds of these roads, in terms both of length and of cost, are directly benefiting the agricultural sector. Thus,

- about 2,000 km are low-cost roads which are virtually part of agricultural development schemes;
- about 5,400 km are rural roads where the benefits to agriculture represent an important part of their economic justification; and
- about 14,400 km are roads where the benefits to agriculture have been identified although not separately estimated.

Investments in other modes of transport, such as railways, have also helped agriculture considerably. But in their case the benefits cannot be so readily assessed in sectoral terms.

The Bank Group has invested significant amounts in *agriculture-related industries*. Such industries include those that use locally-produced raw materials like cotton or forest products, as well as those that produce agricultural inputs like fertilizer for local use. By the end of FY1971, the Bank and IDA had lent about $340 million directly for such industries. The International Finance Corporation (IFC) had invested another $157 million. Over the period FY1968-71, the Bank Group as a whole channeled a further $213 million into agriculture-related industries through local development finance companies. A sub-sectoral breakdown of these investments is given in Annex 12.

Many of the *educational facilities* supported by Bank lending are in rural areas. In addition, since 1968 about $40 million has been specifically lent to support agricultural education, training and research.

Trends in Bank Lending for Agriculture

Diversification of Lending

The most notable trend in the Bank's lending for agriculture, particularly since the early 1960's, has been the diversification beyond basic irrigation infrastructure into on-farm activities, technical services and related rural development (such as rural road construction, processing industries and, so far to a minor extent, education and health services). Increasing emphasis is being given to rain-fed, rather than irrigated, agriculture. The Bank is becoming more heavily involved in storage, marketing, seed multiplication, forestry and fisheries projects. Individual projects of all types are becoming more comprehensive in nature, the stress being on general rural development.

The volume of lending for irrigation projects continues to grow. The annual average has risen from $23 million during FY1948-63, to $53 million in FY1964-68 and $140 million in FY1969-71 (Annex 11). These figures reflect the priority that continues to be given to irrigation projects in those parts of the world (such as East and South Asia, the Middle East and North Africa) where resource conditions require it. On the other hand, the *share* of the Bank's agricultural lending devoted to irrigation projects has declined steadily. It has fallen from nearly 60% in FY1948-63, to 44% in FY1964-68 and 34% in FY1969-71. The decline is even more marked when it is considered that recent irrigation projects have increasingly involved items other than irrigation infrastructure.

The diversification beyond basic irrigation infrastructure results from:

(a) the need to follow-up investments in irrigation infrastructure with credit for on-farm development, so that farmers can take fuller advantage of the water made available to them;

(b) the greater need for the multiplication of improved seeds, and for increasing storage and processing capacity, particularly in Asia, as a result of the "green revolution";

(c) the good export prospects for beef and fresh fruit and vegetables;

(d) the availability since 1960 of IDA funds, allowing investments in many of the poorer countries which typically depend heavily on agriculture. In many of them, particularly in Africa, irrigation has so far had a relatively low priority. Investment in African agriculture has involved mostly small farmers requiring projects specifically designed to overcome the constraints on small farm development[1]; and

(e) population growth has encouraged settlement of new lands, which has often become possible as a result of other developments, such as disease control.

Irrigation Development

Through the 1950's the Bank's lending for irrigation was primarily for the construction of dams and main distributary canals. Governments, farmers and local entrepreneurs were responsible for financing, without further Bank assistance, the complementary investments required to take advantage of the improved water supply[2]. However, it was found that, in many cases, although progress on the major

---

[1] For example, all nine agricultural projects in Africa financed by the Bank in FY1971 involved the small farm sector.

[2] For example, field ditches and drains; land levelling; input supplies; extension services; and additional processing and marketing facilities (including roads and farm tracks).

construction works was generally satisfactory, the complementary developments were delayed. The economic benefits of the capital-intensive works, therefore, were either not fully realized or were realized rather late. This was often attributable to a lack of coordination between various agencies involved in the development of irrigated agriculture and to a lack of appropriate financing.

In recent years, therefore, the Bank has given particular attention to these complementary developments during project preparation and appraisal. It has sought to ensure that the planning of agricultural and ancillary developments has been carried out, and that suitable arrangements have been made for implementation, including those required for proper coordination. In some cases, especially those where the construction and consequently the disbursement periods are long, the Bank has financed irrigation development in phases or, where appropriate, has financed only the major civil works.

But the trend is towards paying equal attention to all aspects of the development and use of water resources, and financing the agricultural and ancillary developments as well as the basic irrigation infrastructure. Some recent irrigation projects have thus provided for the construction of the complete distribution system down to the field level; the construction of roads and tracks; the strengthening of applied research, demonstration facilities and agricultural extension services; the provision of credit to entrepreneurs, cooperatives and farmers for input supply, on-farm investments and storage and processing facilities; and training of farmers as well as of operations personnel.

The broader approach has helped to make it possible to realize more quickly the full economic benefits of the capital works. But often, many other problems have remained, the resolution of which has called for changes in government policies. It is still frequently the case that the organization of government services within irrigation projects is not suitably coordinated. This is particularly true of coordination between the entities directly responsible for infrastructure construction and those responsible for agricultural extension services and applied research; and between the latter and agricultural development banks.

Similarly, governments need to attach much more importance to the efficient control of scarce water. The introduction of double-cropping—which often forms one of the principal economic justifications for the irrigation infrastructure—generally continues to be disappointingly slow, especially where large numbers of small farmers are involved. Some governments still insist on making the water available over as large an area as possible, in order to reach the maximum number of farmers. As a result, individual farmers may be left with too little water for intensive cultivation, and there is the danger that the soil may deteriorate. If cropping intensities remain relatively low, the opportunities for fuller, round-the-year employment also suffer. The scope for increasing cropping intensities by systematic and fully integrated development of surface and groundwater resources deserves greater attention.

The Bank frequently has encountered situations where dams have been constructed, but developments "below the dam" have still to come, leading to a growing number of projects for the improvement and completion of existing systems. In some cases, the projects are for the rehabilitation and redesigning of very old systems; in these, modern methods of water control and drainage are introduced to increase efficiency and thus increase cropping intensity. In other cases, the projects are for completing distribution and drainage systems which have not been developed to their full potential. In yet other cases, the principal objective is to increase the supply of water through an existing distribution system, converting what might have been designed originally as a drought-protection system into one allowing intensive irrigation and double-cropping. Here, systematic and integrated ground water development has an especially important role to play.

The types of projects described in the preceding paragraph generally involve relatively little capital investment, but bring high returns, and are thus of high priority. One reason why governments do not give them priority more frequently is that they involve farmers who have already received some benefits from public investments (e.g., in the original system), whereas governments often prefer to give priority to new schemes which generally are more prestigious, even though such schemes are likely to be more capital-intensive, yield benefits only in the more distant future and bring lower economic returns.

Agricultural Credit

Reference has already been made to the diversification of the Bank's agricultural financing into support for on-farm investments and storage, marketing and processing, usually provided in terms of agricultural credit facilities. Ultimate borrowers have included individual farmers, groups of farmers, cooperatives and public-sector entities. It is not feasible for the Bank itself to invest directly in a large number of small enterprises. So Bank funds provided in support of credit facilities are usually channeled through intermediary institutions within the borrowing countries.

41

These institutions range from agricultural development banks to those parts of the commercial banking system involved in extending medium and long-term credit facilities. Sometimes, especially if there are no suitable intermediaries, it is necessary to establish channels of credit for on-farm development within project authorities, often newly created; the latter may be involved simultaneously in giving technical assistance to participating farmers and in constructing infrastructure.

The share of Bank funds lent in support of agricultural credit has grown very rapidly. It has risen from an annual average of $2 million (5% of Bank lending for agriculture) over the period FY1948-63 to about $56 million (47%) in FY1964-68 and about $258 million (63%) in FY1969-71.

The range of investments financed by the Bank through credit institutions covers practically all aspects other than the transfer of existing resources such as land. The principal items include: on-farm land development (groundwater development, land levelling, field ditches and drains, land clearing); other on-farm investments (tree crop planting, pasture improvement, livestock purchase, farm machinery purchase, building construction, fencing, on-farm processing and storage facilities); incremental working capital needs for initial purchases of additional inputs (such as fertilizers, pesticides and fungicides); and off-farm developments (processing and storage enterprises, fishing vessels and gear).

About half of the Bank's financing of private-sector agricultural investments has been for projects where the provision of medium or long-term credit facilities is the sole or principal element[1]. Of course, this is only possible where the other ingredients essential for agricultural development are already available or are to be provided from other sources. To be successful, such projects depend on active demand for the credit facilities being extended, which means that the policy climate has to be conducive to private-sector agricultural investment.

Other essential prerequisites for effective credit programs are technical advisory services backed up by applied research and demonstration, a well functioning transportation infrastructure, the availability of inputs and a dealer network, including service facilities. On-farm development needs to be backed up by suitable storage, processing and marketing facilities, the establishment of which depends on the scope for increasing marketable surpluses.

Where any of these essential prerequisites for effective credit pro-

---

[1]These are the so-called "credit projects" of Annexes 11 and 13.

42

grams are missing or under-developed, the Bank only finances "credit" within the context of a comprehensive integrated project. For example, "credit" forms a part, sometimes a major part, of practically all lending for integrated rural development and settlement projects.

"Institution building" has been an integral and extremely important aspect of most lending in support of agricultural credit programs. The Bank has actively participated in the creation of new credit institutions, and in the improvement and rehabilitation of many already in existence. Of particular importance has been the adoption of development-oriented lending policies. Existing institutions frequently stress lending against adequate collateral, thus favoring those in possession of assets while not providing facilities to those who offer promising opportunities but inadequate security.

In such circumstances, the Bank has stressed the need for the institutions to rely more on an expert technical appraisal and financial assessment of the incremental earning capacity of a proposed private-sector investment, rather than on the ability of the sub-borrower to provide mortgages and other security. This is particularly important in lending to small farmers, especially tenant farmers and others who have no land to mortgage. The reluctance of many credit institutions to move far enough in this direction is still a major constraint in channeling Bank financing to small farmers, although there is no evidence that the average repayment record of small farmers is any worse than that of larger farmers.

Similarly, the Bank has stressed the need for credit institutions to adopt terms of lending (down payments, grace periods and repayment periods) appropriate to the investments being financed and the financial condition of the potential sub-borrower. Interest rates are frequently subsidized by governments in order to reduce the debt-servicing burdens of the poor farmer. However, because access to institutional credit facilities is frequently limited by collateral requirements as well as by local vested interests, it is usually the wealthier farmers who benefit from such subsidies. The poor farmer is left to the mercy of the moneylender and the exorbitant terms he imposes. For these reasons, the Bank has paid increasing attention to the adoption of realistic interest rate structures and other terms of lending.

Livestock

For the most part, Bank lending in support of livestock development has taken the form of specialized credit programs, although other forms have also been used. Such lending has risen from an annual average of $500,000 (1% of Bank Group lending for agriculture) in the period FY1948-63 to $91 million (22%) in FY1969-71[1]. The rise principally reflects the good export prospects for beef.

Within the overall trend, certain other trends are discernible. Although meat export remains a major objective, a growing number of projects are designed principally to meet local demand.

The scope of livestock projects is being steadily widened. Most of the early projects involved existing private ranch operations in the temperate zones, almost exclusively for beef cattle and sheep. But more recent projects have moved increasingly into: tropical and semi-tropical zones[2]; pigs and poultry for local consumption (often to replace beef, as the price of the latter has risen with the increase in export demand); livestock operations as part of mixed farming operations, including smallholder participation[3]; dairy operations producing for local consumption, usually also involving dairy-beef; secondary industries such as slaughter-houses and meat-packing plants[4]; and state-owned ranching operations in some African countries where this form of organization is preferred by governments and where privately owned ranching has not been established.

Various institutional forms have been tried to bring these developments to the smaller producer. The institutional forms include the establishment of group ranching based on an existing tribal structure, cooperative ranching and ranch corporations owned by smallholders.

In all livestock operations financed by the Bank, the essential elements have been improved management, the transfer of appropriate technology (particularly grassland improvement), training of local technical service cadres, the strengthening of local administering organizations and the application of sound economic and financial lending policies by credit institutions.

Integrated Smallholder Development

Smallholder development frequently takes place within projects for regional rural development, irrigation and settlement. Sometimes

---

[1] These figures, for the most part, are included in the global figures for the credit component of Bank lending mentioned in the sub-section on "Agricultural Credit" above.

[2] This move into tropical and semi-tropical zones has been made practical by the development of new techniques, particularly improved animal health control, use of tropical legumes for pasture improvement and upbreeding of local cattle with improved cattle which are less susceptible to disease and insects.

[3] Beef-fattening and milk production have been found to be practical for smallholder operation (as opposed to breeding, which usually demands larger herds, especially under marginal range land conditions), although milk production by smallholders demands an effective extension service and marketing infrastructure.

[4] In view of stiffer sanitary regulations in the main importing countries, increasing amounts of beef exports are in the form of precooked meats and almost all beef exports now have to be bone-out.

44

it is possible to assist smallholders through the provision of credit alone. But in most cases—especially in Africa—smallholder development has to be of an integrated nature. In other words, it has to provide for such items as technical advice and marketing facilities (including roads), as well as credit for on-farm development and input purchase. Such integrated smallholder development programs are relatively recent (dating mainly from the early 1960's); and patterns of organization and management are not well established in many countries.

The Bank's lending has, therefore, involved a large degree of innovation. While some trends are beginning to emerge, not enough is known yet about smallholder motivation in different environments to make any firm judgments. It is likely that the period of innovation will continue for some time, and will be increasingly based on the applied economic research sponsored by the Bank and the work of the proposed Rural Development Unit[1]. Existing tenurial arrangements may create substantial difficulties in smallholder development. The Bank has, therefore, found it necessary at times to insist on cadastral surveys, and increased permanency in usufruct and/or tenure rights, before financial support is provided.

Two principal strategies of integrated smallholder development have emerged. The first concentrates attention on a specific cash crop of high potential as a focal point for rural development. An example is the Kenya smallholder tea project which provided credit and extension services for smallholders scattered throughout the tea-growing zones, together with complementary tea-processing factories and access roads. For many cash crops, however, the application of this strategy is limited by market prospects, even if particular projects are successful and the climate and soils are suitable over wide areas.

The second strategy is to concentrate attention on the overall development of a specific geographical area which has a high potential and is of manageable size. The activities supported include production both for subsistence and for a marketable surplus, and such aspects as soil conservation, local marketing facilities for food surpluses, input supplies, roads and social services. Recent examples of such a strategy are the Lilongwe and Karonga projects in Malawi, the Wolamo project in Ethiopia and the Casamance project in Senegal.

The principal danger in this strategy is that too many scarce resources, particularly of trained manpower, may be concentrated on a small area. It may become difficult to apply the strategy on a large scale later because of budgetary and manpower constraints. Thus there is a continuing attempt to determine the minimum package of inputs and services which can make a substantial impact on a

[1]See pages 60-61.

large number of widely distributed smallholders farming under varying conditions.

Within both strategies, it is advantageous for small farmers to group together in some way to obtain economies of scale in procuring inputs and marketing their produce. This end has been achieved in a variety of ways in accordance with local traditions and outlook, but no definitive trend has been established. In certain cases, commercial or state-owned estates have formed nuclei for smallholder development, providing smallholders with essential services. In other cases, the service cooperative has been the favored solution. Where cooperatives are unpopular, possibly because of earlier failures, or where they are still in their infancy, semi-autonomous state agencies have sometimes been found to work well. One of the keys to success in all these organizational forms is the quality of the management.

Land Settlement

The settlement of new lands has been supported by the Bank whenever appropriate opportunities have arisen. However, there are not many parts of the world with large areas of suitable and unexploited land. The settlement of new lands has high priority, therefore, only in some countries.

The trend within settlement projects financed by the Bank has been towards reducing the "public" input and relying more on the settlers' own efforts. Otherwise, in countries where the principal initial purpose of settlement is to provide large numbers of families with at least a subsistence income, public budgetary constraints would severely restrict the number of settlers that could be accommodated. Recent settlement projects (e.g., in Colombia, Papua/New Guinea, and Tanzania) thus concentrate on the provision of low-cost access roads, technical advisory services and credit for on-farm development, and construction of drinking water sources.

Estates, Seed Production and Forestry

Some countries continue to seek Bank finance for private and public sector tree crop estates. A start has been made in a small way with the financing of integrated projects covering seed multiplication, processing and marketing. This field of activity should become important as the benefits of modern agriculture are spread more widely.

Another sub-sector which has so far received little Bank lending, but which is expected to grow in importance, is forestry (though forest industries have been extensively helped within the industrial context)[1]. The demand prospects for forest products are favorable.

[1]See Annex 12.

Bank involvement, however, is being restricted at present by inappropriate forest development policies in many countries where viable forest projects have been identified. For example, the need to conserve forest resources may be interpreted as a need to restrict exploitation absolutely, rather than as a need for rational exploitation and resource management through selective cutting and replanting.

A further constraint is that the development periods for forest projects are usually very long. However, new varieties of fast-growing species of tropical woods, particularly pines and eucalypts, are suitable for pulp, paper and chipboard industries and provide a promising base for future projects.

Agricultural Industries

The demand for agriculture-related industries, such as food processing and fertilizer production, is growing. In the case of smaller projects, the most appropriate way of channeling Bank Group funds to such industries is usually through intermediate industrial financing institutions in the borrowers' countries. In the case of the larger projects, such as fertilizer plants, the most appropriate way may be to make industrial, rather than agricultural, loans. Recent Bank Group industrial investments of this type are summarized in Annex 12.

Lending for certain other types of agriculture-related industries is more appropriately handled within the context of general agricultural lending. Projects of this type include private and public-sector grain storage operations, the provision of public wholesale grain markets and the expansion and improvement of grain and feed milling facilities, and crop processing, especially as part of integrated schemes for production, processing and marketing.

Other projects for agricultural industries which have recently been financed—and which possibly point to future trends—involve fresh fruits and vegetables. In such projects it is necessary to integrate investments in on-farm production, sorting and packing facilities and transportation (particularly refrigerated trucks and ships). The amount of such lending has so far been very small; it has averaged about $18 million per annum over the three years FY1969-71, and represents about 4% of total agricultural lending during this period. But it is tending to rise, particularly since marketable surpluses of grains in Asia and elsewhere are increasing.

Fisheries

Although fisheries projects so far account for a very small part of the Bank's agricultural lending—about $24 million since FY1964, representing about 1% of total agricultural lending—support for the development of fisheries is growing and some trends are discernible. The earliest projects involved relatively large and sophisticated operations based on tuna fish for export. But the scope for further lending of this type is limited by the very competitive nature of the industry.

More recent projects have concentrated on smaller-sized operations, based principally on shrimp (mainly for export) and food fish (mainly for local consumption). Expansion of Bank lending for the latter is hampered, however, by difficulties in ensuring the repayment of credits granted to small fishermen in this high-risk industry. Another trend is towards making projects more comprehensive by including shore facilities (wharves, boat repair, ice-making and processing facilities) and technical assistance, as well as the supply of boats and fishing gear. The Bank is currently working on its first project involving fresh-water fish farming, a sub-sector which may be expected to grow in importance.

Training and Research

The widening scope of projects is evident in the tendency to include elements of training and applied research whenever necessary. Moreover, as the importance of these elements has been increasingly recognized, agricultural education, training and research have featured more prominently in the Bank's education lending[1]. The Bank has recently made its first loan exclusively for agricultural research activities (to Spain, at the end of FY1971). Several other countries have meanwhile approached the Bank for technical advice on the formulation of national agricultural research projects.

The need to strengthen the international agricultural research program has been discussed in the earlier section entitled "Challenges Facing Agriculture." To assist in meeting this need, the Bank has taken the lead in co-sponsoring, along with FAO and UNDP, the Consultative Group on International Agricultural Research in order to mobilize finance to continue and expand the work of existing international research centers and to establish new ones. The Bank provides the Secretariat of the Consultative Group. For technical advice, the Consultative Group has established a Technical Advisory Committee (TAC) consisting of 12 distinguished scientists; the Secretariat of the Committee is located in FAO.

Within this context, the Bank is contributing to the financial requirements in 1972 of three centers. The first two are the already existing Centro Internacional de Mejoramiento de Maiz y Trigo

[1]See page 38.

(CIMMYT)[1], located in Mexico, and the Centro Internacional de Papas (CIP)[2], located in Peru. The third center—the International Crops Research Institute for the Semi-Arid Tropics (ICRISAT)—is currently being established; it will be located in India.

Geographical Distribution of Lending

There have been some trends in the geographical distribution of agricultural lending. These are indicated in detail in Annex 11 and are summarized below:

	FY1948-63				FY1964-68				FY1969-71			
	Operations		Amount		Operations		Amount		Operations		Amount	
Area	No.	%	$ million	%	No.	%	$ million	%	No.	%	$ million	%
Sub-Sahara Africa	7	10	60	9	8	17	44	7	32	33	153	12
Asia and Pacific	21	30	255	41	16	35	295	49	35	37	588	48
Europe and Australia	15	21	176	29	—	—	—	—	6	6	119	10
Middle East and North Africa	4	5	42	6	5	11	52	9	4	4	116	10
Central and South America	24	34	95	15	17	37	209	35	19	20	250	20
Totals	71	100	628	100	46	100	600	100	96	100	1,226	100
Average Amount per Operation ($ million)		8.8				13.1				12.8		

Comparisons between FY1948-63 and later periods are distorted by lending in the former period to countries which no longer receive Bank financing. But comparing FY1964-68 with FY1969-71, the share of agricultural lending to Sub-Sahara Africa increased from about 7% to about 12%. Agricultural lending to Southern Europe was resumed in the latter period after a total absence in the former. The share of agricultural lending to Asia, the Middle East and North Africa remained about the same in the two periods, although all these regions showed increases in absolute amounts. On the other hand, the share of lending to Central and South America declined from about 35% to about 20%. This decline is wholly attributable to the South America region, which alone shows a fall in absolute lending for agriculture between FY1964-68 and FY1969-71. The fall partly

[1]International Center for Maize and Wheat Improvement.
[2]International Potato Center.

reflects expanded agricultural lending by the Inter-American Development Bank.

The average size of agricultural loans increased substantially from $8.8 million in FY1948-63 to $13.1 million in FY1964-68, but fell marginally to about $12.8 million in FY1969-71. There are substantial variations by region and sub-sector (see Annex 13). Thus, lending to Sub-Sahara Africa has averaged only $5 million per operation, while most other regions average $10-20 million. The low average for Sub-Sahara Africa reflects the small size of individual countries, the relatively recent introduction of the concept of agricultural investment projects and the relatively small capital investments required for the technologies being introduced. Thus the region's share (33%) of the total number of agricultural projects processed by the Bank is almost three times as high as its share of amounts committed (12%).

Since Bank staff time absorbed by an agricultural lending operation is largely independent of the amount lent, Sub-Sahara Africa's large share of the number of agricultural projects reflects a similar large share of Bank staff time which, in recent years, has about equalled that devoted to Asia. This fact contrasts sharply with the relative population of the two areas (240 million and 980 million, respectively, the latter excluding Japan, Mainland China and Oceania). As another indication of contrast, each man-year of Bank staff time devoted to agricultural project appraisal in FY1969-71 led, on average, to $3.4 million of lending and to assisting some 10,000 farmers in Sub-Sahara Africa; whereas for Asia the figures were $12 million and 40,000 farmers, respectively. This reflects the effort the Bank is making to serve the smaller and poorer countries among its membership.

Technical Assistance and Project Preparation

The technical assistance provided by the Bank for agriculture has increased with the volume of lending, although there has been a conscious attempt to avoid competition with other sources of such assistance. Previously, technical assistance for agriculture was confined largely to broad advice on planning and organization, as part either of general survey missions or of special agricultural missions sent in response to specific requests from borrowers. As the emphasis on agriculture increased, the need to assist developing countries in the identification, preparation and implementation of projects became more apparent.

The establishment of the FAO/IBRD Cooperative Program in 1964 and the posting of permanent missions in Eastern and Western Africa were specific responses to the need for assistance in project identification and preparation. Resident missions in India, Pakistan and

Colombia were also, at least in part, engaged in similar activities, and the resident mission in Indonesia has given particular emphasis to project identification and preparation work. A further trend has been to support project-connected technical assistance—project management, applied research and further project preparation—under loans or credits, in cases where UNDP has been unable to finance it.

In addition, in the course of loan supervision, the Bank has offered advice not only on implementing the project in question, but also on developing new projects. In relatively few cases is the Bank the executing agency for UNDP agricultural projects (e.g., the Yaque del Norte irrigation project in the Dominican Republic, the Khanabad irrigation project and the agricultural credit project in Afghanistan, and the Indonesian Sugar Survey). Nearly always, UNDP looks to FAO as the executing agency for its agricultural projects. In some cases, the Bank has made technical assistance grants for feasibility studies (e.g., for the Jengka Triangle project development in Malaysia).

On UNDP pre-investment projects which are likely to be of interest to the Bank, and for which FAO is the executing agency, there is close collaboration between the three agencies. The Bank comments on the terms of reference and plans of operations for UNDP projects, and makes its views known to FAO during the course of project execution. The proposals emerging from these pre-investment projects thus tend to have a better focus on investment content and implementation plans when they become ready for appraisal.

Activities such as these have made it possible to assist in identifying and preparing promising investment opportunities in sufficient numbers to meet the needs of the Bank's projected agricultural lending program. But "numbers" alone are not enough; there is also the need for improvement in "quality." This is particularly so if projects are to be selected not only because they increase production, but also because they help broader development objectives such as employment creation and income distribution.

One difficulty is that many developing countries do not have a clear and specific set of development objectives against which a potential project's impact can be measured. The inadequacies of their planning organizations also sometimes mean that too many policy matters are left to the agencies providing the project preparation assistance. Within the Bank, a principal handicap is that it needs greater in-depth knowledge of the agricultural sectors of its borrowers, and of the development policies affecting them, than it presently has. Partly for this reason, the Bank has recently instituted a series of in-depth agricultural sector survey missions[1].

[1]See "Agricultural Sector Analysis," page 63.

The Bank has undertaken several major studies in the agricultural field. These include the Special Study of the Water and Power Resources of West Pakistan, the East Pakistan Agriculture and Water Development Program, a Study of African Agriculture, the Gezira Study in the Sudan, an agriculture and irrigation related manpower survey in Morocco, an agricultural credit study in Malaysia, a review of the Master Plan for Medjerda Basin Development in Tunisia and a review of the programs of Colombia's agrarian reform agency, INCORA. The Bank participated in the study of Nigerian Agriculture sponsored by the U.S. Agency for International Development (USAID), and later developed the blueprint for a federal agricultural credit system.

The Bank has also become involved in direct assistance to its borrowers for project management. In lending for agriculture, the weakness of project management often requires the establishment of new public project authorities supported by foreign expertise to manage the project until such time as local staff can be trained to take over. In providing this assistance, great care has to be exercised so as not to stifle local initiative and to ensure that the management training is carried out effectively.

To assist in meeting this problem, the Bank established the Agricultural Development Service (ADS) in East Africa in 1965 to provide a corps of project managers to help governments in the execution of projects. In addition, a number of project managers have been recruited, especially for livestock projects in Latin America, Africa and Europe—through direct hire by the borrowers, through arrangements with UNDP or the Organization of American States (in the Western Hemisphere), under bilateral aid or, as a last resort, as seconded personnel from the Bank.

Through its Economic Development Institute (EDI), the Bank has been helping governments to improve the capacity of their staff to undertake project analyses in the agricultural and other sectors. The EDI offers courses for qualified officials in developing countries, both in Washington and overseas. The number of courses offered each year is increasing, with a higher proportion conducted overseas and/or in languages other than English.

Thus, the EDI has scheduled seven Agricultural Project Courses in FY1973, more than in any previous year. They will be conducted in English, French and Spanish, and four of them will be overseas. Increasingly, the EDI expects to focus its efforts on helping member-countries to develop their own capacity to teach project analysis. For this purpose, it expects more of its efforts to be directed towards cooperation with local and regional institutions. The preparation of

52

teaching materials based on Bank experience for circulation outside the EDI will also assume greater importance.

Since 1964, the contribution made by FAO to the Bank's activities has expanded considerably, particularly in relation to technical assistance. The FAO/IBRD Cooperative Program came into being in mid-1964 with a team of 12 men in Rome. By December 1971, the number had grown to 52. The team is multi-disciplinary, consisting of agriculturalists, irrigation specialists, economists and others working together on project problems.

Most of the work under the Cooperative Program has been concerned with the identification and preparation of projects to be financed by the Bank. At present, FAO staff are participating in some phase of project preparation in the case of about 40% of the projects in the Bank's agricultural pipeline; they are also providing assistance in the preparation of agricultural education projects. The Bank has also called on FAO increasingly to participate in country economic missions and in the appraisal and supervision of projects.

Economic Research Activities

The Bank's economic research activities have two principal aims: to establish a factual or conceptual basis for policy, and to provide general support to operations in the sector. A brief account of the economic research relating to agriculture which is in progress illustrates the current focus. A study is being made of the effects on employment and productivity of the use of tractors in India; this results from the Bank's initial projects to finance mechanization there. Irrigation rehabilitation projects in Mexico have been re-appraised. Similar re-evaluations of two irrigation projects in India and a credit project in West Pakistan are in progress. The farmers' response to new varieties of rice is being investigated in Bangladesh.

A study of rural development in East Africa is being prepared. It will be closely linked with the in-depth agricultural sector surveys that are being carried out in a number of countries and with reviews of a number of ongoing projects. The aim is to improve understanding of smallholder motivation and rural development generally, and to assist in determining the minimum package which may be needed in the future for smallholder development projects covering a wider area.

Other studies which are being conducted or prepared and which are closely related to the Bank's role in rural development include: a study in India of substitution between labor and capital in road-building; a likely extension of this study to the construction of irrigation works; studies of village electrification and water supply; an evaluation of existing experience in non-formal education for rural development; and the construction of programming models of the agricultural sectors of Mexico, Brazil and Portugal.

Some of these studies simply explore the opportunities for raising the productivity of familiar types of agricultural projects—by learning from the experience of past investments and by seeking to improve the theory and practice of measuring project costs and benefits. There is also an "entrepreneurial" aspect—in exploring opportunities for the Bank to support new types of projects. Outside of this formal part of its economic research program, the Bank is endeavoring to expand its research-oriented program of monitoring project performance. So far, a systematic data-gathering and evaluation procedure has been built into only a few projects, such as the livestock projects in Mexico, Uganda and Uruguay and the Kadana irrigation scheme in India.

So much agricultural economic research of relevance to developing countries is undertaken throughout the world that a good deal of attention is devoted within the Bank to reviewing and interpreting studies conducted elsewhere. This is an increasingly important source of new ideas for development policy.

The content of the Bank's own research program is determined by very specific policy needs or by the advantages of working with its own data. Nevertheless, much of it is conducted outside. For example, the Indian mechanization study referred to above is being carried out by two local universities, and many of the other studies are conducted with the help of consultants or cooperating agencies in the developing countries. The Bank has arranged with the FAO/IBRD Cooperative Program for a pilot study of the employment and income distribution effects of the Muda irrigation project in Malaysia, which includes substantial farm mechanization (including private farm machinery pools providing services to small farmers).

Impact of the Bank's Activities

Although Bank lending has been increasing rapidly, it still represents only about 1-2% of the total investment (domestic and foreign) in agriculture in developing countries[1]. The impact of the lending is, however, greater than might be implied by such figures. This is because the capital transfer is in the form of foreign exchange provided on relatively favorable terms (particularly in the case of IDA credits).

---

[1]The basis for this estimate is given at the beginning of the next section entitled "The Bank Group's Future Role."

Furthermore, the Bank carefully considers the development value and appropriate design of the projects it finances.

The overall impact thus extends beyond the capital transfer. For example, the Bank has helped in the introduction or extension of better technologies and in the improvement and strengthening of institutions. Projects have led to improvements not only in farming practices, but frequently also in government policies.

Some ways in which the Bank's agricultural project work has had an impact far beyond the project being financed are indicated below:

(a) introduction or expansion of new techniques such as in the livestock industry[1], bulk handling of grains, improved water control in irrigation schemes, land levelling, low cost settlement methods; and detailed consideration of the appropriate technology (hand versus mechanical methods of forest clearing; pros and cons of on-farm mechanization);

(b) institution building (particularly agricultural credit institutions, agencies handling smallholder development projects, cooperatives and marketing boards); the strengthening of management; and improved coordination between the various entities involved in agricultural development (particularly those responsible for construction and agricultural development in irrigation projects);

(c) improvements in credit policies[2], and the adjustment of interest rates to reflect the scarcity of capital, thereby encouraging labor-intensive rather than capital-intensive methods of production, and promoting resource mobilization through increased savings;

(d) greater attention to particular aspects of project preparation which are frequently neglected (the effects of irrigation on various types of soils, land classification and drainage; fisheries resource estimation; marketing infrastructure and institutions; crop quality control standards);

(e) changes in taxation and other fiscal measures such as water charges (price distortions in the economy may be preventing the development of a particular activity which would be economically advantageous or may be encouraging an activity which is not, as discussed in the earlier section on "Some Major Policy Issues"); and

(f) introduction of project monitoring systems, so that both borrowers and the Bank can learn more from their experience.

---

[1]See pages 43-44.
[2]See page 43.

To a considerable degree, the Bank's influence for change depends on the extent to which it is supported by the sort of detailed knowledge that comes from sector surveys and project activities. Such sector surveys are a fairly recent development, but are scheduled to be expanded greatly in the coming years[1].

Because the data are lacking, it is difficult to estimate the likely impact on employment and income distribution of any but the most recent Bank investments in agriculture. But these aspects are now being regularly investigated during the identification, preparation and appraisal of projects. An analysis can, however, be made of the numbers of farm families directly benefited by Bank agricultural investments over the past three years (FY1969-71) and the average investment per farm. A list of the projects involved, with the pertinent data, is presented in Annex 14.

In approximately 73 of these projects, it was possible to estimate the numbers of farms that could be expected to benefit—about 2 million farms in all, involving a population of about 10 million. The average investment per farm was about $1,100, of which the Bank financed about half. However, the average investment per farm varied widely from one project to another. It ranged from a low of $24 in Niger and $50 in Burundi, to a high of about $120,000 in one case in Iran. A more detailed breakdown is given in Annex 15.

Roughly 80% of all the farms involved were assisted by projects where the average investment per farm was less than the overall average of $1,100. This indicates that a large number of "small" farms benefited from such projects. On the other hand, over 80% of the total investment and over 70% of the operations involved projects in which the average investment per farm was above the overall average of $1,100. Less than 1% of the participating farms benefited from projects where the average investment per farm exceeded $21,000. This category accounted for about 20% of Bank support (in terms of both total project costs and the number of operations). The remaining 80% went to projects in which the average investment per farm was in the range of $20 to $21,000.

The skewed nature of the distribution of the investments implied by these figures reflects the generally skewed distribution of farm sizes referred to in the earlier section entitled "Some Major Policy Issues." It also reflects the ability of the operators of larger farms to undertake investments efficiently, whereas the operators of small farms are usually in greater need of short-term input financing and technical assistance which is being provided under a number of bilateral programs.

---

[1]See sub-section on "Agricultural Sector Analysis" below.

THE BANK GROUP'S FUTURE ROLE

Agricultural investment in most developing countries will continue to receive high priority. The financing of agricultural projects can thus be a useful way of increasing transfers of capital. However, bilateral lending for agricultural projects is comparatively small. There is thus a substantial role to be played by the multilateral aid agencies such as the Bank.

Over the period FY1974-78, the Bank's agricultural lending program is projected at about $4,400 million (compared with $2,400 million in FY1969-73 and $600 million in FY1964-68). This section considers the lending program in the perspective of the total investment in agriculture in the developing countries and of the other agricultural project aid (bilateral and multilateral) likely to be available. It also discusses what the future trends in the content of the Bank's agricultural lending program are likely to be, in the light of the discussions in the preceding sections, and the need for the Bank to improve its agricultural sector analyses.

Overall Agricultural Investment and Capital Transfers

No systematic attempt has been made to estimate the financial resources needed to maintain the momentum gained as a result of the "green revolution." However, some orders of magnitude can be derived on the assumption that present ratios between agricultural investment and agricultural GNP will continue to hold true.

In the 30 developing countries for which the Bank has relevant data, it appears that this ratio averages about 9%[1]. The figure compares with the 7% contained in FAO's Indicative World Plan, which FAO suggests should be a sufficient ratio to sustain a growth in agricultural output of 4% per annum. Agricultural GNP is projected to grow at about 5% per annum in current prices, or from about $100,000-110,000 million in 1969 to about $140,000-155,000 million in 1976. This implies that overall investment in agriculture in developing countries, which may have been of the order of $7,000-10,000 million in 1969, should increase to about $10,000-14,000 million by the mid-1970's.

---

[1] The figure of 9% is used in this paper for want of a better one. The results derived from it (i.e., the estimates of agricultural investment in the developing countries) should be treated with caution. Firstly, the data on investments in the 30 countries are often probably unreliable and, in any case, refer only to a single year. Secondly, the ratio for individual countries varies widely around the average 9% figure, from less than 1% to almost 50%; and only 12 of these individual country ratios lie within the range 6-12%. Thus, it is possible that widening the statistical base to more countries would substantially alter the result.

In comparison with the total agricultural investment in developing countries, the external assistance provided by developed countries and multilateral institutions such as the Bank Group for agricultural projects has been small. Commitments of such assistance for the period 1966 through 1970 appear to have averaged about $630 million annually. Of these, about $220 million have been in the form of bilateral assistance from DAC member countries[1], $170 million from the regional development banks—the Inter-American Development Bank (IADB) and the Asian Development Bank (AsDB)—and $240 million from the World Bank[2].

The trend in bilateral capital assistance for agriculture has recently been downward (it has fallen from $245 million in 1966 to $160 million in 1969); but there was a considerable rise in 1970 to some $300 million. The regional development banks are generally increasing their commitments to agriculture. IADB's commitments reached $236 million in 1970, although they fell sharply to $93 million in 1971. AsDB's commitments started at $24 million in 1969, rose to $31 million in 1970 and then declined to $28 million in 1971.

The rapid increase in the World Bank's commitments has already been noted[3]. In FY1971 they were about $420 million, representing about 40% of the current annual level of such commitments of about $1,000 million from all sources. Considering that, with a rapidly increasing rate of commitments, disbursements lag considerably behind commitments, the World Bank's contribution to overall agricultural investment in the developing countries at present is probably of the order of 1-2%.

Future trends in bilateral capital assistance for agricultural projects are difficult to foresee. Although recently such assistance has been declining, there are indications that some DAC member countries intend to reverse the trend in the future, as evidenced by the recovery in 1970. If the need for food aid decreases as the "green revolution" spreads, donor countries may have to consider increasing their direct project assistance for agriculture.

---

[1]In addition, bilateral food aid is currently running at about $1,500 million per annum; a substantial proportion of the technical assistance (also running at about $1,500 million per annum) is directed to the agricultural sector; some project aid which was for unspecified purposes at the time of commitment ($235 million in 1969) undoubtedly went to agricultural projects in practice; and aid to finance current imports ($884 million in 1969), general purpose loans ($164 million in 1969) and budget support ($260 million in 1969) can generally be expected to involve the agricultural sector to some extent.

[2]Agricultural investments by the European Development Fund (FED) are not included in these computations.

[3]In the section on "Past Bank Group Activities in Agriculture."

However, one constraint may be that the foreign exchange component of agricultural projects is generally low. Another may be that it will take time for the donor countries to build the staff required to appraise agricultural projects. The future trend in agricultural lending by the regional development banks is also difficult to determine, although it seems likely to be upward, perhaps reaching a level of about $350-450 million by the mid-1970's.

Thus the scope for expanding the World Bank's lending in the 1970's is clear. It is proposed to raise the annual rate of such lending from the target of around $500 million for about 40 projects in FY1972 to about $750-850 million for about 60 projects by the mid-1970's and to about $1,000 million for about 70 projects by 1978. This means that the Bank Group's share of external assistance for agricultural projects would probably rise to around 50% by the mid-1970's, assuming that bilateral aid can be raised to about $350-450 million per annum[1].

The World Bank is thus expected to remain the main external source of agricultural project financing. Its contribution to the overall investment in agriculture in developing countries would still be relatively small, but would rise from the present 1-2% to about 4-5%. Part of the increase would result from the fact that the lag in disbursements is expected to be less as the rate of growth of new commitments slows down.

Recent experience indicates that sufficient promising agricultural projects will be identified and prepared as a basis for the Bank's projected agricultural lending program. The various sources of project preparation assistance are now well geared up to this task although more manpower will be needed to achieve the targets, to improve the quality of preparation and to equip the sources of preparation to handle increasingly complex and comprehensive projects, including non-agricultural rural development components.

This situation, which is an improvement over the position in the early 1960's when the lack of prepared projects constrained very much the expansion of agricultural lending, has been brought about in large measure by the establishment of the FAO/IBRD Cooperative Program, the work of the Bank's overseas missions and the provisions for preparation of follow-up projects in loans and credits, which have been described earlier. Other factors contributing to this improvement have been the closer collaboration between the Bank and FAO on UNDP pre-investment studies in the field of agriculture, the in-

---

[1]Even if bilateral capital project assistance remains at the pre-1970 level of about $150-250 million, the Bank Group's share would remain below 60% of total official capital project assistance to agriculture.

59

creasing capabilities of local institutions and consulting firms to carry out project preparation and continuous bilateral technical assistance for project investigation.

The Direction of Future Lending

The direction of the Bank's future lending for agriculture will reflect the progress made in resolving many of the fundamental questions raised earlier in this paper about agriculture's role in the overall development process.

For example, will the agricultural products of the developing countries be given better access to markets in the developed countries? How might protein deficiencies in many traditional and low-income diets be avoided? What constitutes the essential minimum of factors necessary to stimulate broad-based rural development, taking into account the widely varying stages of development reached by different developing countries? Can appropriate intermediate technologies be devised which will make use of abundant supplies of unskilled labor without sacrificing the overall rates of growth which are fundamental to development? What are the trade-offs, if any, between economic growth and more equal distribution of incomes?

In the developing countries, changes in government policies will affect agricultural investment plans, and the direction of Bank support for such plans. Removal or reduction of price distortions could stimulate agricultural development and affect the form it takes. Of fundamental importance will be the attitudes of governments on agrarian reforms generally and on the priority to be given to programs to assist small farmers in particular. The Bank will continue to invest in projects supporting economically sound agrarian reform programs (including land reform, where appropriate), although it does not participate in the financing of land transfers.

At a time when ideas, technologies and socio-economic priorities are changing rapidly, it is essential that the Bank maintain a flexible attitude in its agricultural lending policies and keep abreast of changes. This paper has already referred to the Bank's support for research in agricultural technologies and agricultural economics. The need for improved knowledge of the agricultural policies of borrowers is discussed below[1].

The Bank has recently established contacts with, and provided budgetary support for, the UN Protein Advisory Group. Within the

---

[1] See "Agricultural Sector Analysis."

Bank, a Rural Development Unit is being set up; it will concern itself with all aspects of rural development with a view to identifying agriculture's changing role in the urban-rural polarization as it occurs at different stages of development. The work of this group will have a strong operational bias, and should assist the Bank in giving greater emphasis to the small farm sector.

Project Content

In view of all these factors, it is difficult to predict the longer-term trends in the project content of the Bank's agricultural lending program. But in the shorter term, many of the trends that have become apparent in recent lending may be expected to continue. These include:

(a) a continuing expansion in the scope of projects to cover all investments required to achieve general development objectives in the rural areas concerned;

(b) consistent with governments' ability to provide adequate resources (particularly of qualified manpower), and building on the substantial experience of recent years, an extension of smallholder development schemes (including settlement of landless people) to support larger numbers of small farmers, providing them with a meaningful incremental income at the lowest possible cost per farm;

(c) an increase in the number of projects aimed at producing food crops, livestock and fish for local consumption;

(d) an increase in the number of projects to handle the expected increases in marketable surpluses of food products (e.g., marketing, processing, storage and transportation projects) as well as the provision of facilities for input distribution and related service industries;

(e) basic irrigation infrastructure lending, potentially supporting productive rural works programs, will probably continue to expand in absolute terms although its share of Bank agricultural lending is likely to decline further as increasing emphasis is placed on on-farm investments and agricultural industries; and

(f) as individual developing countries become increasingly conscious of the need to provide employment opportunities and to distribute incomes more equitably, an increasing emphasis on small farmers and projects designed to be labor-intensive.

Geographical Distribution

The aggregate of the agricultural components of the Bank's current country-by-country operations programs for the period FY1972-76 exceeds by far its capacity to appraise projects over that period. However, no other basis exists at present for analyzing the geographical distribution pattern of future agricultural lending. The data are summarized below in relative terms, compared with two preceding periods:

	FY1964-68		FY1969-71		Projected FY1972-76	
	No. of Projects	Amount	No. of Projects	Amount	No. of Projects	Amount
			(percentage of total)			
Sub-Sahara Africa	17	7	33	12	35	17
Asia and the Pacific*	35	49	37	48	29	39
Europe, Middle East and North Africa	11	9	10	20	15	19
Central and South America	37	35	20	20	21	25
	100	100	100	100	100	100

*The FY1972-76 figures for Asia and the Pacific understate the probable position since they do not include lending to Bangladesh or Pakistan, for which projections are not presently available.

The increased rate of lending is also matched by an increase in the number of countries in which the Bank has made, and is expected to make, agricultural investments:

	Number of Countries		
	FY1964-68	FY1969-71	FY1972-76 (Projected)
Sub-Sahara Africa	5	18	33
Asia and the Pacific	7	9	13
Europe, Middle East and North Africa	3	6	16
Central and South America	12	10	21
	27	43	83

The rapid expansion of agricultural lending in the recent past and that projected for the five years FY1974-78 will further tax the capacity of receiving countries successfully to implement agricultural development projects supported by the Bank. Reference has already been made to the need for the Bank and others to provide assistance for agricultural project management. The Bank's project supervision responsibilities will increase even more rapidly and become more complex as the agricultural portfolio is further diversified both in types of projects and geographical distribution; as larger amounts are committed for projects with significant policy reform, rural development and institution building components; and as training programs associated with agricultural project lending receive increased emphasis and in turn require more attention during their implementation. The effectiveness with which projects are implemented not only determines in large measure the benefits the receiving country will attain, but also the rate at which funds committed will be used. Continued expansion of the Bank's lending for agriculture will thus require greatly increased efforts to meet these responsibilities.

Agricultural Sector Analysis

Although most of the agricultural projects at present in the pipeline have been selected without a systematic analysis of the entire agricultural sector, the judgments of the past have probably not been far wrong. This is partly because the choices were rather obvious and were limited by the lack of well-prepared projects. But while the Bank's appraisal procedures ruled out the financing of projects with low economic returns, the projects selected may not always have ranked highest in terms of sector priorities or development goals such as employment creation. With the projected expansion of lending, it is essential that the Bank should improve its knowledge of the agricultural sector in the countries in which it operates. Greater understanding of the policy framework within which a project would have to be carried out should help also to improve its design and execution.

Until quite recently, the Bank's knowledge of the agricultural sector in a particular country was derived largely from two sources. The first was represented by the contacts established in the process of preparing, appraising and supervising projects (sometimes expanded to include subsector reviews, such as the Uruguayan livestock survey). The second source was the agricultural sector work done in the course of economic missions.

But experience has shown that although project-related sector knowledge can be valuable, its focus seldom extends beyond the subsector in which the project is located. Economic mission work, on the other hand, emphasizes the macro-economic aspects; while it is important in providing guidance on intersectoral priorities, it usually cannot provide the depth of sector analysis that is now required to support agricultural lending on the projected scale.

To improve its sector knowledge, the Bank has to depend increasingly on in-depth sector surveys, conducted by expert staff to cover all major aspects of so diverse a sector as agriculture. Such sector surveys can produce guidelines for future lending, particularly in relation to government policies which affect agriculture. They are expected to have a major impact on the selection of investment priorities (and thus also on the selection of projects for Bank financing). They should also facilitate appraisal work and the preinvestment work done by others.

Ten such sector surveys (covering a variety of countries in Eastern and Western Africa, South Asia, East Asia, Europe and South America) have been carried out. One more is scheduled for FY1972 (making five in all for that year). The first five surveys have recently been completed through the stage where the findings have been discussed with governments. Another two reports have been prepared and are scheduled for discussion in FY1972. The remaining three reports are under preparation. The completed sector surveys have clearly helped to identify priorities and further steps in project preparation, and have been well received by governments.

In one case, the survey report has led to a reorientation of the government's irrigation and rural development strategy for an important but depressed region, and to a higher priority for storage and transportation. In another case, the survey has resulted in an extensive revision of irrigation policies and a renewed interest in reorganization of government services to agriculture. A third country has begun serious attempts to reorganize its agriculture along lines recommended in the sector survey report, and to take steps toward land tax reform and more economical use of available lands.

In the other two cases where the results of the survey have been discussed with governments, a positive contribution has been made to the countries' preparations for forthcoming development plans. In all these cases, there have been continuing discussions between the governments and the Bank on major issues, as well as further project preparation activities, based on the results of the sector surveys. Of course, not all recommendations made by sector survey missions are accepted by governments.

The results of sector survey missions have so far been encouraging. It is proposed to expand coverage to other developing countries as rapidly as possible, taking into account the competing demands on the Bank's staff resources. It is planned that, by FY1975, sector survey missions will be mounted at the rate of ten per annum. At that rate, sector surveys would be completed for the prospective 25 largest agricultural borrowers by FY1975, and for the prospective 35 next largest by FY1980.

Indices of Agricultural Production by Level of Development and by Region

	1948-52 Average	1953-57 Average	1957	1958	1959	1960	1961	1962	1963	1964	1965	1966	1967	1968	1969	1970[1]	Annual Growth Rate 1958/60-1968/70 (Percent)
							(1952-56 average = 100)										
TOTAL PRODUCTION ALL AGRICULTURAL PRODUCTS																	
Developed Countries[2]	89	101	106	114	116	114	114	119	124	124	125	128	133	137	136	136	1.75
Developing Countries	86	103	109	114	118	121	125	129	132	135	138	138	144	148	154	158	2.60
Latin America	87	103	111	117	118	120	128	128	132	134	143	140	148	147	153	158	2.58
Far East[3]	87	103	107	111	117	121	127	128	132	136	134	135	141	148	155	160	2.86
Near East[4]	82	104	115	118	122	124	123	135	137	141	145	148	153	159	163	163	2.91
Africa[5]	85	102	107	110	113	121	116	124	128	132	134	134	138	142	147	148	2.42
FOOD PRODUCTS ONLY																	
Developed Countries[2]	89	101	108	115	117	115	115	120	125	125	127	132	138	142	141	141	2.02
Developing Countries	86	103	109	113	116	120	124	127	131	135	136	137	143	149	154	159	2.84
Latin America	87	103	111	116	114	117	124	126	131	137	141	142	151	152	157	166	3.20
Far East[3]	87	103	107	112	118	123	127	129	132	137	134	135	141	149	156	162	2.84
Near East[4]	82	104	115	118	121	122	123	133	135	137	141	145	150	155	159	159	2.73
Africa[5]	86	102	106	108	111	117	113	121	125	127	128	128	132	137	140	141	2.20
PER CAPITA PRODUCTION ALL AGRICULTURAL PRODUCTS																	
Developed Countries[2]	93	100	102	108	108	106	105	108	111	110	109	111	114	117	115	113	0.69
Developing Countries	94	101	102	103	104	105	106	106	106	106	105	103	104	105	106	106	0.16
Latin America	97	100	103	105	102	102	105	103	103	101	105	100	103	99	100	101	−0.30
Far East[3]	95	101	101	102	104	106	108	107	107	107	103	102	103	106	108	109	−0.35
Near East[4]	91	102	107	106	107	106	103	110	109	109	109	108	109	110	110	107	0.16
Africa[5]	94	100	100	100	101	105	98	103	104	104	103	100	101	101	102	100	−0.09
FOOD PRODUCTS ONLY																	
Developed Countries[2]	93	100	103	109	109	107	105	109	112	111	111	114	119	121	118	117	0.92
Developing Countries	94	101	102	103	103	104	105	105	105	106	104	102	104	105	105	106	0.20
Latin America	97	101	103	104	100	99	102	101	102	103	104	102	105	102	103	105	0.23
Far East[3]	94	101	101	103	106	107	109	107	107	108	104	102	103	107	108	110	0.28
Near East[4]	90	102	107	107	106	105	103	108	107	106	106	106	107	108	107	104	0.03
Africa[5]	94	100	99	98	99	102	96	100	101	100	99	96	97	97	97	95	−0.35

(1) Preliminary estimates (2) Includes Japan, S. Africa and Israel and excludes U.S.S.R. and Eastern Europe (3) Excludes Japan (4) Excludes Israel (5) Excludes S. Africa

Source: *The State of Food and Agriculture, 1971*, (FAO, Rome: 1971)

65

Normal Variations in Economic Structure with Level of Development

Structural Characteristic	Level of GNP per capita (in 1964 US$)				
	$50	$100	$200	$300	$400
	Percent				
Share of GDP of					
Primary production	58	46	36	30	27
Industry	7	13	19	23	25
Services	30	35	38	39	40
Utilities	5	6	7	8	8
Percentage of labor force in					
Primary production	75	68	58	50	44
Industry	4	10	16	21	24
Services and utilities	21	22	26	29	32
Urban population, as % of total population	7	20	34	41	46
Exports of primary products, as % of total exports	89	78	68	61	56

Source: Hollis B. Chenery, "Growth and Structural Change", *Finance and Development,* September 1971.

Agricultural Output per Agricultural Worker and Factors Associated with Differences in Output, 19 Countries, 1960

Country	Agricultural Output per Farm Worker	Total Land per Capita of Total Population	Arable Land per Agricultural Worker	Literacy Rate	Infant Mortality Rate per 1,000	Agricultural Workers per Hectare of Arable Land	Fertilizer Used per Hectare of Arable Land	Urban Population as a Percentage of Total Population	Rank of Country in Miles of Road per 1,000 Sq. Miles of Land Area	Agricultural Output per Hectare of Arable Land	Gross Domestic Product per Capita
	Dollars	Hectares	Hectares	Percent	Number	Number	Kilograms	Percent	Rank	Dollars	Dollars
Group I											
Israel	1,825	0.9	3.3	96	32.0	0.31	80.5	77.3	3	557	905
Argentina	1,080	12.5	13.1	86	59.6	.07	n.a.	67.0	16	78	465
Spain	656	1.6	4.4	87	51.6	.23	31.6	n.a.	7	150	372
Poland	616	1.0	2.4	95	74.7	.41	49.0	48.1	2	252	538
Chile	547	9.1	9.3	80	118.0	.11	17.0	67.2	12	59	405
Colombia	531	7.7	1.9	62	100.0	.51	n.a.	n.a.	18	270	248
Venezuela	500	12.5	3.2	52	64.1	.30	3.8	66.1	17	150	650
Japan	402	0.4	0.4	98	37.7	2.39	303.7	63.5	1	961	337
Greece	391	1.6	1.9	80	41.4	.52	38.0	42.5	5	205	297
Mexico	369	5.6	4.1	65	77.7	.30	9.4	50.7	11	110	321
Average	692	5.3	4.5	79	65.7	0.52	66.6	60.3	9	279	454
Group II											
Egypt	365	3.7	0.6	20	130.1	1.76	87.0	37.7	15	643	155
Turkey	326	2.7	2.6	39	n.a.	.39	1.5	37.8	13	127	254
Yugoslavia	250	1.4	1.8	77	98.5	.57	28.0	n.a.	4	141	179
Brazil	229	11.1	1.4	49	n.a.	.45	13.0	45.1	14	104	145
Taiwan	228	0.3	0.6	54	34.2	2.10	203.8	59.5	6	477	97
Pakistan	182	1.0	1.5	19	n.a.	.73	3.2	n.a.	10	133	64
Philippines	181	1.0	1.2	75	82.6	.77	12.5	42.7	9	139	113
India	114	0.7	1.2	24	145.9	.80	2.3	17.9	8	91	70
Thailand	94	1.9	0.9	68	54.8	1.13	2.3	11.8	19	106	84
Average	222	2.6	1.3	47	91.0	0.97	39.3	36.1	11	218	129

Source: *Changes in Agriculture in 26 Developing Nations, 1948-1963* (U.S. Department of Agriculture, Foreign Agricultural Economic Report No. 27, 1965).

67

Compound Annual Rates of Growth in Total Agricultural Production,
Total Agricultural Population, Agricultural Production per Farm Person,
and Crop Area per Farm Person, 25 Countries, Selected Periods, 1950-68

Country and Region	Total Agricultural Production 1950-68[1]	Total Agricultural Population 1950-65[2]	Agricultural Production per Farm Person	Crop Area per Farm Person
		Percent		
Latin America				
Costa Rica	4.2	2.3	1.9	2.1
Guatemala	5.0	3.4	1.6	— .2
Jamaica	2.7	1.3	1.4	1.6
Mexico	5.1	1.7	3.4	1.4
Panama	3.6	2.1	1.5	.4
Argentina	2.0	1.9	.1	— .8
Brazil	3.8	1.3	2.5	3.1
Colombia	3.3	1.3	2.0	.5
Paraguay	2.4	1.8	.6	n.a.
Uruguay	— .1	.8	— .9	—2.8
Venezuela	5.1	2.1	3.0	1.8
Asia and Africa				
Cyprus	4.9	— .8	5.7	n.a.
Iran	2.7	1.2	1.5	n.a.
Israel	9.3	2.2	7.1	n.a.
Turkey	3.4	2.8	.6	— .6
Ceylon	2.9	1.2	1.7	.3
Indonesia	2.3	1.5	.8	.8
Malaysia	4.1	3.1	1.0	—1.5
Thailand	4.5	2.9	1.6	.6
Egypt	2.4	2.2	.2	—1.2
India	2.6	2.1	.5	— .8
Japan	3.3	—4.5	7.8	3.7
South Korea	3.7	.3	3.4	1.2
Philippines	3.7	2.0	1.7	.7
Taiwan	4.5	2.4	2.1	—1.7

[1] Data cover a shorter period than 1950-68 in some instances.

[2] Estimates based on data from several sources. Data on economically active population in agriculture were used for Ceylon, Costa Rica, Egypt, Indonesia, Malaysia and Thailand.

Source: *Economic Progress of Agriculture in Developing Nations, 1950-1968* (U.S. Department of Agriculture, Economic Research Review, 1970).

Actual and Projected Capacity, Production and Consumption of Fertilizers[1] in Developed and Developing Countries

	1967/68			1972		
	Capacity (1)	Production (2)	Consumption (3)	Gross Capacity[2] (4)	Potential Production[3] (5)	Projected Consumption (6)
	Million metric tons					
Latin America	1.6	0.8	2.1	4.0	2.5	3.5-4.0
West, Central and East Africa	—	—	0.3	0.7	0.6	0.5-0.6
Near East and North Africa	1.7	0.6	1.0	3.5	2.4	1.8-2.0
Far East (excluding Japan)	1.9	1.2	3.5	5.3	3.3	7.0-8.0
of which:						
India	(1.1)	(0.6)	(1.8)	(3.3)	(2.0)	(4.0-4.5)
Pakistan	(0.2)	(0.1)	(0.3)	(0.7)	(0.5)	(0.6-0.8)
Total developing countries	5.2	2.6	6.9	13.5	8.8	13-15
Total developed countries[4]	63.0	53.8	46.1	108.4	78.6	65
World Total	68.2	56.4	53.0	121.9	87.4	78-80

[1] In terms of nutrient content (N, P_2O_5 and K_2O).
[2] Gross capacity includes plants in operation and plants and factories under construction, contracted, or in an advanced stage of planning in 1967/68; for the U.S.S.R., production goals have been used.
[3] Potential production has been derived from gross capacity by taking into account closure of old plants, reduced capacity utilization during the first year of operation of new plants, losses in manufacturing and non-agricultural use of primary plant nutrients.
[4] Including Eastern Europe and the U.S.S.R.
Source: *The State of Food and Agriculture, 1970*, (FAO, Rome: 1970).

Area Devoted to High-Yielding Varieties (HYV) in Relation to Area of All Varieties, 1970/71
(Preliminary; subject to revision)

	Area[1]		Proportion
	HYV	All Varieties	HYV
	—acres—		—percent—
WHEAT			
Afghanistan	574,300	(7,329,500)[3]	(7.8)
Algeria	346,300	7,400,000[2]	4.7
India	14,559,000	44,211,100	32.9
Iran	321,200	10,378,000	3.1
Iraq	309,000	5,023,500	6.2
Jordan	300	543,600	0.1
Lebanon	8,600	150,700	5.7
Morocco	49,400	1,230,600	4.0
Nepal	242,700	(959,000)[3]	(25.3)
Pakistan (E)	24,000	311,000	7.7
Pakistan (W)	7,288,000	14,976,000	48.7
Syria	94,000	930,000	10.1
Tunisia	255,000	1,816,200	14.0
Turkey	1,184,000	20,262,200	5.8
RICE			
Burma	496,300	12,295,000	4.0
Ceylon	73,000	(1,609,000)[3]	(4.5)
India	13,593,000	92,494,500	14.7
Indonesia	2,303,400	20,353,600	11.3
Laos	132,500	(1,900,000)[3]	(7.0)
Malaysia (W)	327,100	1,336,000	24.5
Nepal	167,600	(2,900,000)[3]	(5.8)
Pakistan (E)	1,137,000	24,494,000	3.3
Pakistan (W)	1,548,000	3,715,000	41.7
Philippines	3,868,100	7,691,300	50.3
Thailand	(400,000)[2]	18,779,600	(2.1)
Vietnam (S)	1,240,300	6,423,000	19.3

[1] Excluding Communist Asia.
[2] Particularly rough estimate.
[3] 1969/70 area.
Source: *Imports and Plantings of High-Yielding Varieties of Wheat and Rice in the Less Developed Nations.* By Dana Dalrymple. (Foreign Economic Development Service, U.S. Department of Agriculture in Cooperation with U.S. Agency for International Development, Washington, D.C.)

Medium-Term (1974) Forecast for Cereal Production, Utilization and Net Trade in Selected Developing Countries

	Production			Apparent Domestic Utilization			Net Trade		
	Actual		Forecast	Actual		Forecast	Actual		Forecast
	1965-67 Average	1970(1)	1974	1965-67 Average	1970(1)	1974	1965-67 Average	1970(1)	1974
				Thousand metric tons					
NET IMPORTERS									
Far East									
Ceylon	680	1,064	1,364	1,634	2,054	2,034	+ 954	+ 990	+ 670
China (Taiwan)	2,244	2,295	2,410	2,456	3,529	3,696	+ 212	+ 1,234	+ 1,286
India	68,627	91,309	109,400	77,582	94,454	110,000	+ 8,955	+ 3,145	+ 600
Korea, Republic of	5,937	6,788	7,624	6,598	8,764	9,964	+ 661	+ 1,976	+ 2,340
Malaysia (West)	881	933	1,320	1,532	1,655	1,684	+ 651	+ 722	+ 364
Pakistan	17,557	22,814	26,072	19,025	24,500	26,530	+ 1,468	+ 1,686	+ 458
Total Countries Listed	95,926	125,203	148,190	108,827	134,956	153,908	+12,901	+ 9,753	+ 5,718
Near East									
Iran	5,168	6,358	7,245	5,426	6,707	7,385	+ 258	+ 349	+ 140
Iraq	1,892	2,152	2,940	1,926	2,265	3,190	+ 34	+ 113	+ 250
Egypt	5,782	6,642	8,210	7,908	7,293	9,610	+ 2,126	+ 651	+ 1,400
Total Countries Listed	12,842	15,152	18,395	15,260	16,265	20,185	+ 2,418	+ 1,113	+ 1,790
Latin America									
Brazil	17,355	21,993	23,855	18,958	22,307	23,250	+ 1,603	+ 314	— 605
Chile	1,789	1,771	2,357	2,195	2,251	2,750	+ 406	+ 480	+ 393
Total Countries Listed	19,144	23,764	26,212	21,153	24,558	26,000	+ 2,009	+ 794	— 212
Africa									
Algeria	1,383	1,598	2,172	1,920	2,057	2,735	+ 537	+ 459	+ 563
Ghana	527	487	573	638	624	689	+ 111	+ 137	+ 116
Morocco	2,779	4,301	4,519	3,354	4,287	4,902	+ 575	— 14	+ 383
Senegal	663	672	952	898	951	1,342	+ 235	+ 279	+ 390
Tunisia	524	655	515	786	1,228	1,202	+ 262	+ 573	+ 687
Total Countries Listed	5,876	7,713	8,731	7,596	9,147	10,870	+ 1,720	+ 1,434	+ 2,139
Grand Total	133,788	171,832	201,528	152,836	184,926	210,963	+19,048	+13,094	+ 9,435
NET EXPORTERS									
Argentina	16,781	19,166	25,750	7,407	9,287	13,285	— 9,374	— 9,879	—12,465
Mexico	12,276	14,150	17,780	10,727	13,366	16,480	— 1,549	— 784	— 1,300
Thailand	8,713	10,368	12,215	6,020	7,828	8,605	— 2,693	— 2,540	— 3,610
Total Countries Listed	37,770	43,684	55,745	24,154	30,481	38,370	—13,616	—13,203	—17,375

Source: *The State of Food and Agriculture, 1971,* (FAO, Rome: 1971).

NOTE: Net imports are indicated by a (+) sign; net exports by a (—) sign.
(1) Preliminary estimates

70

**Share of Agricultural Primary Products in Export Earnings
of Selected Developing Countries, Average 1967-69**

Country	Total Export Earnings	Share of Agricultural Products[1]
	(US$ million)	(percent)
I. Over 80%		
Ethiopia	106.7	99.1
Ceylon	327.6	98.8
Turkey	518.0	90.7
Uganda	186.7	90.4
Argentina	1,481.5	87.6
Ghana	295.4	83.9
Brazil	1,948.8	82.4
Morocco	453.1	81.7
II. 50-80%		
Thailand	680.7	78.3
Colombia	525.3	77.8
Tanzania	223.6	76.6
Kenya	162.2	75.3
Philippines	890.7	73.3
Mexico	1,277.6	66.0
Malaysia	1,111.9	60.0
Nigeria	713.4	58.8
Tunisia	157.6	53.4
III. 30-50%		
Pakistan	682.2	47.8
Singapore	1,320.1	45.6
Peru	833.8	45.0
Spain	1,621.8	41.7
India	1,758.0	38.0
China (Taiwan)	826.8	33.8
Indonesia	717.9	31.2
Yugoslavia	1,330.1	30.1

[1] SITC 0, 1, 2 (—28), 4.
Source: *Yearbook of International Trade Statistics, 1969* (United Nations).

Indices of Value of Agricultural Exports and Imports, by Level of Development

	1955	1956	1957	1958	1959	1960	1961	1962	1963	1964	1965	1966	1967	1968	1969	1970[1]
								(1957-59 Average = 100)								
Exports																
Developed countries[2]	84	95	106	94	100	110	118	119	136	153	151	159	158	156	164	191
Developing countries	102	102	102	98	100	102	101	102	111	117	118	116	111	114	119	130
Latin America	104	106	105	99	96	99	100	103	112	121	125	123	117	127	128	143
Far East[3]	108	101	101	93	106	109	103	102	112	111	109	106	101	100	103	108
Near East[4]	95	101	110	91	99	102	96	101	113	114	123	127	123	129	135	138
Africa[5]	94	95	96	104	100	100	100	99	107	119	113	113	108	116	117	136
Imports																
Developed countries[2]	95	100	99	97	104	107	110	116	118	119	124	130	129	134	137	142
Developing countries	83	91	100	98	102	116	120	122	129	138	144	154	162	163	154	—
Latin America	101	91	99	102	99	103	108	115	125	140	136	147	144	153	145	—
Far East[3]	74	90	103	98	98	121	117	117	133	143	145	158	173	169	165	185
Near East[4]	77	87	95	94	111	124	137	138	141	149	169	171	174	173	155	—
Africa[5]	87	97	100	95	105	119	131	128	112	116	131	136	151	151	140	—

[1] Preliminary estimates
[2] Includes Japan, Israel and South Africa and excludes U.S.S.R. and Eastern Europe
[3] Excludes Japan and Mainland China
[4] Excludes Israel
[5] Excludes South Africa
Source: *The State of Food and Agriculture, 1971,* (FAO, Rome: 1971)

**Composition of Agricultural Export Earnings
of Developing Countries, 1955-70**

	Competing Products[1]			Non-Competing Products[2]	Total
	Basic Foods	Raw Materials	Sub-Total		
			(percent)		
1955	36.5	31.2	67.7	32.3	100.0
1960-62 (average)	43.0	29.5	72.5	27.5	100.0
1965-67 (average)	47.1	26.2	73.3	26.7	100.0
1970[3]	50.5	23.5	74.0	26.0	100.0

[1] Agricultural commodities produced in direct competition by both developed and developing countries. In the case of agricultural raw materials (e.g., cotton, rubber, hides and skins), the competition taken into account includes that between natural products and synthetic substitutes also.

[2] Coffee, cocoa, tea, bananas, spices, etc.

[3] Estimates.

Source: *The State of Food and Agriculture, 1970,* p. 178, (FAO, Rome: 1970)

Bank and IDA Lending for Agriculture by Area and Subsector for Various Periods
(Amounts in US$ million)

	Irrigation, Drainage, Flood Control		Livestock		Credit		Storage, Processing, Marketing	
	Number	Amount	Number	Amount	Number	Amount	Number	Amount
FY1948-63								
Eastern Africa	3	48.0	—	—	—	—	—	—
Western Africa	—	—	—	—	—	—	—	—
East Asia & Pacific	7	55.4	—	—	—	—	—	—
South Asia	11	182.5	—	—	—	—	—	—
Europe & Australia	—	—	—	—	—	—	—	—
Middle East & North Africa	3	38.0	—	—	—	—	1	3.9
Central America & Caribbean	3	27.5	—	—	—	—	2	.8
South America	1	18.0	1	7.0	3	15.0	—	—
Totals	28	369.4	1	7.0	3	15.0	3	4.7
% of totals	39.4	58.8	1.4	1.1	4.2	2.4	4.2	0.8
FY1964-68								
Eastern Africa	—	—	—	—	2	8.6	—	—
Western Africa	—	—	—	—	—	—	—	—
East Asia & Pacific	4	103.0	—	—	1	5.0	—	—
South Asia	5	103.0	—	—	2	37.0	1	19.2
Europe & Australia	—	—	—	—	—	—	—	—
Middle East & North Africa	—	—	—	—	5	51.5	—	—
Central America & Caribbean	2	44.0	—	—	2	28.0	—	—
South America	2	15.5	9	101.8	1	15.0	—	—
Totals	13	265.5	9	101.8	13	145.1	1	19.2
% of totals	28.3	44.2	19.6	16.9	28.3	24.1	2.1	3.2
FY1969-71								
Eastern Africa	1	5.0	5	13.2	—	—	—	—
Western Africa	—	—	—	—	2	10.1	—	—
East Asia & Pacific	5	117.0	1	7.0	1	12.5	2	21.8
South Asia	8	143.2	—	—	8	188.4	1	6.0
Europe & Australia	2	52.0	3	42.2	—	—	1	25.0
Middle East & North Africa	3	96.0	—	—	1	20.0	—	—
Central America & Caribbean	1	5.0	6	153.8	1	3.7	—	—
South America	—	—	8	56.9	1	17.0	—	—
Totals	20	418.2	23	273.1	14	251.7	4	52.8
% of totals	20.8	34.1	24.0	22.3	14.6	20.5	4.2	4.3
FY1948-71								
Eastern Africa	4	53.0	5	13.2	2	8.6	—	—
Western Africa	—	—	—	—	2	10.1	—	—
East Asia & Pacific	16	275.4	1	7.0	2	17.5	2	21.8
South Asia	24	428.7	—	—	10	225.4	2	25.2
Europe & Australia	2	52.0	3	42.2	—	—	1	25.0
Middle East & North Africa	6	134.0	—	—	6	71.5	1	3.9
Central America & Caribbean	6	76.5	6	153.8	3	31.7	2	.8
South America	3	33.5	18	165.7	5	47.0	—	—
Totals	61	1,053.1	33	381.9	30	411.8	8	76.7
% of totals	28.6	42.9	15.5	15.6	14.1	16.8	3.8	3.1

General Agriculture		Forestry		Fishery		Total		
Number	Amount	Number	Amount	Number	Amount	Number	Amount	% of total
4	12.2	—	—	—	—	7	60.2	9.4
—	—	—	—	—	—	—	—	—
—	—	—	—	—	—	7	55.4	8.7
3	17.1	—	—	—	—	14	199.6	32.2
12	170.2	3	5.8	—	—	15	176.0	28.6
—	—	—	—	—	—	4	41.9	6.5
6	9.0	—	—	—	—	11	37.3	5.8
8	17.8	—	—	—	—	13	57.8	8.9
33	226.3	3	5.8	—	—	71	628.2	100
46.5	36.0	4.2	0.9	—	—	100	100	
5	18.0	—	—	—	—	7	26.6	4.4
1	18.0	—	—	—	—	1	18.0	3.0
1	14.0	—	—	2	13.7	8	135.7	22.6
—	—	—	—	—	—	8	159.2	26.5
—	—	—	—	—	—	—	—	—
—	—	—	—	—	—	5	51.5	8.6
1	5.0	—	—	—	—	5	77.0	12.8
—	—	—	—	—	—	12	132.3	22.0
8	55.0	—	—	2	13.7	46	600.3	100
17.4	9.2	—	—	9.2	2.3	100	100	
9	44.4	2	7.9	—	—	17	70.5	5.7
12	71.1	—	—	1	1.3	15	82.5	6.7
6	67.5	1	8.5	1	3.5	17	237.8	19.5
1	13.0	—	—	—	—	18	350.6	28.6
—	—	—	—	—	—	6	119.2	9.7
—	—	—	—	—	—	4	116.0	9.5
—	—	—	—	—	—	8	162.5	13.3
1	8.1	—	—	1	5.3	11	87.3	7.1
29	204.1	3	16.4	3	10.1	96	1,226.4	100
30.2	16.6	3.1	1.3	3.1	0.8	100	100	
18	74.6	2	7.9	—	—	31	157.3	6.4
13	89.1	—	—	1	1.3	16	100.5	4.1
7	81.5	1	8.5	3	17.2	32	428.9	17.5
4	30.1	—	—	—	—	40	709.4	28.9
12	170.2	3	5.8	—	—	21	295.2	12.0
—	—	—	—	—	—	13	209.4	8.5
7	14.0	—	—	—	—	24	276.8	11.3
9	25.9	—	—	1	5.3	36	277.4	11.3
70	485.4	6	22.2	5	23.8	213	2,454.9	100
32.9	19.8	2.8	0.9	2.3	1.0	100	100	

Bank Group Investments in Agriculture-Related Industries [1]

	Direct Investments By		Investments Channelled Through Local Industrial Development Banks [2]
	Bank/IDA	IFC	
		(US$ million)	
Subsector			
Agricultural Production	—	—	5
Food Processing and Beverages	34	25	34
Textile Manufacturing	13	19	113
Tobacco Processing	—	—	7
Leather and Leather Goods	—	—	2
Wood-based Industries	173	60	32
Rubber Products	—	—	11
Sub-total	220	104	204
Fertilizer, Pesticides and other Chemicals	117	53	6
Farm Machinery	2	—	2
Miscellaneous Products for Agricultural Use	—	—	1
Sub-total	119	53	9
Grand Total	339	157	213

[1] Those industries based on locally-produced agricultural raw materials or supplying local agriculture; through FY1971.

[2] FY1968-71 only.

**Average Size of Agricultural Project by Area and
Subsector over Various Periods**
(US$ million)

	FY1948-63	FY1964-68	FY1969-71	FY1948-71
A. By Subsector				
Irrigation, Drainage and Flood Control	13.2	20.4	20.9	17.3
Livestock	7.0	11.0	11.9	11.6
Credit	5.0	11.2	18.0	13.7
Storage, Processing and Marketing	1.5	19.0	13.2	9.6
General Agriculture	6.8	7.0	7.0	6.9
Forestry	2.0	—	5.5	3.7
Fisheries	—	6.8	3.4	4.8
B. By Area				
Eastern Africa	8.6	3.8	4.1	5.1
Western Africa	—	18.0[1]	5.5	6.3
East Asia and Pacific	7.9	17.0	14.0	13.4
South Asia	14.3	19.9	19.5	17.7
Europe and Australia	11.7	—	19.9	14.1
Middle East and North Africa	10.5	10.3	29.0	16.1
Central America and Caribbean	3.4	15.4	20.3	11.5
South America	4.4	11.0	7.9	7.7
C. Overall Average	8.8	13.1	12.8	11.5

[1] A single project.

Loans and Credits for Agriculture, FY1969-71[1]
Total Cost and Number of Participating Farms

		Loan or Credit		Total Project Cost	Number of Participating Farms[3]
		Number	Amount[2]		
			($ million)	($ million)	
FY1969					
Ecuador	Fisheries	555	5.3	6.6	—
Sudan	Mechanized Farming	556	5.0	8.0	140
Guyana	Sea Walls	559	5.0	7.5	—
Zambia	Forestry	562	5.3	11.1	—
Senegal	Agriculture Credit	584/140	6.0	24.1	90,000
Malagasy	Livestock	585	2.8	4.2	—
Turkey	Seyhan Irrigation	587/143	24.0	63.0	4,800
Cameroon	Oil Palm	593	7.9	14.1	900
Iran	Dez Irrigation	594	30.0	74.3	3,700
Korea	Irrigation	600	45.0	89.9	50,000
Philippines	Agriculture Credit	607	12.5	25.0	6,500
Mexico	Livestock and Credit	610	65.0	200.0	4,600
Ivory Coast	Oil Palm	611/12/13	17.1	29.1	5,500
India	Seeds	614	13.0	22.4	400
Paraguay	Livestock	620/156	8.6	15.5	450
Colombia	Agriculture Credit	624	17.0	42.5	2,500
Zambia	Livestock	627	2.5	5.8	—
Indonesia	Irrigation Rehabilitation	127	5.0	8.8	110,000
Kenya	Livestock	129	3.6	11.4	—
Uganda	Livestock	130	3.0	5.1	56
Tanzania	Livestock	132	1.3	2.0	—
Pakistan	Consultants	136	2.0	6.6	—
Papua New Guinea	Agriculture Development	137	1.5	3.3	580
Dahomey	Oil Palm	144	4.6	9.6	4,000
Burundi	Coffee Smallholders	147	1.8	2.1	44,000
Indonesia	Estates I	155	16.0	32.0	—
Pakistan	ADB III	157	30.0	47.7	18,000
FY1970					
Spain	Livestock	633	25.0	52.0	1,050
Philippines	Irrigation	637	34.0	67.5	17,000
Kenya	Forestry	641	2.6	4.0	—
Morocco	Sebou Irrigation	643	46.0	109.5	15,000
Colombia	Livestock	651	18.3	44.1	970
Ceylon	Mahaweli Irrigation	653/174	18.7	50.0	40,000
Iran	ADFI Credit	662	6.5	16.0	131
Malaysia	Jengka II	672	13.0	28.6	3,000
Malaysia	Forestry	673	8.5	12.4	1,200
Zambia	Commercial Farming	685	5.5	11.1	300
Ivory Coast	Cocoa	686	7.5	13.6	22,400
Uruguay	Livestock	698	6.3	13.1	1,000
Ghana	Fisheries	163	1.3	2.3	—
Ceylon	Drainage	168	2.5	4.1	10,000
Ethiopia	Wolamo Agriculture Dev.	169	3.5	5.1	7,050
Bolivia	Livestock	171	1.4	2.3	110
Ecuador	Livestock	173	1.5	2.5	60
Papua New Guinea	Agriculture Development	175	5.0	8.8	1,020
India	Irrigation	176	35.0	66.7	176,000
Honduras	Livestock	179	2.6	5.2	135
Egypt	Drainage	181	26.0	147.0	250,000
Pakistan	Irrigation	184	13.0	22.7	60,000
Ethiopia	Agriculture Development	188	3.1	4.4	—
India	Gujarat Credit	191	35.0	67.0	26,840

		Loan or Credit		Total Project Cost	Number of Participating Farms[3]
		Number	Amount[2]		
			($ million)	($ million)	
Indonesia	Estates II	194	17.0	31.7	—
Indonesia	Irrigation Rehab. II	195	18.5	37.0	372,000
Afghanistan	Agriculture Credit	202	5.0	7.2	7,000
India	Punjab Credit	203	27.5	40.0	8,000
Ghana	Cocoa	205	8.5	15.6	5,000
Niger	Agriculture Credit	207	0.6	0.9	25,000
Pakistan	Tubewells	208	14.0	45.0	45,000
Pakistan	Irrig. Engineering	S-8	0.8	1.4	—
FY1971					
Israel	Agriculture Credit	709	20.0	49.0	7,000
Jamaica	Agriculture Credit	719	3.7	8.0	140
Philippines	Rice Processing	720	14.3	21.0	—
Guatemala	Livestock	722	4.0	7.8	300
Colombia	Caqueta Land Settlement	739	8.1	21.6	6,300
Mexico	Livestock III	747	75.0	192.5	10,900
Greece	Groundwater Development	754	25.0	50.0	6,000
Ivory Coast	Palm Oil and Coconuts	759/760	7.0	17.6	2,300
Turkey	Fruit and Vegetables	762/257	25.0	44.0	4,500
Nigeria	Western State Cocoa	764	7.2	11.6	8,000
Spain	Personnel and Training	768	12.7	28.2	—
Uruguay	Livestock III Supplement	773	4.0	21.4	3,000
Indonesia	Fisheries	211	3.5	4.3	—
Uganda	Tobacco	212	4.0	7.3	6,000
Malagasy	Alaotra Irrigation	214	5.0	8.2	2,900
Tanzania	Tobacco	217	9.0	14.7	15,000
Indonesia	Irrigation Rehab. III	220	14.5	29.1	260,000
Guyana	Livestock	221	2.2	4.4	—
Ecuador	Livestock III	222	10.0	19.7	575
Upper Volta	Cotton	225	6.2	9.4	46,000
India	Andhra Pradesh Credit	226	24.4	45.0	40,000
India	Agro-aviation	230	6.0	8.8	—
Korea	Livestock	234	7.0	12.6	700
Turkey	Livestock	236	4.5	7.5	300
Mauritius	Tea Development	239	5.2	7.0	3,730
Malawi	Lilongwe II	244	7.3	8.6	52,000
Dominican Republic	Livestock	245	5.0	9.0	260
Afghanistan	Khanabad Irrigation	248	5.0	6.0	6,000
India	Haryana Credit	249	25.0	44.5	20,000
India	Tamil Nadu Credit	250	35.0	62.3	50,000
Senegal	Casamance Rice	252	3.7	4.8	5,000
Senegal	Terres Neuves	254	1.4	1.6	550
Indonesia	Tea	259	15.0	24.9	—
Bolivia	Livestock	261	6.8	11.0	3,000
Indonesia	Seeds	246	7.5	12.0	—

[1] Excludes a multipurpose project in Yugoslavia and a supplemental loan for the Tarbela Dam, Pakistan.

[2] Net of cancellations.

[3] Where no number is given, the concept of "participating farms" is not applicable to the project.

Number of projects: 94

Total cost: $2,500 million

Bank and IDA financing: $1,200 million

Number of participating farmers: 2 million (in 73 projects costing $2,300 million, involving $1,100 million of Bank and IDA financing).

Distribution of Project Investment and Numbers of Participating
Farms by Size of Project Investment per Farm[1]

(For those 73 projects listed in Annex 14 for which the concept of "participating farms" is applicable.)

A. Distribution of Project Investment

Amount of project investment in approximate 20% groupings, ranked by project investment per farm. ($ million)	PROJECT INVESTMENTS PER FARM AVERAGE $	RANGE $	NUMBER OF PARTICIPATING FARMS	NUMBER OF PROJECTS
436.2	43,721	20,910-122,140	9,977	17
468.5	15,513	9,780- 20,080	30,200	9
482.4	5,729	3,430- 9,530	84,200	14
467.3	1,699	1,120- 3,120	275,020	14
456.6	285	20- 1,030	1,602,450	19
(All projects) 2,311.0	1,154	20-122,140	2,001,847	73

B. Distribution of Numbers of Participating Farms

Numbers of participating farms in approximate 20% groupings, ranked by project investment per farm.	PROJECT INVESTMENTS PER FARM AVERAGE $	RANGE $	AMOUNT OF PROJECT INVESTMENT ($ million)	NUMBER OF PROJECTS
399,397	4,643	1,120-122,140	1,854.4	54
367,450	674	410- 1,030	247.5	9
372,000	330	200- 380	122.9	4
312,000	121	110- 160	37.7	2
551,000	88	20- 100	48.5	4
(All projects) 2,001,847	1,154	20-122,140	2,311.0	73

[1] Project investment per farm is defined as the total investment in a project, divided by the number of farms participating in it. The data thus ignore the distributional pattern of investment per farm within individual projects.

Summary of World Bank's Activities in Agriculture, with Projections through FY1976

	Actual			Program		Actual[1]		Program
	1969	1970	1971	1972	1973	1964-68	1969-73	1972-76
Sector Surveys	—	3	3	5	7	—	18	41[2]
Commitments (US$ million)	366	414	446	510	690	600	2,400	3,630
% of Total Bank and IDA	21	19	18	18	24	12	20	22
Number of Countries	24	23	27	35	40	28	74	83
Lending Operations (No.)	28	32	36	42	53	46	190	273
% of Total Bank and IDA	25	27	28	29	32	17	28	32
Projects under Supervision at End of Fiscal Year	87	103	120	141	170	40[3]	124[3]	189[3]

[1] Including scheduled for FY1972-73.

[2] Includes 5 repeat missions.

[3] Annual average over period.

INDUSTRY

Annexes

INDUSTRY
SECTOR WORKING PAPER

● The first part of this paper reviews the stage of industrialization now reached in developing countries, examines the lessons of experience, and explores the principal obstacles such countries are likely to face in advancing their industrial development in the 1970s. It then considers some social aspects of industrial development, and concludes with a brief survey of strategies and policies.

The second part begins with a review of past Bank Group financing of manufacturing industry, with particular emphasis on the period FY1967-71. Projected Bank Group operations in manufacturing for FY1972-76 are then discussed. A final section examines the main tasks and issues faced by the World Bank Group as it extends its capability for assisting industrial development.

The term World Bank Group as used in this paper refers to the International Bank for Reconstruction and Development (World Bank), the International Development Association (IDA) and the International Finance Corporation (IFC). Money amounts are in U.S. dollar equivalents. The Bank's fiscal year (FY) ends June 30.

INDUSTRIALIZATION AND DEVELOPMENT

Industrialization is a key factor in the economic development of most countries. It offers prospects of a growing availability of manufactured goods, increased employment, improved balance of payments, and greater efficiency and modernization throughout the economy. Industrialization is characterized by technological innovation, the development of managerial and entrepreneurial talent, and improvements in technical skills, which lead to rising productivity. Improvements in living standards create a growing and highly elastic demand for manufactured goods. Consequently, industry does not face the same market constraints which affect agriculture, and presents the prospects of a more rapid rate of growth than might otherwise be possible. When promoted along efficient lines, industrialization holds out the possibility of easing balance of payments problems through import substitution and the diversification of exports.

The extent to which industrialization fulfills these expectations and contributes to economic development depends on the strategies and policies which countries pursue. If industrialization is given excessive incentives and is not integrated with overall economic development, it may hinder rather than stimulate economic growth.

Industrialization is not necessarily synonymous with economic growth, nor can it be expected to propel a nation from technological obsolescence to material prosperity and full employment overnight. Such expectations can lead only to disappointment. Industrialization, like other aspects of development, is a slow and complex process.

The impetus to industrialization in today's developing countries stems from the difficulties of colonial and semi-colonial countries in the 1920s, when terms of trade for primary products began to deteriorate and employment problems were experienced in some countries.

The depression indelibly underlined these difficulties, and World War II added new ones by cutting off many predominantly agricultural countries from supplies of manufactured products. The prices of manufactures began to rise in the late 1940s and, after the boom engendered by the Korean War, the terms of trade seemed once again to be turning against primary products. At the same time, development demands aggravated balance of payments problems, and the per capita income gap between agricultural and industrialized countries appeared to be widening.

In many cases, balance of payments pressures led to the emergence of import and exchange restrictions, and to a protected market for local industry. In general, industrialization was easiest with respect to products for which a market had already been created by imports. Import substitution with high protection thus became the principal industrialization strategy. It was frequently supported by various credit and fiscal incentives, as well as protective tariffs.

Such incentives were designed primarily to attract the foreign investment sought by many countries. Governments not only supported industrialization, but sought to control its course to ensure that the available resources were used to their countries' best advantage. This often led to complex restrictions on entry into industry, directly and through the control of imports of capital goods and other industrial inputs.

Social implications of industrialization, such as the structure of ownership and levels of employment, were largely ignored. Japan and Hong Kong, with their emphasis on production for exports, were virtually the only exceptions to the import replacement trend until the 1960s, when a number of other developing countries—notably the Republic of China, Republic of Korea, Singapore and Israel—

began to concentrate on industrialization via export markets. Many more countries are now seeking to re-orient their industrialization efforts to include exports. The employment and income distribution aspects of industrialization are also receiving more attention in many countries.

Stages of Industrialization

Developing countries have had a great variety of experience in industrialization, depending upon population size, natural resource endowments and geographical location, as well as upon the strategies they have pursued. In discussing their present situation and experience, it is convenient to classify countries according to their levels of industrial development.

One approximate measure of this is the proportion of gross value added in manufacturing to gross value added in commodity[1] production. The classification of countries used here and in Annex 1 is based primarily on this approach, although adjustments are made in the case of some countries with large internal markets or other special characteristics.

In this classification, countries with less than 20% manufacturing in total commodity production are defined as "non-industrial," those with 20% to 40% are regarded as "industrializing," those with 40% to 60% as "semi-industrialized," and those with more than 60% as "industrialized."

An adjustment has been made for large countries such as India, Nigeria and Pakistan, where the internal market is large enough for industry to be relatively highly developed although its contribution to total commodity production is still low. Conversely, in certain other countries, e.g., Argentina, Israel, Mexico and Portugal, the classification takes into account the fact that the relatively high estimated proportion of manufacturing (61%) reflects in part the effect of protection in raising prices in the manufacturing sector.

It should be emphasized that these stages of industrialization blend into each other and are significant only in an illustrative sense. The various levels of industrialization are not necessarily indicative of the level of overall economic development. The degree of export orientation and other characteristics, such as the relative importance of heavy as against light industry, also vary as countries move to higher levels of per capita income and industrialization.

---

[1]For purposes of this classification, "commodities" are taken to mean the products of agriculture, mining and manufacturing, and of utilities producing power, gas and water.

"Non-Industrial" Countries

These are countries which are still taking their first steps towards industrialization. Principal opportunities in the early stages usually lie in import replacement in the least technically complicated branches of industry or those based on domestic natural resources. Consequently the incipient manufacturing sector in these countries is engaged mainly in the import substitution of non-durable consumer goods, such as processed foods and leather products, or in the production of simple producer goods such as cement.

These first steps in the industrialization process are very difficult, as such economies are generally deficient in the basic skills and entrepreneurship which industry demands. Many countries at this stage are tempted to use high protection to accelerate their industrial growth, but this usually leads to inefficient development. Since most manufacturing consists of simple processing activities, even low rates of protection for the final product can result in extremely high protection on a value added basis. Costs are raised in other sectors and economic growth can be slowed down.

Most "non-industrial" countries follow the traditional pattern, depending for most of their foreign exchange earnings on specialization in primary exports. In general, new industries oriented toward the export market can develop a comparative advantage only after skills and entrepreneurship have been acquired through production for the domestic market.

"Industrializing" Countries

These are countries that have made considerable advance in the production of consumer goods. They are moving from assembly operations to manufacturing proper, and into import substitution in intermediate goods such as packaging and construction materials and, to some extent, even in capital goods (e.g., pumps, agricultural implements, etc.). Skills and entrepreneurship are being acquired through domestic production, but the injection of intricate technology and capital intensiveness, and the need for economies of scale in production, make this a more complex stage of industrial development.

Many "industrializing" countries have experienced difficulties in making the transition from the simple consumer goods import substitution stage. Frequently, balance of payments difficulties have aggravated these problems, especially where industrial protection has tended to raise costs of primary production, restricting export growth.

Countries with large internal markets can frequently achieve economies of scale and improved efficiency in industry through production for the domestic market, and thus move to an advanced stage of industrialization. Brazil and Mexico are examples. Those with relatively small markets face greater difficulties. Some that have rich natural resources may be able to specialize in primary exports and move to higher levels of per capita income; Malaysia is in this category.

Small countries which lack primary natural resources, however, are forced to adopt a deliberate export-oriented industrial strategy at an early stage of their development in order to ensure sustained growth and overcome their balance of payments difficulties; this pattern was followed by Hong Kong and Singapore.

In general, all "industrializing" countries, large and small, stand to gain by putting greater emphasis on outward-looking industrial policies which promote internal efficiency and keep the manufacturing sector in line with the outside world. Outward-looking policies do not mean mere emphasis on exports; import substitution if efficiently carried out can be equally "outward-looking." Several developing countries which initially relied on a policy of import substitution have begun to move into the export field. Pakistan began to encourage exports from the mid-1960s; others such as Iran and Cost Rica have begun to look in this direction and have already had a measure of success.

"Semi-Industrialized" Countries

These are countries in which the manufacturing base has been deepened and diversified from assembly and finishing operations to the production, in varying degrees, of most product groups, including capital goods. Basically, most of them have continued to be oriented toward import substitution as they have deepened industrial production into more sophisticated intermediate and capital goods, and this has often involved a distortion in the allocation of their resources. Recently, however, a number of countries such as Brazil, Colombia, India and Mexico have begun to stress exports of manufactures.

Rates of industrial growth in "semi-industrialized" countries have generally ranged from six to eight percent. In some cases industry has stagnated, unable to overcome the difficulties of low productivity and high costs, with their limiting effect on the demand for industrial goods. Greater efficiency and export orientation are issues of major concern for most "semi-industrialized" countries, but the export of manufactures on any substantial scale normally requires a reorientation of policy, including changes in the structure of protection and export incentives.

Among the relatively more industrialized developing countries are some, such as the Republic of China, Singapore and the Republic of Korea, which were forced into manufactured exports because of a lack of primary resources and limited domestic markets. There is much to be learned, however, from their industrialization experience.

They based their industrialization efforts initially on products that benefited most from low labor costs and required limited amounts of capital and technology. For example, they were able to become bases for the assembly of electronic components for large international corporations. Since then Singapore, and to a lesser extent the Republic of China, have been able to move to more capital-intensive export products with a higher skill content. Israel adopted this strategy from the start. These small industry-oriented countries enjoyed relatively high rates of industrial output and employment growth during the 1960s.

It should be noted, however, that even an export-oriented industrialization strategy can encounter difficulties if unaccompanied by balanced development of other economic sectors. Aside from the possibility of market restrictions in the developed countries against the importation of manufactured goods, such a strategy can inhibit the growth of agriculture and rural incomes and hence the development of domestic markets for manufactures. These are problems now being faced in the Republic of Korea.

"Industrialized" Countries

These are mostly developed countries which have attained high levels of productivity and where industry makes a large contribution to production, exports and employment. Some developing countries, such as Mexico, are approaching the "industrialized" category, although they still have a relatively low level of per capita income.

The policy framework in "industrialized" countries varies from the relatively strong inward orientation of countries like Australia and the United States to emphasis, as in the small Scandinavian countries, on the achievement of high productivity through specialization in production and liberal trade policies. Japan is a rather special case; it has relied on import substitution behind high trade barriers as the basis for achieving a relatively high level of productivity and export orientation.

The emphasis to be given to industrialization in development strategy, and the resources to be allocated for this purpose, are generally a function of the stage of economic development. Over the last two decades, manufacturing industry has been the most rapidly growing major sector in the developing countries, and its contribution to overall growth has increased with its rising share of the Gross National Product (GNP)[1].

---

[1] Despite this growth, manufacturing remains concentrated in the developed countries. The share of developing countries in total manufacturing production of today's World Bank members (7% to 8%) did not change over the period 1937-1967.

A number of developing countries have built up relatively broad and diversified industrial sectors. Some, such as Brazil, the Republic of China, Colombia, Iran and the Republic of Korea, have made rapid progress in industrialization, beginning virtually from a "non-industrial" stage. In still others, such as Spain, India and Yugoslavia, which after World War II could have been characterized as "industrializing," the manufacturing sector has grown greatly in size and sophistication as they have advanced to "semi-industrialized" status.

Many of the "semi-industrialized" and "industrializing" countries have already made large strides in infrastructure development. Industrialization now holds out for them the promise of rapid gains in domestic production to meet their changing demand patterns; in the progressive injection of modern technology into their economies; and, most critically, in the availability of foreign exchange through exports of manufactured goods to meet the increasing import requirements of their further economic development. Industrialization in the 1970s has become a central issue of development policy for important segments of the developing world.

Obstacles to Industrialization

Countries seeking to increase their rate of industrial growth are faced with various economic and non-economic obstacles. These vary from country to country. Some general patterns of constraint are evident, however, which are broadly related to the levels of industrial development:

- **Shortage of Skilled Labor, Management, Entrepreneurship**

For developing countries, and in particular for the "non-industrial" countries, a lack of skills is frequently the greatest obstacle to industrial development. A serious shortage of skilled and even semi-skilled labor is commonly experienced simultaneously with a superabundance of unskilled labor. There is also usually a critical shortage of entrepreneurship, so that manufacturing opportunities often fail to be recognized and exploited. To resolve this problem, a variety of approaches have been tried and are possible.

Local development banks can undertake promotional activity to assist medium and large scale industries. Specialized organizations are required to assist small scale industries in matters of finance, technology, management and accounting.

Direct foreign investment can also effect an important transfer of management skills and technology, especially through joint ventures. It may also be feasible in many cases to acquire such know-how under contractural arrangements, especially if they provide profit sharing incentives for the sources of technical and management skills.

At times, governments have intervened directly in industry to ensure that important industrial projects are not neglected when private initiative is not forthcoming. These are typically large or complex projects, or those in which the social rate of return appears to be much greater than the private return. Assistance from governments is frequently important in the area of technical education and training, to help overcome manpower deficiencies in industry. The key elements of entrepreneurial and management skills may be fostered by the promotion of business schools and management institutes.

- **Shortage of Capital Resources**

Capital resources are generally insufficient in developing countries, and there are difficulties in mobilizing them for industrial investment. Foreign investment can often make a significant contribution to resource availability, but domestic savings finance by far the largest share of industrial investment in developing countries. As countries industrialize, the shortage of capital tends to become less severe because of capital accumulaton within the industrial sector. This frequently occurs, however, only at the cost of an excessive concentration of wealth and power.

The pursuit of rapid industrial growth together with a broad distribution of industrial ownership requires, among other things, the development of local financial institutions and money and capital markets. The "non-industrial" countries need the establishment and spread of commercial and development banks, and other financial institutions which concentrate on the mobilization of savings.

As the use of financial assets grows in the economy and a more diversified industrial base emerges, creating a demand for specialized financial services, more sophisticated types of financial intermediaries dealing in short and long term securities may be needed. Foreign investment can often make an important contribution in this specialized field.

- **Inadequate Domestic Markets**

Developing countries beginning to industrialize generally have limited domestic markets. Without exceptional entrepreneurial resources and sufficient incentives, their industries do not attempt to break into export markets. Small markets lead to low levels of production and a conflict between the need for an efficient scale of production and internal competition, and often result in low efficiency and high prices.

Countries at low levels of industrial development can do much to avoid such difficulties by selecting an industry mix which will avoid high cost industries. This usually means emphasizing mass consumption goods such as food products, textiles and building materials, rather than luxury and semi-luxury consumer durables. Fostering efficiency in the production of such articles, so that they may be sold at low prices which the bulk of the population can afford, helps to create broad and expanding markets.

The multiplier effects of incomes generated in the production of these articles will further expand consumption, employment and incomes. As countries become more industrialized and develop an efficient industrial base, their industries can more readily enter export markets and thus begin to break out of market and scale constraints.

• Balance of Payments Difficulties

The need to combine export production with efficient import substitution is underlined by the balance of payments difficulties confronted by most developing countries. Often a policy of import substitution fails to reduce the volume of imports, but leads instead to a change in their composition from manufactured consumer goods to intermediate products and raw materials. Furthermore, the resulting dependence of domestic industries upon the availability of imported inputs makes it much more difficult for the authorities to control the balance of payments without adversely affecting industrial plant utilization and employment.

An import substitution strategy without regard to internal efficiency also has a detrimental effect on exports because of the resultant higher costs of protected local inputs, often accompanied by increasingly over-valued currencies. As already noted, there have been exceptions; a number of "industrializing" and "semi-industrialized" countries have devised incentives which make exports as profitable as domestic sales, and sometimes even more so.

Although most countries, especially those in the "industrializing" and "semi-industrialized" groups, are now keenly aware of the advantages of giving an outward orientation to their industry, including greater emphasis on exports, the obstacles to achieving this are formidable. It frequently requires a reorientation of policies and changes in the structure of the economy which are strongly opposed by vested interests.

• Limited Access to Markets

In addition, the extent to which any new policies can generate exports will depend importantly on access to markets in the industrial nations. The system of protection in the developed countries tends to discriminate against imports of manufactures from the developing countries, which bear higher tariffs, on the average, than manufactures traded among the developed countries themselves. Moreover, tariffs tend to rise with the degree of fabrication, discouraging imports of food and raw materials in processed form.

Non-tariff barriers to trade have also been introduced by developed countries with increasing frequency in recent years. Restrictions on market access are reflected in a variety of administrative and fiscal measures including quotas, subsidies, valuation techniques and preferential buying arrangements under government procurement.

Despite these obstacles, the growth in exports of manufactures from developing countries has been rapid in recent years; they increased at an annual rate of about 15% during the period 1962-69. Nevertheless, the share of developing countries in the total manufactured imports of developed countries is still only about 5%, representing only a third of 1% of the latter's GNP.

If the developing countries are to satisfy their projected import requirements in the 1970s, in line with the targets set for the Second Development Decade, they must strive to maintain the roughly 15% rate of growth in manufactured exports which they achieved in the earlier decade.

Application of the general preference scheme tentatively agreed to by the developed countries in October 1970 will be a step toward redressing the tariff discrimination against exports of manufactures from the developing countries. Certain important exports have not been included in the scheme, however, and there is a danger that quantitative restrictions might be imposed when imports in any single category become significant. Consequently the general preference scheme, though representing an advance, does not obviate the need for more comprehensive action on the part of the developed countries to remove discriminatory trade restrictions and other barriers which hinder the entry of manufactures from developing countries into their markets.

While it is in the long run interest of the more developed countries to move out of products in which they have ceased to have a comparative advantage, the expansion of imports of manufactures from less developed countries will inevitably have an adverse effect on some sectors of their economies. This is bound to arouse opposition and resistance on the part of the affected interest groups unless appropriate adjustment assistance policies and programs are introduced concurrently with reductions in tariff and non-tariff barriers. Few developed countries have adopted such policies or programs. Much greater attention to this problem is required to ensure a smooth transition to new production and trade patterns.

There is a tendency on the part of developing countries to concentrate their export efforts on a few labor-intensive products such as simple textiles, footwear or leather goods for which markets in developed countries tend to be limited. There is some danger that the terms of trade of such products could deteriorate relative to capital-intensive goods, just as they turned against tropical commodities in the past.

"Non-industrial" and "industrializing" countries' difficulties in competing in export markets, and their fears that they are being pushed into "cheap labor industries" with deteriorating terms of trade, need recognition. The following steps might ease the difficulties facing developing countries in their efforts to expand exports of manufactured goods, and should lead to an expansion of international trade:

(a) **A gradual shift** by "semi-industrialized" countries from simple labor intensive into more capital intensive industries, thus making room for the "industrializing" countries which have a comparative advantage in the former. "Semi-industrialized" countries are eminently suited for the production and export of capital goods such as machine tools and technologically advanced labor intensive products such as electronics equipment. At present, however, international markets for such products are dominated by exports from developed countries. These are frequently subsidized, both by marginal pricing from relatively large domestic markets and by special medium and long term credit facilities.

(b) **Provision of efficient and competitive export credit** facilities. To develop capital goods exports, manufacturers in "industrializing" and "semi-industrialized" countries usually require subsidized credits in order to compete with exports from developed countries. The question of providing external refinancing for such export credits has figured for some time on the agenda of the United Nations Conference on Trade and Development (UNCTAD). The Inter-American Development Bank (IDB) has established a facility for this purpose, but it has so far been confined to the financing of export transactions between the Latin American countries. Both the Asian Development Bank (ADB) and the African Development Bank (ADB) have been studying this problem for some time, but no decision to mount such a program has yet been taken.

(c) **Phasing out** of existing practices and franchises by multinational companies which effectively limit exports from their associated companies in developing countries.

95

(d) Encouragement of trade in manufactures among developing countries. Regional trade groupings provide one way of benefiting from economies of scale within a multinational framework. The case for such collaboration has often been made on the basis that it would permit the establishment of multinational enterprises designed to operate within the wider regional market and exploit the complementarity of participating economies. While these possibilities are well worth pursuing, such multinational ventures are difficult to organize. Even greater gains in trade are likely to accrue through an increase in the scope for specialization and competition within wider regional markets resulting from the elimination of trade barriers.

- **Inadequate Infrastructure**

The lack of an appropriate infrastructure is another important obstacle to industrial development. Conditions have improved greatly in the last 20 years, but manufacturers still lack many infrastructure facilities and pay more for the services they receive than their counterparts in developed countries. Some countries have been able to minimize the cost of infrastructure for industry by developing appropriately sited and well managed industrial estates. In some cases these have been export-oriented, and have greatly facilitated the growth of industrial exports. Examples are the "free" industrial zones in the Republics of China and Korea.

Social Aspects of Industrialization

The growing concern with the social aspects of development is focusing on employment, a more equal distribution of income, and problems of industrial location. While the allocation of resources between current consumption and investment is an important determinant of the future rate of growth, increased attention to employment and income distribution can help expand internal markets, thereby contributing to the developmental process. A careful selection of investments can ensure that social benefits such as employment and the needs of productive efficiency are mutually reinforcing and conducive to sound industrial growth.

Employment

Although manufacturing has been the largest single source of new urban employment in most developing countries, it has failed to fulfill the widely held expectation that it could resolve unemployment problems resulting from the population explosion. Indeed, the framework of incentives adopted to promote industrialization has in some cases aggravated the problem of unemployment by penalizing the farmer, redistributing incomes in favor of manufacturing, and encouraging an exodus from rural to urban areas.

Manufacturing output in developing countries grew at a rate in excess of 7% per annum over the decade 1955-65, while labor absorption by this sector grew at the rate of 4%. It is, of course, unrealistic to expect industrialization to resolve by itself the employment problems of developing countries. Nevertheless, more could certainly be done at both policy and project levels to expand the employment impact of the industrial sector, possibly along the following lines:

• By developing a pattern of industry, at the earliest stages of industrialization, which encourages the production of mass consumption articles rather than capital intensive consumer durables.

• By phasing out incentives which discourage the substitution of labor for capital, such as credit policies which make borrowing for fixed investment cheaper than for working capital, and preferential foreign exchange treatment and duty exemptions for imported capital goods.

• By ending licensing and other quantitative controls which tend to discriminate against small industrialists because of the administrative problems involved in dealing with them. This is particularly important in "non-industrial" countries which need small scale industries to develop technical skills and management capabilities. Such industries can also play an important role in the production of consumer goods, and as "sub-contractors" for larger industries, both domestic and foreign. Assembly of electronic components in countries with low cost labor is an example of such international "sub-contracting."

• By encouraging maximum utilization of existing industrial facilities through multi-shift production and other appropriate methods, and by greater attention to the process of technological transfer and adaptation, with a view to devising modern but labor-using equipment and production methods.

Income Distribution

Industrialization can contribute to a more equitable income distribution by broadening the middle class group of society and creating a new industrial work force with relatively high incomes. Such groups normally remain small, however, and a growing concentration of economic wealth frequently offsets gains from such trends.

The distribution of income is, of course, affected by the manner in which it is divided between capital and labor, as well as among different sectors and regions within the economy. While there can be an economic argument in favor of high rewards for capital, thereby encouraging capital accumulation for further industrialization, the resulting inequalities in wealth can endanger the prospects for social and political stability, which are critical preconditions for uninterrupted economic development. For these reasons, it is desirable to focus on a policy of more equal distribution of income through increasing employment and lowering prices of manufactured products, rather than trying to protect industry to ensure high industrial profitability and high incomes for factory workers.

Location and Environment

The advantages of geographic concentration of industry have led to some over-concentration of both industry and population. In some countries this is now being followed by a swing to extreme dispersion, which also entails high social costs. Indeed, manufacturers' costs may become so high that they require very high levels of protection.

The developing countries can avoid some of the excessive social costs that have accompanied industrialization in the developed countries. A balanced and planned urban growth, combining investment in utilities, industrial estates and social facilities such as schools, hospitals and housing to make for viable "growth poles" as an alternative to both urban sprawl and rural neglect, presents some possibilities of turning urbanization from a problem to a tool of development. The organizational and resource mobilization problems, however, are formidable.

Developing countries also have reason to be concerned with the impact of industrialization on the environment, and on public health and welfare. A carefully planned and implemented "preventive" strategy in this area, reflecting the particular needs and stage of development of each country, is likely to avoid costly investments at a later stage to overcome the consequences of earlier neglect.

Links with Other Sectors

Where policies affecting industry have been divorced from those for other sectors, industrialization has tended to occur in enclaves, isolated from the rest of the economy. This frequently results in a weakness of linkages between sectors, and in lower overall development. The intersectoral implications of industrial development need careful attention. In many developing countries, excessive incentives for industrialization have resulted in erosion of the comparative advantage in agriculture. An optimal economic strategy requires the balanced growth of agriculture and industry, and special attention must be given to the linkages between these two sectors.

Strategies and Policies

Any consideration of strategies and policies to promote industrialization must take into account the fact that industry in most countries is owned and operated largely by private enterprise. Therefore, a great deal of importance must be attached to policies and incentives which will have the desired impact on the motivations of private entrepreneurs and the investment climate in general.

The predominantly private character of the industrial sector presents certain special problems in the implementation of industrial investment programs. It also has a bearing on the choice of instruments to be used.

It is obviously within the province of every government to determine the relative importance it wishes to assign to the public and private sectors in industry. It should be borne in mind, however, that public manufacturing enterprises tend to be successful when they are left free from political interference and forced to face the pressures of domestic or foreign competition. There is always a danger that excessive government intervention may inhibit the mobilization of entrepreneurial talent and the decentralization of initiatives and decision making which are necessary for rapid industrial growth.

Apart from the predominantly private nature of industry, there are other factors which contribute to the complexity of the industrial sector. The rapid pace of scientific and technological progress which characterizes this field is in itself a complicating factor from the standpoint of industrial policy formulation and investment decisions.

Moreover, like agricultural development, industrialization is not merely a matter of economic evolution but depends on a country's social and political organization and policies. Insofar as the economic aspects are concerned, it is evident that industrial strategy must be part of an overall economic strategy to be successful.

Basically, outward-looking strategies make sense for all developing countries, even those in the "non-industrial" category, which can thereby avoid some of the difficulties now being experienced by the more industrialized countries. An outward-looking policy is not synonymous with export orientation; it means attention to comparative advantage, specialization, and development of the appropriate structure and techniques of industry, so that the sector can develop efficiently and in line with the outside world. A policy of import-substitution based on the utilization of domestic resources could be characterized as "outward-looking" if the efficiency of the industries concerned were comparable to that of similar enterprises elsewhere. Some of the best opportunities for manufactured exports may arise in conjunction with import substitution, but they will be realized only if the import-substitution itself is reasonably efficient and thus outward-oriented.

In many developing countries, at least until recently, there was an excessive shift in emphasis from primary production to industry, and from outward-looking to inward-looking policies oriented toward the domestic market. A reaction against colonial patterns of specialization has frequently been responsible.

The resulting combination of policies has often proved inefficient, slowing down economic growth by penalizing investment in primary production. It has also encouraged undue reliance on instruments such as tariffs and quotas which favor production for the domestic market over exports, in contrast to a more balanced system of incentives including adjustments in exchange rates which would keep domestic costs and prices in line with the outside world.

Import substitution and a certain degree of protection for infant industries is a normal and often indispensable initial phase in the industrialization process. Yet a number of developing countries, particularly those in the "industrializing" and "semi-industrialized" group, are recognizing that further industrial expansion based on a policy of continued import substitution faces critical market constraints.

By contrast, greater emphasis on manufacturing for exports will permit the establishment of larger industrial units with economies of scale, provide access to scarce foreign exchange resources, and give new momentum to industrial development. Progress in this direction obviously depends upon a country's resource endowments, the existing structure of production and protection policies, the available industrial skills, and the time required to bring about the necessary changes.

It is impossible to give a policy prescription for industrialization except in these very general terms, since the appropriateness of a strategy and policy mix varies from country to country and is related in each case to the level of industrial development and the economic and social objectives the country wishes to pursue. Nevertheless, it might be useful to outline briefly some of the principal policies and policy instruments which appear to be successful in fostering efficient and sustained industrialization:

(a) **A policy of moderate protection,** avoiding as far as possible outright import prohibitions and quantitative restrictions. Such a policy is consistent with protection of "infant industries," especially when efficient operations are contingent upon large scale production, but the protection granted should be temporary and manufacturers should be put on notice with respect to a tariff reduction program.

100

Moreover, tariffs should be as uniform as possible, divided at most into a few categories, or "bands." Widely differentiated tariffs, specifically designed to meet the needs of marginal firms, tend to do the most harm by subsidizing inefficiency, misallocating resources and discouraging exports.

Appropriate export incentives should be provided where necessary to counterbalance any disincentives to export created by protection against imports. A rational approach to export orientation, however, does not point merely to extensive export incentives; it suggests instead a program to reduce protection to reasonable levels. The more moderate and temporary the protection, the easier it will be to achieve export orientation.

(b) Minimum use of direct controls, as on the entry of new firms into manufacturing or on pricing of manufacturing output. When there are problems of industrial location or market fragmentation, or when participation by foreign investment is involved, there can be a case for controls over entry of new firms into manufacturing, but such controls should not be extended indiscriminately.

Similarly, price controls should be reserved essentially for those special cases where a monopoly is preferable to market fragmentation, and where abuse of the monopolistic situation cannot otherwise be prevented. For most manufacturing activity, the emphasis should be on the use of market forces to ensure efficiency and low prices.

(c) A fiscal policy framework designed to strengthen the competitive position of industry and to encourage resource use in accordance with comparative advantage. Such an approach would argue generally for moderate direct taxation, "non-cascading" indirect taxation, and the application of excise duties on both imports and local production, instead of placing exclusive reliance on high import duties to control consumption. It would also suggest that accelerated depreciation is a questionable fiscal incentive for industry in most situations because of its tendency to encourage capital intensive projects.

(d) Monetary and credit policies aimed at creating a financial environment conducive to a high rate of savings and the efficient mobilization and allocation of available resources. Aside from the obvious need to maintain reasonable financial stability, this usually means avoiding artificially low interest rates or concessionary credit policies. It also means the creation of appropriate institutional facilities and financial instruments to help mobilize domestic resources for productive investments.

(e) Labor and manpower policies designed to achieve maximum employment. This implies avoidance of labor laws and trade union practices which are inconsistent with employment objectives and encourage capital-intensity, for example by discriminating against night work and multiple shifts. It also implies provision of incentives for training and use of labor. Furthermore, as noted above, it requires the avoidance of financial policies which favor the use of capital over labor.

The implementation of policy is, of course, as important as the formulation of the appropriate policy mix itself. Yet weaknesses in administration are one of the main conditions of underdevelopment, and they take time to overcome. The approach outlined offers no final solutions for the problems of industrialization. Rather, it recognizes the complexities and seeks to identify policies which are likely to contribute to industrialization with least cost and maximum benefit in the 1970s.

MANUFACTURING[1]
AND THE WORLD BANK GROUP

Table 1: Summary of Actual and Projected Bank Group Financing[1] for Manufacturing, FY1969-76

	1969	1970	1971	1972	1973	1964-68	1969-73	1972-76
Sector and Sub-Sector Studies	—	4	8	5	6	1	23	35
Commitments ($ millions)[1]	314	361	347	675	575	786	2270	3115
Percent of Group total	17	15	13	24	20	14	18	20
No. of countries[2]	16	20	19	31	37	39	50	60
Financing Operations (No.)	33	40	30	45	55	114	205	300
Projects under Supervison, end of fiscal year	111	138	145	160	180	92[3]	145[3]	210[3]

[1]Not including credits for industrial import programs.
[2]Does not reflect financing through regional development finance companies for Africa and Latin America.
[3]Annual average.

Main Features of Past Operations

The two main instruments on which the Bank Group has relied since its manufacturing sector operations began in developing countries

[1]The discussion of Bank Group operational activities is in terms of the "manufacturing" sector since this paper excludes consideration of mining operations. In discussing general problems and issues relating to industrialization, however, the term "industrial" is used.

in fiscal 1951 have been the direct financing of projects, and their indirect financing through lines of credit to financial intermediaries known as development finance companies (DFCs). Through these channels, the Group committed a total of $1,314 million to developing countries during the five fiscal years 1967-71. This represented almost 15% of total Bank Group financing in the period, in all sectors.

Table 2 gives comparative figures for the three five-year periods, 1957-71.

Table 2: Bank Group Financing for Manufacturing Projects[1]
In Developing Countries, FY1957-61, 1962-66, 1967-71
(US$ millions)

	1957-61		1962-66		1967-71	
	Amount	%	Amount	%	Amount	%
Direct Financing						
Bank and IDA	38	26	62	12	132	10
IFC	45	31	101	20	305	23
Sub-Total	83	57	163	32	437	33
DFC Financing[2]	63	43	350	68	877	67
Total	146	100	513	100	1,314	100

[1]Does not include credits for industrial import programs.
[2]Includes all IFC investments through financial intermediaries. Excludes DFC financing in developed countries (Finland).

Changes in the composition of Bank Group manufacturing operations in developing countries have reflected mainly the commencement in FY1957 of financing by IFC and a steep rise in commitments to DFCs. Financial operations in the manufacturing sector in the 1950s included lending to such developed countries as Japan, Italy and Australia; these were virtually phased out by the beginning of the 1960s, while those in developing countries showed a steady rise. During the period FY1967-71, direct project financing was more than five times higher than a decade earlier, due largely to the growth in IFC's operations.

Financing through DFCs rose very sharply during the early 1960s, and over the past decade has represented roughly two thirds of the Group's assistance to manufacturing in developing countries. The network of DFCs associated with the Bank Group increased from eight at the end of FY1961 to 40[1] a decade later. In many cases the Group played a critical role in establishing or strengthening these institutions. Although DFCs do not serve the manufacturing sector exclusively, most are heavily specialized in lending to or investing in manufacturing concerns.

---

[1]Includes two DFCs exclusively for tourism and a capital markets development institution.

The Bank Group share of total industrial investment in developing countries has been quite small. Very rough estimates suggest that the direct financial contribution of the Bank Group to total capital formation in the manufacturing sector in developing countries in the five years 1967-71 was on the order of 1.5% to 2%.

Nearly three fourths of total industrial investment was financed from national sources—the reinvestment of profits and reserves, transfers from financial intermediaries, and private non-institutional savings. Nevertheless, the direct financial contribution of the Bank Group represented nearly a third of all foreign official finance available for this purpose, and approximately 10% of the total from external public and private sources combined.

Bank Group operations in manufacturing have had a significant "catalytic" impact. The aggregate cost of Bank Group financed projects was about $7,500 million during FY1967-71. On the average, of every dollar invested in these projects, only 18 cents came from the Bank Group. The participation of associated investors was most pronounced in projects directly financed by IFC, and by DFCs with Bank Group funds. More than three quarters of IFC projects were joint ventures involving technical as well as financial partnership between foreign investors and local sponsors (see Annex 2).

Sectoral and Geographical Distribution
The sectoral and geographical distribution of Bank Group operations in the manufacturing sector does not reveal a consistent industrial strategy, on either a country or a sector basis. When "retailing" its assistance, i.e., through direct project financing, the Group has tended to support relatively large projects, most of them in activities which fall under the heading of "heavy manufacturing," and largely in the "industrializing" and "semi-industrialized" countries at the level of development necessary to absorb such projects.

When the assistance has been "wholesaled" through development finance companies, a shift can be observed towards smaller projects and a more even distribution between "light manufactures" and "heavy manufactures." Most of the development finance companies which have received Bank Group support, however, have also been in the "industrializing" and "semi-industrialized" countries (see Annexes 3 and 5).

In general, direct financing of manufacturing industries in the past has been on a project-by-project basis, with no organized program of project identification and promotion to assist member countries in meeting their industrialization objectives. In the case of IFC, most projects have been referred from outside sources, both domestic and foreign.

The Bank and IDA have financed only a few manufacturing enterprises directly. This reflects the assignment to IFC of the primary role in handling private investment proposals, as well as inhibitions felt until recently by the Bank and IDA in financing government owned enterprises. Other deterrents have been the unwillingness of governments to provide the necessary guarantees, and the unwillingness of some project sponsors to conform to Bank standards of international competitive bidding.

Despite the lack of an organized program of direct financing, many manufacturing projects assisted by the Bank Group have contributed importantly to strengthening or diversifying the manufacturing sector, often introducing for the first time the production of new intermediate and capital goods. More than 85% of direct project financing in FY1967-71 was directed to "heavy manufacturing," including metallurgic and machinery industries, chemicals, non-metallic minerals and pulp and paper (see Annex 3).

Manufacturing operations of the Bank Group during the five years were concentrated in the "industrializing" and "semi-industrialized" countries. From a regional standpoint, the strongest emphasis was on Asia, which absorbed 50% of total project commitments in developing countries[1].

The Latin America and Caribbean area received only 18%, although it included certain countries with rapidly growing manufacturing sectors. There were various constraints on Bank and IDA industrial operations in the area, including non-availability of government guarantees, questions of creditworthiness, and Bank policy precluding loans to government owned DFCs (a policy which was changed in 1968). African countries, most of which fall in the "non-industrialized" category, accounted for only 4% of manufacturing project commitments in developing countries.

Deeper insight is provided by an analysis of a sample of 22 countries which accounted for 75% of total Bank Group manufacturing commitments in developing countries during FY1967-71 (see Annex 4). This indicates that Brazil, Colombia, India, Iran, Pakistan and Turkey have been the major countries in the Bank Group program. Their 50% share in overall commitments is similar to their share in population of developing member countries, though more than their roughly 35% share of GNP. Only Indonesia among the "non-industrial" countries figures prominently in the past program.

[1]Regional percentages shown in the Annexes reflect the inclusion of developed countries (Finland), except where otherwise specified.

Other Principal Characteristics

The channeling of resources for manufacturing through DFCs constituted the bulk of the Bank Group program in many countries during this period (see Annex 4). This was particularly the case in "industrializing" countries (Colombia, Iran, Republic of Korea, Morocco, Nigeria, Pakistan, Philippines, Turkey), and in India among the "semi-industrialized" countries. Lending and investing in manufacturing projects through IFC has also acquired prominence in a number of country situations (Brazil, India, Philippines and Turkey). By contrast, direct project lending by the Bank and IDA was confined to only four countries — Brazil, Indonesia, Pakistan and Yugoslavia — and altogether accounted for only about 10% of total Bank Group commitments.

The majority of projects catered exclusively to the domestic markets of member countries in which they were situated. Import substitution was the predominant characteristic of Bank Group operations, just as it was the prevalent strategy of industrialization adopted by member countries.

More than half the total of Bank Group projects during the five years, accounting for a similar proportion of overall commitments, did not export any part of their output. At the other end of the spectrum were roughly 15% of the number of projects, accounting for a similar percentage of overall commitments, which exported more than half their total output. Available data also suggest a somewhat higher degree of export orientation in projects financed through DFCs (see Annex 2). However, this does not appear to have been the result of deliberate policy.

The bulk of manufacturing projects financed by the Bank Group was in the private sector. IFC is limited by charter to lend or invest in non-government enterprises, although nearly a fifth of its client firms during FY1967-71 had some government participation in their equity. Similarly, DFCs have financed private enterprise, with very few exceptions. Until recently, the Bank as well did not finance industrial units in the public sector. Recent policy decisions have enhanced the Bank's flexibility in dealing with government industrial enterprises directly or through DFC-type operations.

The bulk of Bank Group funds for manufacturing have been directed to the financing of fixed industrial investment, and particularly its foreign exchange component. Permanent working capital and local currency expenditures are financed by IFC, but only when the resources cannot be mobilized domestically. Occasionally, DFCs have also financed permanent working capital requirements.

While the present mix of instruments allows the Bank Group to play an effective role in a variety of industrial and country situations, the Group has not provided much assistance, directly or indirectly, to small scale industry, particularly firms employing less than 20 workers (see Annex 2). A few operations have been carried out for the direct benefit of the small scale industrial sector (industrial estates, etc.), but most have benefited medium and large scale firms.

Until recently, Bank Group operations appear to have had relatively little impact on the broad evolution of industrial policy in developing countries. The excessive inward orientation of industry and distortions in the system of fiscal and other incentives appear to be almost as marked in recipients of Group assistance as in other countries. The shift towards export orientation in countries such as Pakistan seems largely unrelated to Bank Group operations.

While the "project" orientation of operations in the manufacturing sector, plus the predominantly private character of most manufacturing investments, are undoubtedly important elements in this picture, it also appears that the general approach in the past has been to undertake direct financing of projects, or to replenish the resources of DFCs, because the investment appeared worthwhile itself rather than as part of a carefully considered industrial strategy in the country concerned.

It is difficult to make any reliable assessment of the economic contribution made by Bank Group operations to industrialization in individual countries. For example, while there can be little doubt that DFCs have made an important contribution toward widening the possibilities of industrial growth in the developing countries, their performance appears to have been less than satisfactory in developing local capital markets.

Similarly, direct project financing by the Bank Group appears in certain cases to have been directed to projects which have required substantial protection. A strengthened follow-up program, particularly on the economic side, is a prerequisite for arriving at better knowledge and judgment about the economic contribution of past Bank Group operations in the manufacturing sector.

Projected Activities, FY1972-76

The Bank Group does not yet have a coherent industrial sector program designed to meet specific objectives. As explained below, however, the more intensive work initiated in the area of sector studies, industrial policy analysis and investment promotion should assist in the development of a more integrated and goal-oriented program.

An attempt is made in this section to provide a brief account of the activities envisaged in the manufacturing sector by the Bank's Industrial Projects and Development Finance Companies Departments and by IFC over the next five years, under the following headings: Financing of Manufacturing Operations, Sector Studies, Research, Technical Assistance, and Project Appraisal and Supervision.

Information on FY1972-76 manufacturing operations is largely an aggregation of existing programs of the different organizational units concerned. In order to evolve an integrated manufacturing sector program for the period, a great deal of further effort will be required to complete work now under way to:

• Re-define Bank Group objectives in the manufacturing field. Certain operational issues and alternatives are presented in the final section beginning on page 118.

• Prepare a more definitive program of sector and subsector studies pertaining to the manufacturing field.

• Evolve specific programs and proposals for Bank Group manufacturing operations on a country-by-country basis, taking note of the relative priority of the sector and the financial constraints on Bank Group activity in particular country situations.

• Derive the manpower and organizational requirements for implementing the manufacturing sector program.

Financing of Manufacturing Operations

Aggregate new loan and equity commitments for manufacturing are projected at somewhat more than $3,000 million over the five years, almost two and a half times the level of FY1967-71. The share envisaged for manufacturing operations is almost 20% of projected Bank Group operations as a whole in developing countries, compared to 15% in FY1967-71.

Table 3: Projected New Commitments for Manufacturing,[1] FY1972-76

	US$ million	Percent	Percentage Increase Over FY1967-71
Direct Financing			
Bank and IDA	1,200	39	809
IFC	480	15	57
Sub-Total	1,680	54	284
DFC Financing[2]	1,435	46	64
Total	3,115	100	137

[1]Data represent all projected commitments to the manufacturing sector through IFC and the Bank's Industrial Projects and DFC Departments, with the exclusion from IFC and Industrial Projects data of "mining" and "tourism" projects. Data on DFC financing relate to total projected Bank Group commitments to industrial DFCs, part of whose sub-projects will be in non-manufacturing ventures (the proportion was 14% in FY1968-70).

[2]Including IFC investments through financial intermediaries.

Increase in Bank, IDA financing

The outstanding feature of these projections is, of course, the large increase in direct financing of manufacturing projects by the Bank and IDA. This is attributable largely to the change in policy with respect to financing government owned enterprises, and the prospect that an increasing number of such entities may be able to present acceptable loan applications in the coming years. In FY1972, for example, it is expected that eight manufacturing projects calling for direct lending by the Bank and IDA, totaling some $334 million, will be presented to the Executive Directors, all involving government owned or controlled enterprises.

This is an exceptionally large program, much affected by planned loans to three Brazilian steel companies totaling $186 million during fiscal 1972. The pipeline for future years is smaller, and progressively undefined because of uncertainties regarding specific proposals which may be submitted for financing. Nevertheless, the projected figure of $1,200 million over the five years FY1972-76 appears to be a reasonable rough estimate of the volume of lending that may develop in this category.

In the early years, at least, the program is concentrated in large projects with heavy capital inputs, such as steel, fertilizer, forest products, etc. Starting in FY1974, however, it is expected that, as a consequence of more active project identification and promotional work, Bank and IDA financing will be extended into such areas as industrial estates and other projects for assistance to small scale industry, rehabilitation loans for selected industrial branches, and projects oriented especially toward the promotion of export industries.

Financing by IFC

In the case of IFC, the project pipeline is a particularly poor guide for estimating future operations, except to some extent for the remainder of FY1972. The approach adopted has been to estimate the likely volume based on current levels of IFC activity, identifiable prospects for future IFC involvement, an assessment of the country environment for private investment and likely areas where new private investment would be consistent with country economic priorities.

IFC's reliance on the private sector for new investment proposals, the changing climate for foreign private investment, and the incipient stage of IFC's promotional work make programming for IFC a much more tentative exercise than for other Bank Group organizational units concerned with industry. Also the size and range of future IFC operations will depend importantly upon the equity resources available to it through an increase in its capital or in other ways.

As part of its future efforts, IFC will adopt a more systematic program of promotional work, seeking out, in coordination with the Bank, areas of high industrial priority in which IFC may be an effective catalyst for new investment. While an industry breakdown of future IFC activities is not feasible, a number of areas in which the Corporation is likely to be active can be identified. Steel, machinery, chemicals, fertilizers and synthetic fibers are likely to be important in several Asian countries and in Latin America. In Africa, an attempt will be made to encourage domestic resource-based industries.

Financing through intermediaries

The program for supporting intermediaries in financing industrial projects is less uncertain. Repeat operations, involving 36 development finance companies actively associated with the Bank Group, account for two thirds of overall commitments envisaged during FY1972-76. In addition to catering to the needs of DFCs already associated with the Bank Group, it is planned to build new institutional relationships. Forty proposals of this kind are under consideration, but the likelihood is that no more than 23 will mature by the end of FY1976.

The expansion visualized is still ambitious. Two points are particularly noteworthy. First, financial support is expected to be extended to three additional development banks of regional scope. Second, the program implies a large expansion of national DFCs in Africa. This is a formidable undertaking, given the special problems of building or reorganizing institutions in that part of the world, and will require a relatively high component of technical assistance from the Bank Group.

The establishment of new institutional relationships cannot be projected with as much confidence as the "repeat operations." However, if the Bank Group succeeds in consummating the 23 proposals mentioned above, the DFC network associated with the Bank Group will increase its country coverage by 10. Moreover, the coverage would be intensified through the establishment of new institutions in five countries in which Bank-financed DFCs already exist.

Mobilization of savings

An important new element in the FY1972-76 program is more direct assistance to member countries in mobilizing private savings for investment, particularly through the development of capital markets and other appropriate financial institutions. Development finance companies supported by the Bank Group have already made a contribution in this field, but the need is now felt to establish new intermediaries which are equipped to provide specialized financial and technical services to business and industry. IFC envisages direct investment in several new money and capital market institutions; its first investment in this field was in the Korea Investment Finance Corporation (KIFC) in FY1971.

Shifts in lending patterns

In view of the substantial uncertainties regarding the flow of projects to the Bank Group in the industrial field, it is possible to make only very tentative statements regarding the pattern of these projects in FY1972-76. It seems clear that they will be of differing importance in different kinds of countries. In the more industrialized countries, manufacturing projects may constitute 30% or more of total Bank Group financing. On the other hand, there are several "non-industrial" African countries where the share is expected to be less than 10%.

The relatively low share in African countries reflects their earlier stage of development and the fact that technical assistance, rather than finance, is their principal requirement at this time in the industrialization field. Overall, less than 10% of FY1972-76 financing of manufacturing is expected to go to "non-industrial" countries. "Semi-industrialized" countries may account for close to half, and "industrializing" countries are expected to receive the balance.

There will probably be substantial shifts in regional shares from the past pattern of Bank Group manufacturing operations. The proportion of total FY1972-76 financing projected for Asia is about 35% as compared with half during FY1967-71. This reduction will be taken up chiefly by a projected increase in the share of Latin America and the Caribbean from close to 20% in FY1967-71 to about 30% in FY1972-76. Although Africa's share is expected to remain low, the actual amount in FY1972-76 may be several times that of FY1967-71.

Some rough projections have been made of the likely levels of manufacturing investment in developing countries, in order to obtain some quantitative indication of the relative importance of the Bank Group's five-year financing program. They are based mainly on economic projections prepared in the Bank in connection with other studies.

It is estimated that during FY1972-76 Bank Group disbursements will directly finance 2.5% to 3% of total new fixed capital formation in the manufacturing sector in developing countries. As noted earlier, the comparable figure for FY1967-71 is estimated at roughly 1.5% to 2%.

Financial operations do not reflect adequately the promotional or "catalytic" role the Bank Group performs. Assuming that past shares of total project costs financed by the Bank, IDA and IFC remain unchanged, total manufacturing investment likely to be induced by them through direct project financing might be on the order of about 5% of the projected aggregate. Greater uncertainty attaches to DFC sub-projects financed by the Bank. Including these, however, the proportion of total manufacturing investment with which the Bank Group can be considered to be directly or indirectly associated would be about 13%.

It has also been estimated, very roughly, that the contribution of Bank Group disbursements to fixed capital formation in manufacturing might represent some 10% of the total new capital flows from developed to developing countries for investments in manufacturing, excluding petroleum. These estimates are subject to a large margin of error, and are useful only as broad points of reference.

Industrial Sector Studies

Since each country's economic circumstances and industrialization problems are unique in many respects, an expanded program of sector studies is a prerequisite for strengthening the Bank Group's industrial program. Careful study and understanding in depth of the industrial sector in individual countries is required to identify their investment and technical assistance requirements and ensure that Bank Group activities make the maximum contribution to industrial growth.

The principal objective of sector studies may be broadly defined as the acquisition of basic intelligence on which a developmental sector lending program can be based. This means the identification of structural and policy problems in industrial growth to enable the Bank Group to plan its lending operations more effectively and in a longer time perspective than has been possible hitherto in this sector.

Such an approach includes the stimulation of project preparation, early identification of Bank Group financing possibilities, and the evaluation of projects through pre-investment programs to ensure that there is a broad enough base for project selection. Project preparation and selection must take into account not only priorities within the industrial sector, but also the impact of industrialization policies. In the evaluation and design of such policies, the Bank Group might, where requested, provide technical assistance to ensure that members' economies obtain the maximum benefit from given levels of industrial investment.

Sector studies thus have three principal aspects: (a) the provision of a basic data framework on the structure of industry, its relevant factors of production, its growth and, to the extent possible, its relationship to the rest of the economy; (b) an analysis of policies relevant to the functioning and growth of industry; and (c) the identification and selection of projects for Bank Group lending.

An industrial sector study program was initiated in the Bank two years ago. Some half dozen major industry sector reports have so far been completed and another five or six are planned for each of the years FY1972 and FY1973. In addition, the manufacturing sector is treated periodically in country economic reports. These rarely provide the required information base, however, or the analysis in depth necessary for Bank Group technical assistance on policy formulation and project selection.

As soon as sufficient experience has been gained, a comprehensive program of sector studies for FY1972-76 should be evolved in accordance with the emphasis on in-depth, problem-oriented country economic work now being planned. Two important considerations need to be kept in mind.

First is the need to have a comprehensive and reasonably up-to-date study of the industrial sector for all countries which are likely to be major recipients of Bank Group industrial assistance in the 1970s. The focus and depth of such studies will vary from country to country, depending upon the individual situation. The objective should be reasonably comprehensive coverage by the end of FY1976.

The second major consideration is the importance of developing a capability to organize studies in a select group of "non-industrial" countries which request the Bank Group's assistance in the formulation of their industrial development programs and policies.

Research

Bank Group research in the industry field has concentrated in the past on studies of the structure of specific industries. In the last two years, however, there has been a change toward an emphasis on the problems of industrialization and trade, and on industrial lending issues. Much of this newly oriented research is also country focused, so that broad issues may be viewed simultaneously from the point of view of solving a country's particular industrial problems and from a more generalized viewpoint, taking advantage of the Bank Group's unique comparative perspective.

The increase in Bank Group lending activities, together with a growing appreciation of industrialization problems, is leading to increasing demands for research as operational back-up. Greater selectivity is therefore required if the research undertaken is to meet the principal current needs as well as to identify and anticipate problems which are likely to be most important in the future.

A recent review of research proposals has been the first step in improving the relevance of research to the Bank Group's operations, and a proposal to integrate research with country industry sector coverage, together with closer coordination with lending activities, is intended to ensure that close links are maintained between research and operations.

Technical Assistance

The most important aspect of the Bank's technical assistance in industry arises from its sectoral study work. It is more frequently informal than formal in nature, and arises as much in the course of the work of country or research missions as from their resulting reports. The staffing of such missions is to some extent, therefore, a form of technical assistance. In addition, the Bank Group assists countries with specific problems by helping to find, and in some cases finance, appropriate consultants.

The quality and effectiveness of such assistance depends on its continuity and coordination within the Bank Group. For this reason, and to ensure that the manpower devoted to this task is commensurate with both the requirements of technical assistance and the available resources, the sector study program may be seen as central to the technical assistance program in industry.

In a narrower but nevertheless important sense, technical assistance is also a concomitant of direct lending activities. The Bank Group's role in project identification, selection and follow-up can play a seminal role in the development of a country's industrial sector. The institution building assistance provided in the course of lending to development banks and other capital market financial institutions is equally important.

The Bank Group has an important technical assistance arm in the Economic Development Institute. In addition to a general treatment of industrial problems in its development and general courses in Washington and in the various developing countries, it has conducted an industrial projects course for some 25 candidates annually since the mid-1960s[1], and from FY1972 two such courses will be scheduled each year.

Project Appraisal and Supervision

It is generally agreed that industrialization should be oriented to a country's comparative advantage in resource allocation. While the

[1] In FY1971 there were some 150 applicants for this course.

114

series of analyses and judgments reached at a country, sector and project level can contribute to a better understanding of the directions in which such advantage might lie for individual countries, and can thus avoid serious mistakes in investment, there is no operationally foolproof method of evaluating comparative advantage.

The only meaningful approach to ensure that investment operations will be in line with comparative advantage is to improve the analysis and understanding of a country's industrial sector, to arrive at a more informed set of judgments in regard to its industrial priorities, and to initiate project evaluation at a very early stage.

All industrial projects directly undertaken by the Bank Group, and those DFC sub-projects which are subject to "prior approval" by the Bank (roughly a fourth of all sub-projects), are currently reviewed in technical, financial and economic terms. Technical feasibility and a reasonable degree of profitability in relation to the risk involved are, and should of course continue to be, important investment criteria for the Bank Group's industrial operations. In this, the Bank Group has accumulated considerable expertise.

Recently, however, improved methodologies have been developed for the assessment of likely costs and benefits accruing to the economy from investments in individual projects. The Bank Group is now engaged in introducing these new methodologies in its own project evaluation, and in assisting development finance companies to adopt them as well.

The economic rate of return

At the project level, the "economic rate of return" on capital—the rate which equalizes the present value of total economic costs and benefits over the life of a project—provides the most meaningful and comprehensive quantitative indication of the net economic benefits to be derived from the investment. This measure can shed light not only on the contribution of the project to domestic product but also on the protection and balance of payments implications of an investment.

There are several difficult problems in estimating the economic rate of return, however, which need careful attention and require the exercise of judgment. These center around the identification of appropriate long term international prices for project outputs and inputs, the measurement of external economies and diseconomies, the estimation of shadow prices for the primary factors, and the rate at which project efficiency will improve over time.

Since industrial products are generally traded internationally, the availability of reliable international price data is a key element in evaluating industrial projects. Such data are often difficult to obtain, however, because of the multiplicity of industrial products, changing sources and conditions of supply and the prevalence of temporary "marginal" pricing.

Moreover, external economies are generally difficult to quantify and shadow price estimation for wages and capital requires a profound knowledge of a country's economy. Probability and sensitivity analysis can assist in evaluation of these aspects but judgment has to be exercised about the degree to which it is worthwhile extending the analysis for any project.

The issue of protection

An important issue in industrial project evaluation is that of protection. Developments in industrial policies in a number of developing countries make it necessary to take a careful look at this aspect in connection with project evaluation.

Measures of "nominal" protection and "effective" protection of value added can throw useful light on the competitiveness and efficiency of industrial projects. They need careful interpretation, however, in the context of the overvaluation of a country's currency, the financial return on the project in relation to the opportunity cost of capital, and the international prices used as a yardstick for measuring the degree of protection.

In particular, the "effective" protection measure can be very sensitive to small changes in assumptions regarding prices and exchange rates. The economic rate of return, by introducing a time dimension, is a more comprehensive measure of a project's net benefits on the basis of a zero level of effective protection.

Alternative approaches

Since no single economic measure is best suited for all projects and all occasions, alternative approaches to economic evaluation have to be used. Moreover, the results have to be interpreted in the context of the country's economic situation and industrial strategy.

No uniform rules can be formulated with respect to the appropriate degree of protection for individual projects. This is because, among other things, the stage of industrial development of the country, the average level of protection in the economy, and the "maturity" of a particular industry have an important bearing on this matter.

This is not to suggest that the problem of economic appraisal of projects is an insoluble one, but merely to underscore the fact that a number of elements at the country, sector and project levels must be taken into consideration in reaching a final judgment on individual projects. If approached in this way, existing techniques of project appraisal can give perfectly adequate guidance for sensible investment decisions.

Non-economic objectives

Another important problem in project appraisal is to take account of objectives (e.g., employment, the development of backward regions, income redistribution and environment) which are not directly related to growth criteria but which might have particular importance in individual country situations.

These objectives have to be treated primarily in the context of preparing an industrialization strategy for the country. They can also be considered in the context of sector surveys, and in project selection and design.

Attention might be given to the possibility of new types of projects which have as a major objective the creation of direct employment, or similar social goals. At the project appraisal level, the possibility of furthering such goals is more limited. The best methodological treatment of these non-economic objectives in project appraisal is an important area for further research within the Bank Group.

A process of approximations

In summary, economic project evaluation is a process of successive approximations, and it varies with the size and importance of the project. For DFC sub-projects particularly, the introduction of even relatively simple approaches to economic project evaluation can only be a step-by-step process entailing a great deal of effort to ensure progressive improvement.

In the Bank Group's project appraisal work, primary reliance should continue to be placed, in general, on the assessment of the economic rate of return as a measure of the overall economic benefits of industrial projects. In this connection, continuing attention is necessary to test the new methodologies for estimating the economic rate of return and to refine existing techniques, particularly those aimed at assessing non-economic costs and benefits.

There is scope for improving follow-up of existing projects, particularly in the area of economic assessment. IFC has established a separate project supervision unit; the Bank's appraisal reports on development finance companies review the performance of Bank financed institutions, and the Operations Evaluation Division has been organized to undertake economic appraisals of past Bank and IDA investments.

The Role of the Bank Group

The discussion of industrialization in the first section of this paper indicated that industry in the developing countries has changed radically since World War II. Industrialization has become the key element of development policy in many of the more advanced developing countries, and the Bank Group should bring its own policies and operations into line with the new requirements and potential for industrial development.

A more systematic approach to industrial work, based on well-defined goals and on more intensive sector studies and policy work, must form the basis of a more effective, integrated program of action to cope with the new challenges and opportunities in industrial development.

The following appear to be the major issues which deserve consideration in the formulation of such a program:

• Should there be a concentration of financial support for industry in selected "semi-industrialized" and "industrializing" countries? What contribution is feasible in the "non-industrial" countries?

• What can be done to secure improvements in the general policy framework for industrial development in developing countries?

• What can the Bank Group do to encourage developing countries to achieve a more outward industrial orientation?

• What type of operational orientation is suggested by the small share of the Bank Group in total industrial investment in developing countries?

• How can the Bank Group achieve more effective collaboration and division of labor with other international and regional bodies in supporting industrialization?

These issues are interrelated; their resolution will affect the overall volume and pattern of future Bank Group activity in the manufacturing sector.

Need for Concentration of Financing Effort

In view of the serious constraints in the immediate future on the scope and size of any Bank Group program to promote industrialization, there is a strong case for concentrating financial support in the manufacturing sector on selected "semi-industrialized" and "industrializing" countries where the infrastructural base has been sufficiently developed and the manufacturing sector is large enough to have created significant external economies.

This will permit the Bank Group to deploy its resources with maximum effectiveness. Concentration does not mean simply allocating a large share of financing for manufacturing to these countries; it means an organized effort based on detailed country and sector economic studies to assist them in their further industrialization.

Assistance to "Non-Industrial" Countries

This does not imply, however, that the Bank Group will neglect the "non-industrial" countries. On the contrary, a much greater effort will be made to meet their special needs in the manufacturing sector. They are concentrated chiefly in Africa, and many have relatively small internal markets. Frequently, the biggest obstacle to their industrial development is a critical shortage of relevant skills and entrepreneurship. The Bank Group's approach will be along two main lines.

First, assistance will be provided in selected cases to develop and strengthen specialized local institutions concerned with industry, including DFCs. This will frequently involve the establishment of new types of institutions, oriented toward small and medium sized enterprises and actively engaged in technical assistance, including extension and promotion work. Where the prospective local volume of business falls short of the critical minimum required to sustain such entities, the possibility of providing some support through institutions established on a regional basis will be explored[1].

Second, the Bank Group expects to strengthen its activities in certain areas, such as small scale industry, support for extension services, and technical advice on sector priorities and project identification and promotion, which are particularly suited to the needs of the "non-industrial" countries. An effort in these areas will first be of a pilot nature and will be undertaken in close collaboration with other international and regional agencies.

Improvements in Policy Framework

The developmental contribution of Bank Group industrial operations depends critically upon the policy framework in recipient countries. Improvements in industrial policy would facilitate the industrialization process and at the same time enhance the effectiveness of Bank Group financial assistance.

To secure improvements in industrial policies, the Bank Group might link its operations in the manufacturing sector more closely to desired policy changes and improvements. It could, for example, refuse to finance industrial investments in countries where the indus-

---

[1]Projected FY1972-76 operations include a program for expanding local finance companies in Africa and channeling financial assistance to regional banks, such as the Central American Bank for Economic Integration, but there is scope for further expansion of these activities.

119

trial sector benefits from undue protection, or decline support of development finance companies that do not make an adequate effort to raise local resources. Stated more positively, it could indicate its willingness to participate in investment programs and projects which are associated with improvements in sector policies and practices.

The mix of instruments to be employed for supporting industrialization could also be related more closely to the policy frame in different countries. In situations where direct financing promises to be a more effective instrument for advancing desirable policy reforms, the Bank Group could rely on this method rather than financing through intermediaries. In some situations, policy reforms could be facilitated through non-project assistance.

There is much to be said for linking operations in this sector more closely to policy reforms than in the past, as the Bank Group normally does in other sectors. Such a link in this case, however, involves the giving of advice on difficult and sensitive questions to which unequivocal answers are seldom possible. While in some respects the direction of desirable changes may seem clear, it is often difficult to arrive at policy prescriptions in the industrial sector with any degree of assurance.

Furthermore, such a link between finance and policy reform requires a thorough knowledge and understanding of the industrial priorities and requirements of member countries. Such knowledge at present is limited to only a few countries. Advice based on an incomplete grasp of the facts or on a less than sympathetic appreciation of the real problems can often be counterproductive. As the Bank Group's knowledge of the sector improves, it may become increasingly possible to mesh operations in industry with policy goals.

The Bank Group also should make every effort to assist developing countries in defining appropriate patterns of industrial development suited to their resource endowments and to other factors determining their comparative advantage in industrial production and trade. This is not an easy task.

The success or failure of individual countries, especially those in the "non-industrial" category, to develop particular lines of industrial activity, might depend less upon definable measures of comparative advantage than upon the availability in particular situations of the entrepreneurial, management, and technical skills required to launch a successful industrial venture. These might best be cultivated by the maintenance of a general policy regime which will foster investment activities as well as by specific measures for the promotion of technical and management skills.

The Bank Group can, however, carry out a comprehensive program of sector studies and preinvestment work, taking advantage of its ability to view a country's problems in a broad comparative framework. Such studies will also facilitate better identification of the areas and projects where, through direct and indirect financing operations, the Bank Group can more effectively support a country's industrialization plans.

An Outward Orientation for Manufacturing

Import substitution has been the key characteristic of Bank Group operations in manufacturing, just as it has been the dominant industrial strategy in the developing world. An issue confronting the Bank Group now is whether it can make a contribution towards promoting an outward orientation of industry in the developing countries—in other words, whether it can help them achieve a more efficient and internationally competitive manufacturing sector. A strengthened program of advice and assistance in policy formulation, plus greater insistence on the efficiency of industrial production through more rigorous project appraisal, should help in meeting this objective.

The Bank Group can also play a more active role in export promotion. As already seen, a critical problem confronting developing countries in the 1970s is how to increase their manufactured exports in order to secure the foreign exchange they need for future development. In the light of this, the Bank Group will make a special effort in its own operations to provide support for export-oriented projects.

This does not mean, of course, that the Bank Group will not continue to finance projects that result in efficient import substitution. Its willingness to support export-oriented industries will be reinforced, however, by a much more determined and systematic effort. This will be supported through appropriate sector and preinvestment work to identify concrete possibilities for export-oriented industries in individual countries, and to actively promote such investments. It will take time for such efforts to show results, but they should help bring Bank Group operations in industry more closely in line with the industrial priorities of the more advanced developing countries.

A Promotional Role in Industry

The very small share of Bank Group assistance in industrial investment in developing countries highlights the need for the Group to play a strongly promotional role, so that the developmental impact of its contribution can be maximized. There are at least four major areas in which a much more organized promotional effort by the Bank Group can make a real contribution to the industrial development of its members.

Promotion of "growth poles"

The Bank Group will actively promote the creation of "growth poles" for industry, particularly in those developing countries where industrial growth needs new stimulus and direction. Such activity involves complex intersectoral organization and may require application of sophisticated analytical techniques. Large capital outlays may be required in constructing a set of interrelated infrastructure and industrial investments. Projects of this nature are now in an exploratory phase in Iran and Colombia. There may well be other countries in which similar needs exist.

Regional development

Another proposal, touched upon in an earlier part of this paper, is for the active promotion of industrial investment and trade on a regional (multinational) basis. The present status of experiments in regional cooperation is disquieting. It is hardly fashionable to speak affirmatively about the potential for multinational cooperation in the developing world.

Even so, a clear lead by the Bank Group can serve a useful purpose. The present program includes proposals to finance industrial development on a regional basis through a regional development bank, as in Central America and East Africa. The Bank Group will put its weight behind economic integration efforts by supporting policies, programs and projects which further regional cooperation.

Aside from these regional groupings, the Bank Group will assist in the identification and promotion of investment projects involving more than one country which are likely to contribute to the establishment of viable industries and increase trade among developing countries. A number of such possibilities have been identified by the staff in the course of their normal country work. Promotion of such projects in selected cases could yield great benefits to the countries concerned in terms of increased product specialization, economies of scale and exports of manufactures.

Small scale industry

Another promising area for promotional effort is in small scale industry. The development of such industry is an important objective, which should occupy a prominent position in the strategy of several countries. Small scale industry also has a special contribution to make in helping achieve important social objectives, such as employment, income distribution and development of backward regions.

The need in this area is for indigenous organizations which have the facilities to identify potential entrepreneurs, select suitable activities in which small scale production can be viable, prepare feasibility studies, provide technical and managerial guidance, and secure access to finance on appropriate terms.

The Bank Group has so far provided direct support for small scale industry only in Pakistan. It will be essential to develop a small expert group which concerns itself solely with the problem of small scale industry development, since the requirements are very different from those of large scale industrial projects.

The general approach will be to collaborate with specialized local institutions dealing with small scale industry, or to help build such institutions where they do not exist, and to channel the necessary technical and financial assistance primarily through them. A program in the field will be developed in close collaboration with the regional development banks and other specialized institutions.

Improving technology

There is also a strong case for greater support by the Bank Group for improvement of technology in the developing countries. In the past, the Bank Group has been more concerned with the transfer of existing technology. Its adaptation to local conditions is equally important.

The most effective contribution in this area could be made by encouraging countries to adopt policies which result in the emergence of realistic factor prices in the economy and make "intermediate" technology more profitable for entrepreneurs. Assuming progress on this front, specialized domestic institutions could assist in identifying, developing and disseminating appropriate technology.

The Bank Group will explore the desirability of providing assistance toward the establishment or strengthening of institutes working in the area of industrial technology, productivity, design and standards. There are a number of successful institutions, such as those in the Republics of China and Korea, which demonstrate the extraordinary productivity such institutions can attain if properly organized, staffed and financed.

Although the need for assistance in this field is acknowledged in certain country programs, there is no provision in FY1972-76 operations for any specific projects. To prepare an effective program, it will be necessary, as in the case of small scale industries, to develop in-house expertise and to work in the closest cooperation with other international institutions, such as the United Nations Industrial Development Organization (UNIDO) and the International Labor Organization (ILO). Both the Pearson Commission and a Committee of the Economic and Social Council have urged a more active Bank Group role in this area.

Cooperation with Other Agencies

In strengthening its industrial operations, a major concern of the Bank Group must be to ensure that it does not assume responsibilities and burdens which should appropriately be carried by or shared with others. At present, the Bank Group cooperates informally with a number of U.N. agencies in the industrial field. UNIDO is the principal U.N. agency concerned with industrial development. The Bank's Industrial Projects and DFCs Departments and IFC have all established informal operating procedures for cooperation with UNIDO.

While the framework for cooperation exists, instances of meaningful and significant collaboration in industry work between the Bank Group and other agencies concerned have been rare. The difficulties arise partly from the multiplicity of institutions interested in this area, partly from the disinclination of each agency to surrender the lead on projects it has under consideration, and partly from the severe financial and technical constraints under which some of the agencies have to operate.

Nevertheless, the range of problems and requirements in the industrial field is so great that there is obvious justification for a pooling of resources and efforts to the extent permitted by the technical and operational capabilities of each institution. Each agency in this field, including the Bank Group, has its strengths, which can best be utilized if applied in concert with others in accordance with an agreed division of labor between the interested institutions.

There is a strong case for the Bank Group to take the lead in discussing with UNIDO, ILO and the other agencies concerned the basis for collaboration, particularly in regard to activity in the "non-industrial" countries, the development of small scale industry and the promotion of improvements in technology.

Other Issues

There are some other unresolved issues which have an important bearing on Bank Group operations in the manufacturing sector. These have not been treated in this paper, partly because they have been discussed in the past at other levels and partly because they raise complex institutional and procedural issues which justify their separate treatment.

Bank and IDA policy regarding preference for domestic suppliers is one such issue. In a situation where a number of developing countries are beginning to produce capital goods, and should be encouraged to expand such production, the policy on preference for domestic suppliers has important implications from the standpoint of the countries' most appropriate industrial strategy and the effectiveness of the Bank Group's role in industrialization.

Conclusion

In summary, the 1970s present new challenges and opportunities to the Bank Group to assist its member countries in industrial development. The Group is just beginning to develop an integrated program in this field. Industrialization is a complex process, difficult to schedule, but it is a key element in the development strategy of many of the more advanced developing countries. The most effective contribution the Bank Group could make would be to assist its member countries in pursuing sound industrialization policies.

The Bank Group's role should be selective, concentrating its financial assistance on "semi-industrialized" and "industrializing" countries in the context of a continuing policy-oriented dialogue regarding industrialization in these countries. It should concentrate on infrastructure and agricultural investment in "non-industrial" countries, but should develop the capability, in a cooperative division of labor with other agencies, to make a much greater contribution towards meeting their specialized requirements in the industrial field.

The Bank Group's approach should be promotional and innovative, searching for new ways to facilitate the industrial progress of its members, such as investments in "growth poles" and in regional projects.

It is believed that the directions outlined in this paper provide a useful guide for the future, though they will be subject to much testing as additional experience is gained. In moving along these lines, consideration will be given to necessary adjustments in existing organizational arrangements, instruments and procedures, as well as manpower budgets, in order to enhance the effectiveness of Bank Group operations.

Some Indicators of Industrial Development

	Gross Value Added in Manufacturing as a Percent of Value Added in Commodity Production 1968	Average Annual Growth (%) of Real Gross Value Added in Manufacturing 1960-1969	Average Annual Growth (%) of Real GNP per Capita 1960-1969	Percentage Share of Exports of Non-Resource-Based Manufactures[1] in Commodity Exports 1968
Eastern Africa				
Non-Industrial				
Botswana	17.1	---	1.0[5]	---
Burundi	---		0.0[5]	
Ethiopia	13.6	9.8	2.3	2.0
Lesotho	0.9[2]		0.0[5]	---
Malagasy	---	6.8[4]	0.0	---
Malawi	18.8	8.7	1.0	2.1
Rwanda	9.2[2]	---	-0.8	1.0
Somalia	---	---	1.5[5]	3.1
Sudan	11.1	11.1	0.6	0.07
Tanzania	10.8	16.4	1.6	6.0
Uganda	8.4	1.7	1.7	0.7
Zambia	19.0	19.8	5.4	1.0
Industrializing				
Zaire	38.6	12.7	0.2	4.8[6]
Kenya	23.2	6.8	1.5	16.6
Mauritius	35.6	1.9	-0.4[5]	0.0
Swaziland	20.6[3][10]	---	3.2	---
Semi-Industrialized				
Rhodesia	42.0	5.5	0.4	31.6[6]
South Africa	49.2	7.5[4]	3.7[12]	42.3
Western Africa				
Non-Industrial				
Central African Republic	13.5[2]	---	0.0	0.4
Chad	---	---	-1.3	2.8
Congo, People's Republic of	---	---	2.3	15.2[7]
Dahomey	5.2[2]	0.0	0.9	8.3[2]
Gabon	9.0[2]		0.6	7.1
Gambia	---		0.7[5]	0.0
Guinea	3.9[2]		2.6	---
Ivory Coast	19.1	11.2	4.7	12.3
Liberia	8.1	---	1.3	0.1
Mali	13.2	10.0	1.2	2.2[3]
Mauritania	4.9	---	4.6[5]	2.5[3]
Niger	8.5[2]	---	-0.9	1.1[3]
Sierra Leone	9.7	---	1.2	0.02
Togo	15.3[2]	14.4	0.0	3.5[6]
Upper Volta	7.3[2]	17.2	0.1	4.1
Industrializing				
Cameroon	21.7[3]	12.7	2.0	3.1[2]
Ghana	23.5[2]	3.7[4]	0.0	9.7
Nigeria[14]	19.5[2]	10.6	-0.3	1.3
Senegal	29.0	4.3	-0.1	15.3
East Asia & Pacific				
Non-Industrial				
British Solomon Islands	---	---	1.9	0.0
Fiji	---	---	2.7[5]	8.8
Indonesia	13.7	1.2	0.8	4.5
Papua & New Guinea	5.0	9.9	2.0	4.2
Industrializing				
Korea, Republic of	33.8	14.2	6.4	74.3
Malaysia	24.2[8]	12.0[4]	3.8	9.7

	Gross Value Added in Manufacturing as a Percent of Value Added in Commodity Production 1968	Average Annual Growth (%) of Real Gross Value Added in Manufacturing 1960-1969	Average Annual Growth (%) of Real GNP per Capita 1960-1969	Percentage Share of Exports of Non-Resource-Based Manufactures[1] in Commodity Exports 1968
Philippines	32.0	4.3	1.9	13.4
Thailand	27.9	8.1	4.7	8.3
Semi-Industrialized				
China	45.9	13.5	6.3	77.0
New Zealand	55.7[3]	4.7[4]	2.0	8.9
Industrialized				
Hong Kong	87.5	14.3	8.7	91.8
Singapore	65.9	19.0	4.5	11.6
South Asia				
Non-Industrial				
Afghanistan	16.5	4.3[3]	0.3	0.5[3]
Nepal	13.4[2]	1.1	0.4	—
Industrializing				
Burma	20.3[3]	3.5[3]	1.8	1.1
Ceylon	21.4	14.8[4]	2.1	1.1
Iran	37.0[8]	11.0[4]	4.9	3.2[3]
Pakistan[14]	19.2	7.6	2.9	50.5
Semi-Industrialized				
India[15]	20.7	2.5[4]	1.1	51.7
Europe, Middle East and North Africa				
Non-Industrial				
Algeria	17.0[3]	16.3	−2.8	7.8
Iraq	13.9	5.9	3.0	0.8
Industrializing				
Cyprus	27.7	7.2	5.8	12.7
Jordan	21.1[2]	—	4.7[5]	13.3[3]
Morocco	23.4	2.7	3.4	16.2[3]
Syria	20.0[2][9]	—	4.7	13.2
Tunisia	39.4[2]	6.2	2.1	23.0
Turkey	30.9	8.6	3.4	3.9
Semi-Industrialized				
Egypt	41.7[3]	—	1.2	27.0
Finland	58.4	3.7[4]	3.9	67.0
Greece	40.0	6.2	6.2	16.5
Ireland	40.0[2][9]	—	3.5	41.2
Israel[17]	61.5	—	5.3	73.2
Lebanon	48.7[3][9]	—	2.1	25.2
Malta	52.7	6.4	4.1	76.8
Portugal[17]	61.6	7.9	4.9	71.7
Spain	56.8	7.4	6.5	57.7
Yugoslavia	58.1[13]	—	4.6	69.4
Central America and Caribbean				
Non-Industrial				
Haiti	18.8[2]	—	−1.0	—
Industrializing				
Dominican Republic	38.4	3.6	0.4	3.0[3]
El Salvador	38.7	9.0	1.9	34.2
Guatemala	35.4	7.9	1.9	20.6[3]
Guyana	20.9	5.0	0.7	1.2

Some Indicators of Industrial Development

	Gross Value Added in Manufacturing as a Percent of Value Added in Commodity Production 1968	Average Annual Growth (%) of Real Gross Value Added in Manufacturing 1960-1969	Average Annual Growth (%) of Real GNP per Capita 1960-1969	Percentage Share of Exports of Non-Resource-Based Manufactures[1] in Commodity Exports 1968
Honduras	26.7	7.7[4]	1.1	8.3
Jamaica	35.6	4.4	3.0	10.3
Nicaragua	31.0	12.0	3.5	9.5
Panama	37.2	10.7	4.8	2.0
Trinidad and Tobago	30.9[11]	10.1	3.8	12.8[3]
Venezuela	29.7	7.0	2.5	1.2
Semi-Industrialized				
Costa Rica	41.0	—	2.9	19.0
Mexico[17]	61.2[3]	10.0	3.5	19.4
South America				
Industrializing				
Bolivia	29.1	6.4	2.4	0.0
Colombia	32.7	4.5	1.5	9.6
Ecuador	32.3	5.4	1.2	4.6
Paraguay	32.6	4.0	1.0	0.0
Peru	33.9[2]	2.9[4]	1.4	0.0
Semi-Industrialized				
Argentina[17]	61.8	4.3	2.6	21.8
Brazil	56.3	6.6	1.4	11.5
Chile	56.2	5.6	1.7	3.5
Uruguay	51.2[2][9]	—	-0.8	5.0
Selected Industrialized Countries[16]				
Australia	67.0	6.0	2.9	21.0
Canada	65.5[3]	4.3[4]	2.8	53.3
France	78.6	5.9[4]	4.8	74.0
Germany, Federal Republic of	83.7	4.3[4]	3.7	89.0
Japan	73.6	11.6[4]	10.0	95.3
Netherlands	73.4[2]	3.0[4]	3.1	62.3
Norway	69.3	4.0[4]	4.0	58.2
Sweden	76.8	4.6[4]	3.4	72.7
United Kingdom	80.2	2.0[4]	1.8	82.7
United States	80.5	4.6[4]	3.2	68.9

NOTES: The allocation of countries to areas for purposes of this table corresponds to assignments of the Bank's area departments.

[1] Exports of non-resource-based manufactures exclude petroleum and related products, and unworked non-ferrous metals. This column includes goods classified under SITC codes 5, 7 and 8; 6 except part of 68; and parts of 0-4. For non-ferrous metals (code 68) and food products (code 0), the definition of manufactures suggested in *UNCTAD, Trade in Manufactures of Developing Countries: 1970 Review* has been followed, except for refined sugar (code 061.2) which has been included.
[2] 1966.
[3] 1967.
[4] 1968.
[5] Estimates of GNP per capita and growth rate are tentative.
[6] 1965.
[7] Includes industrial diamonds.
[8] 1969.
[9] Includes mining.
[10] Commodity production includes construction.
[11] Excludes oil refining.
[12] 1961-68.
[13] Includes petroleum but no other mining.
[14] Exception made due to the large size of domestic market.
[15] Exception made due to the large size of domestic market, structure of production, and engineering and managerial skills.
[16] Countries in this group with per capita income of $1,300 or more in 1969, and with gross value added in manufacturing as a percent of value added in commodity production of more than 60% in a recent year, are considered "industrialized".
[17] Exception treated as "semi-industrialized" to take into account the effect of protection in overstating value added in manufacturing.

Sources: *U.N. Yearbook of National Accounts Statistics,* 1969, Vol. 1; *U.N. Yearbook of International Trade Statistics,* 1968; World Bank.

Characteristics of Bank Group Manufacturing
Projects by Organizational Unit, FY 1967-1971

Project Characteristics		Organizational Unit	
		World Bank and IDA	
	IFC	Through DFCs(1)	Direct(2)
Average of Total Project Cost ($ millions)	29.0	2.0	14.9
Average Commitment ($ millions)	5.2	0.3	5.5

	Proportion of Projects Bank-IDA			Proportion of Commitments Bank-IDA		
	IFC	DFCs(1)	Direct(2)	IFC	DFCs(1)	Direct(2
Total Project Cost						
Under $200,000	0%	21%	0%	0%	6%	0%
Under $1 million	0%	61%	4%	0%	19%	0%
Under $15 million	51%	98%	84%	21%	90%	28%
Size of Commitment(3)						
Under $50,000	0%	15%	0%	n.a.	n.a.	n.a.
Under $400,000	2%	67%	13%	n.a.	n.a.	n.a.
Under $5 million	63%	100%	79%	n.a.	n.a.	n.a.
Proportion of Project Output Exported						
Zero	73%	54%	21%	74%	50%	66%
Less than 30%	86%	77%	59%	90%	75%	90%
Less than 50%	89%	85%	76%	93%	83%	94%
Less than 100%	93%	97%	100%	94%	94%	99%
Number of Employees in Enterprise(4)						
Under 20	0%	9%	0%	0%	4%	0%
Under 100	2%	39%	0%	3%	21%	0%
Under 500	34%	79%	4%	29%	57%	0%
Proportion of Government Ownership						
Zero	81%	97%	92%	77%	93%	75%
Under 25%	93%	99%	92%	94%	98%	75%
Under 50%	100%	100%	92%	100%	100%	75%
Proportion Involving Foreign Equity(3)						
New projects	85%(5)	23%	100%	n.a.	n.a.	n.a.
Expansion projects	64%(5)	15%	9%	n.a.	n.a.	n.a.
All projects	76%(5)	16%	13%	n.a.	n.a.	n.a.

(1) Figures relate to a representative 1970 sample of Bank Group financed DFC sub-projects.

(2) Excluding import credits and other non-project lending.

(3) Symbol n.a. as used opposite this heading means not readily available.

(4) Includes employees in the enterprise before the project as well as those added.

(5) Involving technical as well as financial participation by foreign partners.

Bank Group Manufacturing Operations by Sector, FY 1967-71
(US$ millions)

I.S.I.C. Industry Category [1] Description	IFC [2] Amount	%	Bank-IDA Direct Financing [3] Amount	%	Total Direct Financing of Projects Amount	%	Indirect Financing of DFC Sub-Projects [4] Amount	%	Total Bank Group Amount	%
Food manufacturing	11.1	3.8	—	—	11.1	2.6	65.4	11.5	76.5	7.7
Textile manufacturing	19.5	6.8	2.0	1.5	21.5	5.1	184.1	32.3	205.6	20.7
Leather and products of leather	—	—	—	—	—	—	11.2	2.0	11.2	1.1
Furniture and wood products	—	—	2.2	1.7	2.2	0.5	19.9	3.5	22.1	2.2
Paper and pulp	36.3	12.6	2.0	1.5	38.3	9.1	19.8	3.5	58.1	5.9
Printing, publishing and allied industry	7.0	2.4	—	—	7.0	1.7	6.0	1.1	13.0	1.3
Chemicals manufacturing	74.4	25.8	62.0	47.0	136.4	32.4	46.2	8.1	182.6	18.4
Petroleum refineries	8.0	2.8	—	—	8.0	1.9	3.3	0.6	11.3	1.1
Manufacture of miscellaneous products of petroleum and coal	22.8	7.9	—	—	22.8	5.4	—	—	22.8	2.3
Manufacture of rubber products	—	—	1.5	1.1	1.5	0.4	26.4	4.6	26.4	2.7
Manufacture of plastic products	—	—	—	—	—	—	4.0	0.7	5.5	0.6
Pottery, china, earthware	2.3	0.8	—	—	2.3	0.6	3.3	0.6	5.6	0.6
Glass and glass products	11.6	4.0	—	—	11.6	2.8	13.9	2.4	25.5	2.6
Other non-metallic mineral products	47.1	16.3	—	—	47.1	11.2	35.0	6.1	82.1	8.3
Iron and steel basic industries	11.3	3.9	8.2	6.2	19.5	4.6	30.4	5.3	49.9	5.0
Non-ferrous metal basic industries	8.6	3.0	27.0	20.5	35.6	8.5	4.7	0.8	40.3	4.1
Fabricated metal products	11.5	4.0	—	—	11.5	2.7	23.1	4.0	34.6	3.5
Machinery, except for electrical	—	—	—	—	—	—	28.4	5.0	28.4	2.9
Electrical machinery manufacture	0.2	0.0	—	—	0.2	0.0	19.1	3.3	19.3	1.9
Transport equipment manufacture	17.0	5.9	20.3	15.4	37.3	8.9	23.1	4.0	60.4	6.1
Other manufacturing industries	—	—	6.8	5.1	6.8	1.6	3.3	0.6	10.1	1.0
Totals	288.7	100%	132.0	100%	420.7	100%	570.6	100%	991.3	100%
Of which:										
Heavy manufacturing	87.0%		90.6%		88.1%		43.7%		62.7%	
Light manufacturing	13.0%		9.4%		11.9%		56.3%		37.3%	

[1] U.N. 1968 International Standard Industrial Classification.
[2] IFC data are qualified as in footnote [1], Annex 8, except that investments in service industries are excluded.
[3] Bank and IDA direct financing data are qualified as in footnote [1], Annex 9.
[4] DFC figures in this table (apart from the total amount of sub-project investments) are not actuals, but are based on percentage distributions obtained from a representative sample of sub-projects in fiscal years 1968-70. Agriculture, mining, tourism and services are excluded.

Pattern of Bank Group Manufacturing Operations in Selected Countries by Organizational Unit, FY 1967-1971
(Percentages)

Countries[1]	Stage[2]	Percent Shares of Bank Group Developing Members		Percent of Total Bank Group Financing of Manufacturing Projects in Developing Countries	Percentage of Bank Group Financing for Manufacturing Projects			
					Bank-IDA			
		Population	GNP		Through DFCs[3]	Direct	IFC	Total Bank Group
India	SI	31.3	16.8	7.3	67.3	—	32.7	100.0
Brazil	SI	5.3	7.1	6.6	28.9	25.4	45.7	100.0
Mexico	SI	2.8	8.1	0.9	—	—	100.0	100.0
Iran	I	1.6	2.7	11.2	94.3	—	5.7	100.0
Pakistan	I	7.4	3.9	10.6	68.3	25.2	6.5	100.0
Turkey	I	2.0	3.3	8.9	77.9	—	22.1	100.0
Colombia	I	1.2	2.0	6.2	96.3	—	3.7	100.0
Philippines	I	2.1	2.0	5.9	64.3	—	35.7	100.0
Morocco	I	0.9	0.8	5.7	100.0	—	—	100.0
Korea, Rep. of	I	1.7	1.7	4.8	89.4	—	10.6	100.0
Nigeria	I	3.7	1.4	1.3	95.2	—	4.8	100.0
Kenya	I	0.6	0.4	1.1	—	—	100.0	100.0
CACM[4]	I	0.8	1.5	0.2	—	—	100.0	100.0
Ghana	I	0.5	0.5	—	—	—	—	—
Indonesia	NI	6.7	3.6	4.0	—	57.6	42.4	100.0
Ethiopia	NI	1.4	0.6	0.7	—	—	100.0	100.0
Tanzania	NI	0.7	0.3	—	—	—	—	—
Uganda	NI	0.6	0.3	—	—	—	—	—
Sub-total		71.3	57.0	75.5	69.6	8.8	21.6	100.0
Other Developing Countries		28.7	43.0	24.5	57.6	14.0	28.4	100.0
Total Bank Group Developing Members		100.0	100.0	100.0	66.7	10.0	23.2	100.0

[1] Countries selected here are the 22 reviewed in detail for the purposes of this paper.

[2] NI, non-industrial; SI, semi-industrialized; I, industrializing.

[3] Includes IFC investments through financial intermediaries.

[4] Costa Rica, one of the five members of the Central American Common Market (CACM), is categorized as a "semi-industrialized" county n Annex 1, but is here combined with the other CACM countries for purposes of presentation.

Sources: Financing data extracted from Annexes 6, 7, 8 and 9, but developed countries (Finland) have been excluded to arrive at percentages in this table. GNP and population percentages, World Bank.

Bank Group Manufacturing Operations [1]
by Organizational Unit and Major Recipient, FY 1967-1971
(US$ millions)

	Stage [2]	Bank-IDA Through DFCs [3] $	%	Direct $	%	IFC $	%	Total Bank $	Group %
Eastern Africa									
*East African Community		—	—	—	—	15	5	15	1
*Ethiopia	NI	—	—	—	—	10	3	10	1
Other		6	1	—	—	—	—	6	0
Sub-totals		6	1	—	—	24	8	31	2
Western Africa									
*Nigeria	I	16	2	—	—	1	0	17	1
Other		—	—	—	—	3	1	3	0
Sub-totals		16	2	—	—	4	1	20	1
Africa Unallocated		1	0	—	—	—	—	1	0
East Asia and Pacific									
China, Republic of	SI	33	4	—	—	10	3	42	3
*Indonesia	NI	—	—	30	23	22	7	52	4
*Korea, Republic of	I	56	6	—	—	7	2	63	5
*Philippines	I	50	5	—	—	28	9	78	6
Thailand	I	—	—	—	—	22	7	22	2
Other		5	1	—	—	5	2	10	0
Sub-totals		144	16	30	23	94	31	268	20
South Asia									
*India	SI	65	7	—	—	32	10	97	7
*Iran	I	140	16	—	—	8	3	148	11
*Pakistan	I	95	10	35	27	9	3	139	10
Other		5	1	—	—	3	1	8	1
Sub-totals		305	33	35	27	52	17	392	29
Europe, Middle East and North Africa									
Finland	SI	42	5	—	—	—	—	42	3
Greece	SI	33	4	—	—	9	3	41	3
Israel	SI	40	4	—	—	—	—	40	3
*Morocco	I	75	8	—	—	—	—	75	6
Tunisia	I	21	2	—	—	—	—	21	2
*Turkey	I	91	10	—	—	26	8	117	9
Yugoslavia	SI	2	0	45	34	17	6	64	5
Other		10	—	—	—	2	1	12	1
Sub-totals		313	34	45	34	54	18	412	30

	Stage[2]	Bank-IDA						Total	
		Through DFCs[3]		Direct		IFC		Bank	Group
		$	%	$	%	$	%	$	%
Central America and Caribbean									
*CACM[4]	I	—	—	—	—	2	1	2	0
*Mexico	SI	—	—	—	—	12	4	12	1
Venezuela	I	12	1	—	—	4	1	17	1
Sub-totals		12	1	—	—	19	6	31	2
South America									
Argentina	SI	—	—	—	—	15	5	16	1
*Brazil	SI	25	3	22	17	40	13	87	6
*Colombia	I	79	9	—	—	3	1	81	6
Other		8	1	—	—	—	—	8	1
Sub-totals		112	12	22	17	58	19	192	14
Latin America Unallocated		10	1	—	—	—	—	10	1
Grand totals		918	100	132	100	305	100	1356	100
Of which									
Industrialized		5	1	—	—	—	—	5	0
Semi-Industrialized		249	27	67	51	137	45	453	33
Industrializing		654	71	35	26	137	45	826	61
Non-Industrial		—	—	30	23	32	10	62	5
Unallocated		10	1	—	—	—	—	10	1

NOTES: The allocation of countries to areas for purposes of this table corresponds to assignments of the Bank's area departments. Totals may not add due to rounding.

* Indicates countries included in the sample of 22 countries reviewed in detail for the purposes of this paper. Ghana was also a sample country but received no Bank Group funds for industry in this period.

[1] IFC and Bank-IDA direct lending data exclude mining and tourism projects and commitments subsequently cancelled. DFC data relate to Bank Group commitments to industrial DFCs though some of their sub-projects are in sectors other than manufacturing. DFCs for tourism ventures are excluded.

[2] NI, non-industrial; I, industrializing; SI, semi-industrialized.

[3] Includes IFC investments through financial intermediaries.

[4] Central American Common Market.

Sources: Annexes 6, 7, 8 and 9.

Bank Group Manufacturing Commitments[1]
by Regions and Countries, FY 1967-1971
(US$ millions)

	Stage[2]	1967	1968	1969	1970	1971	Total 1967-71	%
Eastern Africa								
Ethiopia	NI	—	9.0	—	0.6	—	9.6	1
Kenya	I	—	—	—	14.7	—	14.7	1
Zaire	I	—	—	—	5.8	—	5.8	0
Sub-totals		—	9.0	—	21.1	—	30.1	2
Western Africa								
Nigeria	I	0.8	—	6.0	—	10.0	16.8	1
Senegal	I	3.5	—	—	—	—	3.5	0
Sub-totals		4.3	—	6.0	—	10.0	20.3	1
Africa Regional		—	—	—	—	0.5	0.5	0
East Asia and Pacific								
China, Republic of	SI	—	14.6	—	25.2	2.6	42.4	3
Indonesia	NI	—	—	—	30.0	22.1	52.1	4
Korea, Republic of	I	—	5.7	21.7	5.0	30.7	63.1	5
Malaysia	I	—	3.5	0.2	1.5	—	5.2	0
Philippines	I	37.0	—	—	32.8	8.0	77.8	6
Singapore	Ind.	—	—	—	5.0	—	5.0	0
Thailand	I	—	—	22.1	—	0.2	22.3	2
Sub-totals		37.0	23.8	44.0	99.5	63.6	267.9	20
South Asia								
Ceylon	I	—	2.3	—	6.3	—	8.6	1
India	SI	12.7	25.0	15.9	43.0	—	96.6	7
Iran	I	24.6	24.9	43.9	—	54.5	147.9	11
Pakistan	I	5.2	35.0	75.9	23.0	—	139.1	10
Sub-totals		42.5	87.2	135.7	72.3	54.5	392.2	29
Europe, Middle East and North Africa								
Finland	SI	—	—	22.0	—	20.0	42.0	3
Greece	SI	—	12.5	—	28.6	—	41.1	3
Ireland	SI	—	—	—	—	10.0	10.0	1
Israel	SI	—	15.0	—	25.0	—	40.0	3
Lebanon	SI	—	—	—	—	2.1	2.1	0
Morocco	I	—	—	15.0	15.0	45.0	75.0	6
Spain	SI	0.2	—	—	—	—	0.2	0
Tunisia	I	—	10.0	—	10.6	—	20.6	2
Turkey	I	25.3	—	27.3	14.8	49.1	116.5	9
Yugoslavia	SI	—	10.5	16.0	28.5	9.0	64.0	5
Sub-totals		25.5	48.0	80.3	122.5	135.2	411.5	30

	Stage[2]	1967	1968	1969	1970	1971	Total 1967-71	%
Central America and Caribbean								
CACM[3]	I	—	2.1	—	—	—	2.1	0
Mexico	SI	—	0.4	—	—	12.0	12.4	1
Venezuela	I	—	7.5	2.1	—	7.0	16.6	1
Sub-totals		—	10.0	2.1	—	19.0	31.1	2
South America								
Argentina	SI	—	—	10.0	—	5.5	15.5	1
Brazil	SI	10.7	22.1	9.5	33.4	10.9	86.6	6
Colombia	I	0.9	12.7	26.0	1.9	40.0	81.5	6
Ecuador	I	—	—	0.3	—	8.0	8.3	1
Peru	I	0.01	0.1	—	—	—	0.1	0
Sub-totals		11.6	34.9	45.8	35.3	64.4	192.0	14
Latin America Regional		—	—	—	10.0	—	10.0	1
Grand Totals		120.9	212.9	313.9	360.7	347.2	1,355.6	100
Of which:								
Industrialized		—	—	—	5.0	—	5.0	0
Semi-Industrialized		23.6	100.1	73.4	183.7	72.1	452.9	33
Industrializing		97.3	103.8	240.5	131.4	252.5	825.5	61
Non-Industrial		—	9.0	—	30.6	22.1	61.7	5
Regional		—	—	—	10.0	0.5	10.5	1
Of which:								
Bank-IDA Direct		—	32.5	48.0	51.5	—	132.0	10
Through DFCs[4]		74.9	165.0	194.6	224.5	259.4	918.4	68
IFC		46.0	15.4	71.3	84.7	87.8	305.2	22

NOTES: The allocation of countries to areas for purposes of this table corresponds to assignments of the Bank's area departments. Totals of percentages may not add due to rounding.

[1] Data used in compiling this table are qualified as in Annexes 7, 8 and 9.

[2] NI, non-industrial; I, industrializing; SI, semi-industrialized; Ind., industrialized.

[3] Central American Common Market.

[4] Includes IFC investments through financial intermediaries.

135

Bank Group Commitments to Industrial DFCs[1]
by Regions and Countries, FY 1967-1971
(US$ millions)

	Stage[2]	1967	1968	1969	1970	1971	Total 1967-71	%
Eastern Africa								
Zaire	I	—	—	—	5.8	—	5.8	1
Western Africa								
Nigeria	I	—	—	6.0	—	10.0	16.0	2
Africa Regional		—	—	—	—	0.5	0.5	0
East Asia and Pacific								
China, Republic of	SI	—	14.6	—	18.0	—	32.6	4
Korea, Republic of	I	—	5.7	20.0	—	30.7	56.4	6
Philippines	I	25.0	—	—	25.0	—	50.0	5
Singapore	Ind.	—	—	—	5.0	—	5.0	1
Thailand	I	—	—	—	—	0.2	0.2	0
Sub-totals		25.0	20.3	20.0	48.0	30.9	144.2	16
South Asia								
Ceylon	I	—	2.3	—	3.0	—	5.3	1
India	SI	—	25.0	—	40.0	—	65.0	7
Iran	I	24.6	24.9	40.0	—	50.0	139.5	15
Pakistan	I	—	35.0	40.0	20.0	—	95.0	10
Sub-totals		24.6	87.2	80.0	63.0	50.0	304.8	33
Europe, Middle East and North Africa								
Finland	SI	—	—	22.0	—	20.0	42.0	5
Greece	SI	—	12.5	—	20.0	—	32.5	4
Ireland	SI	—	—	—	—	10.0	10.0	1
Israel	SI	—	15.0	—	25.0	—	40.0	4
Morocco	I	—	—	15.0	15.0	45.0	75.0	8
Tunisia	I	—	10.0	—	10.6	—	20.6	2
Turkey	I	24.3	—	25.4	—	40.0	90.7	10
Yugoslavia	SI	—	—	—	2.0	—	2.0	0
Sub-totals		25.3	37.5	62.4	72.6	115.0	312.8	34
Central America and Caribbean								
Venezuela	I	—	7.5	—	—	5.0	12.5	1
South America								
Brazil	SI	—	—	—	25.0	—	25.0	3
Colombia	I	—	12.5	25.9	0.1	40.0	78.5	9
Ecuador	I	—	—	0.3	—	8.0	8.3	1
Sub-totals		—	12.5	26.2	25.1	48.0	111.8	12
Latin America Regional		—	—	—	10.0	—	10.0	1
Grand Totals		74.9	165.0	194.6	224.5	259.4	918.4	100
Of which:								
Industrialized		—	—	—	5.0	—	5.0	1
Semi-Industrialized		—	67.1	22.0	130.0	30.0	249.1	27
Industrializing		74.9	97.9	172.6	79.5	228.9	653.8	71
Regional		—	—	—	10.0	0.5	10.5	1

NOTES: The allocation of countries to areas for purposes of this table corresponds to assignments of the Bank's area departments. Totals of percentages may not add due to rounding.

[1] Data in this table relate to actual Bank Group commitments to industrial DFCs (net of cancellations), and include funds committed by the latter for sub-projects in sectors other than manufacturing (14% during FY1968-70). Also includes IFC investments through financial intermediaries.

[2] I, industrializing; SI, semi-industrialized; Ind., industrialized.

IFC Manufacturing Commitments[1]
by Regions and Countries, FY 1967-1971
(US$ millions)

	Stage[2]	1967	1968	1969	1970	1971	Total 1967-71	%
Eastern Africa								
Ethiopia	NI	—	9.0	—	0.6	—	9.6	3
Kenya	I	—	—	—	14.7	—	14.7	5
Sub-totals		—	9.0	—	15.3	—	24.3	8
Western Africa								
Nigeria	I	0.8	—	—	—	—	0.8	0
Senegal	I	3.5	—	—	—	—	3.5	1
Sub-totals		4.3	—	—	—	—	4.3	1
East Asia and Pacific								
China, Republic of	SI	—	—	—	7.2	2.6	9.8	3
Indonesia	NI	—	—	—	—	22.1	22.1	7
Korea, Republic of	I	—	—	1.7	5.0	—	6.7	2
Malaysia	I	—	3.5	0.2	1.5	—	5.2	2
Philippines	I	12.0	—	—	7.8	8.0	27.8	9
Thailand	I	—	—	22.1	—	—	22.1	7
Sub-totals		12.0	3.5	24.0	21.5	32.7	93.7	31
South Asia								
Ceylon	I	—	—	—	3.3	—	3.3	1
India	SI	12.7	—	15.9	3.0	—	31.6	10
Iran	I	—	—	3.9	—	4.5	8.4	3
Pakistan	I	5.2	—	3.9	—	—	9.1	3
Sub-totals		17.9	—	23.7	6.3	4.5	52.4	17
Europe, Middle East and North Africa								
Greece	SI	—	—	—	8.6	—	8.6	3
Lebanon	SI	—	—	—	—	2.1	2.1	1
Spain	SI	0.2	—	—	—	—	0.2	0
Turkey	I	—	—	1.9	14.8	9.1	25.8	8
Yugoslavia	SI	—	—	—	8.0	9.0	17.0	6
Sub-totals		0.2	—	1.9	31.4	20.2	53.7	18
Central America and Caribbean								
CACM[3]	I	—	2.1	—	—	—	2.1	1
Mexico	SI	—	0.4	—	—	12.0	12.4	4
Venezuela	I	—	—	2.1	—	2.0	4.1	1
Sub-totals		—	2.5	2.1	—	14.0	18.6	6
South America								
Argentina	SI	—	—	10.0	—	5.5	15.5	5
Brazil	SI	10.7	0.1	9.5	8.4	10.9	39.6	13
Colombia	I	0.9	0.2	0.1	1.8	—	3.0	1
Peru	I	0.01	0.1	—	—	—	0.1	0
Sub-totals		11.6	0.4	19.6	10.2	16.4	58.2	19
Grand Totals		46.0	15.4	71.3	84.7	87.8	305.2	100

137

IFC Manufacturing Commitments[1]
by Regions and Countries, FY 1967-1971
(US$ millions)

	1967	1968	1969	1970	1971	Total 1967-71	%
Of which:							
Semi-Industrialized	23.6	0.5	35.4	35.2	42.1	136.8	45
Industrializing	22.4	5.9	35.9	48.9	23.6	136.7	45
Non-Industrialized	—	9.0	—	0.6	22.1	31.7	10

NOTES: The allocation of countries to areas for purposes of this table corresponds to assignments of the Bank's area departments. Totals of percentages may not add due to rounding.

[1] IFC data relate to original project commitments whether for new or expansion projects. Excluded are: tourism projects and COFITOUR, a tourism financing institution in Tunisia; IFC investments in DFCs and a capital market venture in Korea; mining and ore treatment projects (exclusively ore treatment and/or metals processing projects are included); underwriting commitments, except to the extent that an IFC investment has actually been required; investment commitments subsequently cancelled; and commitments for pre-feasibility studies only. Included are: agro-industry projects involving production, processing and marketing operations (sugar production and refining), and services (utilities).

[2] NI, non-industrial; I, industrializing; SI, semi-industrialized; Ind., industrialized.

[3] Central American Common Market.

Direct Bank-IDA Manufacturing Commitments [1]
by Regions and Countries, FY 1967-1971
(US$ millions)

	Stage[2]	1967	1968	1969	1970	1971	Total 1967-71	%
Eastern Africa		—	—	—	—	—	—	—
Western Africa		—	—	—	—	—	—	—
East Asia and Pacific								
Indonesia	NI	—	—	—	30.0	—	30.0	23
South Asia								
Pakistan	I	—	—	32.0	3.0	—	35.0	27
Europe, Middle East and North Africa								
Yugoslavia	SI	—	10.5	16.0	18.5	—	45.0	34
Central America and Caribbean		—	—	—	—	—	—	—
South America								
Brazil	SI	—	22.0	—	—	—	22.0	17
Grand Total		—	32.5	48.0	51.5	—	132.0	100
Of which:								
Semi-Industrialized		—	32.5	16.0	18.5	—	67.0	51
Industrializing		—	—	32.0	3.0	—	35.0	26
Non-Industrial		—	—	—	30.0	—	30.0	23

NOTES: The allocation of countries to areas for purposes of this table corresponds to assignments of the Bank's area departments. Totals of percentages may not add due to rounding.

[1] Excludes a $30 million loan to India for iron and steel, subsequently cancelled after disbursement of $1.7 million. Excludes also loans for mining projects.

[2] NI, non-industrial; I, industrializing; SI, semi-industrialized.

TRANSPORTATION

Annexes

TRANSPORTATION
SECTOR WORKING PAPER

● This paper outlines the World Bank's lending, technical assistance and research in the transport sector against the background of previous experience. It discusses the role of transport in overall economic activity, reviews what the Bank has done in support of the sector, and summarizes the general lessons derived from that experience.

It should be borne in mind that the Bank's approach to lending in this sector, as in all others, begins with an assessment of the country's economic position and prospects and of the relative priorities of both sectors and projects.

References to the Bank include the International Development Association (IDA) except where the context requires otherwise. Where the term "Bank Group" is employed, it refers to the Bank and IDA but does not include the Bank's other affiliate, the International Finance Corporation (IFC). Money amounts are expressed in U.S. dollar equivalents. The Bank's fiscal year (FY) ends June 30.

CHARACTERISTICS OF THE SECTOR

Role of Transport in Economic Activity

Transportation is a necessary concomitant of the exchange economy and is indispensable to economic growth. Where there is no transportation, economic activity is restricted to hand-to-mouth subsistence levels. Specialization and the generation of surpluses for exchange on the basis of comparative advantage are not possible without the capability to move resources and goods from one place to another. The demand for transport services increases with the extension of the input-output relationships of the economy, and the provision of transportation services can be an important determinant of the pace and locational pattern of development.

In a developed economy the volume of goods and people transported from one place to another is enormous. The contribution of transport to the domestic production effort is usually understated by standard national accounting methods; many transport activities are not included under transport headings. However, in developed economies, transport would typically account for 10% to 15% of Gross Domestic Product (GDP). In developing economies the contribution of transport to GDP varies considerably from one country to another, since the variables which determine the cost and vol-

143

ume of transport are fewer and individually more important in the simpler economy. However, where production is of relatively lower value per ton and transport systems are relatively inefficient or high cost, it is generally also the case that the contribution of transport to market GDP will be higher. For landlocked Chad, the proportion of transport in market GDP is estimated at about 17%. On the other hand, for refined copper-exporting Zambia (before the political situation in that part of the world distorted the transport picture), the comparable figure was only 7%.

Demand for transport is a derived demand depending upon the demand for the commodities carried or for the benefits of personal travel. Likewise, the elasticity of demand for transport is determined mainly by the elasticity of demand for the things being transported, and by the proportion of transport costs in the value of the delivered product. Only to a small extent is demand for transport affected by substitutability of other services (e.g. telecommunications and storage) and only in the longer-run is total transport demand given additional elasticity by locational decisions.

Investigations in developed economies suggest that transportation costs are not a significant proportion of the final price of most manufactured and some mining products (the average is less than 10%), and for that reason the demand for transport is fairly insensitive to the price (or cost) of transport. This inelasticity is reinforced by the highly set locational patterns of production that typically exist in the more developed economies, and by the relatively low cost of transport due to more efficient transport systems.

The situation is radically different in less developed economies where a larger proportion of the economically important movements are likely to be high-bulk, low-value agricultural and mineral products. The thresholds of viable production or export of these primary products are often determined by externally defined prices. Transport costs on the feeder roads, on the trunk road or railway to the coast, through the port, and on the ship to foreign markets often account for as much as 50% of the receipts from these commodities. Maize in Kenya and iron ore in Brazil are cases in point. Where transportation is particularly costly due to a lack of adequate facilities or inefficient operation, the impact on profitability and output can be decisive.

Also, in developing economies where inter-industry linkages are less numerous and less strong, transportation costs are likely to have a much greater role in determining locational patterns of development than in developed economies. In short, price elasticity of demand for transport is likely to be relatively higher in less developed countries, and reductions in transport costs are likely to have a larger impact in terms of bringing into production the marginal piece of land, the marginal worker, or the marginal material resource.

Commensurate with its role in production, transportation absorbs a significant part of total investment, although here again there is great variation from one country to the next. Table 1 gives the results of an attempt to examine the data for 45 countries; it shows the percentage shares of transport and communication in gross fixed investment in the post-1945 years.

Table 1: Percentage of Gross Fixed Investment Allocated to Transport and Communication in 45 Countries, 1945-1965 [1]

Income Levels	No. of Countries	% Range of Gross Fixed Investment	Average %
Over $500 per capita	15	13-36	19
$200-500 per capita	8	14-22	19
$100-200 per capita	7	4-26	15
Below $100 per capita	5	16-50	27
Socialist Countries	10	7-16	12

[1] D. Bejakovic, *The Place of Transport and Communications Investment in Total and Productive Investments in the Course of Economic Development*, July 1965, financed by the Federal Bureau of Economic Planning, Belgrade.

The figures in Table 1 understate the true significance of transport in investment, since they exclude automotive equipment investments which, in many economies, can amount to as much as infrastructure investment. A very rough indicator of the norm of total transport sector investment would be about 5% of Gross Domestic Product (GDP) per annum. However, one is forced to agree with the conclusion of the study mentioned above and of many others, that there are no general guidelines as to the share of national product or total investment that should go into transport investment at any stage of development. The evidence is also unclear as to whether the proportion of resources devoted to transport increases or declines as GNP or per capita income rises. The claim of the transport sector on a nation's resources is clearly very great, however, and the volume of transport investment seems never to taper off.

The aim of investment in the transportation sector is to reduce the costs of production by lowering those of transport, thus facilitating higher levels of production and consumption. When a capacity constraint is eased or a new area is "opened up" by a transportation investment, it is the effects of this upon the costs of production that counts, and the extent to which these savings are translated through consumer and producer surpluses into new output. Thus the real effects of most transportation investment in terms of employment and income growth and distribution are indirect and, to a large extent, depend upon the market and upon policies and conditions in the transport sector and the economy as a whole which affect it.

The safest strategy of investment in transportation is to wait until increases in production or captive productive schemes signal clearly the infrastructure requirements; that is, to wait until bottlenecks appear or solid traffic volumes and clear trends exist, and then to take appropriate action to increase capacity or reduce costs for an assured clientele. Given scarce investment funds, this is a quite common investment strategy and most Bank-financed transportation sector investments follow this approach.

The safest approach, however, is not necessarily the most developmental, especially in the very poor country where the development problem takes on a chicken-or-egg complexity. Furthermore, it tends to reinforce existing patterns of income distribution and geographical patterns of development. Experience shows, and in a rather dramatic fashion, that promotional transportation investments can be the agent of important economic developments.

Having said this, it is important to note that improved transport cannot create development by itself; the area and population served must have the necessary additional resources, and the other investments required to exploit them must be forthcoming. To adopt successfully a more "entrepreneurial" approach to transport investment requires detailed knowledge of the economic environment and of the kind of investment and institutional mix that will stimulate production. There are enough instances where the invitation to produce extended by transportation investment has not been taken up—the uneconomic railway branch line and the overdesigned and underutilized road into the desert or bush—to show that the required degree of knowledge is not common.

Some Characteristics of Transport Systems

Transportation needs can be met by any one or combination of the following modes: aviation, inland waterway, coastal and ocean shipping, pipeline, port, rail or road services.[1] The extent and modal

[1] Although transportation becomes increasingly capital-intensive as economies grow, human effort and animal power are still important in providing transport services over large parts of the world.

structure of a transport system reflects many influences, including the country's geography, terrain, the structure of its economy, and the history of its growth and development. (See Annex I for a basic inventory of transport facilities in 95 countries). Factors such as density of population and the disposition of resources, i.e., the basic supply and demand for goods and travel, are by far the most significant in determining the density and mix of transport modes in the network that has been or will be developed.

Within any system, the modes included both complement and compete with each other. The complementarity aspects may involve a number of necessary steps in the movement of people and goods from points of origin to final destination: e.g., car and bus journeys to railway stations or airports, truck or rail movements from farms, ports, or pipeline terminals to distribution points or market outlets. Complementarity arises inevitably out of the scattered distribution of production, marketing, and residential points as well as technological and economic conditions.

The different modes also compete with each other. Since each mode has different mixes of infrastructure and equipment, different economic sizes of vehicle unit, different speeds and other service characteristics, both transport and total distribution costs incurred in the use of any particular mode can vary widely over different lengths of haul, shipment size, terrain conditions, and volume flows. But shippers' choice and the design of public policy are not exclusively a matter of cost comparisons, in the narrow sense. Important differences exist in the marketing capabilities of the different forms of transportation. For example, one reason for the success of trucking in competition with the railways has been a more decentralized and flexible organization, better able to meet particular shippers' needs.

The situation, therefore, is not one of perfect competition or substitutability or one mode of transport for another. Each mode has certain comparative advantages. The decision to move a specific commodity on a specific route by a specific mode is unique to the circumstances. Nevertheless, some broad generalizations about the advantages of each mode are possible.

The technical and economic advantages of railroads appear first in handling large volume over long hauls. Equipped as mass movement carriers, they are normally the most economic and efficient for bulk traffic on intermediate and long hauls (over 150 miles). Transportation by rail, other than for dense passenger flows in urban areas, is generally uneconomic on short hauls due to relatively high terminal and overhead costs and the need to transship for door-to-door distribution. Most of the railways borrowing from the Bank are saddled with extensive systems built before the advent of the road transport industry, and with public service, employment, and pricing obligations which threaten their financial viability. This has led to patterns of serious underinvestment which in turn have threatened the railways' ability to fulfill their economic roles. This default on the part of railways has tended to inflate the demand for road transport that might otherwise be uneconomic.

Motor transport is generally the most efficient mode for short distance and intermediate hauls. Trucking is equipped to handle commodities of medium and high unit value, and in lots relatively smaller than are advantageous for railway movements. Trucks have a great advantage because they give door-to-door service from shipper to receiver. Motor carriers are generally uneconomic on very long hauls or for high-volume, low-value commodities. The development of the goods transport market in many countries shows, however, that the motor carriers are conquering an increasing proportion of long distance traffic, often, apparently, due to the default of rail transport.

Water carriers are able to move goods—especially bulky commodities—at a relatively low cost per ton-mile over long distances. Generally water carriers have capacity to handle large tonnages, but they are normally much slower than other transport means. Extensive terminal facilities are needed, and port handling costs are an important determinant of the overall costs and competitiveness of this mode. Water carriers are often limited to the hauling of goods of low unit value, except in areas where other means of transportation are less developed.

The primary advantage of air transport is speed. In order to pay for this quality, shipments and passenger movements generally should possess a high unit value. Air transport is primarily aimed at the movement of people where time is especially valuable. The competitiveness of this mode is vitally affected by the capacity and efficiency of terminal operations. Goods having medium or low unit value are not well suited to movement by air, except in special circumstances.

Pipelines are able to move large volumes of liquids and natural gas over long distances and difficult terrain, reliably at a relatively low cost. In the case of land transport of natural gas, there is no economic alternative. The disadvantage of pipelines is that they must operate near capacity to ensure low unit costs. The movement of bulk commodities such as iron ore in water suspension is a recent development in pipeline technology.

Trends in Transportation

Motorization. One of the most important trends in transportation is the accelerating pace of motorized transport. The growth of vehicle fleets on a worldwide basis is of the order of 15% per annum; almost every country in the world is experiencing such growth. (See graph, Annex 5.)

Urban Congestion. The rapid trend toward urbanization throughout the world, coupled with the growth of motorization, is creating problems of urban transport on a wholly new scale for both developed and less developed countries. The future should see a far-reaching shift from the present emphasis on congestion-producing individualized conveyances toward public mass transport—bus and rapid rail transit systems.

Environmental Pollution. The transport sector presents its share of environmental problems, which are just now becoming better understood. Pollution of urban atmospheres by the internal combustion engine is presently the most important. Bringing such pollution under control is likely to create new problems of vehicle regulation. A similar problem—compounded by noise—exists in air transport, although control may be easier to enforce. A special, but important and worldwide, environmental problem exists in petroleum transport; oil spills are becoming so large and so common that special measures seem required to prevent excessive social and economic costs. The growing movement of chemicals, acids, flammable materials, and the like, by road and rail is also posing growing potential hazards.

Railway Reform and Recovery. Almost everywhere, railways are in or threatened with decline as a result of poor financial performance and a long period of serious underinvestment or misinvestment. The emerging problems of indirect economic and environmental costs connected with individualized motorization and, to some extent, of air transport are forcing a review of the role of rail transport and the pricing, regulatory, and investment policies which affect its potential.

Technological Change. The ability of transport investments to continue their cost-reducing contribution to development is being greatly affected by a steady stream of major technological changes. These changes continually alter the investment merit of existing and future transport projects and the competitive position of the various modes. While cost-reducing technological advance has made substantial contributions to developing economies, most of the technological change is consciously or unconsciously in the labor-saving direction, e.g., larger-scale technologies in ocean shipping and air transport, containerization, pipelines, diesel-electrification, computerization, roll-on, roll-off techniques, huge earth moving equipment, etc. This reflects the fact that technological advance tends to originate in higher income, more fully employed economies. In many instances developing countries will be faced with important economic decisions on whether and how to adopt or adapt these technologies to their own situations. In some cases the problems are especially severe because the technologies may be imposed by outside influences regardless of the economic situation of the receiving country; for instance, airports and ports may have to be equipped to handle the planes and ships developed to meet the needs of developed countries, if trade and communications with these countries are not to suffer.

Transportation Planning

Because of the important interaction between transportation and the location, volume and growth of economic activity, and because of the high benefits and costs that can be involved in a transportation policy or investment decision, comprehensive and long-range transportation planning is especially desirable. It is also difficult. First, the overall national priorities on which transport has a direct bearing—economic, social, strategic—are rarely made explicit, which means that from the outset the goals of planning are often vague. Second, since transport demand is derived, good transport planning implies the accurate assessment of activities and targets in other sectors and translation of these forecasts into traffic volumes along specific routes over time, and of the impact of the investment on these flows. Ideally, this requires a systems approach that captures the basic workings of the economy. The necessary tools for such an approach are unfortunately in a rudimentary stage of development. Third, the transport sector involves lumpy infrastructure investments, with long economic lives, which means that forecasting has to be acceptably reliable over long periods.

With respect to the transportation infrastructure, each mode is often the responsibility of a distinct government agency, and even for a single mode there is often a multiplicity of government, business, and labor interests involved, each with its own political constituency. In one Latin American country, for example, seven ministries, six government-sponsored agencies, three international bodies, one foreign government, numerous trade unions, tourist interests and foreign airlines are vitally concerned about civil aviation investment and operations. In other modes and other countries a similar multitude of interests is often found.

150

Lack of comprehensive transportation policy and planning is prevalent in highly developed countries as well as in the less developed. The situation is aggravated in the latter by the lack of data and trained personnel necessary to proper planning, although in some developing countries the impact of these deficiencies may be lessened by the fact that the problems they face are less complex.

The consequences of this difficult and deficient planning situation are often misdirected investment plans and proposals, and transport pricing, investment and regulatory policies that are outmoded or ill-suited to the economic situation. The Bank, therefore, does not start with a clean slate or easy situations in its efforts to obtain an efficient use of resources in the transport sector. The Bank's impact in this sector is in large measure dependent upon its effectiveness in assisting improvement in transportation planning and policy.

PAST ACTIVITIES IN THE SECTOR

Lending

By the end of FY 1971, total Bank and IDA lending for transportation amounted to $6,160 million, divided into $5,220 million (85%) in Bank loans and $940 million (15%) in IDA credits. Table 2 summarizes the history of the expansion and changing modal mix of Bank Group lending for transport.

Transport loans and credits have been the largest single component of Bank Group finance, accounting for more than 30% in terms of both lending volume and number of operations. The share of transport in total Group lending has fluctuated over the years, however, rising from 18% in the pre-1955 period to about 40% in the early 1960s and declining to some 30% in the last five years.

While the Bank Group is one of the major sources of external finance for transportation projects, its lending represents only a small fraction of developing countries' aggregate investment in the sector. If it can be assumed that about 5% of GDP is allocated to public and private investment in transport, the 85 countries currently borrowing from the Group for this purpose are investing more than $16,000 million per year in the sector. At current levels of lending, therefore, the Group's contribution to transportation in these countries would amount to about 4% of combined public and private investment in the sector, and less than 8% of the public component. In financing the general increases observed in borrowing countries in road mileage, paved surfaces, vehicle-kilometers, railway ton-kilometers, berthing space, etc., by far the most important source of investment funds has been domestic savings, both public and private.

Table 2: Bank Group Lending for Transportation [1]

(US$ millions)

	Through FY 1956			FY 1957-61		
	No.	Amount	%	No.	Amount	%
Highways	16	$162.0	24	16	$ 405.0	32
Railways	17	352.0	52	22	644.5	50
Ports	13	112.2	16	9	165.0	13
Pipelines	1	14.0	2	1	50.0	4
Aviation	2	41.7	6	2	14.8	1
Engineering [2]	0	0.0	0	0	0.0	0
Totals	49	$681.9	100	50	$1,279.3	100

[1] The figures understate the full volume of transport lending, since they exclude an unidentified transport equipment element in some of the large post-war reconstruction loans in Europe, as well as the indirect component in the general industrial imports credits to India. In the case of multipurpose transport projects, the full amount has been allocated to the mode

A country-by-country breakdown of past Bank Group transport lending is presented in Annex 2. In about half of the 90 countries and territories in which transport projects have been financed since 1947, the Bank Group's involvement has amounted to less than $25 million. Lending to this large group of countries at such relatively low levels accounts for less than 10% of total Bank Group transport financing. In 15 countries, or a sixth of the total, transport lending exceeds $100 million, and these countries account for about two-thirds of the Group's total financing in the sector.[1] The East African Community and its constituent countries, together with India, Mexico, Pakistan, Spain and Yugoslavia, account for more than a third of Bank Group transport lending to date.

Some important changes have taken place over the years in both the geographic and modal distribution of transport lending. In June 1960, there were 68 member countries in the Bank. A decade later the number had increased to 113, including 33 of the newly independent African countries. The creation of IDA in 1960 gave many of these new nations access to Bank Group financing that otherwise might not have been possible.

Until 1960, the Bank had made loans for transport projects in 33 countries. In the next decade, some 50 additional countries and territories received Bank Group assistance, and half of these were in Africa. The trend has continued in the 1970s, with 13 new coun-

[1] Amounts in millions: India ($780); Japan ($510); Pakistan ($358); Yugoslavia ($305); Spain ($279); E. Africa ($263) — Kenya, Tanzania and Uganda for roads, and the East African Railways and Harbours Corporations; Mexico ($240); Argentina ($225); Colombia ($205); Thailand ($183); Iran ($170); Brazil ($153); South Africa ($150); Nigeria ($136); Peru ($133).

	FY 1962-66			FY 1967-71			Cumulative through FY 1971	
No.	Amount	%	No.	Amount	%	No.	Amount	%
53	$1,069.8	56	78	$1,354.7	60	163	$2,991.5	49
19	674.8	35	20	668.2	29	78	2,339.5	38
14	157.2	8	16	191.2	8	52	625.6	10
1	15.0	1	4	58.0	3	7	137.0	2
0	0.0	0	0	0.0	0	4	56.5	1
1	1.7	nil	10	10.4	nil	11	12.1	nil
88	$1,918.5	100	128	$2,282.5	100	315	$6,162.2	100

accounting for the highest share in the loan or credit.
(2) These are loans and credits exclusively for transport engineering and do not include engineering financed under transport project loans or credits.

tries being added to the list of Bank Group borrowers for transport, of which six are in Africa. Table 3 summarizes the regional distribution of lending over the past five years.

In these five years, about 48% of all transport projects were in Africa, accounting for about 27% of the money volume of transport lending. This relatively large volume is in part a reflection of recently reduced project activity by agencies such as the Fonds d'Aide et de Cooperation (FAC) and the United States Agency for International Development (USAID). The creation of the African Development Bank has not yet had an impact on Bank Group transport operations in Africa comparable to that of the Inter-American Development Bank in Latin America, where only half as many Bank projects have been financed in the five year period. In fact, for two years (FY 1967 and 1968) there were no transport operations in South America, though important preparatory work was being done which led to 14 operations totaling nearly $500 million in the three subsequent years. The low number of operations in Latin America

Table 3: Transport Lending to Developing Countries, FY 1967-71

	Borrowing Countries	Number of Loans	% of Loans	Amount (Millions)	% of Dollar Volume
Africa	31	61	48	$609	27
Asia (Including Australasia)	20	34	26	727	32
Europe	5	10	8	334	14
Western Hemisphere	13	23	18	613	27
Total	69	128	100	2,283	100

reflects in part the increased activity of the Inter-American Development Bank, especially in financing smaller projects. Lending in South Asia, particularly for India and Pakistan, has reflected to a large extent the availability of IDA funds. The Asian Development Bank has financed a few transport projects in the South Asia, East Asia and Pacific Areas, but so far its impact on Bank Group transport activities has been small.

Concurrently with the changes in geographic distribution, there has been a steady trend away from railways and in favor of highways in the modal distribution of transport lending. Up to 1960, railway lending accounted for more than half of all Bank transport loans and amounted to twice that for highways. Much of the pre-1960 railway and port lending was for equipment to make up for the replacement lag caused by World War II and prolonged postwar shortages. There was also a substantial amount of maintenance equipment in some of the highway projects. This emphasis on equipment financing meant relatively quick disbursement of loan funds and limited project supervision problems.

With many of the new members being dependent on highways and the general worldwide growth of motorization, highway financing became the dominant feature of the Group's transport activities in the 1960s. In the ten years ending June 30, 1971, for example, highway lending totaled $2.4 billion compared with $1.4 billion for railways. The growing emphasis on civil works—often in new countries which not only were unfamiliar with Bank procedures but also had less effective civil services or transport agencies—inevitably led to slower disbursements than for equipment financing and required more frequent and continuous staff supervision in project execution.

Lending for ports has been modest in contrast to that for roads and railways. Most of the small amount of lending for pipelines has been in the last two or three years. Bank involvement in aviation and shipping, for a variety of reasons, has been minimal (see pages 173-175). The Group has made no loans for the direct financing of bus or trucking companies. There has been some indirect involvement in vehicle manufacture and assembly, however, via the general industrial import credits to India and in truck and bus company operations through financing of development finance companies. In addition, there was a specific IDA credit to Pakistan for truck assembly and import of buses and spares, and the International Finance Corporation (IFC), an affiliate of the Bank, has made loans to and equity investments in vehicle manufacturing firms in Brazil and Yugoslavia.

154

Physical Aspects of Transportation Projects, 1967-71

By far the largest element in lending for highways during this period represented road building, primarily of relatively high standard paved roads. Bank Group operations helped to finance nearly 25,000 km of such works. Building of new roads accounted for about a third of the route kilometers while various sorts of improvements, including repairing, accounted for the remainder. Though in quantitative terms maintenance has represented a small fraction of lending for highways, equipment for the purpose was purchased under most loans and maintenance was the primary objective of several. Feeder roads represented a small part (estimated at less than 5%) of total kilometers financed by the Bank Group; however, lending for this purpose has been increasing, not only in transport projects as such but as identifiable components of lending in other sectors, such as agriculture. Details of highway construction projects are given in Annex 3, Table 1.

In the past five years the largest single component (more than a third) of railway financing by the Bank Group was for rolling stock —approximately 200 locomotives, 600 passenger cars, and the procurement or fabrication of about 40,000 freight cars. The remainder of the financing for railways included a wide variety of equipment and materials, a large part of which was for track maintenance and renewal. Very little new line has been constructed; projects have concentrated on renewal and rehabilitation. Details of railway projects are given in Annex 3, Table 2.

Port projects have been devoted primarily to the provision of new berthing capacity, which has accounted for 60% of all such lending in the last five years. It is estimated that approximately 22,000 additional meters of berth were constructed and equipped under Bank loans. Other important objects of lending were the provision of cargo handling equipment such as cranes and forklifts and of harbor service craft such as tugs and lighters. Details of port projects are given in Annex 3, Table 3. Bank Group lending for pipelines in the five years comprised four operations which assisted the construction of nearly 1,200 km of new line and increased the capacity of an additional 300 km.

Preinvestment Activities

The Bank has acted as the Executing Agency for the United Nations Development Programme (UNDP) in most of the transportation-oriented preinvestment work financed by that organization. Over the past five years, the Bank has supervised 57 major studies in 33 countries, plus four regional studies costing in total about

$40 million and involving nearly 700 man-years of work in the field by consulting firms and individual experts. These studies ranged from broad surveys of entire transport systems, with a view to devising investment plans and transport policies, to specific project feasibility work.

Technical assistance funded by the Bank or IDA through their lending operations is a common feature of the Group's work. There is seldom a transport loan or credit which does not include important studies or technical assistance needed to help the borrower improve some aspect of its work or to prepare a subsequent project for possible lending. The latter "piggy-back" technique has been very successful in maintaining the planning and project preparation momentum developed by the Group's highway lending. Technical assistance has been an especially important feature of the Group's serial lending approach for railway recovery programs.

The Bank Group has recognized the importance of good sector work for many years. However, while it has promoted and supervised sector surveys in many countries (usually with UNDP finance) and made major transport investigations part of general country economic work in others, it has only recently organized a systematic program of comprehensive in-depth transport sector missions to major existing and prospective borrowers, to be carried out over a period of years. This will give the Bank an opportunity to develop specific preinvestment study programs for some of these countries, identifying and providing guidance to the borrower and the UNDP on the appropriate timing and scope of needed studies in the sector. Equally important, it will give the Bank the basic information and understanding necessary to continue and expand its transport lending, especially in areas where its involvement is reaching important dimensions.

Other Sources of Transport Finance

The main alternative sources of external finance for transportation investment are generally the same as for other types of large capital projects. One of the major sources is private contractor and supplier finance, often without government guarantees. Noteworthy multinational organizations are the regional development banks, i.e., the African Development Bank, the Asian Development Bank and the Inter-American Development Bank. The UNDP is the major source of funds for preinvestment work. In Europe, there is the European Development Fund (FED), the European Investment Bank (BEI) and the European Company for the Financing of Rail Rolling Stock (EUROFIMA), all of which are multinational.

The major bilateral lenders in transport are Canada, France, Germany, Italy, Japan, the United Kingdom and the United States. Most bilateral lenders operate through both official aid and export-promotion agencies. Many agencies specialize in particular types of projects or equipment, or specific areas. For example, the U.S. Export-Import Bank has lent more than 80% of its $1,000 million devoted to transport in the last five years for aircraft financing. EUROFIMA lends for railway equipment purchased in Europe. FED makes grants mainly for technical assistance, and to a lesser extent for capital projects. On the basis of very fragmentary data, it appears that the Bank's lending in the transport field over the past five years is about equal to that of all other multilateral and official bilateral lenders combined.

General Lessons Drawn from Past Operations

Project Re-evaluation and Monitoring. The Bank is conscious of the need for better evaluation of the impact of lending in the transportation sector. In the past, it has been possible to make a full-scale reappraisal of a project's economic results in only a few cases. Furthermore, while the Bank has a system for supervising project implementation, it does not have a wholly satisfactory procedure for monitoring the key economic variables in the post-construction period. It will do so, for example, when it considers further lending for development of the same road, port or other facility, which happens in a significant number of cases. It also monitors the financial results achieved by its revenue-earning borrowers; but these give only a partial indication of economic impact. More frequent project reviews are required, together with a continuous monitoring system designed on the basis of the Bank's appraisal, to illuminate the actual economic impact of each project.

Improved Appraisal Tools. The Bank's research activities in the transport field have expanded greatly in recent years. They have been addressed to the needs of both the Bank and its borrowers for new and better tools of analysis, and for better understanding of certain aspects of transportation policy. In the past five years the transportation research activities of the Bank Group have included some 27 studies, of which five have been published.* The

* World Bank Staff Occasional Papers: Jan de Weille, *Quantification of Road User Savings*, 1966; Hans A. Adler, *Sector and Project Planning in Transportation*, 1967; Alan A. Walters, *The Economics of Road User Charges*, 1968; Herman G. van der Tak and Jan de Weille, *Reappraisal of a Road Project in Iran*, 1969; Herman G. van der Tak and Anandarup Ray, *Economic Benefits of Road Transport Projects*, 1971. A "Central Economic Staff Catalog of Studies," which lists studies completed and in progress and explains how copies may be obtained, is available on request.

external research budget increased from a few thousand dollars for one study in FY 1968 to about $300,000 in FY 1972.

The research output includes computer models for project evaluation, risk and sensitivity analysis techniques, studies on road user costs and pricing, queuing theory applied to port operations, and many other topics. While this has been an important contribution, there is considerable room for further study and research. The Bank still has not solved the inherent problems of evaluating the micro-economics of most railway investment packages, since it is unable to account adequately for the system-wide effects and interdependent nature of particular investments. Highway design options involving large cost differences are not as yet amenable to anything but partial microeconomic analysis, since the Bank is unable to quantify satisfactorily the incremental benefits to highway users or, in terms of savings in maintenance costs, the benefits of such design features as greater road width, stronger pavement and easier curves and gradients. Long-standing questions such as the economically and technically appropriate mix of capital and labor in construction and operation of transport facilities remain unresolved, due to the lack of much pertinent data and problems concerning the use of shadow pricing for labor and foreign exchange where this is necessary to correct for distortions in market prices (see page 169).

Analysis of Developmental Impacts. More important than better microeconomic techniques, however, is the need to refine the Bank's analysis of the developmental effects of transportation investment—the connection between investment and economic output. The major and undoubtedly justified effort to improve the Bank's ability to quantify the costs and benefits of transport investments has had the effect of directing the approach toward one of micro, or engineering, economic and financial analysis, where quantification is more feasible. It has probably also helped to account for the fact that such projects as low standard roads to open up areas of potential production, and similar promotional investments, have not figured large in the Bank's lending program. In short, while the Bank can be fairly satisfied with its assessment of individual projects, the analysis of intra-sectoral and, perhaps more important, inter-sectoral priorities within a development strategy remains weak. If the Bank is to be able to assess priorities in the transport sector rather than merely say "yes" or "no" to an investment proposal, it must go beyond the quantification of user savings and be able to define each project's dynamic effects on the economy as a whole. This is all the more important if transport lending is to go beyond serving established demand and reinforcing existing patterns of economic location and income, and to become more useful in helping to solve the serious problems of unemployment and geographic or sectoral income inequalities by generating new output. Better analytical techniques are necessary if the Bank is to make much headway toward quantification of intra-sectoral and inter-sectoral effects. Even more important is a much better knowledge of the transport sector and of the workings of the economy in particular borrowing countries, to which the sector study program described on pages 161 – 162 is directed.

It should also be noted, however, that the main work to be done in improving this situation must be the responsibility of the governments of member countries. Through periodic missions and special surveys, the Bank should be able to help draw together the results of sector analyses. But this at best can be no more than a review of the situation at a particular point in time, and it can certainly be no better than available statistics permit. The task of gathering and analyzing adequate data on a continuing basis must be performed by governments. The Bank's role should be one of encouraging the creation of suitable sector planning institutions and giving such advice as it can on these continuing operations.

Institution Building and Policy Reform. Another important lesson to be drawn from past lending operations is the importance of policy, management, and institutional development and reform in determining the success of Bank-financed projects, and indeed in bringing projects and institutions to the stage where sound investment is possible. In connection with Bank Group transport lending, railway, harbor and airport corporations or authorities have been set up as autonomous entities in an attempt to improve their efficiency. Systems to promote financial integrity and major accounting, costing and budgetary reforms have been undertaken in connection with Bank lending. Transport planning units have been created and staffed, and equipped with new investment and policy criteria. Highway authorities have been reorganized. Vehicle licensing and road transport regulation laws and practices have been reformed. Pricing policies and specific rates, fares and taxes have been changed, as have procurement and contracting policies and procedures. Policies with respect to hiring and firing of personnel and wages paid have been affected. Limitations have been placed on certain kinds of investments and debt. Individual managements have been appraised and agreements have been reached that borrowers would consult with the Bank on certain appointments. In some cases, the transport sector has been approached as a whole and the Bank has sought to set its lending for particular projects in

the context of agreements on major policy decisions and performance criteria set out in memoranda of understanding related to the
entire sector.

These types of project-associated sectoral reforms are a major
part of the Bank's business. Most of them are backed by implementing studies or technical assistance if necessary. They undoubtedly
have a longer lasting and wider impact on the economy and the
sector than most of the investments being financed. Work on these
institutional and policy matters certainly constitutes the hardest part
of the Bank's field investigations. Such questions also raise the most
serious difficulties in loan negotiations and project supervision. The
aim of all of these attempts at reform is to create the policy and
institutional conditions that will both permit and encourage the borrower and the borrowing country to make the most efficient use of
resources in the transport sector.

While the Bank Group has certainly had a large and positive
impact on transportation institutions and policies in borrowing
countries, the full potential for change in this respect is seldom
quickly realized. Usually the most important reforms—those vital
to sector efficiency—involve difficult political decisions on the part
of the borrowing country, and far-reaching changes which are not
easy to set in motion. Such reforms usually result only from close
and continuing collaboration, at the staff level, between the Bank
and its borrowers.

The implications of this for Bank lending where institutional reform is vital to the success of transport investment are: (a) the Bank
should not get involved unless it is prepared to make a sustained
commitment through a series of loans to see the process through;
and (b) wherever possible, the Bank should adopt a sector, rather
than a modal or project-by-project, approach. The key to a successful sector approach and the ability to assess policies and institutions
tailored to local problems and conditions is, again, a sound knowledge of the sector.

Training. The Bank's past experience has also shown that for
long term transport and general economic development it is not
enough to finance improved transport facilities; the training of people to operate them, and to plan and implement investments, is
at least equally important. This has long been recognized, and most
transport projects include training of one sort or another. Whatever
the source of financing, all technical and project preparation assistance supervised by the Bank includes arrangements for training
local staff. Most programs of this nature include overseas fellowships as well as participation in sector or feasibility studies.

These efforts, however, have been only partially successful. It is often difficult to find suitable domestic personnel who can be assigned to such training programs for sufficient time. It is often equally difficult to find foreign consultants who are not only technically capable but also adept at training and prepared to give adequate attention to the transfer of their skills. For these and other reasons, few transport institutions in borrowing countries have received the assistance they need in the propagation of new attitudes and practices at the staff level. The Bank Group is searching for more effective ways of providing it.

PROJECTION OF FUTURE OPERATIONS
Lending Program

The Bank Group's projected transport program for the five year period 1972-1976 contemplates total lending of about $4,300 million for some 240 projects, not including the transportation elements of projects which are primarily concerned with urban development, tourism, agriculture and industry. This implies a level of lending for transport about 90% above the 1967-1971 period and about 135% above the average for 1964-1968.

Sector Work

The enlarged program of lending will require more complete knowledge of the sector in many countries, and of its relationship to other sectors and development as a whole. Especially where Bank-assisted transport investments play a large role in the development strategies of member countries, a project-by-project assessment is not sufficient. Whenever possible in these cases, an effort will be made to base the transport lending program on comprehensive sector analysis, and to link support for a series of projects to agreed sectoral development strategies and policies.

To raise the Bank's sector knowledge to the level appropriate to operational plans, and then to maintain it, will require a major effort. In addition to the necessary work in countries with the largest programs, it is highly desirable that in-depth sector knowledge be built up in a number of others, where the absolute amounts to be lent may not be so large, but where the Bank Group will be financing a large proportion of total transport investment.

These include a number of relatively poor African and Asian countries where the challenge of using an appropriate mix of transport and other investments to open up new areas or stimulate new agricultural production and rural employment cannot now be fully met for lack of sectoral and general economic knowledge.

The Bank's five year work program to increase its transport knowledge in support of projected lending calls for more than doubling the number of special sector missions. Including expanded transport work in connection with general economic missions, some 45 such studies will be undertaken in about 40 countries. These staff reviews will be in addition to sector surveys to be financed by the UNDP and carried out by consultants in a number of countries where they are most needed.

As already pointed out, the Bank's own missions cannot do the long term spade work that only government departments, and to a lesser extent consultants working on transport surveys, can hope to accomplish. Instead, they will concentrate on the fundamental issues of sectoral objectives and strategy, institutional soundness, and pricing, regulatory and investment policies. They will also attempt to reassess previous Bank Group and other projects to understand better the forces at work in the economy and how and to what extent certain projects make an impact on development under these conditions.

The Bank expects these missions to establish close and, in some circumstances, continuing relationships with overall transport sector planning authorities, in the same way as project preparation and appraisal missions establish close communications with modal planners and managers. Hopefully, this will help the Bank to achieve at the sector level the kind of institution-building success it has had in working with some highway departments and railway administrations.

Transport Policy Questions

There is very little that can be held to be categorically true with respect to transportation pricing and regulation. However, the Bank intends to continue the use of certain general guidelines which have been employed in recent years. These are set out below.

Pricing and Financial Targets. Pricing is one of the most powerful tools of transport policy for achieving efficient intermodal choice and economic utilization of existing and proposed systems, and therefore for contributing to efficient locational and production decisions throughout the economy. As a general point, the Bank believes that this resource allocation or economic function is the central function of pricing.

At the same time, however, pricing must often be used for a number of other objectives, which may or may not be in accord with its primary function but which may, nevertheless, be legitimate and important. These include the achievement of financial viability for

162

transport enterprises in order to ensure adequate resource mobilization, the generation of surpluses for expansion of facilities or for general taxation purposes, and the subsidization or preferential treatment of certain users or regions for economic or social reasons. Often these objectives conflict with that of ensuring the most efficient use of transport resources. Financial analysts and economists working in the transport sector are well aware of these potential conflicts and of the practical barriers to achieving satisfactory compromises. The Bank's general guidelines are as follows:

• For any particular transportation service the price charged to the user should not fall below the relevant economic cost of providing the service. This "relevant economic cost," the short-run marginal cost, may be low, as in a situation of chronically underutilized capacity—a back-haul situation, for example, or a seasonal slack period, or where a major investment mistake has been made. On the other hand, this short-run marginal cost threshold may be a very high one where congestion has set in and the economic costs of accommodating the incremental unit of traffic have begun to soar. Prices set below the relevant threshold would constitute subsidies. As a general proposition the Bank is not persuaded that indirect subsidies through transport pricing are as efficient as more direct ones.

• Since the country's economy must cover the total financial costs in any case, there remains the major question of the financial targets to be achieved by transport pricing. In short, the question is whether to cover the "overhead costs" by user charges or through general or other forms of taxation if the pricing rule of the paragraph above does not yield enough financial resources.

The basic problem stems from the fact that to raise prices above the economic cost threshold, depending upon the elasticities of demand, may dampen justified output in the economy or shift traffic from a low cost to a higher cost service, on the one hand, while to charge marginal cost-based prices may lead to substantial financial deficits and fiscal and cost discipline problems, on the other.

Where financial discipline is not at issue, as is generally the case for highway infrastructure, short-run marginal cost coverage from user charges is the only mandatory economic rule (except where subsidies may be justified; see below). In covering the financial costs beyond that level, ideally one should evaluate the economic impact of any additional user charges vis-a-vis that of other forms of revenue—such as land taxes, or income taxes—taking into account the income distribution, production, locational and administrative or ease-of-collection aspects. The appropriate

163

level of pricing in a case such as highway infrastructure is also affected by the financial targets set for competing modes because the economically desirable allocation of traffic between modes may be unacceptably distorted by different financial targets for one mode as opposed to another.

For revenue-earning entities the Bank believes, in the absence of a convincing economic case to the contrary, that financial viability is a valid target. This means that the entity should be able, from internally generated resources (i.e., user charges) to meet all of its financial obligations and make a substantial contribution to its justified renewal and expansion investments—substantial enough to maintain investment at appropriate levels without a dangerous deterioration of its debt position. This predisposition toward financial viability rests largely on institutional grounds which obviously have a direct bearing on long-term economic efficiency: the need to maintain cost and investment discipline and to ensure adequate self financing for needed renewals and modernization.

Where such financial targets have serious adverse economic implications in terms of dampening or diverting traffic, the first remedy after reaching acceptable levels of operating efficiency is to see what can be done about adjusting the financial burden, such as writing off unemployable assets and discontinuing their depreciation, converting debt to equity, etc., so that all of the unnecessary "fat" in the "financial cost" is removed. If conflicts still exist between financial and economic goals, the question of the extent to which each goal should be pursued has to be faced objectively on a case-by-case basis.

It is important to note that financial viability as defined above says nothing about the level of profitability. A railway with a declining role in the transport economy, with many assets which should not be renewed, and the likelihood of few if any justified expansions in the future, may be financially viable at a very low average return on net fixed assets. To try to achieve a higher return might mean unnecessarily pricing the railway out of markets where it is the low cost mover in terms of true economic costs, or unnecessarily dampening the demand for transportation (output) in general. On the other hand, where the demand for railway, port, or airport services is expanding rapidly, relatively high rates of return on net assets may be required for the entities to be financially viable in the sense outlined above.

Regulatory Systems. In a number of countries a variety of restrictive measures and institutions exist that are ostensibly designed to ensure proper resource allocation in the sector by intervening in the transport market—e.g., by setting "reasonable" prices, avoiding "excessive" competition by restricting entry into the industry, ensuring "rational" coordination, etc.

The Bank has reservations about this type of economic regulation of the transport sector, and believes that caution should be exercised in using it in preference to sound pricing as a tool for allocating resources. The economic case for regulation has been contested by economists and, most recently, in an important Bank research study.[1] The Bank's experience indicates that it tends to become rigid in response to vested interests, is often ineffective, and is prone to many abuses. To be efficient, regulation requires a degree of administrative knowledge and flexibility which may not be easily found. Furthermore, these regulatory systems are administratively expensive, and tend to cramp the development of entrepreneurial talent, technological innovation, and general efficiency by inhibiting competition in the sector. Thus the Bank will continue to review regulatory services with care, and to press for their abandonment where a sound case for them cannot be made.

These general views on regulation and pricing do not exclude recognition that economic cases can be made for important exceptions. While subsidies to certain sectors may be more efficient if made directly instead of through transport sector pricing, there may be cases where this is not true for practical administrative, institutional or political reasons. In some cases, sound policy within the transport sector itself may call for subsidies. For instance, where it is impossible for administrative or other reasons to charge congestion prices on automobile users causing high cost congestion, it may be desirable to subsidize rail or bus services in order to attract commuters away from private cars. The resulting savings to the economy may be large.

In some cases, where the market mechanism is plainly not working and other prices in the economy are also distorted, isolated rationalization of transport pricing and regulatory systems may in fact produce undesirable economic effects beyond the sector. In other cases where massive unemployment and chronic shortages of fiscal and foreign exchange resources exist, it may be rational, at least for a time, to restrict importation of road vehicles, thus protecting a railway from road competition so that its full capacity can be utilized and it can simultaneously operate with redundant labor and earn financial surpluses for support of the government budget.

---

[1] Oort, Conrad J., "The Economic Regulation of the Road Transport Industry," World Bank Report No. EC-177, October 1970.

Directions in Future Lending

Areas of particular concern or emphasis with respect to the major subsectors in transportation for which the Bank Group provides finance are discussed in this section.

(a) Road Transport

The road transport lending program for the next five years will include the same kinds of projects the Bank Group has helped to finance in the past, ranging from low-cost earth and gravel roads to multi-lane limited access highways. However, within that program greater emphasis will be given to "feeder" road development and improvement of highway maintenance, and more effort will be devoted to solving the many training and institutional problems involved in projects of this kind. More must be done also to encourage the development of local civil works contracting capacity, to ensure that design standards fit local conditions, and to substitute labor for capital wherever appropriate.

Feeder Roads. As used here, "feeder road" means a road which depends for its justification upon generated traffic, i.e., new output which would not take place if the road were not built or improved. These are almost always low-standard access roads built at very low cost. They can be justified only within the economic framework of the particular region in which they are located and in terms of the cost-benefit calculus for producing the new output. Therefore, the problem of assessing feeder roads is essentially one of measuring the response of output to changes in transport costs along with and relative to all other inputs, such as land clearance, settlement, storage and marketing facilities, etc. In practice, this often means an agricultural project with a transport element.

One problem is that the measurement of output response is quite complex even in very simple agricultural situations, while the investment costs per mile of road are for the most part so low that expensive preparatory feasibility and design work in each case simply cannot be justified. It would be more economic to make a percentage of investment mistakes than to conduct sufficient localized studies to remove the uncertainties. The Bank proposes to develop a series of selected feeder road projects based on in-depth analysis, which will be monitored carefully in the post-investment period. From this experience, the Bank hopes to develop sound "rule of thumb" criteria for investment and design decisions and guidelines as to the type of local institutions required to plan and implement these projects effectively.

Another problem emerges in building these roads. Most will be of such low standard and low cost that detailed surveys and precise location prior to actual construction are not required and are too expensive. Thus contracting in the manner followed for larger civil works will not be practical. Typically, this is a force-account operation, carried out by a labor-machinery unit not unlike a maintenance unit, with a fixed budget and an area for which to provide roads, and to maintain and upgrade them as required by traffic growth. Force-account construction work has been rare in Bank-financed projects because of the many problems involved in work performance, budgetary and cost control. These problems will have to be overcome if the Bank is to make a worthwhile contribution to this type of road development. This is true even if assistance is restricted to the financing of necessary equipment and technical and management personnel.

Road Maintenance. Maintenance is the "cinderella" of the road business. It is customary for Bank Group loans for highways, whether for construction or maintenance, to include a requirement that the borrower maintain its road system adequately. Much effort has already been devoted to this end. Experience includes cases where it has been possible to bring about improvements. Unfortunately there are also cases where little has been achieved, and still others where, after a period of improvement, a change of government has led to a sliding back to unsatisfactory practices.

The dependence of maintenance on current budget expenditure for which foreign financing is generally not available, and its relative lack of glamor compared with new construction, militate against it when scarce capital and human resources are allocated among competing needs. It is quite obvious, however, that the highest returns on resources can be earned in maintaining existing assets, and that without solid maintenance new investment is a wasteful venture. Establishing maintenance targets, building up road maintenance organizations, training personnel and equipping them properly will receive even more emphasis in the future, and it will be accompanied by efforts to ensure that adequate current budgetary resources are devoted to this purpose.

Local Contracting Capacity. The civil works contracting industry is a fairly basic one, and a logical one for development at relatively early stages of economic growth. In the Bank's view, it is important both for the road sub-sector and for the economy as a whole that this development be encouraged and supported as much as possible. To this end the Bank has for many years tried the technique of "packages" of contracts. Wherever it has seemed appropriate the

Bank has broken road construction projects into the smallest contracts consistent with efficient execution and permitted contractors to bid for single contracts or any "package" of them. The objective has been to achieve a contract within what is often the fairly low capacity of local contractors, while also attracting the larger foreign contractor through packaging, and thus gaining for the borrower the benefits of widespread competition. The Bank has also encouraged, but not required, joint ventures between foreign and local firms and sub-contracting to small local firms. More recently it has tried in one country to assist local contractors more directly by financing consulting services to advise them in bid preparation, costing and the like. In another country it has stimulated an investigation into ways of developing the local contracting industry.

The Bank believes that more could be done. It will explore further what technical assistance might be given to local firms through consultants or in other ways. Recognizing that in some countries shortage of equipment and of the foreign exchange to purchase it have hindered the growth of local firms, the Bank might consider financing equipment for the use of local contractors. This might be possible on a rental or hire-purchase basis through a government department or development bank.

It is clear, however, that member governments must also take complementary measures; indeed, these are more important to development of the local industry than any steps the Bank can take. Local contractors are unlikely to develop unless there is a clear policy of putting road construction and other work out to contract. Similarly there will be a need in some countries to review existing taxation and contracting procedures which are unfavorable to contractors. The Bank has recently started a research study to explore these matters further.

Design Standards. Because of the large changes in motor vehicle dimensions and operating characteristics that are taking place, especially in developing countries where the vehicle fleet is expanding very rapidly, and with the wide differences among countries in the relative prices of factor inputs, there is need for a thorough review of the road design problem. The objective is to develop criteria capable of yielding economic design answers in response to large variations in the relative costs of inputs. Intensive, long-range research into this problem has been started in Kenya by the Road Research Laboratory of the United Kingdom, in cooperation with the Bank. The Bank expects to be able to arrange similar work in Western Africa with the Ponts et Chaussees of France. Controlled experiments are being carried out to develop data on road construction, maintenance and vehicle operating costs, and the trade-offs between them. With the help of consultants connected with the Massachusetts Institute of Technology, the Bank is contributing to the effort by developing computerized models capable of assessing these trade-offs in specific cases and giving guidance toward optimum designs. In the next five years the Bank hopes to disseminate the results of this research and encourage their use in projects it helps to finance.

Labor-Intensive Versus Capital-Intensive Technology. While there are substantial civil works elements in lending for other modes of transport, and the choice of technology obviously goes beyond civil works design and execution, the Bank has chosen road construction as a convenient area for coming to grips with the problem of labor-intensive versus capital-intensive technology. This is because part of the problem is to define the technical substitutability of labor, capital, and other factor inputs within the context of design options with measurable economic characteristics. The Bank will be better able to do this in the highway field because the design studies mentioned above will help to provide this basic context. The substitutability of labor for capital in highway construction is being investigated in a parallel study recently started by the Bank.

In addition to the questions of technical-economic trade-offs, there is the question of what relative prices for factor inputs are valid for use in design, tendering and execution decisions. Where there is a chronic shortage of capital and foreign exchange and a surplus of unskilled labor—and therefore market prices for these inputs do not reflect their true economic cost—the need arises for shadow pricing in designing projects and for methods to ensure that contractors will use the proportions of labor and capital that are most economic on the basis of these notional prices.

The Bank has no illusion that appropriate shadow pricing can be easily determined or that results can be much better than rough approximations. Perhaps until better techniques are available, the best that can be done is to recognize situations where there is a substantial disparity between market prices and economic costs and attempt to allow for them in design preparation and appraisal work, by giving full consideration to local resources and to the possibility of substituting labor for capital. In construction, it may be possible to develop reasonable arrangements whereby governments provide financial incentives to contractors (without discrimination between local and foreign firms) to use labor more intensively. It is primarily for governments to establish the necessary financial and administrative systems, but the Bank is prepared to help in formulating practical arrangements.

Road Transport Industry. Most of the Bank's highway lending operations have been designed to reduce transport costs through improved or more direct roads or better maintenance, but little attention has been given to potential savings from improvements in the vehicle fleet and in the road transport industry generally. In some cases the full potential in transport savings attributable to road improvement is dissipated in the general deterioration of the vehicle fleet. In many countries with balance of payments difficulties, severe import restrictions often result in buses and trucks being kept in service much beyond the point of economic replacement or remaining idle for long periods because of lack of spare parts, thus substantially increasing transport costs. In some cases also, vehicles are not adapted to modern traffic needs and the high costs of operation may dampen economic growth.

The Bank Group's appropriate role in lending for road vehicles is still a moot question. If the operating units are small, such lending might raise difficult problems in terms of international competitive bidding and project supervision. Long term Bank Group loans may also not be well suited to the relatively short economic life of the equipment involved. A more suitable form of Bank involvement might be to support banking institutions designed to finance the purchase of buses and other commercial vehicles. Such institutions could also provide guidance to operators and thus assist the healthy growth of the road transport industry.

In addition to these problems of the mechanics of lending, possible difficulties also arise from the existence in some countries of high cost and heavily protected local manufacturing industries. The Bank does not propose to become active in motor vehicle or road transport industry financing before a great deal more thought is given to the problems entailed. As a part of this examination, as well as for other reasons, the research program includes a series of studies of the trucking industry. The Bank also proposes to give more attention during its sector analyses to this aspect of road transport.

(b) **Railways**

Most of the railways seeking Bank Group assistance can be placed somewhere in the following highly generalized model of decline. Typically, the railway was built in large part prior to the advent of road transport, and was intended to serve all kinds of transport needs. Since the railway began with a virtual transport monopoly, it was easy to assign to it developmental tasks. These tasks were often undertaken through pricing structures that did not reflect railway costs. Traffic was charged according to what it would bear; overall financial targets were met by cross-subsidization, or at least by very heavy differentials in the contribution of particular traffics to overhead costs. Because the railway had no competition, it was also easy to use it as a means of providing employment, with the costs of excess labor borne by the public in the form of higher tariffs. Also, dubious investments could be, and were, undertaken and absorbed without financial disaster. When competition from road transport became a reality, financial targets were immediately threatened. Rather than release the railway from its developmental and employment tasks and its by now traditional pricing system, attempts were made to protect it from the new competition.

Many of the Bank's railway borrowers are to be found in this brittle monopoly stage, propped up by restrictions on road transport operations and road investment. The length of this stage depends on the administrative strength of the restrictions, the degree of identification between government and railway, and the entrepreneurial talent in the local road haulage business. Usually it cannot last long. In most of the countries concerned the situation is rapidly changing and the monopoly stage is about to end. Where the monopoly is perpetuated, the eventual problem will be even larger and more difficult to solve.

Saddled with excess labor and prices in which there are heavy vested interests, the railways begin to lose money once their monopoly is broken and the competition takes away the high-rated traffics which are priced far above railway costs, leaving those that make little or no contribution to overheads. In most cases, resulting deficits must be borne by the state. Because these deficits represent subsidies to industry, agriculture, passengers and labor, ending them poses a major political problem. Nevertheless, the state is usually loathe to bear these deficits, and the railway cannot convincingly defend itself against the inevitable charges of inefficiency.

Self-defeating economies are undertaken: first by slashing depreciation, then by cutting maintenance expenditure, and finally by curtailing renewal and modernization investment. Thus there is a vicious cycle of financial deficits, underinvestments, declining service, loss of traffic and still larger deficits.

The situation is often aggravated by weak railway management which has been protected and demoralized by the effects of public policy and deficit operations. Poor public policy often accompanied by weak management eventually leads to the point where the railway is in grave danger of losing its role in the economy. By this default, major and often excess investment in competing road transport capacity is encouraged, at high economic cost to the country. This stage has been reached in many developed countries, as well as in a number of the Bank's developing member countries which are current and prospective railway borrowers.

The strategy of Bank lending in the railway sector has been to help break or avoid this cycle of railway decline, where the railways have a proper economic role to play in the future development of member countries. While there may be a few projects involving new construction to serve captive demand, by far the majority of railway projects will require a continuation of that strategy. They will focus on rehabilitation, extensive reform, and retreat from over-extended systems with the aim of enabling the railway to fulfill its economically justified role in a competitive environment.

Major emphasis will be placed on transport sector pricing, regulatory and investment policy reforms, the achievement of appropriate financial targets (see pages 162-165), the strengthening of management and the development of better management tools, especially in the marketing and cost-pricing fields. Where necessary, efforts will be made to reform relationships between the railway enterprise and the state. Disinvestment and the elimination of uneconomic services will be important complements to the investment programs. Comprehensive agreement on sector policies and long term commitments through a series of Bank loans are necessary features of this kind of undertaking.

Research activities related to the railway field and the Bank lending program over the next five years will include: (a) a study of the methodology to be employed in making line and service elimination decisions; (b) development and adaptation of existing computer models into flexible tools for use in Bank Group appraisals, with the aim of allowing better quantification of the system effects of investments; and (c) development of railway costing-pricing guidelines which can be adapted by borrowers to their individual needs.

(c) Ports and Shipping

The future lending program for ports and shipping calls for somewhat more emphasis on coastal and ocean shipping than in the past. It will be affected significantly by the rapid pace of change in technology and by the sheer size of ships and loadings now entering into trade.

The main arguments for development of ocean shipping for some countries are that shipping under national flag saves foreign exchange and that it can be an important element in promoting export trade and cutting the economic cost of transporting imports and exports. In some cases these arguments are persuasive; however, there are many prima facie counter arguments which have molded the cautious approach of the Bank Group to the finance of ocean shipping.

First, fuel costs, ship capital costs, crew expenditures, repair and foreign port charges are often foreign exchange costs which cut significantly into expected foreign exchange savings or earnings. Second, the profitability of national flag shipping from an economic viewpoint often depends fundamentally upon rates being charged in the market; these can fluctuate widely from one period to the next, making investment decisions based on them especially uncertain. It is questionable whether capital-poor countries can afford to run the risks of the shipping trade, unless the potential gains are commensurately large.

Coastal and inland shipping are different matters. Here the question is whether to meet demand by water or by land-air transport systems. The investment decision problem is no different from deciding whether to build a gravel or a paved road on the basis of cost-benefit analysis. Shipping is potentially an important mode of transport for many borrowers with long coastlines, navigable rivers and great lakes. For the most part the potential for this mode seems to be underdeveloped in view of the minimum of infrastructure that is usually involved, and the typically large capacity for bulk movement that can be made available at relatively low investment costs. An important problem appears to be in the management and organizational fields, and in ensuring that port operations and procedures do not lead to undue delays and thus to high costs.

As to ports, in addition to building berths and equipping them to handle increasing traffic, future projects will also involve modifications to existing infrastructure and new designs to provide for the recent changes in ship technology. Deep sea, single point moorings with pipeline connections are needed in many parts of the world to handle the behemoth oil tankers now coming into service and relieve congested port areas. The trend toward large ships will probably affect dry bulk operations as well, requiring substantial dredging to deepen harbors, or pipeline arrangements to permit offshore operations.

Probably the most talked-about advance in shipping technology is containerized loading, using specialized vessels and dockside equipment. Containerization is developing rapidly due to the economic advantages entailed, particularly in the North Atlantic, Europe-Australia, and possibly North Pacific trade lanes. Shipping companies are investing heavily in container ships of ever-increasing size. First generation smaller ships are being released to secondary routes.

A major problem of technological adaptation is likely to emerge for many developing countries where containerization economics (labor saving) do not apply, but where containerization is likely to be imposed by the specialized equipment of the developed trading and shipping nations.

When investment in new equipment and capacity speed turnaround time for foreign owned ships and perhaps reduce domestic employment, important questions about the distribution of economic benefits arising from port improvement investment must arise. How these benefits accrue to the country making the investment is a question which has in the past been largely answered by hypothesizing plausible shipping price movements. In the future the characteristics of shipping and port pricing in each case should be analyzed in more depth, to see what can be done with port pricing to retain benefits or to encourage behavior on the part of shippers and shipping companies which will yield maximum benefits to the country. To this end, the Bank is starting an investigation into the pricing practices of ports in relation to shipping and inland customers, and into the potential efficacy of port pricing as an economic tool.

(d) Aviation

Civil aviation, despite its importance in any modern transportation system, is a new field for the Bank Group [1] and one which it is entering cautiously. The Bank's program over the next five years is quite modest, consisting predominantly of airport projects. As in the shipping discussion above, a broad distinction can be drawn between international and domestic aviation and most of the same arguments apply.

International Aviation. Bank involvement in international aviation is expected to be limited to the financing of airports. The Bank is not planning to become active in financing aircraft for international airlines. This is in part because finance is readily available on reasonable terms from bilateral sources, and because there are ques-

---

[1] During the 1950s the Bank made six loans wholly or in part for aircraft procurement to the Netherlands, Australia and India, but made no further loans for aviation until 1971, when it agreed to assist an airport modernization project in Panama.

tions as to the priority of such investment. International airlines in many developing countries are operated as a matter of national prestige; with some notable exceptions, they tend to lose substantial sums of money and often involve net foreign exchange losses as well.

The growth of international air travel and technological change in aircraft confront many developing countries with the prospect of mounting congestion or unsafe operations unless relatively large airport investments are made. The main question the Bank faces in appraising these projects for possible financing has to do with their economic priority—establishing the links between aviation operations, airport congestion, and economic activity. This is not easy to do, especially since relieving or avoiding congestion basically means saving time. Time for capital equipment (aircraft) is relatively easy to evaluate, but often before congestion occurs on the runways and in the airspace around an airport, the situation within the terminal in terms of delays to passengers has become acute.

Time savings for individuals, however, are difficult to assess in terms of their economic benefit to the nation. They may in part amount to a form of non-monetary income (consumption) for the individuals, many of whom are foreigners, that is not translated in any way into further output. Thus while these time savings and increased passenger comfort may be of economic value, it is particularly difficult to trace how and to what extent they benefit the borrowing country until congestion begins to retard traffic development with adverse consequences for the level of business activity or tourist expenditure. To assess adequately these congestion-relieving projects, good market information is required on elasticities of demand to time losses and other costs.

In regard to airport projects the Bank also faces questions of an institutional nature, such as whether or in what circumstances it is important for airport authorities to be set up as semi-autonomous agencies with separate viable financial structures, rather than as government departments as in the case of most highway authorities.

There are also questions as to pricing policy and financial targets in this field, which lacks real competition, serves foreigners to a large extent, and where demand, at least for the use of the airport, is quite inelastic in any reasonable price range. The Bank intends to strive for direct recovery of costs from the users. Where the consumer surpluses accruing to passengers are large, important fiscal surpluses may be available and justified because they help to keep benefits within the country or contribute to public savings and a better income distribution.

Domestic Aviation. Many borrowing countries have geographical or topographical features as well as population distribution that make domestic air transport economically and commercially attractive. In almost every economy there is a distinct and growing role for aviation—from opening up new areas before investment in extensive fixed transport facilities can be justified, to generally enhancing the mobility of scarce entrepreneurial and administrative talent within the economy.

In planning their investments in international airports, the developing countries have largely to react to aircraft types determined by the needs of other countries. But in planning development of their domestic aviation they have some opportunity to select the optimum combination of aircraft, airports, navigation aids and the like. The Bank will try to help in developing some projects with this aim in view. Any Bank finance involved would probably be for airports and navigational aids rather than for aircraft, for which other sources of finance are readily available. At the same time, it should be noted that other sources bring little in the way of critical institution-building, management training, or concern for pricing policies that would accompany Bank lending in this field. Therefore, the Bank intends to keep an open mind toward aircraft lending for domestic aviation, and may be open to persuasion for high priority proposals.

(e) Urban Transportation

Transportation has significant effects on where and how cities grow and how they function. The convergence of transport routes or the transshipment points from one mode to another frequently provide the focus and impetus for urban development. Mobility and accessibility to goods, labor, and markets permit and encourage the urban concentration. Development patterns within cities are, to a large extent, shaped by transportation investment decisions which have a large impact on land values and land uses, just as the latter have an important bearing on transport requirements. Among other important reasons why transportation consistently ranks among the chief concerns of cities is that it is a prerequisite for jobs and business; it accounts for a substantial part of personal and public expenditure; and it typically occupies from 20% to 40% of the city's physical space.

The rise of motorization in cities where land use patterns and intensity of habitation had a prior development, as is the case in most of the big cities of the developing world, creates even more severe problems of congestion than in more modern cities. Whereas the typical Western European or North American city devotes about 25% of urban land area to city streets and highways, the percentage is considerably lower in Asia; for example, it is 14% in Bangkok and 5% in Calcutta. Shortage of road space is often aggravated by competing claims on its use from animal-drawn and other slow non-motorized vehicles, and by the lack of or ineffective use of traffic control equipment.

Those worried about congestion reaching intolerable levels can derive little comfort from the fact that most people in low-income countries cannot yet afford automobiles. Total automobile registration in many of these countries is increasing by 10% to 20% per year, and nearly all of these vehicles are concentrated in a few big cities. Bangkok has 73% of all the automobiles in Thailand and is adding about 15,000 new cars every year. In Sao Paulo, population increased between 1960 and 1967 by 42%; car registration increased 324%.

For many of these cities, the amount of resources that would be needed to transform them to accommodate continued expansion of the private vehicle fleet is enormous. It is clear that for economic and environmental reasons more reliance must be placed on mass transit services to meet the transport needs of cities. In planning urban systems along most economic lines, attention will have to be paid as much to the demand side and how it can be affected by pricing, regulation and levels of service as to the supply of the facilities to meet demand.

The problems of urban transportation are so complex and varied, and so inextricably linked with urban development problems, that there is no single solution for them. The first requirement is to analyze the overall investment needs for the urban area or the region under study and to assess the relative priority of urban transport as compared to other crucial needs such as sanitation, employment or housing. When urban transport ranks among the priorities, there is no prima facie reason to exclude any aspect of urban transportation from consideration by the Bank. The most suitable types of projects, however, appear to be mass transit systems, urban roads, traffic control systems, terminal facilities, and the development of joint uses of transportation rights-of-way to conserve and employ high-value land in city centers.

The figures for future lending mentioned on page 161 do not include finance for projects of a strictly urban nature. The Bank's urban transport lending program and the problems to be faced in its development are to be addressed later in this series in an Urban Sector Working Paper.

Research

It is probably already clear that research is an important part of the Bank's activity in the transport sector. This is true for a number of reasons. First, there has been a general lack of pertinent research work by international bodies in this field, aside from simple analysis and the publication of data. Most have been concerned more with improving operations, furthering technological advances, or exchanging views on practical experiences. Some research is undertaken in the field of ports and shipping by the United Nations Conference on Trade and Development (UNCTAD), by government agencies such as the U.S. Department of Transportation, the U.K. Road Research Laboratory, and Ponts et Chaussees in France, as well as by universities and by some consulting firms.

More important is the fact that most research in transport is geared to the needs of developed countries. The results have to be reexamined and adapted to the needs of the Bank's borrowers. It is here that the Bank can play a constructive role by commissioning selected studies. These may be research into new directions or the testing and development of existing knowledge and techniques, to help the Bank improve the quality of its analysis and strengthen the foundation of its advice. A good example of the lead which can properly be taken by the Bank, supported by appropriate funding, is the cooperation already mentioned with the road research agencies of the British, and probably the French, Government on highway design standards in Africa. In its study of the use of labor and equipment in road construction, the Bank hopes to have the association of the International Labour Organisation (ILO) and some borrowing member countries for data on projects being executed.

In addition to focusing on problems affecting developing countries, it can be noted from the kind of studies described in this paper that the Bank's research activities in transport have turned increasingly to practical subjects. Theoretical issues have been fairly well covered in previous studies, but there are wide gaps between theory and practice, and the Bank must learn more about the actual effects of deviations from "ideal" policies (e.g., economic user pricing) and of distortions in the markets of transport services (e.g., restrictive regulatory systems).

Another important gap is that of data; the paucity of reliable facts often calls into question the use of sophisticated models and the resulting conclusions. Recognizing that these problems may not lend themselves easily to generalization, the Bank feels that the best way of achieving its goals would be through actual case studies in conjunction with its sector work. These require both time and manpower. While theoretical studies can be done relatively quickly and with little manpower, data collection and case studies are expensive.

In the execution of an expanded research program in the transport field, the Bank hopes increasingly to involve the developing countries themselves, especially through grants to universities and other research institutions. A start has been made in this direction. For example, the Bank has contracted with the Asian Institute of Technology to do some analysis of berth operations at the Port of Bangkok. Similarly, it is attempting to bring the University of East Africa into one aspect of the highway design studies and to monitor the results of a Tanzanian feeder road project.

Basic Transport Data

	Mid-1969 Population (million)	Area (Km²)	GNP per cap. (US$)	Road Network Length (Km) Paved	Gravel & Earth	Total
Eastern Africa						
Botswana	0.6	712,195	95	16	4,976	4,992
Burundi	3.5	27,833	48	66	5.000	5,066
Ethiopia	24.8	1,031,647	67	1,957	5,347	7,304
Kenya	10.9	582,601	133	2,489	39,171	41,660
Lesotho	0.9	30,342	83	160	1,680	1,840
Malagasy Republic	6.7	590,520	111	2,900	35,100	38,000
Malawi	4.4	93,492	69	315	10,173	10,488
Mauritius	0.8	1,865	232	1,040	240	1,280
Rwanda	3.5	26,328	52	10	5,990	6,000
Somalia	2.8	637,611	66	900	15,100	16,000
Sudan	15.2	2,505,632	105	281	986	1,267
Swaziland	0.4	17,362	180	205	2,369	2,574
Tanzania	12.8	941,931	97	2,234	31,647	33,881
Uganda	9.5	236,019	113	6,382	17,791	24,173
Zaire	17.9	2,345,227	78	1,900	138,100	140,000
Zambia	4.1	752,560	289	1,579	31,759	33,338
Western Africa						
Cameroon	5.7	475,438	151	1,270	20,230	21,500
Central African Rep.	1.5	611,952	130	75	21,325	21,400
Chad	3.5	1,283,901	66	74	30,651	30,725
Congo, People's Rep. of	0.9	341,973	220	250	8,050	8,300
Dahomey	2.6	112,612	83	765	5,785	6,550
Equatorial Guinea	0.4	28,000	285	396	885	1,281
Gabon	0.5	264,390	324	111	5,444	5,555
Gambia	0.4	10,373	110	260	380	640
Ghana	8.3	237,855	189	3,975	28,200	32,175
Guinea	3.9	245,837	95	862	12,138	13,000
Ivory Coast	4.8	330,251	242	1,300	32,700	34,000
Liberia	1.5	111,361	203	483	2,300	2,783
Mali	4.9	1,201,667	92	1,300	11,700	13,000
Mauritania	1.1	1,085,724	142	575	8,550	9,125
Niger	3.9	1,266,902	79	488	5,875	6,363
Nigeria	64.6	923,701	80	15,300	72,000	87,300
Senegal	3.8	196,177	200	2,046	13,376	15,422
Sierra Leone	2.5	71,735	168	530	7,600	8,130
Togo	1.8	52,832	103	481	6,692	7,173
Upper Volta	5.3	274,180	56	419	16,481	16,900
East Asia & Pacific						
China, Republic of	13.8	35,962	301	5,832	9,449	15,281
Fiji	0.5	18,271	391	181	2,304	2,485
Indonesia	116.6	1,905,743	100	15,650	66,350	82,000
Korea, Republic of	31.1	98,423	213	3,120	34,050	37,170
Malaysia	10.6	332,608	342	13,845	4,607	18,452
New Zealand	2.8	268,676	2230	39,170	54,762	93,932
Papua New Guinea	2.3	475,332	212	100	11,900	12,000
Philippines	35.9	299,658	208	12,371	51,222	63,593
Thailand	35.1	518,343	162	5,400	11,900	17,300
South Asia						
Afghanistan	14.0	657,449	85	2,000	15,000	17,000
Ceylon	12.2	65,605	187	15,297	5,658	20,955
India	526.0	3,267,284	107	324,940	647,390	972,330
Iran	28.5	1,647,872	349	10,200	25,600	35,800
Nepal	10.8	140,787	80	661	2,019	2,680
Pakistan	126.7	946,647	105	27,568	77,093	104,661

180

Railway Route Length (Km)	Vehicles			Road Density (Km÷Km²)	Railway Density (Km÷Km²)	Vehicles per 1,000 Population
	Light	Heavy	Total			
—	2,255	3,426	5,681	.007	—	9.5
—	3,528	596	4,124	.182	—	1.2
781	39,000	12,200	51,200	.007	.001	2.1
2,160	115,000	10,300	125,300	.072	.004	11.9
—	2,111	2,723	4,834	.061	—	5.4
864	38,000	30,500	68,500	.064	.002	10.2
467	8,893	6,654	15,547	.112	.005	3.5
—	12,281	5,324	17,605	.686	—	22.0
—	4,365	742	5,107	.228	—	1.5
—	10,250	5,050	15,300	.025	—	5.5
4,752	27,400	25,000	52,400	.001	.002	3.4
220	4,111	3,475	7,586	.148	.013	19.0
2,400	41,989	20,485	62,474	.036	.003	4.9
1,150	29,163	10,460	39,623	.102	.005	4.8
4,185	79,639	14,700	94,339	.060	.002	5.5
1,120	68,424	15,809	84,233	.044	.002	20.5
949	38,500	16,500	55,000	.045	.002	9.6
—	6,100	2,400	8,500	.035	—	5.7
—	3,299	5,527	8,826	.024	—	2.5
800	6,000	1,500	7,500	.024	.002	8.3
579	6,600	4,400	11,000	.058	.005	4.2
—	4,000	3,000	7,000	.056	—	17.5
—	5,230	4,624	9,854	.021	—	19.7
—	1,800	2,200	4,000	.062	—	10.0
948	29,700	24,300	54,000	.135	.004	6.3
822	7,600	11,300	18,900	.053	.003	4.8
1,173	42,721	7,543	50,264	.103	.004	10.5
344	13,700	7,900	21,600	.025	.003	19.6
640	10,400	3,140	13,540	.011	.001	2.8
650	2,300	3,700	6,000	.008	.001	5.5
—	7,301	2,441	9,742	.005	—	2.5
3,505	63,000	30,000	93,000	.095	.004	1.5
1,032	33,063	20,030	53,093	.079	.005	14.0
500	10,000	6,000	16,000	.113	.007	6.4
442	5,050	750	5,800	.136	.008	3.2
—	5,013	5,879	10,892	.062	—	2.1
976	55,959	26,401	82,360	.425	.027	6.0
676	9,982	4,555	14,537	.136	.037	29.1
7,703	212,124	116,157	328,281	.043	.004	2.8
3,062	56,254	64,070	120,324	.378	.031	3.9
1,933	245,000	78,000	323,000	.055	.006	30.5
4,981	829,672	166,428	996,100	.350	.019	355.8
—	12,935	12,524	25,459	.025	—	11.1
1,190	269,610	177,161	446,771	.212	.004	12.0
3,765	195,200	153,400	348,600	.033	.007	10.0
—	12,040	21,228	33,268	.026	—	2.0
1,989	84,678	39,539	124,217	.319	.030	10.2
59,761	963,605	371,800	1,335,405	.298	.018	2.5
3,510	200,000	73,000	273,000	.022	.002	9.9
103	5,142	3,095	8,237	.019	.001	0.8
11,393	137,406	38,991	176,397	.111	.012	1.4

Basic Transport Data

	Mid-1969 Population (million)	Area (Km²)	GNP per cap. (US$)	Road Network Length (Km) Paved	Gravel & Earth	Total
Europe, Middle East & North Africa						
Algeria	13.3	2,381,741	259	51,700	23,900	75,600
Cyprus	0.6	9,251	965	3,397	4,268	7,665
Egypt, Arab Republic of	32.5	999,992	159	9,334	12,232	21,566
Finland	4.7	336,982	1977	21,828	50,041	71,869
Greece	8.8	131,935	842	12,000	23,000	35,000
Iceland	0.2	102,991	1853	51	11,862	11,913
Iraq	9.4	448,706	306	4,700	4,700	9,400
Israel	2.8	20,700	1573	4,000	5,100	9,100
Jordan	2.2	90,177	284	2,448	348	2,796
Lebanon	2.6	10,398	580	5,800	1,300	7,100
Morocco	15.1	447,605	190	20,735	30,745	51,530
Portugal	9.6	91,964	506	27,688	11,280	38,968
Spain	33.0	504,708	820	82,600	50,400	133,000
Syrian Arab Republic	5.9	187,072	255	7,000	11,000	18,000
Tunisia	4.9	150,208	227	8,300	8,992	17,292
Turkey	34.5	767,876	346	38,000	13,000	51,000
Yemen Arab Republic	5.6	194,983	80	430	1,195	1,625
Yemen, People's Dem. Republic of	1.2	290,058	118	416	4,005	4,421
Yugoslavia	20.4	255,784	575	20,623	69,072	89,695
Central America & Caribbean						
Costa Rica	1.7	50,695	506	1,300	17,300	18,600
Dominican Republic	4.0	48,730	276	5,100	4,900	10,000
El Salvador	3.4	21,392	294	1,200	7,300	8,500
Guatemala	5.0	108,880	353	1,851	8,533	10,384
Guyana	0.7	214,953	340	592	1,932	2,524
Honduras	2.5	112,079	258	900	3,026	3,926
Jamaica	2.0	11,424	548	3,050	1,300	4,350
Mexico	48.9	1,963,739	586	40,333	29,094	69,427
Nicaragua	1.9	139,689	380	1,200	8,800	10,000
Panama	1.4	75,643	662	1,801	4,981	6,782
Trinidad & Tobago	1.0	5,125	885	4,025	2,737	6,762
Venezuela	10.0	911,993	1003	18,000	21,600	39,600
South America						
Argentina	24.0	2,795,741	1061	29,000	107,500	136,500
Bolivia	4.8	1,098,497	163	724	17,485	18,209
Brazil	92.3	8,511,308	269	42,378	897,235	939,613
Chile	9.6	741,708	509	7,000	54,000	61,000
Colombia	20.6	1,179,227	289	5,300	38,900	44,200
Ecuador	5.9	301,116	238	2,450	12,350	19,800
Paraguay	2.3	406,720	237	810	5,499	6,309
Peru	13.1	1,285,116	331	4,900	40,400	45,300
Uruguay	2.9	185,911	562	2,300	7,000	9,300
Selected Capital Exporting Countries						
France	50.3	551,458	2460	629,593	853,146	1,482,739
Germany	60.8	248,477	2190	290,271	124,402	414,673
Japan	102.3	369,660	1430	127,188	878,243	1,005,431
United States	203.2	9,374,826	4241	2,533,374	3,395,420	5,928,794

NOTES: All data are for 1969. They are based on various standard publications, revised according to information available in the Bank. However, many of these figures are inaccurate and should be considered only as orders of magnitude. The weakest information concerns the length of gravel and earth road networks where the distribution between an earth road and a track is

182

Railway Route Length (Km)	Vehicles Light	Vehicles Heavy	Total	Road Density (Km÷Km²)	Railway Density (Km÷Km²)	Vehicles per 1,000 Population
4,241	117,000	88,500	205,500	.032	.002	15.5
—	64,000	12,000	76,000	.829	—	126.7
5,110	123,061	25,414	148,475	.022	.005	4.6
5,636	695,000	57,800	752,800	.213	.017	160.2
2,568	169,985	97,709	267,694	.265	.020	30.4
—	37,304	6,272	43,576	.116	—	217.9
1,635	61,789	40,963	102,752	.021	.004	10.9
692	155,000	64,000	219,000	.440	.033	78.2
366	15,250	6,589	21,839	.031	.004	9.9
417	129,674	16,239	145,913	.683	.040	56.1
2,051	150,000	55,000	205,000	.115	.005	13.6
3,619	458,100	73,600	531,700	.424	.040	55.4
17,510	1,999,000	683,000	2,682,000	.264	.035	81.3
859	29,466	16,081	45,547	.096	.005	7.7
2,461	59,017	33,130	92,147	.115	.016	18.8
8,030	171,000	135,000	306,000	.066	.015	8.9
—	6,900	1,100	8,000	.088	—	1.6
—	24,074	6,389	30,463	.015	—	21.8
16,437	562,500	144,500	707,000	.351	.064	34.7
548	36,000	20,000	56,000	.367	.011	32.9
600	41,734	23,452	65,186	.205	.012	15.5
620	31,300	15,900	47,200	.397	.029	13.9
1,019	33,000	20,500	53,500	.095	.009	10.7
205	14,196	7,924	22,120	.012	.001	31.6
649	14,200	16,600	30,800	.035	.006	12.3
394	60,000	20,000	80,000	.381	.035	40.0
20,207	112,100	524,600	1,636,700	.035	.010	33.5
4,981	14,000	22,000	36,000	.072	.036	18.9
700	41,335	13,785	55,120	.090	.009	39.4
—	67,600	18,800	86,400	1.319	—	86.4
471	498,000	200,000	698,000	.043	.001	69.8
41,148	1,200,000	701,000	1,901,000	.049	.015	79.2
3,626	14,855	19,197	34,052	.017	.003	7.1
35,410	1,537,000	953,900	2,490,900	.110	.004	27.4
9,860	187,483	67,077	254,560	.082	.013	26.5
3,342	141,100	123,200	264,300	.037	.003	12.8
1,121	25,500	35,300	60,800	.066	.004	10.3
522	10,060	13,670	23,730	.016	.001	10.3
2,604	160,000	103,000	263,000	.035	.002	20.1
3,046	142,000	90,300	232,300	.050	.016	80.1
39,660	11,155,000	2,065,000	13,220,000	2.689	.072	262.8
33,660	11,682,556	1,045,297	12,727,853	1.669	.136	209.3
24,140	5,209,319	7,027,538	12,236,857	2.720	.065	119.6
356,619	82,821,000	17,137,000	99,958,000	.632	.038	491.9

an extremely difficult one to make and may vary from country to country. GNP per capita figures are derived from data employed for the World Bank Atlas; the fact that they are not rounded, as in the Atlas, should not be taken as an indication of greater precision.

183

Bank and IDA Lending for Transport Through 1971
(Fiscal Years, US$ million)

	Through 1963	1964	1965	1966
EASTERN AFRICA				
Botswana	—	—	3.6	—
Burundi	4.8	—	—	—
East African Community	24.0	—	—	38.0
Ethiopia	33.5	—	—	—
Kenya	—	—	7.5	—
Lesotho	—	—	—	4.1
Malagasy Republic	—	—	—	—
Malawi	—	—	—	—
Mauritius	—	—	—	—
Rwanda	—	—	—	—
Somalia	—	—	6.2	—
Sudan	39.0	—	—	31.0
Swaziland	2.8	—	—	—
Tanzania	—	14.0	—	—
Uganda	—	—	—	—
Zaire	73.0	—	—	—
Zambia	23.5	—	—	—
Total Bank	184.3	—	—	69.0
IDA	16.3	14.0	17.3	4.1
Total	200.6	14.0	17.3	73.1
No. of Operations	11	1	4	3
WESTERN AFRICA				
Cameroon	—	—	—	—
Central African Republic	—	—	—	—
Chad	—	—	—	—
Congo, Peoples Republic of	—	—	—	—
Dahomey	—	—	—	—
Equatorial Guinea	—	—	—	—
Gabon	—	—	12.0	—
Gambia	—	—	—	—
Ghana	—	—	—	—
Guinea	—	—	—	1.7
Ivory Coast	1.9	—	—	—
Liberia	—	3.25	—	1.0
Mali	1.9	—	—	—
Mauritania	—	—	6.7	—
Niger	—	1.5	—	—
Nigeria	41.5	—	15.5	32.0
Senegal	1.9	—	—	—
Sierra Leone	—	—	—	—
Togo	—	—	—	—
Upper Volta	1.9	—	—	—
Total Bank	49.1	3.25	12.0	34.7
IDA	—	1.50	22.2	—
Total	49.1	4.75	34.2	34.7
No. of Operations	3	2	3	4

1967	1968	1969	1970	1971	Total 1964-68	Total 1967-71
—	—	—	—	—	3.6	—
—	—	—	0.38	—	—	0.38
—	—	—	77.4	—	38.0	77.4
—	21.2	—	—	—	21.2	21.2
5.3	10.7	—	23.5	12.6	23.5	52.1
—	—	—	—	—	4.1	—
10.0	—	8.0	9.6	—	10.0	27.6
0.49	11.5	—	—	—	11.99	11.99
—	—	—	—	—	—	—
—	—	—	9.3	—	—	9.3
—	2.3	0.55	—	—	8.5	2.85
—	—	—	—	—	31.0	—
—	—	—	—	—	—	—
—	3.0	15.0	7.5	—	17.0	25.5
—	5.0	—	11.6	—	5.0	16.6
—	—	6.0	—	7.0	—	13.0
17.5	—	10.7	—	—	17.5	28.2
17.50	13.5	21.20	100.90	—	100.00	153.10
15.79	40.2	19.05	38.38	19.6	91.39	133.02
33.29	53.7	40.25	139.28	19.6	191.39	286.12
4	6	5	8	2	18	25
—	0.55	—	24.2	1.5	0.55	26.25
—	—	4.2	4.3	—	—	8.5
—	—	4.1	—	—	—	4.1
—	—	0.63	1.5	—	—	2.13
—	—	—	—	3.5	—	3.5
—	—	—	—	—	—	—
—	—	6.0	—	—	12.0	6.0
—	—	—	2.1	—	—	2.1
—	—	—	1.5	—	—	1.5
—	—	64.5	—	9.0	1.7	73.5
—	5.8	—	—	20.5	5.8	26.3
—	—	3.6	—	—	4.25	3.6
9.1	—	—	7.7	—	9.1	16.8
—	—	3.0	—	—	6.7	3.0
—	—	6.12	—	5.7	1.5	11.82
—	—	—	35.6	—	47.5	35.6
13.0	—	—	2.1	—	13.0	15.1
—	—	—	—	7.2	—	7.2
—	—	3.7	—	—	—	3.7
—	—	—	—	—	—	—
4.0	5.80	74.10	52.8	33.20	59.75	169.9
18.1	0.55	21.75	26.2	14.20	42.35	80.8
22.1	6.35	95.85	79.0	47.40	102.10	250.7
3	2	9	10	6	14	30

Bank and IDA Lending for Transport Through 1971
(Fiscal Years, US$ million)

	Through 1963	1964	1965	1966
EAST ASIA & PACIFIC				
China, Republic of	2.2	—	20.0	—
Fiji	—	—	—	—
Indonesia	—	—	—	—
Korea, Republic of	14.0	—	—	—
Malaysia	—	—	—	—
New Zealand	—	7.8	—	42.0
Papua New Guinea	—	—	—	—
Philippines	8.5	—	—	—
Singapore	—	—	—	—
Thailand	79.8	—	—	36.0
Total Bank	88.3	7.8	20.0	78.0
IDA	16.2	—	—	—
Total	104.5	7.8	20.0	78.0
No. of Operations	9	1	1	2
SOUTH ASIA				
Afghanistan	—	—	—	—
Burma	33.35	—	—	—
Ceylon	—	—	—	—
India	594.11	—	62.0	68.0
Iran	72.0	18.5	40.5	—
Nepal	—	—	—	—
Pakistan	124.5	106.5	5.25	—
Total Bank	676.46	50.5	40.50	—
IDA	147.50	74.5	67.25	68.0
Total	823.96	125.0	107.75	68.0
No. of Operations	28	7	4	1
EUROPE, MIDDLE EAST AND NORTH AFRICA				
Algeria	50.0	—	--	—
Cyprus	—	—	—	—
Egypt, Arab Republic of	56.5	—	—	—
Greece	—	—	—	—
Finland	—	—	28.5	20.0
Iceland	—	—	—	—
Iraq	—	—	—	—
Israel	49.5	—	—	—
Jordan	—	—	—	—
Lebanon	—	—	—	—
Morocco	—	—	—	—
Spain	—	33.0	65.0	40.0
Syrian Arab Republic	—	8.5	—	—
Tunisia	—	7.0	—	—
Turkey	16.3	—	—	—
Yemen Arab Republic	—	—	—	—
Yemen, People's Dem. Rep. of	—	—	—	—
Yugoslavia	35.0	35.0	70.0	—
Total Bank	207.3	75.0	163.5	60.0
IDA	—	8.5	—	—
Total	207.3	83.5	163.5	60.0
No. of Operations	7	4	3	2

1967	1968	1969	1970	1971	Total 1964-68	Total 1967-71
—	17.5	31.2	—	15.0	37.5	63.7
—	—	—	—	11.8	—	11.8
—	—	28.0	—	34.0	—	62.0
—	11.0	3.5	55.0	54.5	11.0	124.0
—	—	—	—	16.1	—	16.1
—	—	—	—	16.0	49.8	16.0
—	—	—	9.0	—	—	9.0
—	—	—	—	8.0	—	8.0
15.0	—	—	—	—	15.0	15.0
—	29.0	23.0	—	12.5	65.0	64.5
15.0	46.5	54.2	44.5	133.9	167.3	294.1
—	11.0	31.5	19.5	34.0	11.0	96.0
15.0	57.5	85.7	64.0	167.9	178.3	390.1
1	3	4	2	8	8	18
—	—	5.0	—	—	—	5.0
—	—	—	—	—	—	—
—	—	9.8	—	—	—	9.8
—	—	—	55.0	—	130.0	55.0
—	—	—	42.0	—	59.0	42.0
—	—	—	—	2.5	—	2.5
14.5	—	57.5	20.2	—	126.25	92.2
13.5	—	62.4	61.2	—	104.50	137.1
1.0	—	9.9	56.0	2.5	210.75	69.4
14.5	—	72.3	117.2	2.5	315.25	206.5
2	—	5	4	1	14	12
—	—	11.5	—	—	—	11.5
—	—	—	—	—	—	—
—	—	—	—	—	—	—
—	—	—	—	13.0	48.5	13.0
—	—	—	—	4.1	—	4.1
23.0	—	—	—	—	23.0	23.0
—	—	—	—	—	—	—
—	—	—	—	6.0	—	6.0
—	—	—	—	—	—	—
—	—	—	14.6	—	—	14.6
—	50.0	—	—	90.0	188.0	140.0
—	—	—	—	—	8.5	—
—	—	26.35	—	31.5	7.0	57.85
—	—	—	—	—	—	—
—	—	—	—	1.6	—	1.6
10.0	50.0	30.0	40.0	35.0	165.0	165.0
33.0	100.0	59.35	47.3	173.6	431.5	413.25
—	—	8.50	7.3	7.6	8.5	23.4
33.0	100.0	67.85	54.6	181.2	440.0	436.65
2	2	5	2	8	13	19

Bank and IDA Lending for Transport Through 1971
(Fiscal Years, US$ million)

	Through 1963	1964	1965	1966
CENTRAL AMERICA AND CARIBBEAN				
Costa Rica	11.0	—	—	—
Dominican Republic	—	—	—	—
El Salvador	24.1	—	—	—
Guatemala	18.2	—	—	—
Guyana	—	—	—	—
Haiti	2.95	—	—	—
Honduras	18.7	—	9.5	—
Jamaica	—	—	5.5	—
Mexico	116.5	40.0	32.0	—
Nicaragua	10.2	—	—	—
Panama	13.1	—	—	—
Trinidad & Tobago	—	—	—	—
Venezuela	45.0	—	30.0	—
Total Bank	236.90	40.0	73.5	—
IDA	22.85	—	3.5	—
Total	259.75	40.0	77.0	—
No. of Operations	19	1	4	—
SOUTH AMERICA				
Argentina	48.5	—	—	—
Bolivia	—	—	—	—
Brazil	28.0	—	—	—
Chile	25.0	—	—	—
Colombia	162.65	—	—	—
Ecuador	36.6	17.0	—	—
Paraguay	6.0	—	—	4.85
Peru	57.83	3.1	—	42.1
Uruguay	18.5	—	2.2	—
Total Bank	338.58	12.1	2.2	46.95
IDA	44.50	8.0	—	—
Total	383.08	20.1	2.2	46.95
No. of Operations	26	2	1	4
PAST BORROWERS (Pre-1963)				
Rhodesia	9.5	—	—	—
South Africa	147.8	—	—	—
Australia	132.33[1]	—	—	—
Japan	160.0	125.0	100.0	25.0
Belgium	30.0	—	—	—
Netherlands	19.0	—	—	—
Norway	25.0	—	—	—
Total Bank	523.63[1]	125.0	100.0	25.0
IDA	—	—	—	—
Total	523.63[1]	125.0	100.0	25.0
No. of Operations	25[2]	2	2	1
GRAND TOTAL				
Bank	2,304.57[1]	313.65	411.70	313.65
IDA	247.35	106.50	110.25	72.10
Total	2,551.92[1]	420.15	521.95	385.75
No. of Operations	128[2]	20	22	17

[1] Including $123.1 million for the transportation portion of five general development loans to Australia.

[2] Including the Australian loans, referred to in footnote [1], as five distinct operations.

1967	1968	1969	1970	1971	Total 1964-68	Total 1967-71
—	—	—	15.7	—	—	15.7
—	—	—	—	—	—	—
—	2.8	—	—	—	2.8	2.8
—	—	—	—	—	—	—
—	—	—	—	—	—	—
13.4	—	—	—	6.0	22.9	19.4
—	—	—	—	—	5.5	—
—	27.5	—	21.8	—	99.5	49.3
—	—	—	—	—	—	—
8.6	—	—	—	—	8.6	8.6
—	—	20.0	—	—	30.0	20.0
22.0	30.3	20.0	37.5	6.0	165.8	115.8
—	—	—	—	—	3.5	—
22.0	30.3	20.0	37.5	6.0	169.3	115.8
3	2	1	2	1	10	9
—	—	25.0	—	151.5	—	176.5
—	—	—	23.25	—	—	23.25
—	—	26.0	100.0	45.0	—	171.0
—	—	11.6	10.8	—	—	22.4
—	—	35.5	32.0	—	—	67.5
—	—	—	—	—	17.0	—
—	—	—	6.0	—	4.85	6.0
—	—	—	—	30.0	45.2	30.0
—	—	—	—	—	2.2	—
—	—	98.1	172.05	226.5	61.25	496.65
—	—	—	—	—	8.00	—
—	—	98.1	172.05	226.5	69.25	496.65
—	—	5	5	4	7	14
—	—	—	—	—	—	—
—	—	—	—	—	—	—
100.0	—	—	—	—	350.0	100.0
—	—	—	—	—	—	—
—	—	—	—	—	—	—
100.0	—	—	—	—	350.0	100.0
—	—	—	—	—	—	—
100.0	—	—	—	—	350.0	100.0
1	—	—	—	—	6	1
205.00	196.10	389.35	516.25	573.20	1,440.10	1,879.9
34.89	51.75	90.70	147.38	77.90	375.49	402.62
239.89	247.85	480.05	663.63	651.10	1,815.59	2,282.52
16	15	34	33	30	90	128

Selected Statistics[1] on Bank Group Highway Construction Projects, FY 1967-71

	Gravel Roads	Two-Lane Paved Roads			High-Standard Paved Roads[2]	Grand Total
		Improvement	Construction	Total		
Total Length of Roads (km)	2,768	21,480	5,423	26,903	650	30,321
Number of Road Sections	25	120	73	193	19	237
Average Length of Each Section (km)	111	179	74	139	34	128
Total Construction Cost ($ millions)	47	930	788	1,718	628	2,393
Average Unit Cost ($000 per km)	17	43	145	64	966	79
Minimum Unit Cost ($000 per km) for any Road Section	4	5	43	5	140	4
Maximum Unit Cost ($000 per km) for any Road Section	84	883	593	883	2,943	2,943
Total Foreign Exchange Component ($ millions)	33	454	343	797	153	983
Average Foreign Exchange Component (%)	70	49	44	46	24	41
Minimum Foreign Exchange Component for any Road Section (%)	65	23	20	20	12	12
Maximum Foreign Exchange Component for any Road Section (%)	75	75	85	85	65	85
Regional Distribution						
1. Africa						
Total Length (km)	2,628	7,133	1,668	8,801	50	11,479
Total Cost ($ millions)	37	239	140	379	8	424
Unit Cost ($000 per km)	14	34	84	43	160	37
2. Asia, Middle East and Oceania						
Total Length (km)	141	4,404	1,420	5,824	179	6,144
Total Cost ($ millions)	10	185	265	450	356	816
Unit Cost ($000 per km)	71	42	187	77	1,989	133
3. Europe						
Total Length (km)	—	957	546	1,503	135	1,638
Total Cost ($ millions)	—	18	167	185	119	304
Unit Cost ($000 per km)	—	19	306	123	881	186
4. Western Hemisphere						
Total Length (km)	—	8,986	1,789	10,775	285	11,060
Total Cost ($ millions)	—	488	217	705	145	850
Unit Cost ($000 per km)	—	54	121	65	509	77

Note: Totals and averages may not check due to rounding.

[1] Costs given are those estimated at time of project appraisal.
[2] Roads with more than two lanes and limited access.

190

Selected Statistics on Bank Group Railway Projects, FY 1967-71
(Amounts in US$ million)

Country	Loan or Credit Number	Date of Agreement	Amount	Track, Marshalling Yards, Structures and Bridges and Earth Works Amount	Components, Parts and Materials for Rolling Stock	Freight Cars (All Types) Number	Freight Cars Amount	Locomotives (Including Spares) Number	Locomotives Amount	Passenger Cars (Incl. Railcars & Trailers) Number	Passenger Cars Amount	Signalling and Communications Equipment and Materials Amount	Other Railway Equipment, Buildings and Materials Amount	Consulting Services and Training Amount	Interest, Contingencies and Unallocated Amount
Mali	95	9/29/66	9.10	1.66	0.90	107	1.26	9	1.30	22	1.41	0.53	1.32	0.72	—
Senegal	96	9/29/66	9.00	4.19	0.97	16	0.12	7	0.98	19	1.30	0.03	0.67	0.74	—
Pakistan	496	5/26/66	13.50	7.20	4.50	—	—	—	—	—	—	—	1.30	—	0.50
Spain	507	8/4/67	50.00	6.82	—	1,150	14.00	40	13.00	115	9.47	2.77	1.67	—	2.27
Korea, Republic of	110	12/18/67	11.00	—	—	1,050	10.22	—	—	—	—	—	—	0.50	0.28
China, Republic of	524	1/18/68	17.50	1.60	0.40	470	3.60	26	5.10	89	4.60	1.00	—	—	1.20
Yugoslavia	531	3/22/68	50.00	31.30	—	—	—	—	—	—	—	2.60	6.00	0.20	9.90
Colombia	551	7/25/68	18.30	10.50	1.80	—	—	—	—	—	—	0.40	2.60	1.70	1.30
Guinea	557	9/18/68	32.80 (2)	27.61	—	26	0.84	3	0.84	—	—	0.47	0.45	1.97	—
China, Republic of	603	5/29/69	31.20	2.70	0.50	600	5.80	18	4.00	4	0.62	1.00	1.60	0.30	2.10
Tunisia	606/150	6/4/69	17.00	7.96	2.33	—	—	7	1.77	283	13.20	—	0.76	—	2.10
Pakistan	621	6/26/69	14.50	12.00	—	—	—	—	—	15	2.08	—	1.30	0.70	0.50
India	162	9/24/69	55.00	2.40	37.80	2,740	28.40	50	19.50	—	—	4.20	10.60	—	—
Korea, Republic of	669/183	5/14/70	55.00	2.40	—	600 (1)	4.80	—	—	—	—	2.60	—	0.50	1.60
East African Community	674	5/25/70	42.40	23.00	0.60	185	2.18	—	—	—	—	—	5.90	0.40	7.70
Cameroon	687	6/9/70	5.20	1.96	—	800	7.00	6	1.40	—	—	—	—	0.05	1.01
Nigeria	694	6/26/70	11.20 (3)	2.80	—	1,200	11.27	—	—	—	—	—	0.26	—	—
New Zealand	725	3/1/71	16.00	0.27	2.60	—	—	—	—	—	—	0.08	—	0.50	1.02
Argentina	733	4/28/71	84.00	13.90	54.80	160	2.34	—	—	—	—	3.30	1.53	—	12.00
China, Republic of	750	6/11/71	15.00	8.10	—	—	—	—	—	—	—	0.75	0.84	0.90	1.38
Guinea	766	6/25/71	1.80 (4)	1.40	—	—	—	—	—	—	—	—	—	—	—
Spain	772	6/30/71	90.00	36.20	—	565	12.10	34	16.60	60	10.00	1.50	4.50	0.50	8.60
TOTALS:			649.50	205.97	107.20	9,669	103.92	200	64.49	607	42.68	21.23	40.46	9.68	53.46

(1) Estimate.
(2) Total loan amount is $64.5 million of which railway portion is $32.8 million and balance amount of $31.7 million is for port and townsite.
(3) Total loan amount is $25 million of which railway portion is $11.2 million and balance amount of $13.8 million is for highways ($12.4 million) and ports ($1.4 million).
(4) Total loan amount is $9 million of which railway portion is $1.8 million; balance amount of $7.2 is for port.
Source: appraisal reports prepared between 1966 and 1971.

Selected Statistics on Bank Group Port Projects, 1967-71
(Amounts in US$ million)

Country	Loan or Credit Number	Date of Agreement	Amount	Berth(1) Construction & Ancillary Civil Works	Cargo Handling Equipment and Quay Cranes	Transit Sheds Silos Warehouses Misc. Buildings	Dredging & Dredging Equipment	Floating (Except Dredging) Equipment	Breakwater	Contingencies(6) and Unallocated	Consultant Services & Other Training Schemes	Interest During Construction
Singapore	462	8/11/66	15.01	8.10	2.50	—	—	3.01	—	1.00	0.40	—
Honduras	463	8/25/66	4.80	3.19	0.50	0.22	—	—	—	0.03	0.38	0.48
Senegal	493	5/1/67	4.00	1.35	—	—	1.85	—	—	0.53	0.27	—
Guinea	557	9/18/68	31.70(2)	7.15	—	9.95	2.10	1.00	—	5.60	3.10	2.80
Tunisia	573	11/29/68	8.50	0.32	0.87	2.50	2.44	—	0.37	1.15	0.85	—
Liberia	617	6/20/69	3.60	0.20	—	—	1.60	1.15	—	0.43	0.22	—
Cyprus	628	6/30/69	11.50	2.51	1.74	0.92	1.58	—	2.47	1.45	0.83	—
East African Community	638	8/25/69	35.00(3)	15.50	1.55	6.75	0.55	—	—	4.00	2.60	3.30
Gambia	187	5/26/70	2.10	0.96	0.24	0.16	0.34	0.75	—	0.25	0.08	—
Pakistan	S-9	6/10/70	1.00	—	—	—	—	0.07	—	—	1.00	—
Malagasy Republic	200	6/19/70	9.60	3.05	0.90	0.74	—	—	2.17	1.44	1.30	—
Nigeria	694	6/26/70	1.40(4)	—	1.40	—	—	—	—	—	—	—
Thailand	702	8/6/70	12.50	7.68	—	2.04	0.37	—	—	1.15	1.26	—
Cameroon	229	1/14/71	1.50	0.96	—	—	0.20	—	—	0.22	0.12	—
Zaire	255	6/21/71	7.00	—	—	—	1.00	3.00	—	1.08	1.92	—
Brazil	756	6/21/71	45.00	16.67	8.72	3.85	5.88	—	—	9.18	0.70	—
Guinea	766	6/25/71	7.20(5)	2.00	—	2.40	—	—	—	1.00	1.30	0.50
Honduras	767	6/25/71	6.00	3.21	0.63	0.16	0.07	0.42	—	0.94	0.57	—
Malaysia	774	6/30/71	16.10	11.45	0.57	—	—	—	—	2.95	1.13	—
Totals			223.51	84.30	19.62	29.69	17.98	9.40	5.01	32.40	18.03	7.08

(1) Includes offshore tanker moorings and also stacking areas, road and railway inside port.
(2) Total loan amount $64.5 million, of which $31.7 million is for port and townsite and balance of $32.8 million for railways.
(3) Loan amount is $35.6 million. Carryover from Loan 428-EA of $3.33 million brings total to $38.33 million.
(4) Total loan amount is $25 million, of which $1.4 million is for port; balance of $23.6 million is for railways ($11.2 million) and highways ($12.4 million).
(5) Total loan amount is $9 million, of which $7.2 million is port portion and townsite; balance of $1.8 million is for railways.
(6) Mostly for civil works, berth and shed construction.
Source: appraisal reports prepared between 1966 and 1971.

Summary of World Bank Transport Activities, With Projection through FY1976

	Actual			Program		Actual[2]		Program
	1969	1970	1971	1972	1973	1964-68	1969-73	1972-76
Bank Sector Missions[1]	1	8	6	10	9	13	34	45
UNDP-Financed Sector Surveys and Preinvestment Studies initiated	13	7	14	18	20	30	72	98
Commitments (US$ millions)	480	664	651	750	785	1,816	3,330	4,300
% of Total Bank and IDA	27	30	26	27	28	32	28	28
Number of Countries	29	29	28	31	38	75	81	85
Lending Operations (No.)	34	33	30	37	44	90	178	240
% of Total Bank and IDA	31	28	23	24	24	32	25	24
Projects under Supervision[3]	122	131	141	150	164	110[4]	142[4]	181[4]

[1] As of July 1968, the Bank had satisfactory sectoral knowledge of 15 countries.

[2] Including scheduled for FY1972-73

[3] End of Fiscal Year.

[4] Annual average over period.

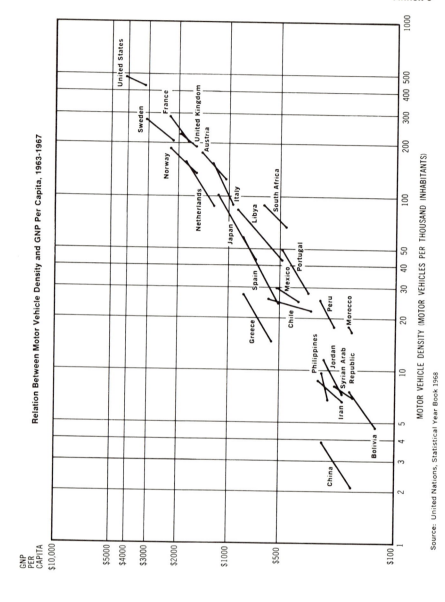

Relation Between Motor Vehicle Density and GNP Per Capita, 1963-1967

Source: United Nations, Statistical Year Book 1968

194

TELECOMMUNICATION

TELECOMMUNICATION
SECTOR WORKING PAPER

INTRODUCTION

Telecommunication networks may be described as the central nervous systems of complex societies, transmitting information and commands between their various parts. Without these facilities, many dimensions of life in interrelated communities, especially government and economic activity, could not function efficiently, if at all.

Wherever public telecommunication services of adequate quality and reliability do not exist, there is widespread recourse to communication systems built by business or government units for their own use. These private links are not only much more costly than public systems; they are also only a partial substitute for they do not provide access to the wider community that would normally be connected to a well-functioning public system. Limitations of access to such private systems imply serious constraints on efficiency and growth in the unconnected parts of the economy.

Telecommunication now encompasses a number of services and facilities for transmission of written messages, voice communication and a variety of other communication modes such as TV and radio programs, data and facsimile transmission, telemetering and telecommand applications. Telecommunication entities provide telephone, telegraph, telex, and data facilities to the public, giving customer service for voice and written communications; in addition, these entities lease telecommunication facilities for private use to meet a wide variety of needs.

All these facilities have one feature in common: they use the same methods of transmission from one point to another. Of these, the public telephone service is the most significant in terms of size and coverage and constitutes the basic telecommunication facility. All others are derived by relatively minor additions of equipment to transform the telephone network to other kinds of communication needs.

The choice of telecommunication as against the other two basic forms of communication—personal meetings and postal service or other means of transporting written messages—depends on the rela-

197

tive cost, speed, convenience and reliability of each form. Transportation is critical to the speed and cost of personal meetings and also of the postal service. Yet improved transportation, rather than reducing the demand for telecommunication, can create a greater demand due to the widening community of interest generated by increased mobility. The three forms of communication are much more complementary than competitive in meeting the total communication needs of a society.

The value of telecommunication services to the users is attested to by unsatisfied demand throughout the developing world, even at prices which generate very substantial money surpluses for reinvestment and thus probably capture a much larger share of user benefits than in any other public service. It is not surprising to find that the economic return on investment in expansion of telecommunication services, when measured by willingness of users to pay for installation and for use, can approximate 50% in some cases.

Such high returns cannot be read as an indication of national expenditure priorities because they cannot be compared with the benefits of expenditures geared to satisfying social needs, which may not be measurable by willingness to pay. We have as yet no adequate technique for comparing intersectoral priorities at the margin: the merits of additional investment in telecommunication vs., say, additional investment in sewerage, education or power. These high returns are consistent, however, with what one would expect to be the expanding communication needs of a growing economy: for efficient administration of government and industry, for effective competition in business, for orderly marketing and the rational movement of goods, for reduction of industrial and business inventories, for tourism, etc. Also, where literacy is low, telephone conversations are more suitable than mail for settling transactions which require checking and bargaining. Telephones provide amenities which some would regard as of questionable priority in poor countries; these amenities, however, are a by-product of the important economic service provided by a good telecommunication system. Telephone facilities in developing countries are useful mainly for government, business and professional purposes.

INTERNATIONAL PERSPECTIVE

At the beginning of 1970, the total number of telephones in the world was estimated at about 255 million. The developing countries of Central and South America, Africa and Asia which have 60.7% of

the world population and about 16.1% of world GNP have some 17
million telephones or about 6.8% of the total. Except for the United
States and Canada, virtually all telephone networks are owned and
operated by governments.

Table 1: World Distribution of Telephones

	Millions of Telephones	Percentage of World Population	Percentage of Total World Telephones	Telephones per 100 Population
Developing countries Latin America, Africa and Asia	17.5	60.7	6.8	1.0
North America	124.0	7.9	48.7	55.0
Western Europe	66.5	13.1	26.1	18.0
Japan	23.0	3.6	9.0	22.0
Oceania	5.4	0.7	2.1	27.0

Among the developed countries, the United States and Sweden
have more than 50 telephones per 100 of population, Switzerland,
Canada and New Zealand over 40, followed by Denmark, Australia
and the United Kingdom with densities above 25. Japan, Germany,
France and Italy, for historical reasons, have lower telephone densities, but theirs are increasing at annual rates of about 10% or more.
Variations between the three developing regions of South and Central America, Asia and Africa are much wider, and there are great
disparities in telephone densities between countries within each of
these regions. Some examples are given in Annex 2.

Within a country, telephones ordinarily are concentrated in the
larger cities. In the industrialized countries, the range of variation in
density as between cities and other regions is small. In less developed countries, however, a large proportion of telephones is usually
concentrated in a few cities, with little or no service for large populated areas.

In developing countries telephone expansion has generally lagged
behind development in other sectors, but recently there has been a
trend towards faster growth. This trend commenced in the late 1950s
in Asia and has now begun to spread to other areas. As a result, the
rate of growth of telephones in service is now higher in many developing countries than in the more developed, as shown by Table 2.

Table 2: Telephone Growth Rate
(Annual percentages)

	1959-1969	1969-1970
Central America	4.9	12.9
South America	5.1	7.8
Africa less South Africa	6.0	5.8
Asia less Japan	11.2	11.0
World	6.6	7.3

There is a large gap, however, between supply and demand for telephone services in the developing countries. The waiting list often approaches the number of telephones in service, and the average waiting time for a new connection may be several years. Likewise, traffic generated by subscribers usually exceeds the network's capacity, giving rise to poor service, particularly on long distance, where calls are frequently delayed many hours.

Typically, investment in telecommunication facilities in developing countries is in the neighborhood of 3% of total public investment.

Table 3: Telecommunication and Total Public Investment in Four Countries
(Millions of U.S. dollars)

	1965-69				1970-74			
	Total Public Investment	Tele-communications Sector	%	Bank Financed Projects	Total Public Investment	Tele-communications Sector	%	Bank Financed Projects
Brazil[1]	5,301	133	2.5	--	7,172	167	2.3	—
Mexico	7,939	191[2]	2.4	—	11,984	296	2.3	—
Colombia	1,450	57	3.9	28	3,190	133	4.2	32
Malaysia[3]	1,082[4]	44.3	4.1	49[5]	1,567	108	6.8	82

[1]Annual averages because historic data not available prior to 1968.
[2]Estimate for 1965 and 1966.
[3]The figures are estimates, since the planning periods are different in Malaysia.
[4]Excludes defense expenditure; figure for 1969 is estimated.
[5]The project covers the period 1968-1970.

SPECIAL CHARACTERISTICS

The most significant feature of this sector is its inherent dynamism. There is a continuous and high demand for facilities, and rapid and continuing technological advances are opening up possibilities for new types of service and for reducing investment and operational costs. Telecommunication systems are unique in that the value of a connection to a single subscriber increases with the number of other subscribers connected to the system. Nevertheless, the prevailing situation in the developing countries is one of gross inadequacy of telecommunication facilities, with obsolete plant and a lack of application of new technology.

These deficiencies are beginning to be corrected in some countries, but greater effort will be necessary to meet the communication needs of economic growth. In many countries this will require wider recognition of the sector's essential role in development, more willingness to free telecommunication management from the day-to-day operating constraints of bureaucracy and a more positive approach by management, as well as steps to provide more adequate funds.

Nature of Expansion and Investment Decision Making

Setting aside complex problems associated with large and sophisticated networks, the criteria for making investment and engineering decisions for routine development of telecommunications are fairly well established; but they require a good management with strong engineering and financial groups to ensure that the necessary disciplines are followed and that decisions are taken correctly and in time. The principal objectives of these decisions are to ensure that expenditures are in line with network development priorities and that engineering designs provide the least-cost solutions to meet given requirements and standards of service.

The fundamental decisions in planning are those which relate to the basic network structure and which remain valid for 15 to 20 years ahead. These decisions involve the location of the principal exchanges, the numbering and routing plans, the principles of charging for local and long distance calls, the choice of a switching system and of a signaling system, and the pattern of broadband transmission system for long distance calls. Decisions on each of these different points must take into account the desired rate of implementation of new facilities and the associated economies of scale, and must be reviewed when new technological alternatives become available.

Within this long term structural development perspective, system managers must decide on the rate at which services should be mechanized. The capital cost of manual exchanges is generally less than for automatic exchanges. However, this differential decreases with the increasing size of the exchange. Also, the continuing operating expenses for telephonists are such that, even with low wages, automation is the cheaper solution for exchanges of more than a few hundred lines. Moreover, in developing countries, literacy and other skills required of a telephone operator are a scarce commodity and probably of greater economic benefit in other occupations. For these reasons, automation is now the accepted objective in nearly all countries, for both local and long distance (trunk) service. Subscriber trunk dialing also brings economies through lower costs for setting up connections and for collection of revenues, higher utilization of trunk circuits and improved service. These lead to cheaper calls, and trunk charges can be directly related to the conversation time rather than charging the subscriber in multiples of three minutes, as is usual with manual trunk service.

The expansion of a telecommunication network is a continuous process. It consists of thousands of installations annually. The design, dimensioning and timing of these installations are done by "in house" planning engineers who follow established plant practices based on economic analysis designed to minimize the initial and subsequent costs of each class of plant or equipment. Many of the optimizing techniques used widely today in other sectors were developed by the telecommunication industry.

In deciding on the components of any program, the first priority is to provide a satisfactory quality of local and long distance service, taking into account the increasing use by existing subscribers and any necessary improvements in the service they receive. The available remaining physical and financial resources are used for new subscriber connections, the objective being the balanced development of all network facilities needed for efficient service.

As in other utilities, telephone users are connected to a network and can use the service at their discretion. The capacity of the system must therefore be adequate to meet the peak traffic. Inadequate capacity results in congestion, rapid deterioration of service and failure of calls. Delay in meeting requests for telephone connections causes the usage of many telephones in the system to become higher than the system was designed to accommodate. Persons trying to reach these telephones get busy signals, try again, tie up other available circuits and thus add to congestion and failure of calls. Congestion also increases costs through increased wear of equipment.

A common result of such unsatisfactory public telecommunication service is the establishment of separate private telecommunication networks by governmental, commercial, industrial, transportation and mining groups to meet their individual needs. The total costs to the national economy of such developments are very high, since these requirements can be served at considerably lower cost, and better, by a well-run public telecommunication network.

The rate at which a system can be expanded is limited by the ability of the enterprise to provide trained staff to plan, install and operate it. Historically, no country has been able to sustain, over long periods, a growth in new subscribers of substantially more than 15% per year, which requires doubling its facilities every five years, even if demand is growing at a faster rate. A higher rate of increase may be achieved for a short period of a year or so, but at the cost of lowering service standards, with subsequent penalties of network congestion and lower quality service.

Impact of Technology

Telecommunication has benefited greatly from recent advances in scientific knowledge and technology. The result has been an ability to provide very large blocks of circuits of extreme reliability and high quality over any distance, at unit costs which have been steadily and significantly decreasing. There are further developments in prospect which promise continuing reductions.

The new coaxial, microwave and other long distance systems permit large increases in the number of circuits on a route with marginal increases in costs; typically a hundredfold increase in the capacity of a route will require about three times the initial investment. Circuits can be brought into commission by the addition of equipment at a relatively small fixed cost per circuit. Similarly, satellite communication offers dramatic possibilities for international service with relatively small expenditure on ground stations and rental of satellite facilities.

Without being as dramatic or spectacular as the advances in coaxial, microwave and satellite systems, steady improvements have been made in the design and manufacture of telephone switching systems. They are now more reliable, require reduced maintenance, permit savings in the costs of distribution networks and provide considerable increase in functional capabilities without increase in costs, so that nationwide automatic subscriber dialing is now not only the better but also the cheaper way of providng service.

Standardization and Local Manufacture

Traditionally, telephone utilities have shown a marked tendency to adopt standard designs and brands and to adhere to these over long periods of time. This is particularly so in the case of switching equipment (local and long distance), which makes up about 30% of the cost of system expansion.

Standardization has the obvious advantages of simplifying technical training and enlarging the flexibility of staff and the interchangeability of supplies and spares. For switching equipment in telephone exchanges, there are additional special and compelling arguments in favor of standardization. Economies are possible by designing the exchange installation for its ultimate capacity and making the initial installation only to meet the immediate needs; future needs can be met by small increments as and when required. If these economies are to be realized, however, further additions must be duplicates of the initial installation. There are similar, though less significant, advantages in adding to the same types of long distance equipment.

A particularly strong reason for standardization of switching equipment arises from the problems of interworking with other equipment. In most other sectors, new additions share the function with existing units, e.g., a new electrical generator produces electrical energy exactly the same as existing units, which will pass through any switch or transformer on the system. In the case of telecommunication equipment, however, the interrelationship is different. The language by which one exchange "talks" to another must be consistent, but only recently have the manufacturers of the world progressed towards adopting common languages. If different brands or "systems" are mixed, an intermediary "translating" station must be installed so that one manufacturer's switch can "understand" someone else's switch. The planning of interworking equipment, drawing up of bid documents for the new additions, procurement of necessary additions to the existing installations, and commissioning of the equipment makes the process complex. As new types are added, the subsequent additions become even more complicated.

The penalty for non-standardization is difficult to quantify, since it increases rapidly with the number of different systems in use and also depends on the proportions of each. However, the advantages of standardization are such that most of the developed countries negotiate bulk supply agreements extending over a number of years, and it is the concerted view that a change in the basic switching system cannot feasibly be undertaken more often than every 10 to 15 years. This is perhaps the main reason for the delay in widespread introduction of electronic exchanges, the imminent use of which was forecast more than a decade ago.

Standardization and bulk supply agreements have also encouraged the establishment of local telecommunication manufacturing industries. At present, the large developing countries such as Argentina, Brazil and India produce a wide range of telecommunication products; and other countries—among them Pakistan, Iran, Israel, Egypt,

Malaysia, Thailand, Singapore, Colombia, Venezuela—produce a part of their needs with foreign collaboration arrangements or in foreign owned local factories. With a few exceptions, these factories are working satisfactorily. Costs of production, net of widely varying import duties and other taxes charged, are generally in line with costs in the industrialized countries. There have been abuses in the name of standardization, but an alert management can protect itself against them.

While a judgment on the setting up of any of these industries in a particular country has to be made on its merits, current indications are that more and more countries will find it advantageous to have domestic manufacturing facilities. These industries are not particularly difficult to set up, have high value added, and thus can lead to sizable savings in foreign costs. They also serve as a training ground or a base for development of other light engineering industries. The establishment of a switching factory contributes to the growth of manufacture of other light metal engineering products; a cable factory, producing a variety of household electric and other wires as well as power cables (telephone cable, power cable and other wires are often made in one factory), and the manufacture of multiplex equipment helps promote the manufacture of other professional and consumer electronic products.

The reasons outlined above for standardization in switching systems suggest that international competitive procurement of this type of equipment should not be carried out in ways which would force borrowers into premature changes in switching equipment. The implications for future Bank operations of standardization are discussed further on pages 209-210.

Pricing and Demand

The tariff structure for telecommunication services varies among countries. In some there is a "flat rate" tariff whereby rental and local calls are covered by a single charge, but in most countries a separate unit fee is charged for each local call. Long distance calls are related to one of a number of mileage categories to which different charges apply; concessional night rate tariffs are traditionally applied to diminish peak loading and increase off-peak revenues.

There is considerable flexibility in structuring tariffs to meet particular objectives, such as altering demand by time of day or subsidizing one group of users by another; for example, by having different charges for rural and urban subscribers. However, telecommunication demand overall is highly inelastic to price: price increases normally cause only a temporary (about one year) depression of demand. In these circumstances, and given the monopoly supply position for this service, most systems set average charges at levels which both fully cover costs and generate substantial surpluses for reinvestment.

Because demand so far exceeds capacity in many countries, various forms of rationing have developed, ranging from explicit priorities for certain categories of users on waiting lists (doctors, businesses, etc.) to unplanned black market pricing for telephone connections, which gives a scarcity windfall to individuals already connected to the system. Some entities have resorted to high installation charges to discourage demand for new connections (and collect the scarcity windfall for the entity) and high usage charges to discourage use of existing connections. Since the value of a telecommunication system derives largely from the access it gives to connected customers, these pricing policies frequently conflict with the objective of maximizing system use by the community and ensuring that increases in capacity, where limited, are allocated to best serve community needs.

MAIN FEATURES OF BANK GROUP OPERATIONS

Finance

The World Bank Group is the principal multilateral source of finance for telecommunication development. Through fiscal 1971, the Bank and IDA provided nearly $600 million for this purpose in 34 loans and credits to 21 countries, or more than 90% of the total from all multilateral institutions. The bulk of external finance, however, has probably been provided through bilateral lending agencies and by suppliers in the industrialized countries.

Well over 70% of the Bank Group's lending in this sector has been concentrated in the last five years, as summarized in Table 4.

Table 4: Summary of World Bank and IDA Lending for Telecommunication, 1949-71

Fiscal Years	Number of Loans	Amount (US$ millions)
1949-60	4	$ 24.4
1961-66	7	139.1
1967-71	23	428.0
Totals	34	$591.5

A full list of telecommunication loans beginning with fiscal 1962, together with the total cost of projects the Bank and IDA have assisted, is given in Annex 1. As will be seen, the volume increased sharply from $40.2 million in fiscal 1967 to $195.5 million in 1971, while the cost of related projects rose from $72.6 million to $889.6 million. The average size of telecommunication loans in this period was $18.6 million; the largest was to India for $78 million and the smallest to Upper Volta for $0.8 million. Table 5 shows the regional distribution of lending during the same five years.

**Table 5: Regional Distribution of Bank and IDA
Lending for Telecommunication, 1967-71**

Region	No. of Countries	No. of Loans	Amount of Loans (US$ millions)	Total Cost of Projects
Africa	5	4	$ 28.7[1]	$ 81.6[1]
Asia	9	13	275.6	1,159.5
Europe	1	1	40.0	95.0
Latin America	5	5	83.7[2]	389.0[2]
Totals	20	23	$428.0	$1,725.1

[1]Two of these loans were to East African Posts and Telegraph, serving Kenya, Uganda and Tanzania.
[2]One loan of $11.2 million to Jamaica was later cancelled at the request of the borrower.

The five-year level of Bank Group lending for telecommunication attained through fiscal 1971 is expected to increase by perhaps 50% in the period 1972-76. (See Annex 3.)

Sector Studies and Research

In the earlier years, telecommunication projects were considered from time to time only as they were presented for financing, instead of as an integral part of country development programs. As a result, the Bank had developed adequate knowledge of the sector only in those countries where projects had been supported.

To overcome this deficiency an enlarged program of sector studies is to be carried out as staff resources permit; of necessity, such work will be limited for several years to countries where lending operations are in prospect, and to the evaluation of sector programs in those with the most acute communication problems. Sector missions for this purpose are not inherently complex, however, since in most countries public telecommunication services are provided by one operating entity and the sector usually comprises a single integrated network.

The five-year Bank Group program through fiscal 1973 calls for a total of 31 sector surveys compared with 18 in the previous five years; and for 34 lending operations involving commitments of about $580 million, compared with nine loans totaling $153 million.

A number of important questions require further research, and a research program is in the process of being formulated. One of the major topics under consideration is the relationships between structure of costs and prices in expanding networks. Other work is contemplated regarding the nature of demand for telecommunication services.

Technical Assistance

In countries where the Bank has been involved in telecommunication development, its participation has often helped operating entities obtain an adequate measure of autonomy in accordance with sound public utility practice, to set tariffs at levels which allow a reasonable percentage of capital expansion to be financed from internal sources, to establish proper accounting systems, and to develop stronger management, planning and engineering capabilities. Good investment planning, designed to produce both balanced and economical expansion plans, is essential in this sector where network development continuously involves large numbers of small additions to the system.

While external finance has been available, much of it has been unrelated to the institutional needs of the operating entities or to the development priorities of the countries concerned. Financing provided by suppliers is oriented, of course, towards the goods financed rather than projects as a whole or the efficient growth of communication systems and the fulfillment of their role in development. In fact, even within the narrow focus of goods, such financing has been further concentrated on switching equipment and microwave systems, largely to the exclusion of cables, which account for about half the cost of most expansion programs.

This did not present serious difficulties in some countries where telecommunication administrations had adequate engineering and planning staffs and strong management, with no inhibitions about resorting to international competitive bidding. These, however, were —and still are—in the minority. In many others, expansion programs were unbalanced as well as unnecessarily expensive, with such results as completed exchanges but no cables to connect subscribers.

The Bank has also been able to help in the introduction of better procurement practices. International competitive bidding has led to considerable reduction in costs—about 30% on average and much more in some cases. Although standardization of switching equipment can have major advantages (see Page 204), there is no case for retaining an outmoded system or paying excessive prices, as many

208

telecommunication entities have done. Especially for cables, radio and transmission equipment, the advantages of standardization are minimal.

What appeared to be lacking in most countries was a means of relating available supplier finance to the more comprehensive approach which characterizes lending by the World Bank, including conditions which both require and facilitate the necessary technical and institutional improvements. Together with the wider use of international competitive bidding, this is the most important contribution the Bank can make in the telecommunication sector.

Ethiopia is a good example of Bank assistance in institution-building. Bank participation commenced in the early 1950's, when the telephone system was run by a government department and consisted of a small obsolete system in bad repair. Four loans and 15 years later, the telephone entity is now an autonomous corporation staffed entirely by Ethiopians, with a sound organization and management, strong planning capability, and a telephone network running efficiently on sound commercial lines. Facilities are expanding by more than 12% per annum, without any financing from the Government.

A more recent example is Colombia, where Bank lending has supported substantial managerial and financial improvements, strengthening of planning capabilities and integration of small, inefficient operating entities. The telecommunication entities of Upper Volta and Nepal, both in an early stage of development, are being reorganized. In Indonesia, the Bank is trying to help improve network planning and balance in investment expenditures.

Procurement

For reasons already explained, too frequent changes of switching systems would give rise to serious long-term interworking and procurement problems and diseconomies in system growth. This special feature of telecommunication systems requires that the normal Bank requirements for procurement through international competitive bidding not be applied in ways that could force the borrower into a premature change in switching systems. Possible approaches to this problem are outlined below.

Where a country is fully equipped to produce its own telecommunication equipment at reasonable prices, the Bank might finance imported raw material and components purchased internationally through open tenders or other methods of international procurement appropriate to the industry, e.g., metal purchases based on international metal market prices. To date this situation has been addressed only in India, where the Bank Group has financed the foreign costs of materials procurement in recent telecommunication loans; the costs of the Indian equipment were in line with international prices.

Where a country does not produce its own equipment, the Bank might find itself considering financing for a project covering requirements for only two or three years, whereas the country might desire to place contracts for a longer period in the interests of standardization. It might be possible in such circumstances to procure equipment under conditions of international competitive bidding and still preserve continuity of supply by placing contracts for the initial period and obtaining options to renew them as needed in later years at prices subject to suitable escalation and review.

A somewhat special case is presented by the country with no local production, which has recently standardized on a new type of switching equipment and has entered into a long term supply agreement with a foreign manufacturer. If the supply agreement were the result of international tender before Bank participation and within the past few years, Bank financing might be appropriate. Where acceptable international tendering did not precede the decision to standardize, Bank financing of switching equipment might still be considered in appropriate cases if the cost of such equipment did not dominate the loan and the Bank were satisfied that the prices paid were reasonably in line with international prices.

Thus the Bank might be willing to finance the foreign costs of switching equipment manufactured locally if the manufacturer were efficient, as judged by prices in comparison with those in developed countries. Where there is no local production, the Bank would expect the borrower to use procurement practices designed to take advantage of the international level of prices, with due regard to the benefits of standardization and the disadvantages of too frequent changes in systems.

Telecommunication Loans and Credits
Fiscal Years 1962-71[1]

Fiscal Year	Country	Signed	Amount	Total Project Costs
			(US$ Millions)	
1962	Ethiopia	5/31/62	Bank 2.9	6.2
1963	India	9/14/62	IDA 42.0	122.0
1964	Costa Rica	7/10/63	Bank 9.9	12.6
	El Salvador	10/7/63	Bank 9.5	13.6
1965	India	7/6/64	IDA 33.0	228.0
1966	Venezuela	12/13/65	Bank 37.0	100.0
	Ethiopia	12/28/65	Bank 4.8	10.8
1967	Jamaica	1/23/67	Bank 11.2	18.3
	East Africa	2/17/67	Bank 13.0	26.7
	Colombia	6/15/67	Bank 16.0	27.6
1968	China, Rep. of	8/2/67	Bank 17.0	50.0
	Singapore	9/15/67	Bank 3.0	9.5
	Papua-New Guinea	6/28/68	Bank 7.0	15.4
1969	Malaysia	9/27/68	Bank 4.4	49.0
	Upper Volta	2/18/69	IDA 0.8	1.2
	Pakistan	3/6/69	IDA 16.0	42.0
	Ethiopia	6/3/69	Bank 4.5	25.4
	India	6/18/69	Bank-IDA 55.0	361.0
1970	Costa Rica	7/10/69	Bank 6.5	9.5
	Nepal	11/10/69	IDA 1.7	4.2
	Singapore	12/19/69	Bank 11.0	37.1
	Yugoslavia	2/20/70	Bank 40.0	95.0
	Pakistan	5/22/70	IDA 15.0	35.3
	East African Community	5/25/70	Bank 10.4	28.3
1971	Indonesia	7/13/70	IDA 12.8	22.1
	Iran	12/18/70	Bank 36.0	149.2
	India	5/3/71	IDA 78.0	290.7
	Colombia	5/28/71	Bank 15.0	39.1
	Malaysia	6/21/71	Bank 18.7	94.0
	Venezuela	6/30/71	Bank 35.0	294.5

[1] Four small loans totalling US$24.25 million were made in the period prior to 1962.

INTERNATIONAL SECTOR DATA—TELECOMMUNICATION

COUNTRY	Gross National Product — Per Capita 1970 (US$)	Gross National Product — Growth Rate 1965-70 (%)	TELEPHONES / National — Population 1970 (000's)	National — Total No. 1970 (000's)	National — Per 100 Pop. 1970 (No.)	National — Growth Rate 1965-70 (%)	National — % Automatic (%)	National — Staff per 1,000 tel.(1) (No.)	Principal Cities — % of Total Pop. (%)	Principal Cities — % of Total Tel.(2) (%)	National Long Distance Service — Quality(3)	International Service(4) Direct Access to: Satellite	International Service(4) Direct Access to: Submarine Cable
U.S.A.	4,235	3.4	206,800	115,222	55.71	5.4	99.9	9	45	51	E	Atl. Pac.	x
Sweden	2,788	3.2	8,050	4,307	53.50	4.9	99.7	n.a.	34	43	E	—	x
Switzerland	2,610	2.4	6,350	2,847	44.83	6.0	100.0	4	37	50	E	—	
Canada	2,720	2.8	21,700	9,753	42.28	5.5	98.8	n.a.	41	49	E	Atl.	x
France	2,288	3.7	51,000	8,114	15.90	7.3	80.1	19	25	50	E	Atl.	x
Australia	2,169	2.4	12,500	3,599	28.79	6.1	89.7	22	64	67	E	Pac. Ind.	x
New Zealand	2,068	1.7	2,950	1,203	40.77	4.6	86.7	18	54	63	F	—	x
U.K.	1,862	2.0	56,050	13,947	24.88	7.0	98.6	20	33	43	E	Atl. Ind.	x
Italy	1,343	4.6	53,600	8,528	15.91	9.0	100.0	n.a.	23	53	E	Atl.	x
Yugoslavia	553	4.2	20,600	623	3.02	11.0	95.9	19	12	49	G	—	
Venezuela	977	1.4	10,650	378	3.54	7.8	97.6	18	35	83	G	Atl.	x
Argentina	836	1.0	24,400	1,668	6.83	2.5	92.7	24	47	86	G	Atl.	
Chile	487	1.8	9,800	348	3.55	6.8	87.2	16	35	76	F	Atl.	
Colombia	319	1.4	21,350	546	2.55	7.4	96.8	n.a.	26	77	G	Atl.	
Brazil	258	1.6	93,500	1,787	1.91	7.2	93.3	n.a.	20	66	F	Atl.	
Mexico	566	3.4	50,950	1,328	2.60	12.9	93.0	n.a.	27	75	G	Atl.	
Costa Rica	469	2.1	1,750	56	3.20	20.5	95.9	13	19	80	G	—	
Guatemala	331	1.7	5,150	38	.73	10.6	95.9	20	15	91	P	—	
El Salvador	292	2.1	3,500	35	1.00	9.7	95.5	33	28	84	G	—	
Singapore	753	3.8	2,100	136	6.47	11.5	100.0	14	100	100	—	Ind.	x
Malaysia	358	4.3	11,050	169	1.52	6.9	89.8	52	3	34	E	Pac.	x
China, Rep. of	305	6.5	14,250	339	2.37	18.0	82.2	39	26	72	F	—	
Iraq	275	2.9	9,100	120	1.31	14.1	81.8	47	54	74	P	—	
Papua-New Guinea	221	2.5	2,400	19	.79	16.1	85.4	34	4	78	P	—	
Ceylon	188	2.3	12,550	61	.48	7.7	98.7	n.a.	5	57	F	—	
Pakistan	106	3.1	129,550	193	.14	9.8	78.2	140	7	75	F	—	
India	102	1.0	550,100	1,160	.21	8.8	75.7	129	4	50	F	—	
Indonesia	102	.8	118,250	182	.15	2.7	49.0	86	8	49	F	Ind.	

212

Zambia	236	3.6	4,300	52	1.20	10.9	98.0	50	13	62	P	—
Ghana	168	−.7	8,850	54	.61	10.3	66.5	n.a.	14	74	F	—
Kenya	134	1.4	10,800	72	.66	7.1	85.1	49(5)	7	73	G	Ind.	x
Uganda	112	1.1	8,550	28	.32	9.2	79.6		5	61			x
Tanzania	82	1.2	13,150	32	.24	8.8	74.4		3	43			x
Nigeria	70	−.3	65,650	81	.12	6.2	79.2	n.a.	3	57	F	Atl.
Malawi	52	2.2	4,500	12	.26	11.4	89.8	n.a.	3	57	P	—
Upper Volta	51	.1	5,400	1	.02	NIL	82.5	107	3	82	P	—

(1) These figures are not strictly comparable. In some cases international, local and long distance services are provided by different organizations in the same country. Telegraph staff may or may not be included and there are wide variations in the use of contract labor for both maintenance and construction work. The number of telephone operators required also varies with the proportion of manual to automatic service.

(2) E.g. in the U.S.A., 45% of the people live in the principal cities and have 51% of the country's telephones.

(3) E = Excellent. Most cities and centers connected by microwave or coaxial systems with extensive subscriber trunk dialing.
G = Good. Principal cities connected by microwave or coaxial systems with subscriber trunk dialing.
F = Fair. Principal cities connected by microwave or coaxial systems but calls handled semi-automatically or manually.
P = Poor. Little or no microwave or coaxial. Calls between inter-connected cities handled manually.

(4) Countries which have satellite earth stations or submarine cable terminals within their borders. Kenya, Uganda and Tanzania are served jointly by a station operated by the East African Posts and Telegraph.

(5) Service provided by a common organization.

Sources: Population and G.N.P., World Bank Atlas, 1970.
Telephone statistics, The World's Telephones, A.T. & T., 1970.
Long distance and international service, World Bank.

213

SUMMARY OF WORLD BANK TELECOMMUNICATION ACTIVITIES
WITH PROJECTIONS THROUGH FY1976

	Actual			Program		Actual[1]		Program
	1969	1970	1971	1972	1973	1964-68	1969-73	1972-76
Sector Studies/Surveys[2]	3	6	5	7	10	18	31	35
Commitments ($M.)	80.7	84.6	195.8	96	123	153.2	580	610
% Total IBRD/IDA	5	4	8	4	4	2.7	5	4
No. of countries	5	6	6	8	9	9	21	22
Lending Operations	5	6	6	8	9	9	34	36
% Total IBRD/IDA	4	5	5	5	5	3	5	4
Projects under Supervision[3]	8	11	14	18	23	4[4]	15[4]	25[4]

[1] Including scheduled for FY1972-73.

[2] In countries where the sector consists predominantly of a single operating utility, which is the case for most tele-communication enterprises, preparation and appraisal of projects includes a sector review, per se. These numbers refer to sector reviews prepared in the course of project work and are thus not comparable with the data on reviews of sectors where the project and sector work is separate.

[3] Borrowers with more than one loan are counted only once.

[4] Annual average.

214

ELECTRIC POWER

ELECTRIC POWER
SECTOR WORKING PAPER

INTRODUCTION

The World Bank[1] has been a major participant in the development of electric power facilities in its less developed member countries for more than 20 years. Its first power loan was made in 1948, to Chile. Since then, power lending has totaled $5,300 million[2], or 27% of the Bank's total commitments. Through these loans, the Bank has been associated with the construction of about a fifth of the estimated 100 million kilowatts of capacity now installed in 41 developing countries and with an additional 16 million kilowatts still under construction.

The earliest objective was to overcome endemic power shortages in many countries, resulting in part from the difficulty of importing equipment and materials during World War II. Subsequently, the focus has been on building a solid institutional, financial and technical base for providing adequate service, without which economic activity would be seriously hampered, especially in large urban communities. The Bank has developed relationships with 55 power utilities in 41 countries. They range from small and simple systems, on the one hand, to very large and complex ones, on the other; thus, they encompass a wide range of problems relating to the development of power institutions and networks.

The Bank's heavy involvement in power development results from the fact that the sector offers an especially appropriate channel for the efficient transfer of a significant part of the capital developing countries require. This is because power systems are so capital intensive; because their rapid expansion (doubling every five to eight years) commands such a high proportion of total investment in developing countries; and because in most countries so much of the equipment has to be imported.

Technical assistance accompanying power loans can help to bring about large economies in the use of resources by improving system planning and operating efficiency. It can also help to mobilize savings through improvements in utility finances.

---

[1] All references to the Bank include the International Development Association (IDA) unless otherwise specified.
[2] Amounts are expressed in U.S. dollar equivalents.

A case for reducing the involvement could be made on the ground that the internationally traded equipment which constitutes such a large portion of power investment is exported by most of the industrialized countries and that financing power projects is one of the most convenient ways of mobilizing development capital from these countries. However, supplier finance is often only a partial substitute for Bank funds. Quite apart from differences in terms of lending and in prices obtained through bilateral and international procurement, supplier finance seldom embraces the institution-building objectives which have been central to the Bank's lending in this field and which remain important in many countries.

CHARACTERISTICS OF THE SECTOR

Electric power, with its unique qualities in terms of convenience and ease of handling, is an indispensable element in the energy economy of all modern societies. In common with other forms of energy supply, electric power production and distribution is accompanied by special problems: availability and transportation of primary fuels; the effects of modifying the regime of rivers; atmospheric and water pollution; encroachment on scarce urban land; infringement on the natural beauties of the environment, etc. Like the industrialized nations, many of the Bank's less developed members are seeking an answer to the question: "What is the alternative to providing electricity in the amounts demanded?" But most societies tend to plan on the premise that a power shortage is liable to affect economic growth very seriously, and that all major demand must accordingly be met.

Some enthusiasts go further. They hold that an abundant, reliable, low-cost supply of electric power, available in advance of market requirements, automatically stimulates industrial development. There is little basis for this view. In some industries, such as electro-chemicals and electro-metallurgicals, electricity is a major raw material. In others, however, electric power generally represents less than 3% of production costs in developing countries. The absence of a reliable central supply may hinder industrial development by forcing producers to install their own generating plants at higher cost, but its presence will not necessarily stimulate this development. The corollary is that the demand for industrial power, which is highly sensitive to levels of economic activity, is within broad limits fairly insensitive to the price of electricity. The same is roughly true of household demand; in this case, the capital cost of wiring houses and purchasing appliances is more likely to affect the growth of demand than the price of electricity.

Throughout the developing world today, most of the agencies responsible for the production and distribution of electricity are publicly owned: federal, state, or municipal. Because it is generally recognized that competition among electricity suppliers in a given area results in wasteful duplication of investment, utilities almost everywhere have been granted monopolies which are regulated by the government. The scope of regulation varies widely.

Load Variation

In common with certain other public services, such as transportation and telecommunication, power systems generally have markets in which demand fluctuates widely from one period to another. Depending on the nature of the market—residential, commercial, industrial, or special electro-intensive users—demand will normally be characterized by a fairly sharp peak or peaks lasting only a few hours each day. The power supply agency must try to meet the peak demands as well as the total energy requirement. When demand exceeds the system's capacity, the quality of service deteriorates: voltages and frequency fall, affecting the performance of all user equipment, especially motors. Beyond certain limits, damage occurs to customers' facilities, and ultimately the power supply itself collapses. Because these peak demands are for a short time, and because it is difficult to store electrical energy, some of the facilities remain idle part of the day.

Much work has been done, especially in the United Kingdom and France, to develop techniques for flattening the demand curve in order to ensure better utilization of expensive plant. Peak demand has been reduced by restructuring tariffs. The introduction of special off-peak tariffs for clock-controlled electric heaters with thermal storage facilities is one method of moving certain categories of heavy demand off the peak. Another approach is simply to refuse to meet the requirements at peak time by cutting off certain consumers, connected separately for this purpose. On the supply side, specially designed peaking facilities, such as gas turbines and pumped storage plants, have been used to save on the investment in generating plant.

Power Systems

The modern power system consists of an integrated network of generation, transmission and distribution facilities. The proportion of investment in each varies between countries due to geography,

219

type of customer, size of system and the degree of sophistication of the economy. Of the total annual investment, the proportion spent on generation can vary from 30% to 50%, on transmission from 10% to 30%, and on distribution from 30% to 60%.

As electrical systems grow, the point comes when it is advantageous to interconnect them by transmission lines. This allows economies of scale, since larger generating units can be used (in relation to the total capacity of the interconnected system) and standby plant capacity (for use in case of breakdowns) can be considerably reduced. Ultimately the transmission lines and generating stations form a "grid" which integrates the electricity systems of a whole country. There are several instances where systems have been connected across political boundaries, e.g., Kenya-Uganda, Tunisia-Algeria, and Argentina-Paraguay. A regional tie connecting Ghana, Togo and Dahomey is now under construction; in due course the line may be extended to Nigeria. Interconnections between Nigeria-Niger, Nicaragua-Honduras, and Nicaragua-Costa Rica are being considered.

Timing of Investment

Careful studies are required to determine the optimum timing for investment. This implies that detailed technical and economic consideration has to be given to alternative strategies for the development of a power system (see page 227). If the commissioning of plant is delayed, it could have serious economic consequences. The risks of delay need to be evaluated at the system planning stage and kept under continual review as the work progresses. Delay in adding a 200 MW hydroelectric unit in a thermal generating system could cause a loss of as much as $250,000 per month in additional fuel consumption. Heavy losses could also be incurred through delays in commissioning large conventional thermal or nuclear units, and sometimes the interconnecting transmission.

Investment Requirements

The rewards of investment economies are especially large in power. The table below illustrates the size of investment in power in relation to total investment in the public sector for a selected group of countries. There is no reason to expect that power investment will in the future be less than a sixth of total public investment, the proportion observed in the recent past.

Power and Total Public Investment in Three Countries
(Millions of U.S. dollars)

	1965–1969			1970–1974		
	Total Public Investment	Electric Power Sector	Power as % of Total	Total Public Investment	Electric Power Sector	Power as % of Total
Colombia	1,450	210	14.5	3,190	550	17.1
Mexico	7,939	974	12.3	12,084	1,580	13.1
India	14,105	2,420	17.2	21,200	3,274	15.5

In developing countries, investment in power facilities has been increasing at an annual rate of about 10% and is expected to continue at a high rate in the future. The chart in Annex 1 shows the actual growth of installed capacity for the three major developing areas of the world during the period 1955–1970, as well as a projection to 1985. The volume of investment needed (at current prices) to accommodate projected demand in the developing countries over the five-year period FY 1971–75 is estimated at about $25,000 million equivalent.[1]

The proportion of foreign exchange required for power investments in developing countries is normally high. In general, such countries can make the largest domestic contribution to hydroelectric plant, for which labor and materials such as cement and reinforcing steel bars figure prominently in the cost. But even here, since heavy construction equipment is usually imported and the contract management experience required may not be available locally, the proportion of foreign costs for hydroelectric work is typically about 50%. In the case of steam electric plant, which is much more dependent on outside fabrication, the proportion of foreign costs is typically 75%. The foreign exchange content of transmission and distribution facilities is also quite high in many countries where the domestic capacity for manufacturing such equipment is limited.

Power projects are admirably suited to achieve large and rapid capital transfers where there are properly planned sectors, well-formulated projects, well-articulated institutions functioning with qualified and experienced managements, and enlightened regulatory policies. One of the principal objectives of the Bank has been to help create such conditions. It has been easier to achieve when there has been a continuing relationship between the Bank, the borrower and government agencies.

---

[1] Based on an average $500 of investment in generation, transmission and distribution for each kW of new generating capacity.

221

RECENT BANK LENDING IN POWER

During the five fiscal years 1967–71, the Bank made 79 loans and credits aggregating $2,046 million for electric power development. Total investment for power in developing countries in the same period was on the order of $15,000 million. The Bank has been one of the major sources of external development finance for this sector, as can be seen from the amount of power loans and credits (exclusive of guarantees) made to developing countries by the following agencies during the period:

Power Loans by Selected Agencies, 1967–1971
(Millions of U.S. dollars)

Agency	Amount	Remarks
World Bank/IDA	2,046	
Inter-American Development Bank	456	Including Fund for Special Operations
U.S. Export-Import Bank	452	Excluding Europe and Japan
U.S. AID	401	Including technical and support assistance
Asian Development Bank	50	Power lending began in 1969
African Development Bank	7	Power lending began in 1969
French Government Agencies	33	Africa only

Significant amounts of financing have been provided by other bilateral agencies, such as the Swedish International Development Authority, the Canadian International Development Agency, the Kuwait Fund for Arab Economic Development and the Kreditanstalt für Wiederaufbau. Some of these funds have been provided through joint or parallel financing operations with the World Bank. These are devices which have facilitated the mobilization of bilateral funds alongside those provided by the Bank.

In joint financing, bilateral lenders agree to provide finance, usually within some specified limit, for supply contracts awarded to their nationals as a result of international competitive bidding. In this way, for example, the 10 largest industrialized countries have committed a third to half of the external cost of certain power sector equipment in Mexico, while the Bank has provided the remainder. In parallel financing, equipment or services for different portions of a project are financed separately by the Bank and bilateral lenders, with international competitive bidding applied to the Bank's portion. An example is the El Chocon project in Argentina, where bilateral "buyer" credits are financing the foreign currency costs of generating and transmission equipment and the Bank is covering those associated with civil works.

The average size of Bank loans for power during 1967–71 was $20 million. The largest single loan was one of $125 million in Mexico, and the smallest $2 million for a project in Trinidad and Tobago. Loans to individual countries are shown in Annex 2. Power operations accounted for 24% of the dollar volume of all Bank lending in this period, as compared with 29% since 1947. Four countries—Argentina, Brazil, the Republic of China and Mexico—accounted for 42% of the lending in terms of dollar volume; loans to nations in the Latin American and Caribbean region accounted for 53% of the total. The regional distribution of lending for the five year period is summarized below:

World Bank Group Power Lending, 1967-71

Region	Number of Loans	% of Loans	Amount	
			In US$ millions	% of Total
Africa	17	21.5	256.7	12.5
Asia	19	24.1	537.8	26.3
Europe	7	8.9	127.8	6.2
Oceania	2	2.5	38.2	1.9
Western Hemisphere	34	43.0	1,085.0	53.1
Total Power Lending	79	100%	2,045.5	100%

The high proportion of lending in the Western Hemisphere reflects the continuity of relationships established over the years with major borrowers in the region. Moving soon after World War II into some of the world's most important urban centers where the shortage of power was acute, the Bank supported the physical and institutional growth of these systems. With the passage of time, the emphasis shifted gradually from eliminating shortages to achieving basic policy and institutional reforms.

In all countries, the adoption of an adequate tariff policy was a key objective. It was not achieved easily. Lending suffered from time to time in cases where agreement on this basic question could not be reached. In most cases, this is no longer an issue of principle; it has increasingly been recognized that only through adequate tariffs (and therefore revenues) can the timely flow of funds necessary for financing large expansion programs be assured. Brazil offers an interesting example in this context. It has one of the largest power investment expenditures in the Western Hemisphere, and at the same time one of the most difficult and persistent problems of inflation. The wider economic implications of adequate tariff policies and adjustment mechanisms have thus been even greater there than in the other countries of the region. Brazil has established a virtually automatic tariff adjustment process to help mobilize resources for its large investment program in the power sector.

223

Tariff policy has been a major element, but by no means the only one, in the broad institution-building objectives of the Bank and its borrowers. Here are two examples:

• In Mexico, a highly fragmented and inefficient power supply has been consolidated under a strong national agency, which has begun to borrow internationally on its own credit. Tariffs have been unified and a consistent revenue policy introduced. Some progress has also been made towards standardizing the frequency of the power supply in the central region.

• In Colombia, the four major power utilities have achieved major economies of scale by integrating the largest systems. They have also adopted a uniform tariff policy.

The Bank has helped to achieve objectives such as these by contributing substantially to the financing of power development in particular countries. In each case it was the stream of loans, rather than any single one, that created new opportunities for achieving, step by step, important improvements in the utility and in the government's regulatory and financing role. Intensive project supervision helped, but experience shows that major improvements can usually be advocated persuasively only within the contractual relationship associated with new lending.

PLANNED BANK ACTIVITIES

Lending

The level of power lending envisaged by the Bank for the five-year period 1972–76 is $2,540 million, about 24% above the actual figure for the previous five years. As a proportion of total Bank financing, lending for power will fall from around 24% to about 17%. However, substantial increases are expected in the number of borrowing countries and of projects. In many countries, the Bank will be assisting the power sector for the first time, and in some of these two or more loans will be made during the same period.

Continuity in lending operations is likely to be especially important for many of the new borrowers, since most will be in the smaller and poorer countries which often confront even more difficult obstacles than have been encountered, and largely overcome, by larger countries with more experience and resources.

Of course, the proper role for the Bank in any country's power sector cannot be defined outside the context of what other financing is in prospect for power and what Bank assistance is being sought for other sectors.

Sector Work

The continual expansion that is characteristic of most power systems means that forward planning is an integral aspect of general operations. Where it is neglected, the results soon become evident in the form of shortages and deteriorating service. The distinction between pre-investment activities, appraisal of specific investment proposals and analysis of system development plans and related policies is thus less sharp than in most other sectors, except telecommunications. This attribute has important implications for the nature of the Bank's sector work. In countries where the sector consists of a single operating utility, preparation and appraisal of loans includes a sector review, per se. The Bank has recently studied 17 of these single-agency sectors in connection with lending operations.

A growing effort in sector work will be required as the number of loans and of countries involved increases, despite the fact that power financing will represent a smaller proportion of total lending. The level of investment is likely to be so large—of the order of $25,000 million during FY 1972–76—that even marginal economies will be important. The Bank's contribution is now projected at about 17% of the foreign exchange required, on the assumption that the foreign component will be 60%. With these stakes, the range and depth of the Bank's sector work in power will have to be increased.

Review of Energy Policy

Decisions in the power sector are greatly influenced by policies affecting the use of energy resources—policies, for example, in the areas of fuel pricing, imports, taxation, etc. Member countries have begun to address themselves to the broader issues of national energy policy, and to seek Bank assistance for this purpose. Such reviews are important not merely because of their implications for the power sector, but also because of the impact of energy policy on the many major investment decisions that are sensitive to the relative costs of fuels. Since the Bank lacks direct experience in this broader field, however, its role will be modest for some time. The aim will be to concentrate on assistance to borrowers in drawing up terms of reference for energy reviews and finding the appropriate persons or firms to help carry them out.

AREAS OF CHALLENGE

The striking institutional improvements achieved by major borrowers might suggest that the Bank's contribution in the power sector has now largely been reduced to financing hardware, albeit on better terms than are otherwise available to most countries. This is hardly the case.

Not only do most of these borrowers require continued financial assistance, but the scope of their need for collaboration in solving non-financial problems of the power sector has expanded. Areas of growing concern include system planning, which encompasses market forecasting and the selection of least-cost alternatives; evaluation of the structure, as distinct from the level, of electricity tariffs; village electrification; nuclear power; and environmental problems. The remainder of this paper touches on these various aspects in turn.

System Planning

Traditionally, the first step in planning the expansion of an electric power system is to forecast the demand for electricity at the time of peak consumption (to determine maximum generating capacity) and for the year (to determine the total amount of energy required annually). This forecast is usually made in the context of existing electricity tariffs, quality of supply, standard of security and plans for adding new consumers to the system.

The second step is to identify the various possible sector development strategies (e.g., varying combinations of hydro and thermal plant in differing sizes and sequences) which would both meet the forecast demand and satisfy the system's technical requirements.

The third step is to select the alternative which has the lowest present value of capital and operating costs at a reasonable test rate of discount. Revenues do not enter this calculation since they are assumed to be equal for all strategies.

Some features of this system planning deserve more attention than they have received so far.

Market Forecasting. The extent to which forecasting can be improved probably depends most on the type of country being considered, or more precisely on the nature of demand. The Bank has under way a program to encourage borrowers to examine periodically their standards and methods of demand forecasting and to improve its own capacity to evaluate these demand projections critically. A recent study indicates that the degree of error in forecasting for developing countries is greater than for developed countries, although the standard of forecasting even for the latter needs much improvement. However, there does not appear to be a consistent bias towards either conservatism or over-optimism. Some of the more sophisticated forecasting techniques have yielded the largest errors, while some of the simpler ones have yielded the smallest. Further investigation is planned to determine what methods of demand forecasting will give the best results in particular circumstances.

Minimizing Costs. Power projects have a long economic life. If different strategies for developing a power system are to be compared, projections of annual investment and operating costs under each strategy must be made for a long period—perhaps as long as 50 years. Frequently, different assumptions have to be made about market development and costs before a particular strategy is chosen. The use of mathematical models is especially suitable for these types of studies.

As power systems in developing countries become more complex and the choice between development strategies becomes more difficult, the use of such techniques by borrowers is likely to increase. They can be extremely useful, provided proper attention is given to the quality of the input data and to the constraints under which electric power systems must operate. Different models are being tested with a view to improving the Bank's capacity to evaluate the quality of this aspect of system planning by major borrowers.

Even the most sophisticated system planning techniques will lead to wrong choices if the cost data employed for alternatives do not reflect real economic costs. Rational project selection requires that critical attention be paid to the appropriateness of the cost measures used in the comparisons. For example, because of official pricing policies, the actual cost to a utility of foreign exchange or of capital may be well below the real economic cost; in fact, this is often the case. In this situation, the actual cost must be adjusted if a bias toward capital-intensive and import-intensive investments is to be avoided. Unfortunately, there is seldom unanimity on the shadow prices to be used in particular circumstances. One can thus only test, where appropriate, the sensitivity of particular decisions to variations in key costs.

Pricing

When forecasting electricity demand, the assumption is normally made that demand is price inelastic. While this is probably broadly true, peak demand could probably be reduced and off-peak demand increased by some form of marginal cost pricing, although the precise amount of the reduction or increase might be difficult to predict. The Central Electricity Generating Board (U.K.) reports peak reduction, attributable to marginal cost pricing, of only 600 MW, or 1.5% of the system demand of 39,000 MW[1]; and Electricité de France reports a reduction of 800 MW, or 3% of system demand of approximately 24,000 MW[1].

The scope for changing the shape of the demand curve in developing countries through the pricing mechanism needs further investigation. Consultants were engaged by the Bank in 1970 to examine this question in West Pakistan, and their findings are now being reviewed. The basic issue is whether use of mechanical devices to control demand is more appropriate than the pricing mechanism.

Care must be taken to avoid cutting the original peak demand in such a way as to form a new peak at a different time of day and season, which could cause greater diseconomies than before, as has already happened in Britain. However, it is probably true that many developing countries could benefit from tariff structures which reflected more closely than at present the structure of system incremental costs. The problem will be considered further after results of the West Pakistan study are evaluated.

Village Electrification[2]

When formulating a demand forecast, it is usually possible to distinguish the increasing requirements of existing customers from the demand created by connecting new customers. In urban areas, these rates of growth can be calculated with a fair degree of accuracy on the basis of a thorough market survey, because the merit of connecting new consumers to a generally well-articulated urban system is seldom in doubt and can be accomplished with relatively little additional investment. The power authority is usually under an obligation to connect all new consumers within a reasonable distance from the main supply. More remote new consumers (mostly industrial estates) are usually willing to pay a capital contribution to the power authority. In both instances, the case for providing service to the customer is clear. Justification for electrifying villages in rural areas, however, is more complex.

Most developing countries have programs of village electrification. Some are quite comprehensive and involve considerable investment. They reflect a mixture of social, political and economic objec-

---

[1] Both in the period roughly 1968/1969.
[2] "Village electrification" is a more accurate term than the more common "rural electrification" because in developing countries it is the electrification of villages and small towns rather than scattered isolated farms which is at issue; the one major exception is ground-water pumping loads for irrigaton.

tives, often concerned with maintaining or changing the rural-urban balance in society. In the past, the Bank has not made loans explicitly for such programs, although it has participated indirectly by supporting utilities involved in them; today the Bank is investigating possibilities for giving more active assistance.

In one country recently, for example, the Bank included in a power loan funds specifically allocated for village electrification. The Government has agreed to undertake a study of the villages involved compared with others not scheduled for early electrification. An attempt will be made to measure the social costs and benefits attributable to village electrification. In two other countries, sampling techniques have been used to a limited extent in connection with Bank-assisted power development programs, in an attempt to measure increased demands—both by type of consumer, and total—in the electrified villages. The Turkish Electricity Authority has been encouraged to initiate a sampling review of its village electrification program. Through a simple questionnaire, the Bank has also requested information from certain member countries that have had village electrification programs under way for some time.

Villages are basically areas of low-density loading. Even if the tariffs there are comparable to those prevailing in the urban high-density loading areas, financial returns on the facilities serving the low-density areas will be low. Financial returns, however, rarely reveal the full benefits of village electrification. Although research is required to determine more precisely which is cause and which is effect, the introduction of electricity into a village appears to foster "cottage" industries, improve agricultural production through irrigation, and slow down migration to crowded urban centers. In order to help develop criteria for better allocating scarce rural electrification funds among rural areas, more of the benefits must be quantified and techniques for doing this need to be developed. A program of research is being prepared for this purpose. The aim will be to study the past, present and likely future development of electrified villages in selected countries, along with "control" villages that are similar in as many ways as possible but have not yet been electrified.

The evaluation of the benefits of village electrification programs is only one aspect of the general problem of evaluating the economic benefits of electric power. As yet there is no reasonable basis for measuring these economic benefits, and thus no basis for defending quantitatively the merit of meeting the expected demand for power at the expense of investment in other sectors of the economy. The financial benefits of power expansion can be readily measured. But revenues are an inadequate measure of economic benefits, and an even less adequate measure of social benefits. Financial returns are thus an unsatisfactory investment test; they reveal more about the effect of pricing policies on (monopolistic) suppliers' ability to cover costs than they do about the merits of particular investments. However, unlike the water supply sector, where the large gap between social and private benefits has probably contributed to serious under-investment, the inability to measure benefits does not seem to have resulted in a tendency to under-invest in power in most countries.

Nuclear Power

Nuclear power is another form of thermal power, and is subject to the same tests of suitability and economy as other forms of generating plant. Until now, nuclear power has not played a significant role in the economies of the developing countries; only three have nuclear power generating facilities in operation. However, others will have them soon. Two countries have nuclear facilities under construction, one is evaluating offers, and several more are in the planning stage. The scope for Bank financing of nuclear plant is being kept under review.

The growth of nuclear power in developing countries will be greatly influenced by changes in the capital and fuel costs of competing thermal power technologies, which are also evolving. Since the capital costs of nuclear plants are higher by about a third than those of conventional steam installations, they are economic only where fossil fuels are unusually expensive. Even there, the minimum economic capacity of nuclear plant is unlikely to be much less than 500-600 MW. This means that nuclear plant can be used effectively only in relatively large power systems. Operating experience indicates that for protection against malfunctioning of the largest single unit in a given power system's network, no unit should have a capacity greater than about 15% of total system demand. That would limit the use of nuclear facilities to systems of 3,000 MW or more. On this basis, only about 10 developing countries could reasonably plan to acquire nuclear facilities by 1975.

The Environment

As the supply of electricity in the less developed world doubles every five to eight years, the impact of expanding power systems on the environment can be expected to increase substantially. Greater attention and publicity are being focused on the environmental consequences of building hydroelectric projects, fossil and nuclear-fueled steam-electric stations, transmission lines, etc. Many utilities in developed countries have learned too late the deep implications of these questions and their impact on public opinion. Henceforth, environmental considerations will have to be evaluated at an early stage when power projects are prepared.

Installed Power Capacity in Developing Member Countries

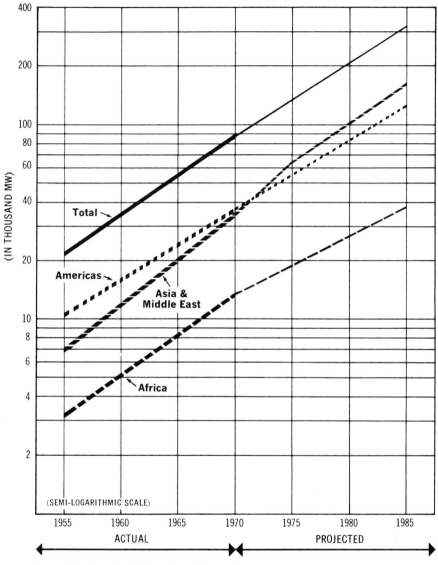

Notes: Chart does not include developing member countries in Europe.

Curves have been drawn through the actual or forecast values at five-yearly intervals.

Sources: Actual capacity, U.S. Federal Power Commission; projected capacity, International Atomic Energy Agency.

233

World Bank Group Lending in the Power Sector, 1948-71*
(US$ millions)

	FY 1948-66	FY 1967	FY 1968	FY 1969	FY 1970	FY 1971	Total FY 1967-71
Africa							
Algeria	10.0						
Botswana					2.5	32.0	34.5
Ethiopia	23.5			23.1			23.1
Ghana	47.0		10.0	6.0		7.1	23.1
Kenya						23.0	23.0
Liberia					7.4		7.4
Malawi					5.2		5.2
Mauritius	7.0						
Nigeria	112.0			14.5			14.5
Sierra Leone	3.8			3.9			3.9
South Africa	74.0	20.0					20.0
Rhodesia	28.0						
Sudan			24.0				24.0
Swaziland	4.2	2.8					2.8
Tanzania			5.2			30.0	35.2
Uganda	8.4						
Zambia & Rhodesia	87.7					40.0	40.0
Sub-Totals	405.6	22.8	39.2	47.5	15.1	132.1	256.7
Asia & Middle East							
Ceylon	41.5				31.3		31.3
China, Republic of				50.0	44.5	55.0	149.5
India	224.2					75.0	75.0
Iran	42.0					60.0	60.0
Japan	178.2						
Malaysia	87.5	37.0		11.5		20.0	68.5
Pakistan	30.2	21.5				23.0	44.5
Philippines	58.7	12.0					12.0
Singapore	15.0	10.0	15.0	20.5			45.5
Thailand	78.6	5.0			46.5		51.5
Sub-Totals	755.9	85.5	15.0	82.0	122.3	233.0	537.8
Europe							
Austria	81.6						
Cyprus	21.0	2.8			5.0		7.8
Denmark	45.0						
Finland	67.7						
Iceland	2.5	18.0					18.0
Ireland				14.5		20.0	34.5
Italy	239.6						
Malta	6.0						
Norway	95.0						
Portugal	57.5						
Turkey	25.7			36.5		31.0	67.5
Yugoslavia	118.0						
Sub-Totals	759.6	20.8		51.0	5.0	51.0	127.8

*Totals in this table include the power component in some multipurpose loans. The amount for Botswana represents industrial infrastructure, including power.

	FY 1948-66	FY 1967	FY 1968	FY 1969	FY 1970	FY 1971	Total FY 1967-71
Oceania							
Australia	100.0						
Indonesia					15.0		15.0
New Zealand	53.0						
Papua New Guinea						23.2	23.2
Sub-Totals	153.0				15.0	23.2	38.2
Western Hemisphere							
Argentina	95.0		55.0	82.0	60.0		197.0
Bolivia	15.0			7.4			7.4
Brazil	367.6	100.6		48.9	80.0	70.0	299.5
Chile	65.4	60.0					60.0
Colombia	205.8		18.0	18.0	52.3		88.3
Costa Rica	20.8				12.0		12.0
Ecuador	10.0						
El Salvador	25.3					5.6	5.6
Guatemala		15.0	7.0				22.0
Honduras	10.3		11.5		11.0		22.5
Jamaica	22.0						
Mexico	374.8		90.0		125.0		215.0
Nicaragua	21.2	5.0	15.2				20.2
Panama	4.0				42.0		42.0
Peru	39.0	10.0	17.5				27.5
Trinidad & Tobago	23.5			2.0			2.0
Uruguay	64.0					18.0	18.0
Venezuela	99.0	15.0		31.0			46.0
Sub-Totals	1462.0	205.6	214.2	189.3	382.3	93.6	1085.0
Totals	3536.8	334.7	268.4	369.8	539.7	532.9	2045.5

International Sector Data—Electric Power

	Country			Sector				
		Per Capita GNP[1]			Annual			Annu Grow
Country	Population Mid-1969 (000)	US$ 1969	Growth Rate(%) 1964-69	Total 1968 Production (GWh)	Growth Rate(%) 1963-68	kWh Per Cap.	1968 Production (GWh)	Rate (1963-
1. Argentina	23,983	899	1.7	17,851	7.5	744	13,451	8.0
2. Austrailia	12,296	2,306	3.4	44,531	8.75	3,625	43,067	8.75
3. Brazil	90,840	272	1.7	38,181	6.5	424	34,437	7.7
4. Ceylon	12,240	204	4.6	650	7.5	53	561[3]	8.25
5. China, Republic of	13,800	304	6.5	10,036	14.0	727	9,802	14.2
6. Colombia	20,463	338	1.6	8,100[6]	6.5	334	7,100[6]	9.2
7. Costa Rica	1,695	493	4.2	833	10.0	490	779	8.5
8. El Salvador	3,390	292	0.5	582	11.25	172	554	11.5
9. Ethiopia	24,769	70	5.1	361	15.25	15	318	15.5
10. France	50,330	2,396	4.3	117,925	6.0	2,340	94,271	7.5
11. Ghana	8,600	180	—.6	2,589	53.0[13]	300	2,560	60.0
12. India	536,983	109	0.2	49,520	10.3	93	45,170	11.0
13. Indonesia	116,000	112	1.2	N.A.	N.A.	N.A.	1,677[3]	1.6
14. Italy	53,170	1,337	4.3	104,011	7.8	1,950	76,660	7.2
15. Kenya	10,506	134	5.6	402	8.9	38	402	8.9
16. Malaysia	10,583	364	4.6	3,076	12.5	290	2,953	13.0
17. Mexico	48,933	612	6.5	22,484	7.9	477	20,074	8.6
18. New Zealand	2,901	2,141	1.4	12,185	6.4	4,200	12,185	6.4
19. Nigeria	63,870	76	—1.8	1,105	4.4	17	1,090	4.3
20. Pakistan	126,353	112	5.5	4,991[3]	11.5	40	4,991[3]	11.5
21. Singapore	2,017	802	6.2	1,639	14.9	800	1,639	14.
22. Sweden	7,978	2,859	2.4	56,237	6.8	7,000	56,237[4]	6.
23. Switzerland	6,230	2,697	2.2	30,552	6.8	4,900	26,676	7.
24. Tanzania	12,926	87	4.5	315	9.5	24	315	9.
25. Uganda	8,340	114	4.1	731	8.0	88	731	8.
26. United Kingdom	55,534	1,906	1.3	223,302	5.2	4,000	204,477	5.
27. United States	203,216	4,242	3.5	1,435,512	7.3	7,000	1,329,443	7.
28. Venezuela	10,035	993	1.1	10,814	9.9	1,004	5,155[5]	6.
29. Yugoslavia	20,351	571	2.6	20,641	8.8	1,002	18,801	8

[1] GNP figures are based on the implicit exchange rate used by the Bank. To be consistent, these rates have also been used to obtain the "fuel cost" and "average revenue" figures quoted, although in countries which import much fuel this may be misleading with regard to the cost of fuel.

[2] Figures for sales are for 1968 unless otherwise noted.

[3] The figure given is for 1967. (In the case of production, the relevant growth figures are for the years 1963-67.)

[4] The figure is for the sector, since public utilities are not differentiated in the data.

[5] The figure is for 1966, and the growth figure for 1963-66.

[6] The figure is for 1969.

[7] Comision Ejecutiva Hidroelectrica del Rio Lempa only.

[8] Kenya consumption figure (for 1967) exceeds production; the balance is imported from Uganda.

[9] Data for 1968.

236

				Public Utilities (excluding 'captive' plant)						
% of Production by Public Utilities	Sales (GWh)[2]	Demand (peak) 1969 (MW)	Fuel Cost Per Million Btu (US Cents)[1]	Installed Capacity (MW, 1969)			Number of Consumers (1969)	Consumers Per Employee (1969)	Average Revenue Per kWh Sold (US Cents)[1] (1969)	
				Total	Thermal	Hydro				
75	12,055[6]	N.A.	23.3	3,965	3,437	528	4,000,000	84	2.44	1.
97	N.A.	N.A.	N.A.	12,153[9]	8,647	3,136	4,000,000	N.A.	N.A.	2.
90	32,000	N.A.	N.A.	7,455[9]	1,633	5,812	N.A.	N.A.	N.A.	3.
86	612	143	55	247	56	191	N.A.	N.A.	2.62	4.
98	10,002[6]	1,850	50	2,245	1,524	721	2,100,000	200	1.35	5.
90	5,750[6]	N.A.	N.A.	1,870	470	1,400	N.A.	N.A.	N.A.	6.
94	678	N.A.	N.A.	213	170	43	150,400	70	1.73	7.
95	500[7]	109	25.6	166	96	70	9,200[15]	N.A.	1.42	8.
88	288[6]	N.A.	N.A.	180	55	125	94,100	46	3.71	9.
80	110,447	19,500[3]	N.A.	25,696[9]	12,210	13,486	15,300,000[10]	N.A.	(11)	10.
99	2,629[6]	378	97	675	87	588	94,500	17	0.62	11.
91	37,800[6]	10,400	N.A.	14,503	8,147	6,356	N.A.	N.A.	2.25	12.
N.A.	1,158[6]	N.A.	N.A.	651[14]	343	308	N.A.	N.A.	N.A.	13.
74	92,139	16,770[3]	N.A.	21,702	9,430	11,060	N.A.	N.A.	N.A.	14.
100	576[8]	112	29	157	63	94	100,900	44	3.29	15.
96	1,939[12]	292		664	265	399	398,600	45	2.1	16.
90	16,705	N.A.	33	4,904	2,471	2,433	4,170,000	122	2.08	17.
100	N.A.	2,544	N.A.	3,023	687	2,336	N.A.	N.A.	N.A.	18.
99	N.A.	N.A.	N.A.	N.A.	N.A.	N.A.	N.A.	N.A.	N.A.	19.
100	4,777[6]	1,090	52	1,873	1,127	746	728,000	127	2.43	20.
100	1,653[6]	321	29.4	524	524	0	245,000	175	2.07	21.
N.A.	50,908	9,675[3]	N.A.	13,731[9]	3,008	10,423	N.A.	N.A.	N.A.	22.
87	22,175	4,090[3]	N.A.	9,500[9]	560	8,940	N.A.	N.A.	N.A.	23.
100	307[6]	69	N.A.	102	54	48	46,100	15	3.32	24.
100	664[6]	128	N.A.	170	0	170	59,700	N.A.	1.75	25.
91	192,431	40,596	54	55,681[9]	53,529	2,158	19,964,000	80	1.72	26.
93	1,317,234	238,000	26.1	309,348[9]	257,478	51,870	55,847,000	N.A.	1.5	27.
48	6,855	1,125	N.A.	1,715	953	762	N.A.	N.A.	N.A.	28.
91	17,000	3,500	34.25	4,865	1,665	3,200	N.A.	N.A.	N.A.	29.

[10] Data are for residential consumers only.

[11] US cents 1.4 for high voltage supplies. US cents 3.69 for low voltage supplies

[12] National Electricity Board only.

[13] The high growth rates and production per capita stem from the heavy power requirements of an aluminum smelter which commenced operations in 1967. This accounted for 75% of total power sales in 1969.

[14] As of June 1968.

[15] CEL (see 7 above) sells power mainly wholesale.

SOURCES:
U.N. Statistical Yearbook, U.N. Annual Bulletin of Electric Energy Statistics for Europe, U.K. Ministry of Power Digest of Energy Statistics, U.S. FPC Electric Power Statistics, Annual Reports of Borrowing Countries, World Bank.

Summary of World Bank Electric Power Activities with Projections Through FY1976

	Actual			Program		Actual[1]		Program
	1969	1970	1971	1972	1973	1964-68	1969-73	1972-76
Sector Studies/Surveys [2]	6	10	7	8	11	8	42	50
Commitments ($M.)	370	540	538	550	525	1613	2523	2540
% Total IBRD/IDA	21	25	21	20	20	28	21	17
No. of Countries	15	14	17	18	19	38	49	50
Lending Operations	17	15	18	19	22	68	91	102
% Total IBRD/IDA	14	12	14	13	12	24	14	11
Projects under Supervision	67	71	77	83	90	60 [3]	78 [3]	95 [3]

[1] Including scheduled for FY1972-73

[2] In countries where the power sector consists of a single operating utility, preparation and appraisal of projects includes a sector review, per se. These numbers mainly refer to sector reviews prepared in the course of project work and are thus not comparable with the data on reviews of sectors where the project and sector work is separate.

[3] Annual Average

WATER SUPPLY AND SEWERAGE

WATER SUPPLY AND SEWERAGE
SECTOR WORKING PAPER

● Urban communities of any size without adequate piped water and sewerage are not viable and thus seriously compromise national development prospects. The Bank stated in the 1970 Annual Report ". . . the economic growth of urban areas, where most modern industry is centered, determines to a very large extent that of the nation; and the problems involved in urbanization will therefore profoundly influence achievement of national development." The purpose of this paper is to elaborate on one dimension of these urbanization problems in developing countries—the need for adequate water and sewerage facilities.

The "sector" discussed below comprises the institutions and physical works associated with the collection, treatment, transmission and distribution of potable water, and the collection, treatment, and disposal of liquid wastes — both domestic and industrial. In the developing countries, these systems usually exist only where population is concentrated even though there is need for similar services in villages and rural areas.

WATER AND SEWERAGE IN URBAN AREAS

Individuals need a minimum amount of water for drinking and preparation of food. Because this minimum requirement is an absolute necessity, people not being served by a piped water system resort to alternatives ranging from carrying water long distances or purchasing water from vendors to use of heavily polluted ponds or roadside ditches. These alternatives are not feasible physically in urban areas beyond a certain size. Moreover, in the case of the purchase of water from vendors, the price is so high (see table below) that only very small quantities are bought.

	Price Charged by Water Vendors ● (US Dollars)		Metered domestic rate to customers served by the city water system	
	Per 1,000 US Gal.	Per m³	Per 1,000 US Gal.	Per m³
Dacca	..20- 8.40	1.11-2.22	.35	.09
Kampala	5.84-14.60	1.55-3.86	.70	.18
Istanbul	3.52	.93	.35	.09
Singapore	—	—	.21	.06
Typical U.S.	—	—	.25-.50	.07-.13
Typical German	—	—	.40-.75	.11-.19

Domestic consumption is only one of the uses of water in urban areas, although it is the major one, typically accounting for 50%-75% of total consumption. Industrial, commercial and government (schools, hospitals, etc.) consumption is frequently also important. Water is vital for many industrial processes. While there is sometimes the alternative available to large industry of developing a private supply, it is seldom cheaper than a well-run municipal system. Economies of scale are important in water and usually favor a central system when all costs are considered. The different time patterns of industrial and household demand also make a central system the least expensive way to satisfy differing peak demands.

Because of the explosive acceleration of urbanization in many developing countries in recent decades, the typical experience is that service which may have been adequate at one time deteriorates as consumers are connected to the system at a faster rate than its capacity is increased. Once a system is operating above capacity, the quality of service deteriorates for all consumers connected to it. A good example of this "network" effect is one large South Asian city which has an extensive and very large water system, but one which has lagged far behind the rapid growth of the urban complex and has not been properly maintained.[1] As a result, an estimated 40% of the water put into the system is lost in distribution. Service is now available for only a few hours a day because the limited water is allocated by rotation to different areas of the city. Consequently, almost every structure has a roof tank and many have pumps to try to suck more water out of the system. The cost of these facilities is enormous, and may exceed the incremental cost of a proper system. A few years ago, when the seasonal rains were inadequate, the very life of the city appeared threatened. Faced with exhaustion of the reservoirs, contingency plans were made to move a part of the population out of the city, and most industry was shut down for weeks. These were the expensive consequences of the failure of the water system to keep pace with the growth of the city.

Even in less dramatic circumstances, the cost of inadequate water facilities in terms of debilitating diseases, associated medical treatment and reduced productivity is undoubtedly high, but the magnitude of these costs is not easily measured. The studies which demonstrate in developed countries the public health benefits of safe water (reduction in enteric disease) do not separate the benefits of

---

[1] This pamphlet offers certain examples of inadequacies in the planning and implementation of projects, or in the quality of service provided by particular water supply and sewerage systems. Such examples have not been specifically identified; to do so would seem invidious when the basic purpose is only to highlight the nature of the problems that are often found in this sector.

adequate piped water from those of adequate medical services, shelter, food, etc. Public health benefits are thus rarely included in quantitative estimates of the benefits of improved water services. As a result, water projects are often penalized inappropriately when compared with the projects in other sectors for which economic returns on investment reflect more comprehensive measurement of benefits; this may account in some degree for the widespread inadequacies of water service in most parts of the developing world.

Water supply contributes to a city's existence in another way: it provides the only satisfactory method of removal of human wastes. Inadequate central sewerage not only raises problems of public health and aesthetics, but usually leads to higher costs. As a practical matter, every city has to provide some waste disposal system. For example, a large East Asia city, which has no sewerage system, is forced to haul away most of its wastes by truck. This is an increasingly expensive and unsatisfactory solution, not only because the volume is growing with the city, but also because disposal is becoming more and more difficult and labor for this kind of work is scarce. Waterborne sewerage systems are normally the most effective means of urban waste disposal, and water and sewerage facilities should thus be considered as part of an integrated system carrying "new" and "used" water. Unfortunately, because sewerage systems may cost as much or more than the water systems and because the value of a sewerage system to an individual is often much less apparent to him than it is to society as a whole, sewerage is often given even lower priority than piped water in developing countries.

SECTOR FEATURES SIGNIFICANT FOR THE BANK GROUP

The water/sewerage sector shares one basic characteristic of other public utilities such as power, gas, telecommunications, etc.: it sells services to the public. But in the minds of many people, it has a stronger "social service" character. It is frequently classified, even in some Bank reports, as "social" rather than "economic" infrastructure, perhaps because no other public utility service more closely affects the daily lives of people. Because of this attitude and the related political sensitivity of water charges, the idea of consumers paying for the full cost of water service is not yet widely accepted in many developing countries. However, in contrast to most "social" services, water and sewerage systems can be capable of paying their way, even after subsidizing reasonable household consumption for the poor.

243

Because most water and sewerage systems are locally managed and locally financed, and therefore normally depend on overburdened municipal budgets, the quality of water supply institutions tends to be underdeveloped in relation to the size of their investments and the importance of their service. This local nature of the service and the relatively low quality of management is one of the major barriers to quick improvement in water supply institutions and systems, and an important reason for central governments tending to pay inadequate attention to improving these services. The facts that benefits are not easily measured and thus tend to be underestimated in production-oriented planning, and that well-prepared programs, including rational study of alternatives and reliable cost estimates, are extremely rare, also contribute to neglect by governments. However, this situation is beginning to change as increasing attention is directed to environmental problems and the quality of life in developing countries. Water and sewerage specialists have been calling attention to growing water pollution problems for years; more widespread and better sewage collection and treatment remain the only technically feasible and proven solution to these problems.

In every country where we have been able to evaluate sector programs, sizable backlogs of needed water supply and sewerage investments have been discovered. The World Health Organization, (WHO), which probably has the best worldwide knowledge of the sector, has suggested the following water supply targets for the second UN Development Decade (1971-1980). These targets underline the present inadequacies of supply in developing countries and the magnitude of the effort necessary to correct them.

Urban Population Served by:	Now	By 1980
Household or Courtyard Service	25%	40%
Public Standpipes	26%	60%
No Service	49%	—

WHO estimates that new capital investment of US$9 billion would be required between 1971 and 1980 to meet these targets in urban areas and another US$1.6 billion to improve rural supplies. If related sewerage works are added, investment requirements approximate US$20 billion. Resources of this magnitude are unlikely to become available for these services during the 1970s.[1] But with growing awareness of the problems and the increasing resources being committed to the sector, the benefits of improved allocation of talent

[1]For comparison, for the period 1961-70, IBRD/IDA and IDB (the largest multilateral lender in this sector) helped to finance projects costing US$1,538 million.

244

and money for these services are large. There is clearly a larger role for the Bank to play here than the very limited role of the past (Bank lending in this sector started only in 1961): to evaluate and help improve the water and sewerage programs of Bank members, to help strengthen institutions, to improve project selection, preparation and execution, and to help finance the more important and complex programs.

Two examples of the kind of benefits that the Bank can sometimes help to achieve are noted below:

(a) In June 1966, a Bank mission examined a proposed project in a Caribbean city. Prepared by consultants, the project included a dam, long transmission line, treatment works, etc. Its total cost was estimated at US$41 million and it was expected to supply 22 Mgd (83,000 m³/day) to the metropolitan area. As a result of the mission's discussions with the authority and its consultants it was discovered that there were possibilities of developing ground-water sources which had not been explored and that utilization of the existing system could be improved. Studies were made and resulted in a project which will supply 17.5 Mgd (66,000 m³/day) at a cost of about US$9 million—about one-fourth of the original cost.

(b) In 1967, a mission visited a prominent African city to make a preliminary study of a project being prepared by consultants. It consisted of a dam, diversion tunnels, transmission and treatment works, but nothing was included for the distribution system. It was designed to increase the city's supply by about 12 Mgd (45,000 m³/day.) The consultants' preliminary cost estimate was about US$25 million; a more realistic estimate was about US$35 million. The mission suggested a re-examination of the scope of the project and the demand estimates. Further studies led to a revised project, which now includes the necessary improvements to the distribution system and is designed to supply 10 Mgd (38,000 m³/day). The revised project is expected to cost about US$12 million, i.e., about one-third of the original estimate. Although the project was delayed by the additional studies, the delay will not cause any water shortage in the city since measures for increasing the utilization of existing facilities were also included in the project.

There is also great scope for Bank assistance in improving the operations and financial policies of poorly managed and inefficient organizations. Strengthened management and better management systems (accounting, budgeting, maintenance, etc.) often lead to more efficient use of present facilities which can reduce or postpone future capital needs. By insisting on reasonable financial performance targets, it is possible not only to help relieve local officials of some of the agony of politically difficult pricing decisions but also to reduce large burdens on the national budget. However, the achievement of institutional reform is much more difficult than improving the scope and design of projects. The difficulties—largely human and political —have been more than amply illustrated by the Bank's disappointing experiences in some of its early loans, and by the time needed to prepare this aspect of more recent projects.

Probably the largest obstacles to adequate levels of investment in the sector have been the inability to prepare projects and mobilize adequate resources locally for them. Encouragement toward more adequate project preparation and pricing may thus be major contributions that an outside lender can make to improve the quality of these essential services.

Foreign costs of projects in this sector vary widely (5% to 50% in sewerage, 10% to 80% in water) depending on the stage of development and size of the country as well as the nature of the project. Also, construction periods are relatively long. Thus, these projects are normally suitable vehicles for large transfers of capital only if lenders are willing to provide substantial local currency financing.

Comprehensive data on external financing of water and sewerage projects are not available, but there is reason to believe that the bulk of external finance in this field has been provided in the form of suppliers' credits and other bilateral loans for pumps, pipes and treatment plants. The principal multilateral source of funds for this sector has been the Inter-American Development Bank (IDB). During 1961-70, IDB lent US$486 million for 85 water and sewerage projects with a total cost of US$1,117 million. This amounted to about 12% of IDB total lending during the period, and was almost 2½ times the amount lent by Bank/IDA for the same period. For 1970, the amount loaned by IDB was US$29.9 million and US$80.0 million is projected for 1971; future lending in this sector is expected to be about 10% of IDB's total lending. The Asian Development Bank has made two loans to Malaysia totaling US$12.2 million and one loan to Singapore of US$8.3 million for water supply; and the African Development Bank has negotiated one loan to Uganda for US$3.2 million equivalent for 20 small water and sewerage systems. The principal bilateral lender in the field has probably been the United States, although French assistance has also been substantial. The Swedish International Development Association has participated in three Bank/IDA loans (Lahore, Tunisia I and II) and has made other loans for rural and village water supplies.

In summary, investment in this sector would seem to be much more suited to the Bank Group's development objectives than the limited Bank involvement to date would indicate. Adequate water and sewerage is a necessary, but not sufficient, condition for the solution of pressing urbanization and public health problems in member countries; the scope for institution building, and for improving investment decision-making and enterprise finance—and the related economies in resource use and increases in public savings—is very large; and the typical problems are such that the Bank can do much to help resolve them.

MAIN FEATURES OF BANK GROUP LENDING
Past Loans and Credits

The Bank's first loan for water supply was made in 1961 to the Republic of China for the Taipei water system. Through FY 1971, 30 loans and credits for US$391.8 million equivalent were made,[1] of which 17 (US$255.8 million) were made in the last three years. This amounts to 2.6% of all Bank/IDA lending for FY 1961-71. Breakdowns by Bank/IDA and by country are shown in Table I. There is no particular pattern in past lending; projects were considered as they appeared. However, our approach has been less passive recently, as increasing sector work and closer cooperation with UN Development Programme (UNDP) and WHO have begun to bring a steadier stream of projects into the pipeline. With a water supply staff that has grown from 13 to 26 in the past two years, the Bank is now in a position to deal with a larger volume of projects, and this is reflected in the projected level of lending discussed below.

Many lessons have been learned since the first loan in 1961 (FY 1962). The most important lesson is that lending in this sector is more difficult than had been expected. Although there is nothing intrinsically difficult about the sector, most borrowers have been poorly organized and elementary principles of public utility management have not been observed. Local and national government officials had first to be persuaded of the need for the fundamentals of good project planning such as thorough study of technical alternatives, design criteria appropriate for the country, financial planning, etc. Then the studies had to be organized and carried out before the project could be appraised. Similar problems have appeared in the procurement and construction stages. Thus delays in the projects have been common, both before and after loans were signed, and more intensive su-

---

[1]US$36.4 million has subsequently been cancelled.

247

pervision has been required than for power and telecommunications.

As mentioned above, institutional improvement is much more difficult to achieve than engineering improvement, particularly where service is bad and deteriorating, as it has been in many projects. Two early projects involved systems which were being ineffectively operated by municipalities, and the credits included several measures intended to help build viable institutions. New autonomous authorities were created, management and engineering consultants were provided, and improved financial policies were established. However, it proved difficult to attract competent management, the consultants were not very effective, and the new financial policies were not observed. The projects had problems from the beginning, and had to be substantially revised and reduced.

Another early loan was made to a national authority which faced many structural and management problems. Again, extensive efforts were made by the Bank and the government during the development of the project to provide the means for improvement. These included, among other things, a management adviser for two years. Despite intensive project supervision by Bank staff, these efforts were not successful. The project was delayed and costs went up due, inter alia, to poor construction planning and execution. Institutional improvements were blocked by militant opposition by two strong unions, top management was inadequate, and financial planning was given little attention. There were recurring legal actions and disputes with contractors and suppliers. The management adviser was ineffective. After these problems were brought to the attention of the government, the government conducted its own investigation and then made certain changes in the water authority; however, major problems still remain. Contact with the project is being maintained but no further lending for water is contemplated until the authority has been effectively improved.

Experience suggests that, with some important exceptions, local officials and water managers are less accustomed to using modern economic, financial, and management methods, and are more exposed to direct political pressure than in higher levels of governments, and in other public utility sectors. This condition is similar to that which existed in some national power sectors when the Bank began lending for power some 20 years ago.

In the work with borrowers the Bank has tried to help develop reasonable financial and engineering solutions to the problems of the projects as they appeared. But, for the reasons already discussed, most projects have appeared in response to a crisis rather than in anticipation of needs. Orderly advance planning is rare, in contrast to power and telecommunications where it is more the norm. One serious lack, both for planning and for appraisal work, is reliable historical data. Borrowers have been encouraged to address themselves to this problem: some of the results are shown in the Comparative Data Sheet in Annex Table 2. These limited data confirm the scope of the problems in this field:

—Urban populations have been increasing by an average 5.9% per annum, reflecting substantial immigration from rural areas;

—In one-third of the cities, the majority of consumers are served by public taps rather than house connections;

—In half of the cities, more than 25% of water produced is unaccounted for; and,

—Average water rates vary by a factor of almost one to ten (US$0.02/m^3 in Palmira; US$0.19/m^3 in Yaounde).

To correct the negative bias towards the sector in many countries, which reflects in large degree inadequate appreciation of the importance of water and sewerage, the Bank is exploring how best to initiate studies to help illuminate public health benefits, price and income elasticity and other characteristics of demand for water and sewerage services in member countries.

Bank initiatives in this sector have been criticized on occasion because they imply concentrating resources on urban areas, which are believed to be better able to help themselves than the poorer rural areas. There are valid reasons for concentrating on urban areas in this field. The need for water and sewerage service increases more rapidly than population in urban areas. Rising population density renders inadequate traditional water sources such as shallow wells, springs, and small streams, and concentrates human and other wastes. At some point, adequate service becomes absolutely necessary to the continued life of the area. Although relatively well-to-do, urban communities must accordingly confront much larger and more difficult problems than their rural counterparts. Also, if a choice must be made, concentrating on urban areas benefits the largest number of people for a given amount of investment. The public health effects are clearly greatest where population is most densely concentrated.

Another reason for the Bank's emphasis on urban areas is that the planning of major water and sewerage projects can have an impact on the broader problems of urban planning. This potentially useful leverage has not been used thus far, but could be available for use as knowledge of and capability for dealing with the complex of urbanization problems increase. The recent Bank urbanization mission to Istanbul found that the proposed water, sewerage, and road projects could be used as incentives to make the rapid growth of the city more orderly.

Well justified rural water projects also merit Bank support, notwithstanding the more difficult institutional and financial problems that would have to be resolved. To date, none has been presented, although a project in Nigeria was under preliminary discussion just before the recent war. Not many such projects are likely to appear unsolicited, however; the reasons which cause governments to neglect urban water and sewerage needs apply with even greater force to rural areas.

The above paragraphs are not intended to suggest that conflicting urban/rural claims on scarce development resources should normally be resolved in favor of urban areas. In certain cases, national development strategies may well be best focussed on the development of rural areas, if only to try to modify migration patterns which aggravate urban problems. The proper urban/rural allocation of infrastructure like water, power, schools, etc., can only be defined in a broad context, to which increasing attention is being given in the Bank's country and sector work.

Future Operations

Bank/IDA activities in this sector are expected to increase sharply in the 1970s. As in the past, most of these activities constitute responses to urgent problems rather than parts of considered sector development programs. But this situation is beginning to change.

	Aggregate FY 1964-68	Projected Aggregates	
		FY 1969-73	FY 1972-76
Number of Sector Surveys	—	23	40
Commitments (US$ million)	127	517	715
Number of Operations	10	34	46

The proportion of "planned" projects based on a knowledge of sector problems in a country and a deliberate evaluation of the merit of Bank involvement is growing and likely to grow further with expanded sector studies. Indeed, it is only through a substantial increase in sector work that country economic missions can evaluate plans for this sector in relation to national programs. Such a perspective is needed whether or not works are to be financed by the Bank.

The amount of sector work that would be desirable unfortunately exceeds the Bank's capacity to carry it out in the near future. Increasing our knowledge of this sector in some 70 countries where it is needed is obviously not a realistic short-term objective. Our actual goal is to do what is necessary to support planned operations and, in the short run, to provide sector support for Bank country economic work in the countries with the most acute sector problems. Sector reviews in other countries will have to be made more gradually.

WHO-World Bank Cooperation

For several years, the UNDP has financed pre-investment studies for water and sewerage projects, with WHO as executing agency. The Bank expresses "special interest" in those projects for which Bank lending appears likely, and follows the progress of the UNDP/WHO project in order to help assure that the project is being prepared in a manner likely to facilitate a prompt financing decision. From this experience it has been observed that there is a need to take a more investment-oriented approach to the execution of UNDP projects in the water supply and sewerage sector. As a result, there have been discussions over the past year between WHO and Bank staff aimed at establishing more effective staff cooperation in carrying out the large work program in prospect. In November 1970, WHO established a new pre-investment planning unit in its Environmental Health Division at WHO headquarters in Geneva to guide all WHO's pre-investment activities in this sector. Since much of the work of this unit could, in due course, replace work that would otherwise need to be done by Bank staff, cooperative arrangements have been negotiated under which the Bank will contribute to the expansion of this group. These arrangements have been approved by the Executive Directors and the Board of Governors and work under the Agreement will begin soon.

Research

The most pressing problem is to develop better criteria for allocating scarce funds among competing projects in this sector. Progress toward this goal depends on developing better measures of economic benefits, which largely depend in turn on developing better data. The Bank is starting to carry out research to this end and expects to intensify it. Other research objectives are to improve water demand analysis and forecasting and to identify pricing policy options for water and for sewerage.

WORLD BANK/IDA LENDING FOR WATER/SEWERAGE
FY 1962-1971

Country	Project	(US$ Million Original Amount) Bank	IDA
FY 62			
CHINA	Taipei Water		4.4[1]
JORDAN	Amman Water		2.0[2]
FY 63			
NICARAGUA	Managua Water		3.0
FY 64			
PAKISTAN	Dacca Water/Sewerage		26.0[3]
PAKISTAN	Chittagong Water/Sewerage		24.0[4]
JORDAN	Three Cities Water		3.5[5]
FY 65			
PHILIPPINES	Manila Water	20.2[6]	
SINGAPORE	Singapore Water	6.8	
FY 66			
BURUNDI	Bujumbura Water		1.1
VENEZUELA	Caracas Water	21.3[7]	
FY 67			
PAKISTAN	Lahore Water		1.7
FY 68			
SINGAPORE	Singapore Water	8.0	
COLOMBIA	Bogota Water	14.0	
FY 69			
SINGAPORE	Singapore Sewerage	6.0	
MALAYSIA	Kuala Lumpur Water	3.6	
TUNISIA	National Water	15.0	
JAMAICA	Kingston Water	5.0	
CAMEROON	Yaounde/Douala Water	5.0	
FY 70			
GHANA	Accra/Tema Water		3.5
COLOMBIA	Cali Water	18.5	
TUNISIA	National Water		10.5
FY 71			
KENYA	Nairobi Water	8.3	
CYPRUS	Nicosia Sewerage	3.5	
CYPRUS	Famagusta Sewerage	1.9	
BOTSWANA	Lobatse-Gaberones Water		3.0
COLOMBIA	Palmira Water	2.0	
COLOMBIA	Bogota Water	88.0	
YUGOSLAVIA	Ibar Water[8]	45.0	
BRAZIL	Sao Paulo Water and Pollution Control	37.0[9]	

NOTE: In addition to the above, a loan to Iceland of US$2 million was made for a hot water supply system used for domestic heating, and a loan to Malta of US$7.5 million for power included US$1.87 million for desalination equipment.

[1] US$0.4 million cancelled.
[2] US$0.5 million cancelled.
[3] US$12.8 million cancelled.
[4] US$17.0 million cancelled.
[5] US$1.0 million cancelled.
[6] US$0.6 million cancelled.
[7] US$4.2 million cancelled.
[8] Multipurpose project for water, power and irrigation.
[9] Two loans. $22.0 million for water supply, $15.0 million for pollution control.

252

COMPARATIVE DATA SHEET

Country and city	GNP of country per capita(1) (US$)	Water statistics data year	POPULATION Million	Five year annual rate of increase (%)	Private connections (%)	Public taps (%)	Water production per capita per day(2)	Total liters	Domestic(4)	Industry(5)	Official	Other	Unaccounted water(6) (%)	Average revenue per m3 consumed (US$)	Sewer connections as percentage of water connections (%)
BRAZIL—Sao Paulo city	250	1969	5.9	5.0	59	—	310	200	NA	NA	NA	NA	36	0.05	57
BURUNDI—Bujumbura	50	1969	0.09(7)	8.0	30(7)	70	95	65	NA	NA	NA	NA	30	0.09	NA
CAMEROON—Douala	140	1968	0.24	5.0	15	85	72	56	22	19	15	—	22	0.15	NA
—Yaounde		1968	0.14	8.0	20	80	83	66	42	4	20	NA	20	0.19	NA
CHINA—Taipei	270	1968	1.89	7.0	71	—	281	183	NA	NA	NA	—	35	0.04	—
COLOMBIA—Bogota	310	1969	2.52	6.7	—97—		215	160	—146—		12	2	25	0.07	NA
—Cali		1969	0.92	7.9	—NA—		295	230	170	30	—30—		22	0.04	99
—Palmira		1969	0.14	6.0	—89—		295	205	NA	NA	NA	—	30	0.02	95
ETHIOPIA—Addis Ababa	70	1969	0.75	6.4	67	20	40	29	27	2	—	—	27	0.19	—
GERMANY, Federal Republic of	1,970														
—West Berlin		1963	2.18(10)	NA	100	—	184	178	109	52	—17—		3	NA	NA
—Hamburg		1963	1.92(10)	NA	100	—	180	167	134	20	—13—		7	NA	NA
GHANA—Accra	170	1970	0.68	7.0	50	50	86	59	34	14	10	1	31	0.12	12
—Tema		1970	0.10	12.0(7)	90(7)	10(7)	36	34	16	18	—	—	7	0.12	NA
JAMAICA—Kingston(9)	460	1969	0.60	4.1	93	7	235	180	119	36	—25—		23	0.08	16
MALAYSIA—Kuala Lumpur(9)	330	1970	0.70	3.9	75(7)	10(7)	271	220	176	44	—	—	19	0.07	21
NICARAGUA—Managua	370	1969	0.34	6.0	73	8	250	205	160	25	20	NA	18	0.09	NA
PAKISTAN—Lahore	100	1969	1.80	4.0	38	26	144(7)	90(7)	NA	NA	NA	—	37	0.03	61
—Dacca		1969	0.80	3.2	32	63	176	81(7)	57	8	16	—	53	0.07	29
—Chittagong		1969	0.35	NA	12	57	62	33(7)	30	3	—	NA	46	0.08	—
PHILIPPINES—Manila	180	1969/70	4.5	NA	—85—		300	135	NA	NA	NA	—	55	0.03	NA
SINGAPORE	700	1969	2.02	2.0	94	5	230	211	101	46	64	—	8	0.03	NA
TUNISIA—Sonede area	220	1969	2.3	5.3	45	55	103	82	67	13	—	2	23	0.12	NA
UNITED STATES:	3,980														
—Baltimore, Maryland		1969	1.49(10)	NA	100	—	619	526	165	361	—	—	15	NA	NA
—Phoenix, Arizona		1969	0.58(10)	NA	100	—	813	729	NA	NA	—	—	10	0.09	NA
—Portland, Oregon		1968/69	0.58(10)	NA	100	—	655	533	NA	NA	NA	NA	19	0.06	NA
VENEZUELA—Caracas	950	1969	2.0	5.0	—100—		280	190	140	45	5	—	32	0.13	NA

CONSUMPTION/CAPITA/DAY FOR POPULATION SERVED:(3)

(1) In 1968 (Source: World Bank Atlas).
(2) For population served.
(3) Water sold for metered systems: estimated consumption for unmetered systems.
(4) Including public taps.
(5) Including commercial.
(6) Percentage of water produced.
(7) Data uncertain.
(8) Data for 1964.
(9) Metropolitan area.
(10) Population served by Water Authority.

NOTE: One cubic meter (m3) = 1,000 liters
= 264.2 US gallons
= 220.1 Imperial gallons

NA = Not Available

SUMMARY OF WORLD BANK WATER SUPPLY & SEWERAGE ACTIVITIES
WITH PROJECTIONS THROUGH FY 1976

	Actual			Program		Actual[1]		Program
	1969	1970	1971	1972	1973	1964-68	1969-73	1972-76
Sector Studies/Surveys[2]	—	3	4	6	10	—	23	40
Commitments ($ M.)	34.6	32.5	188.7	123.7	138.0	126.6	517.5	715
% Total IBRD/IDA	2	1	8	4	5	2	4	4
No. of countries	5	3	6	5	13	7	24	35
Lending Operations	5	3	8	5	13	10	34	46
% Total IBRD/IDA	5	3	6	6	7	4	5	5
Projects under Supervision [3]	13	14	19	28	37	6[4]	22[4]	45[4]

[1] Including scheduled for FY 1972-73.
[2] At the beginning of FY 1969, we had a reasonably adequate knowledge of the sector in four countries.
[3] Borrowers with more than one loan are counted only once.
[4] Annual average over period.

EDUCATION

EDUCATION
SECTOR WORKING PAPER

● This sector working paper considers World Bank lending programs over a perspective of five years and lending policy over a period of approximately a decade. It consists of three parts: (a) a brief review of trends in educational development; (b) a review of Bank policy and operations during the fiscal years 1963-1971; and (c) a projection and recommendations for Bank policy and operations responding to the changing situation of the '70s. All references to the Bank in this paper are to be deemed to refer also to the International Development Association (IDA) unless the context otherwise requires.

TRENDS IN EDUCATIONAL DEVELOPMENT
General

Since about 1950, the movement for political independence, the quickening pace of economic development in the less developed countries with its concomitant emphasis on science and technology, and the related population explosion have provided a powerful impetus and demand for education. The resulting expansion of education systems all over the world has been without precedent in history. The achievement is remarkable although far from complete.

The popular demand for education continues without slackening but there is mounting evidence, on the one hand, that this rapid expansion has created a new set of formidable problems and, on the other, has failed to achieve many of the benefits which were confidently expected of it. Many persons have agreed with Philip Coombs' characterization of this situation as a world crisis.[1] On all sides it is accepted that the continued development of education during the 1970s must be along very different lines from the largely "linear expansion" of the 1950s and early 1960s. The description of the educational development sector which follows attempts to define not only the salient characteristics and problems of educational development at the present time but also to describe them as continuing trends, to which Bank policy must continue to respond and adapt.

---
[1]*Coombs:* The World Educational Crisis, *Oxford, 1968.*

257

Quantitative Expansion

The increase in school enrollments at all levels and among almost all the less developed countries is the most dramatic feature of educational development over the past decade and a half. For the period 1960-1966 in developing countries as a whole enrollment growth rates were 42% at the primary level (reflecting an earlier start), 80% at the secondary level and 93% at the higher (mostly university) level (Annex Table 1). In absolute terms this growth added nearly 55 million primary students, 15 million secondary students and 2 million students in higher education, or an average of 12 million additional students each year. One result of these increases was to achieve in 1968 primary and secondary enrollment ratios, respectively, of 40% and 15% in Africa, 55% and 30% in Asia, and 75% and 35% in Latin America (Annex Table 1).

Two major forces lie behind this dramatic increase in enrollments. First is the strong social and political demand for education. Education is now universally accepted and demanded as essential to participation in the development process and to improvement in the condition of individual life. The fact that the individual economic payoff is often illusory does not diminish the demand since there are important social benefits and in any case education is essential to maintaining one's relative position in the social order. Because most curricula are designed to advance the students to the next level, there is an additional escalating force within the educational pyramid. As enrollments grow at one level, the demand increases for accommodation at the next level.

The second force pushing up enrollments has been the growth of population and, more particularly, the relatively recent increase of population in the developing countries which has resulted in an extraordinarily high proportion of young people. The United Nations estimates that in 1970 the percentage of total population under 15 years of age was 27% in the advanced countries and 41% in the less developed countries. One begins to see here the roots of the dilemma which developing countries face.

Two significant features of this expansion should be noted. First is the narrow concentration by governments and also by external assistance agencies upon the improvement of human resources for the modern economic sector and therefore upon formal education systems. Conversely, all too little attention has been given to the needs of rural populations living in the traditional or transitional economic sectors who, for some years to come, will be the majority in most developing countries. In this connection, President Julius Nyerere has noted of Tanzania:

258

"Although only about 13% of our primary school children will get a place in secondary school, the basis of our primary school education is the preparation of pupils for secondary schools . . . The same process operates again at the next highest level, when entrance to the university is the question at issue."

It is relatively easy to diagnose the problem and enumerate the obstacles to educating rural populations; more difficult, but imperative, is to determine more clearly the characteristics of different learning clienteles, the content of learning which will produce quick and substantial returns and the most appropriate ways to reach hitherto inaccessible learning clienteles.

Secondly, despite the very impressive gains in the numbers of young people enrolled in school, enrollment ratios (percentage of the relevant age group enrolled) remain low in a number of countries. Among 51 countries in which the Bank has had recent lending operations in education, the median primary enrollment ratio is 71%; the range is 6% (Somalia) to 99% (Greece). At the secondary level for the same group of countries in the mid-60s the median enrollment ratio is 13% and the range is 2% (Tanzania) to 54% (Ireland). Twenty-five percent of these countries have less than 8% (Annex Table 9).

Moreover, the composition of these enrollments remains seriously unfavorable from the point of view of economic development. At the secondary level in 50 countries for which data are available, the median percentage of total students studying vocational courses is 11% and in higher education the median enrolled in courses of engineering, medicine, science and agriculture is 21%.

Since almost all countries have a public commitment to achieve universal primary education by no later than 1980, it is likely (whether they achieve it or not) that the '70s will witness a continued pressure for increase at this level and, as a consequence, at the secondary level as well. Hopefully, there will also be a shift toward higher percentages of students following pre-vocational and vocational courses, although as indicated below, there are limits to the ability of the modern sector to absorb the output of technical schools.

Problems of Quality: the efficiency and productivity of education systems

As enrollments have expanded, it has been difficult, and more often impossible, for education systems to maintain the levels of quality and efficiency of the pre-expansion era. Facilities—classrooms, equipment and teaching materials—have not kept pace with the expanding number of students. Teacher training has lagged and the qualification

259

and experience of the teaching force have declined. The most serious gap, affecting everything else, has been in the management capability —organization, planning, evaluation, supervision—needed to meet the challenge of expansion.

The effects of all these factors are reflected in the dropout and repeater rates. In perhaps half of the developing countries, less than half of the students who enter primary school complete the cycle. The resulting inefficiency can be seen in selected cases drawn from the analysis of Bank project appraisals. In the Ivory Coast it requires an average of 12.5 pupil years to produce one graduate of the 6-year primary cycle and 21% of the total primary budget is spent on students who drop out in Grades 1-3. In El Salvador the comparable figures are 15 years and 37%; in Ethiopia they are 14 years and 32% (Annex Table 2).

Of equal importance has been the persistence of institutional forms, school system structures, teaching methods and curricula derived largely from European practice of an earlier era and to a great extent irrelevant to present day needs. In different ways, but with comparable effect, both the former colonies and the historically independent developing countries suffer from a lack of responsiveness to changed conditions. Both types of country have inherited or adopted educational systems designed for an elite—in the historically independent countries usually a landed or commercial upper class; in the former colonies a cadre of civil servants. In both cases, with the change to a mass learning clientele, a substantial proportion of the students in school are being miseducated. The content of primary and secondary courses, heavily dominated by the questions on qualifying examinations, is still drawn to a great extent from the developed world, which is remote from the experience of today's student, especially the rural peasant child, still living in a primitive condition of life. The heavy reliance on examinations encourages rote learning of irrelevant information. Even in technical courses adherence to standards and practices set in the developed countries inhibits the education of students to solve the problems of their own environments in more appropriate ways. The fact that these practices are often the choice of local people does not diminish their bad effects.

Education and the Labor Market

Matching educational growth with the manpower needs of developing economies is likely to become more complex in the '70s. Aspirations of the younger generation and the related expansion of school systems have often greatly exceeded the opportunities for productive employment in the modern sector of the economy, resulting in growing unemployment of the educated. With hardly 10% of the age group in secondary schools and less than 1% in universities, some education systems are already approaching the point of producing graduates in numbers exceeding the effective demand of employers. A long-term development strategy would no doubt call for a continued expansion of the education system to raise the very low educational attainment level of the working population although the short-term reality of increasing unemployment in the rapidly growing younger age group often reduces the economic benefits of such expansion.

When the unemployment problem is of a cyclical or temporary nature, it should be ignored in the development of long-term educational growth targets. Persistently growing unemployment among the educated at progressively higher levels, however, would seem to indicate structural imbalances, which cannot be ignored. In such cases, continued investments in the expansion of education systems without major reforms could become both economically and socially unprofitable. The situation calls for three kinds of action: a continuous reassessment of the economic development, potential and effective manpower demand of the countries concerned, improvements in the functioning of labor markets (particularly the system of incentives and disincentives) and reorientation of the education and training systems. Our knowledge of the problem of unemployment amongst those with advanced education and training (which is of recent origin in a number of countries) is spotty and inconclusive; research in this field deserves high priority and is described in more detail at the end of this section.

Closer attention to the functioning of labor markets is particularly important because the vexing unemployment problem is compounded by labor market imperfections which obstruct the effective utilization of a country's available manpower resources. Often, unemployment among the educated is accompanied by persistent shortages of qualified manpower in fields where work incentives are unattractive. Examples of such pockets of "scarcity in the midst of plenty" are industrial technicians, agricultural extension workers and teachers.

Educational development in the '60s was no doubt imbalanced when compared with these specific manpower needs. Even in those cases, however, where attention was paid to industrial, commercial and agricultural training the result frequently failed to meet employers' needs. Formal technical education and training in schools were often out of step with informal, on-the-job training and employment opportunities. The systems of wages and other incentives are often not conducive to an optimum deployment and utilization of manpower. Public sector salaries, for instance, are normally insensitive to demand and supply. In Africa the high level of these salaries, combined with budgetary constraints, has resulted in a situation where the number of civil service posts expands slowly but at the same time stimulates a demand for education and training for these posts beyond the saturation point of effective demand. In Latin American and Asian countries the low level of public sector salaries may ease the budgetary constraints but it has often made the civil service, including the teaching professions, unattractive to able and qualified school and university graduates and sometimes created an oversized body of less qualified staff. Within the public sector, the rigidity of salary scales often prevents adjustments for those occupations where scarcities persist, particularly for jobs where working conditions are unattractive or competition for specific technical skills is severe.

A reorientation of the education and training systems, with greater emphasis on vocational education and on non-formal training for agriculture and industry, will be required to redress present imbalances. A frequent objection against public investments in vocational training is the fact that most public training schemes have been poorly adjusted to employers' needs and have failed to guide students into the vocations for which they were trained. Since vocational training is considerably more expensive than general education, this situation can therefore lead to misinvestment. From this the conclusion is often drawn that vocational training should be left entirely to in-plant training by industry. There is considerable validity in this view but in many countries it is unlikely that the need for vocationally trained manpower could effectively be met by industry itself. The small scale of the majority of industrial undertakings in developing countries, often working with outdated equipment and without adequate know-how of modern production techniques or interest in staff training does not provide the proper basis for modern vocational training schemes. Industrial development would therefore require that the supply of technically trained manpower, which is greatly inadequate in many countries, be strengthened by institutional public training. To avoid the mistakes of the past, however, there is an urgent need for close cooperation between public training institutions and private industry, e.g. through the establishment of apprenticeship training schemes. Examples of such cooperation are the SENA and INACAP industrial training schemes in Latin America.[1]

The basic causes of rising unemployment in the developing coun-

[1] SENA: Servicio Nacional de Aprendizaje (Colombia).
INACAP: Instituto Nacional de Capacitación Profesional (Chile).

262

tries are of course not to be found within their education systems and the recommendations given in the preceding paragraphs would do little to solve the fundamental problem of the traditional (low income) sector of the population aspiring for a place in the modern (high income) sector, with its narrow employment opportunities. Education can help to reduce the unemployment among certain categories of educated at secondary and tertiary levels but otherwise the unemployment problem requires a concerted inter-sectoral approach to rural and urban development.

To guide the long-term strategy of Bank operations in this field, the Bank's research program includes a study of the functioning of labor markets in developing economies, which should throw more light on the recruitment, employment and utilization of educated manpower, with particular reference to the unemployment problem. The study, which will be closely linked with research undertaken in the framework of the ILO World Employment Program, is expected to be initiated in fiscal year 1972.

Financial Constraints

As indicated previously, rapid school-age population growth and the persistent demand for education mean that enrollments inevitably will increase. In addition, there are upward pressures on unit costs (costs per student). These are largely determined by staff costs, which in most developing countries make up over three-quarters of total recurrent expenditures in education. Teachers' salaries, in competition with wages in the modern sector, tend to rise regardless of productivity. Needed improvements in teacher qualifications, the advance toward seniority by young teachers, who often constitute the majority, and the tendency to raise teacher:pupil ratios are other factors which will act to increase staff costs, and unit costs, in the future.

In the past, public expenditures on education generally have grown at a faster rate than either total public expenditures, public revenue or national income. A comprehensive study of 30 developing countries showed that between 1960 and 1965 the share of education in public expenditures increased, on the average, from 13% to 15%. Similarly, for the same period public expenditures on education rose from 3% of national income to 4% (Annex Table 3). A representative sample of 10 recent Bank appraisal reports indicates that this trend has continued in most cases between 1965 and 1970. Given that both enrollments and unit costs are likely to increase, future increases in expenditures on education are virtually inevitable.

However, the increase in educational expenditures cannot continue indefinitely at a faster rate than that of national aggregates. In 1967, of 50 developing countries for which data were available, 18 devoted more than 20% of total public expenditures to education, compared with just six in 1960. It will be increasingly difficult to obtain an ever greater share of a country's budgetary resources for educational purposes.

Solutions to this dilemma will have to be sought in four inter-related areas. These will include:

—searches for forms of education which will make a more direct and less costly contribution to rural development;

—attempts to improve internal efficiency and increase productivity;

—attempts to identify new sources of educational finance; and

—efforts to help governments plan and control the size and shape of school and university systems.

Dilemma for the Government: how to allocate resources

The above analysis of the quantitative expansion and the problem of quality represents in some respects an outsider's point of view. In the borrower's calculation social, cultural and psychological considerations are merged with the economic to create ultimately a political formulation of the issues in which short-term solutions and benefits sometimes are more heavily weighted than long-term.

The public has increasingly come to consider education as a right and a school place as the entrance ticket to a better life in the monetary sector of the economy. Parents are generally well aware of the growing unemployment among school graduates, but the gap between the subsistence and monetary sectors is so wide that they may still consider that it pays to provide secondary and higher education for their children on the off-chance that one may secure a job that will enable him to help his less fortunate brothers and sisters. To a very large extent these views have been accepted by the governments and are reflected in their education policies.

Cultural and ethnic demands may furthermore force the borrower to establish educational institutions—secondary schools as well as university departments—in areas which for a long time to come will lack the economic resources and the population necessary for a satisfactory development. In some instances schools may be seen as a device for keeping young people out of trouble.

Innovations, which are seen by outsiders as necessary to remedy qualitative and financial problems, may often be resisted by the developing country—and particularly by teachers and ministry officials

—as changes which would downgrade the system and endanger vested interests. They may refuse to participate in experiments which they feel should be tried out in other countries which could better afford failures. They are particularly sensitive to proposed changes in examination systems since these may seem to imply a retreat from accepted world standards. This demand for international equivalence in examinations is undoubtedly hampering the adjustment of secondary and higher education to local needs but it represents a politically vocal requirement which most African and Asian governments find difficult to resist.

In the face of the surging demand for education of the masses as rapidly as possible, it is not surprising that very few leaders have stopped to ask, as President Nyerere of Tanzania has done—What kind of society do we wish to create? What can we realistically expect to achieve with our limited resources? How can we fashion our education system so as to maximize its contribution to these ends? Whom shall we educate, for what and how? Instead most governments have sought to replicate what was at hand as widely and as quickly as they could.

REVIEW OF WORLD BANK POLICIES AND OPERATIONS, 1963-1971

Policies

The basic elements of the Bank's education policy in the initial phase of our educational financing were elaborated in September 1962 when the first education project was presented to the Executive Directors and subsequently in a memorandum from the President on "Proposed Bank/IDA Policies in the Field of Education" of October 1963. In the President's Memorandum, the basic statement of policy with respect to types of projects to be financed reads as follows:

"The Bank and IDA should be prepared to consider financing a part of the capital requirements of priority education projects designed to produce, or to serve as a necessary step in producing, trained manpower of the kinds and in the numbers needed to forward economic development in the member country concerned. In applying this criterion, the Bank and IDA should concentrate their attention, at least at the present stage, on projects in the fields of (a) vocational and technical education and training at various levels, and (b) general secondary education. Other kinds of education projects would be considered only in exceptional cases."

The Bank would thus concentrate on high priority projects within the country's education development plan and fill the most crucial gaps in the system provided they fell within certain a *priori* defined areas of eligibility. Technical assistance and financing of software-curriculum reforms, education planning, production of teaching materials, etc. would comprise very minor parts of the projects, which would consist mainly of construction and equipment of school buildings.

With increased knowledge and experience, the Bank's approach to education widened in the late 1960s. In a Memorandum for the Executive Directors in July 1970, the President reaffirmed the first sentence of the 1963 statement quoted above, but added, "in applying this criterion in future we should broaden the scope of projects considered and we should determine priorities and select projects on the basis of a thorough examination of the education system as a whole rather than by a *priori* designated areas of eligibility which may not relate to the particular country. We should continue to emphasize projects which, like vocational training, produce trained manpower directly but we should also consider for financing other types of projects . . . which should have important long-term significance for economic development." Such projects would be "designed to encourage changes which improve the relevance, efficiency or economy of education systems".

The Bank's education financing in the fiscal years 1963-1971 has thus developed from hardware projects in restricted education sub-sectors to mixed hardware and software projects based on sector analysis aimed at achieving qualitative improvements and meeting crucial manpower needs.

Operations

Up to June 30, 1971, the World Bank Group has approved financing of 57 education loans in 42 countries for a total amount of US$ 431 million. Africa, including North Africa, has received 27 loans and 44% of the total lending volume; Latin America 15 and 22%; Asia 12 and 25%; and Europe three loans and 9% of the volume.

In the beginning most education projects were financed through IDA credits and only 10% of the projects in the fiscal years 1963-1967 were in countries with more than US$ 200 per capita annual income (Annex Table 4). Subsequently, the income range of the borrowers widened and in 1970 and 1971 about 56% of the financing was in countries with more than US$ 200 per capita income. The trend to include countries with a more developed economy has led to increasingly complex education projects designed to meet the need of a diversified labor market in a larger monetary sector and it has often involved major reforms and innovations for the modernization of outdated systems.

So far 72% of the Bank's education financing has been in secondary education. About 23% has gone to universities and post-secondary education and 4% to adult training, while primary education directly (as contrasted to the indirect effect of teacher training) has received little more than 1% of the funds (Annex Table 5). The post-secondary non-university component has increased lately from 8% to 13% of the total. By curricula, general education, including pre-vocational options, comprises the most important project component both in number of student places provided and as a recipient of funds (Annex Table 5). The demand for general secondary education has, however, reached a saturation level in some developing countries during the last years, while important needs persist for teachers, technicians and engineers. Consequently, technical education and teacher training have received 48% of student places provided through the Bank projects in 1970 and 1971, as against a 28% average in the earlier period, while student places in general education are significantly reduced from 64% to 45% (Annex Table 6). The provision of student places for agricultural education has remained at 7-8% and most places have been in middle level agricultural institutes which have had a restricted enrollment and therefore a low output of graduates. Most agricultural graduates are being employed in government extension services and one of the reasons for the low output is insufficient budget allocations for such services leading to limited employment capacity.

As mentioned, Bank education projects have often made significant contributions to educational system building. Practical and pre-vocational subjects have been introduced in the general secondary education curricula on an equal basis with academic subjects in 21 countries. Science teaching has been strengthened and the ratio of science graduates to arts graduates will now be compatible with the market demand in countries such as Colombia and Uganda. The inclusion of curriculum reform studies in recent Kenya and Iran projects will hopefully lead to the practice of continuing reform similar to that in more advanced countries. The instructional television in the Ivory Coast project which is being introduced in the formal education system will be designed to constitute an integral part of the student's learning process as routine as the use of textbooks. The Bank's insistence on having full-time teachers in the Bank-financed schools is intended to discourage the unsatisfactory part-time teaching tradition which is so prevalent in Latin America. It should be said that it is still too early to assess finally the outcome of the above reforms.

Reflecting the Bank policy of relying on other agencies as the primary source for technical assistance in education, the Bank-financed technical assistance component has always been small and amounts to only 5% of the loans. The number of projects which include Bank-financed technical assistance is, however, increasing. Thirty percent of the projects approved in 1963-1967 contained a technical assistance component, while 90% of the 1970-1971 projects do.

Disregarding the small technical assistance component, two-thirds of the loans have been for construction of physical buildings and one-third for provision of equipment (Annex Table 5). Therefore, much attention has been given to the refinement of costing techniques in appraising the physical aspects of projects and improving cost planning measures in implementation of projects. As a result, norms for school construction and basic equipment lists for a variety of types and levels of schools have been developed. A recent preliminary study on unit costs in education projects should also prove useful in our future activities, even though firm conclusions cannot be drawn at this stage due to the slender data base (Annex Table 7).

With increased emphasis on technical education, the equipment component has increased and, consequently, the demand for foreign currency. The main reason for a drop in local currency financing from 40% of the amount of the loans in 1964-1968 to an estimated 18% in 1969-1973 is, however, increased financing of education in relatively more developed countries.

Annex Table 8 contains a complete list of education loans by country, type of project and amount as of July 1, 1971.

Organization, Procedures and Criteria

The organization, procedures and criteria for educational project financing by the Bank are the result of several main factors, from which have developed the length and pattern of the project cycle, the size and composition of educational projects, patterns of disbursement, and various other characteristics of financing in this sector.

Probably the most important of these factors is the character of the sector itself as described in the previous section. The education sector is made up of many elements which interact organically through their effect on the development of human resources and their common dependence on limited sources of revenue as well as on each other. In its organic aspect education is not entirely different from other infrastructure sectors, such as transportation, where intersectoral re-

268

lations and the "investment mix" are of basic importance. In its economic character, however, it does differ from these sectors in one or another respect. Not only is it not directly revenue producing; in the present state of our knowledge, its economic return is not accurately measurable. Moreover, educational investment carries with it an unusually high rate of commitment of recurrent expenditures by the government—perhaps 30 cents per year for each dollar invested. In determining project size and composition, therefore, the recurrent cost commitment rather than the investment cost is often the determining factor.

We have noted other constraints which may also limit the number of new student places which should be created at a given time—the ability of the labor market to absorb persons with different types and levels of training, the availability of qualified teachers and the need for curriculum, structural or management reforms. It is therefore necessary to view the sector as a whole, within the country's development as a whole, and put together an investment package which, at any given time, will help to meet that country's needs in a balanced and economical way without overcommitment of scarce resources.

In addition, even where agreement exists upon educational objectives and needs, there is far less objective and technical consensus upon how to meet those needs than exists in other sectors. In most sectors development assistance is essentially a process of selecting and applying proven technologies which have reasonably predictable results. The results of educational technology even in the advanced countries are difficult to predict and its relation to development is only beginning to be studied.

Our organization and procedures have been strongly influenced by the Bank/Unesco Cooperative Program established in 1964, very early in the Bank's history of educational financing. The program provides for cooperation by the Bank and Unesco in assisting member countries to identify and prepare projects for Bank consideration and in appraising, supervising and, when requested by the country, providing the technical assistance component of such projects. Under the agreement Unesco has "primary responsibility" for assisting countries in project identification and preparation, which it exercises through a separate Educational Financing Division, devoted exclusively to Bank project work. In 1969-71 this unit assisted borrowers in identifying 65% and preparing 80% of the Bank projects.

In the original agreement no provision was made for cost-sharing or other cooperation with respect to services that are closely related to project identification and preparation, such as educational planning, and which might therefore more directly contribute to the efficiency of our operations. During the past year the Cooperative Program has been expanded to provide services of this kind, to be made available by Unesco's Division of Educational Planning and Administration and by its Department of School and Higher Education. These services will include the provision of country education profiles which should help to increase our knowledge of the requirements of this sector.

What then have been the most important practical effects of these factors upon the Bank's organization and procedures for educational financing?

(a) Reflecting its traditional role, the Bank has concentrated upon capital financing and has relied upon the cooperation of other agencies to provide the technical assistance related to the educational and institution building objectives of Bank-financed projects. About 90% of such projects have involved necessary technical assistance from bilateral or other multilateral sources. The Bank will continue to seek such cooperation. However, greater attention by governments to improving the quality and efficiency of their education will require, in the short run, larger inputs of technical assistance. The expanding volume of Bank activity has also, in some cases, exceeded the immediate funding ability of other sources of technical assistance. In such cases we have provided the financing through our loans, while other agencies, at the borrower's request, have arranged for the services.

(b) Educational project identification has depended from the beginning upon comprehensive reviews of the sector which could establish some relative order of priorities—quantitative and qualitative. These sector reviews have been carried on in some cases as parts of the Bank's economic surveys and more often under the Bank/Unesco Cooperative Program by Unesco project identification missions. Unesco identification reports have been useful to both the borrower and the Bank. While they vary in scope and depth and until recently have been largely confined to formal education, they have provided a valuable pilot exercise and example in project identification through a sector approach.

(c) Because of the constraints mentioned earlier and despite the packaging of a number of items in one project, the size of our education loans has been small in comparison with most other sectors. They have ranged from US$ 1.5 million to US$ 20 million and have averaged US$ 7.6 million. The packaging process has also called for larger than ordinary missions made up of a number of specialists. Preparation and appraisal missions, for example, require a number of specialized educators—general, agricultural, technical—as well as an architect and an economist.

WORLD BANK EDUCATION POLICIES AND OPERATIONS IN THE 1970s

Possible New Areas of Lending

Bank policies and lending operations have been adjusted in response to the trends in educational development described above. This adjustment will continue, but changes in the pattern of our lending will be gradual rather than radical. During the next five years the established areas of lending—technical, agricultural, teacher training and improved general secondary—will continue to provide the bulk of our projects. Particular attention will be paid to agriculture and to the close tie between the agricultural training, the agricultural extension activities and the application of agricultural research. We expect also to increase our activity in some areas where we have only recently begun, such as management training, and also to initiate lending in some wholly new areas. Our new and increased activities are likely to fall in the four interrelated areas mentioned above, i.e. the search for less costly education through non-formal training; more efficient and productive education by means of curriculum reform and the coordinated use of new technologies such as radio, television, programmed learning and related teaching materials; exploration of new sources of finance; and management studies to improve the planning and control of educational systems.

(a) Non-formal education and training

As indicated above, the vast numbers of uneducated and miseducated young and older people in the less developed countries, principally in the rural areas, will constitute a major challenge to development for several decades to come. It is true that universal primary education in the 1980s is a major educational policy objective in many developing countries. There is, however, a long way to go before the goal is reached as 46% of the age groups in the developing world are still left outside the formal education system. An illustrative case is East Africa where about 70% of the new entrants to the labor force have had either unfinished primary education courses or no primary education at all. Most of those 70% will remain in the labor force in the year 2000 as unskilled, illiterate subsistence farmers or as equally unskilled, semi-employed urban dwellers, unless major efforts are made to provide non-formal training opportunities. The Bank is therefore concerned to find alternatives to formal primary education and this will include suitable forms of functional literacy programs. The Bank has supported a few projects in non-formal education, notably farmer training centers in Kenya and Tanzania, mobile training units in Somalia and Tanzania and an industrial training scheme in Chile, and we are supporting accelerated vocational training centers in a number of countries. We have also commissioned a research study designed to discover other types of non-formal education which might be assisted by the Bank. We expect therefore that the next five years will see a significant expansion of the Bank's activity in this area and two main categories of programs are envisaged: (a) for children and youth outside the formal system, (b) for adults. The objective and content of those two programs would be similar but the teaching methods, structure and financing would differ. The new mass communication media may have a very high potential for non-formal education.

(b) Educational radio and television

Prudently used as an integral part of the education system, these media can be highly effective in the introduction of new curricula, in upgrading of teachers and in the most efficient use of the best teachers for the mass of students. They do not hold out the promise of lower costs per student but because they can be highly effective innovating forces they can, in some cases, provide a much greater educational return for a moderate increase in expenditure.

Two educational television projects which the Bank has considered —in the Ivory Coast and Niger—bring out sharply the characteristics of this type of development and why the Bank should not rush headlong into it. In the Ivory Coast educational television is being introduced as part of a multi-faceted program of curriculum reform, pre-service teacher training and in-service teacher upgrading. Existing transmission facilities will be used, obviating the need for major investment for transmission, and the expected number of students and teachers to be reached constitutes a sufficiently large market to keep unit costs at an acceptable level. In Niger most of these favorable circumstances do not exist. Although an experimental project in television for 20 classrooms in the city of Niamey had success in exploring new teaching techniques and reducing dropouts, expansion of the project for the education system as a whole would require substantial capital and operating expenditure for a small and widely dispersed market which will not be economically justifiable for some years to come.

A serious danger in educational television is that hardware installation will precede the program planning and production, organization and teacher training and equipment maintenance which are essential to the effective utilization of hardware. This danger is being heightened by the promotional efforts of suppliers and by the tendency of governments to view these media as easy short cuts to educational development, which makes them susceptible to high pressure salesmanship. Wherever it participates in these projects the Bank will exert a counter influence to the emphasis on hardware.

(c) Programmed learning

Programmed learning is a method of organizing the content of a course in progressive steps so as to permit a student to proceed at his own speed with a minimum of guidance by the teacher. It is being used in a number of ways in advanced countries, primarily as a means of freeing the quicker and the slower students from the lock-step pace required for an average class. In the advanced countries programmed learning has often been associated with a high degree of mechanization and automation. Therefore, it has been considered inappropriate for developing countries. Recent research and experience, partly through a Unesco project in Lebanon, indicate that the educational benefits of programmed learning can be delivered through inexpensive workbooks. There may be equally important financial benefits. Although programmed learning requires a substantial investment at the outset for programming and other start-up costs, it promises to reduce the recurrent costs of instruction by allowing higher student:teacher ratios. If applied on a wide scale, this approach conceivably could ease the financial burden of education in many developing countries. Thus, programmed learning might lend itself well to Bank financing, especially in more populous nations.

(d) Teaching materials and equipment

A better and cheaper supply of locally produced textbooks and simple teaching equipment is another of the needs in many developing countries. It should be emphasized that successful production of teaching materials requires more than printing facilities and workshops. A major effort of this kind requires, first, an appropriate curriculum and course syllabi for which teaching aids are to be prepared. On the production side, consideration must be given to the selection and training of textbook authors, equipment designers and audiovisual materials producers. On the consumption side, a market and marketing procedures must be established. In some developing countries it appears that most of these prerequisite conditions exist and that Bank initiative and assistance could provide the catalyst for the solution of a major problem. In a recent loan to Turkey, for example, assistance has been provided to expand and improve an existing center for local production of inexpensive science teaching equipment which will in future reduce the country's dependence on costly, often unsuitable, imported equipment. Although in many countries, it may require time to prepare the way for this kind of development, this type of lending may be expected to increase during the next five to 10 years.

(e) Business administration and management

Only a few institutions in the developing world offer training in business administration and management. A rapid industrialization in some countries, an important development of export and import trades in others, and a replacement of expatriates by nationals in private and public enterprises in most of the former colonies have increased the demand for skilled middle level and high level managers. The Bank expects therefore to finance formal as well as nonformal training institutions in business administration and management, of which the Institute of Management in the aforementioned Turkish loan provides the first example.

(f) Management of education systems

As indicated throughout this paper, perhaps the most pervasive weakness of the education systems is their management. We have already financed within a number of projects the creation or strengthening of educational planning units and we propose now to broaden this approach to include improvement of the full range of management functions at national and provincial levels as well as in the individual schools. This involves the training of supervisors, school principals and other administrative personnel in planning, scheduling, budget and accounting techniques, etc. This type of assistance is appropriate for the Bank and would bring important benefits to whole educational systems.

Project Design, Sector Analysis and Project Sequence

Of major concern in the design of education projects for Bank financing is the need to make education and training systems more responsive to the borrowing country's economic and social needs. The ill-adapted and costly nature of existing education systems, the persistent imbalances between demand and supply in the labor market and the severe limitations of financial and human resources often require fundamental and broad reforms. Projects should therefore not be designed exclusively in terms of meeting manpower needs by expanding and improving specific sectors of the education and training system but should also engender such reforms. While continuing its policy to finance educational investment designed to meet the borrowing country's immediate and most pressing manpower needs, the Bank will encourage more long-term, comprehensive and incisive objectives. Projects will, more and more, be selected on the basis of a thorough examination of the education system as a whole and as part of well designed, comprehensive education plans and reform measures. In some cases this may require projects of longer duration —perhaps eight years for the working out of institutional changes. In other cases we might finance long-term educational programs through repeater projects planned in advance to implement successive stages of the program.

The sector approach was applied at an early stage of the Unesco/Bank Cooperative Program but the methods have varied and will vary depending on the circumstances and on our knowledge of the specific country's education system. Any program of action must furthermore distinguish between:

—sector analysis with the limited objective of serving as a basis for Bank operations only; and

—sector analysis with the widest possible objective of offering solutions to basic national policy issues.

In the first instance our analysis may be based on a number of sources: information gathered through previous Bank projects, Bank economic missions, preinvestment studies, Bank in-depth reconnaissance missions, Unesco and FAO project identification missions, Unesco's collection of country data, reports from bilateral and private agencies, etc. In the second case the in-depth analysis must heavily involve the government of the country if it is to be successful and lead to appropriate follow-up actions. The exercise might be financed through a UNDP grant, a Bank loan or other means. A recent study in the Philippines and forthcoming sector studies in Ethiopia and Northeast Brazil exemplify such comprehensive in-depth analysis.

In order to come to grips at an early stage with the complex problems of an in-depth examination of the education systems and of projects of longer duration as described above, the Bank staff expects to devote more time to sector analysis and other pre-appraisal work.

Projections of Lending Operations in FY 1972-1976

Our projections for the five-year period 1972-1976 envisage the financing of some 80 projects in 56 countries and a total lending of about US$ 800 million. (See Annex Table 10.)

A comparison between the actual and projected lending during the five-year periods of 1964-1968, 1969-1973 and 1972-1976 is shown below:

	FY 1964-1968	FY 1969-1973	FY 1972-1976
Aggregate number of projects	21	64	80
Total lending (US$ million)	157	610	800
Total project cost (US$ million)	266	1000	1400

Analysis of loans by country categories

The content of the projected lending will of course reflect many factors including, most importantly, the borrowers' own investment priorities. On the basis of the approach to educational financing outlined in the earlier sections of this paper, however, the pattern of the Bank's educational financing might be expected to consist of four broad categories of loans.

(a) About 35 loans at $3-6 million each for projects in smaller countries—many of them new borrowers. The projects would form packages of differing items with the objective of meeting overall quantitative as well as qualitative manpower demands. General secondary education of an improved type might be a project item, together with expansion of technical and agricultural education and teacher training. In the poorer countries projects in non-formal education would have a high priority. Construction of physical facilities would continue to form an important part of the projects. Technical assistance for planning, improvement of management and project implementation will often be necessary.

(b) About 30 loans of $7-10 million each to medium-sized countries, for the most part where the Bank has previously been active. In some of these countries, as previously explained, further expansion of the general secondary education system may be questionable because of low employment demand and financial constraints. Projects would be more concerned with qualitative improvements or with special sectors of the education system, such as rural education, use of new media and non-formal vocational training, which would require substantial technical assistance. In many of these countries the strengthening of planning and management capability is urgent.

(c) About 10 loans of $15-25 million each to countries with large populations. Because of the size of these countries and, in most cases, their federal structure, individual Bank projects would probably not attempt to finance large-scale national building programs or comprehensive education reforms intended to cover all important aspects of, e.g., secondary education. To achieve impact our lending would have to concentrate on three major types of projects. One type of loan might finance country-wide projects in instructional radio or television, programmed learning and production of teaching materials. Such projects require a large market of the type available in populous countries to justify the investment. The second type of loan might go to construction of institutions related to specific parts of the labor market such as teacher training schools, polytechnic colleges, agricultural institutes or farmer training centers. The third type might involve the financing of diversified education projects in specific states or provinces with particularly urgent needs.

(d) About 5 loans of $10-20 million each (or in some cases considerably more) to less developed European countries. Countries which see their future within the framework of a common market, urgently need to bring their education and training systems up to the standards of other European countries. Bank lending for this group would point towards rationalizing and modernizing education in the interest of economy and greater output of qualified workers and managers.

Analysis of loans by mode and outlay

A further analysis by mode and outlay of the above lending indicates that more than one million new or improved student places might be provided through the Bank-financed projects. Approximately 60% of those places might be in technical and agricultural education and in teacher training, compared with 42% in the past, while the number of places in general education might be reduced from 58% to 40% of the total. The shares of the lending for non-formal education and for technical assistance might increase from current 4% and 5% to approximately 15% and 10%.

Research and Project Evaluation

Useful research is being undertaken outside the Bank which needs evaluation and adaptation to our operational needs. Within the Bank, a case study of cost-benefit analysis in education (Kenya) and a recent survey of educational financing methods have helped to clarify significant questions involved in our operations. Ongoing studies are: a case study of the external and internal performance of a secondary education system, the use of education planning models and a study of student loan fund schemes. A contract was signed recently between the Bank and the International Council for Educational Development (ICED) under which the latter is undertaking an assessment of existing experience in non-formal education for rural development. ICED is conducting this research with substantial cooperation by Unesco, FAO, ILO and a number of bilateral and private agencies.

A plan for future research, developed last year, covers a wide range of important topics. Important new areas of research which are proposed, in addition to the ongoing studies mentioned above, are:

—evaluation of the functioning of labor markets in developing countries;

—cost/effectiveness of alternative learning technologies;

—improved techniques for project implementation and evaluation.

The proposed labor market study would investigate existing patterns of recruitment, employment, utilization and in-service training of educated and trained manpower in developing countries in the context of existing labor market characteristics: systems of wages and salaries, hiring and in-service training practices, employers' criteria for employment, information deficiencies, job preferences, labor (im)mobility. The objective would be to identify labor market factors which prevent the effective utilization of the output of the education and training system for productive employment. The study would thus form a segment in our knowledge of the design of education for economic development and supplement the manpower forecasting technique used so far. The weaknesses of manpower forecasting are well known and the proposed study would deal with at least one of these weaknesses: that training for correctly assessed manpower needs does not guarantee that students will ultimately be employed in the fields for which they were trained.

Two major technologies are currently used in vocational education: training in vocational schools and on-the-job (in-plant) training. The Bank has so far financed the first category although it has been increasingly felt that the second category might also merit Bank support. In relation to such support the cost effectiveness of the two tech-

278

nologies should be studied and compared. Such comparison would also cover the different teaching methods used, particularly programmed learning, which was originally developed for vocational training and has been widely used in industry, the military services, etc.

Considerably more attention will be given to the evaluation of Bank projects than was possible in the past. This is not only because more of our projects will have become operational in the near future but also because of growing awareness of the need to integrate evaluation mechanisms into the process of project implementation. So far, our practice has been to postpone evaluation until a project has been completed and has become fully operational. To measure the full educational effect of a project as much as eight years may have to pass after its inception. In many cases, however, certain elements of a project (e.g. the results of technical assistance, the training of teachers and other staff) could be subjected to evaluation at an earlier stage. Continuous feed-back of information in the stage of implementation could provide early warnings about the need for project modifications. The proposed third major research project would thus provide the Bank with a methodology to evaluate the education projects of the 1960s and define the frames of reference necessary for a proper and continuous evaluation of future projects.

CONCLUSIONS

A deeper and more continuous dialogue between the Bank and the borrower is necessary if we are to encourage in the borrower a greater willingness to reform and innovate and if we want to succeed with the projected financing of education as indicated in this paper. On the Bank side, more intensive sector analysis, particularly with a longer time perspective, can improve the Bank's understanding of the sector and the credibility of its advice. On the borrower's side, improvement in management and planning practices should lead to a better appreciation of priorities and readier availability of soundly conceived projects. Unesco's present effort to strengthen its planning services for member countries should contribute to this end as well as financial assistance for planning and management analysis for which the Bank has begun to provide financing in selected cases. In all these activities the prime objective is to develop local capability and self reliance.

From this combination of factors, we hope to develop a better basic strategy agreed between the Bank and the borrower within which we can identify a phased sequence of projects covering a period of up to

10 years. In this phased sequence we would expect to find capital and technical assistance financing interspersed so as to constitute a rational and orderly application of resources for development of the sector.

Although we anticipate that the volume of Bank lending will continue to increase rapidly as it has done since 1968, it is a major point of this paper that the success of the Bank's efforts in the education field is not to be measured primarily by the amount of money we lend but rather by the effectiveness with which Bank and country resources are deployed to meet crucial needs. We expect the Bank to become the largest financer of educational assistance and to continue in most cases to finance projects of such size that a qualitative and quantitative impact is secured. However, since all external assistance to education will probably continue to be less than 10% of total expenditure by developing countries, the motivating and multiplying effects of external assistance will be the principal test of success.

Enrollment Growth Rates by Educational Levels and Regions
(1960-1966)

Number of Pupils (Thousands)

	1960/61 Academic Year				1966/67 Academic Year				Percentage of Increase 1960-1966			
	1st Level	2nd Level	3rd Level	Total	1st Level	2nd Level	3rd Level	Total	1st Level	2nd Level	3rd Level	Total
Africa	18,931	2,115	192	21,238	26,748	3,893	334	30,975	+41	+84	+73	+45
Latin America	26,973	3,885	567	31,425	36,653	7,468	978	45,099	+36	+94	+72	+45
Asia [1]	74,645	12,186	1,432	88,261	111,986	21,421	2,911	136,300	+50	+76	+103	+54
DEVELOPING COUNTRIES	120,549	18,186	2,191	140,924	175,387	32,782	4,223	212,374	+42	+80	+93	+51
WORLD	248,486	63,927	11,174	323,587	311,700	96,713	19,992	428,405	+25	+51	+79	+32

Note: Figures may not total due to rounding.
[1] Excluding Japan, Mainland China, North Korea and North Viet-Nam.
Source: Office of Statistics, Unesco.

Comparative Enrollment Ratios at First and Second Levels 1967/68

(Percentage)

	Enrollment Rates of Primary School Age Population[1]	Enrollment Rates of Secondary School Age Population	Combined Primary and Secondary Enrollment Rates[1]
Africa	40	15	28
North America	98	92	96
Latin America	75	35	55
Asia [2]	55	30	45
Europe and USSR	97	65	85
Oceania	95	30	67
(Arab Countries)	(50)	(25)	(38)
TOTAL DEVELOPING COUNTRIES	54	23	44
WORLD	68	40	56

[1] Regardless of the School they attend. [2] Excluding Mainland China, North Korea and North Viet-Nam.
Source: Estimates of the Office of Statistics, Unesco.

281

Inefficiency in Primary Education

	Years to produce Primary School Graduates		Primary Education Expenditures spent on Students who drop out in Grades 1, 2, or 3 (Percentage of Total)
	Ideal	Actual	
Latin America			
Venezuela	6	10	19
El Salvador	6	15	37
Africa			
Ethiopia	6	14	32
Ivory Coast	6	12.5	21
Kenya	7	8	6
Asia			
Malaysia (East)	6	7	4
Ceylon	7	10.5	10

Source: Bank Economic and Education Appraisal Reports.

Table 3

Public Expenditure on Education as a Percentage of the Budget and National Income 1960 and 1965

	1960		1965		1960		1965	
	Percentage of Budget	Number of Countries[1]	Percentage of Budget	Number of Countries[1]	Percentage of National Income	Number of Countries	Percentage of National Income	Number of Countries
Africa	14.5	23	16.4	36	3.0	21	4.3	22
America, North	15.6	10	17.6	18	3.9	15	4.1	14
America, South	12.6	7	15.4	10	3.1	11	4.0	11
Asia	11.8	17	13.2	28	3.3	16	4.0	16
Europe and								
USSR	13.5	13	15.0	23	4.2	25	5.3	24
Oceania	10.4	4	15.7	10	3.7	2	4.4	2
WORLD	13.5	74	15.5	125	3.6	90	4.5	89

[1] Including territories.

Source: Unesco questionnaire on statistics of educational finance and expenditure.
F. Edding, *International Developments of Educational Expenditures 1950-1965,* Unesco.

World Bank/IDA: Education Loans by GDP/Capita at Time of Loan
FY 1963-1971

GDP/Capita at Factor Cost	Number of Loans									Total	Millions $	
	63	64	65	66	67	68	69	70	71		Total Amount	Average Size
Below $100		3	2	2	1	1	2		4	15	101.2	6.7
$100 - 200	1		1	1	4	1	1	4	3	16	118.9	7.4
200 - 299							1	2	2	3	8	59.6	7.5
300 - 399						2	4	2	2	10	82.3	8.2
400 - 499				1	1			2		4	20.75	5.2
500 - 599									1	1	13.5	13.5
600 - 699												
700 - 799												
800 - 899							1	1	1	3	35.2	11.7
900 - 999												
1,000 +												
Total Number	1	3	3	4	6	5	10	11	14	57	431.45	7.6
Total Amount	5.0	17.6	29.5	33.95	51.8	24.2	81.8	79.9	107.7	431.45		
Average Size	5.0	5.9	9.8	8.5	8.6	4.8	8.2	7.3	7.7	7.6		

Analysis of World Bank/IDA Education Lending
Table 5
FY 1963-1971

A. **By Levels**

	Million US$	Percentage
Primary	4.90	1.1
Secondary	309.65	71.8
Post-Secondary	56.08	13.0
University	43.24	10.0
Adult Training	17.58	4.1
Total	431.45	100.0

B. **By Curricula**

	Million US$	Percentage
General[1]	190.77	44.1
Technical[2]	126.48	29.3
Agricultural	63.03	14.7
Teacher Training	51.17	11.9
Total	431.45	100.0

C. **By Outlay**

	Million US$	Percentage
Construction	262.17	60.8
Equipment	148.16	34.3
Technical Assistance	21.12	4.9
Total	431.45	100.0

[1] Includes comprehensive education
[2] Includes industrial and commercial

283

World Bank/IDA Education Projects, FY 1963-1971
Student Places Provided or Improved

No. Student Places Provided or Improved	1963-1969 Number	%	1970-1971 Number	%	1963-1971 Number	%
General and Comprehensive	433,000	64	120,000	45	553,000	58
Technical	159,000	24	91,000	34	250,000	27
Agricultural	55,000	8	18,000	7	73,000	8
Teacher Training	30,000	4	36,000	14	66,000	7
Total	677,000	100	265,000	100	942,000	100

Boarding Places and Staff Housing

	1963-69	1970-71	1963-71
Number of Boarding Places Provided	82,000	35,600	117,600
Boarding Places as % of Total Places Provided	12	13.4	12
Total Education Project Costs (US$ Millions)	429	245	674
Total Cost of Boarding and Staff Housing	100	38	138
Cost of Boarding and Staff Housing as a % of Total Project Costs	23	16	20

World Bank/IDA Education Projects
Cost of Physical Facilities per Student
(Median Cost—US$)

	Primary	Secondary General and Teacher Training	Secondary Agricultural, Technical and Vocational	Post Secondary General and Teacher Training	Post Secondary Technical and Vocational	Adult Education	Secondary	Post Secondary	Staff Housing
			Academic and Communal				Boarding Facilities		
Sample Size									
(No. Institutions)	31	161	30	27	14	11			
Construction									
Cost/Student	365	475	641	661	1381	1164	538	1116	—
Furniture									
Cost/Student	39	58	46	81	96	62	86	123	—
Equipment									
Cost/Student	50	110	829	241	906	1073	—	—	—
Total Cost/Student	450	648	1400	1047	2416	2318	652	1258	14,283

285

World Bank/IDA Education Projects   Approved as of July 1, 1971

Fiscal Year	Country	Main Purpose	Total Project Cost	Amount of Loan (US$ Million) Bank	IDA
1963	1. Tunisia I	Secondary General, Technical and Teacher Training	9.2		5.0
1964	2. Tanzania I	Secondary General	6.0		4.6
	3. Pakistan I	University Agricultural, Post-Secondary Technical and Teacher Training (T.A.)	9.0		4.5
	4. Pakistan II	University Agricultural, Post-Secondary Technical and Teacher Training (T.A.)	17.0		8.5
1965	5. Philippines	University Agricultural	11.7	6.0	
	6. Afghanistan	Secondary Technical, Agricultural and Teacher Training (T.A.)	4.7		3.5
	7. Nigeria	Secondary General, Technical, Adult and Teacher Training	30.0		20.0
1966	8. Chile I	Adult Training	3.8	2.75	
	9. Morocco	Secondary General, Technical and Agricultural	16.2		11.0
	10. Ethiopia	Secondary General, Technical and Teacher Training	10.7		7.2
	11. Pakistan III	University Agricultural and Post-Secondary Technical (T.A.)	21.7		13.0
1967	12. Kenya I	Secondary General, Technical and Teacher Training	9.7		7.0
	13. Tunisia II	Secondary General and Agricultural	19.8		13.0
	14. Jamaica	Secondary General, Post-Secondary Agricultural, Technical, Adult and Teacher Training (T.A.)	19.4	9.5	
	15. Thailand	Secondary Technical and Agricultural (T.A.)	21.0	6.0	
	16. Uganda	Secondary General	14.3		10.0
	17. Malawi	Secondary General and Teacher Training	7.0		6.3
1968	18. Malagasy	Secondary General, Technical and Teacher Training	7.2	4.8	
	19. Nicaragua	Secondary General and Teacher Training	8.0	4.0	
	20. Gabon	Secondary General and Teacher Training	3.6	1.8	
	21. Sudan	Secondary General, Post-Secondary Agricultural and Teacher Training (T.A.)	15.4		8.5
	22. Ecuador	Secondary General, Agricultural and Technical and Teacher Training (T.A.)	10.2		5.1
1969	23. Colombia I	Secondary General	15.2	7.6	
	24. Chad	Secondary Agricultural and Teacher Training (T.A.)	2.1		1.8
	25. Trinidad and Tobago	Secondary General and Teacher Training	18.8	9.4	
	26. Guatemala	Secondary General, Post-Secondary Agricultural and Teacher Training	12.6	6.3	
	27. Guyana	Secondary General and Teacher Training (T.A.)	10.0	2.9	2.9
	28. Zambia I	Secondary General, Technical and Teacher Training	36.2	17.4	
	29. Malaysia	Secondary General, Technical, Agricultural and Teacher Training	16.4	8.8	
	30. Tanzania II	Secondary General and Teacher Training	7.2		5.0
	31. Korea	Secondary and Post-Secondary Agricultural and Technical (T.A.)	26.8		14.8
	32. El Salvador	Secondary General, Technical and Post-Secondary Agricultural (T.A.)	8.4	4.9	

Fiscal Year	Country	Main Purpose	Total Project Cost	Amount of Loan (US$ Million) Bank	IDA
1970	33. Cameroon	Secondary General, Technical, Agricultural and Adult and Teacher Training (T.A.)	14.0		10.5
	34. Zambia II	University Technical and Teacher Training	7.4	5.3	
	35. Sierra Leone	Secondary General, Technical and Teacher Training (T.A.)	4.5		3.0
	36. Chile II	Adult Industrial and Agricultural Training	3.0	1.5	
	37. Ivory Coast	Primary, Secondary General, Technical, Post-Secondary Technical, Agricultural and Adult and Teacher Training(T.A.)	19.1	11.0	
	38. Chile III	Secondary Agricultural and Teacher Training (T.A.)	14.0	7.0	
	39. Kenya II	Secondary Technical, University Agricultural and Adult and Teacher Training (T.A.)	9.3		6.1
	40. Colombia II	Secondary General (T.A.)	13.0	6.5	
	41. China	Secondary and Post-Secondary Technical and Agricultural and Teacher Training (T.A.)	15.0	9.0	
	42. Pakistan IV	University Technical (T.A.)	12.8		8.0
	43. Spain	Primary, Secondary General and Teacher Training (T.A.)	24.0	12.0	
1971	44. Iran	Primary, Secondary General, Technical and Agricultural; Teacher Training; and University (education) (T.A.)	41.7	19.0	
	45. Indonesia	Secondary Technical (T.A.)	7.6		4.6
	46. Greece	Post-Secondary Technical (T.A.)	24.0	13.8	
	47. Dominican Republic	Secondary General and Teacher Training (T.A.)	8.1		4.0
	48. Tanzania III	Non-Formal Rural Training and Post-Secondary Agricultural (T.A.)	4.7		3.3
	49. Jamaica II	General Secondary; Teacher Training; Vocational Training; ITV (T.A.)	28.2	13.5	
	50. Congo (B)	Secondary General and Technical Teacher Training; Non-Formal Rural Education (T.A.)	4.1		3.5
	51. Ethiopia II	Secondary General and Secondary Technical and Agricultural	13.4		9.5
	52. Brazil	Secondary Technical and Agricultural, Post-Secondary Technical (T.A.)	21.0	8.4	
	53. Chad II	Secondary Technical and Agricultural	3.1		2.2
	54. Somalia	Secondary General, Technical; Teacher Training and Non-Formal Agriculture (T.A.)	3.7		3.3
	55. Turkey	Secondary and Post-Secondary Technical; Technical Teacher Training; Non-Formal Management and Adult Technical Training; Science Equipment Production; Mass Media (T.A.)	17.9	13.5	
	56. Senegal	Secondary General and Secondary Technical and Agricultural	2.3		1.8
	57. Uganda II	Secondary General and Technical; Post-Secondary and Non-Formal Agricultural; Health and Medical Training (T.A.)	10.4		7.3
		TOTAL	755.6	212.65	218.8
				431.45	

Explanatory Notes:
"Secondary General" = Includes Comprehensive and Pre-vocational Courses
"Technical"   = Includes Industrial and Commercial
"(T.A.)"   = Technical Assistance

287

Comparative Education Indicators

Comparative education data are useful in the evaluation of various education systems and the analysis of relative stages of educational development between various countries. However, on the basis of the present data, cross-national comparisons should be approached with great caution. Data presented in the following table have been collected largely by the Bank missions from government sources; the remainder are staff estimates or data from Unesco. Efforts have been made to standardize definitions and, within limits, to check the accuracy of the data. Nevertheless, such data are still imperfect in several respects and the Bank is working to improve them progressively on the occasion of its operational work. In the use of these data the following qualifications should be borne in mind:

1. "Education" as defined in the table includes all education and training, formal and non-formal;

2. "Primary" education refers to education at the first level and "secondary" education refers to all education at the secondary level regardless of type (e.g. general, technical, agricultural);

3. "Vocational" education (Col. 10) includes enrollments in technical, commercial, agricultural, vocational and home-economic courses;

4. "Literacy rates" (Col. 3) are usually obtained from country censuses. In many countries they are only approximations and it is doubtful that any uniform definition of "literate" has been followed consistently;

5. "Public expenditure in education" (Columns 4 and 6) refers to all capital and recurrent expenditures devoted to education by public and quasi-public agencies;

6. "Enrollment ratios" (Columns 7 and 9) refer to school year and mean the percentage of eligible children enrolled full-time in the appropriate school, public and private by level. They are often subject to a wide margin of error in the developing countries owing to variations in the accuracy of basic data (i.e. age-specific population and enrollments). Enrollment figures frequently are higher than the number of students actually in school. Overage students whose inclusion is indicated by footnotes also can inflate the ratios.

	Year	Population (Millions) (1)	GNP/Capita at factor cost (Constant 1968 US$) (2)	Literacy Rate (% of Adults) (3)	Public Educ. Expenditures per Capita (Market Prices US$) (4)
ADVANCED					
Austria	1969	7.4	1,498 F	99	73
Canada	1969	21.2	2,420 F	91	265 C
Germany, Fed. Rep.	1968	60.8 E	2,315 F	99	85
Japan	1969	102.3	1,505 F	99	50 C
Netherlands	1968	12.9 E	1,730 F	99	154
New Zealand	1970	2.8 E	2,209	.	90 C
Norway	1969	3.9	2,064 F	99	153
Sweden	1969	8.0	2,884 F	99	250 D
United Kingdom	1969	55.5	1,831 F	97	94
U.S.A.	1968	203.2 E	4,000 F	98	228 C
Europe					
1. Greece	1969	8.7	855 F	82 C	23
2. Ireland	1969	2.9	1,067 F	98	58
3. Spain	1970	34.0	822	94 D	20
Africa					
4. Algeria	1970	13.1	266	25 B	35
5. Cameroon	1970	5.9	153	...	6
6. C.A.R.	1970	1.5	124	...	5
7. Chad	1970	3.6	90	7	3 D
8. Congo, Peop. Rep.	1970	0.9	221	50 ?	14
9. Ethiopia	1970	24.8	66	7	2
10. Gabon	1968	0.5 F	297 F	30 D?	11 C
11. Ghana	1970	8.5	184		13
12. Ivory Coast	1968	4.9 E	243 F	9 A	10
13. Kenya	1968	10.9 E	135 F	30	7
14. Liberia	1970	1.5	263	15	8
15. Morocco	1970	15.5	216	20	9
16. Nigeria	1971	68.0	104 F		3
17. Senegal	1969	3.8	195 F	10	11 P
18. Sierra Leone	1968	2.5 E	160 F	7 YA	4
19. Somalia	1971	2.8	49 D	5	1
20. Sudan	1968	15.8 G	100 F		4 A
21. Tanzania	1969	12.6	80 F	15 ?	3
22. Uganda	1970	9.5	123	25 A	6
23. Zaire	1970	18.5	94	13	8
24. Zambia	1968	4.0 E	262 F	41 A	20
C. America & Caribbean					
25. Dominican Republic	1968	4.0 E	274 F	55	6 E
26. El Salvador	1969	3.4	281 F	49 YA	10 BV
27. Guatemala	1968	5.0 E	343 F	38 YA	6 B
28. Jamaica	1969	1.9	535 F	86	24
29. Mexico	1970	48.4	605	76	18
30. Nicaragua	1969	1.9	389 F	53	10
31. Trinidad & Tobago	1971	1.0	836 F	90	40
South America					
32. Brazil	1969	92.3	272 F	65 D	10
33. Chile	1969	9.6	485 F	90	32
34. Colombia	1968	20.5 E	286 F	73 A	12
35. Ecuador	1968	5.9 E	238 F	68 A	8 V
36. Guyana	1968	0.7 E	327 F	83 A	15
37. Paraguay	1970	2.4	232	79	5
38. Venezuela	1970	10.8	986	81	45
Asia					
39. China (Taiwan)	1971	14.6	310 F	73	15
40. Indonesia	1970	124.2 G	113	43 A	2
41. Iran	1971	29.8	339 F	37	11
42. Iraq	1970	9.4	301	26	19
43. Jordan	1970	2.2	267	55 A	12
44. Korea	1970	31.5	219	85 B	8
45. Lebanon	1971	2.6 F	551 F	86 F	21 F
46. Malaysia	1970	11.0	340	89 B	17
47. Pakistan	1968	58.0	108 F		
48. Philippines	1971	39.4	195 F	72	6
49. Singapore	1970	2.1	843	75	30
50. Thailand	1971	37.6	158 F	70	8 V
51. Turkey	1969	34.5	340 F	49 A	9
SUMMARY FOR DEVELOPING COUNTRIES					
Number of Countries				45	50
Range				(5-98)	(1-58)
Quartiles: Upper				76	15
Median				50	10
Lower				25	6

Symbols:
. Data unavailable
— Magnitude nil or negligible
0 Magnitude less than half of unit employed
? Questionable

Notes: A = 1965 or before
B = 1966
C = 1967
D = 1968
E = 1969

F = 1970
G = 1971
M = Current Prices
N = G.D.P.
P = Including foreign aid

288

% of GNP Devoted to Educ. (Public Expenditures only) (5)	% of Total Public Expenditure Devoted to Education (6)	Primary Enrollment Ratio Net (7)	Primary Students per Teacher (8)	Secondary Enrollment Ratio Net (9)	% Secondary Enrollment in Vocational Schools (10)	Secondary Students per Teacher (Full-time equiv.) (11)	% Higher Enrollment in Agriculture and Engineering (12)	Annual Output from Higher Education per 100,000 Population (13)
4.3	9.9	99	24	46	60	12	24	77 B
7.2	19.6 C	99	26	51 YD	12	17	9	266
3.5	9.1	99	32	66 Y	52	22	25	145 C
3.9	20.5	99	26	90	20	21	21	308
7.0	23.3	99	31	64	50 C	20	20 C	204 A
4.4	14.3	99	32	71		19	21	189 B
5.5	18.8	99	23	82	22	16	15	64 C
7.1	14.6	99 D	16	75	34	11	10	180
5.8	13.8	98	28	58	5 C	18	16	188 B
4.8	15.1	97	26	80		20		515 C
2.2	11.7	99	33	53	16	31	17 D	90
4.8	11.4	95	33	54 YC	25	17	13 B	133 A
2.4	12.5 E	91	35	29	22 C	30	19	31 C
10.5	20.0	51	42	9	22	20	6	6
3.0	20.0	74 F	48	8	23	25	4	7
4.0	20.0	73 X	64	4 X	18	30	...	...
4.3 N	14.3 D	33	72	2	8	30	...	...
5.8	23.2	80 X	59	13	10	28	...	...
4.0 P	20.0	17	51	5	2	34	10	4
3.3 C	13.7 C	75	40 E	10	18	18 E	1	
4.7	21.7 Q	74	29	8	4	18	15 E	13 E
4.2 C	20.4	44	46	6	8	23		
6.3 V	18.4	65	32	8	2	22	29	5 A
3.7	11.7	50 X	31	12 X	6	16	12 C	9 C
4.1 N	17.4	54	35	12	3	22	3	7 A
3.2 N		34 X	37	4	18	23	16	6
3.5	20.1	43 X	46	8 X	27 B	25	2 C	8 A
2.9	19.5 C	32	30	13	7 C	25	17	7 C
	6.7 E	6	30	2	5	20	20	0 A
3.5 B	22.0 B	31 X	48 A	2 A	3 C	17 A	23 B	10 C
5.8 V	18.9	35	38 C	2	6 C	21 B	2	0 A
5.2 N	24.3 Q	46 EU	36 E	4 EU	11 E	21 E	10	5
5.7 N	19.0 E	78	44	8	20	24	10	2 B
6.2	15.0	84 X	56	11	5	22		2
2.9 F	17.0	80	56	17	1	26	10	16 C
3.0 B	25.4 CQ	63 C	31	15 C	32 E		15 C	7 A
2.5 B	17.6	43	38	6	22	26	10	6
4.4	19.1	86 X	52	43	9 A	19		11 A
2.6	17.1 Q	71	46	19	23 C	23	26 C	22
2.4	19.8	80	36	13	8	23	20 C	15
5.1	18.9	95	35	49	11	25	19	14
3.2	14.0	64	31	16	17		18 C	35 C
5.4	29.0 F	89	40	35	31	32 A	28 C	41 A
4.0	13.6 B	70	40	21	22 C	13	29 C	20 B
3.2 V	21.5 C	71	38	18	29 D	13 A	29 C	21 C
5.0	14.4	90 X	33 A	18 C	3 C	28	3 C	
2.2	6.3	89 X	26	17 X	5	15	12	12 A
4.9	22.0	80	33	35	32	22	18	59
4.2	19.0	98 F	52 F	50 F	16 F	35 F	27 F	179 F
	16.0	71 X	40	13 X	21	22	15 C	
3.1	10.8	62	33	23	3	34	23	41 F
6.1	16.3	64	22	25	3	26	17	80
4.4	9.8 Q	90	40	54 X	3	25	1	46
3.8	18.4	107 X	57	42 X	19	38	37	114 E
3.3	18.0	79	23 U	34	26	18	4	120
4.7	18.5 E	89 X	31	29 X	3	25	16	74
		45 X	35	15		38		
3.6	29.0	93	30	42	8	36	10	457
3.4	16.1	90	32	40	16	25	18	182
4.1 V	17.1	90 X	34	13 X	13	25	15	37
3.5	17.1	92 X	42	25 X	14	33	26	41
48	49	51	51	51	50	49	45	43
(1.4-6.3)	(6.3-29.0)	(6-107)	(22-72)	(2-54)	(1-32)	(13-38)	(1-38)	(0-457)
4.8	20.0	86	42	25	20	28	19	41
4.0	18.0	71	36	13	11	24	15	13
3.2	14.3	46	32	8	5	20	10	6

Q = Central government only
U = Public only
V = Including private expenditure
X = Including overage students
Y = Unesco sources

Sources: Columns (1) and (2) : World Tables (IBRD) Figures Provisional
Columns (3)—(9) & (11) : IBRD Missions
Columns (10), (12) & (13): Unesco Statistical Yearbook and IBRD Missions

Summary of World Bank Education Activities with Projection Through FY1976

	Actual			Program		Actual[1]		Program
	1969	1970	1971	1972	1973	1964-68	1969-73	1972-76
Sector Reviews[2]	—	2	2	2	2	—	8	14
Commitments ($ M.)	82	80	108	180	160	157	610	800
% Total IBRD/IDA	5	4	4	6	5	3	5	—
Number of Countries	10	10	14	14	15	19	52	56
Lending Operations	10	11	14	14	15	21	64	80
% Total IBRD/IDA	9	9	11	10	9	7	9	—
Projects under Supervision	24	31	42	56	68	11	44	76

[1] Including scheduled for FY1972-73.
[2] At the end of FY1968, the Bank had an adequate knowledge of the sector in 15 countries.

POPULATION PLANNING

POPULATION PLANNING
SECTOR WORKING PAPER

● This paper describes the Bank's efforts to help member countries reduce population growth rates and sets out its future program of activity in the field, as now envisaged.

To give perspective to this discussion, the paper also outlines the economic effects of reducing population growth in developing countries and summarizes available information on the global demographic situation, world population trends and projections, and the accomplishments and potential of family planning programs.

References to the Bank or the World Bank Group include the International Development Association (IDA) but not, for purposes of this paper, the International Finance Corporation (IFC). Money amounts are expressed in U.S. dollar equivalents. The Bank's fiscal year ends June 30.

INTRODUCTION

The purpose of economic development is to make possible higher living standards for individual men, women and children. A rising standard of living means a growing ability to afford both the material and non-material benefits which a modernized economy makes possible. For most people in most countries, however, the first requirements are more and better food, improved access to education and health care, and more opportunity for gainful employment.

Despite its limitations, one of the best available measures of economic progress toward these goals is the growth of per capita income. This is the growth of national income, adjusted for growth of population. Thus the relationship between the growth of a nation's income and that of its population is fundamental to the improvement of human welfare.

While neither the causes nor the effects in this relationship are fully understood, one central fact is clear: the higher the rate of population growth, the more difficult it is to raise per capita income. Today the world's population is growing much faster than at any time in history. This simple fact led the Pearson Commission to say, in 1969, that "No other phenomenon casts a darker shadow over the prospects for international development than the staggering growth of population."

The problems created by the large numbers and high growth rates of population concern both the world as a whole and individual countries. Both more and less developed countries confront such universal questions as the ultimate size of population the world can sustain and the rate at which the limit will be approached. The earth can undoubtedly support substantially more than the 3.6 billion people now living on it. But there is great doubt about its ability to sustain unlimited numbers at decent standards of living, which a majority do not have even now.

The World Bank's concern, however, is not with ultimate numbers, but with the developmental impact of population growth. Development does not mean more people, but higher living standards and greater welfare for however many there may be. The Bank entered the field chiefly because it became convinced that the attempt to raise living standards in a great many developing countries was being seriously undermined if not thwarted. The Bank has no fixed ideas as to how large the population of individual countries ought to be. But it is convinced that in the great majority of developing countries, the faster the rate of population growth, the slower will be the improvement of living standards. Within the last few years, the governments of more than 26 countries have indicated that they share this belief by adopting official policies to slow their population growth.

There is another important reason for the Bank's entry into the population field. It concerns human welfare, and particularly health. There is strong evidence that where children have been well spaced, both they and their mothers enjoy better health and experience lower mortality rates. It does not follow, of course, that parents will necessarily choose to space their children or to have fewer of them, if given the chance to do so.

Many governments feel, however, that people should be given the choice if it is possible to bring it to them, and the Bank is prepared to help them do so. Experience suggests that if couples are given this voluntary choice their own family-size decisions will tend to slow the rate of population growth. Yet no one can predict whether the general response will develop strongly or quickly enough to give governments substantial help in attaining their development objectives.

The Demographic Situation

It took more than 1,800 years for the world's population to increase from 210 million to one billion. The second billion required about a century and a quarter, and the third only 30 years. It is now taking only 15 years to add the fourth billion (see Table 1). If present growth rates

294

Table 1: World Population Trends, Zero A.D. to 1970

A. Population Size[1] (millions)

Area	About 0 A.D.	About 1000	1750	1800	1850	1900	1950	1960	1970
World	210	284	750	960	1,240	1,650	2,518	2,995	3,632
Europe	39	63	120	155	195	293	392	425	462
Soviet Union			30	45	70	130	180	214	243
Asia	138	165	480	630	810	930	1,381	1,660	2,056
U.S. and Canada			1	6	26	81	166	199	228
Africa	33	56	100	100	100	150	222	278	344
Latin America			12	20	35	65	163	213	283
Oceania			2	2	2	2	13	16	19

[1]Totals may not check, due to rounding.

B. Average Annual Rates of Growth (%)

Area	1750-1800	1800-1850	1850-1900	1900-1960	1960-1970
World	0.5	0.5	0.6	1.0	1.9
Europe	0.5	0.5	0.8	0.6	0.9
U.S. and Canada	—	3.0[1]	2.3[1]	1.5	1.4
Soviet Union	0.8	0.9	1.2	0.8	1.4
Asia	0.5	0.5	0.3	1.0	2.5
Africa	0	0	0.8	1.0	2.4
Latin America	1.0	1.1	1.2	2.0	2.9
Oceania	0	0	0	1.6	2.0

[1]Includes a high rate of adult immigration.

Sources: UN World Population Conference, Vol. II, pp. 21-22; and Population Council, Reports on Population/Family Planning, December 1969.

were to continue, the current population of more than 3.6 billion would double in 35 years, and by the end of this century it would be increasing at the rate of a billion about every eight years.

It is becoming increasingly difficult to raise living standards and maintain even the present quality of life in the face of these huge annual increases in population. This is especially true in the developing countries, where two thirds of the world's population live and where five sixths of the 1970-80 increase will occur. Such increases impose heavy economic and social burdens.

In the mid-1960s, about two thirds of total annual investment in a sample of 22 developing countries was required to maintain per capita income at a constant level, leaving only about a third to raise living standards. The corresponding figures for a representative sample of 19 developed countries were one quarter and three quarters. It is clear that present rates of population growth in developing countries are penalizing the hundreds of millions who live on the margin of subsistence. If developing countries are to achieve sustained social and economic development, population growth must be reduced.

The high rates of population growth in most developing countries result from their traditional high birth rates and declining mortality rates. Improved health services and medical technology will cause further mortality declines, which will require fertility rates to be reduced from present levels simply to avoid further increases in population growth rates.

The evolution of populations through the three stages of (1) high fertility/high mortality, (2) high fertility/low mortality, and (3) low fertility/low mortality is what demographers refer to as the historical demographic transition. Both the first and last are periods of modest population growth; the middle stage is one of rapid growth. It is in this middle stage that the world as a whole now finds itself, because the total rate of growth is heavily influenced by what is happening in the less developed countries where two thirds of the world's population live.

The demographic transition describes what happened historically in the now-developed countries. The causes of fertility declines that carry countries into stage three are complex and not yet fully understood. They include such influences as increases in the age of marriage, urbanization, the gradual spread of education, reduced infant mortality, the high living standards that accompany rising incomes, the spread of old age pension systems, the prohibition of child labor, and rising equality for women.

There is no guarantee that the same set of forces affecting decisions on family size will emerge with equal force in today's developing countries and lead them inevitably into stage three. They have not done so to date. Eventually they may, although no one knows how long it might take. The provision of family planning services can do much to speed up, perhaps by many decades, a transition that otherwise might occur only very slowly. The difference in the pace of this change might make the difference between development and non-development.

It is important to note that the Bank's interest in "population" is wider than family planning, which is directed at the spacing of children and limiting fertility. The Bank's concern also embraces many other aspects of population and its effects on development. Its periodic analyses of the development prospects of member countries normally include the main demographic variables of births, deaths, and migration. Population issues are central to the Bank's long standing interests in education, employment, and rural development.

These other aspects of the population question lie outside the scope of this paper, which is concerned only with the problem of limiting fertility and with the Bank's contribution to that objective.

However, enabling and persuading man to limit his fertility is itself a much broader problem than the provision of family planning services.

WORLD POPULATION TRENDS

In the pre-industrial era, world population grew slowly. Disease, famine and breakdowns in the social order resulted in mortality rates which were normally high, and occasionally very high. Epidemics sometimes wiped out large proportions of a population in a few years. For example, in the two years 1348-50, bubonic plague (the Black Death) reduced the population of Europe by 25%. Under these conditions, fertility had to be consistently high to ensure the survival of families and of the population. Societies whose cultural, religious and legal codes did not place a high value on fertility would not have survived.

The Demographic Transition

Population growth rates in Europe began to increase during the late eighteenth century. This was the result of a decline in mortality which accompanied the agricultural and industrial revolutions, but which was not matched for many years by any corresponding decline in fertility. Before the decline, death rates were around 28 to 32 per thousand. By the mid-1800s, death rates in England and Scandinavia were about 10 points lower than they had been a century earlier. The decline spread over most of the continent, and the rate continued to fall until in Europe today it is about 10 per thousand. Thus in many European countries the transition to present death rates took more than 100 years; the transition occurred more quickly in countries where it started later.[1]

Three factors are considered basic to the historical decline in mortality rates: improved nutrition as a result of higher agricultural and industrial productivity; better sanitation and personal hygiene, which reduced parasitic and infectious diseases, particularly water-borne diseases; and improvements in medical care. As a result of the differential trends in mortality and fertility, the long term growth rate of Europe's population doubled, from about .5% to 1%.

[1]One of the more dramatic cases of a rapid fall in fertility occurred in Japan after World War II. Both birth and death rates rose between 1875 and 1920; thereafter the birth rate fluctuated at the intermediate levels of 26-36 per thousand, standing at 33 in 1949. The death rate, on the other hand, fell to about 12 in 1949, giving Japan a rate of natural increase of more than 2%. Between 1948 and 1952, abortion on medical or social grounds was legalized and contraception encouraged by the passage of new legislation. During the subsequent 20 years the birth rate fell 15 points to 18, and the death rate continued its drop to about seven per thousand in 1969, giving a rate of natural increase just over one percent.

297

In most European countries a decline in fertility did not begin until the second half of the nineteenth century. It has continued, with minor interruptions, until the present. In the mid-1700s European birth rates were high (35-40 per thousand in most countries), but not as high as in many of today's developing countries (often 40-50). The sharpest declines in fertility occurred between 1870 and 1930, when they leveled out at around 20, and most European countries today have rates between 15 and 20.

The motivation for reduced fertility appears to have arisen from the spread of education, the progress of urbanization, and a realization that reduced death rates would lead to larger families unless fertility were checked.

Population Trends in Developing Countries

Prior to World War II, the developing countries also were characterized by high birth and death rates, and thus had low rates of natural increase. The demographic transition began with a rapid postwar decline in death rates unaccompanied by a corresponding decline in birth rates. Growth rates began to increase. Today, the average is 2.8%, with the level in some countries as high as 3% and even 4%.

There are wide variations, of course, and different developing countries are at different points along the path of the demographic transition (see Table 2). In some, both fertility and mortality remain high.

Table 2: Population Distribution in Developing Countries by Fertility and Mortality Levels, 1970

Stages	Deaths per 1000 Population	Births per 1000 Population	Population					
			Africa[1]		Asia[2]		Latin America	
			Number	Percent	Number	Percent	Number	Percent
1 (a)	High (over 25)	High (over 25)	27.0	8.0	17.0	1.4	—	—
(b)	Falling (15-25)	High (over 40)	307.0	90.1	978.5	82.6	24.0	8.4
2 (a)	Low (less than 15)	High (over 40)	5.0	1.5	76.0	6.5	112.5	39.9
(b)	Low (less than 15)	Falling	1.5	0.4	112.0	9.5	145.5	51.7
Totals			340.5	100.0	1,183.5	100.0	282.0	100.0

Note: Population figures are approximations. For purposes of this table, they have been rounded to the nearest 500 thousand.

[1] Excluding five African countries with a total population of 42.4 million.

[2] Excluding People's Republic of China and four other countries with populations totaling 26.1 million, due to incomplete data.

Sources of basic data: United Nations, *Population and Vital Statistics Report*, January 1971; *Monthly Bulletin of Statistics*, August 1971; and Population Reference Bureau, *1970 World Population Data Sheet*.

In others, mostly in Asia and Africa, fertility is high and the death rate is falling. In still others, notably in countries with two fifths of Latin America's population, fertility is high and death rates are already low. In a few countries of temperate South America, East Asia and parts of Oceania, death rates are low and fertility is declining.

The postwar demographic experience has differed from the earlier experience of developed countries in several important respects:

• The decline in mortality has been much more rapid, occurring over one or two decades. For example, between the five-year periods 1945-50 and 1955-60, life expectancy at birth increased in India from 32 to 45 years, in the Republic of China from 41 to 61 years, and in tropical South America from 44 to about 52 years. Consequently, growth rates in the developing countries today are higher than were ever reached in Europe.

The difference is not merely in degree, but in kind. A European country with an annual rate of growth of 1% would double its population in 70 years; the average developing country with a growth rate of 2.5% will double its population in 28 years. If a 1% rate of growth were reduced to .5%, the doubling time would be extended by another 70 years to a total of 140. But an identical reduction of half of one percentage point when the growth rate is 2.5% would extend the doubling time by only seven years—a tenfold difference.

• Many of today's developing countries lack the open spaces and wealth of natural resources which characterized the areas of European settlement and enabled them to support high rates of population growth more easily.

• To some extent, the earlier growth in today's developed countries was attributable to adult immigration, leading to significant differences between their age structure during development and that of today's developing countries. By 1900, for example, only about 44% of the population of the United States and Canada was below the age of 20, while in developing countries today that age group commonly accounts for 50-55%.

• When mortality began to decline in many of today's developing countries, the levels of economic and social development were not comparable to those prevailing in Western Europe before the industrial revolution.

• The postwar decline in mortality has been occurring in many societies in which non-traditional economic practices and social attitudes, which normally accompany development, have not yet taken root. Unlike the reduction of fertility, a decline in mortality encounters no cultural and ideological opposition and does not require a large measure of continuous and active participation by the population. In the earlier experience of today's developed countries, however, the technological means for similarly rapid reduction of mortality did not exist.

Thus, the current demographic situation in the developing countries does not have historical precedents from which they might take comfort. The considerably more rapid decline in mortality has created a greater imbalance than ever existed in the developed countries. This is the heart of "the population problem" in today's developing countries.

The solution depends on how fast and by how much fertility will decline in the next 20 to 30 years. The objective of population programs is to bring about declines in fertility more rapidly than would otherwise occur, primarily by supplying information and services to those willing to use them. To the extent that additional government policies and activities can influence voluntary fertility decisions, they too deserve to be considered as part of a country's population strategy. Much more needs to be learned, however, about both the effects and the efficacy of other instruments.

WORLD POPULATION PROJECTIONS

Table 3 suggests a range of possibilities over the next 30 years for the population of the world, the developing countries collectively, and a number of large developing countries individually. These are based on alternative projections showing what is likely to happen under optimistic assumptions (Projection A) and very slowly changing conditions (Projection B).

Projection A illustrates a type of population growth which could develop over the next 30 years if maximum efforts were made to develop family planning programs and take any other reasonable measures that might be effective in curbing fertility. On the basis of results achieved in the most successful programs to date, a "net reproduction rate" (NRR) of 1.0 could be expected by the year 2000.[1] This is a possible but unlikely achievement.

Projection B can be conceived of as an illustration of population growth trends if family planning efforts remain as modest as they are at present. Even under these slowly changing conditions, some decline in fertility can be expected because of family planning and some

[1]The net reproduction rate is a measure of population replacement, in terms of the number of girl children born over the reproductive life of a hypothetical age group of women, after allowance for mortality. A population will not stop growing when the NRR of 1.0 is reached. It will maintain momentum for two or three generations, depending mainly on its age structure. Usually there is a relatively higher proportion of women in the child bearing ages than would be required for a stationary (non-growing) population. Therefore, even with a sustained NRR of 1.0 these populations would continue to grow for about 60 to 70 years until their age structure became stationary.

improvement in socio-economic conditions. In this case a NRR of 1.0 would be reached by about 2040.

These alternative projections, discussed in detail in Annex I, have the following major implications:

(a) **Population size and distribution.** World population, which totaled more than 3.6 billion in 1970, would reach 5.9 billion under projection A and 6.7 billion under projection B by the year 2000, a difference of about 770 million. Under projection A, world population would level off during the last quarter of the next century after having reached 8.4 billion. Under projection B, population would become stationary half a century later, at about 15.3 billion, or 7.4 billion more than under projection A.

The figures for developing countries alone are not very different. These countries would increase their population from 2.5 billion in 1970 to 4.5 billion in the year 2000 under projection A and to 5.3 billion under projection B. The difference is in the neighborhood of 800 million. The ultimate levels for today's developing countries would be about 6.7 billion people under projection A and twice as many, or 13.4 billion, under projection B.

(b) **The key role of large countries.** What happens to world population will depend very much on fertility trends in a few large developing countries. Comparing projections A and B for developing countries, half the difference in population size is accounted for by 12 of them: seven in Asia (India, Iran, Malaysia, Pakistan, the Philippines, Thailand and Turkey), two in Africa (Kenya and Egypt), and three in Latin America (Brazil, Colombia and Mexico).[1] This suggests the importance of giving priority to efforts to reduce fertility in countries where maximum impact can be achieved.

(c) **Fertility trends and births to be averted.** If projection A were achieved, the birth rate would be 7.1 per thousand lower in 1995-2000 than under projection B (21.1 instead of 28.2). For developing countries, the difference would be 9.3 per thousand (23.7 instead of 32). To achieve projection A rather than projection B, it would be necessary to avert about 840 million more births between 1970 and the year 2000 in the developing countries than projection B assumes; almost half of these would have to be in the 12 countries listed above.

While present programs give little promise of achieving a NRR of 1.0 by the year 2000, a substantially increased effort now should bring this goal within reach by about 2025. To reach a NRR of 1.0 by the year 2000 would require a maximum effort, something it is probably not realistic to expect.

---

[1]Two large countries, Indonesia and Nigeria, are omitted from this list due to lack of sufficient data.

Table 3: Alternative Population Projections,[1] Birth Rates, and Births Omitted

Regions and Countries	Projec- tion	Population (in millions) 1970	2000	c. 2075 A c. 2125 B	Birth Rate (Per 1,000 Population) 1965-70	1995- 2000	2020-25	Additional Births Omitted 1970-2000 (in millions)
World Total	A	3,652	5,916	8,348	34.0	21.1	16.3	882
	B	3,652	6,690	15,306	34.0	28.2	23.1	
Developed	A	1,122	1,388	1,622	18.8	15.8	14.0	45
	B	1,122	1,431	1,931	18.8	17.4	15.6	
Developing	A	2,530	4,528	6,727	41.8	23.7	17.2	837
	B	2,530	5,259	13,374	41.8	33.0	24.6	
Asia								
India	A	536	948	1,402	41.4	23.6	17.1	174
	B	536	1,100	2,799	41.4	32.9	24.6	
Iran	A	28	56	88	45.0	24.3	17.2	13
	B	28	68	213	45.0	36.5	26.8	
Malaysia[2]	A	9	18	27	36.0	21.2	16.1	4
	B	9	21	54	36.0	30.1	22.8	
Pakistan	A	126	260	408	42.3	24.2	17.0	62
	B	126	316	982	42.3	36.4	26.6	
Philippines	A	38	79	122	45.2	24.1	17.3	18
	B	38	95	282	45.2	35.9	26.2	
Thailand	A	37	72	108	41.1	22.4	16.7	15
	B	37	86	234	41.1	33.1	24.7	
Turkey	A	34	62	91	36.0	22.0	16.5	10
	B	34	71	173	36.0	30.6	23.2	
Africa								
Egypt	A	33	62	94	44.5	24.0	17.1	13
	B	33	74	205	44.5	34.8	25.6	
Ghana	A	9	17	25	49.2	25.6	18.0	4
	B	9	20	58	49.2	37.7	27.4	
Kenya	A	11	21	31	49.6	25.1	17.6	5
	B	11	25	70	49.6	36.7	26.5	
Tunisia	A	5	10	15	45.3	24.0	17.4	2
	B	5	12	34	45.3	35.8	26.1	
Latin America								
Brazil	A	94	181	273	38.6	22.1	16.5	31
	B	94	209	529	38.6	31.1	23.5	
Colombia	A	21	41	62	38.0	22.1	16.6	8
	B	21	48	120	38.0	31.3	23.6	
Mexico	A	51	109	172	44.6	23.7	17.0	27
	B	51	131	397	44.6	35.7	26.1	

[1]For Projection A, a linear decline in gross reproduction rate (GRR) is assumed to a level which corresponds to a net reproduction rate (NRR) = 1 by the years 2000-2005; this decline is equated with maximum effective fertility control. Projection B represents population trends under the assumption that the GRR will decline linearly to make NRR = 1 in the year 2045; this situation is considered likely to occur if efforts for fertility control continue at the present levels. Both projections assume the same mortality which is supposed to have different declines in the future, for different countries. The full explanation of the assumptions is found in Frejka's introduction to his projections.

[2]Excluding Sabah and Sarawak.

Source: The table is computed on the basis of data from Tomas Frejka (Population Council), in "Alternatives of World Population Growth," a monograph in process of publication.

302

ECONOMIC EFFECTS

Relative Growth Rates of Population and Income

Rapid population growth is a comparatively recent phenomenon. It has accompanied economic development, and it is clear that the possibility for more people to live longer and fuller lives has been one of development's more important results. Past history, however, is a misleading guide to action, because the present situation does not offer a comparable possibility. As noted above, new forces are producing unprecedentedly high rates of population growth, while special circumstances which gave peculiar impetus to economic growth in the earlier period do not prevail.

There is no reason to believe that current rates of growth will fall fast enough to relieve the pressures on developing countries arising from the need to use significant and rising proportions of their resources simply to maintain the average standard of living of growing numbers, leaving less for further improvement. It is not that countries cannot have both growing per capita incomes and growing populations; the growth record of many developing countries in the last two decades shows that this is not impossible. What is at issue is the maintenance of per capita income growth at acceptable levels over longer periods, when the population may be doubling every two to three decades.

The decline of mortality in most developing countries has resulted in the survival of more adults, who would otherwise have had a shorter life span, and an increase in the number of surviving infants. The respective contributions of these two groups to the postwar population increase cannot be accurately calculated, but probably they are about equally significant.

The economic impact of their survival is quite different, however; more adults living longer increase the potential labor force and create an immediate demand for jobs and supporting services. They also add to the numbers in the reproductive age group, with a potential impact upon fertility. More children surviving mean a rise in the dependency burden and, at a later stage, a further relative increase in the reproductive age groups. Thus while any fall in the infant mortality rate is to be welcomed on humanitarian grounds, it adds burdens to weak economies which can be lessened only by reducing fertility. To do so, and thus lessen the dependency burden, leads to large economic benefits. This is the heart of the economic case in favor of programs to limit fertility.

The other component in high population growth rates has been the continued high level of fertility. In the longer run this can be

303

expected to decline everywhere. However, cultural and social factors are significant enough to make for important differences in fertility levels among areas of the world. In the face of continuing success in reducing mortality, no developing country has yet experienced a fertility decline sufficient to reduce the rate of population growth to the average level of 1% per annum characteristic of the developed economies of Europe, North America and Japan.

Falling fertility is the only factor that can accomplish such a reduction—except, of course, a return to much higher mortality rates. The issue is not whether the reduction will take place, but how soon, by what means and at what cost. The question is whether it can be initiated and accelerated through appropriate policy actions, in order to reap more quickly the economic benefits that can be linked with lower rates of growth.

Effect on Per Capita Incomes

The most certain, immediate, and measurable benefit of slowing population growth is the increase in per capita income. The immediate impact of falling fertility is a decline in average family size, reflected throughout society in a smaller dependency ratio.[1] In the short run there is no change in the labor force or other resources, so that the same national income will be available to a smaller number of people. At the same time, proportionately less of the national income will have to be used to maintain the capital stock per person at a constant level, making it possible to apply more resources to increasing capital per worker, thus raising productivity and per capita income.

The higher per capita incomes permit higher savings which could finance higher levels of capital accumulation, both physical and human. This, in turn, leads to further increases in the national income. There is nothing automatic about such a process, however; it is made possible by falling fertility, but the possibilities have to be seized and used for purposes which promote economic development. Such development may be accelerated as much by the investment in human resources—notably improvements in the quality of education—as by other kinds of capital improvements.

The effects of the decline in fertility will be felt in the labor market, which will have fewer entrants approximately 15 to 20 years later. The impact of this decline upon the national income will depend

---

[1]The ratio of people not in the labor force to the total population. Since all persons depend on the production of those in the labor force, a lower ratio means that producers do not have to share their output with as many non-producers, yielding both producers and their dependents a higher per capita income.

mainly upon whether the opportunities made possible by lower population growth in the previous 15 years or so have been used to increase the quantity and quality of the capital stock. Many factors are involved, including labor productivity, the composition of the labor force, and improvements in health and education made possible by rising per capita incomes.

Employment and Income Distribution

Problems of unemployment and inequality in the distribution of income will always be eased by reductions in fertility. Continuing high fertility results in large numbers of young people entering the labor force each year. Employment opportunities have to expand fast enough to absorb them. At high rates of growth of population, where the numbers involved may be doubling every 25 years, the absorption problem is severe.

Any country with a problem of long run unemployment cannot fail to benefit from the slower growth in the labor force which results from reduced fertility. Where large numbers of people are entering the labor force to compete for jobs, wages are depressed, while those who own or control capital earn high returns, as do the owners of land and other resources in fixed supply. In any social or political system, high fertility tends to worsen the distribution of income and wealth. A reduction in the rate of growth of population makes it easier to redress these inequities.

Estimating the Effects

The longer term cumulative economic effects of lowering population growth rates are clearly profound, although it is difficult to isolate them from those of other economic forces. Since there is no basis for estimating such effects historically, attempts have been made to indicate their orders of magnitude by the construction of simulation models. With these models it is possible to work out the implications of varying fertility reductions over several decades, and to compare the results with the situation assuming no fertility decline.

While the quantitative results depend upon assumptions made about the economic relationships involved, they indicate substantial benefits in growth of per capita incomes, with a cumulative effect over time. Typically, if fertility is halved in a generation, by the end of that period per capita incomes can be 20% to 40% higher than if fertility had remained constant. The indicated benefits become more impressive as projections are extended into the future, but results in the shorter period are more persuasive in terms of current policy.

This account of the economic benefits to be expected from a reduction in population growth rates places its main emphasis on the attainment of a higher per capita national income. The national income, however, has long been recognized as an incomplete measure of welfare, even in strictly economic terms. It needs to be supplemented by taking account of other benefits of reduced fertility.

Some of these appear as social benefits, but they have economic consequences which may themselves be measurable, at least in principle. They include an increase in the spacing between pregnancies, bringing benefits to the family in the form of improved health for mothers and children, fewer maternal deaths, and fewer retarded and handicapped infants. Improved nutrition and family care is more likely with smaller family size. A reduction in the number of illegal and unsafe abortions also follows as knowledge of contraception spreads.

It is possible to place many of the above conclusions in a cost-benefit framework, relating the value of the benefits to the costs of programs required to bring about reductions in fertility. There is as yet no fully agreed basis for estimating some of the key values to be employed, and even the use of this approach has aroused controversy. But there can be no question that the economic benefits of lower rates of population growth are considerable, and would prove to be all the greater if proper account could be taken of those which are not easily quantified. Calculations have consistently shown a level of benefits that exceed costs by a very wide margin.

Other Implications of Population Size

Much of the concern about current population growth stems from anxiety about its implication for the future size of population, whether in the world or in a particular country, in relation to the availability of natural resources. The growth of population, however, accounts for only about half the growing annual drain on the world's resources. The other half, or more, arises from the growth of per capita incomes.

Thus, except perhaps in the case of food, it is both rising levels of income and expanding populations that create pressures on the use of natural resources. These seem bound to intensify even if population growth slows down, despite man's ingenuity in overcoming technological problems with new agricultural methods, new sources of energy, new ways of combating pollution, and new, increasingly dense modes of urban living.

Even if many of the difficulties concerning the environment and resource availability stem as much or more from income growth as from population growth, the wealthier a country is in per capita terms, the easier it will be to mobilize resources in order to cope with such problems. For example, an economy of 20 million people with an average income of $2,000 might have the same problems of pollution or scarcity of resources as one of 400 million with a per capita income of $100. There is little doubt that the smaller country could more easily tackle such problems, because of its greater taxing power and the more developed research and production capabilities that are associated with higher incomes.

Against the disadvantages of larger population size one potential advantage is sometimes mentioned: countries with large populations may be able to take advantage more readily of the economies of scale that undoubtedly exist in many activities, particularly in manufacturing. Market size, however, is more a question of aggregate income than of population size per se. There may historically have been countries which could have been considered under-populated, in terms of the economy's ability to make effective use of its natural resources. Perhaps the United States was in this position at some point in the past. However, instances when the addition of more people to the labor force led to increases in labor productivity and income per head must have been few in the past and are virtually nonexistent today. Developing economies will be able to increase per capita incomes more rapidly if their population growth is low than if it is high.

FAMILY PLANNING EFFORTS

While efforts to reduce population growth rates are still dwarfed by the magnitude of the problem, there has been a notable—even dramatic—increase over the last decade in both public and governmental interest, concern and action. In 1960, only three countries had official policies designed to slow the rate of population growth; by 1971, 26 countries, with more than two thirds of the population of developing areas, had announced such policies or started official programs; and some 24 others, with 12% of the developing world's population, supported private family planning programs without announcing official policies (see Table 4).

By 1970, 30 heads of governments, including those of 19 developing countries, had signed the U.N. Declaration on Population, which characterized "unplanned population growth" as one of the world's "great problems" and called on national governments to recognize family planning as one of their "vital interests."

Table 4: Official Positions of 48 Developing Countries on Family Planning

Population Size (Millions)	Policy and/or Program	Support but No Announced Policy
400 and more	People's Republic of China (1962) India (1952, reorganized in 1965)	
100-399	Indonesia (1968) Pakistan (1960, reorganized in 1965)	
25-99	Egypt (1965) Iran (1967) Republic of Korea (1961) Nigeria (1969) Philippines (1970) Thailand (1970) Turkey (1965)	
15-24	Morocco (1965)	Colombia South Africa
10-14	Republic of China (1968) Kenya (1966) Malaysia (1966) Nepal (1966)	Ceylon Tanzania Venezuela
Less than 10	Barbados (1967) Botswana (1971) Dominican Republic (1968) Ghana (1969) Jamaica (1966) Mauritius (1965) Puerto Rico (1970) Singapore (1965) Trinidad and Tobago (1967) Tunisia (1964)	Bolivia Chile Costa Rica Cuba Dahomey Ecuador El Salvador The Gambia Guatemala Haiti Honduras Hong Kong Nicaragua Panama Rhodesia Senegal Western Samoa

Source: Lapham, R. J. and Mauldin, W. P., "An Assessment of National Family Planning Programmes," unpublished paper presented to OECD's Fourth Annual Population Conference, October 1971.

Program Results

About 20 million women in 18 countries with programs, or 10% of the married women of reproductive age in those countries, have become "acceptors" during the last five years, the average period the programs have been in effect (see Table 5). It is important to distinguish between the total number of "acceptors" and the annual increase in that number (and to distinguish between the gross and the net increase, i.e., after allowing for those who cease their participation). The figure of 20 million acceptors overstates the number of women practicing contraception, because in every country many acceptors leave the program and those who reenter are again recorded as "new acceptors."

Countries with population programs usually establish population goals, or targets. They may aim at reducing the existing crude birth rate to a specified lower rate over five to 10 years, or at recruiting specific numbers of acceptors into the program (sometimes even classified by methods) over a certain number of years.[1]

An examination of these targets will show that a number of the programs which began five or more years ago, after declines in fertility for a few years, appear now to have reached an annual peak of acceptors; the number of new acceptors seems to have stabilized, while the decline of the birth rate appears to have slowed down or

[1]See Annex 2 for population targets.

Table 5: Number of Acceptors by Method, and Coverage Achieved by Programs of 18 Countries (000s)

Country	Year	IUDs	Oral Contra- ceptives	Sterili- zation	Other Program Methods	All Program Methods	All Program Methods as a Percentage of Women 15-44[7]
Ceylon	1966-69	68	55	18	19	160	>8.2
Colombia	1965-70	209	97	u	11	316	u
Ghana	1969-70	5	3	0	3	11	1-2
Hong Kong[1]	1964-70	76	55	4	149	284	51.
India	1964-70[5]	3,799	0	8,659	2,098[6]	u	14.9
Indonesia	1968-70	88	59	0	28	175	u
Iran	1966-70	36	627	0	u	662	>9.3
Kenya	1969-70	49	24	u	u	u	2.
Korea, Rep. of	1964-70	1,713	597	150	u	u	42.
Malaysia[2]	1967-70	3	196	9	12	220	8.
Morocco	1964-70	41	25	0	0	67	3.
Pakistan[3]	1964-70	3,277	6	189	u	u	4.
Philippines[4]	1970	84	193	—	85	362	u
Singapore	1965-69	10	82	4	51	147	35.
China, Rep. of	1964-70	779	150	1	u	979	44.
Thailand	1964-70	248	207	34	0	489	>9.6
Tunisia	1964-70	66	24	9	20	108	12.
Turkey	1965-70	250	32	0	0	282	u

Symbols: u, unknown; >, greater than total.

[1]Non-sovereign territory.

[2]Excludes Sabah and Sarawak.

[3]Annual number of acceptors is an estimate based on units of contraceptives supplied, the assumed relationship being one acceptor equals 130 units per year. Because of the arbitrary bias of this estimate, the cumulation of acceptors is not considered warranted.

[4]Acceptors for years prior to 1970 when a population policy was announced represent clients attending clinics that currently participate in the government program.

[5]To March 31, 1971.

[6]Users of conventional contraceptives, based on figures of distribution.

[7]This column refers to current acceptors of all program methods as a percentage of women aged 15-44 as of January 1971 except for India, for which the date is January 1970.

Source: Population Council, *Population and Family Planning Programs: A Factbook,* No. 2 (1971 edition), June 1971, New York.

even to have been reversed. The long-established programs in the Republic of China, Hong Kong, Republic of Korea and Singapore are in this situation.

In a number of countries—India, Malaysia, Pakistan and Tunisia among others—programs have been in operation for five or more years and a substantial operational infrastructure has been built up; however, performance has been uneven and there has not yet been a significant or demonstrable impact on their fertility rates. But even in the case of the more successful programs, it is clear that more effective education and motivation efforts and more and better family planning services could increase significantly the proportion of women practicing family planning, with consequently lower fertility levels.

Other countries are just beginning their programs and the number of acceptors is still increasing. These newer programs include those in Ghana, Indonesia, Iran, Philippines and Thailand.

In addition, many countries are moving gradually from limited voluntary efforts in urban centers to a larger scale of services but without any national population policy, although government health facilities may offer family planning services. As their scale of activities expands, these countries can learn from the experience of others and develop not only their delivery systems for contraceptives but also their programs of information, education, and the evaluation of results. Such countries include many of the 34 which have pioneering private associations affiliated with the International Planned Parenthood Federation (IPPF).

One estimate of the number of births averted by family planning programs was made by the Development Center of the Organization for Economic Cooperation and Development (OECD) in 1970. It indicated that 2.3 million births had been averted in 1968. Compared with what is needed to bring down the rate of population growth to acceptable levels within a reasonable period, this is far from adequate. Approximately 4.8 million births would have to be averted annually between 1970 and 1975, and more than ten times that many, or 60.5 million annually, between 1995 and 2000 if the population of developing countries were to reach a net reproduction rate of 1.0 by the year 2000 (Annex 1, Table 6).

Constraints on Family Planning

There is considerable unevenness in the strength of commitments to population control in developing countries, ranging from mere pronouncements to firm policies and programs with varying degrees

310

of budgetary support. This may reflect in part some of the difficulties which have limited the effectiveness of many family planning programs.

Politically, there is sometimes concern that support of population programs may be a liability, especially since the results of any program will not be immediately demonstrable but unfavorable misconceptions may be widespread: a belief, for example, that there is a correlation between population size and military power; a fear that ethnic balances within a country will be upset; or a suspicion that the advocacy by rich countries of lower growth rates for the poor is merely a new form of colonialism and an excuse for not providing adequate development aid.

Cultural and religious objections to family planning are still serious, even in areas where national programs exist. In some countries a family planning program would imply a complete reversal of practice, tradition and mores. Furthermore, where infant mortality is high and children are needed for the family work force, high fertility is to be expected.

Various administrative and organizational difficulties commonly beset governments in launching new programs. These are often serious limitations. No matter how earnest the political commitment, a family planning program cannot be effective unless there is an organizational structure capable of bringing the available technology to those prepared to make use of it. Family planning programs are inherently difficult to administer, since they must maintain continuing contact with married couples over a long period.

The difficulty is increased when services must be carried to a widely dispersed, and often illiterate, rural population. Moreover, there is seldom enough trained personnel to carry out a program of the required magnitude. Finally, there is the handicap of limited administrative experience on the part of many persons in the medical and social service professions, who in most developing countries are responsible for administering family planning programs.

There are also important technological constraints. Although contraceptive technology has made considerable progress in the last 15 years, so far there is no perfect contraceptive: highly effective, safe, inexpensive, easily used and reversible, and one which would not necessarily have to be delivered under medical surveillance. Oral contraceptives and the intrauterine devices (IUDs) are likely to be the best available means of contraception for some time to come, although experience has demonstrated that both have their limitations.

While research is producing variations and refinements of both "the pill" and the IUD, any radically new technique of fertility control must come from basic research in reproductive physiology, which is expensive, complex and uncertain. For the present, family planning programs will have to operate with essentially the same methods known today. Improvements are on the horizon, but radical breakthroughs toward the "ideal" are not expected soon (see Annex 3).

Family planning programs normally include education and information components, although the exact type of activities carried out must be carefully tailored to allow for cultural sensitivities and religious beliefs. Education consists of the preparation of curriculum materials on family life and sex and their introduction into school curricula after suitable testing and training of teachers. The target group is principally the next generation of potential acceptors.

Information, or communication, activities are directed mainly to the present generation of potential acceptors. These may be reached through various forms of mass communication (radio, cinema, newspapers, posters, etc.), as well as through face-to-face contacts established by health personnel, social workers, or specially trained field workers. The education and information components are vital parts of any well conceived family planning program.

A final constraint on effectiveness is inadequate evaluation. Although considerable work has been done on the measurement of results of family planning programs, there is everywhere a long way to go before adequate reporting systems exist to provide information for management decision-making and program evaluation. Inadequate evaluation machinery limits assessment of a program's effectiveness in reducing fertility, the ultimate test of its success.

An adequate information system for evaluation would address itself to three questions in particular: (a) The structure and level of demand, to provide guidance for determining the priorities of the program's efforts among areas and population groups; (b) The effect of varying the level and mix of various program inputs, to suggest the combination likely to achieve best results; and (c) The effect of the program on reducing fertility, to provide a measure of effectiveness.[1]

Program Costs

Financial expenditures on family planning programs have been modest in relation to national budgets (averaging about 1%) and, as noted in the previous section, very low in relation to the economic benefits of reduced fertility. To date, external assistance has carried a sizable proportion of the costs, usually more than 30%. Tables 6 and 7 give data for selected countries. The relatively low costs are

[1]See Annex 4 for discussion of a desirable management information and evaluation system.

partly explained by the use of existing health services as the main delivery system.

In many cases, even when a population policy exists, program expenditure is too little in relation to the need. Because national family planning efforts are so recent, cost trends are available for only a few countries; in some (e.g., India, Republic of China) expenditures are increasing; in others the data show decreases. Cost projections and the level of foreign assistance needed in the next decade cannot be assessed with confidence on the basis of such limited experience, but informed estimates have been made which suggest orders of magnitude.

Table 6: Budgetary Position of Family Planning Programs in Selected Countries, 1968-1969 (US$ millions)

Country	National Budget	Health[1] Program	Family Planning Program	Foreign Aid for Family Planning	Foreign Aid as % of Family Planning Budget	Family Planning as % of Health	Family Planning as % of National Budget
China, Rep. of	823.0	64.4	0.6	0.5	87.1	1.0	0.1
India	3,141.9	70.8	49.3	18.9	38.3	41.1	1.6
Indonesia	646.3	n.a.	4.0[2]	n.a.	92.5	n.a.	0.1
Jamaica	218.3	18.5	0.5	0.2	31.7	2.9	0.3
Korea, Rep. of	984.8	7.7	4.1	2.0	48.8	52.8	0.4
Pakistan	996.6	46.0	19.1	14.9	77.9	41.5	1.9
Trinidad and Tobago	188.6	13.5	0.1	0.03	30.2	0.8	0.1

[1]These data are not comparable on a country basis. Some countries do not show family planning costs independent of expenditures for health programs or do so to varying degrees. In some countries it is considered politically inadvisable to publish precise figures. Also, the data do not include the costs of private programs.
[2]Data for 1970-71.

In a staff study, the United Nations Fund for Population Activities (UNFPA) has estimated that it would be necessary for developing countries, if they were to carry out reasonably complete family planning programs on a broad national basis, to spend approximately 65 U.S. cents per capita per year. This figure increases to $1 per capita if the costs of educational, motivational and system evaulation activities are included. These amounts are not small when translated into the proportions of national budgets they would represent, e.g., somewhere around 5%. Five percent is a much lower proportion than most governments normally spend on education (15% to 30%) or on national security, but it is about the proportion of total Ministry of Health expenditures in many low income countries.

Not even the most committed governments with the most successful programs are spending as much as half the per capita figures mentioned in the UNFPA study, and most are spending much less.

Table 7: Annual Per Capita Expenditure of Selected Family Planning Programs[1] (US cents)

China, Republic of	6.0	(1971)
India	7.72	(1968)
Indonesia	4.1	(1970)
Jamaica	37.0	(1968)
Korea, Republic of	10.4	(1969)
Pakistan	9.4	(1969)
Tunisia	16.8	(1969)

[1]Based on funds from all sources—government, international, bilateral, and private.

Source: Population Council, Population and Family Planning Programs: A Factbook, No. 2 (1971 edition), June 1971, New York.

It is clear that population programs require important shifts in government priorities, which will frequently require fairly significant changes in budget allocations. Successful programs require substantial increases in both national and international inputs, public and private.

The Potential for Family Planning

How successful can family planning efforts be in reducing fertility over the next generation? No one knows. Not enough experience to serve as a guide has been accumulated in existing programs, most of which began only four or five years ago. Large areas of ignorance surround such key questions as the potential number of acceptors, since relatively little is known about the determinants of family size decisions and how open to change they may be among various social groups.

There is much debate among experts as to whether the present numbers of acceptors can be increased (a) primarily through the extension of services (an approach which assumes the existence of large numbers waiting to participate); (b) whether much more intensive information, communication and family life education activities would be more productive; or (c) whether much larger numbers of acceptors can be recruited only after basic socio-economic changes have taken place. Both research and further experience are needed to throw light on this fundamental question. Some inferences may be drawn, however, from recent experience:

• There does appear to be a correlation between a national program's supply capacity (i.e., the number of service facilities) and the number of women who make use of the program. This suggests that as a program's capacity is increased, it does gain additional acceptors, particularly in the early stages when those who can be most easily recruited are becoming acceptors. But there is also evidence that

314

programs in which insufficient attention is given to education and motivation do not succeed in recruiting anything like the proportion of women needed to reach national population goals. It seems clear that governments will have to give equal attention to both the supply and demand sides of the problem.

• Everywhere there are constraints to program expansion because of the already heavy demands on the medical services, inadequate numbers of trained personnel at all levels, inadequate and insufficient physical facilities, etc. But given the political will, such problems are not insurmountable over the long run (and, as indicated in the next section, these are areas in which the Bank can assist). Over the short run, there are possibilities for making use of non-medical personnel, in particular social workers, and using paramedical personnel more effectively in providing family planning services.

• As to long term demand for family planning services, three kinds of evidence suggest that it exists or can be developed:

(1) Various knowledge, attitude, and practice (KAP) surveys indicate that most couples in developing countries want fewer children than they now have. The average number of children that a family "desires" is between four and 4.5, compared to actual family size of five to 5.7. In particular, many families which already have at least three children do not want more: in Hong Kong and seven developing countries,[1] 60% of respondents who already had three children and 70% of those with four said they did not want to increase their families (see Table 8).

These surveys have their limitations. For example, the replies of older respondents are influenced by their actual reproductive history. Moreover, an expressed preference for a given number of children does not necessarily mean that contraceptives will be used on the requisite sustained basis. Nevertheless, studies suggest that younger and better educated women want smaller families than their mothers did. If the evidence of the studies is accepted, it does appear that there is an unsatisfied demand for expanded family planning services.

(2) The appallingly high incidence of illegal abortions in many countries, particularly in Latin America, clearly indicates an unmet need for family planning services.

(3) The most successful family planning programs to date—in the Republic of China, Hong Kong, Republic of Korea and Singapore— have been conducted in countries were social pressures and the level of socio-economic development had already led to some decline in

[1]Hong Kong 1967; Thailand 1965; Philippines (urban) 1969; Turkey 1963; Republic of Korea (urban) 1964; Tunisia 1964; India 1960-61; Indonesia 1963.

fertility. Preliminary results of the 1970-71 census in many countries of Asia and Latin America indicate a population size smaller, though admittedly to a minor degree, than had been projected by the United Nations. To the extent that the lower-than-expected population level indicates that a decline in fertility has begun in these countries, it may be an encouraging indication of the results that might be achieved by inaugurating or intensifying family planning programs there.

Table 8: Survey Findings on Actual and Desired Family Size

A. Average Desired Family Size and Percentage of Persons Reporting They Do not Want More Children, For Selected Countries

Area	Type of Sample	Average Number Children	Percent not wanting more children among those with		
			4	5	6
Ceylon	Rural	3.2	69	88	44
China, Rep. of	Urban	3.9	76	88	—
Ghana	Urban	5.5	—	—	—
India			75	85	37
Central India	Urban/Rural	3.8			
Mysore a	Urban	3.7			
b	Urban	4.1			
c	Rural	4.7			
d	Rural	4.6			
New Delhi		4.1			
Indonesia	Rural	4.3	37	41	19
Jamaica	Urban/Rural	3.4-4.2	80	84	—
Korea, Rep. of	Rural	4.3	—	—	—
Pakistan[1]	Urban	4.0			
East			57	54	45
West			68	71	41
Philippines	Urban/Rural	5.0	68	85	50
Thailand		3.8	86	96	70
Turkey	National Population	3.8	44	66	—

B. Completed Family Size by Region

Region	Completed Family Size[2]
World Total[3]	4.7
Developing Regions[3]	5.5
Africa	6.1
Asia[3]	5.5
Central and South America	5.7
Developed Regions	2.9
Europe	2.7
United States and Canada	3.7

[1]Before political events of 1971-72.

[2]Average number of children born per woman living through reproductive period.

[3]Excluding the Soviet Union and People's Republic of China.

Source: Mauldin, W. Parker, "Fertility Studies: Knowledge, Attitude, and Practice" in *Studies in Family Planning*, Number 7, The Population Council, New York.

In the long run, fertility reduction can be achieved only with the right combination of social and economic development, cultural and political attitudes, and easy availability of contraceptive facilities. No one yet knows the required mix, which will probably differ from country to country. However, the limited experience available has already shown that if an adequate service can be provided, including public information and a variety of acceptable methods, the results will be demographically significant even if inadequate to achieve the desired reduction in fertility. The initiation of movement in the right direction also provides hope that more rapid progress will be possible as programs are extended and improved.

THE BANK'S PROGRAM AND APPROACH

Program Projections

Table 9 summarizes the Bank's actual and projected lending for population projects in the seven fiscal years 1970-76. It also shows the number of sector missions already mounted and contemplated.

**Table 9: Summary of World Bank Population Activities
By Fiscal Years, with Projection through FY1976**

	Actual			Program		
	1969	1970	1971	1972	1973	1972-76
Sector Missions	1	3	3	4	5	24
Commitments ($ million)		2.0	8.0	29.0	30.0	150.0
% Total Bank and IDA		0.1	0.3	1.0	1.1	1.0
Number of Countries		1	2	3	4	19
Lending Operations (No.)		1	2	3	4	20
% Total Bank and IDA		0.8	1.6	1.9	2.2	2.0
Projects under Supervision[1]		1	3	6	10	14[2]

[1] End of Fiscal Year.
[2] Annual average.

The number of projects, the number of countries involved and the volume of lending anticipated are all relatively minor when compared with the Bank Group's total operations. This should not, however, be taken to reflect the importance attached to the population sector by the Bank or by increasing numbers of its borrowers, nor do such projections serve as a full measure of the Bank's growing activity in this field.

As now envisaged, projects assisted by the Bank and IDA by the end of FY1976 will be in countries with about 70% of the population of the Bank's developing members. Many of the projects will be considerably larger than the first few that have been financed while the Bank has built up its staff, gained experience in the field, established close working relations with governments, other international institutions and private organizations concerned with population questions, and mounted nearly a dozen missions to accumulate detailed knowledge of the sector in individual countries.

Beginning with FY1972, Bank Group operations will focus increasingly on the larger countries where a downward shift in fertility rates would be most significant. For planning purposes, it is assumed that roughly half the 20 projects foreseen over the period 1972-76 will involve commitments of between $5 million and $10 million, while half the remainder will be above and half below that range.

The Bank's strategy in the five year period will be to establish the usefulness of its project approach in dealing with the population problem, primarily through experience with about 25 family planning programs, including as many as possible in countries with large populations. At the time of drafting this paper, for example, projects in India and Indonesia were nearing the final stage of consideration, and a number of others involving major population groups were already well advanced.

The projections in Table 9 are based on an assessment of practical possibilities in specific countries, in the light of both government and popular attitudes prevailing in 1972. They are unlikely to be revised downward, but experience may well show them to be overly conservative. Attitudes toward population questions have already changed dramatically since the Bank entered the field three years ago, thanks chiefly to the pioneering work of a few governments and several leading private organizations. The momentum of change is increasing. As awareness of the problem spreads and the Bank's capacity to assist becomes better known, further acceleration of the five year program may become possible.

Fact Finding and Institution Building

Leaving that possibility aside, however, it should be emphasized that project numbers and amounts in money terms are a less accurate barometer of Bank involvement in the population field than are similar figures for most other sectors. This is because, in most cases, a lack of foreign exchange is not the principal constraint on effective implementation of population policies. Often, in fact, the greatest need and the Bank's most useful contribution is not finance, although this can be critically important, but technical assistance in any or all

318

of its many forms.

One of these is education, in the most strategic sense. In many countries, the general implications of population growth in terms of development may be known by the professional and political elite, but understanding may not be sufficiently widespread to support decisive policies or action. In these cases, the Bank can often help governments through its capability for fact-finding and analysis. It can do so effectively, of course, only at the Government's invitation or, at the least, with its acquiescence. Given one or the other, however, the Bank's help in collecting, organizing and analyzing facts about a country's demographic position and its meaning in terms of development can sometimes be crucial.

One medium for this is the Bank's regular economic reports on borrowing countries. As a matter of policy, each of these reports is now supposed to include an analysis of the country's demographic situation and of its population policies or program. Unfortunately, this policy objective has not yet been fully realized; in fact, demographic analysis was included in only half the country reports completed in calendar years 1969 and 1970. This situation can be expected to improve, however, steadily increasing the effectiveness of such reports in providing the basic facts governments need to identify their own population problems and generate the political will on which action must depend.

Far more detailed knowledge of the demographic situation and of population problems, policies and programs in specific countries is provided by the Bank's sector missions. Because of staff limitations and the shortage of qualified independent consultants in this field, the number of such missions will increase only gradually over time. They can be extremely valuable, however, both to the Bank itself and to the countries concerned.

As of January 1, 1972, population missions had been sent to Colombia, Egypt, India, Indonesia, Jamaica, Malaysia, Mauritius, Trinidad and Tobago, and Tunisia. Missions to Ghana and the Philippines were planned during the remainder of fiscal 1972. In addition, pre-investment studies in population planning have been completed for Iran, Kenya, Tanzania, and Uganda; hopefully, at least two of these will lead to projects in the near future.

Each of the three projects thus far financed by the Bank Group, in Jamaica, Tunisia, and Trinidad and Tobago, was preceded by a sector study. These three relatively small countries have given the Bank invaluable experience in a new sector. A fourth successful sector mission was one in 1969 to Indonesia, involving the United Nations, the World Health Organization (WHO) and the Bank. This mission's work led to the Government's adoption of a five year plan and facilitated reorganization of the Government's Family Planning Board. In Mauritius, the work of a fifth sector mission led to an increase in the Government's financial support, and provided the basis for an integrated family planning maternal and child health program which was subsequently financed by UNFPA.

Proposals for a large scale pilot project in India, including a management information and evaluation system, have been accepted by the Government and will form the basis of a Bank project which has already been appraised. No project has emerged as a result of the mission to Colombia, since the Government does not feel able to accept a project justified solely in terms of family planning.

Results of some of these sector missions illustrate another facet of the Bank's technical assistance capability which may often be more important than external finance: help to governments in building the exceptional types of institutional structures which are required to plan and administer successful family planning programs.

This institution-building form of assistance involves a wide range of activities. It may include help in the organization and top-level staffing of national family planning agencies; the assessment of a program's manpower needs; the planning or provision of training for medical, social and demographic personnel; the design, collection and processing of service statistics; the evaluation of a program's performance; the design of research projects; the conduct of attitude surveys; the development of education materials for use in school systems, adult education activities or public information programs; the functional and economical design of buildings used in providing family planning services; the organization of recruitment activities; the procurement and distribution of contraceptive supplies; or other facets of planning, administration or training.

The Bank, of course, is not equipped with either the staff or the expertise required to provide assistance in all such areas directly. A number of these matters are the primary responsibility of other agencies in the United Nations system. In some specific fields, the principal reservoir of competence and experience may be found in other international institutions, bilateral agencies or private organizations. The Bank maintains close working relations with all these sources of expert assistance, and can often play an important coordinating and catalytic role, with or without financial involvement.

The relative emphasis to be placed on fact-finding and analysis, on the one hand, and institution building, on the other, will vary from country to country, depending upon the government's attitude toward population planning. The first role is likely to be dominant in countries which are hospitable or permissive with respect to family planning activity but which have no official programs; institution building will play a larger role in countries which have adopted population policies or programs and which welcome the Bank's assistance.

As in other sectors, the Bank's lending for population projects will also be accompanied by help in building institutions and by other forms of technical assistance. One of the most basic of these is assistance in identifying those projects which command the highest priority and preparing them in sufficient detail for the Bank, IDA or other agencies to consider their financing. Many other aspects of technical assistance will be incorporated in the projects themselves, with their costs included in Bank loans or IDA credits.

Constraints

Government commitment to population planning is a prerequisite to Bank activity. In those of its member countries which have not yet recognized that a population problem exists or which have expressed opposition to family planning programs, and which accordingly do not seek the Bank's assistance, the Bank cannot expect to operate. It may seek to educate and persuade, but it cannot hope to develop projects. This constraint, very real where it exists, may nevertheless become less severe with time, since political support for population planning appears to be spreading while commitments already made are becoming stronger.

At present the lead time for project development is long, since the Bank does not possess the basic sector knowledge in most countries which allows projects to be identified rapidly. Every project is a "first," in a new country. The field itself is a new one so far as large scale government programs are concerned, and there is no firm body of experience to give clear leads as to what activities are needed and will be successful. When project proposals have been worked out, they frequently have a number of components that require preparation with several ministries and agencies which may have no experience of working together in the population field.

The large number of external agencies providing assistance in the field also presents a problem of coordination in each country as well as internationally, especially since some of the basic relationships among key agencies are still in the process of being sorted out. Finally, almost all governments are new in dealing with population problems; they too are inexperienced and uncertain about the kinds of projects they want and need and about what types and sources of external assistance can help them most. For all these reasons, the number of Bank and IDA lending operations is bound to grow fairly slowly.

Population Projects

Population programs typically embrace much more than the provision of family planning services. In addition, they may include information and educational activities, research on the determinants of fertility and family-size decisions, adjustments in the social and welfare legislation affecting the age of marriage or the size of families, the improvement of vital statistics, and training in demography, nutrition and related activities. Nevertheless, the core of population projects is the provision of effective family planning services, including not only supply-oriented activities but also demand-oriented activities designed to motivate and recruit acceptors.

Family planning services are provided through a system that can be described in terms of the following nine components:

(a) **Program organization, management and administration:** i.e., designation of the responsible program agency and its location within government, the qualifications of key individuals, and the agency's internal organization and functioning.

(b) **Physical facilities:** buildings, equipment and vehicles used for dispensing services and for training, research, and program administration;

(c) **Staffing and training:** the medical, paramedical and other staff required and their training in family planning work;

(d) **Contraceptive methods and supplies:** the methods made available in the program and the existing arrangements for procuring and distributing necessary supplies;

(e) **The "delivery system":** the channels through which contraceptive methods are made available to acceptors. This will depend mainly on how the facilities and staff used for family planning are related to the regular health services, and the way the latter are organized. The use made of the private sector, including voluntary agencies, physicians, pharmacists and other retail distribution channels, is an important aspect of the delivery system;

(f) **Information, education and the recruitment of acceptors:** the kinds of public information and communication programs used to explain program objectives, plus the mechanisms relied on to establish contact with the target population (husbands and wives in the child-bearing years); also family life education built into school curricula.

322

(g) **Evaluation:** trends in activity levels as revealed by service statistics; demographic trends as revealed by census data and special research studies; bio-medical effects as revealed by special studies;

(h) **Finance:** program costs, including capital and operating expense, and arrangements for meeting them;

(i) **The program:** the action plan, or strategy, for expanding and improving family planning services.

While this is not an exhaustive list, it serves to identify those aspects of a program which the Bank examines when making a sector survey as background for project identification. Weaknesses or gaps in the set of activities outlined above, as found in a particular country, automatically suggest the contents of a project. They may also suggest steps the borrower will be asked to take before the Bank is prepared to finance a project.

Projects as well as programs normally include both tangible and intangible elements. The tangible—or "hardware"—elements usually account for the principal capital expenditure. These are items such as buildings, vehicles, furniture and equipment, office machines, training aids, printing equipment and machinery for contraceptive manufacture, etc.

Most "software" items also require additional expenditures. They may include training, the preparation of materials for schools and adult education, applied contraceptive research, attitude surveys, demographic research, foreign study fellowships, technical assistance services, or additional operating costs arising from program expansion.

Project components which may or may not require funds include necessary legal or organizational changes, the improvement of service statistics, the installation of improved accounts, revisions in arrangements for procuring contraceptive supplies, or the working out of an action plan for three or four years in the future.

The mix of project components in the Bank's initial population projects has already shown considerable variety. The first three, in Jamaica, Tunisia, and Trinidad and Tabago, include a high construction component (about 80% of total project costs), although there are significant differences in the types of facilities financed in the three projects. The much larger Indonesia project consists of only 40% construction, the rest being distributed among advisory services, technical assistance, vehicle purchase, demographic research, training stipends, and incremental operating costs.

"Software" components of the first three projects are also widely varied, and there are considerable differences in the organizational and administrative changes agreed upon with the borrowers. In the proposed India project, an experimental nutrition component will be introduced in order to test the relationship among nutrition, infant mortality and fertility.

Thus, while population projects consist of a certain number of identifiable "building blocks," the relative importance of each element can differ greatly from project to project. Furthermore, the importance of a particular component may bear little relation to the amount of money earmarked for it in the project cost table.

While facilities financed by the Bank for family planning purposes will frequently include buildings used for other health needs as well, their justification is solely in terms of their contribution to family planning objectives. In other words, the Bank does not currently finance health facilities per se.

Areas of Emphasis

Certain aspects of the problems of broadening the scope and improving the effectiveness of population programs demand special attention, and will be given greater emphasis in the Bank's work. These include:

• **Training.** The effective use of family planning facilities depends to a large extent on the quality of the training of personnel available to staff them. Most developing countries suffer from shortages of adequately trained personnel in the three most relevant fields: medical, paramedical and social service. Paramedical personnel play a key role in family planning through provision of services in clinics, in the field, and in maternity hospitals. In rural areas they are often the only persons with whom villagers come in contact; they are therefore a critical class of family planning workers. In addition, voluntary social workers can be trained and mobilized for field work.

Besides the local training needed for most operational workers, support frequently needs to be given for external training of personnel in the various disciplines at suitable overseas centers. Bank projects have provided for such training of selected personnel to strengthen the programs.

• **Physical Facilities.** Most developing countries have a substantial need for the development of physical infrastructure. This is true of health services and institutions for training, education and research. In the current stage of contraceptive technology, health facilities will continue to be the main vehicle for delivery of services and for the training of personnel involved in family planning. A large number of governments with population policies have committed themselves to provide family planning services only within the context of maternal and child health (MCH) services, for practical as well as political reasons. The successful programs in East Asia are in countries with developed MCH services.

Thus the provision of physical facilities in population projects will often be designed to enable family planning services to be delivered within the existing framework of a government's health services. Recent studies have suggested a close relationship between declines in infant mortality and, with some time lag, declines in fertility. Some of the contraceptive methods now in use and others likely to become available in the future require the support of a health infrastructure. These facilities also provide an important base for postpartum motivation.

There will also be need to expand other types of physical facilities required for such functions as communication, information and education, the production of educational materials, and research on socio-economic and technical problems.

• **Communication Strategy.** More emphasis will be given to the stimulation of demand for family planning services, especially in the larger of the less developed countries. These include the provision to individuals of information about family planning, group motivation, and face-to-face communication, particularly through social workers. Some existing programs will need a review of their communication strategy, since present approaches, adequate to reach the most responsive acceptors, appear less effective in penetrating deeply.

Information may be provided through existing channels of communication, for example by incorporating family life education into the school curriculum. In addition, influential older people may need to be reached by incorporating family planning information in literary, handicraft, or community development programs.

In some countries, and especially for rural areas, it may be more effective to develop a program of home visitors—trusted local persons trained in social work and community development — who would work closely with local family planning and MCH centers, serving as a link between them and the community.

• **Commercial Sector and Private Groups.** Often the commercial sector and private groups have not been adequately utilized in government programs, though they have been in some and much can be learned from their experience. The utilization of these groups for delivery of contraceptives and for promotional work will be built into programs where opportunities exist.

• **Measures for Social Welfare.** There are indications that reductions in fertility and acceptance of the small family concept may be promoted by measures which have little or no relation to the direct provision of family planning services. These include steps to improve

325

the status of women and expand their opportunities for education and a wider choice of occupational and intellectual pursuits. Other examples are changes in the lawful age of marriage, in benefits provided by old age insurance, in the payment of children's benefits under insurance or welfare programs, and changes in allowances or exemptions for children provided by personal income tax law. Although research on these topics is now going on, the field is new and little firm guidance yet exists. The Bank will try to keep abreast of findings in the field and will use them as appropriate.

• **Reduction of Infant Mortality.** In assessing attitudes toward family planning, it is important to differentiate between women in the subsistence and monetary sectors of the economy. Among the former especially, a convincing reduction of infant mortality rates may be essential before the majority can be effectively motivated to practice family planning. The Bank intends to take full account of government policies and plans to achieve this result, for example through nutrition programs and the provision of maternal and child health services.

• **Research.** In virtually all areas involving population questions there is need to improve the state of knowledge by means of well conceived, well implemented research. It is the Bank's intention to promote research in areas where the need is most pressing.

Research in the population sector covers a wide variety of topics. These can, however, be classified into four main groups. There is first of all basic demographic research, aimed at improving the data base for the main variables—fertility, mortality and migration. Second, there is economic research into the implications of population trends and their interrelationships with other economic variables. Included in this group would be studies of the economic effects of population programs.

The third area is bio-medical research, involving contraceptive technology and reproductive biology, basic to the increase in knowledge required before improved contraceptives can be devised and tested. Finally, there is a variety of operations research topics, all of which are directed to questions in various disciplines involving population policies. These include, for example, research on management questions, evaluation procedures, the role of communications, and motivation and educational techniques. One subject that needs considerably more research in nearly all countries is the set of motivations that determines the fertility and family size objectives of dissimilar socio-economic groups.

In view of the nature of the Bank's involvement in the financing of family planning programs, its main interests in research are likely to be those related to the operations of such programs. The methodological aspects of family planning programs, including, for example, cost-effectiveness and cost-benefit questions, or techniques of evaluation, are likely to be of particular concern to the Bank.

In addition, analysis of the wider relationships of population growth and movement to economic development requires support through appropriate research. In carrying out general economic analyses of the development prospects of member countries it is necessary to study the demographic aspects which form the underpinnings to economic planning.

Population research is usually best pursued in the country concerned, by domestic institutions which can draw upon well informed local research workers. The cross-disciplinary nature of the work requires skills and knowledge which normally go beyond the competence of the Bank. In these cases, such as biomedical research, the Bank is unlikely to be involved directly. It will maintain a continuing interest, however, and will encourage other appropriate national and international organizations to pursue such work.

In such areas as economic and operationally oriented studies, the Bank's involvement may be more direct. It might initiate research projects or encourage national institutions to carry out studies. It is also hoped that the Bank's own operations will yield material which can help to illuminate research undertaken by others.

Cooperation with Other Agencies

The Bank works with a number of other agencies operating in the family planning field (Annex 5). This cooperation has been both formal and informal. It is certain to increase, in depth and in scope.

The United Nations, WHO, UNFPA, the Pan American Health Organization (PAHO), the International Planned Parenthood Federation (IPPF), the International Development Research Centre of Canada, the Population Council and the Ford Foundation, as well as several academic institutions, have cooperated with the Bank in providing experts for missions.

The Bank itself has participated in missions with other institutions. The UN-WHO-Bank mission to Indonesia, which the Bank initiated, helped the Government establish its population policy and prepare its Five Year Plan. The UNFPA participated in a second mission to Indonesia. The Swedish International Development Authority (SIDA) sent an observer on an appraisal mission to India.

Cooperation with other agencies has extended beyond sector studies into the project implementation stage. In the Jamaica project, two studies bearing on the management aspects of the program were financed by the U.S. Agency for International Development (U.S. AID). PAHO will provide some of the advisory services in the Trinidad and Tobago project. WHO may undertake some health studies related to the project in Tunisia. In Indonesia, the project will be jointly financed by UNFPA. SIDA may join in financing the Indian project.

Within the United Nations system, the major expertise in the population field is not with the Bank but is spread among a number of agencies: WHO for the medical aspects, the United Nations for demography, Unesco where education is concerned, etc. Accordingly, the Bank's work in this sector must be carried out in close cooperation with the other international agencies concerned, as well as with bilateral agencies, such as AID, SIDA, the Canadian International Development Agency (CIDA), and with private organizations such as the Population Council and IPPF.

Cooperation with the large number of development assistance organizations involved presents some difficulties, particularly in cases where basic approaches to the subject may be different. Moreover, there are many kinds and degrees of cooperation, ranging from projects formally organized as joint financing operations to informal arrangements for separate but complementary projects in the same country. Only after considerably more experience has been gained will it become clear precisely which patterns or sets of patterns of cooperation are likely to be most effective.

POPULATION PROJECTIONS, 1970-2100

Future size of population in the various regions of the world will depend ultimately on the trend of fertility in the next 20 to 30 years. Other determinants are the present age and sex structure and the mortality schedule. As for mortality, after a further substantial decline in developing countries over the next decade or so, it may reasonably be assumed that the downward trend will level out, as it has in the developed countries.

For this analysis, a recently developed model[1] has been used to prepare illustrative projections for the entire world, the less developed countries (LDCs) considered as a whole, and for large countries and regions of Asia, Africa and Latin America. This model permits calculations and demonstrates the interaction, at five year intervals, of future population size, age structure, and several demographic indices and rates, such as the average annual growth rate, crude birth and death rates, total fertility rate (sum of age-specific fertility rates multiplied by interval length), expectation of life at birth, and gross and net reproduction rates.

The basic data for these projections are the age distribution of the population of a region or country in or around 1965 and the mortality and fertility levels of the late 1960s. Only one set of mortality assumptions, implying an orderly decline, is used for each region or country; in the calculations, a series of assumptions has been used, differing from each other by speed of fertility decline.

For the purpose of this illustration, two projections for each population under consideration have been selected. These are provided for the whole world, more developed regions, less developed regions, and for regions and countries selected on the basis of their absolute size and their present favorable disposition to measures of fertility control.

Projection A assumes that fertility will decline to a level corresponding to a net reproduction rate (NRR)[2] of unity by the period 2000-2005. For this decrease to be possible, an effort of "maximum effectiveness" is assumed.

Projection B represents population trends in the future if efforts to achieve NRR of 1 by the year 2000 are unsuccessful, and the level of replacement is not achieved until 40 years later (i.e., by 2040-2045).

The measure of the effort required to decrease fertility to NRR of 1 by the year 2000 is the result of comparing absolute numbers of births

[1]Tomas Frejka (Population Council), "Alternatives of World Population Growth," monograph in process of publication.
[2]For definition see footnote, page 10.

through the years, under assumptions A and B and applying the same mortality rates.

The arbitrary choice of NRR of 1 as a goal of fertility decline is based on the generally accepted view that populations will have to stop growing some time in the future. Fertility patterns corresponding to NRR of 1 lead eventually to stationary populations. A NRR greater than 1 results in compounded population growth. The consequences of continued growth for a long period are extremely large populations, difficult to conceive as functioning societies in terms of present standards.

Table 1 presents the results of projections A and B for the entire world and for the less developed regions to the year 2100. Other demographic indicators of the resulting populations at different dates between 1970 and 2100 are included in the table, as supplementary evidence to describe the consequences of rapid or slow fertility decline.

World population was estimated to be at a level of about 3,700 million in 1970. Projection A, which resulted from assuming that fertility would decline after 1970 and achieve NRR of 1 by 2000, indicates that the size of the population in that year would reach 5,900 million. This growth may be considered a minimum. It is a target which can be attained only if considerable effort is applied to changing present attitudes toward high fertility among peoples of less developed countries, where world population trends will be chiefly determined.

The contribution of the developed countries to population growth may be considered negligible. As a group, they had 30% of the world's population in 1970 and a net reproduction rate of 1.25. By 2000, under the assumption of effective fertility control in the world as a whole, their share of population would be reduced to 23%.

Therefore, in analyzing the alternatives of world population growth in the next 30 to 70 years, it will suffice to concentrate on alternative changes in fertility in the less developed countries, and especially on likely developments in a few large countries.

The total population of developing countries in 1970 was estimated to be about 2,530 million people. Under assumption A (effective control) for fertility decline, by the year 2000 there would be 4,500 million inhabitants of those areas, an increase of almost 80%. This would require a decline in the crude birth rate (CBR) from the level of 42 per 1,000 in 1970 to 24 in 2000 (Table 2), or an annual average decrease of 0.6 per 1,000. If fertility trends decline less rapidly during the next 30 years—that is, if efforts to achieve NRR of 1 by 2000 are unsuccessful and the population reaches this rate some 40 years later—the

Population Projections and Other Demographic Indicators—World, Developed Countries, Developing Countries, 1970-2100

Region	Assumption[1]	1970	1975	1980	1985	2000	2050	2075	2100
World Total									
Population (millions)	A	3,652	4,019	4,402	4,796	5,916	8,136	8,348	8,386
	B	3,652	4,042	4,475	4,956	6,690	13,444	15,306	15,815
Percent Increase (base, 1970)	A	—	10	20	31	62	124	129	130
	B	—	11	22	36	83	268	319	333
Average Annual Growth Rates (%)[2]	A	1.99	1.91	1.82	1.71	1.20	0.28	0.06	0.00
	B	1.99	2.03	2.04	2.04	1.96	0.82	0.31	0.04
Percent under 15 yrs.[3]	A	37.0	—	—	34.5	29.1	20.3	19.8	19.8
	B	37.0	—	—	36.6	34.7	23.7	20.3	20.3
Dependency ratio[4]	A	0.74	—	—	0.66	0.55	0.52	0.57	0.57
	B	0.74	—	—	0.72	0.60	0.52	0.53	0.53
Developed Countries	A	1,122	1,169	1,217	1,263	1,388	1,610	1,622	1,623
	B	1,122	1,171	1,222	1,274	1,431	1,853	1,931	1,952
Developing Countries									
Population (millions)	A	2,530	2,850	3,185	3,533	4,528	6,525	6,727	6,763
	B	2,530	2,871	3,253	3,682	5,259	11,591	13,374	13,863
Percent Increase (base, 1970)	A	—	13	26	40	79	158	166	167
	B	—	13	29	46	108	358	429	448
Average Annual Growth Rates (%)[2]	A	2.6	2.4	2.3	2.1	1.4	0.3	0.1	0.0
	B	2.6	2.6	2.5	2.5	2.3	0.9	0.3	0.0
Percent under 15 yrs.[3]	A	41.6	—	—	38.2	31.4	20.8	19.9	20.0
	B	41.6	—	—	40.6	38.2	24.8	19.7	19.7
Dependency Ratio[4]	A	82.0	—	—	72.0	56.3	50.4	56.1	56.0
	B	82.0	—	—	79.2	73.0	48.2	51.1	51.1

[1] For projection A, a linear decline in the GRR is assumed to a level which corresponds to NRR=1 by 2000-2005; this decline is equated with effective fertility control.

Projection B represents population trends under the assumption that NRR=1 will not be achieved until 2045; this situation is considered likely to occur if efforts for fertility control continue at the present levels.

[2] Annual growth rates for preceding five-year period.

[3] For the female population.

[4] Ratio of female population under 15 and over 65 to population 15-64 years.

Source: Tomas Frejka (Population Council). "Alternatives of World Population Growth," monograph in process of publication.

LDCs will be inhabited by 5,300 million people in the year 2000. The possibility of an additional 800 million in the year 2000 under assumption B, however, is less significant than the difference in total numbers under the two assumptions by the time a stationary population is arrived at. By 2050, assumption A would result in total population in the LDCs of 6,500 million, compared with 11,600 million under assumption B. It would still grow to 6,700 million under assumption A, or to 13,400 million under assumption B, before becoming stationary by approximately 2075. Population trends for the years 1970-2075 are presented for main world regions and large countries in Table 3.

The consequences of slow fertility decrease have to be measured in terms of the unavoidable ultimate size of the population. Although

Projected Birth Rates[1] per 1000 Population—World, Developing Regions—Selected Countries, 1965-2025

Region	Assumption[2]	1965-70	1970-75	1975-80	1980-85	1985-90	1990-95	1995-2000	2020-2025
World Total	A	34.5	32.4	30.4	28.5	26.6	24.3	21.8	16.5
	B		33.6	32.9	32.1	31.3	30.5	29.6	24.0
Developed Countries	A	18.8	18.6	18.2	17.8	17.2	16.4	15.8	14.0
	B		18.8	18.9	18.7	18.2	17.7	17.4	15.6
Developing Countries	A	41.8	38.2	35.3	32.5	29.8	27.0	23.7	17.2
	B		39.9	38.3	36.9	35.7	34.4	33.0	24.6
East Asia	A	34.5	32.2	29.8	27.5	25.3	23.3	21.2	16.4
	B		33.3	31.9	30.4	29.2	28.3	27.4	21.3
South Asia	A	44.1	39.9	36.6	33.7	30.8	27.6	23.8	17.1
	B		41.7	40.1	38.7	37.5	36.1	34.5	25.4
India	A	41.4	38.1	35.4	32.9	30.1	27.1	23.6	17.1
	B		39.7	38.4	37.3	36.0	34.4	32.9	24.6
Iran	A	45.0	40.8	38.5	36.4	33.1	28.9	24.3	17.2
	B		42.8	42.5	42.1	40.8	38.6	36.5	26.7
Malaysia[3]	A	36.0	34.4	32.9	30.6	27.7	24.5	21.2	17.0
	B		36.1	36.0	35.1	33.4	31.6	30.1	22.9
Pakistan	A	42.3	41.1	40.0	37.3	33.2	28.8	24.2	17.0
	B		43.2	44.0	43.0	40.9	38.4	36.4	26.6
Philippines	A	45.2	41.3	38.2	35.6	32.5	28.5	24.1	17.3
	B		43.4	42.1	41.2	39.9	37.9	35.9	26.2
Thailand	A	41.1	37.9	35.2	32.4	29.5	26.2	22.4	16.7
	B		39.8	38.6	37.5	36.2	34.7	33.1	31.5
Turkey	A	36.0	34.2	32.9	31.2	28.5	25.3	22.0	16.5
	B		35.7	35.8	35.4	34.0	32.2	30.5	23.2
Africa	A	45.8	41.9	38.5	35.7	32.7	29.2	25.3	18.1
	B		43.8	42.0	40.6	39.2	37.5	35.7	26.2
Egypt	A	44.5	40.3	36.7	33.7	31.1	27.9	24.0	17.1
	B		42.1	40.2	38.7	37.6	36.4	34.7	25.6
Ghana	A	49.2	44.7	41.0	38.3	34.7	30.3	25.6	18.0
	B		46.7	45.2	44.1	42.2	39.9	37.7	27.4
Kenya	A	49.6	44.3	40.2	36.5	32.9	29.3	25.1	17.6
	B		46.3	44.0	41.9	40.1	38.1	36.7	26.5
Tunisia	A	45.3	41.2	37.9	35.1	32.0	28.3	24.0	17.4
	B		43.3	41.7	40.6	39.3	37.6	35.8	26.1
Latin America	A	39.4	36.4	33.8	31.5	28.9	25.9	22.5	16.6
	B		37.9	36.9	35.9	34.6	33.3	31.9	23.9
Brazil	A	38.6	35.9	33.5	31.1	28.4	25.4	22.1	16.5
	B		37.4	36.5	35.5	34.1	32.6	31.1	23.5
Colombia	A	38.0	36.4	34.9	32.8	29.5	25.8	22.1	16.6
	B		38.0	38.1	37.4	35.4	33.1	31.3	23.6
Mexico	A	44.6	40.6	37.4	34.4	31.5	27.9	23.7	17.0
	B		42.6	41.2	40.0	38.7	37.3	35.7	26.1

[1] Female birth rates resulting from projections multiplied by factor 1.025.
[2] Assumptions used for projections: See Footnote (1), Table 1.
[3] Not including Sabah and Sarawak.

Source: Tomas Frejka (Population Council), "Alternatives of World Population Growth," monograph in process of publication.

332

Alternative Population Projections 1970-2075—World, Developed Countries, Developing Countries, Selected Large Countries (Millions)

Region	Assumption[1]	1970	1975	1980	1985	1990	1995	2000	2050	2075
World Total	A	3,652.1	4,019.3	4,401.9	4,796.4	5,191.9	5,571.9	5,916.1	8,135.7	8,348.4
	B		4,041.7	4,474.8	4,956.1	5,485.9	6,064.2	6,690.1	13,443.6	15,305.6
Developed	A	1,122.2	1,169.4	1,216.7	1,263.2	1,309.0	1,350.6	1,388.1	1,610.3	1,621.7
Countries	B		1,171.1	1,221.9	1,274.0	1,327.6	1,379.8	1,431.3	1,852.9	1,931.2
Developing	A	2,529.9	2,849.9	3,185.2	3,533.2	3,882.9	4,221.3	4,528.0	6,525.4	6,726.7
Countries	B		2,870.6	3,252.9	3,682.1	4,158.3	4,684.4	5,258.8	11,590.7	13,374.4
East Asia	A	940.8	1,034.6	1,129.6	1,223.5	1,315.2	1,403.5	1,485.0	2,001.7	2,053.4
	B		1,039.9	1,146.4	1,259.2	1,379.1	1,507.8	1,645.5	3,010.9	3,358.0
South Asia	A	1,102.7	1,253.1	1,413.0	1,582.1	1,755.4	1,925.0	2,079.3	3,076.6	3,153.5
	B		1,263.4	1,447.0	1,658.1	1,898.2	2,168.7	2,468.9	5,915.8	6,896.0
India	A	534.3	598.3	666.7	739.0	812.4	883.5	948.3	1,365.5	1,402.0
	B		602.5	680.5	769.6	869.3	979.5	1,100.2	2,431.8	2,799.0
Iran	A	27.9	31.9	36.5	41.5	46.7	51.8	56.2	85.9	88.1
	B		32.2	37.4	43.7	51.1	59.4	68.4	179.8	212.9
Malaysia[2]	A	9.4	10.7	12.2	13.8	15.4	16.9	18.3	26.8	27.4
	B		10.8	12.5	14.5	16.6	18.9	21.3	47.3	54.2
Pakistan	A	126.2	144.9	166.7	190.7	215.1	238.4	259.6	398.9	408.4
	B		146.2	171.3	201.3	235.3	273.3	315.8	831.0	981.8
Philippines	A	37.8	44.0	50.6	57.8	65.1	72.3	78.6	118.6	121.9
	B		44.4	52.0	60.9	71.2	82.6	95.2	239.7	282.0
Thailand	A	36.6	42.1	48.0	54.2	60.5	66.6	72.1	105.5	107.6
	B		42.4	49.2	56.9	65.6	75.4	86.0	202.2	233.7
Turkey	A	34.5	38.5	43.0	47.8	52.7	57.4	61.6	88.4	90.8
	B		38.8	43.8	49.7	56.3	63.4	70.9	151.4	173.3
Africa	A	344.2	386.9	432.4	480.5	529.6	577.2	620.2	899.2	929.0
	B		389.9	442.2	502.3	570.2	645.9	729.1	1,663.6	1,931.6
Egypt	A	33.5	37.9	42.7	47.6	52.8	57.8	62.4	91.7	93.8
	B		38.3	43.7	49.9	57.0	65.1	74.0	176.3	205.1
Ghana	A	9.0	10.1	11.4	12.8	14.2	15.6	16.8	24.8	25.4
	B		10.2	11.7	13.4	15.5	17.7	20.2	49.8	58.2
Kenya	A	10.9	12.5	14.1	15.8	17.6	19.2	20.7	30.3	31.0
	B		12.6	14.5	16.6	19.1	21.8	24.8	59.7	69.5
Tunisia	A	5.0	5.8	6.5	7.4	8.3	9.2	9.9	14.7	15.1
	B		5.8	6.7	7.8	9.0	10.4	12.0	29.5	34.5
Latin America	A	283.2	323.8	366.7	411.3	456.4	500.0	539.7	797.3	818.8
	B		326.2	374.5	428.7	488.8	554.7	625.9	1,396.4	1,614.3
Brazil	A	94.0	107.6	122.1	137.3	152.7	167.5	180.9	265.9	272.8
	B		108.3	124.7	143.0	163.3	185.4	209.3	459.3	528.9
Colombia	A	21.1	24.1	27.5	31.1	34.7	38.1	41.2	60.3	61.7
	B		24.3	28.1	32.5	37.2	42.3	47.7	104.8	120.4
Mexico	A	50.7	59.5	68.9	79.1	80.4	99.6	108.7	167.9	172.5
	B		60.0	70.8	83.3	97.5	113.6	131.3	335.4	396.8

[1] Assumptions used for projections: See Footnote (1), Table 1.

[2] Not including Sabah and Sarawak.

Source: Tomas Frejka (Population Council), "Alternatives of World Population Growth," monograph in process of publication.

assumption B implies also a decline in the CBR of developing countries from 42 in 1970 to 33 in the year 2000, and a drop in total fertility[1] from 5.7 in 1970 to 4.3 in 2000 (see Table 4), this would not be enough to stop growth for at least 60-75 additional years. By then, the absolute size would exceed 13,000 million persons—twice as many as under assumption A.

Accepting the desirability of achieving population trends nearer to projection A in the LDCs, one can elaborate on the process of fertility change which would be necessary and on the likelihood of such change taking place.

In the LDCs, under assumption A the population would achieve NRR of 1 by 2000 and would stabilize some 75 years later at approximately 6,700 million. For this situation to occur, the total fertility rate would have to decrease from a level of 5.7 in 1970 to less than three in 2000 (2.8 children per woman, see Table 4). As indicated above, the resulting birth rate would decline at a speed of 0.6 per 1,000 per year, reach a level of 24 by 2000, and further stabilize at about 17 per 1,000 25 years later (Table 2).

What would make the difference between a situation conducive to changes in fertility from assumption B to assumption A? This question may be answered by showing how many live births would take place annually in both situations, indicating the magnitude of the difference, and estimating the number of women who would need to practice contraception yearly in order to prevent the excess births. Table 5 shows projected live births for the world, the LDCs, and several regions and countries.

The difference between the numbers of births under assumptions A and B may be taken as an estimate of the additional number of births which would have to be averted annually by expanded population planning programs to accomplish population trends similar to projection A. This has been summarized in Table 6. Thus, in the five year period 1970-75 it would be necessary to avert 4.8 million births per year in the LDCs; these annual averages would increase to 11 million by 1975-80 and up to about 60.5 million births by the year 2000.

Since population growth in the developed countries is already slow, and in these projections it is assumed that it will stop in the near future, it may be expected that after the year 1985 birth prevention beyond the levels of present contraceptive practice will have to take place in the LDCs. During the period 1970-2000, half the magnitude of birth prevention to achieve projection A instead of B would

---

[1]Sum of five-year interval age-specific fertility rates multiplied by five; it is interpreted as an indicator of "children per woman."

Projected Total Fertility Rates per Woman[1]—World, Developed Countries, Developing Countries, Selected Large Countries, 1965-2025

Region	Assump-tion[2]	1965-70	1970-75	1975-80	1980-85	1985-90	1990-95	1995-2000	2020-2025
World Total	A	4.74	4.38	4.02	3.66	3.30	2.94	2.58	2.15
	B		4.56	4.39	4.21	4.04	3.86	3.69	2.81
Developed Countries	A	2.66	2.58	2.50	2.42	2.34	2.26	2.18	2.08
	B		2.63	2.59	2.55	2.51	2.47	2.43	2.24
Developing Countries	A	5.74	5.25	4.77	4.28	3.79	3.31	2.82	2.20
	B		5.50	5.26	5.02	4.78	4.54	4.30	3.09
South Asia	A	6.15	5.60	5.04	4.49	3.93	3.38	2.82	2.16
	B		5.88	5.61	5.35	5.08	4.81	4.54	3.20
India	A	5.55	5.08	4.62	4.16	3.69	3.23	2.77	2.19
	B		5.32	5.09	4.86	4.63	4.41	4.18	3.04
Iran	A	6.76	6.12	5.47	4.83	4.18	3.54	2.89	2.15
	B		6.46	6.15	5.84	5.53	5.22	4.91	3.36
Malaysia[3]	A	5.31	4.86	4.40	3.95	3.49	3.04	2.58	2.10
	B		5.09	4.88	4.66	4.45	4.23	4.02	2.94
Pakistan	A	6.53	5.91	5.30	4.68	4.07	3.45	2.84	2.14
	B		6.23	5.94	5.64	5.35	5.06	4.76	3.29
Philippines	A	6.77	6.12	5.48	4.84	4.19	3.55	2.90	2.17
	B		6.46	6.15	5.84	5.53	5.22	4.91	3.35
Thailand	A	6.15	5.58	5.02	4.45	3.88	3.32	2.75	2.15
	B		5.88	5.61	5.34	5.07	4.81	4.54	3.19
Turkey	A	5.30	4.86	4.43	3.99	3.55	3.11	2.67	2.16
	B		5.09	4.88	4.66	4.45	4.24	4.02	2.95
Africa	A	6.35	5.80	5.24	4.68	4.12	3.56	3.01	2.28
	B		6.08	5.80	5.52	5.24	4.96	4.68	3.28
Egypt	A	6.14	5.59	5.04	4.49	3.94	3.39	2.83	2.17
	B		5.88	5.61	5.34	5.07	4.81	4.54	3.20
Ghana	A	6.97	6.32	5.68	5.03	4.38	3.74	3.09	2.26
	B		6.65	6.33	6.01	5.69	5.37	5.05	3.45
Kenya	A	6.75	6.13	5.51	4.89	4.27	3.65	3.02	2.23
	B		6.45	6.14	5.84	5.53	5.22	4.92	3.38
Tunisia	A	6.77	6.13	5.49	4.85	4.21	3.56	2.92	2.19
	B		6.46	6.15	5.84	5.53	5.22	4.91	3.36
Latin America	A	5.54	5.07	4.60	4.13	3.66	3.19	2.72	2.20
	B		5.31	5.09	4.86	4.64	4.41	4.19	3.06
Brazil	A	5.38	4.93	4.48	4.03	3.58	3.13	2.68	2.20
	B		5.16	4.95	4.74	4.52	4.31	4.09	3.02
Colombia	A	5.56	5.08	4.61	4.14	3.67	3.20	2.72	2.20
	B		5.33	5.10	4.88	4.65	4.43	4.20	3.07
Mexico	A	6.54	5.92	5.31	4.69	4.07	3.46	2.84	2.19
	B		6.25	5.96	5.66	5.37	5.08	4.79	3.33

[1] Sum of age-specific fertility rates multiplied by 5; it is interpreted as an indicator of "children per woman."
[2] Assumptions used for projections: See Footnote (1), Table 1.
[3] Not including Sabah and Sarawak.
Source: Tomas Frejka (Population Council), "Alternatives of World Population Growth," monograph in process of publication.

Projected Annual Average Number of Live Births[1]—World, Developed Countries, Developing Countries, Selected Large Countries, 1970-2000 (Thousands)

Region	Assumptions[2]	1970-75	1975-80	1980-85	1985-90	1990-95	1995-2000
World Total	A	124,090	128,160	131,260	132,758	131,052	125,200
	B	129,170	139,954	151,238	163,560	176,272	188,548
Developed Countries	A	21,255	21,761	22,120	22,147	21,808	21,608
	B	21,511	22,566	23,287	23,726	24,001	24,485
Developing Countries	A	102,835	106,399	109,140	110,611	109,244	103,592
	B	107,659	117,388	127,951	139,834	152,271	164,063
East Asia	A	31,789	32,276	32,320	32,137	31,628	30,643
	B	32,991	34,847	36,616	38,536	40,835	43,149
South Asia	A	46,966	48,780	50,501	51,485	50,738	47,611
	B	49,354	54,313	60,153	66,707	73,366	80,098
India	A	21,593	22,366	23,125	23,376	22,946	21,593
	B	22,547	24,657	27,052	29,482	31,836	34,213
Iran	A	1,220	1,318	1,420	1,460	1,424	1,312
	B	1,287	1,480	1,709	1,934	2,135	2,332
Malaysia[3]	A	345	377	398	404	396	373
	B	365	419	474	520	561	606
Pakistan	A	5,572	6,228	6,668	6,738	6,531	6,023
	B	5,877	6,980	8,021	8,928	9,774	10,718
Philippines	A	1,689	1,808	1,928	1,996	1,958	1,817
	B	1,781	2,030	2,326	2,633	2,916	3,190
Thailand	A	1,492	1,584	1,655	1,693	1,668	1,557
	B	1,571	1,770	1,990	2,216	2,450	2,672
Turkey	A	1,249	1,341	1,414	1,432	1,394	1,311
	B	1,307	1,474	1,653	1,804	1,927	2,051
Africa	A	15,327	15,786	16,283	16,516	16,166	15,157
	B	16,063	17,482	19,166	20,995	22,809	24,523
Egypt	A	1,438	1,479	1,522	1,559	1,542	1,441
	B	1,512	1,647	1,813	2,011	2,221	2,417
Ghana	A	426	443	464	469	452	415
	B	449	495	554	610	662	714
Kenya	A	518	534	545	549	539	501
	B	544	596	652	715	788	855
Tunisia	A	222	234	244	251	247	229
	B	234	260	294	330	365	400
Latin America	A	11,043	11,677	12,241	12,539	12,400	11,722
	B	11,556	12,929	14,407	15,895	17,382	18,817
Brazil	A	3,616	3,850	4,027	4,117	4,069	3,857
	B	3,784	4,251	4,747	5,228	5,683	6,130
Colombia	A	822	902	961	972	940	877
	B	863	999	1,134	1,232	1,316	1,407
Mexico	A	2,236	2,402	2,548	2,509	2,509	2,455
	B	2,360	2,695	3,080	3,502	3,938	4,368

[1] Births estimated on the basis of projected population and resulting birth rates in model (shown in Table 2), under assumptions A and B.

[2] Assumptions used for projections: See Footnote (1), Table 1.

[3] Not including Sabah and Sarawak.

Estimated[1] Average Annual Number of Births Omitted if Projection A
Instead of B is Achieved, 1970-2000 (Thousands)

Region	1970-75	1975-80	1980-85	1985-90	1990-95	1995-2000
World Total	5,080	11,794	19,978	30,802	45,220	63,348
Developed Countries	256	805	1,167	1,579	2,193	2,877
Developing Countries	4,824	10,989	18,811	29,223	43,027	60,471
South Asia	2,388	5,533	9,652	15,222	22,628	32,487
India	954	2,291	3,927	6,106	8,890	12,620
Iran	67	162	289	474	711	1,020
Malaysia[2]	20	42	76	116	165	233
Pakistan	305	752	1,353	2,190	3,243	4,695
Philippines	92	222	398	637	958	1,373
Thailand	79	186	335	523	782	1,115
Turkey	58	136	239	372	533	740
Africa	736	1,696	2,883	4,479	6,643	9,366
Egypt	74	168	291	452	679	976
Ghana	23	52	90	141	210	299
Kenya	26	62	107	166	249	354
Tunisia	12	26	50	79	118	171
Latin America	513	1,252	2,166	3,356	4,982	7,095
Brazil	168	401	720	1,111	1,614	2,273
Colombia	41	97	173	260	376	530
Mexico	124	293	532	993	1,429	1,902

[1] Estimates obtained by difference between the number of births under projections A and B, shown in Table 5.
[2] Not including Sabah and Sarawak.

have to take place in South Asia. In India alone the share of birth
prevention would be more than 20% of that required for the entire
group of LDCs.

Table 7 gives the total number of live births during the 30-year
period 1970-2000 in the world as a whole, in the less developed
countries, and in several large countries under alternative assumptions A and B, and the number that would need to be averted to
achieve projection A instead of B. During that period about 840 million live births would have to be prevented in the LDCs. Of that
number, almost half (46%) would have to be prevented in the 14
countries mentioned in Table 7.

In order to accomplish projection A, the number of women who
would have to practice contraception each year through the period
1970-2000 has been calculated and presented in Table 8. In 1970-75
it is estimated that an average of about 19.3 million women (or 3.3%

Projected Number of Births and Births Omitted, 1970-2000 (Millions)

Region	Total Number of Births 1970-2000		Births Omitted	Percent[2]
	Projection A[1]	Projection B[1]		
World Total	3,862	4,744	882	100.0
Developed Countries	653	698	45	5.1
Developing Countries[3]	3,209	4,046	837	94.9
South Asia	1,480	1,920	440	49.9
India	675	849	174	19.7
Iran	41	54	13	1.5
Malaysia[4]	11	15	4	0.4
Pakistan	189	251	62	7.0
Philippines	56	74	18	2.0
Thailand	48	63	15	1.7
Turkey	41	51	10	1.1
Africa	476	605	129	14.6
Egypt	45	58	13	1.5
Ghana	13	17	4	0.4
Kenya	16	21	5	0.6
Tunisia	7	9	2	0.2
Latin America	358	455	97	11.0
Brazil	118	149	31	3.5
Colombia	27	35	8	0.9
Mexico	73	100	27	3.1

[1] Assumptions used for projections: See Footnote (1), Table 1.

[2] Ratio of births omitted in each subdivision to world total.

[3] During the 30-year period, there would be 4,325 million births in the LDCs under conditions of almost maximum human fertility (constant fertility at the levels of 1965-70, or about 200 live births per 1,000 women 15-44 years); in all, 1,116 million births would have to be averted to make projection A a reality. Of that number, it is expected that about 279 million will be avoided if present contraceptive practices are maintained. Projection A instead of B will be achieved in the LDCs only if about 837 million additional births are avoided in the three decades.

[4] Excluding Sabah and Sarawak.

of all women 15-44 years of age) would need to be practicing contraception each year in the LDCs in order to prevent 4.8 million live births. The number of women practicing contraception in a year would have to increase to 117 (13.9% of those 15-44 years old) in 1985-90 and to 242 million (22.5%) in 1995-2000.

These calculations were made on the basis of the projected age structures produced by the model, and on the assumption that four women receiving protection for one year are needed to prevent one live birth. If fertility is assumed to continue constant[1] at present levels to the year 2000, it is estimated that the proportion of the female

[1] Almost equivalent to a low estimate of maximum human fertility, or 200 live births per 1,000 women 15-44.

**Total Average Annual Number of Women 15-44 and Estimated
Proportion of Contraceptors Required to Achieve Projection A,
1970-2000 (Thousands)**

Region	1970-75			1985-90			1995-2000		
	Women 15-44[1]	Contraceptors[2]		Women 15-44	Contraceptors[2]		Women 15-44	Contraceptors[2]	
		Number	%		Number	%		Number	%
World Total	820,840	20,320	2.48	1,123,684	123,208	10.96	1,381,432	253,392	18.34
Developed Countries	240,618	1,024	0.42	272,010	6,316	2.32	293,040	11,508	3.93
Developing Countries[3]	576,982	19,296 (26,700)	3.34 (5.0)	841,728	116,892 (130,000)	13.89 (16.2)	1,076,165	241,884 (320,000)	22.48 (30.8)
South Asia	249,125	9,552	3.83	375,470	60,888	16.22	494,530	129,948	26.28
India	120,622	3,816	3.16	176,860	24,424	13.81	225,312	50,480	22.40
Iran	5,920	268	4.53	9,790	1,896	19.37	13,528	4,080	30.16
Malaysia[4]	2,125	80	3.76	3,358	464	13.82	4,355	932	21.40
Pakistan	26,702	1,220	4.57	45,450	8,760	19.27	62,748	18,780	29.93
Philippines	8,365	368	4.40	14,010	2,548	18.19	18,938	5,492	29.00
Thailand	8,245	316	3.83	13,048	2,092	16.03	17,232	4,460	25.88
Turkey	7,628	232	3.04	11,508	1,488	12.93	14,698	2,960	20.14
Africa	77,315	2,944	3.81	115,150	17,916	15.56	148,178	37,464	25.28
Egypt	7,498	296	3.95	11,300	1,808	16.00	14,875	3,904	26.24
Ghana	1,988	92	4.63	3,085	564	18.28	4,035	1,196	29.64
Kenya	2,522	104	4.12	3,775	664	17.59	4,988	1,416	28.39
Tunisia	1,108	48	4.33	1,778	316	17.77	2,388	684	28.64
Latin America	63,888	2,052	3.21	98,268	13,424	13.66	126,842	28,380	22.37
Brazil	21,420	672	3.14	33,205	4,444	13.38	42,505	9,092	21.39
Colombia	4,802	164	3.42	7,715	1,040	13.48	9,812	2,120	21.61
Mexico	11,185	496	4.43	17,705	3,972	22.43	25,725	7,608	29.57

[1] Female population 15-44, estimated on basis of projected age structures as obtained by model (projection A).

[2] Number of women who would need to practice contraception during year (couple-years of protection), in order that projection A is achieved instead of B, is obtained by assuming that four couple-years of protection are needed to avert one birth.

[3] Numbers in parentheses represent the total contraceptors needed to achieve projection A, as compared to a situation of constant fertility at 1965-70 levels.

[4] Not including Sabah and Sarawak.

Source: World Bank, computed on the basis of data from Tomas Frejka (Population Council), "Alternatives of World Population Growth," monograph in process of publication.

population in reproductive ages who would have to use contraception during the year to achieve projection A in the LDCs as compared to potential maximum human fertility would be 5% in 1970-75 (26.7 million), 16.2% in 1985-90 (130 million), and 30.8% in 1995-2000 (320 million).

The estimates in Tables 7 and 8 give an indication of the magnitude of the task required in the next 30 years to reduce fertility in the less developed regions of the world to the levels implied by assumption A.

A second important consideration is the changes in age structure of the population which alternative fertility declines A and B would bring about. In Table 1 the proportions of female children under 15 are given for the world and the LDCs. Also, the dependency ratios which would result at different points in time are presented. The proportion of the female population under 15 is a consequence of prevailing fertility conditions. In the LDCs the proportion is high— on average in excess of 40%. If in the next 30 years fertility decreases are of the magnitude stated in assumption A, the proportion of females under 15 will gradually decrease to 38% by 1985 and about 31% by 2000, stabilizing at about 20% in the following years. If fertility declines are closer to assumption B, changes in age structure will be much less noticeable, and by 2000 the population under 15 years will still be 38% of the total.

The slow change in age structure will also have implications for the dependency ratio. In the developed countries this ratio indicates an age structure more favorable to the growth of productive activities; therefore, changes in age structure resulting in a decrease of this ratio are considered desirable for development and improvement of economic conditions. If assumption A can be made a reality in the next 30 years, the dependency ratio in the LDCs will drop from 82% at present to 72% in 1985, and to 56% in the year 2000. These ratios would be similar to those prevailing now in the developed countries. If assumption B dominates the trends, however, the change in the dependency ratio will be considerably more moderate, remaining almost unchanged up to 1985 and decreasing to 73% by 2000.

Specific or General Population Targets in 27 Countries

A. Countries with Specific Goals or Targets

Country	1970 Population (Millions)	Estimated 1970 Crude Birth Rate[1]	Specific Goal or Target
Africa			
Egypt	33.3	37	Reduce CBR by one point per year in 1970s.
Mauritius	0.8	26	Reduce CBR from 30 to 20 by 1975.
Morocco	15.5	50	Reduce CBR (from about 50 in 1968) to 45 by 1972 and 35 by 1985.
Tunisia	5.0	41-42	Reduce CBR from 43 in 1968 to 34 in 1975.
Western Hemisphere			
Barbados	0.3	30	Enlist 60,000 women in program in 3 years.
Dominican Republic	4.3	45-48	Reduce CBR to 28 in 10 years.
Jamaica	1.9	32	Reduce CBR from 34.2 per 1,000 in 1968 to 25 per 1,000 by 1976.
Trinidad & Tobago	1.1	28	Reduce CBR to 19 per 1,000 by 1977.
Asia			
China, Republic of	14.7	27	Initial target was to reduce the rate of growth from 3% to 1.9% by 1973. Current target is to reduce the CBR from 27.1 at end of 1970 to 24.4 by 1976.
Korea, Republic of	31.9	30-32	Achieve a 2% population growth rate by December 1971 and 1.5% by 1976.
India	552.0	40	Reduce CBR to 32 by end of Fourth Plan (1974) and to 25 six to eight years later.
Indonesia	118.0	40-45	Reduce birth rate. Current five-year plan sets a target of six million acceptors.
Iran	28.7	46	Decrease annual population growth rate from 3% to 2%.
Malaysia	10.4	37	Achieve 2% population growth rate by 1985.
Nepal	11.1	n.a.	Tentative target of 2% population growth rate.
Pakistan	134.0	45-50	Recommended goal for Fourth Five-Year Plan (1970-75) is to reduce CBR from estimated 41-43 in 1970 to 33.2 in 1975, with 31% of fertile couples effectively using contraception.
Singapore	2.1	22	Reduce CBR from 32 in 1964 to below 20 in the five year National Family Planning Program, 1966-70.
Thailand	35.7	40-45	Reduce population growth rate from 3.3% in 1970 to 2.4% by 1980.

(continued)

B. Countries with General Goals

Country	1970 Population (Millions)	Estimated 1970 Crude Birth Rate[1]	General Goal
Africa			
Botswana	0.7	n.a.	Reduce population growth rate.
Ghana	9.0	50	(1969) Reduce the population growth rate and give Ghanaians choice of family size.
Kenya	10.8	50	Provide family planning services to combat malnutrition, improve maternal and child health, and slow rate of population growth.
Nigeria	66.4	50-55	Provide information, facilities, and services to families to enable them to achieve desired family size.
Western Hemisphere			
Puerto Rico	2.8	26	Provide services through the Family Planning Association.
Asia			
Ceylon	12.5	32	Government's position has shifted from reducing birth rate (1965) to support for family planning programs in the interest of maternal and child health.
China, People's Rep. of	750-950	36-40	Degree of expressed official interest varies, but fertility control services are widely available. Government advocates late marriage and small families.
Philippines	38.4	44-50	All agencies providing services are to cooperate in making family planning efforts effective.
Turkey	35.5	40	Population Planning Law No. 557 states that every Turkish couple should have the number of children it wishes.

[1] All crude birth rates (CBR) are per 1,000 population per year.

n.a. = Not available.

Sources: United Nations, 1970 Demographic Yearbook.

Nortman, Dorothy, "Population and Family Planning Programs: A Factbook," 1971 edition, *Reports on Population/Family Planning*. The Population Council, New York, June, 1971, tables 4 and 5, pp. 5-15. A few of the crude birth rate figures and goals are based on recently available information.

CONTRACEPTIVE METHODS

Of all the species, only man can control his fertility. This unique ability is exercised by interfering with the biological consequences of sexual intercourse at any one of several steps in the process of conception, fetal development and birth.

Various methods of preventing conception have long been known and practiced: coitus interruptus, male sterilization through castration, and various folk preparations of uncertain effect and reliability. Within recent years, there have been significant advances in knowledge of reproductive biology and in the development of contraceptive technology. The two most widely known and used of the newer methods are, of course, "the pill" and "the loop," but other promising methods are under trial or development. With increased research, still more and better methods can be expected.

Family planning, or birth control, is the application of scientific knowledge by couples to regulate the number and spacing of their children. It makes birth a process of choice rather than chance. All scientific methods of accomplishing this—whether surgical, medical, mechanical or behavioral—rely on interference at some point in a complex series of events which must occur in perfect harmony to result in pregnancy.

This can be done by blocking the passages through which the ovum and sperm must travel to meet, by changing the hormonal balance to prevent ovulation or sperm formation, by altering the wall of the uterus so that it becomes nonreceptive to the ovum, or by limiting sexual intercourse to times when no ovum is exposed to fertilization.

Some methods, such as male or female sterilization, diaphragms, oral contraception and intrauterine devices, require medical supervision. Others, such as the condom, rhythm, vaginal creams, jellies and suppositories, do not.

A good contraceptive must be reliable, effective, and simple to use. It should not interfere with sex activity or be harmful to either partner. It should not affect fertility unless used as a terminal method. Finally, it must be inexpensive and easily supplied to large numbers of people. All methods now known have some disadvantages, and all have their failures. There is no perfect contraceptive. The method chosen must therefore be a matter of compromise and personal preference. Each of the main categories of methods is described below.

Oral Contraceptives (The "Pill")

From ancient times, there has been speculation about the use of medicines taken by mouth to prevent childbirth. It was not until the early 1950s, however, that a scientific oral method became available. Pincus and Rock had worked on experiments with hormone preparations and developed their "pill," which was first tried out in Puerto Rico beginning in 1956. This work was based on experience in the use of certain hormones in the treatment of women's diseases, for regulation of the menses, for severe pain during menstruation, and for subfertility.

During normal pregnancy, the ovary produces certain hormones which help the fertilized egg to continue to develop in the womb. These hormones in the blood stream decrease the capacity of the pituitary gland to produce other hormones which cause the ovaries to develop eggs; the absence of the pituitary hormones causes ovulation to be suppressed. The "pill" produces a hormonal condition similar to pregnancy, in that no egg cells are released. The original "pill" was a combination of two types of hormones—one stops egg production, the other helps menstruation to occur. Several brands now on the market vary slightly in composition but also employ two hormones to achieve the same results.[1] The routine requires that 20 or 21 tablets be taken orally every month, beginning on the fifth day of the menstrual cycle (counting the first day of the period as day one). A "sequential" pill has also been developed which is taken every day of the month without interruption.

When the course is finished, menstruation will occur within two to three days, and the course will be repeated again from the fifth day of its start. For women who faithfully take these pills, success is 100%. Side effects such as nausea and vomiting, fullness of breast, and headaches have been reported, but most of these cease to occur in time. Weight changes may also occur. Medical complications in association with the use of these oral progestagens, e.g., thrombo-embolic conditions, etc., are worth attention, but it has still to be shown that they occur more frequently among pill users than among other women of similar age and history.

Other contingencies, largely hypothetical, are also much discussed, but these questions will not be resolved until enough experience of prolonged use by women and other species has accumulated. The "pill" is already aesthetically acceptable, however, because its use is removed from the time of the sex act. It is the most widely used contraceptive among women in developed countries, and in some of the

[1]There are newer varieties being developed with other action; these are discussed below under "Prospective Methods."

national programs of developing countries. The discovery of oral contraceptives has revolutionized family planning methods.

The Intrauterine Device (IUD)

The use of small devices inserted and left in the womb is a revival and modernization of older methods, such as metal buttons, stems and Grafenburg Rings, which were used about 40 years ago. They were frowned upon by most medical people on the ground that they might cause infection or cancer.

Modern IUDs are made of stainless steel or plastic impregnated with barium sulphate, which makes them visible under x-rays. They are made in a variety of shapes. The more well-known are the Margulies Spiral, Lippes Loop, Birnberg Bow, and Ota Ring. These devices are threaded through an inserter which straightens them for easy introduction into the uterus; after they are released in the womb, they regain their original shape which helps to keep them in place. Insertion is usually quite easy, and no anesthetic is needed for women who have had children (IUDs are not recommended for others). Removal normally requires medical attention.

The IUD is fairly effective, with a pregnancy rate of 4% at the end of one year of use. The failure rate declines with subsequent years of use. It is superior to more conventional forms of contraceptives and is inexpensive, with no recurrent cost. Once fitted, it can be left in place for at least two years; in fact, no ill effects have been reported from cases of much longer use.

The IUD is a simple method, once inserted, and requires no further motivation. It is also the only reversible form of contraception which does not rely on the user for its success, and therefore is more suited for couples who are not constantly motivated. The IUD, like the pill, does not require any precoital or postcoital preparation. The main disadvantage, aside from the rather small chance of pregnancy, is that some women who cannot tolerate the presence of foreign bodies in the uterus suffer cramps and various degrees of bleeding. Some women also cannot retain the IUD, and expel it.

Permanent Methods

Sterilization renders a person incapable of reproduction, and the result is usually permanent. Although there are many ways to render a person sterile, in practice the methods most commonly employed are to cut and tie the fallopian tubes in women (tubal ligation) or the spermatic ducts in men (vasectomy).

Sterilization may be advised in cases of ill health as well as a means of family limitation. Because of the method's finality, it never gained much acceptance until the recent awakening to the population problem. Even today, the acceptability of both male and female sterilization varies greatly among different countries.

Both popular and professional views as to how many children a couple should have before considering sterilization have changed in recent times. Whereas formerly doctors in many areas were loathe to agree to such operations for families with less than six or eight children, it is likely that most today would accept three or four as a more realistic figure. Sterilization below the age of 30 is generally discouraged. Each case must be considered on its merits, taking account of all relevant factors: the number, sex and health of the family's children, the couple's economic circumstances, and experience with other family planning methods.

The exact legal position varies in different countries, but generally voluntary sterilization is permissible if the couple fully understand the nature and permanency of the procedure. Cases considered for sterilization are those of couples who have reached the desired family size and where both partners give their unequivocal consent. The operation must be done in good faith and for the welfare of the family concerned.

In men, sterilization is performed by blocking the seminal duct through which the sperm move out of the testicles to join the seminal fluid. This simple operation is called vasectomy and does not require a general anesthetic or hospitalization. It can be completed within 10 minutes under a local anesthetic on an outpatient basis. Only a half inch incision is made on each side through the skin in the scrotum to cut and tie off the vas deferens, just under the skin. Nothing is removed and there is no change in sexual drive or capacity.

In women the operation, though not a serious one, does necessitate hospitalization and is done under general anesthesia. It is conveniently performed within 24 hours after delivery—ideally as a postpartum procedure. A small abdominal incision is made in order to tie the fallopian tubes which carry the ovum to the womb. The patient is usually discharged from the hospital in four to six days, and can gradually resume her normal activities after the usual recovery period advised after childbirth, i.e., about two weeks. The woman's chemistry is not affected and she will continue to have her menses normally. Nothing has been removed and her physical well-being and sexual characteristics are not affected.

It is possible to carry out this operation intra-vaginally, but the procedure is more complex and requires highly competent surgery; it is not yet suited for general use. Research is under way to develop techniques for blocking the tubes by chemical injection through the cervical canal.

Traditional Methods

Other contraceptive devices of varying efficiency, depending on the motivation, knowledge and interest of the user, are the condom for men and the vaginal diaphragm and spermicides for women.

The diaphragm, which was used most successfully in developed countries before the advent of the pill, has several disadvantages, such as the need for a suitable housing environment, pelvic examination and fitting by a physician, and elaborate preparations for use.

Spermicides are chemical products in the form of jellies, creams and foams which have the effect of immobilizing the sperm on contact. These are preparations relatively easy to use, but they are not so effective.

Rhythm Method

In virtually all societies, it has been known that women could conceive only during a certain part of the menstrual cycle. This fact is the basis of the rhythm method of avoiding conception. Early ideas about the fertile and sterile periods of the menstrual cycle, however, were often mistaken. Much has been learned about them in recent years.

Two varieties of the rhythm method are now practiced: calendar rhythm and temperature rhythm. Calendar rhythm, developed in the 1920s, depends upon estimation of the day of ovulation by a formula based on the individual woman's menstrual history recorded over a number of months. Abstinence is prescribed for a few days before and after the estimated day of ovulation.

More recently the temperature rhythm, based on the principle of the rise of basal body temperature at the time of ovulation, has been used to determine that ovulation has occurred; marital relations are permitted during the postovulatory phase only. The rhythm method is based on the avoidance of coitus when it could result in the simultaneous presence of a fertilizable ovum and mobile sperm.

The contraceptive effectiveness of the rhythm method has been the subject of much controversy. Correctly taught and understood, and consistently practiced, it may be quite effective, especially the method based on temperature records. Successful practice, however, requires considerable self discipline and an equally strong desire to control fertility. Self-taught rhythm, haphazardly practiced, is a very ineffectual method of contraception. It has never been used on a mass basis.

Abortion

Abortion is any termination of pregnancy before the 28th week, the stage before the fetus is regarded as viable and capable of an independent existence. Pregnancies can be medically terminated for medical and social reasons. Pregnancies can also abort spontaneously (if before the 28th week, an abortion; if later, a miscarriage); it is estimated that about 10% terminate this way, usually in the third month or earlier.

The traditional method of terminating early pregnancy (before 12 weeks) is by the operation termed dilation and curettage (D and C), which involves the scraping of fetal contents from the uterine wall. This operation is usually done under surgical operating conditions, though it can be done as an outpatient procedure if the pregnancy is of less than 12 weeks. More modern is the use of a "suction method" to evacuate the uterus. This relatively simple and safe outpatient method was developed in Eastern Europe. Its use is increasing rapidly in many countries where abortion laws have been liberalized.

Therapeutic abortion is sometimes permitted if doctors of consultant status agree that a woman's life might be jeopardized or her health endangered or seriously impaired should the pregnancy continue. Social abortions are usually authorized by regulatory tribunals, although recent legislation in the United Kingdom and some jurisdictions in the United States allows the procedure to be practiced almost "on demand."

Since the last war, Japan has brought down its birth rate to a very low level by legalizing abortion on medical or social grounds. The idea behind more liberal abortion laws is that a woman should have the right to decide whether to give birth, and that legal abortion in a hospital will be much safer than an illegal one.

The rate of illegal abortions is difficult to estimate but ranges from 10% to 30% of births, depending on the country. The incidence of such abortions, which cause much maternal morbidity and even death, can be reduced by more liberal attitudes towards abortion itself and by encouraging contraceptive practice. In some countries, there are so many illegal abortions that strong efforts are now being made to encourage family planning as an alternative.

Prospective Methods

There is common agreement that additional research on the biomedical basis of contraception is needed. The world total of expenditure in this area is now in the range of $50 million a year. Biomedical research is of two main types, both of which are essential to further progress:

1. Reproductive biology covers the anatomy and physiology of reproduction. This work, which is largely fundamental and not applied in nature, is often unrelated to population control objectives. It nevertheless provides the basic knowledge of the full chain of events involved in reproduction. Such knowledge is far from complete.

2. Contraceptive development is goal-oriented applied research. Even though not all links in the reproduction chain are delineated, many areas are sufficiently well understood to support present contraceptive techniques and to suggest some promising new leads. These can be translated into contraceptive products if they meet standards of safety and acceptability. They point to the following future possibilities:

a) **Hormonal method:** a monthly pill, a postovulatory progestin that induces menses; a weekly pill which affects the lining of the uterus and prevents ovum implantation; a precoital pill which acts by causing thickening of cervical mucus which acts as a barrier to sperm passage; a long-acting injection which provides a more satisfactory performance than reported with medroxy progesterin acetate and related hormones; and a long-acting skin capsule, a progestin implant which causes infertility for up to one year.

b) **Mechanical method:** a high-performance, low-side-effects IUD —e.g., the copper T intrauterine device.

c) **Postconceptive method:** Prostaglandins—a vaginal insert which causes termination of pregnancy.

A number of these developments are in various stages of trial and testing They include:

• **Progestagen Skin Implants.** Delivering progestagens to the system on a long term basis by under-skin implant offers promise. A method now in the intermediate stage of development requires the injection of capsules containing progestagen under the skin of the arm or hip. A quick, painless outpatient procedure, this method offers promise because it is economical and convenient, requiring implantation only once a year.

• **The Copper T IUD.** This is a T-shaped IUD with a strand of fine copper wound around the stem; in trials it seems not to have some of the main disadvantages of other IUDs. Its users have been reported to be free of bleeding and cramps. Because of its shape it is not expelled and the reported pregnancy rate is close to zero. The exact mechanism of copper's effect on the endometrium to prevent pregnancy is not known. Like all IUDs, the "T" does not interfere with either ovulation or menstruation.

349

• **Prostaglandins.** A new type of contraceptive is provided by prostaglandins, a body chemical of many uses. One of its characteristics is that it acts as a chemical abortifacient; it is therefore a postconceptive method. Its action in producing abortion has been amply demonstrated, but it seems on the basis of present information that side effects and toxicity still need to be regulated. Prostaglandins offer the best promise when used intravaginally. One advantage of this or a similar contraceptive is that it can be used after a pregnancy has occurred, when motivation is high. It also requires no regulation of sex activity and greatly reduces the need for education.

Medical Supervision and Assistance Required

Contraceptive methods differ in the extent to which they need to be supervised and carried out by medically trained personnel. Some methods (e.g., the condom, foams, jellies, etc.) require no medical supervision and can be made available in outlets unconnected with health services. Other methods, e.g., abortions and sterilizations, require highly trained, highly specialized medical personnel working under hospital operating room conditions.

Between these extremes are methods for which some degree of supervision and assistance by medical or paramedical personnel (nurses, midwives, health visitors, etc.) is necessary, and contraceptive delivery normally relies heavily on the general health system. These conditions apply to both "the pill" and IUDs; well trained personnel are required to examine for possible contraindications, and to insert the IUDs. There is room for judgment, however, as to the degree of medical supervision and assistance required at delivery points in the system. This is an important point that affects the planning and staffing of a program's various delivery systems and the design of training courses for the different categories of staff involved in the provision of services.

EVALUATION OF FAMILY PLANNING PROGRAMS

As with any action program designed to produce attitude changes and influence behavior in population groups, the evaluation of family planning programs is based on the following general principles: a) Definition of program objectives; b) Selection of appropriate criteria to judge achievement; c) Decision on the design of evaluation; d) Collection and analysis of data; and e) Interpretation of findings for use by program administrators.

The frame for the evaluation process is built upon the definition of a hierarchy of objectives. It comprises the ultimate objective, fertility reduction, and an array of descending and branching subsidiary objectives. The ultimate success of the program will depend on the extent to which the established targets are met and the validity of assumptions on which the various goals are based.

In the evaluative process of a family planning program, the following progression may be identified: a) Evaluation of program efforts or inputs (personnel-years, visits, clinics, costs, etc.); b) Evaluation of intermediate results (number of new acceptors, continuing users, etc.); c) Evaluation of program efficiency (relation of intermediate results to various physical or financial inputs; this stage corresponds to an evaluation of process); and d) Evaluation of effect on the ultimate goal, fertility decline.

Independent of the administrative arrangements under which an evaluation system operates, both continuous and periodic data collection will be required to develop quantitative measures and indicators of program achievement. The system should provide a steady flow of information for judgment of program performance, for stimulating new approaches tending towards program improvement, and for testing procedures, on a demonstration basis, before adopting them as standard for the whole program.

In order to carry out the different stages of evaluation, a system combining continuous data collection with periodic sample surveys will be required. This Annex describes the technical means to accomplish evaluation at all indicated levels. The accompanying diagram relates the various levels with the data collection mechanisms and gives an indication of time frequency and phasing of activities. A clear understanding of the functions of all the means of measurement indicated in the diagram will help considerably in designing and administering family planning programs in which decisions will be based on concrete knowledge about what is more efficient in rela-

351

Components of Evaluation of a Family Planning Program

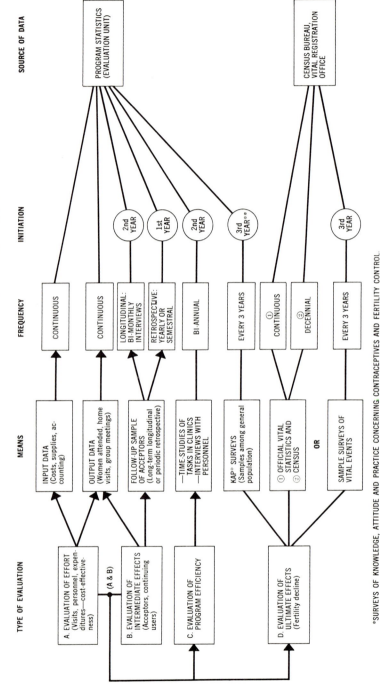

TYPE OF EVALUATION

MEANS

FREQUENCY

INITIATION

SOURCE OF DATA

PROGRAM STATISTICS (EVALUATION UNIT)

CENSUS BUREAU, VITAL REGISTRATION OFFICE

2nd YEAR

1st YEAR

2nd YEAR

3rd YEAR**

3rd YEAR

CONTINUOUS

CONTINUOUS

LONGITUDINAL: BI-MONTHLY INTERVIEWS

RETROSPECTIVE: YEARLY OR SEMESTRAL

BI-ANNUAL

EVERY 3 YEARS

CONTINUOUS

DECENIAL

EVERY 3 YEARS

INPUT DATA (Costs, supplies, accounting)

OUTPUT DATA (Women attended, home visits, group meetings)

FOLLOW-UP SAMPLE OF ACCEPTORS (Long-term longitudinal or periodic retrospective)

—TIME-STUDIES OF TASKS IN CLINICS
—INTERVIEWS WITH PERSONNEL

KAP° SURVEYS (Samples among general population)

① OFFICIAL VITAL STATISTICS AND CENSUS
②

OR

SAMPLE SURVEYS OF VITAL EVENTS

A. EVALUATION OF EFFORT (Visits, personnel, expenditures—cost-effectiveness)

(A & B)

B. EVALUATION OF INTERMEDIATE EFFECTS (Acceptors, continuing users)

C. EVALUATION OF PROGRAM EFFICIENCY

D. EVALUATION OF ULTIMATE EFFECTS (Fertility decline)

°SURVEYS OF KNOWLEDGE, ATTITUDE AND PRACTICE CONCERNING CONTRACEPTIVES AND FERTILITY CONTROL.
°°ASSUMING THAT A SURVEY WAS CARRIED OUT PRIOR TO INITIATION OF FAMILY PLANNING PROGRAM.

tion to the intermediate and ultimate goals of program acceptance and fertility decline.

Evaluation of Program Effort

Statistics maintained on clinic operation, number of visits, sessions, personnel time, materials and expenditures are measures of the effort made and should be considered as guides for the administrator in terms of cost controls, methods of storing and distributing contraceptives to clinics, personnel requirements, etc. Also, to an extent, data on the numbers of acceptors and their characteristics give a measure of the effort by field personnel to encourage women to attend clinics and adopt a contraceptive method.

Record keeping of new acceptors and revisits is necessary for establishing a follow-up system through which women may be reminded of their next appointments and home visits may be scheduled by field workers for women failing to keep appointments. A simple form to keep records of new and returning patients should be designed by the evaluation unit. A summary sheet of daily activities, keeping new and returning patients separate, will be needed as a basis for preparing a monthly report to the district or state headquarters.

The monthly reports are usually designed to be filled with precoded information for punching. Tabulations may then be produced at the central level with mechanical equipment or computer. Prompt distribution of monthly reports (within three weeks) as feedback to districts and clinics as well as summaries for the whole country are important for effective use of the information. Detailed cross-tabulations at the state and national levels could be produced annually. A system along these lines, once in operation, will provide current information about program performance and will also serve to establish a follow-up of patients. In addition, it will be used as a frame for the periodic sample surveys referred to below.

Until now, in the absence of better information, data on new acceptors have been generally used as a main indicator of "program success." It is recognized, however, that the important fact in a family planning program is not so much the acceptance of a method of contraception by a woman, but continued use, or retention in the case of the IUD.

Evaluation of Intermediate Effect

The extent to which women in reproductive ages accept contraception, and the rate at which they continue to practice it, may be determined from sample groups of acceptors, followed up in longitudinal studies for relatively long periods, or from periodic retrospective surveys among acceptors. An estimate of the relationship between extent of contraceptive use and pregnancy prevention may be derived from these follow-up studies of acceptors by matching, i.e., by including in the study a control group of other women outside the program, with socio-demographic characteristics similar to those of women in the family planning program. Controls in this case, as in medical investigations, pose sensitive problems to be tackled by the evaluator with great caution.

The relationship between contraceptive practice and pregnancy prevention may also be assessed by comparing subsequent fertility of women in the program with an estimate of their "expected" fertility performance in the absence of contraceptive practice. Follow-up sample surveys among clinic acceptors will provide a measure of use-effectiveness of contraceptives; also, they will allow calculation of rates of discontinuance, determination of reasons for discontinuance and explanations for failures, and will help in correcting procedures and redirecting efforts for recruiting acceptors.

A system of evaluation must be set up and conducted under the same principles ruling scientific research, with constant awareness that results are to be utilized by the administrator to increase efficiency in relation to the established goals. The ability of the administrator to make purposeful use of these results is a key issue in the whole exercise of evaluation.

Evaluation of Program Efficiency

In the diagram of components of evaluation, the assessment of program efficiency is a separate activity ascribed to the evaluation unit. Its objective is to obtain a measure of the adequacy of the services. The proposed mechanism for this measurement is a special study to be made every two years to determine effectiveness of the family planning personnel in meeting the needs of the public and performing the intended tasks. Time studies in which skillful individuals observe portions of tasks for short periods of time and take note of all movements and details of service performance, are appropriate for this assessment.

As in the case of follow-up surveys, rules of scientific research apply to these studies. They should be based on a sampling scheme of clinics, personnel, and time intervals during the day, and should strive for representativeness and minimum bias. A time study of this type may require as much as a year for design, development of methodology, actual surveying and analysis. In the last few years, however, some universities in the United States have carried out studies of this type in several developing countries, and a methodology has been developed which, with proper alterations for particular situations, may allow replication of the study in approximately three months. Thus, it might be feasible to perform one time study every two years as part of the general evaluation system.

In a large-scale family planning program, there is pressure to operate within a limited budget. Efficiency of the program, i.e., getting the job done well at the most reasonable cost, is important. Cost-effectiveness is measured by the ratio of input to output; inputs are given in monetary units and outputs in units of work in the program, e.g., number of acceptors for the clinics, number of visits made for the field workers, number of meetings held, number of persons attending meetings, etc. In order to allow for analysis and comparison of costs per unit, it is helpful if activities are classified in broad groups for accounting purposes. For instance, the groups may be: a) Administration; b) Clinic and medical services; c) Field work and community organization work; d) Public information and mass communication; e) Training of personnel; and f) Research and evaluation.

Some of the major categories above could be subdivided into a few sub-categories for principal types of expenditures, e.g., personnel (medical, non-medical), maintenance of buildings and equipment, contraceptive and medical supplies, and other supplies. This information from the accounting system would give the nominator for calculation of the cost-effectiveness ratio, using as denominator data on number of "units" produced by the major activities of the program. Comparisons of cost-effectiveness ratios between clinics, districts (for field work), and training centers, would provide evidence to pinpoint operational problems. These data would also serve to calculate overall cost-effectiveness ratios for the program.

Evaluation of the Ultimate Effect—Fertility Decline

Information about existing fertility levels and patterns in a country are obtained from the following sources: a) Censuses; b) Registered vital statistics; c) Sample surveys of vital events; and d) Sample surveys on knowledge, attitude and practice concerning contraceptives and fertility aspirations.

Censuses provide valuable material for the calculation of fertility measures, through the application of special demographic techniques. In many developing countries with deficient vital registration systems, censuses taken around 1970 will be the main source of information for establishing changes in fertility and mortality that have taken place during the decade 1960-70. Detailed census tabulations needed for these analyses are delayed in many countries, however,

355

due to problems of enumeration, requiring manual verification of questionnaires, and to scarcity of computer programming ability.

In many developing countries, the registration of vital statistics is incomplete or lacking entirely. In recent years, efforts have been made to remedy this deficiency by carrying out sample surveys which are also used as a basis for establishing or improving permanent registration. Detailed tabulations on births by age, sex, parity, and other socio-economic characteristics are important to calculate refined measures of fertility, such as age-specific fertility rates, gross and net reproduction rates, total fertility rates, etc.

Very few countries have good registration systems, however, or timely processing of data. Sample surveys for registration of vital events are the most expedient solution to this problem, but their design and implementation are costly and time consuming operations requiring trained personnel. Recent surveys carried out in developing countries with U.N. assistance are producing estimates of vital rates on the basis of area and household representative sampling and periodic interviews (one every three or four months) to register all vital events in the household during the interval. Usually, each household in the sample is interviewed four or five times during a period of 12 to 15 months.

Knowledge, Attitude, and Practice (KAP) Surveys

In the last few years, several countries have conducted special surveys on the knowledge, attitudes, and practices of people concerning reproduction and contraception (KAP surveys). These surveys play an important role within the system of evaluation of a national family planning program. Data on the fertility, attitudes and contraceptive practices of the population in general are essential as measures of control and comparison with the results obtained from studies of acceptors. Therefore, KAP surveys should normally be an integral part of any evaluation system.

Main groups of variables to investigate, common to KAP surveys and follow-up studies of acceptors of family planning programs, have been set up by an international committee of experts convened by the International Union for Scientific Study of Population and the United Nations[1] (1966-70). These variables may be grouped as follows:

- Data on fertility (complete marriage and reproductive histories).
- Measures of the "intermediate variables" (according to the analytic framework developed by K. Davis and J. Blake), that is, those through which any social variables should work to affect fertility.

[1]United Nations, *Variables and Questionnaire for Comparative Fertility Surveys,* Department of Economic and Social Affairs, Population Studies No. 45, New York 1970.

These include, for instance, age at marriage (or at first sexual union), periods of separation, use of contraception, fecundity and its impairments, and natural or induced abortions.

• The social norms about these intermediate variables, as well as the norms about family size and child spacing.

• The elements of the social and economic organization which affect the norms, the intermediate variables and fertility itself (education, rural-urban background, women's economic activity, husbands' occupation, religion, ethnic language, extended versus nuclear family, income, etc.).

Fertility Indicators

Several indicators of population dynamics are derived from the data of censuses, vital statistics, and sample surveys of vital events. They serve to define the fertility of a population in terms of magnitude, trends and differentials. The most common and elementary measure of fertility is the crude birth rate; it represents the number of live births in a population group during a given year divided by the population at mid-year (person-years of exposure). More refined measures of fertility are obtained by restricting the denominator of the rates to the population actually at risk (number of women in reproductive ages, or, even more specifically, women married or in consensual unions).

The general fertility rate (number of live births over female population 15 to 44 or 49 years) represents an improvement over the birth rate as a measure of fertility. However, since the frequency of childbirth varies markedly with the age of women, age-specific fertility rates describe even better the fertility pattern of a population. A more synthetic measure, based on the age-specific fertility rates, is the total fertility rate, which results from adding the former and multiplying the results by the age interval used (usually five years). It represents the average number of children born to each woman during her reproductive life. The gross reproduction rate (GRR) is constructed in the same way as the total fertility rate, but is restricted to female births, thus being an estimate of the average number of daughters born to women during the whole reproductive period. The net reproduction rate is based on the same principle as the GRR, but it takes into account the mortality of the female population.

The indicators mentioned above are some of the conventional measures of the level of fertility. They permit making comparisons between geographic areas as well as observation of changes through time. For the latter analysis, a series of observations at successive dates is needed. Interpretation of fertility changes through time is complicated by the fact that in response to especial conditioning, couples sometimes advance or delay their bearing of children. This may cause sharp movements of yearly rates, with little or no effect on the total size of family that they eventually attain. In other words, a change in annual rates may not be permanent, but reflect a shift in the scheduling of births. This is particularly so in societies where contraception is practiced to a large extent.

Analysis of the fertility of cohorts of women (age-specific birth rates derived from an actual group of women completing childbearing) is being used increasingly in fertility studies of developed countries with good statistical information, dating back many years. For the less developed countries, however, data on reproductive histories are rare and comparisons through time will have to be based on periodic measures for a long time to come. Awareness of the usefulness of cohort analysis, however, is important to stress improvement of registration of vital events, anticipating the need for more complex measures of fertility as contraception becomes an accepted practice.

Impact of the Family Planning Program on Fertility

Reference has been made to the measurement of program effect on the fertility of women attending clinics. A separate problem is the measurement of program impact on the level of fertility of the population in general. That is, if fertility indicators show a declining trend, the problem consists of explaining the fall in fertility in terms of several interrelated factors. A multivariate analysis with fertility as the dependent variable and program activity as one of the independent variables is appropriate in this case. Such analysis is, of course, conditioned to the availability of data. For this evaluation, a thorough understanding of the determinants of fertility is necessary in order to select pertinent variables, with explanatory power. One possibility would be to use geographical divisions in a country as units of analysis, with and without family planning programs or with measurable accomplishments in family planning. Information on vital events would also be necessary for each unit.

Again, the problem of census data availability, with detailed tabulations by socio-economic characteristics of the population, is evident for evaluation purposes. For further refinement, a multivariate analysis could be performed, using as units of analysis individual couples in and out of the program. The sources of data for this analysis could be a KAP survey in the general population and a follow-up survey of clinic clients. A convenient way of dealing with the nominal character of client status and other unquantifiable variables is the use of dummy variables, applied often in sociological studies. Regression analysis offers the technical tool to judge the significance of the contribution of several variables (including clinic attendance) to the fertility level.

Other less sophisticated ways to estimate what would have happened in the absence of a family planning program may be suggested. One possibility is to compare actual present fertility trends with those estimated before the family planning program began, or with trends projected on the basis of experience in the past 10 years (which in some developed countries are showing slight declines).

Still another way of assessing program impact would be to compare the socio-economic characteristics of clinic clients with those of the general population. Demographic evidence indicates that rising urbanization, literacy, income, etc., are major factors accounting for increasing contraception. Family planning programs have as their main objective promotion of the practice of contraception in spite of rural traditions, illiteracy, low income, etc. A test can be made by comparing groups practicing contraception outside and within the program. If clinic clients are disproportionately among the poorer classes, then the program can be considered effective in terms of goal achievement.

This brief outline of alternative ways of learning the effect of a family planning program on the fertility of a population suggests the mass of information and technical knowledge required of the evaluation unit. The first step in tackling the problem of evaluation is recognition of the magnitude of the task, and review of the possible means available.

Administrative Aspects

In most family planning programs now underway, evaluation is gradually being recognized as a necessity, but very few countries have adopted effective systems to provide it. In fact, due to the improvised fashion in which many of these programs originated (usually in the private sector, with undefined goals but great enthusiasm and faith in the cause of preventing pregnancies), the need for evaluation became clear only after governments began to develop national family planning programs, and investment of resources in these programs had to be justified in terms of results related to goals. Even then, the concept has often been limited, at least in part, to the evaluation of effort and of progress toward the intermediate goal (most often, number of acceptors only).

The main obstacles to establishing a system capable of covering all evaluational needs can be summarized:
- Insufficient understanding or recognition on the part of program

administrators and governing bodies of what evaluation really is, what is required to implement it, and how it can be used to improve the program.

• Unavailability or scarcity of professional expertise.

• Reluctance to accept technical assistance, which sometimes has been better designed to benefit the research programs of foreign institutions than to build effective evaluation systems for national purposes.

• Lack of adequate demographic information from censuses and vital statistics registration.

Once the obstacle of insufficient understanding is overcome and evaluation is accepted by administrators of the program as a useful tool for their activities, suitable expertise must be brought to bear on the problem. Often this can best be done by arranging for an expert team in demography, evaluation and social research to plan a system, with clear provisions in their contract concerning the national character of the operation. If foreign experts are employed, it will still be necessary to arrange for a team of national professionals, to be trained in all aspects of evaluation and research in an appropriate institution. Where foreign technical assistance is used, the national team should of course take over the operation after training, with an overlap of the two teams working together (for perhaps a year) before the total transfer of responsibilities. The whole process, from the planning stage to the complete take-over by the national team, may take as long as five years.

Given the availability of professional staff, a fundamental question is the place this evaluation team will occupy in the system. The following possibilities may be considered:

• An external body, outside the family planning program, partially devoted to family planning evaluation but also engaged in other activities (e.g., a department in a local university).

• The evaluation unit might be part of the national family planning organization, partially utilizing the same personnel and facilities.

• A separate unit, completely dedicated to evaluation and research in the field of population and family planning—a population center or institute, along the lines of the center in the Republic of China.

The first possibility should be treated with reservation. It implies a situation of ambiguity, in which evaluation might be diverted to other research or become too remote to the needs of administration. The second alternative runs the risk of not being objective enough to exert effective criticism from within. A separate unit appears to be the most workable and effective solution, provided that a strong link is established with administration of the program.

BILATERAL, MULTILATERAL AND PRIVATE AGENCIES

Twelve years ago, bilateral, multilateral and private organizations together devoted a total of about $2.8 million to activities related to family planning; in 1971, the amount was about $225 million.

The proportion of such resources going directly to developing countries has steadily increased, reaching about 70% in 1969, compared with some 45% three years before.

The most important components supported with external finance have been training and technical assistance (including salaries, allowances, etc., of foreign advisers); together, they accounted in 1969 for about 80% of the external resources allocated to family planning programs in developing countries.

A wide range of technical assistance is provided. It includes medical, paramedical, educational and administrative personnel directly involved in the distribution of family planning services; assistance in undertaking social, technical, psychological and demographic studies necessary to determine the kind of program which will be best accepted by the population; assistance in collecting information and in program evaluation; and assistance in training local personnel in all fields of family planning.

Another major component has been the supply of small equipment and contraceptives. This represented about 18% of the total in 1969.

The balance—about 2% in 1969—has been allocated to buildings, schools, vehicles and fixed equipment. In the same year, $18 million was spent on bio-medical and social research and $6 million in support of university training programs in the population and family planning fields in developed countries.

A summary of principal agencies and their programs follows:

Bilateral Programs

Canada. The government of Canada began assistance to family planning in developing countries after repeal, in 1969, of legislation against advertising or encouraging the use of contraceptives. In December 1970 the Government announced its first official support for family planning activities abroad. Assistance includes funding the work of international organizations (e.g. expanded medical research by UNFPA) and direct assistance in priority countries. Grants have been made to Barbados and Colombia, and to WHO for contraceptive research.

Denmark. Since the mid-1960s, the Danish Government has provided multilateral family planning assistance through a number of agencies, cooperated in family planning training courses, and supported contraceptive research. It has also provided bilateral assistance in family planning to India, Egypt, Thailand and Uganda.

A total of $807,000 has been granted to the IPPF, both for special projects and for its general program. The UNFPA received $400,000 during the 1967-71 period.

Family planning training courses are given for students from developing countries in collaboration with the Danish Family Planning Association. In 1968, Denmark made a grant of $72,000 for activities of the Egyptian Family Planning Association and provided $135,500 worth of raw materials for production of oral contraceptives.

Federal Republic of Germany. The Government allocated $1.5 million to the United Nations Fund for Population Activities in 1970 and 1971. Other financial support has gone to the United Nations Development Programme, which was granted $250,000 in 1969, and to the population group in the OECD Development Center. The Government supported a multi-functional training and research center in Tunis in 1971.

Japan. The Japanese Government, whose assistance to family planning in developing countries began only recently, expanded its efforts considerably in 1969. A grant of $100,000 was made to the International Planned Parenthood Federation in 1969 and 1970; in 1971, the grant was increased to $500,000. In 1971 Japan pledged $2 million to the UNFPA. In October 1970, it sent a family planning mission to Indonesia. Following the mission's recommendations, the Government began receiving Indonesian trainees and sending advisers and materials to that country.

The Family Planning Federation of Japan, Inc., established in April 1968, provides contraceptive materials, equipment and other commodities to the Republic of China, Indonesia, Republic of Korea and Nepal.

Since 1967, seminars on family planning have been held for doctors, nurses and government officials from southeast Asian countries. They have been conducted by the Government's Overseas Technical Cooperation Agency and the Family Planning Federation.

The Netherlands. The Government of the Netherlands has contributed to the United Nations Fund for Population Activities and is providing about $1.7 million to assist family planning activities in Indonesia, Kenya, Pakistan, and Tunisia.

In Pakistan, the Netherlands supports research to gather data on motivation of the rural population towards family planning and to help implement Pakistan's family planning program. Under a three year project begun in 1968, five Netherlands nationals did research in selected villages.

A 1968-73 project in Kenya includes training of local personnel in contraceptive uses, and clinical research on the applicability of various family planning techniques and the causes and treatment of sterility. A two year project including clinical research and training of medical personnel in Tunisia will help to implement the Tunisian Government's family planning program. Two grants have been made to Indonesia; one was for the National Training Center, the other for the National Family Planning Institute and two Indonesian universities for social and clinical research.

Norway has given assistance to family planning activities since 1964. Since 1970, its aim has been to allocate approximately 10% of total aid appropriations to such activities in developing countries, divided about evenly between multilateral and bilateral programs. Bilateral aid, primarily financial, will go mainly to Norway's priority countries that request assistance.

In 1971 Norway provided $1.5 million to the UNFPA. It has also contributed to the IPPF and UNICEF for family planning purposes. Under the bilateral program, $1.1 million was granted to the postpartum family planning program in India. Norway also contributed clinical equipment to Kenya for the establishment of 50 family planning units in health centers.

Sweden. Family planning has been assigned the highest priority in Sweden's development aid program. Aid is extended through the Swedish International Development Authority (SIDA), and has grown from a single project in Ceylon in 1958 to assistance in materials, finance, and personnel to numerous developing countries. Disbursements in 1969-70 amounted to approximately $5.3 million. They rose to about $6.4 million in 1970-71, and were expected to total some $11 million in 1971-72. The share of Sweden's bilateral aid for family planning has increased from a few percentage points in the early 1960s to about 10% today.

SIDA now furnishes supplies and equipment to some 14 countries. In three of these (Ceylon, Kenya and Tunisia) it also provides expert personnel for government programs. SIDA also has a special arrangement permitting governments and organizations to buy contraceptives at reduced prices, made possible by volume purchases. The Government provides substantial allocations to the International Planned Parenthood Federation and various United Nations organizations. Assistance has also been given to WHO for research in human reproduction.

The United Kingdom. The United Kingdom has recently increased its aid to population programs through both multilateral and bilateral channels. The allocation for 1971 was $4 million.

Grants were made to the United Nations Fund for Population Activities and to the International Planned Parenthood Federation. At the meeting of the Consortium on aid to India in May 1970, the United Kingdom pledged an interest-free loan of $2.4 million for local costs of the Indian family planning program. Technical assistance is being given to some 10 or 12 countries.

A Population Bureau was set up in 1968 by the Ministry of Overseas Development. The Bureau encourages training and research and helps to provide operational and advisory personnel for overseas programs. A fertility research unit was established at the London School of Hygiene and Tropical Medicine in January 1970. A graduate course in medical demography, at the same school, commenced in September 1970. Both programs receive assistance from the Government.

United States. The largest budget for population assistance is that of the United States, operating chiefly through its Agency for International Development (AID). AID's budget increased from $50 million in 1969 to $75 million in 1970 and $100 million in 1971, compared with $4 million in 1966 and 1967.

AID has supported bilateral programs in 33 countries and helped finance activities in many others through organizations such as the International Planned Parenthood Federation (IPPF), the Pathfinder Fund, the Population Council and the United Nations. Assistance covers all major disciplines concerned—information, education and communication, demography, social research, and research in fertility control methods. The Agency assists in manpower development, including leadership and specialized technical training in evaluation and analysis. It also promotes institutional development. In 1971, AID provided contraceptives for family planning programs in more than 70 countries and made available supplies and equipment to a number of institutions.

In addition, research on population and family planning in developing countries is carried out in the U.S. Department of Health, Education and Welfare, largely by agencies under the Public Health Service. Some 100 Peace Corps volunteers have worked in population programs overseas.

Multilateral Programs

The Food and Agriculture Organization of the United Nations (FAO) is becoming involved in the population field in two areas:

policy-oriented research into the implications of population trends for agricultural development (food consumption and nutrition and their effects on fertility and mortality), and integration of family planning into home economics education programs.

The International Labour Organization (ILO) has a mandate to promote information and education activities on population and family planning and to conduct policy-oriented research on the demographic aspects of social policy in such fields as employment promotion, social security, and enterprise-level medical services in family planning.

The United Nations. On the basis of resolutions adopted over the last several years, all major United Nations agencies have authority to undertake action programs in population and family planning.

In 1969 several of these agencies took the first steps to develop and pursue operational programs, with financial support from the United Nations Fund for Population Activities (UNFPA). This Fund was established by the Secretary-General in 1967 to finance an expanded United Nations program in population and family planning. During 1969, the Secretary-General turned over management of the UNFPA to the Administrator of the United Nations Development Program (UNDP), the central technical and development assistance agency for the United Nations.

By the end of 1969, more than $5 million in contributions had been pledged to the UNFPA, of which $4 million was provided by the United States. Other contributors were Denmark, Finland, the Netherlands, Norway, Pakistan, Sweden, Trinidad and Tobago, and the United Kingdom. In 1970 the Fund received pledges of $15.4 million, and in 1971 $28 million. By the end of 1971, about 60% of these funds had been received for disbursements. Most were obligated for projects involving support for demographic training activities, research on demographic and population questions, advisory missions and technical services to member countries, national program support for non-conventional equipment and supplies, information and documentation, and infrastructure costs within the United Nations system.

The Population Division, within the United Nations Secretariat, continues its program of demographic research and projections, technical information services, and support for conferences and technical meetings, funded from the regular budget of the United Nations. In addition, the Population Division executes for the UNFPA, as do other elements of the United Nations system, the provision of technical assistance to countries in areas within its competence.

United Nations Educational, Scientific and Cultural Organization (Unesco). Population programs are a new area for Unesco, and the work program is developing rapidly. Unesco's population and family planning activities increased from less than $500,000 worth of UNFPA-financed projects in 1970 to an estimated $3.5 million in 1972.

The Organization's mandate covers the development of curricula and teaching materials, teacher training, the use of communications and related training, and research in population-related education, motivation, evaluation, etc. Unesco has sent advisory missions to a number of countries, provided consultants and advisors for national education and communications programs, conducted regional meetings and training courses and, through its regional office in Bangkok, produced sample population education materials. Proposed projects include seminars and workshops and an expanded program of research, including the development of simulation studies on demographic growth and educational opportunity.

The United Nations Children's Fund (UNICEF) has provided assistance for family planning since 1967, as part of its maternal and child health programs. Its contribution has been in the form of vehicles, equipment and supplies, salaries for teaching staffs, and stipends for trainees. Under an Executive Board decision in 1970, UNICEF is also able to furnish contraceptive supplies to countries on request.

The World Health Organization (WHO) has a key role in carrying out an effective United Nations family planning effort. WHO has a mandate to work in the health aspects of human reproduction, family planning, and population dynamics, and is expected to assist countries in the development of family planning activities within the context of health services.

Private Agencies

The Ford Foundation. The Ford Foundation has contributed substantial funding for population work. Since 1952, it has committed about $147 million for this purpose, and has been an important force in three areas concerned with problems of population: research and training in reproductive biology, establishment and expansion of university population study centers in the United States, and assistance to family planning programs in developing countries.

Major emphasis has been on reproductive biology, with some $80 million in grants going primarily for fundamental research and training programs in 93 institutions around the world. Grants have been made to a dozen university centers focusing on population problems. While two thirds of the Ford Foundation's population expenditures have gone to American institutions, their activities in the field are mainly directed toward population problems in developing countries.

Since the mid-1960s, resources devoted to population work in developing countries have grown significantly. The Ford Foundation has financed family planning work in 26 developing countries. In Asia and Africa it is assisting family planning action programs as well as training and research. In Latin America, emphasis is placed on the study of population problems and reproductive biology.

The International Planned Parenthood Federation (IPPF). The IPPF assists the formation and effective operation of family planning associations and institutional affiliates throughout the world. It encourages and supports the training of medical and paramedical workers, sponsors workshops and seminars, and promotes and organizes international and regional meetings and conferences. The Federation also stimulates scientific research in the fields of biology, demography, sociology, methods of contraception, fertility and subfertility, sex education, and marriage counseling.

Established in 1952, IPPF is an association of autonomous national family planning associations. One non-governmental family planning association in each country is eligible for full membership, provided it is a national organization. In 1971 there were 79 members, including associate members and two affiliates. Information and assistance have also been given to non-member associations. The IPPF has six regional offices, and representatives for Africa in Nairobi and Accra.

IPPF is financed largely by foundations, individuals and grants by governments. It has also received assistance from the UNFPA. Indicative of the growth of the Federation in recent years was the increase in its annual budget from $325,000 in 1962 to nearly $20 million in 1971 and its estimated program of $25 million in 1972.

The Population Council. The Council was established in 1952 and is financed primarily by the Rockefeller and Ford Foundations. It promotes research, training and technical assistance in the social and bio-medical sciences, and serves as a center for the collection and exchange of information on significant ideas and developments in the field. Its activities include an extensive publication program.

The Council initially confined its activities chiefly to fellowships and small demographic and bio-medical research grants. In the early 1960s, however, it began to give technical assistance to family planning and population projects in developing countries. Its budget in 1970 totaled $17.2 million. It had a staff of about 230, of whom 30 served in 18 foreign countries. Through its Technical Assistance Division, the Council provides support to family planning programs in 17 countries. It also seeks to evaluate the effectiveness of programs.

The Council's Demographic Division has assisted the United Nations Demographic Centers in Bombay, Cairo and Santiago, and national centers in 15 countries. Grants have been made to numerous university departments and study centers in developing countries. The Demographic Division also conducts research on fertility, estimation of rates of population growth, population policy, and related topics.

The Bio-Medical Division has focused much of its resources on specific research leads in various methods of contraception. In 1967 it began a project to establish fertility regulation by continuous progestin therapy. The progestin—in this instance megestrol acetate—is being field-tested in 10 countries. Research on a number of other contraceptive leads is being done by an international panel of experts in six countries. Basic research on reproductive biology and other aspects of fertility regulation is also being conducted.

The Council started its International Postpartum Family Planning Program in 1966 in 25 hospitals in 14 nations. The program has grown to include 150 hospitals and clinics operating in 14 countries in Asia, Africa, Latin America and the Middle East.

The Postpartum Program is an international demonstration effort to provide family planning information and services immediately after childbirth to urban women of low socio-economic status, in settings where delivery is institutionalized in public hospitals and clinics. A world-wide follow-up survey has been completed.

The Rockefeller Foundation. Although the Rockefeller Foundation gave support to bio-medical research in fertility control in the early 1930s, it was not until the late 1950s and early 1960s that the Foundation made major commitments to help solve population problems. Since 1963 it has provided more than $45 million, including more than $15 million in 1970.

The Rockefeller Foundation concentrates increasingly on the interaction of social, medical and biological sciences. It finances research, training and experimental programs in a broad range of fields relevant to population and, like the Ford Foundation, is making a major effort to stimulate basic research in reproductive biology.

At the University of North Carolina, a grant was made to finance research on applying techniques of modern cellular and molecular biology to problems of fertility control. A new building to house the Harvard Laboratory of Human Reproduction and Reproductive Biology was made possible by a Rockefeller Foundation grant of $2 million to equip the Laboratory and provide staff over the next 10 years. Grants were made to Tulane, California, Columbia and Georgetown Universities. The Foundation has also supported research at the London School of Economics and in universities in Chile, Colombia, Indonesia, Mexico, Thailand and Turkey.

RESEARCH

Research in population is as varied as the disciplines concerned. It can be classified into four groups:

- **Demographic research.** Research related to the basic demographic variables—fertility, mortality, migration, and implications for the size, structure, and rate of growth of populations. A growing but specialized aspect of this research concerns the demographic assessment of the effects of fertility control programs.

- **Economic research.** Economic implications of population trends, including the economic effects of programs, and the economic analysis of programs (cost-effectiveness, for example), etc.

- **Bio-medical research.** This covers the entire field of contraceptive technology and reproductive biology, including related clinical trials. It involves basic physiological research, research on products and agents and their action, and also applied field trials for clinical testing, evaluation of side effects, etc.

- **Operational research.** This involves research directed to operational problems in selected disciplines, e.g., management, evaluation, communications, educational methods, and media.

Research in all these areas has increased as interest in population matters has grown and more money has become available. The spectrum of interests is very wide, not only in its interdisciplinary scope, but also in its range from purely theoretical topics to narrowly focused projects designed to solve day-to-day applied problems. Much of the planned and ongoing research is not directly relevant to operational needs. However, in a rapidly expanding field where research has been neglected in the past, it is not always possible to assess the longer term significance of research topics that may appear, in the short run, to be of no direct operational relevance. There is a clear need to expand the boundaries of knowledge about population matters in all directions, while recognizing that only a limited range of topics is likely to fall within the immediate interests of the Bank.

It is useful to distinguish three kinds of research interests for the Bank. There is a wide range of population matters which do not fall within the competence of the Bank, and are not a direct concern of day-to-day operations, but in which the Bank has an interest in seeing that knowledge and understanding are expanded through research. This can be done by making the Bank's interests known and encouraging other, more appropriate, institutions to plan and finance the research. The most important group of subjects in this category covers the fields of basic research in human biology and reproduction, con-

369

traceptive development, and other medical and health topics. It will be necessary to follow the progress of this kind of research and to consider, at an appropriate time, whether the Bank can make a contribution in a coordinating role. Initiatives being taken by WHO and the Population Council through its International Committee on Contraceptive Research, in addition to those of the industry, represent an expanded effort in this field.

Second, there are research topics that the Bank has an interest in pursuing but where the work cannot be done easily within the Bank, either because of staff commitments or because the work is not feasible with facilities available. As in other areas of activity, such research can be contracted out under staff supervision. In this respect some aspects of population research would be no different, in principle, from other areas in which the Bank has undertaken work through consultancy arrangements. An additional reason for such arrangements, however, may be the need to encourage the development of research institutions and capacity in the developing countries. This may be as important in the population field as obtaining actual research results.

The third area of research activity covers those studies which can and should be done by Bank staff. This group is not always sharply distinguished from the kind of topic that might be handled on a consultancy basis. It will normally be identified by the criteria that it can be best pursued within the context of project, sector and country economic work, and will focus on problems of operational interest to the Bank.

The objective of most Bank-sponsored research will be to provide information which will ultimately lead to the improvement of Bank operations. This objective suggests that research projects which are to be useful in this sense must be linked closely to population programs and relate to program needs, including the generation of appropriate data for this purpose. It will often be the case that the most effective research will be done through local talent, which is likely to be most sensitive to local needs and priorities. This would in no way preclude the use of expatriate assistance in the planning and undertaking of many aspects of research. The essential need is for a partnership rather than a paternalistic relationship. Experience with family planning programs so far strongly suggests that a minimum of three to five years may be necessary before research can lead to meaningful conclusions. The planning, collection and analysis of the data required set the minimum period before research results can be used to improve program performance and measure results.

One of the Bank's main objects in the field of research will be to build into projects it finances a strong management evaluation component, linked in the most appropriate way to program administration. The usefulness of data generated in such projects will be enhanced if it is collected in such a way as to make possible meaningful comparative studies. This is particularly important if progress is to be made in understanding the relationship between costs and results of family planning services in terms of the number of people served and possible effects in reducing fertility. This information does not now exist on any basis which makes possible sound generalizations about the scale of expenditures needed to produce a given reduction in fertility.

Part of the research program of the Bank, therefore, both internal and as contracted through consultancy arrangements, will focus on key aspects of the management of family planning programs. In particular, it is proposed to study the methodological aspects of family planning programs including the cost-effectiveness, evaluation and cost-benefit aspects. Of equal importance is the need to study the cost patterns arising from different variations in family planning programs, including the resultant budgetary implications of program development. A third area of research of interest for program operation covers the role of the commercial sector in the provision of family planning services.

These topics are those most closely related to the operational needs of the Bank, insofar as lending for family planning is concerned. However, there are other areas of population research equally relevant for operational purposes but not directly connected with project activity. These include studies to support general economic analysis of the development prospects of member countries, and related sector analysis. They include the demographic and macro-economic aspects of development.

In choosing topics to be pursued through consultancy arrangements, special attention will be paid to proposals for collaborative research with institutions in member countries. An important role in country project development will be to support related social research through national institutions; this could range from the provision of positions, support to programs, and establishment of centers for this type of supportive research. The objective of these proposals is to provide support for strengthening research capabilities in the developing countries and, at the same time, ensure that research of importance to both the country and the Bank is carried out by local talent.

TOURISM

TOURISM
SECTOR WORKING PAPER

● This paper describes the growth of tourism throughout the world, the various factors which have affected this growth, and the prospects for developing countries to benefit more fully from tourism. Focus is primarily on vacation travel since business travel is far less responsive to an expansion of tourism facilities and is, therefore, of less interest for Bank Group operations. The paper recounts the role of the World Bank Group in encouraging the establishment and extension of the tourist industry in developing countries and outlines its plans for the future.

The term World Bank Group includes the International Bank for Reconstruction and Development, the International Development Association (IDA) and the International Finance Corporation (IFC). Money amounts are expressed in U.S. dollars. The Group's fiscal year (FY) ends June 30.

REVIEW OF THE SECTOR
Recent Growth Trends of International Tourism

Since the early 1950s international tourism[1] has grown rapidly, particularly after the liberalization of foreign exchange and travel restrictions which characterized the years following World War II. In the early 1960s international tourism, which in Europe had been mainly limited to neighboring countries, spread more widely and developing countries began to benefit increasingly from its growth. From 1950 to 1970 international visitor arrivals (including vacationers[2], business and other visitors) in all countries grew from 25 million to 168 million, an average yearly growth rate of 10%, while international tourism receipts rose from $2.1 billion to $17.4 billion, 11% per year. In some of the developing countries much higher growth rates have been recorded in recent years (see Annex Table 1), as these more distant destinations have become increasingly accessible with the expansion of air transport.

There are three major tourist generating areas: North America (United States and Canada), Western Europe and Japan. About three-

---

[1] An international tourist, as defined by the United Nations and the International Union of Official Travel Organisation, is a person who visits a country other than that of permanent residence for at least 24 hours, whatever his motive for travel.

[2] A vacationer, whether international or domestic, is defined by major European tourist services as staying away from home for at least four nights on any one trip and may in some instances include tourists traveling for a combination of business and pleasure. An excursionist is a person who stays in any one destination for less than 24 hours.

375

quarters of all international visitor arrivals, including the great majority of arrivals in developing countries, are accounted for by 12 countries—United States, Canada, United Kingdom, France, Germany, Sweden, Denmark, Belgium, Netherlands, Switzerland, Austria and Italy. Until 1967, foreign travel from Japan was severely limited but with the easing of restrictions in subsequent years, foreign holiday travel particularly has grown very fast.

Factors Affecting Vacation Travel

Only a few countries have tried to analyze the factors affecting the various types of tourist demand and this only in recent years. The studies, usually based on sample surveys, indicate that levels of income, income distribution, educational levels, social structure, changing vacation habits, the degree of urbanization and geographical location, are the main determinants of the growth of vacation travel.

The following table shows the proportion of the population in the more developed countries which travel on vacation, both at home and abroad. The table shows that the correlation between per capita Gross National Product (GNP) and vacation travel is not very close. In the U.S., with the highest per capita GNP, the proportion of the population traveling on vacation is considerably lower than in some European countries, and countries with similar per capita GNPs within the same region vary considerably in their travel patterns. In some highly industrialized countries like Great Britain and the nations of Scandinavia the proportion of the population traveling on vacation has reached 60% and more of the adult population and this proportion is unlikely to rise much further. In many others, however, including such major tourism generating countries as the U.S., Germany and France, it is only around 40%. There appears to be a large potential for further growth in vacation travel.

The extent of foreign travel depends in part on income levels, levels of education, etc., but it is also heavily dependent on the size of the country of origin and its geographic location. A European vacationer is much more likely to cross an international frontier than a North American vacationer though the latter may travel a longer distance. Even in Europe, however, the bulk of vacation travel is domestic.

Although statistical data are incomplete, the broad pattern of present and prospective vacation travel is fairly clear. The bulk of vacation travel is over relatively short distances within and between the developed countries. Over somewhat longer distances there are substantial numbers of vacationers from the U.S. and Canada visiting

376

Table 1: Vacation Travel in Major Tourist Generating Countries, 1967[1]

Countries	Population	GNP per Capita	Proportion of Population Traveling on Vacation	Proportion Traveling only at Home	Proportion Traveling to Foreign Countries within the region[2]	inter-regional	Inter-regional Travelers
	million	$	%	%	%	%	thousand
Sweden	7.87	2,500	77.0	52.0	22.2	2.8	172
Switzerland	6.07	2,310	57.0	28.5	28.5	n.a.	n.a.
France	49.55	1,950	41.0	35.0	5.1	0.9	267
Denmark	4.84	1,950	66.0	40.0	22.6	3.4	123
Norway	3.78	1,860	78.0	67.0	10.2	0.8	23
Germany, Fed. Rep. of	57.70	1,750	39.0	20.0	18.4	0.6	277
Belgium	9.58	1,740	34.3	16.5	16.9	0.9	65
United Kingdom	54.98	1,700	60.0	50.0	9.3	0.7	295
Netherlands	12.60	1,520	54.0	38.0	14.7	1.3	92
Austria	7.32	1,210	40.0	26.0	14.0	n.a.	n.a.
Italy	52.35	1,120	19.5	18.7	0.7	0.1	32
Yugoslavia	19.84	530	12.0	10.0	2.0	n.a.	n.a.
Western Europe							1,346
United States	198.63	3,670	36.0	33.8	0.8	1.4	2,240
Japan	99.87	1,000	n.a.	n.a.	0.3	0.3	241

[1]Since most data are results of sample surveys they can only be considered as estimates. Data on vacation travel of persons 18 years of age and older.

[2]Regions are the following: North America, Europe and East Asia.

Source: "Problems of Tourism for Selected Countries in the Mediterranean Area with Special Reference to Local Conditions" 1969, Institute for Tourism, University of Munich.
"1967 Census of Transportation", U.S. Department of Commerce, with own adjustments.
"Statistical Bulletin of International Tourism", 1966-69, Japan National Tourist Organization.

Mexico and the Caribbean and larger numbers from Western Europe visiting the Mediterranean. The figures of inter-regional vacation travelers shown in Table 1 are approximations, but they provide a reasonable estimate of orders of magnitude. As a proportion of all vacation travel, inter-regional travel is small, and within the absolute total of such travel the share of the U.S. is large (almost 60%). The majority (52%) of U.S. travelers leaving North America visit Western Europe.

Analysis of the European travel market indicates that for the next decade an increase of some 40 million in the number of vacationers (approximately a 45% increase over present levels) can reasonably be expected. A similar relative increase, if not higher, is likely for the U.S. and Japan. Only a part of this growth will result in foreign travel and only a fraction in long-distance travel; it can be assumed that those already traveling will tend to go farther afield in the future while newcomers to the travel market may seek their first experience in domestic tourism.

The costs of transport are a key element in determining tourist flows. In almost all tourist generating countries the private car ranks first as a means of transport and is likely to gain further ground. Rail travel, once the most important mode of transport in tourism, is steadily declining; its share in European travel is hardly more than 30% and in the U.S. much less. With declining tariffs (at least in real terms) and better and faster service, air transportation, while still used by only 6% to 10% of all vacationers, shows the fastest relative growth. The growth of air charters especially has made possible rapid increases in traffic from North America to Europe, from northern Europe to the Mediterranean—e.g. Majorca and Tunisia—and on a more limited scale from Europe to more distant destinations such as Kenya, Thailand, Ceylon and the Caribbean.

Long-distance travel by air, which is virtually the only mode of travel to the more distant developing countries from the major tourist generating centers, will continue to account for a relatively small share of total tourism travel in the foreseeable future. Nevertheless, considering the likely growth of income in the main tourist generating countries and the rising proportion of the population earning higher incomes and enjoying higher levels of education, the absolute number of vacationers traveling long distances by air should increase very considerably in the next decade.

Likely Future Tourist Flows to Developing Countries

The factors which influence demand point to the likely development of tourism by areas of destination. The bulk of vacation travel will continue to be within and between the developed countries but there will be large increases in flows of visitors to the developing countries in the Mediterranean Basin and to Mexico and the Caribbean. These countries will include:

Mediterranean Basin: Spain, Yugoslavia, Greece, Morocco, Algeria, Tunisia, Egypt, Israel, Lebanon, Syria, Turkey and Cyprus. The growth of tourism in some of these countries (Egypt, Syria, Israel and Lebanon) has been hampered by the political situation.

The Caribbean: most of the Caribbean islands; Central American countries and Mexico; as well as Colombia and Venezuela in South America.

From studies made of the European market, and from data available on the United States, rough orders of magnitude can be given of the likely potential increase in vacation visitor flows to these two regions over the next decade. For the Mediterranean this figure would be about 10 million additional visits, nearly doubling the 1968 total and for the Caribbean and Mexico an additional three to four million, compared with about three million in recent years.

For long-distance travel, the areas of greater interest among developing countries are likely to be Eastern Africa (Kenya, Tanzania, Uganda and Ethiopia) and South East Asia (Iran, Afghanistan, India, Ceylon, Nepal, Thailand, Indonesia and Singapore). In these countries multi-destination circuits have developed, for example through Eastern Africa, South and East Asia and the Pacific. With appropriate air fares and increased facilities such circuits might also be developed further in Western Africa and South America.

The magnitude of the likely visitor flows to each of the more distant destinations is difficult to predict. They are competing destinations and much will depend on the success of each in providing tourist facilities of the right type and at the right price. Overall, the growth in long-distance vacation travel is likely to be fast, but in absolute terms will probably not exceed two to three million additional vacation travelers over the next decade—approximately doubling the levels of recent years.

Regional tourism can also be expected to expand. The greatest growth is likely from Japan to nearby destinations such as Korea and the Republic of China, but more distant destinations—Thailand, Singapore and Indonesia—will also benefit from the fast growth of the Japanese market. Other areas of regional tourism will continue to be in South America, between Argentina and Brazil and from these two countries to Paraguay, Uruguay and Chile; in southern Africa, from South Africa to Lesotho, Swaziland, Malawi, Malagasy and Mauritius; and in the South Pacific, from Australia and New Zealand to Fiji, New Caledonia and Tahiti. A number of these countries will also be the destination of visitors from distant countries but in relatively small numbers.

Patterns of Tourism Expenditure

As a rule of thumb, vacationers are likely to spend an amount equivalent to one month's income per family on annual leave, although this varies according to the living standards, not only from country to country but also within each country. Generally speaking, tourists will respond to price incentives. They have demonstrated strong price consciousness not only about accommodation and other services offered but also in choosing modes of transport and travel distances. Changes in tariffs have quite often resulted in considerable redirection of tourist flows. Moreover, changes in relative air fares have meant increasing price competition even between regional destinations such as Western Europe and the Caribbean where price levels had until recently been relatively independent. This empirical evidence that demand for vacation travel, both domestic and foreign, is strongly price-elastic has been confirmed by the limited amount of serious research carried out to date. The studies also suggest that expenditures on long-distance foreign travel are highly income-elastic.

A tourist's daily expenditure may vary from a very low amount (i.e. when camping and visiting friends and relatives) to large sums for luxury vacations. Tour operators, especially in Europe, exercise a certain price leadership in their market which indicates at what prices supply can be offered. For example, European tour operators at the present time regard a daily expenditure of about $9.00 for full board as a ceiling price, which will be exceeded only in exceptional cases. The individual tourist very often orients himself by comparing prices of total holiday packages (including transportation) offered by tour operators and therefore will not easily be prepared to spend more. With long-distance travel, not only do travel expenses increase but daily expenditure also tends to go up, since most vacationers prepared to travel long distances are likely to demand relatively high standards of accommodation. This, of course, limits the number of potential tourists.

The data on average daily expenditure by foreign tourists in Table 1 of the Annex reflect the differences in the types of market for different developing countries. Mediterranean destinations such as Spain, Yugoslavia, Greece and Tunisia appeal to a broad spectrum of middle-income tourists. In these markets the role of tour operators organizing package tours and budget holidays is very significant. This is also increasingly true of such distant destinations as Kenya, Ceylon and Thailand. On the other hand, travel on the part of relatively well-to-do vacationers or business travelers and those who combine business and vacation travel predominates in most other distant destinations. Vacation travel to most Caribbean islands (other than Puerto Rico and the U.S. Virgin Islands) has until recently been dominated by relatively high-income North Americans—most individual vacationers—at least during the main winter season.

Excluding travel costs, normally from 60% to 75% of tourists' expenditures goes on food and accommodation. The balance is spent on excursions, entertainment and shopping. In some tourist destinations shopping accounts for a much larger part of expenditures—notably in Hong Kong and Singapore, both internationally famous duty-free ports—but in virtually all destinations tourists buy souvenirs and local crafts, thus providing an addition to exports which might not otherwise occur. Travel costs as part of the total cost of the holiday vary greatly according to distance and mode of transport. For long-distance destinations by air, travel costs can amount to 50% to 60% of total costs.

In the light of the patterns of tourism expenditure which have been described, it is clear that in a number of countries a really significant expansion in demand can be achieved only by increasing the supply of moderately priced accommodations, particularly if suitable arrangements can be reached with tour operators and airlines to reduce the costs of air travel. Some countries, distant from the main centers of tourism generation, might be better advised to concentrate on the high-income part of the tourist market.

"Seasonality"

School holiday patterns, industrial vacation customs and climatic and geographic factors in both tourist generating and receiving countries cause most vacation tourism to be highly seasonal. There is, however, a growing trend to two or more holidays in some of the most highly developed countries, particularly where winters are very severe such as the Scandinavian countries, Canada and the northern United States. This mitigates to some extent the seasonal peaks in some tourist destinations such as Majorca, Morocco, Mexico and some Caribbean and Pacific islands. Business travel has little relation to seasons and to a limited extent offsets variations in vacation travel. Other travelers, whose motivation might be for personal reasons, may travel at any time.

The possibilities of offsetting fluctuations in business and holiday travel are quite limited. Tourism facilities for vacation travel are often not suitable for business travel. City hotels usually show their lowest utilization during the peak holiday season and holiday resorts experience rather slack business during the rest of the year. Apart from the attempts to stagger school holidays, which have not been notably successful, there have been other attempts to lessen seasonality. The most promising seem to be in the creation of new demand, such as convention business and in price policies that induce tourism through preferential tariffs in the off-peak season. However, there are limits to price elasticity and also to the number of conventions to be arranged. Seasonality can never be fully balanced out. This is most important in planning tourism facilities since a project must be designed for specific occupancy rates.

The following yearly bed occupancy rates can reasonably be expected:

(a) **Business Travel**—60% to 90%; there is a tendency for declining utilization of business accommodation with the shortening of the work week.

(b) **Vacation Travel**—20% to 60% and higher, if the climate is very favorable in the tourist receiving country. Mediterranean resort hotels usually have occupancy levels between 30% and 45%; in a few exceptional cases this may go as high as 60%. In some of the Caribbean and Mexican resort hotels as well as some East African and South Sea resorts which cater mainly to vacation travelers, occupancy rates may go up as high as 80% and 90%. This, however, is only possible with a very select clientele whose holidays are not tied to any particular time of the year.

Tourism Facilities

Tourism facilities do not consist only of accommodation like hotels and boarding houses. They include also recreational and sports facilities of great variety and, of course, all the necessary infrastructure like transportation and utilities. In countries of cultural interest, historical monuments may also be regarded as part of tourism infrastructure, and the preservation, restoration, or better accessibility of these monuments may be critical for the future of the sector in these countries.

The composition of superstructure, mainly accommodation, has undergone considerable changes in the last 20 years. New types of accommodation, particularly holiday villages suitable for family-type tourists, condominiums and apartment houses, private villas and camping facilities, have proved successful and to some degree are replacing traditional hotels and boarding houses. These changes reflect changes in demand with new, often younger, groups entering the international travel market and also new approaches to the problem of providing facilities in a very competitive industry with a highly seasonal demand.

It is typical of the tourism industry that individual units are of rather moderate size. Hotels in general range from 150 to 500 beds, while holiday villages may offer as many as 1,000 beds. Considering an average investment per bed to be in the range of $5,000 to $10,000 depending on quality and location, the total investment required for each unit could be in the order of less than $1 million up to $5 million and more. There are, of course, exceptions whenever the implementation of a whole complex is being considered; this type of development provides potential economies in construction and in marketing which are likely to be particularly significant in some less developed countries.

In almost any developing country a need exists for some basic tourist facilities to accommodate business travelers. In these cases individual investments will be of relatively moderate size. By comparison, the supply of accommodation needed to meet demand for vacation tourism will call for relatively large investments in the regions likely to attract the largest tourist flows (i.e. the Mediterranean Basin and the Caribbean area) and for rather sizable investments even in those not close to the major tourist generating areas (e.g. Bali).

Financial Aspects of Investment in Accommodation

Although international experience indicates that over the longer term well-conceived investments in tourism accommodation facilities show satisfactory financial rates of return, the supply of accommodation has often failed to increase in line with the growth of demand. In many countries starting the development of tourism, it has been difficult to interest the private sector to invest in hotels and other forms of accommodation. Apart from lack of experience in the sector, two features of hotel investment in particular seem to account for the reluctance of investors: (a) the fact that relatively large amounts of capital have to be tied up in fixed assets over a long period (up to 20-25 years) with all the risks of changes in market conditions, the political and social framework, etc., involved; and (b) the strongly seasonal demand which is particularly pronounced in resort areas. This gives rise to concern that it will not prove feasible to achieve sufficiently high occupancy rates to make satisfactory profits. All the more so since, contrary to a widely held impression, only a small proportion of hotel operating costs—the equivalent of 15% to 25% of total sales—are variable in the short term. With fixed costs relatively high, there is little flexibility to adjust to low seasonal demand.

Many governments in both developed and developing countries have attempted to overcome this reluctance of private investors to finance hotels and other forms of accommodation through a variety of incentive schemes. These include providing cheap or free land, equipment grants, exemption from import duties, liberal depreciation allowances and tax holidays, loan guarantees, long-term government loans and interest rate subsidies. The different incentives are being provided in varying combinations. In some cases they are made to apply to investments in all new accommodation, in others they are used selectively in an attempt to direct investment to certain areas or for accommodation serving a specific market. In the Mediterranean Basin equipment grants and interest rate subsidies are the most common subsidy schemes in effect at the present time, while in other parts of the world, notably the Caribbean, tax holidays and tax exemptions are the most widely used incentives. The question of incentives is discussed further on pages 397 - 398.

Planning for the Tourism Sector

In the majority of developing countries tourism has only recently attracted the attention of government as a sector warranting special economic policies and institutions. Too frequently, expertise in this sector is not presently available in government. Often and despite a sizable tourist flow, the private sector as well as the public lacks the know-how that would maximize benefits from tourism. Although training programs are increasingly available from different institutions and the United Nations Development Programme (UNDP), the International Labour Organisation (ILO) and various bilateral programs have already made a significant contribution, the need for training and technical assistance in tourism will remain a constraint on the growth of the sector in developing countries for some time to come.

The need for an improvement in planning techniques for the sector is being increasingly recognized. Lack of expertise in market analysis, in construction techniques for hotels and other accommodation and tourist facilities, in appropriate financing for the sector, in tourism infrastructure requirements, in promotion techniques and in means to reduce the adverse effects of seasonality, can lead either to over- or under-investment in supply of accommodation, as well as to inappropriate construction in relation to the market. Furthermore, the tourism sector can develop adequately only when given an appropriate government and semi-government institutional framework. In many countries such a framework does not exist and tourism is quite inadequately represented in high policy-making bodies where decisions are made on such topics as aviation policy and exchange rate policy which are critical for the industry. A major task of governments that have an important or potentially important tourism sector is to design and implement an integrated development plan for that sector. Many governments require outside assistance in formulating such a plan.

Foreign Exchange and Employment Effects of Tourism in Developing Countries

The data in Table 1 of the Annex show that for a number of developing countries tourism has become a leading foreign exchange

384

earner. In many cases gross tourism receipts amount to more than 20% of the total value of merchandise exports and in some—Spain, Lebanon, Mexico and many Caribbean islands—tourism has become the most important export of goods and services. Between 1960 and 1968, while exports from developing countries (other than oil exports) rose by 7.6% a year, receipts from tourism increased at an annual rate of 11%. In view of the dubious world market prospects of many primary products and the uncertainty about the extent to which the industrialized countries will permit increased imports of manufactured goods from developing countries, this trend may continue and the dependence on tourism by many of these countries may well tend to increase in the years to come. In any event, it provides for many a useful element in diversifying their sources of foreign exchange earnings and, for some, one of the very few export opportunities available.

The *net,* as a percentage of *gross,* foreign exchange earnings of tourism by developing countries vary considerably but tend to be high relative to many other exports. The countries fall roughly into three groups. Tourist facilities in such major tourist destinations as Mexico, Yugoslavia and Spain are constructed, equipped and supplied largely from local resources and staffed by local labor. Many of them are locally owned and operated. The *net* foreign exchange receipts are in excess of 85% of the gross foreign exchange earnings of these countries. At the other extreme are some of the islands in the Caribbean and the Pacific and some of the relatively undeveloped countries of Africa. In many of them, operating supplies such as many foods and beverages come from abroad; specialized management, equipment and a major part of construction materials have to be imported; and ownership of tourist facilities is often foreign. Even for these countries the *net* foreign exchange earnings are estimated to be seldom less than 45% of gross receipts. In most other developing countries which are less heavily dependent on imports, *net* foreign exchange receipts from tourism range from 60% to 80% of gross earnings.

Available data indicate that even for many developing countries where tourism has become a leading foreign exchange earner, the sector's output constitutes a relatively small portion of the GNP and employs directly only a small part of the labor force. It is often claimed that tourism is relatively labor-intensive but the available evidence is not conclusive on this point. Studies in Mexico and Kenya suggest that the relative amount of employment generated for each unit of capital invested has tended to be higher in tourism than in most other private sector activities. However, similar studies in Yugoslavia and Israel, carried out by the United Nations Conference on Trade and Develoment (UNCTAD) Secretariat, were far less conclusive.

385

Since tourism can often be developed in the less developed regions of a country, it may become a significant factor in redressing regional imbalances in employment and income. The extent to which this may be so will vary greatly from country to country. In some of the least developed countries the rapid growth of tourism may even lead to the creation of acute economic and social disparities between the areas where tourism has its most direct impact on money incomes and employment and the rest of the economy.

Some Social Effects of Tourism Development

The rapid development of international tourism in some of the developing countries has given rise to social problems which must be of concern to governments and outside bodies. One such problem is the attitude of the local population to tourists and their reaction to the tourists' requirements for accommodation and service, which by local standards are luxurious. Another problem may arise from foreign ownership and management of tourist facilities and the feeling that indigenous people perform only menial tasks. Tourism may be regarded as a threat to the indigenous culture and mores, and there is a real possibility of a serious deterioration in standards of local arts and crafts as efforts are made to expand output to meet the tourists' demands. Not infrequently, resort development has resulted in local people being denied access to their own beaches. All these factors can give rise to serious problems in the reception of tourists and to demands for limitations on the flow of visitors. A further problem may be the demonstration effect of foreign visitor standards on the consumption expenditure patterns of the local population, and the dissatisfaction which can result if new wants cannot be satisfied.

While these possible negative effects of international tourism cannot be ignored, positive effects may be the increase in international contacts and in cultural exchanges which occur. The demonstration effect may also provide a stimulus to effort on the part of the population of the receiving country, while the growth of tourist traffic may open up needed economic opportunities.

The balance between the negative and the positive effects of international tourism varies in different countries. The effects are complex and little work has so far been done to try to assess the full impact of tourism development in particular destinations. By careful planning and regulation, the negative effects can be mitigated and it is important that the responsible public authorities should take this into account in formulating development policies and programs for the sector.

WORLD BANK GROUP OPERATIONS IN TOURISM

Financing

Recognizing the important role of the private sector in tourism development, the main forms of World Bank Group assistance to tourism were, until mid-1971, directed to the investing and lending operations of the International Finance Corporation, and the financing of hotels through development finance companies. A number of Bank/IDA financed infrastructure projects, such as the Adriatic Highway in Yugoslavia, had also made a significant contribution to tourism development. As is evident from the data presented in Annex Table 2, IFC operations in the tourism sector, which started in 1967, have thus far consisted of nine operations for a total of $24 million. Of the investments held by IFC in tourism projects at the end of 1971, $4 million was in the form of equity participation and $16.5 million in loans. These investments and loans have contributed to total investments appproximating $70 million.

Two of the IFC operations deserve special mention. One was a recent loan in East Africa which is designed to promote regional tourism circuits in Kenya and Uganda. This loan is to be used both to finance hotels in the two countries and also ancillary facilities such as vehicles for the associated touring company. The second, by far IFC's largest operation in tourism to date, was assistance to a privately owned tourism promotion and financing company in Tunisia — Compagnie Financière et Touristique, S.A. This company with total funds of $40 million linked important private Tunisian investors with foreign private interests involved in tourism. The company is engaged in the planning of new tourist areas and is financing besides hotel projects, ancillary facilities such as golf courses, marinas and camping sites.

Through its loans to intermediary institutions, the Bank has provided $32 million for 79 tourism projects in five countries. Until August 1970 these loans were made through development finance companies whose main business was lending for industrial projects and two of them—the Banque Nationale de Développement Economique in Morocco and the Société Nationale d'Investissement in Tunisia—accounted for the overwhelming share of such financing. In August 1970, a loan of $10 million was approved for hotel financing through the Crédit Immobilier et Hotelier of Morocco, which in the last few years has been mainly engaged in financing tourism projects.

The first direct Bank loans for tourism projects were made only in mid-1971 with two loans for large integrated projects, both in Yugoslavia. In December 1971 a third loan was made to support the provision of infrastructure for a new resort to be developed on Mexico's Pacific coast, and in March 1972 an IDA credit for two moderate-sized hotels in Nepal was granted. Direct financing for tourism by the Bank and IDA has thus far amounted to $56.2 million. Negotiations have been completed for the financing of a project which would provide infrastructure to six principal tourist zones in Tunisia.

Preinvestment Activities

While the amount of Bank/IDA lending for tourism has been limited so far, preinvestment studies have been made in a considerable number of member countries. Comprehensive surveys of the tourism sector have been carried out in 10 countries. Less comprehensive reconnaissance surveys have been made in another 21 countries.

The Bank has been the Executing Agency for a UNDP financed preinvestment study for tourism development in Bali (Indonesia) and is currently Executing Agency for studies in Afghanistan, the Dominican Republic, Fiji and Venezuela. The studies in Bali, Fiji, Dominican Republic and Venezuela are designed to provide the planning framework for the development of new integrated tourist beach resort areas. In Afghanistan the purpose of the study is to recommend the location, scale and type of tourist accommodation needed over the next five years. The Bank is providing technical assistance for tourism studies under way or planned for Colombia, Korea, Kenya, Yugoslavia and Mexico and for regional tourism development in Western Africa.

Lessons Drawn from Past Operations

During the relatively short time that the Bank Group has been actively involved in tourism development, a number of important issues have emerged. Among these are the appropriate strategies of tourism development in particular countries with special reference to market possibilities and to the types and location of tourist facilities; the appropriate air transport policies; the environmental, ecological, cultural and social impact of tourism development in particular areas; and the ownership and use of land for tourism purposes.

In its evaluation of tourism projects to date, the Bank has paid particular attention to the assessment of market demand, still a difficult task where the necessary data are fragmentary and where rapid changes in the organization of the travel trade and in the development of air travel can have a major impact on traffic to particular destinations. In view of the many uncertainties, countries should avoid committing themselves too firmly to catering for one type of traffic. Experience has shown that developments in air transport (e.g. air charter flights) have brought quite distant destinations within the reach of much broader market segments, and this can provide the basis for an advantageous diversification and broadening of the national tourism industry.

Within the framework of market possibilities and the tourist attractions of a particular country, tourist facilities should be developed with due regard to the costs both of the hotels themselves and of the necessary supporting services and infrastructure. The development of well-planned resort areas at priority sites to serve relatively large concentrations of visitors is likely to be much more economical than more scattered development which would require infrastructure to be provided over wide areas. Moreover, the former type of development is likely to be more in accord with market preferences as the tourist can enjoy a wider variety of activities and services. These considerations have weighed heavily in the Bank's projects in Mexico and Yugoslavia and also in the consideration of tourism development plans for Bali, the Dominican Republic and Fiji now being formulated.

The issues in air transport policy are highly complex, and no full treatment of these issues is possible in this paper. Insofar as tourism is concerned, however, one issue is preeminent. Tourist traffic to a number of countries has been severely restricted because air charter operations have been limited in order to safeguard the position of national airlines. This is not necessarily in the country's best interests, and it is essential that the potential advantage to the national economy from the development of tourism should be fully considered in devising rational air transport policies.

The importance of the environmental and cultural impact of tourism development looms especially large in some countries, for example the island of Bali, where one of the principal tourist attractions is the rich cultural life of the population. Here it is critically important that tourist accommodation and other facilities should be located appropriately and tourist flows regulated so as to minimize the disruptive impact on the daily life of the people.

The preservation and improvement of the physical environment either in new or established resorts requires the provision of adequate infrastructure and the enforcement of appropriate land-use patterns, zoning and building regulations. In the evaluation of the Mexican and Yugoslav projects, particular importance was attached to these aspects. In the proposed Tunisian project, the preservation of the environment and the safeguarding of existing assets and new investments by the provision of adequate infrastructure, particularly sewerage, is a principal objective.

In many areas of the world tourism development has produced great disparities in the standards of amenities provided for the visitor and for the local population. This cannot be entirely avoided, but in the longer run the improvement of standards for the local population is probably a condition of successful tourism development. The upgrading of amenities to be provided for the local population is an integral part of the Mexican project.

The development of a new resort by the provision of infrastructure costing perhaps millions of dollars has a great impact on land values in the area affected. Were these benefits to accrue largely to a few private landowners, the Bank would have difficulty in financing such a project. The acquisition of land by government or a public agency prior to development, as in the case of the Mexican project, eases the problems of planning on an integrated basis, and of enforcing proper zoning and building regulations. It also helps to ensure that windfall gains do not accrue solely to private land owners and provides the opportunity for the public agency to offer serviced sites to hotel developers at prices which can include if necessary an incentive element. There is a very close relationship between land prices and building densities, and by appropriate land pricing the development authority can help to ensure that acceptable physical planning and density standards are maintained.

While projects consisting of hotels alone are relatively straightforward, though they of course involve a thorough examination of market, architectural and engineering, managerial, staffing and training, financial, legal and economic aspects, tourism infrastructure or integrated resort projects have proved much more complex. Such projects normally include several kinds of infrastructure—roads, water, sewerage, electric power, telecommunications, and sometimes airports—and they also involve questions of area and urban planning and architecture, complex ecological questions and problems of land tenure, as well as most aspects of hotel projects though in some respects in less detail. The preparation of the project in the borrowing country is, therefore, often very complicated and requires the co-operation of many government agencies as well as of private investors. Difficult problems of coordination arise which can sometimes be resolved only at the highest level.

Due to the complexity of the projects, close involvement by the Bank in the project preparation stage is essential. Project feasibility studies submitted by potential borrowers thus far have sometimes lacked a realistic analysis of tourism demand. Plans for area development and accommodation facilities have tended to over-stress physical factors with insufficient regard for economic and financial viability. Some hotel projects have been poorly designed from a functional point of view. Consulting firms are still largely inexperienced in this field though gradually a body of expertise is being built up, and an improvement in the quality of consultants' work is already evident.

The Economic Evaluation of Projects

The Bank attempts to evaluate projects in the context of the tourism sector, assessing the range of the country's tourism assets and the value to the economy of the sector as a whole. In this last respect, tourism's particular value may be as an earner of foreign exchange or in some cases as a creator of employment. However, foreign exchange earnings or employment creation are not in themselves a sufficient reason for investing in tourism facilities. The economic benefits of such investments must be related to costs as in any other sector, and the Bank employs broadly the same criteria in evaluating a tourism project as in evaluating a project in, for example, agriculture, mining or manufacturing. A tourism project is considered appropriate for Bank financing when the economic rate of return is at least equal to the opportunity cost of capital in the country in which the project is located.

Revenues (benefits) are derived from all expenditures by tourists resulting from the project, and costs are the value of all the inputs needed to produce these revenues. Expenditures made outside the project area (e.g. on travel costs to the country) are normally excluded. In cases, however, where the project would have a significant and measurable impact on the utilization of capacity elsewhere in the economy (e.g. of the national airlines) these benefits should be taken into account. Conceptually, the costs and benefits properly attributable to the project may be clear, but there are often great practical difficulties in obtaining even an approximation of the relevant data.

Whether the project consists of hotels or infrastructure or a combination of these, its economic evaluation is made in terms of the investment in the project itself together with essential supporting investments in local transport, entertainment, shopping facilities, and other services for the tourist. Some of the facilities to be provided would serve and be paid for directly by the tourist, while others would be compensated for only indirectly. Accordingly, great care has to be exercised in estimating the costs and the benefits, so as to avoid any double counting. Cost and benefits may be evaluated in appropriate cases by the use of shadow prices, particularly for foreign exchange, labor and land.

Although overall a tourism project may be economically justified, appropriate shares of the benefits may not be captured by the different investing agencies. For example a new airport serving a tourism development may not be self-supporting for many years, and charges for some other basic utilities may be below economic levels. This might in some exceptional cases be justified in the broader project framework, but care must be taken to ensure that charges for public utilities are normally not subsidized for the benefit of the private investor.

Reasonably precise estimates of expenditures by tourists in hotels can be made on the basis of comparable past experience. Similarly, operating costs of hotels can be estimated on the basis of past data for comparable hotels in similar locations. Data on expenditures by tourists outside the hotels are less easily obtained. Such data can only be established by periodic sample surveys, which in many countries are not available. Even if national estimates of different categories of tourist expenditure are available, the net benefit to the economy of these expenditures is still difficult to establish. Bank practice so far has been to assess as accurately as possible the supplementary investments required and to apply the typical gross operating profit of each relevant economic activity to each category of tourist expenditure.

Besides tourist expenditures on accommodation, food and entertainment, internal transport, shopping and other services, a project will also yield net benefits to the national economy from payments for visas, insurance, port fees, landing rights, etc. made by tourists directly or indirectly in their country of origin to the country in which the project is situated. However, these benefits are generally excluded altogether from the calculation, since it is impossible to determine the share attributable to any one project rather than to another located elsewhere on the tourist's travel route. Payments of commissions of travel agents in the tourist originating country are of course also excluded.

In the case of a new resort to be developed in more or less virgin territory, provision has to be made for the permanent population which will be attracted to the area. Basic services such as roads, water, sewerage, health and education, must be provided. To the extent that economic charges are made for such services, no charge need be made against the tourism project as such. To the extent that similar services (e.g. health and education) would have to be provided elsewhere for the same population in the absence of the project, only the additional costs of providing the services in the particular resort area are conceptually properly chargeable to the project. In practice the determination of such additional costs is likely to be very difficult. The provision of greater amenities for the permanent population will produce benefits which should also be taken into account. To the extent that these benefits are reflected in the prices paid for the services, some measure of value is available, but there is likely to be a residual of services for which no direct charge may be levied. Here also, the practical difficulties of including these benefits in the cost/benefit calculation are very great.

OTHER EXTERNAL FINANCIAL AND TECHNICAL ASSISTANCE

Data on tourism financing from external sources other than the World Bank Group are rather fragmentary since most financing has been done privately, often in the form of suppliers' credits, commercial bank loans and investments from international hotel companies. Financing of tourism by regional development banks has been relatively limited thus far. The Inter-American Development Bank has reserved portions of industrial lines of credit to intermediate credit institutions in a number of countries for the financing of small and medium-sized hotel and motel projects and has made a loan to finance site development and infrastructure for a new beach area on the Caribbean coast of Mexico. It has also sponsored a number of tourism preinvestment and feasibility studies which it is financing by both loans and grants. The Asian Development Bank has financed some tourism studies but has not yet made loans directly in the sector although some of its loans for infrastructure, e.g., improvement of the airport at Kathmandu, Nepal, will be very helpful for tourism development. The African Development Bank has sponsored a useful survey of tourism in 15 countries of Western Africa. The Bank for Central American Economic Integration has begun to finance a number of tourism projects in Central America on the basis of a special line of credit from the U.S. Agency for International Development. Finally, the European Investment Bank is becoming increasingly interested in financing tourism projects in states associated with the European Economic Community. To tourism projects in associated states it provides loans on particularly easy terms.

Bilateral official assistance for tourism development has taken the form of technical assistance, sector surveys, preinvestment studies and training programs financed with grant funds, as well as loans and guarantees from official credit institutions. Belgium, France, Germany,

Italy, Netherlands, the Scandinavian countries, United Kingdom, South Africa, United States, and recently Japan, have furnished an increasing amount of such assistance. The French and German official lending institutions have been particularly active in this field. Among agencies concerned with preserving open spaces for recreation the programs carried out by the United States and Canadian National Park Services deserve special mention.

While there has been some technical assistance by the United Nations and the Organization of American States in the tourism sector over the years, the financing of specific preinvestment and feasibility studies with UNDP funds is a relatively recent development. The physical development plan for the South Adriatic region of Yugoslavia financed by UNDP was the single most important preinvestment study with strong emphasis on tourism carried out prior to the study of tourism development in Bali, Indonesia, for which the Bank was Executing Agency, and the other preinvestment studies, presently under way, to which reference has been made.

The International Labour Organisation is acting as Executing Agency in education and training programs in the tourism sector. Largely as a result of ILO's initiative, a number of comprehensive education and training programs have been started in countries such as Cyprus, Iran, Lebanon, Singapore and Tunisia, largely financed with UNDP funds.

The U.N. Educational, Scientific and Cultural Organization (Unesco) has in recent years financed a number of studies of historic monuments and sites and their potential tourism aspects, including plans for their restoration and preservation. Unesco has also given advice and financial assistance to member governments in their efforts to restore and preserve historical monuments.

The United Nations and UNCTAD Secretariats, as well as the Organisation for Economic Cooperation and Development (OECD), have produced valuable studies of worldwide tourism trends and tourism developments in individual member countries. In the area of data collection, the key role is played by the International Union of Official Travel Organizations (IUOTO), whose legal status is being changed to that of an international inter-governmental organization under the name of World Tourism Organization. Composed of 109 countries and 96 national and international organizations, its operation is based on six Regional Commissions. The Bank has been working closely with this organization, including providing some financial assistance for a study sponsored by IUOTO.

FUTURE BANK GROUP OPERATIONS

Financing Program

The Bank Group's projected financing program for the period 1972-76 contemplates total investing and lending of about $404 million for 44 tourism projects (including loans to development finance companies lending significant amounts for tourism projects).[1] This does not include the tourism element of projects in the fields of air transport, highway construction, water and sewerage and vocational training.

Sector Work

This sizable investment program will require increasing the Bank's knowledge of the tourism sector in those countries and areas in which the bulk of operations is scheduled. Major sector reviews are scheduled for Yugoslavia, Morocco, Mexico, Brazil, India, Tunisia and Turkey. Less comprehensive sector surveys will be made in many other countries, among them Kenya, Indonesia, Thailand, Malaysia, and countries in Western Africa and the Caribbean.

The following table summarizes the Bank Group's actual financing of tourism projects and that projected through FY1976. It also shows the number of major sector studies already mounted or planned.

Table 2: Summary of World Bank Group Tourism Activities by Fiscal Years, with Projections Through 1976

	Actual			Program		Actual[1]		Program
	1969	1970	1971	1972	1973	1964-68	1969-73	1972-76
Sector Studies	3	2	3	1	3	1	12	7
Commitment ($ million)	14	5	42	55	59	3	175	404
% of Total Bank Group	1.0	0.2	1.6	2.0	2.1	0.1	1.4	2.4
Number of Countries	4	2	6	6	8	1	19	22
Number of Financing Operations	4	2	7	6	8	1	27	44
Projects under Supervision (End FY)	5	7	12	18	25	1	14[2]	42[2]

[1]Including scheduled for 1972-73
[2]Average for five years

---

[1]Cf. Annex Table 5.

Directions of Bank Group Financing

While the Bank Group still has limited experience in financing tourism projects, conditions in different developing countries point to the need for flexibility in considering the types of projects it may finance. Until now, consideration has been given mainly to financing hotels or infrastructure, or a combination of the two, and the main emphasis has been on international tourism. Essential tourism infrastructure may include the restoration and better presentation of cultural attractions and such work may be included in a project provided the economic return on such investments is adequate.

In many of the developing countries there are reservations about the desirability of developing tourism on the basis of private foreign ownership of hotels. If such foreign ownership is linked with interests promoting and organizing the flow of visitors from the main market countries, it can contribute significantly to the success of a project. The Bank Group might be able to promote various forms of joint ventures whereby the developing countries would retain majority ownership of the facilities while the foreign investors would have a large enough commitment to ensure their interest in the success of the venture.

In the richer of the developing countries, domestic tourism is expanding quite rapidly. In the Yugoslav and Mexican projects domestic visitors make up part of the projected traffic flows. Domestic tourism can contribute significantly to the success of a project by supplying a demand in the off-peak seasons and securing better average occupancy rates. Provided that economic returns are satisfactory, there appears to be no *prima facie* case for the Bank to exclude from consideration projects catering to a significant extent for domestic tourists.

A further area in which the Bank Group may expand its operations is in financing related projects in two or more countries. In several tourist destination areas (e.g., Eastern Africa, Western Africa, East Asia) the attractions of one country alone may be insufficient to draw visitors from distant markets, and tourist circuits through several countries have been developed. The IFC is already participating in a project which includes hotels and lodges in both Kenya and Uganda. The development of tourist circuits may significantly expand the tourist flow to Western Africa and a regional project has already been submitted for consideration by the Bank Group. Increasing attention will be given to such proposals in the future.

The large increase in tourist flows to the developing countries has for the most part occurred in the past 10 to 15 years. The industry is still young. Traditions of visitor reception and hotel management are only now developing. Skilled personnel at all levels are in short supply. With the large prospective increases in visitor flows, the problem of providing skilled manpower in the numbers required will be serious. In these circumstances the Bank Group will need to pay greater attention to training and, where appropriate, include funds for training in its lending for tourism projects. A start in this direction was made in the case of the Yugoslav and Mexican projects.

In its lending operations in tourism the Bank Group aims, as in other sectors, to combine financing with technical assistance. Besides advice on the technical aspects of the project itself, emphasis will be given to broader questions of planning, including the organization of the industry, the structure of planning in the public sector, regional and area planning, and planning the preservation of the environment. For effective action in developing tourism, which impinges on many economic sectors and areas of responsibility, a strong organization either in government or elsewhere in the public sector is essential, and the effective coordination of all public sector agencies responsible for the implementation of a tourism development program usually requires attention at the highest level of government. Tourism cannot develop under a policy of benign neglect. In regional and area planning, also, the active support of top government is needed, for the implementation of soundly conceived regional plans with adequate zoning and building regulations may meet strong opposition from powerful private interests. Here the support of the Bank Group may be of considerable value in bringing the type of development which does not destroy the physical environment but preserves irreplaceable assets for future generations.

Investment Incentives

The successful development of tourism requires the cooperation of government and private investors. Conditions must be created to attract the private investor. The various kinds of investment incentives which many governments offer have been noted on page 383. A case can be made for incentives to hotel investors in certain circumstances. The hotel is only one, though a key part, of the total "package" bought by the tourist. Because a substantial part of tourist expenditures is made outside the hotel, the hotel investor may be unable to capture all of the benefits flowing from his investment. Hence the prospective financial returns on the hotel may be unattractive. In these circumstances, assistance to the hotel investor may be justified, but the case for incentives of wide applicability is not proven.

Each system of investment incentives has its specific advantages and disadvantages. For example, the size of the once-and-for-all demand on public sector resources made by the capital grant incentive system is one of the major disadvantages of this type of incentive for governments. The tax rebate system has been an important inducement to invest, but has been difficult to suspend. Tax holidays are normally offered for part of the life of the project only, so that the project's cash position can change unfavorably once they are terminated. Moreover, it is very difficult to estimate the costs to governments.

Subsidization of interest rates has appealed to governments as it can be easily administered. A major advantage is that the cost of an interest rate subsidy is calculable compared with a tax holiday. A disadvantage is the stimulus provided to investors to increase the proportion of debt in the project's capitalization beyond a prudent level. The major disadvantage of all types of incentives is that they may lead to over-investment and a waste of scarce capital.

If assistance to the tourism sector through investment incentives is provided, experience to date points to the desirability of limiting such assistance in time and providing it selectively. The danger exists that in some countries such selectivity may be poorly and corruptly administered. The need for special assistance may, however, be avoided or greatly reduced if capital for tourism projects, particularly hotels, can be provided on extended terms related to the economic life of the assets and with adequate grace periods. The absence of such terms has frequently caused cash squeezes which have resulted in poor service and maintenance and inadequate replacement expenditures. Because loan funds on suitable terms are frequently not available in developing countries, the contribution which financing from the Bank Group can make may be of particular value.

In evaluating tourism projects, the Bank Group will continue to pay close attention to the overall impact and justification for investment incentive systems. There are formidable conceptual and practical problems in assessing such systems and research here will be needed to provide a basis for discussion with member countries where incentive systems are in effect. It must be recognized, however, that even if a case against such incentives in a member country is established, any change in the system may be very difficult to bring about or may not be justified if investment incentives are offered in competing tourist destinations.

Research

Reference has been made to the need for research into the scope and impact of investment incentives. It is proposed that attention should be focused first on the Mediterranean area and the study would begin with a comprehensive review of the legislation and practical operation of the incentive schemes operating in Morocco, Tunisia, Spain, France, Italy, Yugoslavia and Greece. This would provide the basis for formulating guidelines for Bank Group operations in countries where important incentives for tourism investments are provided.

To provide fuller information on hotel operations in different countries, the Bank will continue to finance the work of a German research institute which collects comparative hotel operating statistics for about 479 hotels in 28 countries. This research will be expanded, the objective being to include additional hotels in the developing countries.

A third area of study will be the Caribbean. The major markets for all Caribbean destinations are the same, and the development of capacity in one destination will affect others. A study is proposed of the tourism development programs of all Caribbean destinations, including Venezuela, Colombia and Central America, in relation to the prospective market. It is hoped that this study can be carried out in cooperation with the Caribbean Development Bank.

More basic research into income and price elasticities of demand for vacation travel, into the likely trends of air transport costs, and into patterns of tourist expenditures in developing countries will be carefully considered. It is hoped that some of this work could be carried out in cooperation with selected developing countries which have already become important tourist destinations.

Comparative Data on International Tourism
in Selected Developing Countries, 1970

	Estimated Foreign Visitor Arrivals (000)	Growth of Foreign Visitor Arrivals Index 1969 (1965 = 100)	Average Length of Stay of Foreign Visitors (Nights)	Gross Foreign Tourism Receipts ($ million)	Average Daily Foreign Tourist Expend. ($)	Gross Tourism Receipts Compared to Merchandise Exports (%)
East Africa						
Ethiopia	53	—	4.0	6	28.0	4.9
Kenya	344	—	8.8	52	16.8	24.0
Tanzania	63	—	9.0	14	24.8	5.6
Uganda	80	—	9.7	19	24.0	7.7
West Africa						
Ivory Coast	42	—	4.0	5	30.0	1.5
Senegal	40	—	3.5	4	25.0	2.6
East Asia & Pacific						
China, Rep. of	472	352	4.9	89	38.8	6.2
Hong Kong	927	228	3.8	293	83.2	11.7
Philippines	144	171	7.2	32	30.5	3.0
Thailand	629	280	4.8	104	30.0	14.9
Indonesia	129	—	5.0	16	25.0	2.0
Fiji	110	275	7.0	28	29.4	27.5
Korea	173	524	4.0	19	27.0	5.6
Europe, Middle East and North Africa						
Cyprus	127	385	5.2	20	30.4	18.3
Greece	1,408	166	10.9	194	13.0	30.2
Israel	437	168	8.3	104	28.7	13.4
Lebanon	822	137	7.4	132	14.1	76.7
Malta	171	356	14.2	29	12.0	74.4
Morocco	747	197	9.0	136	15.0	27.9
Portugal	3,343	221	3.9	222	16.8	23.5
Spain	24,105	197	7.0	1,681	15.7	71.7
Tunisia	411	248	9.3	55	14.6	30.2
Turkey	484	154	7.7	51	13.7	8.8
Yugoslavia	4,748	179	4.8	275	12.2	16.4
South Asia						
Afghanistan	100	909	9.1	6	7.8	7.1
Ceylon	46	230	10.6	4	8.2	1.2
India	281	190	22.7	51	8.0	2.5
Iran	299	220	7.0	42	20.1	1.8
Nepal	46	511	4.0	2	13.0	9.1
Pakistan	122	165	8.9	10	9.3	1.4
Central America and Caribbean						
Bahamas	916	212	5.3	221	45.5	248.3
Jamaica	309	163	8.1	95	40.0	28.2
Mexico						
Tourists	2,246	187	13.6	575	21.0	41.0
Border Travel	—	—	—	879	—	—
*Colombia	143	180	7.0	30	30.0	4.9
*Venezuela	108	200	13.0	46	30.0	1.8

	Estimated Foreign Visitor Arrivals (000)	Growth of Foreign Visitor Arrivals Index 1969 (1965 = 100)	Average Length of Stay of Foreign Visitors (Nights)	Gross Foreign Tourism Receipts ($ million)	Average Daily Foreign Tourist Expend. ($)	Gross Tourism Receipts Compared to Merchandise Exports (%)
South America						
Argentina	695	233	6.8	77	16.2	4.3
*Brazil	173	168	n.a.	28	n.a.	1.2
Paraguay	119	476	4.0	14	29.0	21.9
*Uruguay	620	103	7.5	45	10.0	18.0

*1969 data.

NOTE: The above statistics are mainly from official sources, supplemented by semi-official estimates. In view of the many different definitions and methods of collection used, the above figures should be taken as indicative only, reference being made where possible to the most recent official sources available.

Sources: IUOTO, International Travel Statistics
OECD, International Tourism and Tourism Policy in OECD Member Countries
IMF, Balance of Payments Yearbook
IMF, International Financial Statistics
World Bank, Various Reports

Tourism Financing by the International Finance Corporation

Country	Project	Original Amount of IFC Commitment or Approval ($ thousand)	FY of Original Commitment or Approval	Investment held by IFC as of December 31, 1971 ($ thousand)			Comments
				Equity	Loan	Total	
Kenya	Hotel Properties	3,204	1967, 1968	561	1,550	2,111	Part-financing of 200-room hotel in capital city, some game lodges and 100-room beach hotel.
Jamaica	Pegasus, Hotels of Jamaica	2,913	1969	679	1,280	1,959	Convention hotel in capital city.
El Salvador	Hotel Miramonte	933	1969	333	600	933	224-room first class hotel in capital city.
Tunisia	Cie. Financière et Touristique	9,905	1969	1,905	6,891	8,796	Tourism development and holding company.
Colombia	Hoturismo	6	1969	6	—	6	Participation in hotel development company.
Colombia	Pro-Hoteles, S.A.	1,045	1970	238	800	1,038	225-room business and tourism hotel in provincial capital.
Mauritius	Dinarobin Inns & Motels Ltd.	600	1971	—	600	600	Financing of two beach hotels comprising 360 beds.
Panama	Corp. de Desarrollo Hotelero, S.A.	1,473	1971	267	1,206	1,473	256-room hotel in capital city.
Kenya & Uganda	Tourism Promotion Services Ltd.	2,420 } 1,180 }	1971	—	3,600	3,600	Financing of 6 hotels and lodges comprising 950 beds and 138 vehicle touring service.
Total		23,679		3,989	16,527	20,516	

**Commitments for Tourism Projects Under World Bank Loans
to Development Finance Companies**

Country	Name of Company	No. of Projects	Bank Funds Committed by DFCs as of Dec. 31, 1971 ($ thousand)
Malaysia	Malayan Industrial Development Finance Limited	1	325
Tunisia	Société Nationale d'Investissement	32	14,510
Morocco	Crédit Immobilier et Hotelier	22	8,131
Morocco	Banque Nationale de Développement Economique	22	7,871
Thailand	Industrial Finance Corporation of Thailand	1	260
India	Industrial Credit and Investment Corporation of India	1	972
		79	32,069

**Direct Bank Loans and IDA Credits
for Tourism Projects, FY1971-72**

Country	Type of Project	Date of Agreement	$ Million
Yugoslavia (Slovenia)	Integrated Resort Complex (Bernardin)	6/18/71	10.0
Yugoslavia (Croatia)	Integrated Resort Complex (Babin Kuk)	7/21/71	20.0
Mexico	Tourism Infrastructure	1/18/72	22.0
Nepal	Hotels	3/22/72	4.2
Total			56.2

**Projected Bank Group New Commitments
for Tourism[1] FY1972-76**

Direct Financing	$ Million	%
Bank/IDA	294	73
IFC	37	9
	331	82
Development Finance Company Financing	73	18
	404	100

[1] Excluding loans to industrial development banks which do only minor tourism financing.

URBANIZATION

URBANIZATION
SECTOR WORKING PAPER

INTRODUCTION AND SUMMARY

Problems of urban poverty and unemployment, of inadequacy of housing and urban infrastructure, have been recorded throughout history. What most distinguishes the current urban problems of the developing countries is their scale and intensity. The severity of the problems reflects primarily the rapidity of overall population growth and the acute shortage of resources with which to equip the additions to urban population.

The proliferation of squatter settlements and slums, and the rising backlog in urban services, have been accompanied by growing recognition that "development" implies much more than just expansion of output. Yet with few exceptions, measures so far undertaken have signally failed to reverse these trends or produce more efficient patterns of urban growth.

In recognition of the importance of these issues, the World Bank[1] recently decided to supplement its activities in individual sectors with a more direct focus on problems of urbanization. As this is a new field for the Bank, the discussion and policy proposals contained in this paper are more tentative than for fields in which the Bank has many years' experience.

The first section outlines the broad dimensions of the problem. The combination of a 5% urban population growth with historically rapid expansion in rural population appears unprecedented. About half of the additions to urban population are migrants from rural areas. However, the migrants represent only a fraction of the natural increase in rural population. Existing trends provide no expectation of an early alleviation in total or urban population growth rates.

Even if the totality of the net savings of the poorer countries were devoted to this purpose, only $500[2] to $800 per head would be available for equipping the additions to their population. Much the same

---

[1] All references to the Bank include the International Development Association (IDA) unless otherwise specified. References to the World Bank Group include the International Finance Corporation (IFC) as well as the Bank and IDA.

[2] Amounts are expressed in U.S. dollar equivalents.

level applies to the urban centers where higher savings are offset by more rapid population growth. In practice, a large slice of the savings will inevitably go to other purposes. Municipal revenues in relation to population growth are substantially lower and are largely preempted by current expenditures.

By contrast, capital costs per head for minimum conventional housing and for education, water and sewerage, typically total over $500. Capital costs for providing employment vary from perhaps $400 per worker for "traditional" to upwards of $1,500 in "modern" occupations. Many other investments, in transport and electricity for instance, are also required to provide infrastructures for the urban population growth. In the poorer countries at least, the resources available are quite evidently insufficient to equip the additions to urban population at customary standards.

The next section considers the possibilities of relieving urban pressures by measures to restrain migration from the countryside. The arguments for greater emphasis on rural development as against urban development, and on smaller towns as against major cities, are inconclusive. Cases undoubtedly exist where urban biases should be corrected. Of much greater potential importance, however, are policies to promote better use of national resources, particularly labor, by reducing factor price and other distortions. Such policies will affect the composition of investment in both town and country and may lead to either greater or less priority for urban development according to the differing conditions existing in individual countries.

Greater emphasis on development in rural areas or the smaller towns is, in any case, unlikely to cause significant reduction in the rapidity of growth in urban population or the problems of the larger cities over the next two decades. Rural development in the circumstances indicated in the text may even accentuate migration to the towns, and from the smaller towns to the larger.

The third section accordingly turns to consideration of the problems within urban areas and the associated opportunities to economize in use of resources and increase urban efficiency. Such opportunities arise from the extensive interrelations between urban sectors inadequately taken into account in decision making, from customary standards of urban services not appropriate to prevailing conditions and, closely connected, from inappropriate pricing and taxation policies. Nowhere are these factors more evident than in the trilogy of urban transport, land use and housing which together play a leading role in shaping urban growth.

The population and area of many of the cities will triple within 20 years, necessitating heavy investment in roads, other transport infrastructure and equipment for the mass transit of the majority of the population who cannot afford automobiles. Private automobile use is rising rapidly. The resultant congestion greatly complicates provision of mass transit. A strong case exists for bringing automobile user charges more into line with the high marginal costs of providing for additional vehicles in congested urban areas, and for other steps to limit their growth in numbers.

No less important are the possibilities provided by future extensions to the urban areas which in much less than 20 years will be larger than the existing areas. These urban extensions offer opportunities for promoting more economical urban patterns than would be achieved by continued laissez-faire growth. While transport facilities play a large part in determining urban growth patterns, transport requirements can be greatly reduced by appropriate siting of employment and residence. Strong interrelations also exist between different transport modes, necessitating their consideration in the context of the urban transport system as a whole.

The shortcomings of existing land use regulations, and methods of public acquisition of land present a serious obstacle to more rational urban development. Shortage of resources for extending urban service networks restricts the availability of "urbanized land" and adds to the already strong forces of population growth and increased income in pushing up land values. The heavy costs of acquiring land in turn impinge on municipal financial resources. Public acquisition of land and other measures can greatly facilitate a more integrated urban development. Reform of urban land taxation can play a crucial role in strengthening municipal finances.

Housing needs are being met to a large degree, though inadequately, by the rapid growth of squatter settlements which in many cities already accommodate over a third of the population. At present income levels, it is impossible for most urban inhabitants to afford even minimum standards of conventional permanent housing. Given the limited resources available, there is no prospect of adequate provision of subsidized housing for the new additions to population, at least in the poorer developing countries. In these circumstances, more emphasis on "site and services" type schemes providing urbanized land for self-help housing is indicated. Indeed, for most developing countries, the harnessing of the self-help and savings potential provides the only realistic possibility for substantial alleviation of nousing conditions.

"Trade-offs" between levels of urban services and corresponding costs have not yet been adequately analyzed in relation to resource availability. Possibilities of significant economies may well exist. A

10% reduction in capital costs of electric power generation and distribution, if attainable, would provide a saving of over $1 billion a year by the 1980s. A choice may often exist between services at conventional standards for a limited proportion of the population or for a larger proportion at somewhat lower levels but lower unit costs.

Early attainment of comprehensive, and at the same time effectively policy-oriented, urban plans and models, is precluded by the unsatisfactory state of methodology and the rapidity of change, not only in population but also in social patterns and economic functions. In these conditions, pricing policies and taxation incidence acquire a critical importance in harnessing market forces to produce more rational patterns of urban growth. Better charging of marginal costs of peak loads and of social costs of private investment could result in substantial economies. The multiplicity of local governments and autonomous agencies greatly complicates the problem. In assessing advantages of greater centralization and the closer relation of planning with budgeting and political decision making, the importance of promoting local initiative and self-help should not be neglected.

It would be unrealistic to expect the degree of coordination, and of planning and executing capacity, needed to take into account fully all the complex urban interlinkages. Rather a sub-optimization approach seems indicated based on rough alternative patterns of urban growth, and initially taking into account only major interlinkages. The framework for evaluation of projects on such an approach will vary according to the type of project. Calculation of economic costs/benefits should be supported by an assessment of other aspects such as impact on income distribution and employment. A similar step-by-step approach is indicated towards institution building. It is difficult to perceive a better practical alternative to the present ad hoc decision making.

The final section considers the role of the World Bank. Although the Bank has only recently undertaken explicit consideration of problems of urbanization, it is already involved as a result of the high proportion of its lending that is related to urban areas. In extending its activities in the urban field, several types of problems have become evident, ranging from institutional difficulties where several agencies, often relatively weak, are involved, to development of new methodologies and pricing policies. Such difficulties make preparation of projects specifically directed to the underlying problems of urbanization particularly time-consuming and arduous. Experience in this field both in the Bank and elsewhere is scarce.

In view of the large number of developing countries which are members of the Bank and the far greater number of their urban centers, a policy of selective concentration both as regards countries and types of urban project is indicated. Advantages will stem from both continuity and complementarity between projects. Some new types of urban projects addressed to particular urban problems, such as provision of site and services to low-income groups, should be undertaken in a wider range of urban centers.

A program is outlined of urban projects for FY1972-76[1] and of other activities to complement the more traditional work of the Bank in such fields as public utilities. The program encompassing some 40 projects and a roughly estimated $700 million of lending, is necessarily more tentative than in fields where the Bank has longer experience and extended connections with borrowing agencies. To increase the impact of the program, collaboration will be sought with other agencies with experience in the field.

The Bank's system of economic missions, economic reports and country programs will be progressively extended to help national authorities provide a focus for consideration of urbanization problems. Technical assistance on programming and institution building is foreseen in connection with the urban projects. Improvement of urban management is particularly important.

A number of projects for mass transit are included in the program with particular emphasis on bus systems. Interlinkages both between modes of transport and with the pattern of urban growth will be an important aspect of evaluation, including policies towards restraint of private automobile use. Similar considerations apply to the urban road projects. Wholesale market projects, which can make a large contribution to urban efficiency, are also included in the project program.

It is recognized that the Bank's contribution in terms of resources to solution of the housing problems of urban centers can only be small. The several projects in this field included in the program are designed accordingly for maximum demonstration impact and institution building. For several reasons, direct lending for house construction appears of lower priority than for site and services type projects which can mobilize self-help, reach the poorer levels of population and stimulate savings and employment. The project program is therefore concentrated on this type of scheme. Other projects in this field include improvement of low-income settlements and integrated urban extension areas that can both produce economies within the areas selected and promote more economical patterns of urban growth.

---

[1]The Bank Group's fiscal year (FY) ends June 30.

While direct lending for house construction is not contemplated at this time, the Bank Group is prepared to consider lending for seed capital to develop housing finance institutions. The emphasis here is on the leverage effect in promoting savings and developing capital markets in a form which will lead to amelioration of the overall housing and employment situation. Particular attention will be paid to the income groups for which housing is proposed, the mobilization of small savings and the possibilities for supporting improvements to substandard housing.

More generally, throughout the field of projects in urban areas, the consideration already being given to ensuring project designs appropriate to the local resource availabilities will be further extended. In this connection, the research program, which will be undertaken in collaboration with other agencies, will contain some specific studies of relations between costs and levels of services. Municipal finance, and urban transport interdependencies, will also be prominent in the research program.

It should be recognized that this is a preliminary stage of the Bank's efforts to relate its work more closely to the problems of urbanization, unemployment, poverty and congestion. The changes may appear cautious in comparison to the mounting urban crisis. But from the review of activities in the field of urbanization has come an acute awareness of the paucity of knowledge and methodology on how best to cope with the problems. A policy of learning while doing and readiness to adapt policies with experience is therefore strongly indicated.

DIMENSIONS OF THE URBANIZATION PROBLEM

The Growth of Urban Centers

To assess the implications of the rapid growth in urban centers in developing countries, it is necessary to distinguish between the rise in the proportion of urban to total population and the growth in absolute numbers of urban population. The rise in the urban proportion does not appear exceptional. The urban proportion in the industrialized countries rose at much the same rate during the initial periods of their technological revolution and when their urban proportion was similar.[1] As the following table and the chart in Annex 1 indicate, a

[1]Kingsley Davis estimates the rate of growth in the urban proportion for 171 developing countries between 1950 and 1960 at 2.29% per annum. For 18 developed countries during their decades of fastest urban growth, the average was 3.09% per annum, but the rate was somewhat lower during initial periods of accelerated growth from the new technologies.

strong correlation exists between degree of urbanization and level of income per capita.

Table 1: Urban Population in Developing Member Nations of the World Bank

	by GNP Per Capita (1970)					
GNP Per Capita	Under $100	$100 to $199	$200 to $349	$350 to $574	$575 to $1,000	Over $1,000
Percent of Total Population in Urban Areas	9.5	17.7	39.5	45.3	53.6	69.0
Percent of Population in Communities of More Than 100,000	4.6	10.1	19.2	22.2	27.2	31.7

What *is* exceptional is the rate of increase in absolute numbers of urban population and, even more, the accompanying growth in rural population. The underlying cause is obvious—much higher natural rates of total population growth than ever reached by today's developed countries. The urban population is currently growing about 5%[1] a year, or doubling in about 15 years, a rate only occasionally reached by the developed countries for short periods at a much later stage of economic development.

For such growth in urban population to occur accompanied by a rapid increase in rural population appears unprecedented. Rural population grew by over one-third between 1950 and 1970. Compared with the first half of the century, the growth rate accelerated faster than did that of the urban population. At comparable periods in the developed countries, rural population, with few exceptions, showed very slow growth or absolute decline.

As much as half of the urban population expansion is accounted for simply by natural increase—rather more than half in South and Southeast Asia and probably somewhat less in Africa. Not only are birth rates considerably higher than in, say Europe in the early nineteenth century, but life expectancy is now much longer.[2]

---

[1]1950-60 estimate for urban agglomerations of over 20,000 inhabitants, "Growth of the World's Urban and Rural Population, 1920-2000," United Nations, 1969, Table 11. Unless otherwise indicated, "urban" data in this paper follow the UN definition of "over 20,000 inhabitants."

[2]Despite the squalid conditions of the city slums and generally far greater poverty, medical progress has ensured a much lower death rate particularly during infancy than in the cities of Europe at comparable periods. Even for countries with income per capita below $200 per annum, expectation of life at birth in cities of over 100,000 habitants is now on average appreciably higher than in London as late as the mid-nineteenth century.

413

No early alleviation of this component of urban expansion can be foreseen. As incomes rise, large families are more likely to become an economic liability to their parents than in rural areas. Together with the expansion of birth control programs, this influence can be expected to reduce urban fertility. But such trends are slow to develop. In the short term, their effect may well be offset by other influences, including further declines in mortality rates.

Migration from rural areas accounts for the other half of urban population expansion.[1] The many studies on the causes of this migration have shown so many "push-pull" aspects and such variety in its composition, not only between countries but also between regions of the same country and over time, as to make generalizations hazardous. Differences in social norms, including the degree of "emancipation" which the towns offer, in existing links with urban families, in prevailing conditions in the towns and the countryside, particularly the dynamism of urban economic growth and the availability of additional agricultural land, all influence the flow.

That greater opportunities are seen in the towns primarily in terms of income seems clear enough. There is considerable evidence that the migrants, or at least those who stay, are generally successful in this respect, even though there may be a period of waiting during which support is received from friends and relatives. Unemployment among migrants of a few years' residence is generally noticeably lower than urban averages.

The attraction of amenities as such seems of less immediate significance. Use of amenities generally requires payments and is therefore conditional on earning a sufficient income. Conversely, attempts to restrain migration by deliberate policies of restricting the growth of urban services appear to have been unsuccessful. Migrants generally seem to regard living conditions even in squatter settlements as no worse than those they have left. And certainly the life-style is generally considered more attractive. Surprising to the town dweller the neon lights and billboards may also appear more beautiful to the migrants than the countryside.

As a very tentative generalization, the migratory movement has slowed significantly only when the absorptive capacity of the towns in terms of economic growth remains stagnant and urban unemployment is persistently high. There are, however, isolated cases such as Taiwan where prolonged and successful rural development of a

---

[1]This broad discussion abstracts from consideration of urban population growth recorded as a result of villages growing to exceed the lower urban limit of 20,000 habitants. This statistical factor accounts for around 10% of the apparent urban population growth.

labor-intensive nature has been accompanied by significantly lower than average migration.

The marginal nature of rural to town migration deserves emphasis. Important as the migration is in relation to existing urban population, it is nevertheless equivalent to only a fraction even of the *increase* in rural population. If the population of the rural areas is six times the population of the urban areas (as in the most populous of the developing countries), and the rate of natural increase the same as in the towns, then migration equivalent to only one-sixth of the additions to rural population will double the urban population growth rate.[1]

These considerations throw some light on the variations in urban growth rates between countries and regions of the developing world. Urban population growth is most rapid where total population growth is particularly high as in South America, or where, as in Africa, a somewhat more modest population growth is accompanied by a particularly high proportion of rural to total population. The unexpectedly slow rate of urbanization in India in the 1960s appears to be associated with very slow economic growth and very heavy unemployment in some of the major towns, such as Calcutta. Additional information on urban growth in individual countries is given in Table 3 of Annex 1.

Projections of future urbanization levels depend on the assumptions made as to changes in population and urbanization trends as the process of development continues, and as to the speed of the rise in income levels. The estimates given below are from United Nations sources. Comparisons with other estimates do not indicate important divergencies over the next two decades due to the strong influence of the existing age structure and the limited potential for changes in birth rates over this period. Even for the year 2000, the differences can be considered marginal in relation to the size of the problem— similar levels of urban population would be reached a few years earlier or later. Thereafter divergencies become much more marked.

The projected increase in the urban population of the developing countries in the 40 years from 1960 to 2000 is over one billion, more than four times the increase in the previous 40 years and about three times the total urban population of the developed world in 1960. If this appears scarcely plausible, the projected increase in rural population appears equally so. The one and a half billion increase foreseen is three times that of the previous 40 years and almost as large as the

---

[1] In countries such as most of those in Africa with still lower proportionate urban population, even a relatively small migration of rural population can thus have a dramatic effect on the rate of growth of urban population. In the more highly urbanized Latin American countries, migration of a similar proportion of the rural population will have much less impact.

Table 2: Urban/Rural Population of Developing Countries

	1920	1940	1960	1980	2000
Urban (above 20,000) Population (Millions)	69 (6%)	128 (9%)	310 (15%)	693 (22%)	1,436 (31%)
Rural and Small Town Population (Millions)	1,118 (94%)	1,346 (91%)	1,705 (85%)	2,431 (78%)	3,235 (69%)
Annual rate of increase —in urban population	3.1%	4.5%	4.1%	3.7%	
—in rural population	0.9%	1.2%	1.8%	1.4%	

Source: Table 32 in "Growth of the World's Urban and Rural Population, 1920-2000." UN 1969. Estimates are an average of four alternative series based on existing trends and weighted for each region according to the assumptions judged most relevant.

total rural population in 1960. An increase of at least 50% in the ratio of rural population to agricultural land may be implied for many countries. Yet there is no indication that total population will increase less than assumed so as to be able to reduce either rural or urban estimate without increasing the other.[1]

Perhaps the most striking feature of the urbanization process in the developing countries has been the rapidity of growth of large cities. Many are more than doubling in population and perhaps tripling in area within a decade. This phenomenon is not confined to any region. Abidjan grew from 69,000 in 1950 to well over 500,000 today; Lagos from under 250,000 to 1,500,000; Bangkok from less than 1,000,000 to 3,000,000; and Bogota from 650,000 to over 2,500,000.

No close relationship has been established between city-size distribution and either relative economic development or degree of urbanization. It is perhaps hardly surprising that the developing countries show considerable variation in the growth pattern of different urban types and sizes. They contain many of the world's most ancient cities and urban cultures as well as youngest. In some countries such as India intermediate size cities appear to be growing faster than others. In other countries, both the smallest and largest urban centers are growing appreciably faster than those in the middle of the

[1]Such evidence as exists suggests that both total and urban population in 1970 were somewhat higher than the projections. For the developing world as a whole, the *increase* in urban population between 1960 and 1980 may equal the *total* urban population of the developed world in 1960. It may be noted that the projected rural population of the developing countries would still approximate about 70% at the end of the century and the 30% urban population would correlate with a national income per capita average of only a little over $200.

range. In others the smaller are growing the fastest. In some, seaports are declining in relative importance, in others growing.

Dominance of one primate city is, however, much more evident than in the developed countries, the capital city often being several times the size of the next largest. Such primacy, with significant exceptions, tends to be associated with such factors as low income, small densely populated countries, high population growth, relatively strong agricultural exports and colonial history. Not surprisingly, in view of transport and communications constraints, very big countries such as India have several large centers; but physical features, such as the separated valleys of Colombia, may also lead to several large cities in smaller countries.

Notwithstanding these differences, there is considerable evidence that after a certain stage of development a tendency exists towards a less top-heavy distribution of urban size. The largest cities continue to grow, but less fast than intermediate ones. The slowly downward trend in the growth rate for total urban population, indicated in Table 2, also leads to some expectation of a gradual decline in growth rates of the large cities. Such a trend seems likely, however, to be a compound of slower growth rates for large urban centers of the richer developing countries as urbanization approaches or passes the 50% mark, and still rising growth rates of big cities in countries at early stages of development, particularly those where total population growth rates have not yet peaked.

It is not, however, necessary for the purposes of this paper to attempt sophisticated projections of large city growth.[1] Foreseeable difference in growth rates among urban categories would generally not bring about major changes in the urban patterns of individual countries over the next one or two decades. This is particularly true of primate cities. Even significantly higher rates of growth in smaller towns would have little effect in the medium term on the size of the primate city because of the low level from which the secondary cities start.[2] Changes in relative rates of growth can be very important in the

---

[1] To illustrate magnitudes, if (in rough conformity with past observations) one-half of the projected urban population increase accrues to big cities, the developing countries are likely to have well over 300 million people in cities of over 500,000 by 1980 compared with 130 million in 1960.

[2] In Thailand, for example, if Bangkok's growth is reduced by the equivalent of an extra 2% on the growth rate of the nine next largest cities, the effect will be only to reduce Bangkok's population in 1990 from 7.6 million to 7.1 million (the present population is 3.4 million)—and the difference would be made up by 1993. If the nine cities achieve 3% additional growth, the difference for Bangkok in 1990 would be about one million or some five years further growth.

417

long run and hence for policy decisions now. But for most developing countries they are likely to have only marginal significance in the context of the overall urban problems of the next two decades.

Urban Employment, Income Distribution and Living Conditions

The malaise of urban centers in the developing countries is only too evident in the squalor of the rapidly growing slums and unauthorized settlements, the deterioration in many public services, the extreme shortage of housing, and the congestion in the streets. Less immediately evident, but certainly no less important, are the growth of unemployment and the worsening of income distribution.

Data on urban employment are sadly inadequate partly because the wage-paid element of the labor force is generally very low and the conceptual difficulties in defining "unemployment" and measuring "income" for the remainder are considerable. Scattered evidence suggests that unemployment in urban areas, as variously defined, is much more often above 10% than below, and is over 20% in some countries and, more frequently, for the 15 to 24 age group. There are again, however, a few significant exceptions both among countries with a strong record of rural development, such as Taiwan, and among those with particularly high urban and industrial growth, for example, Korea. For large cities, the position appears worse than for the smaller urban centers. In some major African cities estimated unemployment exceeds 30%.

The urban unemployment situation appears generally to have worsened over the last two decades, though it is by no means clear whether unemployment plus underemployment is worse than in the countryside.[1] The limitations of modern industry as a means of absorbing the available manpower have become increasingly evident. The growth rate in industrial employment tends to be only about half that in industrial output. Nor does this take into account the repercussions that expansion of modern industrial output may have in reducing employment in small-scale handicrafts—though this may in some cases be more than offset by employment directly created in associated service industries.

Estimates by the International Labour Office (ILO) indicate that even after allowing for a decline in participation rates, the total labor force

---

[1] It is to be noted that the data usually underestimate the seriousness of the problem, particularly the degree of underemployment and involuntary withdrawal from the labor force as a result of poor employment possibilities, of activities in brief well below the economic potential.

of developing countries will expand by at least 25% between 1970 and 1980.[1] Such a rate is unprecedented even in countries which had large-scale immigration, such as the United States. This surge in the labor force derives from the lagged effect of the earlier surge in life expectancy at birth. With few exceptions a continuance of this trend in labor force at least until the middle 1980s is implied by the pattern of birth and mortality rates over the last two decades.

Growth in urban labor force is likely to be particularly rapid. The natural increase will be high as a result of past immigration which has tended to raise the average age in the countryside and lower it in the towns.[2] Moreover, in many developing countries, and in large regions within others, the availability of suitable land for agriculture is already very restricted and the median size of farms small. In such cases, any acceleration in the growth of rural labor force can be expected sharply to increase pressures to migrate, further intensifying urban employment problems.[3]

The wide divergence between urban employment patterns in developing countries and those in developed countries deserves emphasis. "Dualism" in the countryside between modern and traditional agriculture is paralleled in the cities by a dualism between the small modern wage-paid sector and the much larger traditional or "bazaar" sector. A large part of this latter group is covered in conventional terminology under the "service sector"; yet its functions are much wider than the nomenclature indicates. A multitude of small enterprises generally exists in shantytowns as in older areas of the cities. Casual labor and petty trading are highly important not only as a source of employment but also for the economic functioning of the cities and the economizing of scarce resources, in re-use of products as well as in reduced needs for equipment and buildings. Though productivity is low compared to the modern sector, it is far superior to unemployment and in all probability exceeds productivity in marginal employment in agriculture.

Unfortunately, concentration of attention on industry has resulted in little analysis of the much larger "service" sector of urban employment. Little is known of its composition and functioning or its linkages with the modern sector. Yet there is no evidence that it will

[1] As workers in urban centers enter the labor force later and retire earlier than in agriculture, the urbanization trend of itself tends to reduce participation in the labor force.

[2] Where migration has been predominantly of unaccompanied male workers, the impact on future labor force may not occur.

[3] Where, as in many African countries, additional cultivable land is relatively abundant and a large part of rural migration is to colonize new areas, the increased rural labor force may have less urban impact.

decline in importance in the near to medium future. Even looking further into the future, employment in manufacturing seems most unlikely ever to attain the levels of 40% or more of the total reached in the developed countries. The reason is simply that advances in technology are progressively reducing the proportion of labor in the manufacturing process. Machines are more efficient than they were and power is more readily available.

The functions of the city and composition of employment are thus likely to remain very different from the present or earlier situation in developed countries. There is no inevitable technical connection between industrialization and urbanization. Solutions based on historic Western typology are most unlikely to be appropriate for the urban employment problems of the developing countries. In the developing countries, the service industry predominates over manufacturing industry in the majority of urban centers and is likely to continue to do so.

Closely associated with the employment problem is that of income distribution. It is widely recognized that a large gap exists between incomes in the towns and those in the countryside. Average Gross Domestic Product (GDP) in the major urban centers of the developing countries may be three to five times that of rural areas, with a somewhat lower differential for the smaller towns. Even allowing for higher prices in the towns, the gap is wide and, on somewhat scant evidence, appears to be widening. A similar situation of polarization of incomes has developed within the urban centers with a small and increasingly wealthy group separated socially and often physically from the poorer mass of the population.

In large part, this situation reflects the impact of the technological revolution, an impact much sharper than it was in today's developed countries. The differences between productivity in the modern and the traditional sector are much greater than they used to be—for production of non-agricultural goods, for agriculture, and for services. Not until modern technologies have spread much more widely in both town and countryside will the underlying causes abate. While the choice of technology alternatives will play a large part in the speed of diffusion of impact, the time required must be measured in decades for most developing countries.

Present trends and the pressures of population and labor force thus indicate a further worsening of income distribution over the near future at least. Sharp gains in the small modern sectors of both urban and rural areas will be paralleled by more rapidly rising numbers in the more traditional sectors. Not only are considerations of equity and social unrest involved. A more even income distribution would also create the basis for mass markets for manufactured goods of lower import content and provide a stimulus to growth and urban employment.

With a few notable exceptions, the high natural growth of urban population, the inflow of poor rural migrants, and the increasing unemployment and imbalance in income distribution, have been reflected in a deterioration in urban living conditions. The shortcomings of present living conditions are, it is true, generally less for the migrants than those they have left in rural areas. Parallels can, moreover, readily be found in many industrial cities of the nineteenth century, in the inadequacy of sewerage for instance. What is most disturbing is rather the scale of the problem and the prospect of urban populations increasingly outdistancing the urban services and housing available.

Many big cities are experiencing shantytown population growth in excess of 20% a year and a doubling of slum and shantytown population within the next four to six years is now in prospect. The shantytown population already accounts for a third or more of the total population in many cities. Such settlements are therefore very quickly becoming, if they have not already become, the major part of the city in terms of living conditions and urban pattern. Though varying widely in type, social structure and the degree of poverty, they are in large part characterized by absence of even minimal standards of housing, water supply, sewerage, streets, and social facilities.

Housing conditions are generally poor in the extreme. The case of Calcutta where more than two-thirds of families are reported as living in one room is only slightly more drastic than for many other cities of Asia, Africa and Latin America. Housing construction is typically running at a quarter or less of estimated minimum requirements.[1] The World Health Organization (WHO) estimates that only a quarter of the urban populations currently receive public water supply in house or courtyard and only a further quarter is supplied from public standpipes.[2] The situation for sewerage is certainly worse with the backlog of requirements rapidly growing.

The position with regard to other public services is more varied. A distinction is necessary between the proportion of population served and level of service provided. On both counts, electricity supply probably has the highest rating. Even in squatter areas without water and sewerage, some system of electricity supply is usually obtained. Though often illicit, make-shift, and far below prescribed

---

[1] UN Document A/8037—21 August 1970.
[2] WHO Document A23/P&B/5, 10 April 1970.

standards, the systems function. Public transport presents a more mixed picture with marked variations in adequacy of service and probably, overall, an appreciably deteriorating trend. Although school enrollment continues to increase, average education standards in many urban areas may now be declining, judged by the proportion of children of relevant age reaching various grade levels. Facilities for health have greatly improved in the treatment of illness and, for many illnesses, in prevention.

Traffic congestion has greatly increased in the last decade and is itself a major factor in the deteriorating level of public transport services. In many cities, congestion is also seriously affecting the transport of goods. The rapidity of the increase in private car ownership presages an intensification of the trend in the future.

Resources for Urban Development

The acuteness of the shortage of resources in relation to urban growth has probably not yet been fully grasped. On the one hand lie the basic limitations of total resources available for development, on the other the heavy costs of providing urban services, particularly long-life infrastructure to support the rapid increase in urban population. For countries with low income levels and high population growth, the squeeze between these constraints has become intense.

A level of net savings of 10 to 15%, fairly typical of the developing countries, implies net savings per head below $25 a year for the majority of them, and below $15 for many. Even if the *totality* of these savings could be mobilized for the benefit of the additional population, the amount per head of the additional population, assuming a 3% annual growth rate, would average from $500 to not much more than $800. By contrast, net national savings per head of population growth in the richer countries of Latin America may exceed $4,000. Obviously, the problems for such countries though serious enough are of a quite different order.

Such illustrative figures may appear unduly pessimistic in the context of urbanization problems since urban incomes and savings are well above the national average. However, though savings in the major towns are typically two or three times the national average, so also is their rate of population increase. Net savings in the towns per head of urban population increase are accordingly likely to be of the same order of magnitude as the national average. Relative rates of population growth between town and country in other words tend roughly to parallel relative levels of saving.

Comparative information on costs of urban infrastructure is scarce. Available data indicate incremental costs of water supply averaging around $100 per head and sewerage about the same. There are considerable variations, but these appear to depend much more on physical conditions than income level. Conventional "low income" housing costs range from a minimum rarely below $1,000 per family unit for the house construction alone to double this figure or more; $200 per head is perhaps a typical minimum. Primary school capital costs for projects with which the Bank has been associated range around $450 per student place, or $90 per head assuming one-fifth of the population in this age bracket. Capital costs for employment vary widely from perhaps around $400 per worker in the more traditional urban sectors to over $1,500 in the modern sector and several times this amount in the more capital intensive advanced technology occupations. With a labor force of one in four of the population, which may be low for many of the towns on which migration is concentrated, this would give a range of $100 to upwards of $400 per head for employment facilities. Large investments are also needed for transport infrastructure and equipment, health services, electricity, police and fire protection, garbage collection and other urban services.

It is thus evident that the total capital requirement for services at existing standards greatly exceeds resource availability for the poorer developing countries, even were the totality of net savings to be devoted to providing such infrastructure for the additional population. In practice, of course, the resources effectively available to equip the additional population with basic economic and social infrastructure are, even after making allowance for foreign aid, much more limited. Strong pressures for higher living standards by many groups, particularly those which the modernization process favors, and improved replacements for existing equipment and structures, make heavy calls on the nation's savings. Taxation measures sufficient significantly to offset such pressures have yet to be devised. In most developing countries income redistribution by taxation is quite limited.

The municipalities, in particular, find themselves increasingly short of revenue to meet both capital and current expenditures required to maintain even existing levels of service, let alone to reduce the backlog. Municipal revenues for all purposes amounted to no more than $84 million in Bombay in 1970, or roughly $330 per head of the increase in population. Even in the much richer Caracas, municipal revenues of $120 million, amount to little more than $1,000 per head of the population increase. In practice, a major part of these revenues is committed to the continuation of existing services to the present population.

The information available is inadequate to make any generalization on the extent to which the municipalities receive financial subsidies from, or provide subsidies to, the rest of the country. While transfers are customarily made from the national budget to municipalities for various services, what is not clear is how far these offset, or more than offset, the national taxes raised on the urban economy.[1] What does seem clear is that the taxation base of the municipalities is generally less responsive to growth in income than that of the nation, implying a greater relative stringency at the municipal level as economic growth and urbanization continue.

Several conclusions follow from these considerations. The first is the obvious importance of concentrating on ways of economizing in resource use, including maximizing use of existing urban service capacities. Closely related is the question of standards. If only a fraction of the urban population can be supplied with basic infrastructure at conventional standards, the choice has to be faced of leaving the rest without basic services or of designing lower, less costly levels of service for a larger part of the population.

It is difficult, however, to avoid the conclusion that even with strenuous efforts to economize in use of resources, to modify design standards, and to improve municipal finance, some continuing deterioration in average living and working equipment for city population in the poorer developing countries may be in prospect until incomes rise appreciably above present levels and population growth slows. The importance of sufficient information to enable the choice of priorities to be made against a clear understanding of the practical alternatives for the urban population as a whole is correspondingly increased.

In these conditions, it is also obvious that considerable emphasis should be placed on "self-help" projects. The personal initiative and work stimulated by such schemes adds both to output and savings in a sector where resource limitations are so evidently crucial.

A further deduction is that much more attention should be paid to shorter life structures with provision for future amelioration. In large measure, urbanization problems derive from the long-life nature of housing and other infrastructure of high initial cost. Whereas a 3% population growth will increase food consumption by roughly 3% compared with a stable population, it will increase house construction needs by roughly four times if housing has an average life of a hundred years (i.e. 1% requiring replacement with a stable population). With continued growth in income, the resources per head

---

[1] Some Indian studies purport to show a considerable net subsidy from the major towns to the rest of the state in which they are located.

available to future generations for such purposes will be greater than at present, the more so as population growth is curbed. The relative social costs of providing now rather than later for future generations are correspondingly high.

Finally, the wide variations in income levels among the developing countries involving very considerable, almost quantum, differences in relative resource availabilities, have important policy implications. The proportionate difference between say Pakistan and Chile is much greater than between Chile and the United Kingdom. Costs of providing comparable urban services do not vary to anything like the same degree. Indeed construction costs may at times be higher in the lower income country. The appropriate mix of urban investment and level of services supplied are, for both reasons, likely to vary widely according to the income level of the country.

THE NATIONAL/REGIONAL SETTING

It is clear that urbanization problems have reached a magnitude and importance necessitating explicit consideration in overall national development policies. It is no less clear that considerations of social policy, equity and regional balance—in large part involving value judgments—as well as more narrowly defined economic considerations, must play a considerable role in determination of national urbanization policies.

One school of thought holds that much greater emphasis should be placed on creating jobs and improving amenities in the countryside. Urban pressures would thereby be lessened through a reduction in migration. Income disparities between town and country and between different regions would also be narrowed, and help provided to the rural poor, who have as yet received little or no benefit from economic development. And if, unfortunately, it has to be accepted that large-scale unemployment is inevitable for at least several years to come, "Planners should ask themselves: Where is it more convenient for the unemployed to be, in the country or in the city? In the country, of course."[1] Both infrastructure and welfare requirements will be less in rural areas than in the cities not only because costs may be lower, but also because lower standards are accepted. The foreign exchange element of the infrastructure and of the spending from rural incomes will also be lower.

---

[1] Professor Edmundo Flores, "Economic Growth and Urbanization," Rehovot Conference paper, 1971.

Those who hold this view contend that the existing urbanization trend, particularly to big cities, is biased by a number of influences. Costs of relocation of migrants are not sufficiently taken into account in considering urban employment, nor in assessing the benefits of labor-saving investments in agriculture. Failure to charge industrialists with the full social costs of their operations, including pollution and congestion, biases location and investment towards the big city. Above all, the concentration of political power produces a very favored position for big cities in the allocation of investment resources. Such influences operate through the allocation of development funds and favored treatment for various types of permits. Perhaps more importantly, policies such as those towards exchange and interest rates swing the terms of trade between town and country in favor of the former.

On this view, in short, attention and investment have been unduly concentrated on urban areas and on accompanying capital intensive projects which, while they may provide the greatest returns on outlay, do not maximize the use of the nation's total resources. Or more extremely, the urban population is increasingly a parasitic growth, its privileged position based on exploitation of the rural surplus. What is generally implied is that a given total of local resources and foreign exchange can, with appropriate policies, achieve more in the countryside than in the cities in creating employment, raising living standards, and also possibly in output. By reducing migration, cities will be relieved of a corresponding burden of expenditure.

The opposing view sees the solution of rural poverty in accelerated migration to the towns. Urbanization is expected to continue to offer the most important opportunities for increasing employment, output and savings, and thus also the possibilities for increased future investment in both town and country on any but a short view. Concentration of activities in towns provides the basis for specialization, and for increased productivity in manufacturing and supporting services. Large, flexible labor markets with diversified skills are needed to match changing patterns of production. Cities provide concentrated markets for the output and are the link with the outside world through which technological know-how flows. The concentration of population also permits standards of education and health not possible in the countryside if only on account of distances. The informal spread of knowledge of modern methods can be as important as the more formal training possibilities.

Urbanization is considered a necessary condition for increasing productivity in rural areas by providing markets for agricultural products and, most importantly, stimulating specialization of agriculture

426

between regions. Urban activities provide agricultural inputs and incentive goods, and indirectly promote use of modern techniques. Only by rapid migration can the population of rural areas be brought into balance with rural resources and productivity, incomes raised, and the poverty of the lowest income rural groups, the landless and marginal farmers, reduced. The dualism between "modern" and "traditional" sectors existing in the countryside will inevitably increase as commercialized agriculture and new techniques spread until the countryside as a whole enters the modern sector. This situation is a long way away and will be retarded by anti-migration policies.

That migration of rural labor to higher incomes in the towns may increase disparities between regional average income levels is not denied. But the relevance of such statistical measures of income balance is questioned if the persons who move are better off while those left in the rural areas are at least marginally better off. Reduced densities as a result of migration should, in most circumstances, result in higher average productivity per man in the rural areas since there will be less fragmentation and fewer inhabitants in the less productive areas. The national, as opposed to regional, income distribution should be improved.[1] Higher incomes of the remaining rural population will, moreover, provide additional markets for urban products.

On this view, in brief, the real problem is rural overpopulation not urban overpopulation. The question which should be posed is accordingly not how many should be in towns, but how few are needed in agriculture. As for the basic problem of harmful population growth, the greater the urbanization, the sooner a declining rate can be expected.

The relative concentration of national investment on the towns is therefore not considered surprising. The towns provide probably about half of total GNP from a fifth of the population, and higher levels of infrastructure investment are appropriate in the context of more rapidly growing populations, now and in the future, which relieve rural areas of a burden. By contrast, agriculture provides considerably less than half of GNP in most developing countries and will continue to grow more slowly and with lower productivity than other sectors. The urban development protagonists accordingly feel that

---

[1]For greater inequality on a national basis to be produced by migration, it would be necessary (i) for rural production to increase more than proportionately with increases in population and (ii) the returns to population growth to be lower in urban than in rural areas. Such a combination appears generally remote. Income distribution *within* regions may also be improved by migration providing an outlet for the rural unemployed and underemployed.

within limits of ensuring adequate national food supply, agriculture deserves lower priority. Attempts to reverse or delay the process of urbanization will only lead to dissipation of the very scarce resources.

This dilemma between rural and urban priorities has led to increasing attention to the possibility of accelerating the development of small- and medium-size towns or creating new urban growth centers. At least *prima facie,* such an approach appears to combine many advantages. It would relieve population pressures both in the major cities and the countryside, increase the modernization spin-off which urban centers provide to surrounding rural areas, provide less congested and polluted urban living at an infrastructure cost no greater and possibly less than in the main cities. It should also reduce regional imbalances and capture to a greater extent the potential initiative from regional decentralization.

Such generalized approaches to the balance of rural and urban development do not, however, appear particularly productive. No satisfactory basis of facts, experience or theory exists, or may ever exist, for a generalized solution to the opposing arguments. Not only are the interrelationships highly complex. Physical conditions vary greatly, as do existing patterns of urbanization which greatly influence the benefits of alternative future policies. Models to simulate existing patterns have not yet proved possible. Construction of dynamic models for future growth, which would allow alternative policies for changing existing spatial trends to be adequately tested, does not appear attainable in the near future even in developed countries. For the more rapidly changing social and functional structures of developing countries, the problem is much more complex. The underlying springs of development, of entrepreneurship and organization, or inter-occupational impacts, are still at best imperfectly understood.

It is evident, nevertheless, that the three approaches each contain important elements warranting consideration in a national urbanization strategy. Attention generally *has* been centered more on urban investment opportunities than on the rural development potential. Cases of very extensive and expensive investment programs in rural areas are, however, not lacking. In some countries, political pressures certainly bias the allocation of resources towards urban centers and distortions in factor prices may seriously compromise rural development. The social costs of individual units of production in urban centers may often significantly exceed the private cost on which decisions are made. It is less clear than these "diseconomies" offset socio-economic advantages of agglomeration not fully reflected in the benefits to decision makers.

The impact of rural development in reducing migration can easily be exaggerated. Policies which provide incentives for agricultural output, for example through correction of inappropriate terms of trade between agricultural and urban products, can certainly often provide a marked stimulus to rural production. The effect on rural employment and in narrowing the gap between rural and urban wages may however be marginal. Much depends on local conditions including the unit value of crops grown, land tenure arrangements and the stimulus given to adoption of new techniques.

Evidence of the impact of programs promoting green revolution techniques is somewhat contradictory. In areas of relatively good land, which benefit most from the new technologies, higher productivity per man and per acre has been accompanied by a somewhat higher total of persons employed, particularly where double cropping is introduced. In some areas, however, the introduction of farm machinery, even if limited to the minimum required to exploit the new technologies, may reduce labor requirements. Machines required to prepare land in the short period between crops or for difficult soil conditions are, rationally, used for other labor-saving purposes. The position of marginal farmers and landless laborers has often been depressed. In some countries, land reform can provide important opportunities for increasing agricultural output with greater employment. But the process is typically slow due to inherent administrative as well as political difficulties. With rare exceptions, the impact on overall employment and migration appears likely to be small.

In brief, accelerated expansion of agriculture, though obviously important for national development, seems unlikely to go far in reducing migration. Indeed, for many countries, the impact of the foreseeable growth in agricultural production seems unlikely to offset acceleration in growth of labor force. Even if rural employment grows by 2% a year, an increase in urban employment of 4½% a year will still be needed to provide sufficient jobs for the additions to the national labor force, assuming growth rates of 20% in the urban population and 2½% in labor force; a 7% urban employment increase is needed if the labor force grows by 3%.[1]

The influence on migration of providing greater amenities to the rural population is also problematic. To have a significant impact on the marginal fraction of population that migrates to the town would require very large and prolonged efforts to improve conditions

[1]The absolute number of jobs required in the rural areas with a 2% expansion rate, will of course still be much larger than that required in the towns with a 4½% or 7% rate due to the much smaller starting base in the towns.

throughout the rural areas. Provision of housing and many utilities at a level judged acceptable in rural areas is likely to be appreciably cheaper in the countryside than conventional urban standards.[1] However, except perhaps for some richer developing countries, the total number of units needed to obtain a general improvement in conditions is many times the number required in the towns to accommodate the small fraction which migrates. Administrative as well as resource constraints set limits to any feasible policy, however justified such policies may appear.

Greater social amenities in rural areas may even promote migration, at least initially. So far as can be judged from limited studies, extension of education, improved transport facilities, the spread of national information media, and increased contact with urban-type amenities tend to increase rather than decrease the impetus to migrate to urban centers and from the smaller centers to the larger.

A faster growth of small- to medium-size urban centers relative to the largest has obvious attractions. A rapid growth of market and servicing centers can be expected to accompany modernization of agriculture. Marketing requirements are highly geared to the margin of production above subsistence and to the expanded use of fertilizers and other inputs.

Specific promotion of new manufacturing centers is another matter. For the poorer countries in particular, concentration of their sparse physical and entrepreneural resources in one, or at most two or three, large cities may have considerable advantages during initial stages of development. Economies from scale of operation and specialization, contact with foreign capital and dissemination of technology may thereby be maximized. The primate city at the hub of a radial transport network may also at this stage result in economies in the national transport system. Whatever the historic reasons for location, it would be unwise to assume without explicit evidence that the continued growth of primate cities is not well based on considerations of efficiency. Though social considerations may favor decentralization, it is important that the probable economic cost is realized.

Experience in a variety of developing countries, ranging from India and Pakistan to Venezuela and Brazil, shows that promotion of assumed "growth centers" can be very expensive both in terms of financial and administration resources. In practice, great difficulties have been encountered in choosing appropriate new "natural" growth centers. It is generally much easier to chose an appropriate location

---

[1]Electricity is an important exception; education and health may be. For the *same* standards, more people can generally be served per investment and operating dollar in urban than in rural areas.

430

for an individual industry than to identify a group of industries that can be attracted to, or generated in, a given area. Dangers of investing in infrastructure which proves to be underutilized are easily demonstrable.

There are several reasons for the difficulties encountered. Most small urban centers in developing countries lack the basic infrastructure of transport and services which in developed countries permits manufacturing units readily to locate away from major centers. Management and professional staff are unwilling to move from the major cities. There is, moreover, no clear evidence that costs of urban services for the same quality of service are less in the smaller centers.[1] Even if lower urban service costs in the smaller centers were proved, it would still be necessary to show that the differences exceed the net advantages that the larger cities provide from concentration of population and economic activities.

Completely new towns seem particularly expensive. A fairly large "minimum mass" is needed for the town to operate as an efficient largely self-contained unit.[2] In the process, considerable underutilized capacity has to be created. In existing towns such "lumpy" investments are staggered as capacity limits in each utility are reached. Some "over-capacity" utilization both of services and housing customarily occurs before new investments are undertaken. Lacking the hard-to-define but nonetheless important organization "infrastructure" of existing centers, the administrative requirements of new towns are particularly heavy.

Such problems appear noticeably less for centers where above average growth is already apparent. Removal of specific and evident constraints can in such cases lead to accelerated growth at relatively small expenditure. Towns within a narrow radius of large cities, where intermediary services of the metropolis can be utilized and public utilities more readily linked, can also offer favorable opportunities.

---

[1]Even looking at the growth of individual urban centers (perhaps a clearer indication of scale economies since towns of a similar population vary so greatly in density, urban layout and physical constraints), there is little indication in most cases of significantly higher incremental costs with growth. Many urban services can be duplicated without increase in costs. For others, such as electricity and various types of health and education facilities, economies of scale continue up to very large populations. For a minority of services including water (if more distant supplies have to be tapped) and passenger transport, marginal costs rise after a certain size. However, the greatest constraints on economic efficiency as the cities grow appear to lie in the field of the growing complexity of administration.

[2]Widely differing views are held on the size of the minimum mass. In the developed countries, the minimum size for a viable new town has been progressively increased and 300,000 is now often held as the lower limit. The relevance of Western experience is, however, dubious.

In the circumstances described, a pragmatic approach to a national urban strategy, based on general policies to reduce distortions and a deeper evaluation of identifiable practical alternatives for both rural and urban development, would appear the most productive. Such an approach would seek to analyze and reduce underlying biases towards urbanization in such fields as taxation and price policy, and in the inadequate charging of social disutilities to private and public decision makers. It would place greater emphasis on investigation of the development potential in rural areas. It would seek to identify smaller or medium size towns already demonstrating above average growth potential where removal of specific constraints should lead to acceleration of growth without heavy prior infrastructure investment.

Even more important appears the need for a new perspective towards employment, both urban and rural. The availability of surplus labor should be regarded as an opportunity for undertaking relatively labor-intensive investments rather than simply as a problem. At a later stage of development, as employment and wages rise, such investments are likely to represent a much higher "opportunity cost". In general terms, the need is to promote a better combination of the scarce resources of capital, land, skills and foreign exchange with the increasingly abundant supply of labor. There appears, indeed, little prospect of reducing unemployment unless the pattern of demand is changed by policies towards exchange and interest rates, taxation and subsidies, and investment programs, in the direction of goods, services and production processes in which the relative share of unskilled labor is higher. Only by such an approach does it appear possible to make economic growth compatible with social balance in the existing conditions of most developing countries.

How such a reformulation of policy will affect the balance of rural and urban development cannot be decided in the abstract. The widely varying conditions will produce different answers for different countries. Neither increased emphasis on rural development, nor on urban development will, however, by itself produce a panacea. Farms, rural villages, market towns, intermediate centers, and major cities form a continuum in which complementary action is required to make the best use of national resources. The dichotomy between urban and rural development is to this extent false.

Difficult reconciliations between higher returns on projects as conventionally evaluated and greater equity appear inevitable. The unfortunate reality is that the best economic returns for further investment tend to be where conditions are already relatively favorable and prosperous—within sectors such as farming as also between regions or between urban centers. This does not however mean that increasing GNP is at variance with reducing unemployment. On the contrary, the evidence suggests that maximization of use of total resources, including labor, rather than maximizing returns (as narrowly defined) on individual projects can often provide the best prospect for growth in total output.

In not a few developing countries, particularly where growth of agricultural output is already adequate and rising faster than population, the policy review suggested may indicate the desirability of greater concentration of investment in the towns—though, as the next section indicates, by no means necessarily of the present pattern. The costs of providing additional urban employment compared to resulting output, evaluated from both economic and social aspects, may in such circumstances prove more attractive than for rural projects. The arguments against very capital-intensive industrialization should not be identified with urban occupations as a whole, since only a small percentage fall into this category.

Even, however, where the approach suggested leads to stronger emphasis on rural investments, it should be recognized that the problems of urbanization are unlikely to be significantly reduced in the shorter term. Indeed, it should be accepted that success in stimulating overall national development, through green revolutions in agriculture for example, may lead, even with more appropriate technology, to an intensification of urban pressures.

THE PROBLEMS OF URBAN CENTERS

The despondency surrounding the task of ameliorating urban conditions in the developing countries arises primarily from the speed of urban growth and shortage of resources, human as well as financial. There are further contributing factors which, though also apparent in developed countries, operate with much greater force and are less amenable to solution due to the shortage of resources. For instance, experience has shown that the provision of more and better urban highways provides by itself no more than temporary alleviation and does not solve traffic congestion. Metros or urban railways tend to have their major impact in diverting passengers from buses. Investment in transport facilities accordingly can appear of dubious permanent value.

Housing also appears as a "bottomless pit", individual projects being too marginal to have any real impact and the costs of major programs beyond the realm of possibility. In most developing countries, "low-cost housing" tends inexorably to provide shelter for the medium rich rather than the more needy poor whose payment of indirect taxes often subsidizes it. The "trickle down" of space freed by better-off inhabitants moving to new houses proves to be negligible. Water supply and sewerage projects often appear to be fighting a losing battle, the backlog growing faster than it can be filled. Soaring urban land prices make urban projects increasingly expensive. Comprehensive urban plans have tended to be unrealistic in terms of resources and implementation capacity, and out-of-date by the time they are completed. They have had little influence on decision making. Urban administration is woefully lacking in capacity to deal with the problems and highly fragmented. The list could be readily extended.

Yet within less than 20 years, the present populations and areas of urban centers will account for less than a third of the total; the same is true of employment and of housing and urban services. Inevitably many new roads and transport facilities, dwellings and utilities, employment sites, markets, and social facilities, will have to be provided. Equally obvious, much can be done to promote more efficient use of public and private resources and to generate additional resources. Here, the urban centers of the developing countries have some advantages. The rapidity of their growth, and the still small number of industrial plants and private automobiles, offer the opportunity to develop a more rational urban pattern and avoid the necessity of very costly reconstruction which now confronts most major cities of the industrialized world.

The opportunities for improvement derive principally from three sets of considerations. The first set concerns the important and extensive interactions between investment decisions usually undertaken in an unrelated manner either by individuals or by various public entities. Because of these interactions, private benefits, or benefits of individual public enterprises, may vary considerably from the social benefits.

The possible "externalities" or social "disutilities" of industrial location have long been recognized in terms of pollution and other nuisance imposed on the community. Fortunately for the developing countries, these effects are generally much less than in the past and many more industries can now be closely integrated with residential areas. The impact of industrial location on transport and utility requirements, and the similar impact of business and residential location and densities, have received less attention. Even within residential areas, private development of small lots can result in great

434

waste of space, particularly for roadways.[1] Similarly, uncoordinated investment in different transport modes can result in large unnecessary expenditures.

The second set of considerations concerns the extent to which levels of urban services and housing can be tailored to the resources available, both public and private. Poor housing in the urban centers is primarily a reflection of the basic poverty. Attempts, such as have often been made, to set housing standards out of line with the resources of the inhabitants and the community cannot succeed. Similarly, the scarcity of resources means that decisions on the level of public services provided are tantamount to decisions on the proportion of the urban population to be served. Closely connected to this question of standards is the highly important opportunity to stimulate self-help.

The third set concerns pricing, including charging by way of taxation. Considerable opportunities certainly exist for using pricing mechanisms better to harness market forces in producing a more efficient pattern of urban development, as well as to increase the total of resources available for public purposes. Since private investment customarily accounts for over two-thirds of urban investment, and detailed physical regulation by public authorities is at best weak, pricing policies must inevitably occupy a central role in measures for increasing urban efficiency.

In the context of the concentration of population and economic activities in the towns, these considerations provide the main rationale for treating the urbanization problems of developing countries as a separate field from the more general problems of poverty and underemployment or of individual sectors. Nowhere are the problems and opportunities better illustrated than in urban transport, urban land use and housing, three fields which together play a leading role in determining the patterns of urban growth.

Urban Transport and Urban Patterns

Despite many studies, no simple physical patterns have been established as optimal for the cities of developing countries. Existing facilities and topography as well as differences in functions, and in social values and organization, necessitate considerable variety. Some considerations do, however, appear to have general application. Up to a certain size, generally well below one million inhabitants, higher densities can result in considerable economies in the provision of

[1]The new town of Milton Keynes in England is illustrative of the potential. Even with 90% of residents owning cars, congestion will be avoided with only 11% of its area taken by transport and communications facilities compared with 30% and over in many American cities.

transport and utilities.[1] For the larger cities, general urban spread based on concentrated employment in a single central district is clearly uneconomical in resource use. An urban pattern with several nuclei of relatively high densities connected by major transport arteries, and with considerable open space or low-density development preserved between them, can offer considerable advantages.

Close location of residences and employment, which with city growth requires the establishment of new employment groupings away from existing centers, can secure considerable economies. Further opportunities exist in the development of new urban areas on a sufficiently large scale to enable economies of road and utility layout as well as better environment to be achieved. The appropriate emphasis in developing the cities is in general likely to be on largely self-contained urban areas which substantially reduce transport needs with adequate mobility between them to reap the benefits of specialized services.

The importance of transport to the pattern of the urban centers and the efficiency of their functioning is such that it is difficult to discuss other urban problems meaningfully without becoming involved also in urban transport. The existing urban pattern, particularly of housing and employment, largely determines present transport needs; the provision of new transport facilities largely determines the future pattern of the city. Deficiencies in urban transport facilities add substantially to the costs and difficulty of moving both goods and workers within and through urban areas; transport access is a prerequisite of urban development. Transport constitutes moreover a major item of public capital expenditures in urban areas, often to an extent that significantly limits the availability of funds for other purposes. It is also a sector where large economies appear attainable, not least in utilizing more fully existing transport facilities.

Similarities between traffic congestion in the business centers of the major cities, particularly the richer ones, and congestion in developed country cities should not obscure some fundamental differences. The much higher rate of population growth means that whatever solutions are sought, a high level of investment in transport will be required on grounds of population growth alone. Secondly, despite the rapid rise in the number of private automobiles, usually over 10% a year, in most developing countries the number of automobiles is still very small. Less than 10% of the world's automobiles are in de-

---

[1]The point at which congestion, not only of transport but also in providing utilities such as sewerage funnelled through narrow arteries, causes rising unit costs with increased density, obviously varies considerably according to existing layout, physical conditions and costs of reconstruction of properties.

veloping countries. For many years to come, the great majority of the city populations will, on account of their income level, have no option but to rely on walking, bicycles or some form of public transport. The rise in private automobile use at this early stage of development greatly intensifies the problem because of the high ratio of road space per passenger involved and the generally low proportion of road space to urban area.[1] But even with a curb on private automobile use, investment costs of providing roads and other expensive long-life transport infrastructure and public vehicles on an adequate scale will remain high.

Nevertheless, since roads represent the largest part of transport infrastructure investment and private automobiles are the most obvious cause of congestion, it is here that attention is understandably centered. The balance between personal and mass transport, between vehicles and roads, is not only at the heart of the urban transport problem. The decisions taken regarding this balance will fundamentally affect the quality of urban life in the future. The developing countries are still in a position to avoid exaggerated dependence on the private automobile from which many developed countries are now trying to escape.

In considering the relation of private automobile to road expenditures, generalizations based on national totals are of little help. On highways between towns, additional private vehicles cause little congestion or road maintenance. The marginal costs incurred through vehicle use are likely to be below average costs. In city centers, where each road user imposes costs and delays on others, the reverse is true. Widening of existing city streets is very expensive, provision of urban highways even more so, typically costing well above a million dollars per lane-mile. For a 10-mile stretch, the cost per car is likely to be in excess of $2 per day.[2] Additional urban parking space represents a further important investment, particularly if costed on an "alternative use" value. The growing use of private cars also slows down and increases the cost of public transit and goods traffic. Outside of peak hours, the marginal costs of private cars are much lower. However, the costs of additional roadways and public utilities incurred in "city sprawl" resulting from private automobile use also have to be taken into account.

---

[1] The typical Western European-North American city devotes 25% or more of urban land area to streets and highways. In developing country cities the proportion is often only half as much.

[2] Assuming that a new expressway lane can accommodate an additional 3,000 cars during a two-hour peak period then, on a conservative costing of $1 million per lane/mile and a 10% rate to cover interest, amortization and maintenance, the public cost of a ten-mile highway per automobile round-trip at peak periods is about $2.50.

The conclusion appears inescapable that the urban motorist is generally charged well below the social costs incurred. Considerations of national priorities and the use of foreign exchange reinforce this viewpoint. Expenditure on automotive equipment often equals that on road infrastructure. It has a high foreign exchange content and is concentrated on the upper income group in the large urban centers. Though much more extensive analysis is required, there appears to be a considerable element of truth in the contention that a continuation of present trends in allocation of resources for the private automobile may seriously undermine the possibilities for more general economic and social development.

Congestion can be relieved by staggering working hours to reduce peak travel. Road capacity can also often be increased at relatively low expenditure by better traffic controls, particularly synchronized traffic signals, and by construction of short highway links to complete major circuits. With such obvious exceptions, investment in urban highways in heavily built-up areas is difficult to justify unless and until complementary steps are taken to restrain private automobile use. Traffic congestion is a method, albeit a poor one, of restricting the growth in private car use and of providing incentives to locate new employment away from existing central business districts. Insofar as steps are not taken to charge automobile use with the costs incurred, it appears better, given the sparse resources available for other critical needs, that restriction by congestion should occur at lower rather than higher levels of inner-city highway investment.

The logic of the traffic congestion situation is to tax the urban motorist much more heavily, particularly at peak hours. Several schemes for peak hour charging are under consideration in developed countries, but none has yet been introduced. In developing countries it is perhaps more realistic to attempt a progressive increase in private vehicle taxes, with a surcharge for congested cities, combined with the prohibition of private vehicles in central areas at peak hours, and much stricter parking enforcement with higher parking charges. But it should be recognized that—as for many other policies such as those to reduce births—the prospects for effective measures are greatly enhanced if underlying conditions can be improved to reduce the demand. Adequate provision of alternative transport and development of urban patterns that reduce trip requirements must be regarded as a partner in policies to control private automobile use.

The main problem is the provision of transport facilities for the greater majority of the population, rapidly increasing in numbers, who cannot in any case afford private cars. Better facilities for walking and bicycles are both important and usually neglected. However,

438

mass transit must play a much greater role than in most cities in developed countries. It is an essential component in linking workers with jobs. Several alternative and often complementary modes need to be considered—buses, jitneys, taxis, urban railways and metros. One general point, however, deserves note. Improved mass transit in the developing countries' cities is unlikely of itself, even if offered free, to wean a significant number of passengers away from private automobiles unless automobile user charges are raised considerably. Social and income differences between the two classes are generally too great.

Buses are, and seem likely to remain, the most important type of mass transit. They have many advantages. Capital costs and road space requirements are low in relation to passenger capacity. Running costs can be readily reduced by taking buses off the roads in off-peak periods. Routes are flexible and can be altered as cities grow and change. The frequency of stops to meet the needs of the large number of passengers and limited maneuverability, however, cause greater dislocation of traffic flows than the smaller "jitney-type" vehicles with a handful of passengers. Jitneys are also more effective on less populated routes and provide greater convenience for individual origins and destinations. Both, the buses more than jitneys, suffer from idle capacity during off-peak periods though to a lesser extent than other modes of passenger transport except taxis, which are more expensive but can convert into jitney-type service during peak periods.

Faced with both mounting requirement for mass transit and increasing congestion—which slows buses and streetcars even more than it does automobiles—attention is increasingly turning to systems of priorities for buses. Separate lanes for buses can provide great improvement in service while lowering operating costs. Unfortunately, in heavily congested inner-city areas, the practical difficulties of exclusive surface rights-of-way are great. On existing roads, serious underutilization, difficulties at intersections and stops, as well as enforcement difficulties, are likely to arise. New lanes for buses are very expensive. However, when bus traffic is sufficiently heavy to permit near capacity utilization of separated lanes, at least four times as many passengers may be accommodated as a lane of private automobiles. Table 9 in Annex 1 provides some estimates. Unfortunately, little experience is available to provide reliable guidelines on practical systems.

At the opposite extreme, capital and foreign exchange costs of metros and urban railways for infrastructure as well as rolling stock, are very heavy[1] and routing is inflexible. Capacity of rapid rail trans-

---

[1]Excavation costs for metros vary greatly but are typically above $15 million per route/mile; total costs may be upwards of $20 million per lane/mile.

port is large at 30,000 to 40,000 passengers per hour per track. This represents 10 to 20 times the capacity of urban highway lanes used for private cars and at least four or five times an exclusive bus lane. The combination of high capacity and inflexibility, however, necessitates coordination with lesser capacity modes as feeders and distributors and also more passenger interchanges. Unless fares are coordinated among transport modes, charges per passenger trip tend to be correspondingly higher.

Generally speaking, due to the high capacity and expense, a multimillion population with relatively high density both of residence and employment centers appears a prerequisite for consideration of the metro alternative. In such cities, a metro may be viable when surface congestion reaches a point that necessitates further extensive high cost urban highway construction to provide for essential traffic movement even with feasible restriction of private automobiles. It will not remove congestion from the streets but it can, in appropriate circumstances, provide the minimum peak load transport facilities required more cheaply than by additional highway construction and surface transport.[1] Several cities in developing countries are considering metro construction ranging from Calcutta to Caracas, Singapore to Sao Paulo, and many more can be expected to do so with the future growth to multi-million populations.

Such considerations emphasize the need to consider urban transport as a system covering all the various modes both in terms of economizing total resources and in the closely connected aspect of pricing policy. Providing for peak load traffic by whatever mode is more expensive, as a result of unutilized off-peak capacity, than providing for traffic levels at other periods. The relief given at times of peak load compared with other alternatives for the urban transport system as a whole is, therefore, of central importance in evaluation of projects such as metros.

The feasibility of alternatives cannot, however, be adequately assessed without consideration of pricing policy throughout the system. Almost all rapid transit systems throughout the world lose money and require heavy financial subsidies by public authorities. Such financial subsidization — whether or not justified on socio-economic grounds—together with the heavy initial costs, may exclude serious considerations of metros by the poorest cities unless they are very large and have high densities. Meeting peak load needs adequately with buses in heavily congested conditions with corresponding low

---

[1]This conclusion is generally supported on the basis of present road use. Some experts believe, however, that metros cannot compete with the new road/exclusive bus lane alternative if private vehicles are strictly controlled.

levels of service is also likely to result in deficits for bus companies. A general increase in fares may cause the familiar downward spiral of lower utilization, declining service and increased deficits. To raise fares for peak hours without a corresponding charge on other modes, particularly the private automobile, is likely to be politically difficult as well as discriminatory.

"Ideal" conditions of full user charges on private automobile and coordination of public transport might well permit fare levels both politically acceptable and sufficient to cover costs. Private bus companies do make profits though often not carrying a significant part of the peak load. There are evident possibilities for economies from better coordination of routes. However, even with heavier taxation of private automobiles, some compromise on public transport pricing may be inevitable. Shortage of resources restricts possibilities of expanding the transport infrastructure. Historic patterns of services and pricing cannot quickly be radically changed. The multiplicity of operating agencies, both public and private, greatly complicates coordination. In practice, the question tends to become one of minimizing the financial burden while ensuring that the most economical pattern of transport modes in terms of overall resources is progressively attained.

It should be recognized, however, that holding of urban transport charges below costs may not only increase congestion and day time densities in central business areas to levels where increasing marginal costs of facilities apply. It may also induce dispersed and much lower densities elsewhere, causing unnecessarily high roadway to population ratios and expensive utility connections. Unless attention is focused on this longer term context of interlinkages, attempts to solve the urban transport problem based on existing needs can easily aggravate the future situation.

The greatest scope for economizing in urban transport and relieving congestion in the longer term lies indeed in influencing the growth of the cities in ways which reduce the need for transport, particularly to and from the present central business and industrial districts with their already determined and usually insufficient and inefficient road network. The provision of a highway between two distant cities obviously does not affect the location of the two cities and to only a limited degree, at least in the short term, the location of population between them. An urban highway can vitally and quickly affect the pattern of a city, the location of its occupations and its dwellings, and its growth potential. Traffic generated by transport facilities is as important a consideration as the meeting of existing demand.

Too often consideration of existing transport demand, or that projected on the basis of existing trends, precludes consideration of how the pattern of demand could be changed and reduced by better siting and coordination of transport facilities and by better transport pricing. Conversely, haphazard regulation of urban land use can multiply travel requirements. The two are intimately connected. Similarly, scarcity of housing leads to immobility in residence change and unnecessary cross traffic, while the development of new housing areas is dependent on provision of transport facilities. Consideration of urban transport, accordingly, cannot be separated from that of land use guidance and housing.

Land Use Guidance

Measures to guide and direct land use are of obvious importance to the growth pattern of urban centers. Nowhere perhaps are social and individual interests likely to be at greater variance. Greater or lesser powers to control land use exist in almost every city in the world. They comprise specific measures such as zoning, physical building regulations and permits, controls on pollution and public purchase of land, as well as more general measures such as taxation of land, property and betterment values, and rent controls. The problems to which these measures are addressed range from efficient zoning of different activities, particularly industry and housing, and consolidation and acquisition of land for specific purposes, to the reduction of land speculation and the raising of tax revenues.

In the urban centers of developing countries, the problems of land use are particularly acute. Land values are in many cases mounting precipitously[1] to levels often in excess of similarly situated sites in cities of the developed world. Sites with, or readily accessible to, urban services remain unoccupied often to a much greater degree than in developed countries.[2] Effective regulation of location by user type is frequently minimal, and collection of land and property taxes only a fraction of a realistic assessment. Stocks of undeveloped public land suitably located are meanwhile often rapidly diminishing.

Many attempts have been made by municipal authorities to improve their land use powers and programming. It cannot be said, unfortunately, that the progress to date has been great. The legal bases for acquisition of land, control of type of use, building permits,

[1]For example, in Taipei land values are reckoned to have increased roughly 1,000% in under 15 years.
[2]Unbuilt land within metropolitan areas frequently exceeds 40%, e.g., as shown by a survey of 103 cities and towns in India; also Bangkok, Buenos Aires.

taxation powers related to unexploited land and betterment values, are more often than not quite inadequate. Nor are those that are available energetically used. This is not merely a problem of national or local politics, though this aspect is often a major contributory factor. In the dire straits in which the city authorities find themselves, it is difficult for them to turn down proposals for construction that yield immediate additional employment and increased tax revenues even if they cause considerable disutilities.

The rapid increase in population, in income level, and corresponding advantages of central sites would in any case lead to increased urban land values, particularly in central areas. The trend is reinforced by investment and speculative advantages of urban land in the absence of comparable investment avenues, a situation often exacerbated by quasi-monopolistic land ownership. Perhaps even more important is the relation between population growth and supply of urbanized land with adequate services. Compared with the developed countries, a considerable scarcity value attaches to urbanized land due to the financial difficulties of municipalities and utility agencies in extending their networks at a rate commensurate with population growth.

When to such tendencies are added the inherent divergencies between private decisions and social benefits in urban land use, the very limited public financial resources, and the importance of land costs in public projects, it is abundantly clear that market values are usually not an efficient allocator of urban land. Also obviously, the capacity does not exist, either now or in the foreseeable future, for efficient detailed land planning by public authorities, and even less for effective implementation. In practice, a compromise has to be sought in which controls and public acquisition of land or development rights provide a framework which allows the price mechanism to play a still important role in detailed allocation.

The policies should also seek to augment public financial resources by taxes on land profits exceeding levels necessary to provide the desired incentives. Charges for utilities higher than those necessary to cover costs may constitute a form of such taxation. Given the present exiguous levels of municipal budgets, more adequate land taxation is generally an essential element in programs for bringing about an overall amelioration of urban conditions.

An initial review of the measures, ranging from simple regulatory controls to land nationalization, which various countries are using is given in Annex II. Land acquisition by public authorities and subsequent development by, or in cooperation with, private developers, may provide the most effective route to establish efficient urban patterns and also the easiest means to capture a large part of the value created by provision of urban services and by the growth in total population and income. Supplementary measures can improve the functioning of the land market.

In this connection, development of limited new urban areas on an integrated basis appears to offer particular advantages, social as well as economic. Low-income housing, or "site and services" projects can be combined with a variety of other land uses, including employment places and community service centers. Prices, or rents, obtained from land associated with the higher income, commercial and manufacturing uses, together with the economies realizable from marginal additions to utility capacities, can then permit much lower charges, compatible with income levels, for the land devoted to low-income housing. Segregation of the rich and poor can be reduced in a manner compatible to both.

Physical controls and building regulations provide an important method of generalized control. However, in many cases, existing regulations are often inappropriate to prevailing conditions and can easily do much harm. Housing standards or zoning regulations based on Western concepts which take little account of prevailing customs of business/residence mix provide examples. Taxes on betterment and on unutilized urban land, more rigorously defined and implemented, can direct the growth of the urban centers in more rational directions as well as adding to financial resources. Selected provision of urban services can further influence urban growth with transport occupying a leading role. The denial of urban services to localities not in accordance with the general framework for urban development, though so far little used and politically difficult, could also be effective, particularly if adequate services are provided in localities chosen for development.

Indeed, expansion in the supply of land with adequate urban services for generally defined purposes at appropriate new locations appears as a central objective to which individual land control and taxation measures need to be specifically related. The new urban extension areas require even more attention than the old which will soon constitute only a minor part of the total and are much more expensive to alter. The importance of the new areas lies not only in conserving resources by better urban patterns but also in relieving the pressure on the older sectors. At a later stage, with more wealth and municipal resources, and lower population growth, the remodelling of older areas can be more effectively tackled.

Urban Housing

Food, clothing and housing constitute basic necessities for living. "Progress" accordingly appears questionable if it takes the form of higher production of less essential goods accompanied by acute and growing shortage of housing for the poorer mass of the population. Such considerations add further point to the importance of housing as customarily the largest component of urban investment. Housing typically represents well over 10% of total private and public national gross investment, with by far the largest part in urban centers[1]. It is probable that over 200 million new dwellings will be needed in the urban centers of developing countries between now and the end of the century simply to house the additions to urban population. This total is almost equal to all the urban dwellings of the world in 1960.

Perhaps the most salient feature of the housing situation is the stark fact that typically well over half of the urban population cannot afford minimal "permanent construction" housing, even if financing arrangements are made available or limited subsidies given. An example, purposely on the high side, will illustrate the point. With a family income of $400 a year perhaps 15% may be available for housing (excluding services and maintenance) after allowing for food, clothing, transport to work and other necessary expenditures. On this basis, the capital cost of the house which can be afforded with a 20-year loan at 12% is only $450, or at 7% $640, compared with minimum costs for conventional housing usually exceeding $1,000[2].

Nor, in prevailing conditions of acute shortage of housing and resources, can public subsidization provide a solution. Total savings of the countries and even more of the municipalities are quite inadequate. For at least the poorer countries, encompassing the great majority of the people of the developing world, basic resource constraints preclude public provision of new housing for the urban poor directly or indirectly. There is, moreover, ample evidence that housing provided for a relatively small proportion of the poor families at standards appreciably above what they could normally afford quickly tends to be occupied by higher income groups. Either the selection

---

[1] For new towns, housing may exceed 40% of the total investment.

[2] A rule of thumb for housing that can be afforded is 2 to 2½ times family annual income. This is probably excessive at prevailing interest rates and for large families, or where incomes are so low that food and clothing preempt a very high proportion. Inflation and high interest rates cause additional difficulties; in real terms, the payments during initial years are much higher than in later years—but the high initial levels are likely to be prohibitive.

445

process is subverted, or informal arrangements are made by the nominal tenants[1].

A second major feature is the extent to which dwellings, albeit of "substandard" quality and subject to great overcrowding, have in fact been provided by the unaided self-help efforts of migrants. In many of the rapidly growing cities, over half the population has secured accommodation by such efforts and many others will reach this position within the next decade. Because the sites are often illegally occupied and the construction supposedly "temporary," no note is generally taken of this output and investment in national accounts. Yet in total, such activity undoubtedly represents a major share of dwelling construction. The situation is less one where provision of housing attracts migrants—of which there is little evidence—than one where the migrants provide the housing for themselves. The migrants appear at least as much to be providing a solution as to be creating a problem.

The wide variety of shantytown conditions deserves attention. The densely crowded inner-city slums to which migrants, in many countries at least, initially gravitate in their search for work, are usually quite distinct from the shantytowns of the urban periphery in the problems posed and possible solutions. The shantytowns themselves are widely dissimilar in density, income level, and type of location. Of particular note, many shantytowns of some years standing show evidence of self-generated upgrading. Dwellings of more permanent materials appear along with a proliferation of small enterprises. Commercial and social organization improves. Rudimentary urban facilities are improvised. The essential conditions for such dynamic amelioration are imperfectly understood; but certainly security of tenure and development of community organizations play essential roles.

Populations of shantytowns often appear to place more emphasis among their wants on the provision of minimal utilities and services, particularly water supply and health facilities, than the provision of more adequate dwellings as such. For shantytowns on the periphery of large cities, transport to areas of employment is of great importance. There are several instances of under-utilized public housing or "site and services," simply because the location has been too far from employment centers and the transport facilities inadequate or too costly.

Such considerations pose a series of dilemmas to the public authorities. Initial reaction to the shanty settlements has often been to tear

---

[1]There is also evidence of considerable difficulties of upkeep and rent collection even in subsidized public housing. Moreover, with housing shortage also existing at higher income levels, the "trickle-down" of vacated housing space to the large mass of poor families is negligible.

them down as both illegal and an urban blight. It is by now generally appreciated that such action provides no solution. New shanty settlements appear more quickly than the old are removed, and all that is usually achieved is destruction of useful capital investments. Much the same considerations apply to pulling down and reconstructing central slums. Unless the city is wealthy enough to provide in advance for relocation of the inhabitants at a cost they can afford, the immediate loss of dwelling space will compound the problem and tend to offset potential future advantages. For the poorer majority of developing countries, large-scale reconstruction of central areas appears a luxury that cannot yet be afforded.

Improvement of existing squatter settlements raises similar, if less intense, questions of priorities. If resources are concentrated on improving existing settlements, at the end of a few years new settlements duplicating the poor conditions of existing ones but of larger area will have sprung up. If measures are taken to restrict new settlements, the growth of population density in the existing settlements will be intensified, compounding the problems there. Settlement improvement, in brief, does not add to the stock of housing, the basic problem. Moreover, the difficult sites of existing settlements, often on mountain-sides or swampy land, their restricted access and low proportion of unbuilt area, tend to increase the cost of improvements.

In such a situation, it may seem more logical to concentrate on providing services and achieving a better layout in new settlements specifically designed to allow for future amelioration. Much, however, depends upon local conditions. Cases certainly exist where, with relatively small public expenditures combined with local self-help, major improvements can be achieved in living conditions without preempting much public resources otherwise available for creating new urbanized areas.[1] The benefits may then clearly justify the allocation while reducing pressures to demolish the settlements with consequent waste of existing capital.

Over the last decade, considerable experience has been gained in "site and services" projects providing urbanized land on which low-income groups can construct their own dwellings often with organized technical assistance. While the scope of such projects in relation to population growth is still very small, there is growing recognition that this type of approach deserves greater emphasis. A considerable variety exists in space allocated per family, in provision of

---

[1] For example, the Kampong improvement program now under consideration in Djakarta would entail costs of only about $15 per head. Difficulties may arise from substantial improvements producing a jump in land values if the occupiers of the land are not the owners.

utilities and social services, in the assistance given, in the type of tenure, in stipulated standards for construction of dwellings, and in the participation of private development enterprises. The schemes may or may not be subsidized, though any subsidy element is likely to be much less per family than for public low-cost housing.

Considerable variation in the organization of site and services projects is hardly surprising in view of the differences in income levels, social values and organization, climate and topographical features. The more conspicuous successes, however, tend to demonstrate the importance of securing involvement of the population concerned through community groups, not only for initial implementation but also in creating a momentum for further amelioration, in provision of communal facilities and in the collection of payments.[1]

Typical costs per urbanized family plot, including provision of water and sewerage, roadways and street lighting, and reservation of space for social facilities, commercial and cultural activities, may be of the order of $300 to $600.[2] Where community labor is organized and given technical assistance, costs may be further reduced.[3] Economy in costs of site and services and low-cost housing projects is however only one aspect of their contribution. Properly planned in relation to employment, social services and environment, they can lead to a marked improvement in general living conditions while reducing costs of supplying urban services.

Placing the major stress on the "site and services" approach does not imply that possibilities of low-cost housing should be ignored where action in this field would be appropriate. In the richer Latin American cities, low-cost housing schemes can make a significant contribution. Even for their poorer income groups, over 20% of income may be devoted to housing needs against probably less than 10% in India. Singapore, with its rapid economic expansion, limited population growth, and well above average income for the region, provides a further, obviously successful example.

[1]Rent collection appears generally easier than for public housing. The amounts assessed on "site and services" schemes are much lower and the families, with their own capital involved, have a greater interest in maintenance. Community group organizations can more readily apply sanctions, or provide help in deserving cases, than can public authorities.

[2]Dakar "site and services" project now under appraisal by the Bank will result in costs of about $300 (excluding land costs) for the relatively large families concerned. The average cost per housing unit for 16 public housing programs in the same city is over $4,000.

[3]In one El Salvador program, the overall costs per family in small planned units of development, including land and the self-help construction of houses with individual water supply and toilet, the materials being bought on a bulk basis, appears to have been brought down to below $800 for a 44 m^2 floor space house.

In this connection, a far greater effort in cheap building techniques using local materials appears called for. Little effective use seems to have been made of local building research centers. Though results with prefabricated dwellings have so far not been particularly encouraging, scale economies for various components including on-site fabrication, appear to offer brighter prospects. Much more analysis is required of the relative merits of high-rise apartments in reducing land use and, if appropriately located, also transport needs, compared with lower density housing.

There has been a tendency to minimize the contribution of housing to national output and welfare because of its high capital to output ratio. Such a simplistic approach, however, may considerably underestimate the importance of housing partly because both "capital" and "output" are ambiguous in this context. In the developing countries, construction of housing and supporting utilities makes little call on capital equipment but has a relatively large input of labor, mainly unskilled. Shortages of skilled labor for certain tasks may occur; but the training required to overcome such shortages is relatively simple. For low-income group housing, individual or small entrepreneur effort predominates. Indeed construction appears as one of the easiest occupations for surplus labor to enter. Building materials for low-income housing can generally be developed relatively easily within the countries from local raw materials[1], and here the overall capital to output ratios are generally favorable. Again considerable employment is created. For other materials, such as timber, a contribution may also be made to development in poorer areas of the country.[2]

Investment per house is high in relation to output as valued by rent obtainable, though the high rents charged in overcrowded developing country cities may produce a lower ratio than in the developed countries. The ratio is certainly substantially lower for less permanent buildings. Nor, in terms of welfare, does rent appear to be an adequate measure of output.

Perhaps more importantly, the savings required are largely generated by the house construction. There is ample evidence that people building a house at all income levels save more, and thus reduce their other consumption calls on resources which are likely to be more capital and foreign exchange intensive. Scattered evidence from

---

[1] In some African countries, however, the proportion of building materials imported appears to be very high.

[2] It can be argued that for some countries at least, stimulation of building provides a better route to industrialization than specific promotion of import-substituting industries that, on experience, are likely to be very costly or premature and, because of higher import content, are much more limited by foreign exchange scarcities.

site and services projects indicates that the initial investment in urbanizing the land is at least doubled by the efforts of the families in constructing dwellings on the land provided. Indeed, only a system which mobilizes this savings/investment potential is likely to succeed in substantially alleviating the housing shortage.[1]

The importance of stimulating savings by way of housing suggests the need for greater attention to the financial mechanisms for providing housing credit. The extreme stringency of public resources, including foreign aid, does not indicate a high priority for subsidizing the housing of the relatively well-to-do either directly or through artificially low interest rates. But the success of certain countries, such as Brazil, in mobilizing savings through housing finance institutions with a modicum of seed capital and technical assistance demonstrates a wider potential. For the poorer income groups, the need may be more for credit for construction materials organized through community groups.

Looking at housing as a separate urban sector does not, however, provide a sufficient basis for determining an appropriate strategy. The opportunities for economies and increased efficiency are usually dependent on action in other urban sectors. The provision of new areas for low-income settlements for instance, raises problems of acquiring suitable sites, of segregation of rich and poor, of higher costs of transport with increased distance, of higher costs of some public utilities and reduced costs for others with lower densities, and the more general problem of the level of services to be provided.

Levels of Urban Services

The fundamental shortage of resources for urban infrastructure to equip the additions to population, let alone to ameliorate existing conditions, poses in acute form the quality of services to be provided. The possible extent and implications of lower levels of service as a "trade-off" to lower costs represent a critical element in determining the proportion of the population that can be provided with the services. Also of great importance is the relation between original capital cost and maintenance, and the degree to which variations in this relationship affect the proportions of domestic labor and materials involved.

---

[1]The output from provision of dwellings stands in urgent need of a deeper analysis of direct and indirect impact on available national resources and foreign exchange. With the exception of one study in Japan which tends to confirm the much higher rating to be given house construction if the linkages are taken into account, and a more general analysis in the case of Colombia, the overall impact of housing does not appear to have been carefully investigated.

Some consideration has already been given to such aspects in the case of housing. In the case of urban transport, restriction of private automobiles can be regarded as a choice between high levels of service for the few and adequate levels for the many. Levels of service in mass transit can also be widely varied including the degree of overcrowding and discomfort tolerated at peak hours. The choice of alternative transport modes besides influencing total costs also greatly influences the proportion to labor of capital costs and the foreign exchange component of both capital and operating expenses. For a single transport mode, for example a metro, there are trade-offs between degrees of sophistication in equipment and speed, and between machines and labor, for instance in fare collection. For buses, vehicle replacement and expenses of maintenance are directly related. It is most unlikely that the best pattern for a developed country will be appropriate for a developing country, or that for a richer developing country appropriate for a poorer one with perhaps a fifth of the level of income. It should be possible to develop some general guidelines. The particular features of each individual city, especially the existing infrastructure, will nevertheless require significant variations around any "norm".

In other sectors, considerable opportunities may exist for lower cost services of minimum "utility" quality. Electricity distribution is often being designed at standards approximating those of developed countries. Simpler systems would increase the risks of loss of supply but could provide appreciable savings of costs and foreign exchange. In some non-industrial areas, the supply of electricity to more customers at lower cost with somewhat increased failure rate may well appear preferable to higher costs for a better quality of service to a smaller proportion of the inhabitants.[1] Greater attention to measures to reduce peaks and to the relation between lower reserve capacity and the risks and costs involved also appears appropriate. Electric power customarily represents about one-sixth of total public investment. A 10% saving, if attainable, would represent over half a billion dollars a year at projected rates of power investment in the developing countries for 1971-75, or over a billion dollars a year by the 1980s.

For water and sewerage, "trade-offs" of both convenience and health are involved. Undoubtedly reducing water pressure or filtering processes augments health hazards to the consumers affected; and

---

[1]See also Sector Working Paper on Electric Power. The comparison may in practice be between systems *designed* for lower service levels and costs, and systems designed for higher levels which because of overutilization (and poor maintenance) still incur high risks of outages. Out-of-date or otherwise inappropriate safety regulations can be an important factor in over-design.

451

in the former case may result in higher capital costs for individual storage tanks and deterioration of the transmission and distribution system. Poor intermittent service also creates difficulties in collecting or raising charges and in management. On the other hand, a larger proportion of the population supplied with lower quantities, rationed by restricted outlets or higher charges, may improve overall health and also reduce the risks of contagion spreading from previously unserviced areas. In countries where expenditures on medications are a significant item in family budgets, charges at economic rates for good quality water supply may be lower than the savings on medicaments.[1]

Sewerage presents other trade-offs. Depending on soil and topographical features, lower densities of housing may permit cesspools for all or part of a development area. Evidence on economies through communal provision of water and sewerage facilities is contradictory. Individual supply appears generally to lead to much better maintenance. But much depends on local community spirit and habits. Other possibilities of economizing resources arise from the fact that many water-using devices, such as toilet flush tanks, are not designed for high water economy, principally because water has traditionally been so cheap and charges inadequately related to volume used.

Institutional, Planning and Pricing Problems

The problems arising from the multiplicity of agencies dealing with urban growth, weak planning and management, inadequate policies on pricing, land regulations and taxes, and the scarcity of municipal finance are inextricably interwoven. As many as five levels of government—national, state, metropolitan, regional, municipal or local—may be involved with often little communication between them. More than 30 municipal authorities may partition a single metropolitan area as is the case in Calcutta. The boundaries of local govern-

---

[1] The wide range of possible combinations of quantity and quality of water is indicated in the range from a minimum of under 2 liters to over 200 liters per capita per day in usage. Investigations in East Africa indicate that communal standpipe supply typically works out at less than 20 liters per capita per day; for a single tap per family without indoor waste disposal at 30 to 40 liters; while for multiple tap and waste disposal the range may be as wide as 60 to 600 liters with mean use of the order of 100 to 180 liters. Costs of construction for piped water per capita may vary by a factor of 30. The variations in charges appear to be much less. Charges for carried water in areas without public facilities are generally much higher than for piped water. (They may absorb as much as 10% of family income compared with typically less than 2% for upper income classes with piped water.) A significant proportion of urban water may go to industrial and other nonconsumptive uses and could be recycled or returned for other uses if treated. In such conditions, simple projections of demand are likely to be an inadequate base for investment decisions.

ment jurisdictions are slow to respond to fundamental changes in urban configurations in all countries. The exceptional speed of large city growth in the developing countries poses particularly acute problems of adaptation. The number of individual uncoordinated agencies under a single authority is no less a problem. Creation of autonomous agencies to ensure better management of individual services while improving some operations may, in the absence of a similar strengthening of municipal administration, compound the problem of integrating policies and determining appropriate priorities of the urban center as a whole.

Urban planning has a long history; but it is a history centered on physical and architectural planning. Only recently, even in the developed countries, has the focus changed substantially to incorporate economic and social objectives and constraints, and inter-sector linkages, in the context of dynamic growth. To date, no satisfactory comprehensive models have emerged. Even the transport/spatial models, on which most work has been done, remain essentially static in concept with little in the way of feedbacks to incorporate the alternative impacts of the transport mode patterns tested. The more complex the models, the fewer the alternatives it has proved possible to consider. For various reasons, the alternatives have not been radically different in the sense of recognizing the potential for structural transformation, and consequently have produced remarkably uniform cost/benefit results. There is little evidence of their having had a significant influence on decision making. More generally, descriptive models based on observed relationships are of limited use for analyzing changes in public policy designed to alter fundamental bases, such as price relationships in transportation and housing.

In the developing countries, the lack of adequate attention to restraints on resources and implementation capacity greatly reduces the utility of most of the "comprehensive" town plans. Lack of explicit consideration of policies for pricing and land use, for example, and of specific short and intermediate run realistic programs, limit their effectiveness. There are additional reasons for the current disillusionment with comprehensive urban planning. Income redistribution effects are frequently mentioned but rarely studied in depth. Quantification of social indicators, moreover, does not solve the problem of choosing the parameters for defining the development sought. The planners have been largely isolated from the policy makers whose decisions are involved. Moreover, inadequacy of data and the rapidity of change of the urban centers, and in their social structure and economic functions, makes the determination of relationships, now and for the future, much more difficult than in developed countries. Already by the time comprehensive plans are produced, they tend to be sadly out-of-date.

Similar difficulties are faced in the evaluation of individual urban projects. Methodology even in the developed countries is weak, particularly in the evaluation of benefits. Because of the linkages with other sectors and the importance of social considerations, both the boundaries of relevant results and the weighting to be given them are difficult to decide. It is often difficult to determine unequivocally the relevant levels of demand when, as for many social services, the user may not be the purchaser in the sense of the taxpayer. In urban transport projects, differences in financial setup between municipal and various types of private or mixed public/private finance, makes comparison of alternatives more difficult. More generally, techniques evolved for evaluating projects in the complex urban context tend to be weak in generating them.

Nowhere are the shortcomings of existing urban development policies and planning more evident than in the field of pricing in respect both to individual urban sectors and, perhaps even more, to their interactions. Failure to take into account such linkages often produces a conflict between the twin objectives of pricing policy—to secure a rational allocation of resources for urban development and to mobilize resources for this purpose. The appropriate pricing for one mode of urban transport is dependent on the pricing policy towards other modes. The price to be charged for providing a utility service to a specific locality, though it covers the costs, may not be appropriate if it involves the costly provision of other facilities such as roads. More generally, a failure to take into account marginal costs rather than average costs in pricing policies is widely evident.[1]

As in the national context, there is an absence of clear guides to optimal allocation of resources and strong practical limitations to administrative regulation. The reduction of pricing anomalies so as to allow market mechanisms better to play a leading role in allocating resources accordingly assumes special importance. In this connection, taxation of benefits resulting from city improvement expenditures, and charges to obtain compensation for social diseconomies attributable to private actions are of central concern in attaining a closer balance between private and social costs and benefits. Yet there has been remarkably little analysis of municipal taxation and its economic incidence. The great variety of tax and rate structures,

---

[1]Also of a general nature is the difficulty of establishing an appropriate "opportunity cost" for pricing capital for municipal undertakings when overall resources are so limited and when different types of projects have a widely differing impact on the tax base.

and the wide divergencies between theoretical incidence and actual collections, preclude a simple formulation of policy measures required.[1] Analysis is needed on an individual city basis. If one field more than others should be singled out, it is probably the modernizing of property taxes and their implementation to capture more of the gains resulting from public action and population growth.

The need for greater coordination of urban development programming to take into account the intersector linkages and permit better overall establishment of priorities is now widely acknowledged. The prevalent ad hoc decisions at the time of municipal or agency budgets quite evidently do not lead to preferable growth patterns. The decisions can be demonstrably counterproductive, accentuating longer term problems and making their solution more difficult. There is much less agreement on the form or degree of centralization which should be attempted. A concensus seems apparent on the need to relate urban programming and planning much more closely with municipal budgets and the decision makers. General objectives, priorities which are necessarily politically determined, and financial allocations can then condition from the start the programming effort and make it more realistic. At the same time, however, there is increasing recognition of the vital need, if the urban problems are to be countered, of stimulating local effort and self-help which require rather small organizational units.

It appears of little practical value to contend that the extensive interlinkages between sectors require a highly complex system of analysis and models projecting detailed future consequences; or that a high degree of coordination between all the agencies involved is a requisite for preparation and implementation of projects and programs. To make achievement of such a situation a condition for introducing improvements would indefinitely delay effective action towards solving the mounting problems.

The immediate need seems to be formulation of more general objectives and priorities, based on a cross-sectoral examination of broad alternatives of future patterns of urban growth, resource limitations and feasible implementation. Within these broad limits, alternative packages of definite projects and policy proposals can be evaluated, using a restricted analysis encompassing major indirect as well as direct benefits and costs. Aspects that can be quantified in economic cost/benefit terms should be separated from others, such as the im-

---

[1]It is in the context of overall taxation incidence that remedial action on the details needs to be considered. Dependence on indirect taxation resulting in a regressive general tax structure may be partially offset by subsidies, for example to mass transport. At present such offsets are more likely to be unintentional than deliberate.

pact on income distribution. Both groups of considerations are relevant to decision taking. But it is a fallacy to imagine that they can be adequately combined in a single measure, at least at this time. Rough calculations of orders of magnitude of key variables can provide sufficient quantitative insight to narrow substantially the field of practical alternatives for more intensive study.

The framework required for reasonable evaluation varies according to the type of project or program. Leading dynamic sectors, such as major urban transport projects, deserve particular attention and require greater depth of analysis than others. Detailed consideration of overall urban growth patterns and social and economic structure is not, however, necessary for taking a reasonable decision on installation of traffic lights. The framework needed for evaluating a new wholesale market may be quite limited if, as usually the case, the transport network indicates only a few possible focal points. A single "site and services" project, depending on site and relation to other areas, may not need to wait for an overall urban plan. The development of a limited area of urban extension, while requiring consideration of overall city growth patterns, may in many cases be sufficiently obvious as to warrant a fairly narrow framework of analysis if new basic decisions on alternative strategies of overall city development are not involved.

In other words, it would seem that within such frameworks the emphasis should be primarily on an incremental approach, based on relatively short-run programs explicitly linked to individual projects, budgets and the political decision process, particular attention being given to the sectors primarily shaping the pattern of future urban growth. That some imbalances will result requiring correction is inevitable. But it is difficult to perceive a better practical alternative to the present ad hoc urban decision making. Some imbalance is, in any case, a natural concomitant to dynamic growth and can provide the spur to further action. The experience gained should however produce progressive refinement of techniques and also the flexibility in adjusting objectives necessary to cope with the rapidly changing conditions of the urban centers.

A similar approach to institution building appears to be called for, centered on the links between political decision-making, municipal budgets and programming/project preparation activities. The trilogy of urban transport, housing, and land policy appear to merit particular attention due to their role in determining patterns of urban growth.

The problem of coordination of the wide variety of public urban activities is one with which all major urban centers of the world are contending. It would be unrealistic to assume that it can be easily

456

and quickly solved in the developing countries. But an incremental approach based on a definite program for the more dynamic activities seems to offer the greatest hope of progress. This implies that the pattern and degree of coordination must be expected to differ considerably from one city to another; local traditions and norms, and the need to stimulate local initiative and self-help, should be taken carefully into account in evaluating feasible organizational improvements.

THE BANK'S ROLE

A large part of Bank lending has been urban-oriented. Most of the lending for power, water and telephones, as well as the lending for port facilities, urban expressways and industry has been for urban purposes. The major part of transport and telecommunications lending has been to link urban areas. Bank lending in these various categories which has been directly urban-related totals roughly $13 billion, or over three-quarters of total lending to the developing countries.[1] On a more restricted definition, excluding inter-urban transport and telecommunications, the proportion is still nearly half.

Much of this lending has been concentrated on major cities. Over $2 billion, or more than 10% of all Bank lending, has been absorbed by 13 cities, each receiving $100 million or more. Projections for the next five years indicate no diminution in this effort.

In its early years, limited resources, emphasis on projects of high priority in terms of output, and on strong borrowing organizations (strong both administratively and financially), restricted the types of the Bank's urban-oriented projects. Electricity supply has represented over a third of the total and inter-urban transport nearly 40%.

In more recent years, the pattern has been changing. For example, for the 13 major cities, some 70% of the lending has been for electric power. This proportion declines to 40% for the projections for 1972-76. The financing of water supply operations began in the early 1960s and though still relatively small is beginning to represent a substantial portion of Bank lending to a number of cities such as Bogota, Singapore, Caracas and the Moroccan coastal towns. In the mid-sixties, the first loans were made for road projects within metropolitan areas. These, however, have remained a small proportion of the total.

The nature of past lending for urban purposes has had two consequences. The borrower has generally been an existing or newly set up

[1]Current borrowing countries, excluding Europe. Loans for services to both rural and urban areas have been split in proportion to the urban use. Annex 4 gives some details of the Bank's urban-oriented lending.

national or autonomous agency, rather than a municipality or traditional agency. Secondly, the limited scope of the Bank's contribution made it natural to concentrate on the particular field of activity of the project concerned. While it was recognized that the projects represented only part of a wider complex of activities, it could generally be assumed that necessary complementary action would be undertaken by other parties. To a large extent this approach implied a fairly rigid and constrained view of the "externalities," or wider repercussions, of the projects. Rate-setting and cash flow analysis could be considered largely in isolation from overall considerations of municipal finances and welfare.

Experience in lending to local agencies indicates that this is generally much more difficult than for national agencies. Local officials tend to be less qualified and local organizations less efficient and perhaps more often subject to political pressure. In such conditions, considerable staff time has been required to ensure that the funds lent are effectively used, that construction is carried out and subsequent operations are conducted with a reasonable degree of efficiency. A large measure of institutional reform has been both a requirement and a result of some of the Bank's lending for municipal water systems. In some cases, suitable organizations simply do not exist and must be created before any operation is possible.[1]

Rate problems, varying from one utility to another, have been involved in placing urban services on a financially viable basis. Resistance to rate increases in water supply appears greater than for telephones and power. Urban mass transit rates appear still more difficult to adjust. A subsidy to the poorer class of subscribers is common in the case of power and water.[2] Differentiation of this sort while maintaining an overall financially viable system seems likely to be much more difficult in mass transit. More generally, experience indicates that concentration on overall financial viability may not lead to sufficient attention to the *structure* of rates in the context of either social considerations or marginal costs.

A limited number of cases have arisen where it has been considered acceptable practice to combine the earnings of several utility services

---

[1]This has been the case where the rational organization of a project involves a number of independent jurisdictions, particularly where the interest of the parties involved are not identical. In the case of the water and sewerage system in Calcutta, for example, the Bank recommended formation of a Metropolitan Water Authority as necessary in order to devise and execute a rational plan for the area.

[2]However, the definition of subsidy may be based on an arbitrary allocation of common costs, and charges may be little connected with volume, particularly at peak periods. The marginal costs of adding low income users may in such cases be below the charges made.

to achieve a satisfactory yield—when, if each were taken singly, all would not give a satisfactory yield. For a few projects, it has been considered acceptable for a particular class of consumers to be subsidized out of general revenues paid by the state. Rural electrification and urban water supply to slum areas provide examples.

The physical standards of Bank-financed projects have also raised problems. A change from local standards and local ways of doing things is generally involved, for example regarding road standards, use of equipment in construction, or use of foreign consultants. While the authorities of developing countries are sometimes more aware than foreign consultants of the need to tailor standards to local conditions, the reverse situation of local agencies favoring the highest standards in use in developed countries appears more general.

The successful operation of projects outside of urban areas have occasionally been jeopardized, or at least limited in their benefits, by failure to develop complementary activity within the urban area. A few cases have arisen of city distribution systems not capable of handling the increased generation from a power project. Inter-urban highways or ports may sometimes have contributed to increased congestion in urban areas.

Although the Bank's lending covers only a small fraction of total national and urban investment, experience indicates that it can have an influence out of proportion to its size. The progressive extension of Bank activities has accordingly been accompanied by more comprehensive approaches to lending than in the Bank's early days. Work on country programming and individual economic sectors has already been considerably extended. With problems of urbanization becoming increasingly severe, attention is now being devoted to how the Bank's operations can be more consciously and effectively related to improving the efficiency of the urban centers both for production and for living.

The preceding discussion has focussed on the problems involved in ameliorating urban conditions in the developing countries. The situation is far too complex, variations between countries and between urban centers too great, information and methodology too poor, and institutional framework too weak to permit any simple determination of appropriate urbanization policies. To these limitations must be added a recognition that policy changes concerning major investment programs in developing, as in developed countries, are likely to be incremental in nature. That solutions will be difficult to achieve is obvious. On the other hand, the very weaknesses and often chaotic conditions of organization of urban growth, and the wide field for new types of policies, programming and projects, offer prospects of achieving substantial improvements even by measures appreciably short of optimal.

Many opportunities for Bank assistance are evident. To at least as great an extent as in other fields, the Bank can supplement the direct contribution of its lending to the total of resources by focussing attention on major issues and introducing new concepts, by suggesting ways to economize in resource use, by stimulating policies to reduce price distortions or improve controls and by assisting in the building of institutions.

Before turning to consideration of future Bank activities in this field, some limitations with which the Bank is confronted deserve mention. The most obvious is shortage of experience and expertise on the urbanization problems of developing countries both within and outside the Bank. Only relatively recently have the acuteness and magnitude of the problems, deriving as they do from the post-war upsurge in populations and economic development, come to be recognized. Other aid providers, like the Bank, have concentrated primarily on individual projects or sectors rather than a cross-sectoral approach combining both socio-economic and physical aspects. Few of the developing countries themselves have yet come to grips with the problems of formulating urbanization policies. Consultants experienced in the field are rare. When set against the number of the Bank's developing country members, and the number of their urban centers—more than 500 have populations over 100,000—it is obvious that the shortage of expertise available involves difficult choices in country and city selection.

Shortage of expertise relates not only to formulation of general urban strategies but also to individual projects. The possible range of projects contributing to urban efficiency is very large. However for many types, including such important sectors as mass transport, the expertise available is very limited. Techniques so far used to appraise metros in developed countries do not, for instance, appear adequate to evaluate overall benefits and opportunity costs in cities of developing countries.

The problem is less acute for types of projects in which the Bank already has considerable experience. Their influence on the pattern of urban development, however, differs widely. A wrong decision, wrong in the light of the priorities of an appropriately structured urban investment program, on a telephone or many other utility projects is unlikely seriously to affect the longer term pattern of urban growth. The project may be too soon, may not be of the highest priority, but it is likely to be beneficial and unlikely to prejudice desired future urban patterns. At the other extreme, an urban transport

460

project, an expressway for example, will radically affect the future development of the city and may involve much higher total urban expenditure than other solutions. In between, there are many projects of sufficient size to raise the problem of the proportion of development funds preempted.

A further limitation stems from the dearth of effective local urban agencies with which to collaborate and of projects adequately prepared for financing. The concentration of foreign aid on national or autonomous agencies has resulted in an absence of financial and techical assistance to major fields of urban investment. The development of municipal institutions and channels capable of dealing with the broad problems of urban areas and of preparing projects in this context has been slow. Judging by experience in other sectors, a combination of technical assistance with project lending may be the most efficient method of assisting in the critically important task of reinforcing, or at times creating, appropriate agencies. Shortage of municipal finance, exacerbated by inadequate tax structures, is a further serious limitation.

Because of these limitations, the Bank's activities specifically directed to the complex of urbanization problems will be initially focussed on a relatively small number of urban centers providing continuity of involvement over several years. In view of the inherent difficulties, the readiness of both national and urban authorities seriously to commit themselves to working out more rational urban policies and develop appropriate institutions must very strongly influence the choice. To gain experience, the selection will, however, contain both large and smaller cities, and cover both relatively wealthy and poorer countries. It is recognized that such a policy of concentration entails risks of changes in local conditions involving substantial parts of the program.

Shortage of expertise also indicates a need for selectivity in the types of project undertaken. Particular attention will be given to projects that exert a catalytic or dynamic influence on the pattern of urban growth through the project itself, or through the linkages with other sectors and the overall planning involved. Looked at from a different viewpoint, attention will be directed to projects which obviate, or substitute for, more expensive or lower priority alternatives.

For similar reasons, projects will be linked to policies which affect their functioning in the wider context of urban development. The Bank's lack of experience and the general limitation of knowledge must be clearly acknowledged. With local conditions so important in determining appropriate and feasible policies, extensive dialogue with local authorities and experts, and the possibility of use of local consultants will necessarily be involved. It is also recognized that less ambitious projects undertaken with more restricted evaluation either singly or as part of a package may provide the basis for building up collaboration with municipal authorities while studies for longer term urban development are being undertaken. This approach can guard against the search for "ideal" projects precluding good projects in the interim. It is also proposed to undertake some projects of new types of special relevance to developing country urban conditions, such as site and services projects, on a wider geographical basis if particularly favorable opportunities for gaining experience present themselves and the possibility exists of repeat loans of a similar type.

The Bank is now developing a program along the general lines indicated above. Preliminary economic reviews have been made of seven cities—Bombay (in some depth), Istanbul, Singapore, Bangkok, Kingston, Taipei and Djakarta. Specific urban project preparation has been undertaken also in six cities—Caracas, Istanbul, Dakar, Sao Paulo, Kuala Lumpur, Georgetown; and more general project identification in four—Bombay, Kingston, Djakarta and Seoul. Urban transport has been the principal project field in three cities, overall urban development (including transport) in two. A "site and services" project has been appraised in one city. Technical assistance for transport and land use planning studies has been extended in seven cities, Singapore, Kuala Lumpur, Bangkok, Nairobi, Teheran, Amman and Bogota. Reviews have been made of experience in the urban field, particularly "site and service" schemes and urban land control measures.

The Program of Urban Activities

A program of project activities directed specifically to urbanization problems has been established for FY1972-76. It involves some 30 urban centers and around $700 million of Bank lending and is summarized in Table 3. The program is necessarily more tentative than for longer established sectors of Bank lending where close connections have already been built up with borrowing agencies. Several of the projects are not yet specifically identified, being dependent on the results of initial studies. Some may be dropped and others substituted as part of this process and in order to bring the overall program more closely into line with the general approach to selection outlined above.

The supporting study program is extensive. In four city areas—Bogota, San Jose, Klang Valley (Malaysia), and Singapore—the Bank has already agreed to be executing agent for the United Nations

462

Table 3: Urbanization Projects FY1972-76

Major Element of Project	1972	1973	1974	1975	1976
"Site and Services," Urban Extension Areas, etc.	1	2	7	7	12
Integrated Urban Region		1		4	4
Roads and Traffic Improvement	1		1	2	1
Mass Transit		1	2	3	2
Wholesale Markets		1	1		1*
Other Urban Infrastructure and Land Development	1	1	1		1*
Gross Total	3	6	12	16	21
Net Total Allowing for Eliminations and Slippage	2	4	8	10	14

*Not yet identified.

Development Programme (UNDP) for studies of transport and urban pattern requirements designed to lead to identification of specific projects. Technical assistance will be provided to several other municipal and central government agencies for similar studies, including Nairobi, Teheran, Bangkok and Amman. The preliminary phases of more general studies to assist urban and national authorities in defining appropriate priorities for urban projects now under way in the five countries indicated earlier will be extended and studies in some other cities are contemplated. In the virtual absence of "ready made" projects conforming to the requirements of an overall urban strategy and ready for appraisal, considerable Bank assistance of this type appears a prerequisite for building a pipeline of suitable projects. Some of the projects identified are expected to be financed by other agencies.

The program of urbanization projects is being coordinated with programs of projects in more traditional sectors of Bank lending. In Istanbul, for example, an overall program related to priority investment needs has already been initiated, involving water supply and electricity distribution as well as urbanization projects including a wholesale market, land development and urban transport. Public utility projects are scheduled for almost all of the cities in the 1972-76 urbanization project program.

The Bank is coordinating its work with other agencies. The general shortage of experience and the desirability of a package approach to maximize the impact of urban projects accentuate the need for such effort. The United Nations Centre for Housing, Building and Planning (UNCHBP) is performing most valuable work in, for instance, devising housing programs compatible with technical and financial resources and on the social organization of site and services schemes. Two joint

463

programs with the UNCHBP are already under way.[1] Several other agencies are involved in specific areas of urban growth (See Annex 3). The Bank is assisting the UNCHBP in instituting regular inter-agency exchanges of information on activities with a view to sharing information and completing necessary studies by the most appropriate agency, avoiding duplication of effort, and reducing the burden on developing country administrations resulting from numerous uncoordinated missions. An area of Latin America has been selected for trial exchange of information. In the field of water supply and sewerage, a joint program has been established with the World Health Organization, in education with Unesco.

Formulation of National Urbanization Policies

The Bank will take further steps to help developing countries focus attention on urbanization problems and alternative courses of action, including the balance between rural development and the development of urban centers of differing sizes. It is the governments of the developing countries who must assume the responsibility of solving their urbanization/unemployment problems. Without strong commitment on their part, the difficulties of surmounting the obstacles to a more rational approach can hardly be overcome.

National development programs, budgets, and pricing and taxation policies largely determine the pattern of use of national development resources. The supplementary finance provided from the national budget to augment local resources, and the programs negotiated with foreign aid agencies, affect both the regional balance of resource allocation and the composition of investments. The incidence of national taxes, foreign exchange and interest rates, import and investment permits, and price controls are of no less importance.

The problems of urbanization have seldom been explicitly examined in this context of total national resource allocation. Responsibilities for preparation and implementation of development programs affecting the urban balance are usually split among many ministries and agencies. As a broad generalization, none has been ready to provide the leadership for a general policy in respect of urbanization—or to concede it to others. There is, however, rapidly growing recognition that analysis of the problems of urbanization should be part of national development programming and policy-making.

---

[1]The world-wide review of site and services experience, and community organization of the Senegal site and services project.

Attention to these basic problems will be progressively incorporated in the Bank's system of economic missions, economic reports and country programs. It is believed that the focus provided for specific examination of the problems through discussions with national authorities and local experts can serve to stimulate interest and action. It should also help in orienting the Bank's own program. Determination of precise objectives in the urbanization/unemployment field may be a chimera, at this stage at least; growing awareness and progress towards new decision patterns are not.

Technical Assistance in Urban Programming and Institution Building

Where interest shown and readiness to take action are apparent, the Bank will consider in association with other agencies—bilateral or private, as well as international—the provision to planning agencies of technical assistance on urbanization problems. The Economic Development Institute (EDI) of the Bank will also provide help in overcoming one of the worst bottlenecks, the critical shortages of personnel in developing countries capable of performing the programming tasks relevant to the urbanization problems at both national and municipal level. A first EDI course in this field is now under preparation.

The improvement of management in municipal agencies, or "institution building," is obviously crucial to the success of attempts to produce more efficient urban growth. In the Bank's public utility and other lending, an important element of technical assistance is often provided for this purpose. Technical assistance of at least comparable degree is envisaged in the new fields of urbanization project lending outlined below.

Urban Transport

The importance of mass transit to the movement of the labor force within the urban centers and its central role in determining urban growth patterns merit the inclusion of mass transit projects in the Bank's urbanization program. However, for such projects to contribute fully to solution of the urbanization problems, evaluation must be in the context of the urban transport system as a whole, and the impact on urban patterns and different income groups. Policies towards restraint on private automobile use have particular relevance to evaluation of the projects (see pages 436-441).

An extension of Bank lending to *bus systems* as the main form of mass transit is contemplated. The studies of transport systems noted on page 462 are expected to lead to between five and ten projects incorporating improvement of bus systems within the FY1972-76 period. Terminals and maintenance facilities may be included as well as buses. Weaknesses in present bus systems are a compound of inadequate equipment, poor administration (including lack of coordination between different bus entities) and inappropriate pricing policies. All three elements will necessarily be involved in project preparation and appraisal.

Provision of bus equipment under suppliers' credit has often contributed to a less than thorough analysis of operations and the needs for complementary investments and policies. Differences in terms of the credits, rather than suitability and performance, have often been deciding factors in the choice, with little relation to policies affecting transport demand or overall transport programming. Incorporation of suppliers' credit within an overall bus system improvement project may be possible. The possibility also exists of lending through the intermediary of an urban bus agency or metropolitan development agency, particularly when several independent bus operators are involved.

Urban railways, particularly the improvement of facilities which already exist, are also expected to form part of the urbanization program as it develops, as may light railways or *tram systems* with rights-of-way. As in the case of metros, improved methods for recovering some of the benefits reflected in increased urban property values are likely to be important to financial viability.

Urban Roads. Highways and streets carry virtually all intra-urban freight and most of the passenger traffic. While the development potential of roads between urban centers has received strong attention by the Bank in the past, little attention has been devoted to the corresponding intra-urban road development potential. As noted earlier, populations and areas of many of the cities are tripling within 20 years. Heavy investments in urban roads cannot be avoided. Good intra-urban distribution networks are required if the full benefits of intra-urban road projects are to be realized. Similar considerations apply to extension of port facilities.

The discussion on Urban Transport and Urban Patterns (pages 435, 442) indicates that well conceived road projects can contribute greatly to the efficiency of urban centers and promote patterns of urban growth which economize in use of total resources. But an ad hoc approach to relieving congestion may be not only expensive and ineffective but also compound future problems. The Bank's approach to lending for urban roads will accordingly require particular attention to the influence of the roads on alternative patterns of urban growth, to the main beneficiaries, to interdependencies with mass transit, and to policies towards restraining the use of private automobiles and guiding land use.

Several urban road projects are included in the program of urbanization projects for FY1972-76, either as the main element or as part of urban extension areas or the wider urban region projects. In one case, the project would provide a diversion route for a rapidly expanding port, in another an improved link between a major city and a satellite town as part of a wider urban region development. Two other "urban corridor" development projects are contemplated which are likely to include road construction.

Almost every city investigated could benefit greatly from comparatively inexpensive *traffic engineering and controls*. Capacity of existing streets could in many cases quickly be increased by 50 to 100% by installation of modern coordinated signal control systems, intersection redesign and other control measures. Besides providing almost immediate improvements in traffic flows and reductions in user costs, such measures can in some cases postpone or even eliminate the need for other much more costly projects. In some cases, traffic movements on an entire central street system might be substantially improved for less than the cost of building a mile of urban expressway. In other cases, short links between existing arteries could substantially reduce congestion by increasing effective capacity of existing roads or obviating the need to enter congested central districts.

One project involving traffic signals and other improvements is included in the program and another in this general category may be added. While the general considerations indicated above are relevant, the inter-linkages with mass transit improvements are likely to be particularly important. Projects may include technical assistance and training in traffic control.

Terminals. Freight terminals which economize on sorting and consolidation of goods shipments are of particular importance to the efficiency of urban areas. The number of trucks carrying goods on city streets may be reduced to a small fraction of their previous number by the construction of freight terminals at appropriate sites. At present, most cities in developing countries are suffering from inadequate and poorly sited terminals as a result of their rapid expansion. Besides improving the efficiency of freight handling and reducing costs, including those of distribution, new freight terminals can result in substantial benefits by reducing traffic congestion.

Two projects are under study for *wholesale markets* in cities where facilities are quite inadequate. Some retail distribution facilities and housing (above the commercial facilities) are likely also to be involved. One project has been identified in which the major element would be an *inter-modal passenger terminal* serving railways, buses and taxis. It would permit transfers between regional and urban-suburban rail and bus lines and could be instrumental in achieving effective coordination among these services and eliminate much congestion. Because of its inter-modal character, construction is outside the range of any single-mode transport agency.

Housing and Urban Works Projects

The problem of housing in urban centers is distinguished from other urban problems not least by the magnitudes of the needs and investment involved. Bank projects cannot realistically be expected to make a major direct contribution to the resources required. Moreover, the resources required are primarily of a local nature, and housing does not yield foreign income. For most developing countries, to incur foreign debt to cover more than a small operational housing expenditure would rapidly result in serious foreign debt servicing problems.

It is recognized, however, that less direct methods to stimulate housing construction, particularly for low-income groups where the need is greatest, can provide a very important contribution not only to social well-being but also to the growth of national output and employment. Moreover, the siting of new housing and its relation to the siting of employment can greatly facilitate urban patterns which economize in total resource use. These considerations, more fully developed on pages 445-450, point to Bank lending for relatively small projects in the housing field which can have a catalytic impact on local programs, particularly in their influence on institution building.

In line with these considerations, the urban project program in this field is concentrated on *"site and services"* and similar projects to provide urbanized land on which the occupants can build their own dwellings using self-help methods. One project is already being appraised in Senegal and several others are envisaged. The first project is illustrative. The land provided by the Government will be equipped with roads, water, sewage and power facilities. Most water and sewage facilities will be provided on a community basis. Education and health facilities are included in the project as well as sites for industrial, commercial, recreational and other developments. Exclusive of the social facilities and power grid, charges to occupants are expected to cover costs which will be only a small fraction of those of minimal housing schemes in the city.[1] A new institutional organization will be built up with technical assistance to form the basis of a national program on similar lines. The emphasis on use of local labor and employment will result in a somewhat higher proportion of local costs than has been customary in Bank lending.

As noted on page 445, public schemes for minimum housing, at least in the poorer countries, do not effectively reach the poorer groups forming a majority of the population even though they generally involve heavy subsidies either directly or indirectly through low interest rates. As other agencies have found, there are also considerable difficulties of management. The possibility is not excluded at a later stage when more experience has been gained, of direct financing of permanent housing where the particular circumstances warrant for example a pilot scheme. Such housing may also form a limited integral part of a wider urban project. Generally, however, direct financing of housing is not contemplated at this time. Indirect lending for housing through financing institutions is considered below.

One project has so far been identified for *improvement of low-income settlements*. Generalizations on the appropriate composition of such programs is difficult. Provision of minimum services of water, drainage, sewage (often cesspits), streets and street lighting, construction materials, schools and vocational training centers, may all constitute elements. As for site and services projects, security of tenure is an essential factor. Some elements may be provided directly out of public finances and be revenue earning, for example water supply. Others can be provided on a loan basis, for example construction materials. But in general, the benefits whether the obvious ones of improved living conditions and stimulation of self-help output and savings, or the more indirect ones of increased economic value of land, will not be directly revenue producing. The local element of expenditure will be high. However, a few Bank projects on a pilot basis appear justified in view of the low costs involved in relation to overall impact. Bank assistance for such programs or portions of them can be linked to action to improve the position of municipal finances through administrative and land tax reforms which are often involved, and be directed also to securing economies of overall urban development.

The rapidity of extension of urban areas offers great opportunities for economizing in resource use by more rational development of

---

[1]In some cases, public subsidies may be justified, but at much lower levels than those customarily involved in public housing schemes.

new areas. *Integrated extension areas* also offer the possibility of capturing a large part of the increase in land values produced by public action and growth of population. The rationale for such projects has already been outlined in greater detail on page 444. Bank assistance can play an important role in stimulating well organized and managed schemes. Preliminary investigations are proceeding for identifying two or three such projects for inclusion in the lending program. "Site and services" type schemes may form a part of such projects.

While direct lending for housing construction is not at present contemplated, indirect Bank assistance to housing through the stimulation of *housing finance institutions* more clearly fits the general considerations outlined on page 468. The non-availability of adequate housing is a serious cause of discontent among skilled labor and white-collar groups who must frequently live far from their jobs or accept high rents and poor housing closer in. Immobility due to shortage of housing and poor locations may greatly increase transport demands. Absence of financing institutions to collect savings and extend loans for housing for these and for the lower income groups often presents a major bottleneck. Experience shows that the volume of new savings collected by such institutions is a multiple of the amount of "seed capital" initially needed to start them.

The International Finance Corporation is prepared to consider "seed capital" for independent housing finance associations and similar institutions providing mortgage facilities where such projects form part of a program to stimulate savings and develop the capital market, and where subsidization of housing for relatively richer groups of the population is not involved. Discussions are at present being held with three countries. The Bank can also lend indirectly for similar purposes through local development corporations. Particular attention will be paid to the income groups for which housing is proposed, the mobilization of small savings and the possibilities for supporting improvements to substandard housing.

Urban Region Projects

Evaluation of many of the projects discussed above will necessarily involve consideration of a region considerably wider than the municipal limits. The interactions between growth in cities and that in surrounding areas extending 20 miles or more have a direct relevance to projects such as major urban roadways. Similarly the growth of satellite towns has repercussions on the major city with which they are intimately connected. The program contains three or four projects which are concerned with a package approach to the development of such urban regions or corridors. The elements of the package, however, are likely to fall under the previous headings.

The Design of Urban Projects

The Bank is already involved in detailed appraisal of standards of construction and services and frequently succeeds in introducing changes in project design which cut costs without endangering efficiency.[1] Further emphasis will now be given to opportunities for low-cost urbanization services of minimum "utility standards." Bank projects should occupy a leading position in this field. Urbanization projects such as "site and services" and urban extension areas will provide evaluations of alternative basic service systems that can have much wider applicability for Bank projects in urban areas.

The relation of capital costs, particularly the foreign exchange element, to local costs and employment will be given increased attention. Projects which would reduce *current* urban public expenditures will also merit particular consideration. Projects which would cut current costs of education per student through new techniques of teaching and capital costs through more intensive use of existing buildings are of particular moment in view of the large and rising share of education in total public expenditures and the opportunities provided by urban concentrations.

The difficulties of achieving such economies should not be underestimated. The initial definition of public utility projects by municipal agencies, and the stress laid on the maintenance of high standards by the authorities concerned, national leaders, consultants and others, often makes the suggestion of alternative lower-cost systems and of pricing policies—for example to restrict peak demand—a highly sensitive issue. Many normative judgments may be involved both related to the existing socio-political structures and to the balance of near-term to long-term benefits.

In these conditions, close working association and discussion of alternatives over a series of projects may provide a more fruitful influence than an attempt to impose conditions at an early stage too greatly at variance with what is locally acceptable at that time. However, appropriate clauses will be included where possible in terms of reference of consultants to cover evaluation of alternative lower levels of services and the risks of failure of supply and maintenance costs involved. More intensive consideration of the flexibility of demand in

---

[1]See for example the Sector Working Paper on Water Supply and Sewerage.

relation to costs, and feasible peak-pricing policies, may also serve to ensure adequate consideration of the wider issues. Sector review missions and reports will provide a particularly opportune occasion for discussion of such issues and the position of the sector in the general urban development policy.

Research

Research of operational significance is required in many fields. Given the limitations of staff, the Bank's contribution can comprise only a very small portion of the total. The objective accordingly is a blend comprising analysis of project experience, an "intelligence" function designed to keep abreast of research being conducted elsewhere and limited original research to fill gaps not covered by others when needed to support project activity. Collaboration with other agencies is particularly important for economizing in staff and avoiding dissipation and duplication of effort. The following paragraphs outline areas of particular concern rather than attempting to delineate at this time those aspects which should be chosen for a direct research effort by the Bank.

Strong emphasis is placed on the highly important but neglected field of analysis of *municipal financing and tax systems* in relation to development. The analysis should cover existing sources and expenditure patterns, elasticities of revenues to income variation and to rate increases, the regressivity or progressivity of tax structure, the influence of taxes on location and land values, the scope for capturing rent and betterment values, the possibilities for financing public involvement in the land market, relations with state and national revenues, and the impact of alternative development patterns. *Municipal expenditure patterns* have also been remarkably little investigated. Both fields are of cardinal importance in assessing alternative strategies for tackling urbanization problems or taking advantage of opportunities for economies. The Bank has already initiated some studies of the impact of provision of utilities on land values.

Many difficulties will be faced by governments in moving from a growing awareness of problems towards new decision patterns until more is known about *urban and inter-urban structure and economics*. A considerable amount of work, most of it of quite recent origin, is being conducted to develop satisfactory analytical frameworks in various institutions. As in the field of national and sectoral economics, a considerable effort will be required within the Bank to keep abreast of developments elsewhere and, in conjunction with work on eco-

472

nomic missions and country programs, to complement this with appropriate adaptations or innovations.

Closely allied to both the above subjects is the analysis of methods for more closely equating *private and social costs*. Systematic collection of data is a prerequisite for such studies, and the Bank has under way one study to provide information on the extent to which appropriate data for these purposes are available. Important questions for such analysis include the ways and costs of providing tax and credit incentives for smaller growth centers and of improving the sectoral and spatial allocation of investment packages within metropolitan areas.

Private automobiles represent a particularly acute case of divergencies between social and private costs and benefits. The Bank has begun a general study of this. The first phase is designed to collate existing studies and information on experience in the control of urban automobile use. The second phase is intended to be a cooperative effort in which other agencies as well as the Bank will review in greater depth the problems and policy alternatives for developing countries. A study in greater detail of vehicle user costs and charges has been made in Central America[1] and another is under way in Venezuela.

Also in the field of *transport,* continuing research is required on mass transit, urban roads and the location and design of ports and other inter-modal terminal facilities, including wholesale markets. The field includes least-cost means of reducing average commuting times, feasible means of financing mass transit systems and the effects of large existing ports and other major terminal facilities within major cities.

Site and services projects, both as individual programs and in the wider context of integrated urban extension areas represent a further field for cooperative effort including analyses of employment and savings aspects. A first joint review of experience by the Bank and the UNCHBP is already in progress. A considerably wider effort is needed, as is research into certain other aspects of urban *housing* such as the extent to which costs vary with living space, and quality and "completeness" of construction.

Urban *land* and land policies have been identified as of central importance in the urbanization process. The UNCHBP has already commissioned and conducted substantial investigations and intends to continue its work in this field. In addition, some further research may be necessary in order to provide a basis for judgments on allocation of funds to infrastructure services for improvement of low-income settlements, urban renewal or urban land extension.

---

[1]"A Study of Road User Charges in Central America" by A. Churchill and others. World Bank Occasional Paper No. 15.

The Bank can help assure adequate attention to the stimulation and assessment of *new techniques*. The construction and construction materials industries appear particularly in need of a concerted effort to develop new materials and evolve new techniques to improve productivity in developing countries. The Bank might aid directly in the assembly and comparison of data on incremental costs and benefits in urban development. Such information would be particularly valuable for judgment on alternative strategies and appraisal of specific projects. Much information is likely to be available in consultants' reports and municipal files as well as in individual studies. An appreciable effort of interpretation and analysis is required, for example of the overall differential in urban costs between different densities of housing, and the identification of the more variable elements of distribution of urban services. In a few fields, the Bank will itself undertake more intensive research on the relation between levels of service and their costs and benefits.

The development of *urban employment* analysis through examination of interdependencies among economic activities has great importance for the definition of appropriate urban policies and projects. Considerable gaps exist in knowledge of the operation, finance and distribution of earnings of small-scale activities, even though they affect a large proportion of the urban population. The indirect as well as direct employment effects of housing stand in need of greater analysis. The effects of legislative tax measures and legal or customary work restrictions (e.g. on double-shift working) on urbanization problems present a further field for study. It is a paradox that use of capacity of expensive investments often appears lower in the cities of developing countries than in developed ones. Inevitably, the return on Bank investments and feasible national urbanization/employment policies are affected. Much more information is also desirable on the pattern and causes of migration, and the experience of new migrants.

BACKGROUND DATA ON URBANIZATION

Chart 1: Degree of Urbanization Compared with GNP Per Capita

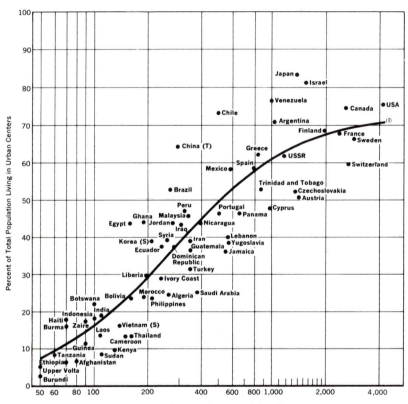

Sources:
1. GNP per capita—World Bank Atlas, 1971.
2. Urban Area Population—Kingsley Davis. World Urbanization 1950-1970, Vol. I, University of California, Berkeley, 1969. Definition of "urban" is based on differing national standards.
3. Percent of population in communities of more than 100,000 for Table 1 in main text are from UN Demographic Yearbook: 1970, New York, 1971, Table 9.
4. Figures based on most recent census or estimated from sample surveys ranging from 1960 to 1970.

(1) Curve fitted to type $y = \dfrac{a}{1 + be^{-c(\log \text{GNP})}}$

Table 1: Past and Projected Total and Urban Population of the Developing Nations of the World Bank 1920-2000

(1) Total regional population of Bank's developing nations (millions).*
(2) Total urban (20,000 and over) population (millions).*
(3) Annual rate of total population growth (%) for 20 years preceding.
(4) Annual rate of urban population growth (%) for 20 years preceding.

Developing Region		1920	1940	1960	1980	2000
East Asia and	(1)	131.5	182.8	268.7	450.3	730.6
Pacific[1]	(2)	5.7	15.3	41.3	104.6	232.7
	(3)	—	1.6	1.9	2.6	2.4
	(4)	—	5.1	5.1	4.8	4.1
South Asia[1]	(1)	333.1	422.2	579.9	941.7	1,381.2
	(2)	18.2	34.6	76.6	168.9	343.9
	(3)	—	1.2	1.6	2.5	1.9
	(4)	—	3.3	4.0	4.0	3.6
Southern Europe	(1)	111.5	140.0	176.6	234.8	314.0
and the Middle	(2)	24.5	36.2	59.4	91.1	141.1
East[2]	(3)	—	1.1	1.1	1.4	1.5
	(4)	—	2.0	2.5	2.2	2.2
Africa[3]	(1)	135.1	179.8	255.4	419.3	716.9
	(2)	5.7	11.2	30.8	76.7	189.5
	(3)	—	1.2	1.4	2.5	2.7
	(4)	—	3.4	5.2	4.7	4.6
Latin America	(1)	89.5	129.9	212.4	378.4	638.1
	(2)	12.9	25.5	69.7	163.4	342.0
	(3)	—	1.9	2.5	2.9	2.6
	(4)	—	3.5	5.2	4.4	3.8
Totals for all	(1)	800.7	1,054.7	1,493.0	2,424.5	3,780.8
countries	(2)	67.0	122.8	277.8	604.7	1,249.2
above	(3)	—	1.4	1.8	2.5	2.2
	(4)	—	3.1	4.2	4.0	3.7

*Source: UN Population Studies, No. 44, *Growth of the World's Urban and Rural Population, 1920-2000*. United Nations, New York, 1969. (ST/SOA/Series A/44.) Regional totals have been combined where possible to approximate World Bank groupings of developing regions.

[1] Burma is included in the totals for East Asia and the Pacific and not South Asia. North Korea and North Vietnam (not Bank members) could not readily be separated and are included in East Asia; they do not significantly affect the trends shown.

[2] Including Italy and Portugal which could not readily be separated. In mid-1969, the combined populations of these "developed" countries was 62.7 million (World Bank Atlas 1971) or approximately 31% of the regional population at that time.

[3] Excludes South Africa.

476

**Table 2: Growth of City Population (100,000 and over) in
Developing Nations of the World Bank 1920-1960**

(1) Total city population (millions).
(2) Annual % growth rate over preceding 20 years.

Developing Region		1920	1940	1960
East Asia and	(1)	3.4	10.3	30.7
the Pacific[1]	(2)	—	10.1	9.9
South Asia [1]	(1)	8.1	17.7	45.8
	(2)	—	5.9	7.9
Southern Europe	(1)	11.5	18.9	34.9
and the Middle East[2]	(2)	—	3.2	4.2
Africa[3]	(1)	2.4	5.7	19.4
	(2)	—	6.9	12.0
Latin America	(1)	4.9	11.1	35.6
	(2)	—	6.3	11.0
Total of all	(1)	30.3	63.7	166.4
countries above	(2)	—	5.5	7.3

Sources and Notes: See Table 1.

477

Table 3: Growth in Total Urban and Principal City Population 1960-1970 in Bank Developing Countries

Country	Total Population 1970 (thousand)	Annual Growth Rate 1960-70[1] (%)	Urban Population 1970 (thousand)	Annual Growth Rate 1960-70[1]	% Urban 1960	% Urban 1970[1]	Principal City	Population (thousand)	Annual Growth Rate 1960-70[1] (%)	Principal City Population as % of Urban Population
A. Eastern Africa										
Botswana	626	3.0	140	3.3	20	22	Gaberones	—[2]	—	—
Burundi	3544	2.0	93	7.2	2	3	Bujumbura	—	—	—
East African Community	32655	3.0	2661	7.6	6	8				
Kenya	10861	3.0	1000	5.1	8	9	Nairobi	500	6.0	50
Tanzania	13252	3.4	1049	8.6	5	7	Dar es Salaam[3]	350	9.0	33
Uganda	8542	2.5	612	9.2	4	7	Kampala	325	9.2	53
Ethiopia	24754	1.9	1643	2.4	6	7	Addis Ababa[3]	631	3.9	38
Lesotho	946	2.9	16	7.9	1.0	2	Maseru	—	—	—
Malagasy	6864	2.4	891	4.3	11	13	Tananarive[3]	432	5.6	48
Malawi	4429	2.5	240	10.1	3	5	Blantyre Limbe[3]	174	—	73
Mauritius	857	2.7	469	5.3	42	55	Port Louis	146	—	31
Rwanda	3624	3.2	10	8.3	.2	.3	Kigali	—	—	—
Somalia	2941	3.9	713	6.0	20	24	Mogadiscio	200	—	28
Sudan	15631	2.9	1303	4.3	7	8	Khartoum	452	3.4	34
Swaziland	419	4.9	18	9.4	3	4	Mbabane	—	—	—
Zaire	17405	2.1	3000	3.9	15	17	Kinshasa[3]	580	10.0	19
Zambia	4326	3.1	1137	6.4	19	26	Lusaka	225	—	20
B. Western Africa										
Cameroon	5839	2.2	748	6.8	8	13	Douala	229	4.0	31
Central African R.	1585	2.6	1207	8.4	14	24	Bangui	180	—	15
Chad	3562	1.6	275	7.9	4	8	Fort Lamy	—	—	—
Congo Peop. R.	895	1.5	345	5.4	26	39	Brazzaville	190	4.0	—
Dahomey	2732	2.9	438	6.0	12	16	Cotonou[3]	175	—	—
Gabon	485	1.0	101	6.5	12	21	Libreville	—	—	—
Gambia	364	2.0	37	3.8	9	10	Bathurst	—	—	—
Ghana	8808	2.8	2990	6.8	23	34	Accra	752	6.8	25
Guinea	4011	2.7	451	6.6	—	11	Conakry	220	7.0	49

Ivory Coast	4289	2.9	1244	9.3	16	29	Abidjan	550	11.0	—
Liberia	1168	1.7	344	10.4	13	30	Monrovia	—	—	—
Mali	5010	2.0	439	5.7	6	9	Bamako	225	5.6	—
Mauritania	1161	1.9	28	2.4	2	2	Nouakchott	—	—	—
Niger	3845	3.0	118	2.4	3	3	Niamey	—	—	—
Nigeria	66000	3.9	13826	6.0	17	21	Lagos[3]	800	6.0	6
Senegal	3958	2.5	1081	4.0	24	27	Dakar	600	—	52
Sierra Leone	2500	1.4	360	3.8	11	14	Freetown[3]	175	—	49
Togo	1851	2.5	305	8.2	10	17	Lome	180	—	59
Upper Volta	5363	2.2	253	5.1	4	5	Ouagadougou	—	—	—
C. East Asia and Pacific										
British Solomon Islands	153	2.1	6	4.7	3	4	—	—	—	—
China (Taiwan)	14402	3.0	9272	4.1	59	64	Taipei	2150	4.7	23
Fiji	540	3.2	106	3.9	18	20	—	—	—	—
Indonesia	118184	2.3	21136	4.2	15	18	Djakarta[3]	4500	4.7	21
Khmer R.	6850	2.3	878	4.8	10	13	PhnomPenh	700	7.6	80
Korea, South	32168	2.6	12547	4.1	28	39	Seoul[3]	4661	8.0	37
Malaysia	9376	3.1	4291	5.9	35	46	Kuala Lumpur[3]	650	4.0	15
Papua and New Guinea	2348	1.2	29	7.3	7	1.2	—	—	—	—
Philippines	38290	3.5	8867	4.3	22	23	Manila	4100	4.3	46
Singapore	2113	2.6	2113	2.6	100	100	Singapore	2113	2.6	100
Thailand	31239	3.0	4659	4.5	11	13	Bangkok	2100	6.0	45
D. South Asia										
Afghanistan	16715	1.8	1128	2.3	6	7	Kabul	500	3.2	44
Ceylon	12685	2.5	2100	3.6	15	17	Colombo	1250	2.8	60
India	544621	2.4	102433	2.9	18	19	Calcutta	5153	1.8	5
Iran	28805	3.0	11306	4.8	33	39	Teheran	3250	6	29
Nepal	11143	2.0	552	8.0	3	5	Katmandu	440	7.9	80
Pakistan	114191	2.1	18178	4.3	13	16	Karachi	3246	5.6	18
E. Europe, Middle East and North Africa										
Cyprus	631	.9	302	3.9	36	48	Nicosia	112	—	37
Egypt, Arab R.	33283	2.4	14544	4.0	38	44	Cairo	5600	4.1	38
Finland	4768	.7	3259	2.7	56	68	Helsinki	757	3.2	23

Table 3: Growth in Total Urban and Principal City Population 1960-1970 in Bank Developing Countries (continued)

Country	Total Population 1970 (thousand)	Annual Growth Rate 1960-70(1) (%)	Urban Population 1970 (thousand)	Annual Growth Rate 1960-70(1)	% Urban 1960	% Urban 1970(1)	Principal City	Population (thousand)	Annual Growth Rate 1960-70(1) (%)	Principal City Population as % of Urban Population
Greece	8876	.7	5552	1.6	57	63	Athens	2425	3.0	44
Iceland	212	1.8	152	2.7	67	72	Reykjavik	—	—	—
Iraq	9089	2.9	3954	4.0	39	44	Baghdad	1250	4.4	32
Israel	2908	3.2	2365	3.7	77	81	Tel-Aviv	900	3.0	—
Jordan	2421	3.6	1064	4.8	39	44	Amman(3)	350	4.5	33
Lebanon	2600	2.1	1034	4.0	33	40	Beirut	600	3.4	58
Morocco	15519	2.9	5484	4.9	29	35	Casablanca	1462	4.2	27
Portugal	9723	.9	3549	1.7	34	37	Lisbon	1500	1.2	42
Southern Yemen	1000	2.6	325	4.2	28	33	—	—	—	—
Spain	32958	.8	19369	1.7	44	59	Madrid	2990	2.8	15
Syria	6101	2.9	2351	3.4	37	39	Damascus(3)	670	2.4	28
Tunisia	4882	1.6	2118	3.2	37	43	Tunis(3)	700	.8	33
Turkey	35225	2.5	11007	4.2	27	31	Istanbul	2600	5.0	24
Yemen Arab Republic	5000	—	301	5.9	3	6	—	—	—	—
Yugoslavia	20649	1.2	7986	4.8	27	39	Belgrade	1165	3.7	15
F. Central America and Caribbean										
Costa Rica	1767	4.2	640	4.6	35	36	San Jose	435	5.4	68
Dominican Republic	4324	3.6	1601	5.7	31	37	Santo Domingo(3)	650	5.9	41
El Salvador	3499	3.6	1392	4.0	38	39	San Salvador	375	4.6	27
Guatemala	5172	3.1	1892	4.9	31	37	Guatemala City	770	5.0	41
Guyana	737	2.8	221	3.2	29	30	Georgetown	200	3.1	41
Honduras	2703	3.4	700	5.2	22	26	Tegucigalpa	281	5.9	40
Jamaica	2020	2.2	727	4.3	29	36	Kingston	560	5.0	77
Mexico	50624	3.8	29468	5.2	51	58	Mexico City(3)	3541	5.0	12

Nicaragua	1989	3.5	869	4.6	39	44	Managua	350	5.9	40
Panama	1465	3.1	685	4.4	41	47	Panama	440	4.9	64
Trinidad & Tobago	1106	2.9	589	6.0	40	53	Port of Spain	—	—	—
Venezuela	10390	3.5	7934	5.6	62	76	Caracas	2147	5.5	27
G. South America										
Argentina	24089	1.9	16978	2.4	57	71	Buenos Aires	9410	3.0	56
Bolivia	3956	1.4	1002	2.4	23	25	La Paz	500	2.3	50
Brazil	93545	2.8	50025	4.6	45	54	Sao Paulo	8405	6.4	17
Chile	9510	2.0	7007	3.4	65	74	Santiago	2600	3.1	37
Colombia	21168	3.2	11648	5.0	46	55	Bogota	2500	7.0	22
Ecuador	6089	3.4	2238	4.7	33	38	Guayaquil[3]	800	5.9	36
Paraguay	2378	3.1	852	3.5	34	36	Asuncion	445	3.6	52
Peru	13581	2.1	6256	3.3	41	46	Lima	2500	5.1	40
Uruguay	2889	1.3	2433	2.9	72	84	Montevideo[3]	1530	4.7	63

[1] Source: Kingsley Davis, *World Urbanization 1950-1970, Vol. I*: Basic Data for Cities, Countries and Regions, University of California, Berkeley 1969. The 1970 figures are projections. The annual growth rates for these principal cities where recent data is available have been adjusted.

[2] When no population figure is given for principal city, the population is under 100,000.

[3] Figures refer to the city area as opposed to the metropolitan area.

Table 4: Estimates of Migrants as a Percentage of Recent Population Increases

City	Period	Total Population Increase (Thousands)	Migrants as a Percentage of Total Population Increase
Abidjan	1955-63	129	76
Bogota	1956-66	930	33
Bombay	1951-61	1,207	52
Caracas	1950-60	587	54
	1960-66	501	50
Djakarta	1961-68	1,528	59
Istanbul	1950-60	672	68
	1960-65	428	65
Lagos	1952-62	393	75
Nairobi	1961-69	162	50
Sao Paulo	1950-60	2,163	72
	1960-67	2,543	68
Seoul	1955-65	1,697	63
Taipei	1950-60	396	40
	1960-67	326	43

Sources:

Etude Socio—Economique de la Zone Urbaine D'Abidjan, Societe d'Economie et de Mathematique Appliquees, Paris, 1967.

Bogota Transport and Urban Development Study, Phase I (draft report), Vol. 1, Freeman, Fox, Wilbur Smith and Assoc. Restrepo y Uribe Ltda., Bogota, 1970.

Report on the Development Plan for Greater Bombay 1964, Municipal Corp. of Greater Bombay, Bombay, 1964.

Caracas 1990, Plan de Desarrollo Urbano, 1 Etapa Del Estudio, Consejo Municipal del Distrito Federal Oficina Municipal de Planeamiento Urbano, Caracas, 1968.

R. Oliver, "Greater Djakarta, The Capital City of Indonesia", Washington, D.C. 1970.

"Istanbul Metropolitan Alan Planlama Calasmalari", Mimarlik Special Issue, May 1970, 55-77.

Urban Government for Metropolitan Lagos, B. A. Williams and A. H. Walsh, Praeger, N.Y. 1968.

"Population, Employment and Earnings," (draft report), Nairobi Urban Study Group, 1971.

Caracterizacao Preliminar Da Regiao Da Grande Sao Paulo, Gegran, Sao Paulo revised edition 1969.

Yoon, Jong-Joo, "A Study on the Migration Magnitude of Seoul," Journal of Population Studies, No. 2, Seoul, 1966.

Taipei City Statistical data, Taipei Municipal Government, Taipei, 1950, 1960. 1967.

Table 5: Percentage of Urban Population in 1970 of 138 Countries Grouped by GNP per Capita in 1968

Per Capita GNP in 1964 in US$

Less than 100		100-200		200-500		500-1000		1000-2000		2000 and more	
Rwanda	0	Mauritania	2	Fiji	20	Romania	39	Libya	28	Switzerland	60
Burundi	3	British Solomon Islands	3	Rhodesia	20	Hungary	43	Puerto Rico	48	Sweden	66
Niger	3	Papua & New Guinea(1)	4	Gabon	21	Bulgaria	47	Austria	51	Canada	75
Malawi	5	Swaziland	4	Korea, North	22	Panama	47	Italy	51	U.S.A.	75
Nepal	5	Mozambique	6	Saudi Arabia	25	Cyprus	48	Czechoslovakia	52	Kuwait	80
Upper Volta	6	Uganda	7	Honduras	26	South Africa	50	Norway	55		
Yemen	6	Kenya	9	Zambia	26	Ireland	51	Netherland Antilles	58		
Afghanistan	7	Angola	11	Ivory Coast	29	Trinidad & Tobago	53	Luxemburg	66		
Ethiopia	7	Khmer R.	13	Guyana	30	Poland	56	New Zealand	68		
Tanzania	7	Cameroon	13	Turkey	31	Spain	59	Finland	68		
Chad	8	Thailand	13	Albania	35	U.S.S.R.	59	France	68		
Sudan	8	Sierra Leone	14	Costa Rica	36	Greece	63	Belgium	69		
Mali	9	Ceylon	17	Jamaica	36	Argentina	62	Iceland	72		
Guinea	9	Philippines	23	Paraguay	36	Venezuela	71	Netherlands	76		
Laos	11	Central African Rep.	23	Portugal	37	Hong Kong	100	United Kingdom	79		
Malagasy	13	Bolivia	24	British Honduras	37	Singapore	100	Denmark	80		
Burma	13	Viet-Nam, Rep. of	25	Dominican Rep.	37			Israel	81		
Dahomey	16	Senegal	26	Guatemala	37			Germany, Fed. Rep. of	82		
Pakistan	16	Liberia	27	Ecuador	38			Japan	83		
Togo	17	Southern Yemen	30	Surinam	38			Germany, East	84		
Zaire	17	Ghana	33	Congo, Peop. R.	39			Australia	88		
Haiti	18	Morocco	34	Yugoslavia	39						
Indonesia	18	Algeria	35	El Salvador	40						
India	19	Syria	37	Iran	39						
Nigeria	21	Korea, Rep. of	38	Lebanon	39						
Botswana	22	Tunisia	39	Iraq	43						
China (Mainland)	23	Egypt, Arab R.	43	Jordan	44						
Somalia	24			Nicaragua	44						
Viet-Nam, North	24			Barbados	45						
				Malaysia(2)	46						
				Peru	46						
				Mongolia	52						
				Brazil	54						
				Colombia	55						
				Mauritius	55						
				Cuba	58						
				Mexico	58						
				China, Rep. of	58						
				Chile	64						
				Uruguay	74						
Median 13		23		38		55		68		75	

Note: The percentage of urban population is the proportion of the population defined as urban by the country's own definition to the total country population shown in percentage.

(1) Percentage of urban population in Papua only.
(2) Percentage of urban population in West Malaysia only.

Source: Per capita GNP from World Bank documents.
Percentage of Urban Population from Kingsley Davis, *World Urbanization 1950-1970, Vol. I*, University of California, 1969.

Table 6: Extent of Slums and Uncontrolled Settlements
in Various Cities in Developing Countries

				Uncontrolled Settlement	
Country	City	Year	City Population (Thousands)	Total (Thousands)	At Percentage of City Population
Africa					
Senegal	Dakar	1969	500	150	30
Tanzania	Dar es Salaam	1967	273	98	36
Zambia	Lusaka	1967	194	53	27
Asia					
China (Taiwan)	Taipei	1966	1,300	325	25
India	Calcutta	1961	6,700	2,220	33
Indonesia	Djakarta	1961	2,906	725	25
Iraq	Baghdad	1965	1,745	500	29
Malaysia	Kuala Lumpur	1961	400	100	25
Pakistan	Karachi	1964	2,280	752	33
Republic of Korea	Seoul	1970	440 (d.u.)	137 (d.u.)	30
Singapore	Singapore	1966	1,870	980	15
Europe					
Turkey	Total Urban Population	1965	10,800	2,365	22
	Ankara	1965	979	460	47
		1970	1,250	750	60
	Izmir	1970	640	416	65
North and South America					
Brazil	Rio de Janeiro	1947	2,050	400	20
		1957	2,940	650	22
		1961	3,326	900	27
	Brasilia	1962	148	60	41
Chile	Santiago	1964	2,184	546	25
Colombia	Cali	1964	813	243	30
	Buenaventura	1964	111	88	80
Mexico	Mexico City	1952	2,372	330	14
		1966	3,287	1,500	46
Peru	Lima	1957	1,261	114	9
		1961	1,716	360	21
		1969	2,800	1,000	36
Venezuela	Caracas	1961	1,330	280	21
		1964	1,590	556	35
	Maracaibo	1966	559	280	50

Source: U.N. General Assembly, *Housing, Building and Planning, Problems and Priorities in Human Settlements,* Report of the Secretary General August 1970, Annex III, p. 55. Definitions vary. Additional details are given in the source quoted.

Note: d.u. = dwelling units

Table 7: Public Transportation in Selected Cities

City	Population (Thousands)	Type of Public Transport	Number of Units Owned	Average Daily Passengers (Thousands)	Average Daily Public Transport Trips per Habitant
Abidjan (1970)	550	Buses	200	220-250	0.45
Addis Ababa (1968)	500	Buses	135	80	0.16
Bombay (1967)	5,200	Buses Suburban rail	1,338 1,160 trains/day	1,810 2,130	0.35 } 0.76 0.41 }
Caracas (1966)	1,719	Buses Por Puestos[1]	925 6,000	1,300	0.76
New Delhi (1966)	3,000	Buses Suburban rail	820 110	750 35	0.26
Sao Paulo (1967)	5,253	Buses/Trolley Suburban rail	7,000	4,718	0.90
Tehran (1966)	2,711	Buses	1,600	1,900	0.76
Calcutta (1965)	7,200	Buses Suburban rail Trams	886 450 trains/day 459	1,500 650 850	0.21 } 0.09 } 0.42 0.12 }
Bogota (1969)	2,340	Buses	4,170	3,782	1.62

Source: World Bank documents.
[1] Collective taxis operating on regular routes

Table 8: Automobile Registrations in Selected Cities

City	Year	Population National	City	Registered Automobiles National	City	Persons per Car National	City	City's % of National Total Population	City's % of National Total Automobiles
		(millions)		(thousands)				Popu-lation	Auto-mobiles
Abidjan	1968	4.1	0.51	43.9	30.9	93	16.5	12.5	70.4
Bangkok	1966	31.7	2.50	99.0	72.0	320	34.8	7.9	72.8
Bogota	1969	20.2	2.34	146.0	52.0	138	45.0	11.6	35.6
Bombay	1966	475.0	5.00	420.0	61.0	1,131	82.0	1.1	14.5
Caracas	1966	8.9	1.72	420.0	151.5	21	11.3	19.3	36.1
Djakarta	1969	118.0	4.50	212.2	77.2	557	58.0	3.8	36.6
Nairobi	1965	9.5	0.45	70.0	41.6	135	10.8	4.7	59.4
San Jose (C.R.)	1966	1.5	0.19	27.2	13.0	56	14.2	12.3	48.1
Sao Paulo	1967	86.6	5.25	1,417.9	366.1	61	14.4	6.1	25.8
Tehran	1966	25.1	2.71	174.0	85.5	144	31.7	10.8	49.1

Source: Automobile Manufacturers Association Facts and Figures and World Bank documents.

Table 9: Alternative Estimates of Passenger Capacity—
Peak Hour Volumes/Track or Lane

		Rail Rapid Transit	Bus Rapid Transit	Private Auto on Expressway
	1.	40-60,000	47,000	7,500
	2.	62,000	23,000	7,500
	3.	40,000	20,000	
	4.	25,000	4,000	1,100
	5.	28,000	9,000	2,250
	6.	35-40,000	22,500 (6,000)	3,200-3,600
	7.		28,000	
	8.	(see Table 10)	90,000	10,000
	9.	36-48,000	14-18,000	4,000
	10.	30-72,000	6- 7,500	

Sources:

1. Highway Research Board, *Highway Capacity Manual,* Special Report No. 87, 1965, p. 345. Calculations are theoretical, not based on actual experience. The assumptions are:—Rail: Headway of 1.5 minutes 40 10-car trains, 24,000 seated passengers plus standing passengers. 940 buses per hour per bus lane, headway—3.8 seconds, bus seating capacity—50, speed—33 mph. Auto: 1,500 automobiles per hour, seating capacity—5. If 1.6 people per car is assumed the number of passengers would be 2,400.

2. Wilbur Smith & Associates, *The Potential for Bus Rapid Transit,* February 1970, Tables 8 and 10, and p. 147. Rail: Actual peak-hour passenger load on IND-8th Ave. Express, New York. This is the greatest volume among the seven different lines surveyed by the Institute of Traffic Engineers in 1965. Bus: Actual passenger load on the exclusive bus lane, the ramp to bus terminal, New York—the highest volume carried on the 14 expressways and local streets surveyed by the Institute of Traffic Engineers. Auto: Actual peak-hour passenger volume on Chicago's Congress Expressway.

3. Wilbur Smith and Associates, *Future Highways and Urban Growth,* 1961, p. 143, adopted from Hornburger, Wolfgang S., "Rapid Transit: Present and Future," *Traffic Quarterly,* Volume XIV, April 1, 1960.

4. D. J. Reynolds, "Urban Motorways and Urban Congestion," in George A. Smerk (ed.) *Readings in Urban Transportation,* Indiana University Press, Bloomington, Indiana, 1968, p. 225.

5. Walter S. Rainville, "The Importance of Urban Transit and Its Effective Passenger Capacities," in George A. Smerk (ed.) *Readings in Urban Transportation,* Indiana University Press, Bloomington, Indiana, 1968, pp. 176-177. Subway: A rapid transit train of eight cars operating on a 2-minute headway. Bus: A transit bus on an expressway lane operating on a peak-hour headway of 30 seconds (120 buses per hour) at 1,500 load factor. 1 bus lane = 4 auto lanes. Auto: An expressway lane operating at a rate of 1,500 vehicles per hour and carrying an average of 1.5 occupants.

6. Wilbur Smith and Associates, *Future Highways and Urban Growth,* New Haven, 1961, pp. 144-147. Rail: Includes standing space and assumes 10-car trains, 50 seats per car, and 90-seconds headways. Bus: Assumes use of 400-450 fifty-seat buses with no stops and unimpeded use of freeway lanes. If buses stop at stations along freeways, an estimated 120 buses with 6,000 seats can be accommodated. Auto: Assumes an occupancy of 1.8 persons per car.

7. U.S. Dept. of Transportation, *Resource Book on the Federal-Aid Highway Program,* Sept. 1971, p. 322. Actual operations on a freeway lane have shown that close to 660 buses carrying almost 28,000 persons in one hour are possible with capacity to spare.

8. U.S. Department of Transportation, *Resource Book on the Federal-Aid Highway Program,* Sept. 1971, pp. 335-336. Calculations of theoretical possibilities. Rail: See Table 10. Bus: Based on maximum bus capacities established by different experts for an exclusive bus freeway lane (Texas Transportation Institute—1,250 buses/hour, FHWA —1,450 buses/hour, General Motors—1,200 buses/hour. Auto: 2,000 automobiles per hour on a freeway lane under maximum flow conditions. Assumes an occupancy of 5 persons per car. The estimate is for the maximum figure based on the lowest alternative, with an average of 50 seats and 25 standees possible per bus.

9. Walter S. Rainville, *"The Importance of Urban Transit and Its Effective Passenger Capacities,"* in Smerk (ed.) pp. 175-178. Rail: Rapid transit 10-car train, 90-120 passengers/car at headways of 1.5 minutes and 40 trains per hour. Bus: 240 transit buses on a freeway operating on a peak-hour headway of 15 seconds. Auto: 2,000 vehicles per lane per hour with an occupancy of 2 persons per vehicle.

10. Wilbur Smith & Associates, *"Center City Transportation Project: Urban Transportation Concepts,"* September 1970, Table 28.

486

Table 10: Capacities of Subways

a. Passenger Capacities on Actual and Proposed Subway Systems

City	Seats/Car	Standees/Car	Cars/Train	Trains/Hr.	Theoretical Capacity (Persons/Hr.)
New York	50	250	10	32	99,000—16,000
Toronto	83	217	6	30	54,000—14,940
Rotterdam	80	210	4	30	34,000— 9,600
San Francisco	72	—	10	40	28,000—28,000
Montreal	40	100	9	24	30,200— 8,640
Pittsburgh	28	42	10	30	21,000— 8,400
Washington, D.C.	81	94	8	30	72,000—19,440

b. Maximum Passenger Capacity vs. Actual Usage

City	Capacity	Volume	Present Usage
(Existing Systems)			
New York	99,200	61,400	0.62
Chicago	37,500	10,373	0.28
Cleveland	11,200	6,211	0.55
Toronto	54,000	35,166	0.65
(Planned Systems)			
San Francisco	88,800	28,000 (est.)	0.32
Washington, D.C.	42,000	31,900 (est.)	0.76

c. Reported Peak-Hour Track Loads

City	Persons per Track per Hour
Toronto	30,000
Chicago	28,000
Philadelphia	20,000
Boston	18,000
Cleveland	10,000

Sources: Tables a and b from the U.S. Department of Transportation, *Resource Book on the Federal Aid Highway Program,* Sept. 1971. pp. 338-339 and Table c from Wilbur Smith and Associates, *Future Highways and Urban Growth,* New Haven, 1961, p. 126.

URBAN LAND POLICY

Introduction

Three principal problems affect policies on the use of urban land in the developing countries—the difficulty of acquiring land for development within the urban areas, the inefficient pattern of urban development and land use, and the severe limitation of resources for further urban development.

The severity of these problems varies greatly between cities because of the great diversity of urban patterns around the world—differences in cultures and in the organization of society; in legal and communal tenure of land; in major economic activities and political-economic organization; and in historical patterns of development. All of these factors have influenced, and have in turn been affected by, patterns of land use and land ownership.

In virtually all cities of developing countries there are problems of underutilization of existing serviced land and of constraints on urban land extension. Underutilization frequently results in part from historical patterns of development—the types of buildings constructed, the layout of streets, etc.—and withholding of land from the market for investment speculation, to which may be added deficiencies in zoning laws and/or their enforcement. Development is restricted by the poverty of the bulk of the population and the paucity of municipal government resources. If a substantial proportion of the land is owned by a small number of large landowners, their monopoly/oligopoly behavior may further retard inner city development and extension of the urban area. High and rising land prices, though partly an inevitable result of rapid urban population and economic growth, are accentuated, perhaps greatly, by such factors. Rising prices encourage speculative withholding of both serviced and unserviced land, which aggravates all three basic problems. Other factors retarding urban land extension are constraints on public sector provision of infrastructural support for private sector development either *ex ante* or *ex post* or simple failure of owners to perceive suitable investment returns from urban land development. As a result, substantial areas of unplanned vacant land and low density development are common features, with the percentage of vacant land reportedly ranging as high as 75%.

In some cities substantial tracts of land are owned by government and in a few of these (of which Singapore is a notable example) this "opportunity" has been seized with vigor and no little imagination. In most cities, however, because such land falls under the control of many ministries or government entities, because there is no development program, or for some combination of these and other reasons, the land is not brought into productive use. Many other factors may have an impact on curtailing development or contribute to undesired patterns of development. Particular difficulties arise, for example as in Bombay, where rent controls inhibit the construction of medium and low income housing in or near the center city where most jobs exist, the absence or inadequacy of public services (e.g. water and telephones) discourages the location of economic activities in outlying areas of the city where many workers live, and heavy subsidization of the transport network tends to fossilize this historically determined pattern.

Objectives

The more commonly identified problems of rapid rise in land prices and speculative withholding need to be viewed against this background of scarcity of land readily available for construction, inefficient patterns of urban development and severe resource limitations.

Rather extensive legal powers frequently exist on paper to deal with these problems. However, a lack of clarity as to objectives has meant that these have not always been appropriately designed. Even where they have been, they have usually not been used with great frequency or determination. The objectives would seem to be fivefold:

1. To increase the supply of urban land for development.

2. To mobilize the necessary financial (and other) resources for development.

3. To influence development so as to improve patterns of land use and the spatial and sectoral allocations of investment.

4. To achieve a greater measure of distributional equity on both the resource and the expenditure side, keeping in mind externalities and secondary income effects.

5. As part of 2 and 4, to obtain for public use a satisfactory portion of betterment values in private land which are induced by public investment.

Instruments[1]

A number of attempts have been made to develop a taxonomy for the instruments or measures for achieving these objectives. None have proved free from problems. To record experience in the market economies to date, however, three types of measures may be distinguished.

---

[1]This section draws heavily upon the very useful papers prepared for the United Nations Interregional Seminar on Urban Land Policies and Land Use Control Measures held in Madrid, 1-13 November, 1971.

A. Non-tax Measures designed to influence private development.

B. Tax Measures designed to influence private development and/or raise revenues for public development.

C. Direct Public Involvement in the land and land development market designed to substitute public for private sector development, to encourage certain private sector development and/or raise revenues.

It should be pointed out, at the outset, that for purposes of brevity and clarity these measures are discussed individually. However, in practice many are highly interdependent and the use of one alone may be ineffective. Similarly, they vary greatly in the administrative burdens imposed and their practical usefulness should be assessed with this in mind.

A. Non-tax Measures

Non-tax measures cover regulation of land ownership, trading and use and public assistance for development. The most important regulations affecting land ownership are those having to do with a forced transfer of ownership rights when land is required for public purposes. Others seek to improve the functioning of the land market by forcing vacant land into use and facilitating trading. Regulation of land trading has generally been confined to the establishment of price controls. Land use controls exist in most countries, whether or not any formal planning exists, and include zoning and sub-division regulations; building regulations and development permits; and planning concepts such as controlled areas and urbanized or "urbanizable" limits. Various schemes of public assistance for land assemblage and joint adjustment of land use planning have been adopted in recent years.

1. Regulation of Land Ownership

Almost every country has adopted regulations which limit private ownership rights in cases involving the general public welfare. In North America eminent domain and police power are the devices. According to *eminent domain,* the government may assume ownership of private land for the benefit of the community, provided just compensation is paid. *Police power* refers to the right of the authorities to limit the exercise of private rights in real property without compensation if the health, safety, morals or general welfare of the public is enhanced thereby. Similar laws exist in Western Europe. Generally, the individual landowner may challenge the decision to make his land available for a public project. It is then up to the courts to examine the issues and decide whether the authorities' proposed action is justified.

In France the *preemption* right gives the authorities priority in buying land from private owners. In India, New Delhi has embarked upon a land purchase program based on *compulsory sale* of private land. So far half the designated 66,000 acres falling within the urbanized limits defined in the master plan have been acquired. This land cannot be resold, but may only be leased for development purposes specified in the plan.

Expropriation of vacant land has a long history. In the Ottoman Empire, for example, the concept of *Machlul* provided that uncultivated agricultural land becomes state property after three years. The power to expropriate vacant land has been legislated recently in Cuba, Chile, Ceylon and Spain. In China (Taiwan) a law provides that, if an owner's land exceeds a maximum prescribed area, he must sell the excess portion within two years. Otherwise, the local authority may purchase the land. In such cases of *compulsory sale,* the land ownership regulations in Taiwan and a number of other countries forbid payment to owners of prices higher than those obtaining prior to announcement of the intention to use the land for public purposes.

2. Regulation of Land Trading

The most frequently used land trading regulations have been price controls and price freezing. Both are intended principally to restrain speculative increases in land values.

Cuba has established a ceiling on the maximum allowable unit price of land; in addition, the sale of real estate is banned to prevent accumulation, although units can be exchanged. France and Spain have adopted land-price freezing in connection with plans for priority development zones.

General registration and evaluation of land prices can be found in Australia, Denmark and Japan. Japan has established a "guidepost" system of price control which involves periodic official announcements of land values for selected standard tracts of land. A similar system exists in Spain. In South Korea the law establishing the transfer tax requires posting by government, at least twice a year, of "standard market prices."

The Netherlands has pioneered in controlling land values through active participation in the market. Feeding their own substantial land holdings into the market at appropriate times, municipalities have achieved quite remarkable results. Consequently, the most densely populated country in Europe has had the lowest rate of increase of urban land prices, and the weight of land in urban construction costs has remained stable for 50 years.

3. Regulation of Land Use

Land use regulations are intended to guide the physical growth of the city according to a master plan or whatever other framework for development exists. As with all control measures, interest groups are bound to exert pressure on decision makers, influencing them to adopt plans consistent with their diverse interests. Thus, in addition to planning considerations, such master plans as exist reflect socio-economic and political realities prevailing at the time of their adoption.

Zoning and subdivision laws vary between countries. A particularly restrictive version is found in North America where, among other things, zoning regulations have typically been used to "protect property values" in higher income residential areas. In Britain and other countries of Western Europe much broader concepts of zoning have been in use for many years.

Among Latin American countries, Chile and Venezuela have significant land use controls. In Venezuela the subdivision developer must cover the costs of infrastructure services provided by local government. Before a subdivision can be approved, the Municipal Council must confirm that the city has not designated the area for other uses. In Chile, the central government exercises control over land use on a national scale. In theory, this enables government to direct physical development not only within city limits but also on the peripheries and throughout the country.

In France and Japan the national plans specify zones of priority development and deferred development. One function of this system is to exercise some control over the urbanization process by defining urbanizable limits. In India, the city of Chandigarh has adopted a Periphery Control Act under which the area within five miles of the city boundaries on all sides is declared a controlled area. Development of this territory must proceed in accordance with a periphery land use plan intended to prevent squatting and uncontrolled development.

Other land use regulatory devices are building regulations, including codes and by-laws, and development permits. Where such regulations exist, developers are required to submit plans to the authorities for approval to ensure that they conform with building codes. Without such approval, work cannot commence. Development permits have been employed effectively in Britain where the permit covers the type and timing of development. Once an appeal for a permit is filed the authorities must respond within a period not exceeding two months. This time limit is important in light of long delays experienced in such countries as Nigeria, Ghana and Malaysia. In Italy and Spain the central government exercises final control over the granting of building permits. In the United States the states handle building permits and related regulations. As a result, regulations vary widely and this has been a factor preventing the development of industrialized housing.

The controlled development of infrastructure is another potential policy tool which, particularly if incorporated into a comprehensive land development plan, would assist municipalities in directing land into desired use patterns. To be sure, land can be brought into use without prior or adequate provision of power, water, sewerage, roads and other services; and developers frequently are motivated to provide infrastructure as part of a development scheme. However, there is no doubt that government participation in the financing and/or provision of infrastructure can be an important factor encouraging development according to desired patterns. By the same token, the withholding or proscription of infrastructure can effectively discourage development where it is not desired. It is somewhat surprising that conscious application of such policies has been so infrequent; however, such methods have been used as part of the general planning process in Britain and in some towns of Canada.

4. Land Regulations Related to Public Assistance

Some countries have adopted regulations designed to facilitate development schemes through public assistance. The main idea behind this approach is that cooperation between the private and public sectors may remove difficulties associated with the raising of capital, land assemblage, and improvement of land use patterns.

Again, programs have varied from country to country. In India, a "pooling" technique has been utilized in assembling large tracts instead of negotiating with each owner—a long and costly process. The land is assembled, given a new layout, provided with infrastructure services and redistributed among the original owners. Since this process raises land values considerably, values before and after development are taken into account in compensating the owners. Also, the reduced size of plots as a result of provision for parks and other public space is considered for the purpose of determining just compensation and ownership rights. A similar method, called land readjustment, has been used extensively in Japan since 1909 and was introduced more recently in South Korea.

In Western Europe several forms of public assistance in land development exist. In France, Spain, Italy, and the Federal Republic of Germany the demand for land in different municipalities has resulted in the creation of landowners' associations. These bodies attempt to coordinate with the public authorities the implementation of land development programs. Another frequently used technique for mutual benefit is the mixed private-public company. The landowners' association pools the land of a group of owners, and the joint company undertakes development of the land according to plans approved by the municipality. The private landowners retain collectively some ownership rights in the form of leasing privileges and development rights.

B. Tax Measures

All taxes have as one objective the raising of revenues. Given the limited resources of municipalities, this must be regarded as a most important feature of the overall fiscal system if not of individual taxes. In addition, taxation of vacant land, particularly at penal rates, is designed to bring the land into productive use. Other tax measures are used to influence the desired location and type of land development, to improve distributional equity and/or to discourage speculation.

The betterment tax is of special interest since it operates on rising land values; and, if properly applied, can be a very important source of revenue. However, there are difficulties in attempting to establish betterment tax policies. These difficulties stem from differing views as to the causes of increases in real property values. For example, increases in land values may occur as a result of the general increase in demand (resulting from population and economic growth), from publicly financed betterment and/or from privately financed betterment. The rationale for and methods of taxation differ correspondingly. Basically, it is the betterment values arising from the first two factors that one would like to "capture" for public sector use. In so doing, it is necessary also to attempt to distinguish between real increases in value and those caused by inflation.

1. Taxation of Vacant Land

The main purpose of a tax on vacant land is to bring land into productive use to meet the needs of a growing urban population and economy. Ideally, the tax would motivate landowners either to develop their sites (in accordance with a master plan if one exists), or to sell the property to interested private or public concerns willing to undertake development.

A number of countries have such taxes. In China (Taiwan) vacant land which is not developed within a prescribed period is subjected to a tax ranging from three to ten times the land value tax, which is the standard real property tax. In South Korea there is a "Real Property Speculation Check Tax" applicable to "untransferred unoccu-

494

pied" land. The law includes in the definition of unoccupied or vacant land lots with structures that cover no more than one-tenth of the total area, thereby encouraging also the development of under-utilized land.

In Chile municipalities levy a tax based on the assessed values of all vacant land in urban areas. This rate begins at 3% and is increased annually to a maximum of 6%. In Uruguay, in addition to a tax on vacant land, there is a special tax on "unused" lots where the value of the land is greater by a factor of 4.5 or more than the value of structures on the land. Both taxes are on a progressive scale. Syria also has adopted a progressive tax that increases from 1% to 5% of assessed value.

Although in principle a very well-conceived instrument, in most countries the vacant land tax suffers from a number of deficiencies—including (1) improper and outdated valuation, (2) widespread tax evasion, and (3) inefficiency of the tax administration generally.

2. Taxation to Influence the Location and/or Type of Development

Land taxation has been recognized as a potentially effective means of achieving desired patterns of land development in urban areas. However, it has not been fully utilized as yet in most parts of the world because of inexperience, political hesitation and the pressure of interest groups. As the urbanization process continues and urban problems mount, it can be expected that municipalities will increasingly resort to land taxation as a policy tool to influence the location and type of urban development. In principle these taxes should be highest in areas which attract investments and lower in second choice areas. Hopefully this would contribute to a more balanced distribution of land uses, providing the population with employment centers, commercial and cultural facilities in the areas where they live.

In France, under a law aimed at discouraging land development not in accordance with recommended uses, a developer is taxed 90% of the added value accruing to his property following additions or renovations not in conformity with the municipal plan. A similar law in Spain imposes an 8% tax on the added value to the property in urban areas, and 2% in rural zones. These low rates can be expected to be considerably less effective than those in France, provided the latter are enforceable. The land tax system in the State of Hawaii—following a different approach—establishes tax rates according not to the existing land use patterns, but rather in conformity with their approved use in the master plan. Though not perfect, this system provides considerable incentives to reduce discrepancies between actual and desired land use.

3. Land Transfer Taxation

The rapid rise in land values in urban areas has no doubt encouraged speculation and the development of land markets involving, usually, a small group of traders controlling substantial resources. As public authorities have become aware of this situation and, in particular, of the fact that land prices in many cities of developing countries currently exceed those in developed countries, there have been attempts to devise instruments to exercise a measure of control over the land market, so that the growing need for urban land can be satisfied at more reasonable cost.

A popular tax measure aimed at checking speculative land transactions has been the land transfer tax. In principle it discourages speculative trading by cutting into speculators' profits, at the same time providing the public with a share of market values. On the other hand, the tax does nothing to discourage speculative withholding, and—unless the tax is confined to, or the rate is much higher for transactions taking place within a short period of time—discourages all transactions, including those which would bring land into productive use.

The rate of the land transfer tax varies from country to country. In Afghanistan and Jordan it amounts to 1% of the sales price of land, in France 1.25%, Lebanon 3% (5% for foreigners), West Germany 5% and Spain 7.4%. In most if not all countries the low rates imposed have had little or no success in discouraging speculative land transactions.

In South Korea the law imposes a special tax payable by the seller on the transfer of land. This is not so much a transfer tax as a capital gains tax applicable only at the time of transfer. The tax rate is based on a complicated formula involving the difference between acquisition and sales price, capital expenditures made during ownership and administrative costs involved in the sale. The tax figure is further adjusted in accordance with the "wholesale commodity price index." The result is that the tax approaches 50% of the capital gain.

4. Taxation on the Income from Real Property

Urban real estate produces income in the form of rentals. In cities with high rates of automobile ownership, even vacant land may provide income if used for commercial parking.

Taxation of income from real property is an important source of revenue for most governments. In countries as diverse as the United States and India income taxes apply equally to income from real estate. However, these taxes operate as well in a reverse way. Expenses

496

deductible against total income include: maintenance costs on buildings, service charges and local taxes, costs of collecting rent, mortgage interest and (in the United States) accelerated depreciation. It is reasonable to assume that laws so favoring landowners are bound to increase speculative pressures and do violence to commonly held concepts of equity.

The British tax system distinguishes between income earned from employment ("earned income") and that from real property or other wealth ("unearned income"). The latter is taxed at a higher level with a minimum rate of 40%. In Nepal the urban property tax is increased by 50% if the land is used as an income source. In Iraq there is a tax and progressive surtax ranging from 1% to 16% on real estate income. In Jordan there is a tax of 17% on the rent earned from real property.

5. Taxation on Real Property and Betterment Values

Taxation on real property normally constitutes the principal source of revenue from land. As urbanization proceeds, real property and betterment taxation are viewed equally as a control measure and an indispensable financial source for municipal governments. A well-designed tax program would provide the municipal authorities with a fair share of the benefits accruing to landowners, while encouraging the latter to maintain and develop their property in accordance with the interests of the community.

The forms and rates of taxation on real property and betterment values vary widely. In Taiwan, there are two taxes: (1) the Land Value Tax, and (2) the Land Value Increment Tax. The basis for the former is the unimproved value of land, with assessment on the basis of the owner's self-declaration of value. The local government reserves the right of compulsory purchase at the owner's declared value; this power serves as a deterrent to tax evasion through understatement. This tax is annual and progressive from 1.5 to 7%. The Land Value Increment Tax is levied on the net increment in land value at the time of its transfer or after a lapse of ten years since the last assessment. This tax too is progressive, rising from 20 to 80%. Two other taxes may be levied to cover betterment values: (1) the Annual Tax on Constructional Improvement, and (2) the Constructional Benefit Charge. The first applies to improvements brought about by the owner's investments. The second covers increases in values attributable to public works. Though in principle this appears to be a marvelous combination of taxes, there are severe problems with assessment and enforcement.

In India, municipalities levy property and betterment taxes, but the income from these sources has been far below expected levels be cause of deficiencies in the assessment system and collection machinery. As a result, many municipalities have refrained from levying these taxes.

In Latin America, inflationary pressures have contributed to spectacular increases in property values. In fact, investment in land has become one of the most attractive means of protection against inflation. This situation requires more frequent assessments of real property values in order to adjust taxes to new market values. However, municipalities have generally failed to do this, utilizing unrealistically low values for the tax base.

C. Direct Public Involvement

The case for direct public involvement in urban land markets derives from the fact that the desired results cannot be achieved solely by seeking to influence private sector behavior—even by the use of substantial tax and non-tax incentives. It would seem that this involvement should be developed with three principal objectives in mind:

1. Increasing the supply of adequately serviced urban land at a rate sufficient to reduce land prices and/or reduce their rate of increase to a "tolerable" level;

2. Economizing on total resources by bringing about a better pattern of development; and

3. Capturing a substantial share of the betterment values associated with provision, by the public sector, of urban infrastructure and services.

These objectives correspond closely to the three problems described at the outset. To be successful, such intervention should be so arranged as to permit public authorities to enter or leave the market at any stage—as dictated by circumstances. But, first, it is necessary to deal with the problem of acquisition subject to fiscal constraint. Acquisition can take place in a number of ways. To the aforementioned means of eminent domain, compulsory purchase and the exercise of preemption rights, should be added such non-compulsory means as purchase on the free market.

In addition, the problem of finance must be overcome. It seems likely that, once a public market for the purchase, development and resale or rental of land is developed, the process can be financially self-sustaining. To start such a process in a situation where fiscal resources are slight, it might be worth considering exchanging bonds for property—in much the same way that the Japanese financed their rural agricultural land reform in the last century. In any case, public involvement in urban land markets must be comprehensive. The "package" of policy inputs might include appropriate combinations of the following: declaration of value by owners (in the knowledge that this declaration will be used for both tax and expropriation purposes); the designation of zones of priority and deferred development with appropriate time limits and price-freezing provisions; an "appropriate" rate of annual property tax; annual expropriation of significant amounts of land; a "balancing" of expropriation quantities and tax rates to create incentives for the "declared value" to be as near as possible to actual value; public development of the expropriated land; and a mechanism for capturing betterment values.

1. Acquisition

The best known examples of this far-sighted approach are provided by the municipalities of several Western European countries. Most of these countries currently acquire land for a variety of purposes—the leading examples being Sweden, Norway, the Netherlands, Germany, France and Spain.

The Swedish approach began in Stockholm before the end of the 19th century and is now approved for all municipalities. It involves purchases in the private market, supported by the right of municipal preemption. The city council of Stockholm has accumulated enough land about the city to effect housing developments for the working population and entire satellite towns, and has found this policy extremely rewarding financially. This has enabled it to build up reserves almost from the start of the program. As already indicated, a similar situation exists in the Netherlands.

In West Germany, in the period 1948-1965, public authorities invested $4 billion in land acquisition, considerably increasing existing municipal land reserves. In 1963, 31% of the land in towns of 100,000 population or more was under public ownership. In cities of one million and over, the municipalities controlled 37% of the land.

In less developed countries, the situation varies widely. In Asia, Hong Kong, Singapore, China (Taiwan), Afghanistan and India have programs. In Latin America, with the exception of Cuba and Chile, few countries have a positive policy of public land ownership. In Argentina, the state owns substantial tracts of valuable land in Buenos Aires and elsewhere, but no development program exists for this land. In fact, there has recently been a tendency to sell off tracts to meet the immediate fiscal problem. Ecuador, which built up a reserve of publicly held land during the 1940's, has recently not only ceased to acquire land, but begun a systematic process of donating substantial quantities of public land to social institutions. In Brazil, the majority of urban real estate is in private hands, except in the new capital of Brasilia.

The experience in land acquisition points to many advantages of creating a Public Land Bank, which perhaps explains an accelerating trend in the developing countries, as in the world generally, towards increased public ownership of land. In developing countries in which the private land ownership concept is not firmly established, as for example in some areas of Africa, there would seem to be a strong case for municipalities to clearly define in law their control over this land.

2. Development

Public investment in the land market covers, in addition to acquisition, development for such purposes as low and moderate income housing, schools, green belts, etc. However, the two aspects are strongly interrelated. Expropriation, by whatever means, has been gaining favor in recent years largely because an increasing number of countries have come to regard housing, particularly for the urban poor, as an extremely important social and political matter—an important public service that fully warrants the power of condemnation. Housing and roads provided the main stimulus for the development of land acquisition policies around the world, though the United Kingdom (where new towns were also an important factor) and the Netherlands (where public land has been used to regulate urban land prices for general planning purposes) provide at least partial exceptions to the rule. Initially, in most countries, expropriation was limited to the right of eminent domain and the latter applied only to specific —and of these often only important—development schemes. These restrictions are rather rapidly being relaxed in most countries. In the U.S. and Canada the concept has been stretched gradually to cover first housing and then general development uses (including private sector uses). In Spain and Italy, all that is needed to use this technique is general plan approval to develop a certain area; and in France, acquisition by expropriation is explicitly permitted in order to build up reserves.

Land acquisition and development is administered at the local level in most countries of Europe and North America, though this may be about to change in favor of regional concepts. National institutions are responsible in Britain and Spain, and regional institutions in France. Elsewhere, control is generally at the national level. However administered, acquisition and development are encumbered by lack of information, confusion or disagreement concerning title and/or assessed value. In many cases, the process is substantially delayed while litigation on such matters is proceeding. Recently, some countries have tackled this issue by taking possession first and dealing with such matters later. Ceylon has attempted to convert confusion over title from a liability into an asset by specifically providing for land with defective titles to be expropriated for public use.

In the United States, different programs exist under federal legislation providing for federal aid to cities for urban renewal, including low and moderate income housing. In Western Europe, many municipalities actively engage in residential construction for low income citizens. Hong Kong, Singapore, and Israel provide additional examples of public involvement in general land development and housing. The United Kingdom was the first country to adopt a national new town policy as a means of easing congestion in the older cities.

3. Redistribution

Acquisition, development and redistribution of public land follow different paths in different countries. The financial aspects of public land acquisition, development and resale or lease take on major importance, since no plans can be executed without adequate resources. Most countries rely upon some combination of "prior financing" and the realization of profit upon resale or lease. However, since there is no case where public sector financing provides adequate funds for accumulating reserves, primary emphasis has been placed upon the latter approach.

Sweden, United Kingdom, France and Spain have recently budgeted some funds for the purposes of reserve accumulation, but the amounts involved are almost derisory compared to the requirements. Norway has adopted a rather unique practice of public sector rental of private lands, which helps to mitigate the financial problem. Other countries have relied to some extent upon borrowed capital.

In France and Sweden, short and medium-term financing are utilized for land acquisition in cases where the public authority buys land for early resale to construction firms. If the land is intended to be kept in public ownership for possible lease to private developers, the financing is based upon long-term credit. The more favorable financing terms given in this case are designed to encourage leasing of land so that it may be retained in public control. In some instances municipalities adopt a policy of selling for housing but leasing for commercial and industrial uses. The wisdom of such a distinction has recently received considerable testimony in Britain where the expiration of long-term residential leases has caused severe personal and political problems.

As for redistribution, in some countries, e.g. the Netherlands, land is resold to the private sector in its undeveloped state. In the bulk of countries (particularly among developing countries), most land is turned over to housing corporations. But in a fair number of instances it is turned over to general development institutions. Examples in the developing countries are the Bombay and New Delhi Development Corporations in India and the Guayana Development Corporation in Venezuela. These new multi-function institutions work on a range of problems extending from housing to unit development in urban areas to new town development.

Redistribution of land to the private sector is by sale in most countries, by sale or lease in Sweden. In Hong Kong and Singapore, where much of the land started out under public control as Crown Lands, the authorities have kept it under public ownership, leasing it (and whatever public facilities have been added) to the private sector. This has obvious advantages, particularly since the period of the leases is shortened to a point where it is much easier to capture "unearned increments" and bring about appropriate changes in land use patterns.

INTERNATIONAL ASSISTANCE IN
URBAN DEVELOPMENT

International assistance, both multilateral and bilateral, has been slow in focussing on the need of less developed countries for help in dealing with urbanization. In part, this has been due to a lack of understanding of the gravity of conditions and the fact that cities have not been perceived as positive integral parts of the national development process. The scarcity of funds has also mitigated against allocations for urban development *per se,* a new, relatively undefined area of development investment. While these attitudes in part still exist, there is a growing awareness of both the magnitude of the urbanization phenomenon in the less developed countries and the need to act upon its inherent opportunities and dangers for development.

Available information on the kind and amount of international assistance in urban development, especially financial data, is fragmentary. However, while incomplete, the information presented here is sufficient to demonstrate that to date the amount of involvement has been quite limited.

A. Multilateral Assistance

According to estimates made by the United Nations Centre for Housing, Building and Planning (UNCHBP), in the 1966-1967 biennium a total of $700 million was expended for international programs in housing, building and planning. Of this total $570 million was actually reported by international agencies, and an additional $130 million was added by UNCHBP to account for those agencies which did not respond to their inquiry. The estimate for unaccounted expenditures represents 22.5% of the total which was reported. The average expenditure of $350 million annually is also approximately what UNCHBP estimated for the 1963-1965 period.

United Nations

The United Nations undertakes several different kinds of activities in the area of urban development. These include the collection, analysis and dissemination of information; research on specific problems; training programs and pre-investment projects. The Centre for Housing, Building and Planning is the UN unit that undertakes these activities at the headquarters level, and the regional economic commissions do similar work within their respective regions, with the exception of pre-investment studies. The special UN agencies, such as WHO, FAO

503

and ILO, also are involved in these activities. The United Nations Development Programme (UNDP) is responsible for the programming and financing of most technical assistance and pre-investment projects of the UN parent body. The special agencies undertake their own activities and, along with the Office of Technical Cooperation of the agencies for UNDP pre-investment projects. Projects vary from urban and regional development planning and training undertaken by an expert team of 10 to 15 members lasting three years to the appointment of a single housing finance advisor for several months.

Urban development has received a relatively low level of commitment in both staff resources and technical assistance funds in the UN. However, although the amount continues to remain small, there is evidence of an increasing trend. In 1963 expenditures of the UN regular budget and the UNDP together for housing, building and physical planning was about $1.35 million; in 1970, it was about $3.86 million. The following table summarizes the amount of funds expended by the UN bodies in international programs for housing, building and physical planning.

Table 1: UN Funds Expended in International Programs for Housing, Building and Physical Planning
(Amounts in $ thousands)

UN Source	Total Amount 1963—1970	Average annual amount in 1966—1969
Un regular budget	12,817[a]	1,681
UN extra-budgetary (UNDP, Funds in Trust)	16,109	2,837
UN special agencies (WHO, FAO, ILO)[b]	—	6,950
Total	28,926	11,468

[a] This does not include operating expenditures of the administrative agency (UNCHBP) for 1963, 1964, 1965.
[b] UN special agencies not included: Unesco, UNICEF, UNIDO, World Bank Group.
Source: Centre for Housing, Building and Planning, UN, New York, June 1971.

Aside from the above information on housing, building and planning, in the available data on UN projects, the urban development component is not specifically identified. The following table of the UNDP Special Fund capital commitments during the First Development Decade (1960-1970) indicates the magnitude of projects in housing, building and physical planning in comparison to other UN designated sectors, and Table 3 contains a selected list of ongoing UNDP Special Fund projects.

The UN has recently expressed a considerable interest in greater coordination of its pre-investment studies and technical assistance with World Bank lending in the field of urban development.

504

Table 2: UNDP/SF Capital Commitments 1960-1970
(Amounts in $ thousands)

UN Project Sector	No. of Projects[a]	Total Project Cost	UNDP Contribution
Agriculture	457	1,010,078	429,930
Education and Service	106	468,510	341,369
Health	15	51,331	39,164
Housing, Building and Physical Planning	21	48,410	29,843
Industry	323	664,685	387,311
Multi-Sector	69	150,521	64,323
Public Administration and Other Services	57	134,405	81,383
Public Utilities (including transport)	180	354,728	188,615
Social Welfare	6	9,204	5,753
Total	1,234	2,891,872	1,567,691

[a] Excludes cancelled projects.
Source: *Status of Approved Projects in the Special Fund Component As of December 31, 1970, DD/SF/Reports UNDP, New York, 1971.*

Regional Political and Economic Bodies

European Economic Community (EEC)

EEC through Fonds Européen de Développement has given some assistance for urban development in African, Asian, and Latin American countries in the form of technical assistance and capital loans. Between 1964 and 1969 urban development-related aid from this source amounted to approximately $39.7 million. This includes expenditure on water supply and drainage, sites for dwellings, improvement of central marketing facilities and airports.

Organization of American States (OAS)

Six years ago OAS established a Division of Urban Development for the purpose of giving technical assistance in two areas to member countries: the formulation of urban development policy and the transmission of housing and construction technology. In 1970 the Division's budget amounted to some $2.2 million and its projected budget for 1975 amounts to $2.8 million.

Regional Development Banks

Inter-American Development Bank (IDB)

Since its establishment in 1960, IDB has played a major role in international aid for urban development. Drawing on funds primarily from the Social Progress Trust Fund ($575 million, contributed by the United States), IDB began its urban development activity by financing

Table 3: Selected On-Going UNDP/SF-Financed Studies in Urban Areas—1970

Country and Project	Executing Agency	UNDP/SF Contribution	Commencement Date of Project
AFGHANISTAN			
Central Authority for Housing and Town Planning, Kabul	UN	$ 865,000	1966
BRAZIL			
Assistance in Strengthening the Operations Research and Control System of the National Housing Bank (BNH)	UN	546,500	1969
CHINA			
Urban and Housing Development	UN	727,800	1967
Sewerage Planning in the Greater Taipei Area	WHO	517,400	1969
The Preparation of a Consolidated Community Development Programme	UN	405,000	1969
COLOMBIA			
Transport and Urban Development Study, Bogota	IBRD	207,000	1969
GHANA			
Preparation of a Master Plan for Water Supply and Sewerage for the Accra-Tema Metropolitan Area (Phase II)	WHO	1,726,400	1967
IRAN			
Pre-Investment Survey of Sewerage Needs and Facilities in Teheran	WHO	1,110,000	1969
IRELAND			
National Institute for Physical Planning and Construction Research	UN	725,000	1964
IVORY COAST			
Water Supply and Sewerage for Abidjan	WHO	503,100	1970
NEPAL			
Development of Water Supply and Sewerage, Greater Kathmandu and Bhaktapur	WHO	752,400	1970
NIGERIA			
Master Plans for Wastes Disposal and Drainage, Ibadan	WHO	867,500	1969
PAKISTAN			
Location and Planning of Cities in the East	UN	1,009,700	1967
Master Plan for the Metropolitan Area of Karachi	UN	1,208,100	1970
PERU			
Experimental Housing Project, Lima	UN	1,065,500	1968
PHILIPPINES			
Master Plan for a Sewerage System for the Manila Metropolitan Area	WHO	714,000	1967
SENEGAL			
Establishment of a Master Plan for Water Supply and Sewerage for Dakar and Surrounding Areas	WHO	2,170,300	1968

Table 3: Selected On-Going UNDP/SF-Financed Studies in Urban Areas—1970 (continued)

Country and Project	Executing Agency	UNDP/SF Contribution	Commencement Date of Project
SINGAPORE			
Assistance in Urban Renewal and Development	UN	$1,576,400	1967
SYRIA			
Centre for Housing and Construction, Damascus	UN	681,000	1969
TOGO			
Building Construction Centre, Cacavelli	UN	1,132,700	1968
TURKEY			
Master Plan for Water Supply and Sewerage for the Istanbul Region	WHO	1,222,900	1966
UGANDA			
Master Plans for Water Supply and Sewerage for the Greater Kampala and Jinja Areas	WHO	616,800	1968
VENEZUELA			
Urban Research and Planning	UN	767,300	1968

two types of projects: water and sewerage, and housing construction (excluding land and administration costs). Subsequently, its housing finance policy changed to one of supporting housing in combination with related water, sewerage and road facilities, and at present IDB finances housing only within the framework of integrated urban development programs. Housing projects *per se* are no longer being considered by the IDB. Recently, IDB has initiated technical assistance, including pre-investment studies, for several large urban food

Table 4: IDB Urban Development Assistance, 1961-1970
(Amounts in $ thousands)

Project Type	Completed Projects		Ongoing Projects[a]		Total Capital Commitment	
	No. Projects	Amount	No. Projects	Amount	No. Projects	Amount
Electric Power	2	12,822	8	170,632	10	183,454
Food Marketing Facilities	1	600	1	6,300	2	6,900
Housing and Related Community Services[b]	20	113,214	12	105,280	32	218,494
Manufacturing Plants	12	31,562	1	4,587	13	36,149
Water & Sewerage	31	158,403	38	261,308	69	419,711
Totals	66	316,601	60	548,107	126	864,708

[a] As of December 30, 1970.

Source: *Banco Interamericano de Desarrollo Undecimo Informe Anual 1970,* Washington, 1971. Aggregated amounts for project types, particularly housing, electric power and water and sewerage may be lower than actual due to difficulties in distinguishing between urban and rural investments.

[b] This includes local roads, water and sewerage, and some community development technical assistance as integral parts of housing developments.

marketing facilities. In the ten years (1961-70) of lending activity, approximately 21% of IDB's capital commitment, some $864.7 million, has been for the following urban development-related projects.

Based on the principle of securing 50% participation by governments in its lending, IDB has been responsible for approximately $800 million investment in housing and related community services in some 16 countries. In addition, through technical assistance it has helped Latin American Governments establish five national housing agencies and reconstruct several other national housing agencies and banks. In the field of housing finance, IDB has developed saving and loan systems, mortgage insurance schemes, and secondary mortgage markets in several Latin American countries.

African Development Bank (DBA) and Asian Development Bank (ADB)

The other two more recently established regional development banks, the African Development Bank and the Asian Development Bank, are also involving themselves in urban development. In 1970, the DBA was financing one water supply and sewerage study ($300,000) and had several other similar projects in the pipeline. The ADB, by the end of 1970, had made three loans for water supply totalling $20.5 million, and a loan of $18 million for a metropolitan freeway.

B. Bilateral Assistance

Information collected by the United Nations indicates that bilateral aid for housing, building, and physical planning is about five times that of multilateral aid. Information from this source also indicates that the aggregate expenditure of France, the United Kingdom and the United States for recent years equals about 95% of total bilateral aid in this area of development assistance (see Table 5).

Agency for International Development (AID)

Most of the US Government aid to developing countries is channelled through the US State Department's Agency for International Development (AID). Information from AID indicates that between 1949 and mid-1970 approximately 4%, some $459.4 million, of its capital commitment has been for the urban development related projects shown in Table 6.

AID assistance for housing is conducted mainly through the Office of Housing (OH) and the Latin American Housing and Urban Development Division of the Office of Development Resources. The OH was established in 1970 to administer the Housing Investment Guarantee Program (HIG) and to provide other housing services as requested by AID regional bureaus. The HIG program accounts for most of present US Government commitment to housing assistance. Its basic purposes are, *inter alia*, to support in developing countries local institutions which mobilize local savings, specialize in providing long-term housing credit, and to stimulate housing demonstration projects. For this program the US Congress has authorized some $780 million to guarantee the housing investments in developing countries of US private lending institutions such as insurance companies, commercial banks, and federally chartered savings and loan associations. Of this amount, $67 million has been committed for Africa, $106 million for Asia, and about $346 million for Latin America. In spite of the high interest rates (8¾% to 10⅞% to the institutional borrower and 11% to 13% to the individual) the demand for the program is said to be growing.

Table 5: Bilateral Assistance in International Programs for Housing, Building, and Physical Planning of Selected Countries [a]
(Amounts in $ thousands)

Donor Country	Average Annual Amount 1966-1969	As Percentage of the Total Official Development Assistance Given to Developing Countries (1968)
Australia	1,587 [b]	—
Austria	53	0.1
Denmark	178	2.1
France	57,645	7.7
Japan	120	0.03
Sweden	1,714	2.0
United Kingdom	31,254	6.1
United States	88,383	2.6

Source: Funds Expended in International Programs for Housing, Building and Planning (E/C.6/110), UN, New York, 1971 (forthcoming). Information submitted by the governments of donor countries, and L. B. Pearson, *Partners in Development, Report of the Commission on International Development*, Praeger, N.Y. 1969.

[a] Other countries have also provided assistance to developing countries but data are not available. In comparing the expenditures of the various countries it should be kept in mind that countries differ in their policies toward assisting through bilateral or multilateral means. For example, of its total development assistance the US channels only 6.4% through multilateral means, and France 4.5%. On the other hand, Denmark channels 48.6% and Sweden 52.8% through multilateral means.

[b] Average of 1966-1967 and 1969-1971.

Since the creation of the Alliance for Progress in 1960, the Latin America Division has made bilateral loans of approximately $190 million and has made available about $60 million in local currency for housing.

AID loans for housing and urban development have generally been on soft or concessional terms which at one time were at such favorable terms as ¾ of 1% for forty years but today are at around 3%

Table 6: AID Urban Development Assistance, 1949-1970
(Amounts in $ thousands)

Project Type(a)	Capital Grants and Loans						Technical Assistance						Total Capital Commitment	
	Completed Projects		On-going Projects(d)		Total		Completed Projects		On-going Projects		Total			
	No. Projects	Amount	No. Projects	Amount	No. Projects	Amount	No. Projects	Amount	No. Projects	Amount	No. Projects	Amount	No. Projects	Amount
City and Regional Planning	—	—	—	—	—	—	2	128	1	32	3	160	3	160
Environmental Sanitation	33	54,511	15	63,233	48	117,344	70	28,661	5	1,879	75	30,540	123	147,884
Highways(b)	1	131	8	30,390	9	30,521	—	—	—	—	—	—	9	30,521
Housing(c)	25	71,989	10	87,558	35	159,547	76	11,272	21	16,159	97	27,431	132	186,978
Project Support for Housing	2	13,698	—	—	2	13,698	3	74	—	—	3	74	5	13,772
Potable Water	2	1,832	15	66,422	17	68,254	1	141	9	8,719	10	8,860	27	77,114
Urban Transit and Traffic Engineering	1	306	1	2,000	2	2,306	7	315	1	402	8	717	10	3,023
Totals	64	142,067	49	249,603	113	391,670	159	40,591	37	27,191	196	67,782	309	459,452

(a) The categories of environmental sanitation, housing, and project support for housing may include some assistance to rural areas.
(b) Inter-city highways.
(c) The housing investment guarantees are not included in this category.
(d) As of June 30, 1970.
Source: Technical Assistance Completed Projects; Capital Assistance Completed Projects; Capital Assistance Projects, Office of the Controller, AID, W253, 6/30/70.

per annum for forty years with a period of grace of ten years and 3% interest during that period.

While more than half of AID's loans for housing have been to public bodies for low-income housing, AID's interest has been on the creation of capital generating institutions for middle income families and on cooperative techniques. Recently, however, serious consideration has been given to AID's earlier concern with aided self-help techniques and low-income housing and the use of cooperative techniques for that purpose. Financial assistance for "site and services," "core" housing, and "shell" housing will undoubtedly ensue.

AID has also made substantial contributions in the form of grants for technical assistance, again primarily in Latin America.

The Office of Engineering's urban development unit is presently formulating strategy for coordinating separate infrastructural projects and building complexes to better support development goals and result in more integral assistance. That office also has initiated a study in labor-intensive construction technologies for low-income housing and supporting urban infrastructures.

The AID approach to housing and urban development has not been central policy directed. The Urban Development staff of the Bureau for Technical Assistance has been assigned the task of helping the Agency to determine what role, if any, is appropriate for US technical assistance in further support of developing country efforts to address the problems of rapid urban growth. An intensive international survey of urban development problems, approaches, resources, and opportunities has been concluded, and a study is in preparation, in consultation with other elements of the Agency, including field missions. A policy decision is anticipated early in fiscal year 1973.

Apart from a $29 million urban sector loan to Colombia, capital assistance in urban development has been project specific, focusing on physical infrastructure. However, there are several capital assistance projects under review in the Latin America Bureau which incorporate a more comprehensive approach to infrastructural development, including a technical assistance component.

Caisse Centrale de Cooperation Economique (CCCE)

CCCE is the disbursement agency for a large portion of the French Government's investment funds in Africa, Indo-China and the French overseas territories and departments. CCCE also works as a delegated agency for aid of the Fonds Européen Développement (FED) to Madagascar, the thirteen African countries where CCCE has offices, and the French overseas territories and departments. At this time investment figures are only available for housing. Between 1966 and

511

1969 CCCE lent approximately $28.94 million for housing; $5.58 million in 1969 alone. The four-year aggregated amount aided in the construction of some 27,700 housing units.

Commonwealth Development Corporation (CDC)

CDC, a Government statutory corporation established in 1948, is an important channel for British development assistance. It is empowered to undertake, either alone or in association with others, projects for the development of a wide range of economic enterprises, including agriculture, forestry, fisheries, mining, factories, electricity and water supply, transport, housing, hotels, construction and engineering. The corporation was initially empowered to operate only in developing Commonwealth countries, but since 1969 its operation has been extended. The corporation operates under borrowing powers of up to $612 million: it borrows principally from the United Kingdom Exchequer. At the end of 1971 it had 210 ongoing projects representing a total estimated commitment of about $496 million. The following types of urban development-related projects accounted for approximately 65% of this amount, or some $324 million.

Table 7: CDC Urban Development Aid, 1971

Project Type	Capital Commitment ($ million)
Housing	117
Electricity, Power and Water	121
Transport	19
Industrial and Property Development Companies[a]	67
Total	324

[a] Includes housing and other property development, development of industrial estates and the building of factories for sale.

Source: *Commonwealth Development Corporation*

In the area of housing finance, CDC has aided in establishing 21 mortgage finance companies in African, East Asian and Caribbean countries. These companies finance up to 90% of the value of mortgage loans. Some of the companies also develop and build housing projects when necessary. There is also a wholly-owned CDC subsidiary, Commonwealth Housing Corporation Ltd (CHCL) which combines the functions of technical adviser to CDC and to CDC's housing projects and also of acting more generally as consultants on the promotion, planning and execution of housing developments in overseas territories.

BANK LENDING FOR URBAN PURPOSES

Table 1: Bank Lending[1] for Urban Purposes as of January 31, 1972

		$ million
Total Bank and IDA lending		20,000
of which to developing countries	17,300	
to developed countries	2,800	
Total lending urban-related[2]		15,770
of which to developing countries	13,610	
to developed countries	2,160	
Total lending urban-related excluding inter-urban transport and telecommunications to developing countries		7,920
Urban lending as % total to developing countries	79%	
Urban lending (excluding inter-urban transport and telecommunications) as % total to developing countries	46%	

[1] Bank and IDA including $220 million Bank loans to IFC but not the total of IFC investments ($550 million at end-1971). Figures are rounded and are net of cancellations, refundings and terminations totalling $477 million of Bank loans and $70 million of IDA credits.

[2] Power, Industry, Development Finance Companies, Water Supply and Sewerage, Education and Tourism, Transportation and Communication, and IFC operations.

Table 2: Urban Projects of the World Bank in Selected Cities

Cities	Past Lending thru January 31, 1972	$ million
Buenos Aires	power, water supply, industry	292
Lagos	power, port, urban roads, industry, education	180
Sao Paulo	power, water supply, industry, port	260
Teheran	industry, power, telecommunications	175
Bogota	power, water, industry	260
Caracas	power, water, telecommunications and urban expressways	170
Bombay[1]	industry, power, port	135
Rio de Janeiro	power, commuter railway	135
Karachi	power, port, industry	128
Calcutta[1]	power, port, industry	120
Kuala Lumpur	power, water, industry, telecommunications	113
Istanbul	industry, power, port, education	100
Medellin	power, industry	100
TOTAL		2,168

[1] Totals for Calcutta and Bombay are substantially underestimated since no satisfactory basis exists for apportioning to them parts of the $500 million for industrial imports, the $265 million for development finance companies, the $180 million for telecommunications, and $651 million for Indian Railways (which include commuter lines into these cities).